KU-794-386

CIVIC QUARTER LIBRARY

International Marketing Strategy

LEEDS BECKETT UNIVERSITY
LIBRARY
DISCARDED

03

Leeds Metropolitan University

17 0221548 8

International Marketing Strategy

THIRD EDITION

FRANK BRADLEY
UNIVERSITY COLLEGE DUBLIN

PRENTICE HALL EUROPE

LONDON ● NEW YORK ● TORONTO ● SYDNEY ● TOKYO

SINGAPORE ● MADRID ● MEXICO CITY ● MUNICH ● PARIS

First published 1991
Third edition published 1999 by
Prentice Hall Europe
Campus 400, Maylands Avenue
Hemel Hempstead
Hertfordshire, HP2 7EZ
A division of
Simon & Schuster International Group

LEEDS METROPOLITAN
UNIVERSITY LIBRARY
1702215488
BT-B
925658 13.4.99
658.848 BRA B
658.84 BRA 22

© Prentice Hall Europe 1991, 1995, 1999

All rights reserved. No part of this publication may be reproduced, stored
in a retrieval system, or transmitted, in any form, or by any means,
electronic, mechanical, photocopying, recording or otherwise, without
prior permission, in writing, from the publisher.

Typeset in 9½/12pt Stone Serif with Stone Sans
by Hands Fotoset, Ratby, Leicester

Printed and bound in Great Britain by Redwood Books

Library of Congress Cataloging-in-Publication Data

Bradley, Frank, 1942–
    International marketing strategy   /Frank Bradley. – 3rd ed.
      p.   cm.
    Includes bibliographical references and index.
    ISBN 0-13-010057-9 (alk. paper)
      1. Export marketing–Management.   I. Title.
    HF1416.B72   1998
    658.8'48–dc21
                                                        98-33968
                                                        CIP

British Library Cataloguing in Publication Data

A catalogue record for this book is available from
the British Library

ISBN 0-13-0100579

1 2 3 4 5   03 02 01 00 99

This book is dedicated to my wife Breda,
my daughters Síobhán and Maedhbh and my
sons Jonathan and Simon with love

Contents

PART IV
The international marketing programme

PART V

====== **Implementing the international** ======
marketing programme   459

Acknowledgements

Several people helped with the third edition of this book. I am grateful for the stimulation and challenge provided by my students at University College Dublin. I also acknowledge the contributions of colleagues, Larry O'Connell in particular, and students at universities and business schools in Europe, North America and the Far East where I have had the privilege to teach and where parts of this edition were tested. I owe University College Dublin and my colleagues there a great degree of gratitude for their professional and personal support over many years. I am also indebted to a number of reviewers who provided very useful contributions regarding content and structure at various stages in the preparation of the third edition. I am particularly grateful to them for their detailed and most useful suggestions which are much appreciated. My editor Julia Helmsley, at Prentice Hall International, provided extensive and continuous advice and support at all stages, which was much appreciated. I am also very grateful to Pat Kenny who helped with the background research and the accumulation of research materials. He was also most helpful in sifting through recent research and contributed to the final editing process. Thanks are also due to Evelyn Corrigan whose talent and patience were very much in evidence as she prepared the figures used throughout the text, and to Fiona Walsh who was most thorough in preparing much of the typescript changes and the new exhibit material. The people I owe most gratitude to are the students and lecturers who have used the previous two editions and have in a most practicable way supported the preparation of this edition. I look forward to a partnership with them and others in the future. While these and others have helped in many ways, I remain responsible for any errors and other shortcomings in the book. Nevertheless, I hope that colleagues, students and managers will find the book valuable as they prepare for the challenge of international markets.

The author and publisher would like to thank the American Marketing Association, the Regents of the University of California, and Prentice Hall, for permission to use copyright material.

Every effort has been made to trace all copyright holders, but if any have been inadvertently overlooked, the publishers will be pleased to make the necessary arrangements at the earliest opportunity.

Frank Bradley
University College Dublin

Introduction

International marketing is no longer the preserve of large international companies, commodity traders and a few pioneering high-technology companies. With increased globalization of consumers and markets managers in most industries are now concerned with developments in domestic and international markets: banks; communications and transport; manufacturing; retailing. Small and large companies are affected, as are companies in traditional and high-technology industries and many service businesses. There are very few companies that are not affected by trends in international markets. More open and integrated international markets create opportunities and competitive challenges for the firm seeking profitable growth. To succeed in such an environment students and managers must be flexible and able to develop and implement dynamic international marketing strategies. It is necessary for students and managers to acquire a detailed knowledge of international markets to be able to develop successful international marketing strategies. This book has been prepared for them. A study of international marketing strategy is concerned with the strategic and operational marketing issues arising in the management of the firm's international operations. The firm in international markets develops its marketing strategies and implements them in the context of a complex and changing environment. In doing so it must also respond to the needs and demands of its customers while coping with competition. Of special interest, therefore, is the role of the firm in mediating the international environment through corporate marketing strategies. The material in this book is presented from the perspective of the firm that is attempting to develop and grow in international markets.

Objectives

Having studied this book the reader should be able to understand the full range of tasks facing the firm in international marketing and integrate the various market entry and development strategies into a series of decisions which reflect an interplay of the international marketing environment, technological forces and the strength and weaknesses of the firm. The book should enable the reader:

1 to examine and develop international marketing strategies for consumer products firms, industrial products firms and services firms, irrespective of size or ownership structure;
1 to integrate a wide range of material written on various aspects of management with an emphasis on the international dimension;
1 to assist students and managers to develop analytical frameworks suitable for the design and implementation of international marketing strategies;
1 to analyze management problems facing the firm in international markets, to select and evaluate appropriate conceptual frameworks, to identify courses of action, to develop appropriate international marketing strategies and to know how to implement them.

Target audiences

The text is designed for people interested in understanding the changing international business environment, in particular the question of how international business affects our daily lives and the unique and changing role that the firm has played in international markets. Included in this readership would be senior undergraduate students of marketing, international marketing and international business and postgraduate students specializing in international business or international marketing who are likely to work with firms active in the international arena. In addition, students in business, economics and organizational behaviour with research interests in the evolution and growth of the firm in international markets would have a general interest in the book. The book should be of special interest both to the manager who thinks strategically about the development and growth of the firm in international markets and to those managers who wish to keep abreast of the most recent thinking in their specialized field.

Features

This book has three important content features:

1 Current research and management practice related to the discipline of international marketing have been consolidated and integrated, with a focus on the strategic development of the firm in international markets.
1 Conceptual and theoretical aspects are illustrated in two ways: examples of the practice of international marketing by actual companies are used throughout and a series of chapter exhibits, drawn from actual reports of international marketing in action, provide further detail.
1 The book is international both in terms of the sourcing of its material and in the treatment of the subject matter. It is not a book on marketing management to which an international emphasis has been added. The material has been written from the point of view of the firm competing in international markets irrespective of country of origin. It is strongly research based and reflects the most significant contributions of recent research and managerial literature.

Changes in the third edition

The third edition contains a number of important changes which improve the content and structure. The same five-part structure is maintained as it provides strong pedagogic support but there are many important changes made to individual chapters, many of which have been completely re-written, some of which have been modified considerably and all of which have been updated to include relevant recent research thinking. The underlying philosophy of the book is that for the firm to survive in international markets it must add value to the business system in which it operates.

All chapters in this edition have been updated and new research material has been included. Most of the new material has gone into Chapters 12–17 with Chapters 12, 14, and 16 receiving most attention. The more important changes are as follows:

- Chapter 1 is now written with a much stronger international marketing emphasis with a focus on the firm and Chapter 2 preserves what is useful from international trade theory but develops comparative advantage theory into international marketing theories based on company competitive advantage.
- Chapter 3 develops these points and shows how the firm leverages its resources and managerial assets, particularly its knowledge-based assets, to profitable effect in the international arena. The changes in Chapter 4 reflect a focus on how the firm may use its competitive advantage to compete abroad and shows that the firm may be constrained in its choice of strategic options.
- Chapter 8 has been re-written and now appears as Chapter 5 as it presents an overall view of the international competitive environment. Chapter 6 on culture has be re-structured and updated while the following two chapters on public policy and the creation of competitive advantage have been shortened and focused specifically on the firm.
- The material in Chapter 9 has been re-organized and updated while Chapter 10 has been completely re-written with much new material on how firms compete internationally. Chapter 11 has been shortened but with a much greater emphasis on the strategic choices to be made in entering international markets. Chapter 12 has been extended to include new material on pricing, financing of exports and payments. Chapters 13 and 14 have been re-organized and include much new research material.
- Chapters 15–17 have been extensively re-written, especially Chapter 16 which has been given a greater focus on the international aspects of industrial marketing. There is a much greater emphasis on building the global brand in Chapter 15 and recent research findings are included. Chapter 18 has been re-organized and much of it re-written. The material on negotiations and selling in Chapter 19 has been linked much more strongly with the earlier material on culture in international marketing. Chapter 20 remains much as before with some minor changes; it has also been shortened.

Outline

The material is developed from the perspective of the firm attempting to grow and develop in international markets. The book develops and evaluates international marketing strategies for firms at different stages of their development – firms new to internationalization, firms at the growth stage and the experienced firm attempting to extend into many additional markets using a multiplicity of entry strategies to suit the circumstances faced by the firm. This is viewed as a five-stage process of internationalization of the firm. The situations facing the firm at these five stages of its development are examined:

1. the decision to internationalize – why, how, when and where (Chapters 1–4);
2. coping with international marketing environments – global and regional markets, sociocultural environment, political environment and how to convert country comparative advantage into competitive advantage (Chapters 5–8);
3. deciding how to enter international markets – which combination of entry modes to use – exporting, strategic alliances or foreign direct investment and acquisitions (Chapters 9–14);
4. how to develop appropriate marketing programmes for different kinds of firm: consumer products, industrial products and services (Chapters 15–17);
5. implementation and control in international markets – distribution and negotiation of operational issues and implementing and controlling the international marketing effort (Chapters 18–20).

The focus is on the firm, not on individual elements of the marketing programme. The following schematic outline of the book shows how each chapter and part fits together in a logical and structured way.

Stage 1: decision to internationalize
• international marketing in the firm
• theories in international marketing
• resources and managerial capacity
• strategic options for the firm

Stage 2: analysis of international marketing environment
• global, regional and emerging markets
• sociocultural environment
• public policy environment
• creating competitive advantage

Stage 3: entering international markets
• international markets and customers
• analysis of international competitors
• entering international markets
• exporting
• strategic alliances
• foreign direct investment – acquisitions

Stage 4: international marketing programme
• consumer products firm
• industrial products firm
• services firm

Stage 5: implementing the international marketing programme
• managing international distribution channels
• selling and negotiating in international markets
• managing international marketing operations

Five stage process of internationalization of firm

1
International marketing in the firm

The corporate context of international marketing involves understanding how the firm responds to environmental opportunities and threats in markets of very different configurations and underlying behaviour. In such circumstances the firm responds by developing new products or by adapting existing products to the needs of consumers in domestic and international markets. International marketing also means deciding which markets to enter and develop and the sequence and timing of entry. A most important issue is the firm's decision as to how to enter international markets. The nature and significance of international marketing for the firm are described in this chapter. The performance and growth of the firm as it diversifies into new international markets are also examined. Central to the argument is the role of the firm's competitive marketing strategies for success in international markets.

International marketing environment

The international marketing environment is a complex mixture of macro and micro forces which must be considered. The environment facing the international firm consists of the constellation of demands and constraints to which the organization must adjust in order to survive and grow. This environment consists of a number of elements, the underlying characteristics of which are that they lie outside the control of the firm (Figure 1.1). The successful firm caters for its customers within the context of a competitive environment which has become increasingly international. It is not the marketing environment itself that is important but the firm's ability to cope with it. In the rapidly changing technological environment that characterizes international markets there are few isolated market niches. Attention must be focused on the missing link in developing a competitive strategy for success in international markets: investment in marketing to produce an international orientation and an ability to compete successfully in international markets.

Figure 1.1 The international marketing environment

International marketing strategy

The distinctive attribute of the strategic development of the firm in international markets is that the firm transfers products and services, packages of tangible and intangible assets or resources, across national boundaries. In some circumstances the transfer is through exporting or selling. In other situations ownership or management control over the transfer is retained by entering into alliances with like-minded companies, or the firm may invest directly in foreign markets to transfer the assets or resources. In making the transfer, the firm in international markets responds to many pressures, among which the most important are pressures originating in the home country, such as saturated markets or the opportunity to exploit new products, lower production costs, the attraction of incentive packages offered by host country governments, the attraction of large and growing foreign markets for the firm's products and shortening product and technology life cycles and growth aspirations in the firm.

In more recent years, the function of the firm in international markets has been to combine international marketing decisions with newer forms of resource transfer, thus blurring the distinction between the equity and contractual form of international asset transfer. What is needed, therefore, is a way of examining the activities of the firm which encompasses the selling activities associated with exporting and the investment activities associated with the other modes of resource transfer such as licensing, joint ventures and other forms of competitive alliance and foreign direct investment. Concern for international marketing is concern for these issues from both a descriptive and a normative point of view.

This book examines the unique and changing role of the firm in international markets and seeks to judge how established firms, firms new to international marketing and policy makers in home and host countries approach dynamic international markets and the evolving modalities of international resource transfer. The primary unit of enquiry is the firm and the effect on it of the changes required in response to internationalization.

Process model of internationalization

In order to examine the firm in international markets, a five-stage process model of internationalization is proposed (Figure 1.2). In the first stage, the firm decides whether to internationalize. In order to make such a decision, it is necessary to understand the role of the international marketing in the firm. It is also necessary to explore the value of the various theories of the firm in international markets. Next, it is necessary to understand the impact of organizational issues on the process. Here, we examine the firm's resource base and managerial capacity. In deciding to internationalize, the firm will also examine the strategic options available to it. Some strategic options may be successful while others are not. Indeed, the firm's resource base and the requirements of the market may constrain the firm in its selection of a feasible international marketing strategy. These issues are examined in Chapters 1–4 of the book.

In the second stage, it is necessary to examine the international marketing environment. Four chapters are devoted to this stage of the process. First, it is necessary to understand the context of international markets (Chapter 5). Then, it is important for the manager to understand the sociocultural environment of international markets (Chapter 6). The influence of the public policy environment and the role of governments and other regional institutions affect the fortunes of the international firm (Chapter 7). The last

Figure 1.2 Five-stage process model of internationalization

chapter in this section is devoted to examining the ways countries and companies have in creating advantage to compete internationally (Chapter 8).

In the third stage, the ways of entering international markets are examined. However, first, it is necessary to understand customer and market behaviour and how competitors respond (Chapters 9 and 10). The concept of entering foreign markets is examined in Chapter 11 and the following three chapters are devoted to the principal modes of entry: exporting, competitive alliances and foreign direct investment.

In the fourth stage, the dimensions of the international marketing programme for three different types of firms are examined. Chapter 15 examines international marketing strategies followed by consumer products' companies, while the situation facing industrial products and services companies is examined in Chapters 16 and 17 respectively. These three sets of circumstances cover the broad range of experiences facing the international firm at any one time or at different stages in their evolution.

In the last stage of the process, ways of implementing the international marketing programme are examined. This means examining the way that goods and services are delivered to international customers through distribution channels (Chapter 18) and how the firm sells and negotiates in international markets taking account of the cultural and business factors already examined (Chapter 19). In Chapter 20, the overall operations of the firm are examined with the objective of ensuring that objectives and strategic targets established for the firm are attained.

The firm in international markets

Firms exist where an organizational or hierarchical solution to the allocation of resources is superior to a market solution. Firms come into existence when markets fail. Firms attempt to internalize within themselves firm specific advantages such as brands, service quality, marketing skills and an understanding of the business system. By bringing these assets within the firm they create added value which gives them a competitive advantage in the marketplace (Hymer, 1970; Caves, 1996). The growth of the firm may be conceived as the replacement of markets or the creation of an internal market within the firm where none existed previously. The motivation for growth by internalization of markets may be attributed to a number of factors.

Production and distribution take time, and delays in the provision of inputs or services when and where necessary may require control of market for these inputs and services: backward integration of raw materials markets, the forward integration into distribution and marketing of branded products and the control of information by financial institutions across national borders are good examples. Internalized markets avoid the bilateral concentration of market power; instability is avoided in a joint venture or internal market.

The buyer uncertainty problem which adversely affects the market transfer of information is avoided in internal markets. This is particularly true in international markets where marketing information is such a vital asset. In such circumstances the buyer is unaware of the value of information until he or she has possession of it, at which point he or she has no incentive to pay for it. Such outcomes are avoided when the buyer and seller join together in an internal market formed as a joint venture, licensing arrangement or full equity participation in foreign direct investment. In an internal market within a firm, transfer prices may be adjusted to achieve the firm's objectives; arm's length pricing is only one alternative.

Other price factors must also be recognized. Price discrimination among foreign subsidiaries may be used by firms to increase profits or to minimize the impact of national taxes. Firms also shift funds between currency areas to avoid the adverse effects of changes in currency values. While these activities may be legitimate, the discretion left to the international firm is a major cause of concern to governments and transnational regulatory bodies (Buckley, 1987, pp. 16–17).

There are costs, however, of establishing an internal market within the firm. The market is an economizer of information; only price and quantity signals are necessary. The information burden of an internal market is greater and communications costs are higher than those experienced in the open market. Skilled management is required to run an internal market and is expensive. The cost of foreignness, including lack of knowledge of local conditions and costs of adverse discrimination, is a disadvantage.

Nature of the international firm

Until the mid-1960s, there was little treatment in the literature of the firm in international markets. Also, there was not much examination of internationalization as a process culminating in foreign direct investment (Teece, 1986). Teece suggests that the international company is one that exports capital, moving products and equity from countries whose returns are low to markets whose returns are higher, earning the profits of arbitrage while simultaneously contributing to the more efficient worldwide allocation of capital. However, the predictions of capital arbitrage theories are quite different from the resource transfer activities of international firms, who invest, borrow, buy and sell in different markets. There are considerable cross-flows of investments and products between markets, which make the task of the international firm both interesting and challenging.

A more plausible theory of foreign direct investment appeals to oligopoly theory and suggests two major reasons why firms should operate beyond their borders (Hymer, 1970). The first reason is to bypass competition by acquiring it or displacing it, and the second is to employ the firm's special competitive advantages abroad, such as financial skills, access to capital, entrepreneurship and marketing skills. There are various ways to ensure that the benefits accrue to the firm. The product in which the competitive advantage is embodied could be exported or the technology used to make the product could be licensed to, or produced under a joint venture with, a foreign firm. The firm will, however, prefer to invest abroad in many situations to avoid technological misappropriation and to prevent the costly bargaining between licensor and licensee, on the one hand, and the inherent instability and danger of technological misappropriation of joint ventures on the other (Hymer, 1970; Killing, 1982). It is the costs associated with these forms of transfer and the extent of control under each which decides the hierarchical mode of organization. These insights shift emphasis away from international trade and finance toward industrial organization and marketing.

Competitive advantage in the international firm

Where the capacity and incentive to internationalize are strong enough, the firm is likely to concentrate on those products that seem in most demand in the home market. Later the advantage is exploited internationally in a series of stages. The assets which provide a competitive advantage for the firm in international markets may be subsumed under seven headings (Table 1.1). Once a firm establishes a technological lead in some product it will be faced with the question of how best to exploit the lead. Exporting the product will sometimes be sufficient. Exporting to exploit a technological lead is likely because, at the early stage of the development of a product, managers are not acutely concerned with production cost. Later on, however, costs do become a concern.

Firms that place heavy weight on technology as a basis for their strategy typically adopt very different patterns in the way they enter foreign markets (Vernon and Wells, 1976, Chapter 1). Successful firms with very narrow product lines (IBM, SKF) are generally committed to an effort to maintain their lead in a limited, well-defined market. Confined to that market they have a high stake in maintaining quality standards, in holding their technological skills close to the chest and in maintaining tight control over market strategy

---

Table 1.1 Assets which create competitive advantage for the firm

1. Proprietary technology
    Product and process
2. Management know-how
    Multicountry operations
    Experience of different countries
3. Multinational distribution network
    Sales subsidiaries
    Portfolio of markets
4. Access to scarce raw materials
    Ownership
    Long-term contracts
5. Production economies of scale
    Low unit costs
6. Financial economies of scale
    Access to low-cost funds
7. Possession of a strong brand or trade name
    Reputation for quality

Source: Grosse, R. E. (1989) *Foreign Investment Codes and the Location of Direct Investment*, New York: Praeger.

to be applied to their products. Strategic decisions may be relatively few but each is highly important and each affects the firm as a whole. Such firms show a strong preference for wholly owned subsidiaries. They usually enter and stay in foreign markets through foreign direct investment.

Successful firms with very broad product lines which exploit technological leads see themselves as comparatively efficient at developing those technological advantages. Because they know that such advantages are perishable, their strategy is to make the widest, and presumably the quickest, application of any technological lead they may develop. Since such leads can be exploited over many products in many markets, these firms rely on others to provide the specific market information and specialized distribution needed to exploit them. Because of the need to penetrate markets quickly, they are more tolerant of joint ventures as the means of entering and staying in international markets.

An alternative means of internationalizing the firm is to exploit a strong brand name. In the modern world of easy international movement and communication, brand names can sometimes gain strength without much conscious effort on the part of the firm that owns the name. Strength of a foreign brand name is associated with the fact or illusion of superior or predictable performance. The expectation of this performance is often strengthened and fortified by extensive promotional expenditures, as is commonly the case for branded pharmaceuticals and foods, beverages and tobacco products. With regard to predictable performance, the strong brand may rest on some technological capability, e.g. delivering a packaged food product such as Nestlé, or Jacob–Suchard confectionery in a reasonably standardized condition on a reasonably reliable basis can be a technically exacting job that has been mastered by only a limited number of firms.

While brand names endure, their ability to command a premium erodes with time. If the product underlying the brand in packaged foods, soft drinks, cosmetics and similar products does not change, national producers learn either to match the performance of the foreign product or to overcome the illusion of a difference that was never there. Foreign firms tend to lose market share or face a complete closure of the market in time unless they continue to innovate.

To ensure a continued presence in international markets in the early 1980s, Swatch created a low-price prestige segment in the quartz analog watch market. Using its production skills and adroit product positioning, the company built up a large share of the market. The company combined its high volume production experience to deliver a technological breakthrough at a very low cost, which gave the company protection against competition. The Swatch was positioned as a quality product which was shock resistant, while the time-keeping features were not emphasized. The watch concept was effectively repositioned to being a fashion accessory that happens to tell the time, as a second or third watch, using the occasion to segment the market.

A brand name applied to a very narrow range of products such as cars, e.g. Ford, Fiat or Nissan, is intended to convey a narrow and explicit set of expectations about a particular product. A brand name applied to a broad range of products, e.g. 3M, Heinz, Hoechst or Heinkel, is intended to convey only a general aura of reliability. Firms with a broad product range have less need for tight control of production and marketing. For such firms, the risks of weakened control associated with operating through joint ventures and even looser alliances are more tolerable.

Even narrow product range companies may use joint ventures and other 'less control oriented' modalities. Coca-Cola works with local distributors as partners in its foreign bottling plants because Coca-Cola, until recently, totally controlled the vital marketing functions: trade name, advertising programme, flavour and the bottles. Competing in international markets is not for the faint-hearted as Pepsi-Cola discovered when it tried to match Coca-Cola outside the US (Exhibit 1.1). Coca-Cola's competitive advantage is sufficient to sustain it against aggressive competitors in most markets throughout the world.

▬▬▬▬ Exhibit 1.1 ▬▬▬▬
Battered PepsiCo licks its wounds

PepsiCo's decision to close down its Pepsi-Cola operations in South Africa marks a humiliating retreat for the world's second largest soft drinks company. Battered by the competition from Coca-Cola, PepsiCo is carrying out an examination of its international markets to determine whether it has a viable future in countries where Coca-Cola is the dominant player.

Until recently, Pepsi-Cola had been determined to vie with Coca-Cola for world domination. It ploughed money into what many saw as a quixotic attempt to beat Coca-Cola in some of its strongest territories. But last year Pepsi-Cola's biggest international bottler, Baesa of Argentina, ran into financial difficulties; the company's Venezuelan bottler defected to Coca-Cola; and Pepsi-Cola International's losses began to climb.

In September 1996, Pepsi-Cola announced a drastic change in strategy: from now on it would make the best of life in second place, concentrating on markets where it could prosper alongside Coca-Cola rather than trying to defeat it. PepsiCo's decision to pull out of South Africa was the first evidence of this new strategy: it had less than 5 per cent of the market compared with 81 per cent for Coca-Cola.

So is Pepsi-Cola doomed to oblivion? 'Far from it,' says John Sicher, editor of *Beverage Digest*. 'There will be more markets like South Africa, where Pepsi-Cola may not compete, but I think in India, China, Eastern Europe and the Middle East, they will be a major factor.'

Some indication that the strategy was taking effect came in this year's first quarter, when PepsiCo produced better-than-expected results from its soft drinks business and indicated that it was on track to cut operating losses on the international side from $846m in 1996 to about $50m this year. Meanwhile, Pepsi-Cola is fizzing satisfactorily in its biggest market, the US. Although Coca-Cola is number one with a 43 per cent share of the soft drinks market, Pepsi-Cola commands a robust 31 per cent share.

Source: Adapted from *Financial Times*, Friday, 30 May 1997, p. 26.

The globalization debate

There has been an extensive debate on the issue of globalization in the literature and in the popular press which raises the need to examine its elements. Globalization means different things to different people. Many elements affect globalization and its impact on countries, companies and people. The technological capacity of a country and its ability to adapt to changing needs is a major element in globalization of business. Another factor which underlies the concept is access to large integrated markets, such as the United States or the European Union. The competitiveness of people and enterprise, increasingly dependent on their ability to create new assets, provides an attraction for mobile foreign investment, which, when combined with a political capacity to adapt and change, is an additional element to be considered in the globalization debate. Related to these is the need to establish and promote international institutions which provide the necessary framework for globalization of business to take place. This in turn increases competition between firms and industries. Lastly, there is the role of governments which is becoming increasingly important in influencing the location decisions of companies, particularly those engaged in mobile foreign investment.

Causes of globalization

Governments have progressively lowered trade barriers internationally through the Uruguay Round of the GATT and within countries through groups such as the European Union (EU), the North American Free Trade Agreement (NAFTA) and MERCOSUR in Latin America.

Until recently, globalization meant a slow global roll-out by a large company of a product. Nowadays, relatively small companies engage in global marketing even of sophisticated products. However, the word globalization refers to different aspects of business: organizing the company for worldwide production, a worldwide marketing programme or the demise of national borders. As a result, attention focuses on concepts such as global products, large matrix organizations and a world without trade barriers. The result is an increased pressure on companies to compete for international markets by innovating and developing new products and upgrading existing products. It may also mean reducing prices by removing cost elements.

There have been a number of geopolitical developments which have contributed to the globalization debate. The re-unification of Germany and the collapse of communism have ushered in a market orientation in Eastern Europe, the former Soviet Union and former COMECON countries. The emergence of these new markets and other newly emerging markets in the Far East, Africa and Latin America have re-distributed wealth and increased the demand for industrial and consumer goods.

Three aspects of globalization are of interest here: the impact of industry structure, influences on the business system and country market interdependence (Ohmae, 1989, 1990; Solberg, 1997). Some industries such as services, building materials and furniture are highly fragmented and serve fragmented niche markets which are very segmented. Other industries such as consumer electronics, soft drinks and tobacco are highly consolidated and firms serve mass markets. Competition in fragmented markets is diffuse with the result that small, poorly resourced firms can survive. Consolidated industries and markets tend to be dominated by high-technology multinational firms with low-cost facilities. The type of industry structure is determined by entry barriers and their resistance to attack. Scale economies, product differentiation and blocked distribution channels are barriers to market entry and help to determine industry structure.

The most important influences on the business system include market liberalization, technological developments, communications, homogenization of demand and concentration of distributors and customers. Changes in these factors affect the way firms can compete internationally and help to develop an international marketing presence.

Market interdependence refers to the consequences of the firm's actions in one market in other markets. Even when a firm is active in only one market it recognizes that its actions there may be felt in many other markets owing to the interdependence which has arisen in recent years among countries. A most common manifestation of this element of globalization is the extent of strategic alliances and price competition which exists in certain industries in international markets.

Technology and trade liberalization

Two forces have been driving the increased international flow of goods and capital: technology and trade liberalization. The natural barriers of time and space have been reduced as the cost of communications and computing falls. These developments allowed Yip (1992) to refer to a general set of 'globalization drivers' which included market drivers, cost drivers, public sector drivers and competitive drivers. The globalization debate must take account of each of these factors.

Cheap and efficient communications allow firms to locate different parts of their production processes in different countries while maintaining close contact. Modern information technology reduces the need for physical contact between providers and consumers which allows previously untradeable services to be sold internationally. Any activity that can be conducted on a computer screen or over a telephone, e.g. writing software or selling tickets, can be carried out anywhere in the world linked to head office by telecommunications and computer technology. Medical and educational services are now sold at a distance through the use of such technology.

For Levitt (1983), the introduction of new technologies helped to create large global markets in which standardized products with universal brand appeals would dominate consumer choice. According to this argument, the new technologies would enable companies to concentrate on producing advanced, functional, reliable and low-priced products which would deliver benefits such as the 'alleviation of life's burdens and the expansion of discretionary time and spending power' (Levitt, 1983, p. 46), rather than worrying about the details of what everyone thinks they might like, or so the argument goes. In this way, producers would gain global scale economies and experience curve benefits in production, distribution, marketing and management. Global companies would drive down unit costs which would allow them to price penetrate markets and force non-global competitors out of the markets. 'The global corporation operates with resolute constancy, at low relative cost, as if the entire world, or major regions of it, were a single entity; it sells the same things in the same way everywhere' (Levitt, 1983, pp. 39–40). The idea that the same product can be sold everywhere in the same way has, however, been discredited. Most large consumer products companies exploit national differences. Even well-known brands, such as McDonald's, make concessions to local tastes in order to succeed in international markets. McDonald's hamburgers are served with teriyaki sauce in Japan and with chilli peppers in Mexico. Levitt assumes that customer needs and interests are becoming increasingly homogenous worldwide but there is no clear evidence that this is a universal trend. Furthermore, timing of market entry and market barriers may allow incumbents to develop strong local brands which sometimes form an antidote to the charms of strong aggressive international brands as McDonald's discovered when they made a late entry into South Africa (Exhibit 1.2). Even within markets, there is great diversity of behaviour and tastes.

In the past decade, trade has increased twice as fast as output and foreign direct investment three times as fast. However, product-market integration still has a long way to go. A measure of such integration is the extent to which prices converge across countries. In theory, free trade should converge prices. However, for many consumer products, at least, prices are consistently lower in North America than in Europe or Japan. This reflects differences in tastes, transport costs, taxes and inefficient distribution, but it also is due to the persistence of import barriers. Product markets, therefore, are still not as integrated across borders as they are within countries, but even here there are great differences of opinion regarding the impact on international marketing. A cursory examination of the academic and management literature shows that the entire thrust of marketing has been to segment customers rather than treating them as homogenous.

Contrary to expectations, Craig *et al.* (1992, p. 779) discovered that the 18 industrialized countries they studied experienced divergent development in regard to the key macroeconomic indicators, such as population density, real income per person and living expenses. Earlier, Douglas and Wind (1987) and Boddewyn (1981) had indicated that there were limits to standardization in regard to income parity, but especially in regard to behavioural patterns. Clearly there are differences in different markets; high-technology markets are highly standardized especially in product categories such as consumer electronics whereas in high-touch sectors circumstances dictate the extent of standardization: teenage clothing, food and music are highly standardized while food in general is highly culture bound and not standardized. Having analysed private consumption expenditures from 1985 to 1990 in the European Union, Wenke (1994, p. 17) concluded that consumption patterns were not converging although at a broad macro level there is evidence of some convergence (Leeflang and van Raaij, 1995, pp. 373–4). Furthermore, the recent recognition in the United States of African, Chinese and Spanish influences has encouraged large US companies to recognize their domestic market as a series of markets rather than a single large homogeneous market. Furthermore, the advance of new information technologies allows companies to use data collected from a wide range of sources to identify smaller groups who may be reached with customized products.

===== Exhibit 1.2 =====
Johannesburgers and Fries

Managers at McDonald's pride themselves on knowing how to adapt the Big Mac to local markets (teriyaki burgers in Tokyo etc.), while promoting the same basic idea: good fast food served in clean surroundings by a company with a strong family brand. By the time the first McDonald's restaurant opened in South Africa in 1995, it was clear that the American giant was entering a rather unusual market. However, South Africa did not fit the typical formula: it had already developed a first-world consumer industry in almost complete commercial isolation, behind sanctions and tariffs. Nobody at McDonald's realized how difficult it would be to break in.

Over the years, South Africa's fast-food industry had developed its own strong brands: Nando's, a spicy Portuguese-style chickenburger chain, Chicken Licken, a mass-market chain, and Steers, a fast-food burger chain. 'People think it's an easy market,' comments Robert Brozin, head of Nando's, 'but it's not: there are a lot of very successful South African brands'. Not only were South Africans relatively isolated from the advertising of global brands, but they had grown to know and love their own. Even with a lavish television campaign, with the slogan 'It's MacTime Now', it is clear that South Africa is not succumbing in the way that McDonald's assumed that it would.

Anecdotal evidence suggests that McDonald's fare is not quite what its customers want. For many blacks, a McDonald's chickenburger is pricey: 30 per cent dearer than Chicken Licken's equivalent. Meanwhile, through white eyes, even McDonald's biggest burgers, the Big Mac and the quarter pounder look puny next to, say, Steers's 'Big Steer', which packs 200 g (7 oz) of beef. 'In South Africa, it's a man's red-blooded meat country,' says Jeremy Sampson, who runs Interbrand in South Africa. 'McDonald's comes here with a small, thin burger and people laugh'.

McDonald's experience in South Africa shows how even the strongest brands cannot expect to trample all before them, particularly when consumers can choose established local alternatives. Given that the owner of 'the world's leading brand' has had such trouble, companies with a less recognizable trade mark might think twice before following its example.

Source: adapted from *Economist*, 27 September 1997, pp. 79–80.

Levitt's second assumption that people around the world are willing to sacrifice preferences in product features, functions and design for lower prices and higher quality is also challenged by the evidence available. A number of price-sensitive markets exist, but differentiation is still a valid strategy. A major source of differentiation in international markets derives from brand loyalty which is unlikely to be a major consideration in price sensitive market segments. Branding is an effective basis for competition in international markets. Furthermore, in recent years, there has been an increased emphasis on product variety and service.

Company size and scale effects

Company size is no longer much of an impediment to success in international marketing. With deregulation, the decline or removal of trade barriers and the fall in transport and communications costs, a company does not have to be large in order to serve global markets successfully. The new communications technologies enable every company to participate in world markets. A new service economy based on communications has arrived. Furthermore, large companies no longer have a monopoly on managerial abilities since modern management techniques are also accessible to smaller companies.

Companies active in international markets have access to a much larger pool of management resources than a small local firm and experience a wider range of environmental changes, consumer needs and competitive reactions. By integrating and using this information effectively, the international firm is better prepared for global markets. In many instances, the successful international firm's most valuable resource is a culture reflecting its ability to integrate and use diverse marketing information. Information about information has become a key resource. Communication technologies injects a supplier into the business processes of customers, which ensures closer communication and efficiency.

The production scale economies are of themselves of little value but, if they can be combined in a marketing system that integrates knowledge from different countries, they are much more important. Two types of integration, simple and complex, must be considered. In simple integration, companies keep their most sophisticated operations at home but contract out other production to low-cost countries. Smaller multinationals seem to favour this strategy, whereby product development and marketing are performed in the home base while production takes place in numerous overseas subsidiaries. These subsidiaries are highly mobile and their location is often dependent on wage rates.

In complex integration, companies site their production activities according to the dictates of the market. Decision making is dispersed throughout the company, irrespective of location, and the entire company is held together as an information system. Knowledge management within a company is complex and integration of activities on the basis of information across different countries is particularly difficult. Many companies have attempted complex integration but have failed. Others, such as Ford, have failed on numerous occasions but have returned to the task and persist in their attempt to reach the goal of complete international integration of complex production and marketing.

Regional markets not global markets

The extent of geographic expansion is a feature often discussed. Many multinational companies are properly regional organizations in that they expand only to markets of close business distance. European companies, typically, expand to other nearby European countries, US companies expand into Canada and Mexico, and Japanese companies concentrate their overseas ventures in Southeast Asian region.

For many years, large well-known international companies were in fact a series of national entities held together in ownership, but not for any strategic reason. These companies coped with high tariffs, high transport costs and very restrictive local content rules by establishing subsidiaries in each country in which they operated. The lowering of trade barriers, transport and communications costs ended all that. For example, by 1997, about 25 per cent of Unilever's ice-cream production in Europe was sold across borders compared with about 3 per cent in 1990. This consolidation and trade expansion resulted in the closure of many production plants. By producing regionally for local markets, Unilever achieves production scale economies. Unilever ice-cream brands are different in most markets, indicating that market convergence is yet to manifest itself in a major way. Unilever recognizes this diversity in international markets but attempts to balance local and global demands primarily through the astute management of its brands (Exhibit 1.3).

═══════ **Exhibit 1.3** ═══════

World of many markets – Unilever succeeds by balancing local and global demands

Unilever is one of the world's largest consumer goods businesses with more than 1,000 strong and successful world wide brands. The company's total sales make it one of the top industrial companies in the world. Sir Michael Perry has been chairman of Unilever PLC since May 1992. His career has been filled with geographical and product diversity. Well-known writer and broadcaster Professor Alan Watson met with Sir Michael to discuss Unilever's success as a multinational company as well as its future marketing obstacles and opportunities.

WATSON: Does the future lie with the multinational or with smaller, speedier businesses with simpler lines of control?

PERRY: To survive as a multinational in the future one has to be much more agile. Agility particularly has to do with local strengths. We consider ourselves to be a local company everywhere – that is the definition of Unilever's competitive advantage. Over the past 60 or 70 years, we have built strong local businesses, with strong local management, owning their own marketplaces and dominating them with strong brands, leaders in each of their category fields. It is that which gives us our strength.

WATSON: There always has been in Unilever a balance between the central direction and local initiative. How has that balance been altered by the information technology revolution?

PERRY: Information technology has not altered our belief that decisions should be taken as close as possible to the consumer. The task of the Unilever centre, however, is to enable the local decision maker to make better, higher-quality decisions. That sort of 'push–pull' between the centre and the periphery has become much more multi-directional and much more frequent as a result of information technology.

WATSON: Is that 'push–pull' between centre and periphery vital to Unilever's competitive advantage?

PERRY: Yes, speed of response now is something that has to be looked at globally, not just locally. Competitive pressure means that our strategic moves in continent A must be understood in continent B. To that extent, there is more central direction strategically than there was, but none of this must get in the way of recognising that preference is very local.

WATSON: In the future, will Unilever be confronted in each sector by other transnational global competitors?

PERRY: It is likely that the major international companies will increase in size and scope, disproportionately. But it is also true that one ignores strong local players at one's peril.

WATSON: Looking to the next century, do you see other technologies, other approaches beginning to stand alongside television advertising as a way of getting your brand across?

PERRY: Every piece of new technology, the Internet for example, will, in the end, be used quite differently from the way in which its proponents first imagined. The important thing is to understand what is in it for consumers. We are by no means convinced that some of the direct selling into homes, through television, personal computers and so on, will go the way that is predicted.

WATSON: Identifying core competencies of business increasingly is seen as the glue that holds the whole business together. What would you say are the core competencies of Unilever?

PERRY: Clearly our internationality is one. Another is our unchallenged reputation for strong, ethical business principles. Our personnel training process is second to none. But above all, our brands.

Source: adapted from 'Outlook 1996', *Andersen Consulting Magazine*, pp. 31–2.

Access to intangible resources

Different countries have different competitive strengths. Germany excels in sophisticated engineering industries and chemicals, Japan in electronics and miniaturization, United States in computers and the cinema and the British in books, theatre and television drama programmes (Porter, 1986). Local roots appear to be important; a German company does not necessarily become better at engineering if it globalizes. Three reasons are cited for the benefits of being local: the abilities to cultivate good suppliers, to recruit good workers and to respond daily to challenging competitors, facing the same customers and markets. Areas and regions which immediately fit this description are the Prato region of northern Italy for design and fashion, Silicon Valley in California for computers and the Valencia area in Spain for ceramics. For example, there are roughly 150 packaging machinery firms in the Bologna area of Italy, there are about 100 firms in the Sassuolo area which produce about 35 per cent of the world's ceramic tile output and two towns, Arezzo and Valenza

Po, account for a combined total of more than \$2 billion in precious metal jewelry exports each year (Enright, 1995, p. 4). The resources which form the basis of the economic strength of these regions are immobile and the skills and competitive advantages are intimately bound to the local culture and are not easily copied.

Influence on the international firm

Arising out of the globalization debate there are two important sets of factors which influence the performance of the international firm. First are the geopolitical influences which refer to technology advances, the emergence of new markets and the market orientation of the former Soviet Bloc of countries. These geopolitical forces are now all pervasive. Open markets and liberalization of industry and trade have fostered innovation and technological advances in western-style economies. The increased wealth and improved human development conditions associated with these new technologies have encouraged former socialist and less developed countries to seek to share these benefits. Second are the international trade and investment influences which refer to the liberalization of international markets, the integration of regional markets throughout the world and the growth in foreign direct investment (Figure 1.3).

According to research carried out by Morgan Stanley, only five countries have 10 or more companies which possess a global competitive advantage. According to this research there are 125 such companies in the US, 21 in the UK, 19 in Japan, 12 in France, and 10 in Germany. There are many countries which have only one such company and most countries have none (Table 1.2)

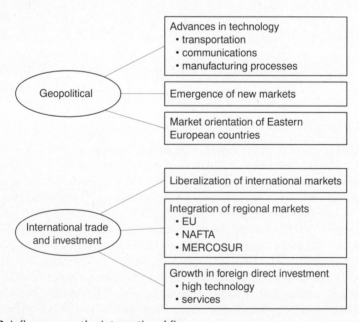

Figure 1.3 Influences on the international firm

Table 1.2 Companies with a global competitive advantage

Countries	Number of companies
US	125
UK	21
Japan	19
France	12
Germany	10
Netherlands	7
Canada, Switzerland	6
Sweden, Finland, Brazil	3
China, Korea, Hong Kong, Italy, Australia	2
Denmark, Belgium, Ireland, Spain, South Africa, Chile, Indonesia, Thailand, Malaysia, Singapore, India, Taiwan	1

Source: *The Competitive Edge*, Morgan Stanley, 25 October 1996 (and updates through 15 July 1997).

Strategic thinking in international marketing

Markets are continually fragmenting and companies face the task of consolidating them. It is difficult to deal with markets which are highly fragmented but the nature of the innovation and expansion processes of firms necessarily involves fragmentation. The development of new product markets introduces fragmentation into existing stable markets. When the firm decides to expand abroad into new international markets it usually discovers that the markets for its products and services are fragmented. At the other end of the product life cycle when markets have reached maturity, innovation is again necessary. Mature markets are typified by numerous product extensions and a break-up of traditional product markets. These three factors tend to introduce fragmentation into markets. Faced with such circumstances firms attempt to develop new product-market strategies, new business strategies and new market entry strategies to consolidate markets again, and so the process continues.

The process of market fragmentation followed by consolidation presents firms with growth and development opportunities in the context of foreign product-market development. Market fragmentation is caused by low entry costs and high exit costs, no experience curve effect, atypical cost structures and government interference in the market. Persistent differences in consumer tastes, differences in culture and language and variation in technical standards also contribute (Figure 1.4). Consolidation of markets is achieved when low-cost, standardized products are introduced, marketing expenditures are systematically raised, a spate of acquisitions occurs and large capital investments raise the minimum scale to be efficient. Other factors which promote the consolidation of markets are attempts by companies to rationalize production capacity across a number of

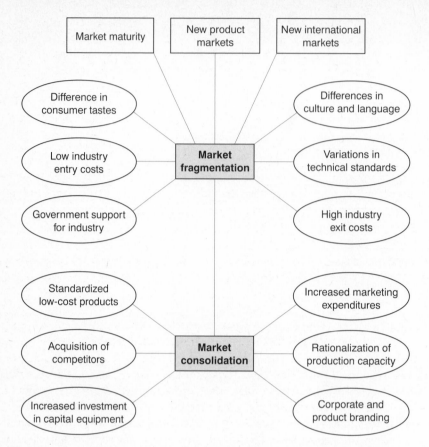

Figure 1.4 Causes of market fragmentation and forces for consolidation

markets and increases in investment in knowledge to raise labour productivity. The consumer electronics business in Europe had been very fragmented. In recent years there has been an attempt, principally by Philips, to consolidate the market to compete with the Japanese. The growth of the firm in international markets is conditioned by these factors.

With regard to the corporate context of international marketing the key issues for management include the direction and behaviour of competitors in domestic and international markets, the needs and wants of customers and how to gain sustainable competitive advantage in those markets in which the company decides to operate. For the firm in international markets the strategic thinking menu consists of carrying out an analysis of the industry or industries in which they compete, determining the best sources for components, raw materials and other resources, identifying and specifying their competitive advantage and analysing the strengths and weaknesses of competitors. The firm must then determine an appropriate competitive position in each of its markets, evaluate the strategic alternatives open to it and specify a set of operational and concrete courses of action.

Firms in different parts of the world respond to different value systems. Even within a country the corporate culture of firms influences the approach to strategic thinking. In particular the time horizon of market investments differ. Not all firms emphasize quarterly earnings which can sacrifice their future well-being for the present. Many firms confuse strategic control of operations with tactical control. Diffused and unfocused strategic control which must percolate through unwieldy hierarchies inhibits initiative and frustrates decision making. In such circumstances strategic control can easily turn to tactical control. Strategic strength derives from organizational consensus whereby the corporate culture of the firm encourages a thorough understanding throughout the company of its mission, thereby making close tactical control unnecessary.

Marketing orientation for the international firm

Marketing means starting with customer needs to focus the firm's resources on these needs to serve them at a profit. Profit, profit growth and cash flow are normally the objectives of the firm, not just sales. A marketing orientation helps to define the firm's business since marketing is concerned with problem solving and customer benefits. Customers face problems and seek solutions in products and services which are of value to them. A marketing orientation also means matching the firm's resources with the needs of the market (Figure 1.5). The marketing function identifies and manages the area of overlap between the firm's resources and market and customer needs to ensure that the customer obtains the product and service benefits desired when and where wanted at an acceptable price while producing a profit for the firm.

It is important, especially in regard to international markets, to recognize that needs and wants are not the same thing. Needs are often universal but the means of satisfying them are frequently parochial. Wants reflect the customer's education, culture and personality. The housekeeper may need the carpets cleaned but may or may not want an Electrolux to do the job. Depending on the country and circumstances there may not even be carpets to clean, other forms of floor covering being more common. It is important, therefore, that the firm closely examines the potential match between what it can provide

Figure 1.5 Matching the firm's resources with market requirements

and customer needs and wants while recognizing that international markets are highly variable. In some circumstances there will not be a match between the two and so it may be better not to attempt to serve those markets. Sometimes it is sufficient to develop a different marketing mix or strategy customized for the new international market.

A standardized approach to the domestic market is frequently adequate because buyers and conditions may be relatively homogeneous. To succeed in international markets it is necessary to develop multidimensional strategies. It is usually myopic to consider exporting as the only or primary way of entering foreign markets. By ignoring licensing, joint ventures and direct investment as ways of entering foreign markets, many firms effectively limit their international strategic options to those markets which are best served by exporting. Increasingly, however, other foreign market entry modes are being used. Foreign direct investment and equity joint ventures, licensing and other alliances are now quite common.

Strategic marketing process

Irrespective of focus, domestic or international or both, the modern firm must adopt a value orientation in its marketing activities. This means providing value to customers, communicating and delivering the value, having first identified the values desired by society and having decided which values to provide and which markets to serve (Figure 1.6). In international markets the tasks of identifying customer values require a sophisticated understanding of many influences, especially those which are culture related. Similarly, the task of communicating the values provided and their delivery in international markets is a complex task requiring a great deal of understanding of the environment and its determinants. There are a number of preconditions for successful marketing in the international firm, which means recognizing that marketing exchanges are characterized by the convergence of the company's marketing process and the customer's purchase decision process. In this context it is important to recall that a market is the total of the actual and potential buyers of a product, service or idea, and that marketing is about understanding the behaviour of people and firms on the buying and selling sides of the equation. Also implied is the expectation that marketing deals with existing and potential products and services.

The firm must, therefore, be outward looking. It must attempt to understand its own strengths and limitations in a world of customers with different needs and wants and in a world of competition from other firms located in the domestic market and, increasingly, abroad.

While most successful international firms attempt to operate in the context of strategies developed for international markets, some will also successfully exploit opportunistic markets. In working in opportunistic markets successful firms attempt to avoid opportunistic cost traps, which usually involve providing customized capacity, high front end design and engineering costs to obtain the first order, the opportunity cost of unsuccessful bidding and the opportunity cost of resources devoted to opportunistic business. Firms operating in such markets avoid opportunistic cost traps by setting conser-

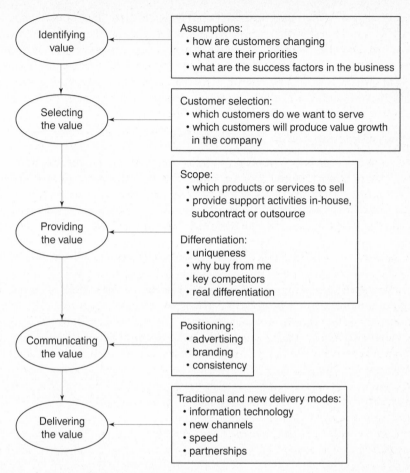

Figure 1.6 Value orientation in marketing
Source: adapted from Bradley, F. (1995), *Marketing Management: Providing, Communicating and Delivering Value*, London: Prentice Hall.

vative capacity levels for such business, separating core markets both organizationally and procedurally and implementing tight screening processes throughout.

Summarizing, the meaning of strategy for the international firm refers to an integrated set of actions taking account of the firm's resources, aimed at increasing the long-term well-being of the firm through securing a sustainable advantage with respect to its competition in serving customer needs in domestic and international markets. The key words in this definition of strategy are as follows: integrated; actions; sustainable; competition. Within this approach to describing strategy, marketing mix strategy refers to the development of specific marketing mixes geared to the unique characteristics of selected target markets to achieve marketing objectives.

Performance and growth of the firm

Ways of improving the marketing performance of the firm and growth in the firm over time are factors closely monitored by management. The more important dimensions and meaning of growth in the context of international markets are, therefore, key considerations for the profitable expansion of the firm in international markets.

Improving marketing performance in the firm

The international firm has a number of choices available as it attempts to improve marketing performance (Figure 1.7). First, it may adapt existing products or develop new products. Second, it may develop new markets. Third, it may decide on a combination strategy of new products for new markets. In examining these issues firms sometimes fail to recognize that they must make another set of decisions which are central to success in international marketing: on the modes of entry to international markets. There are many ways of entering international markets but for our purposes it is sufficient to consider three broad sets of circumstances: those where licensing or joint ventures are appropriate; those where exporting is appropriate; those where foreign direct investment, acquisitions or mergers are appropriate. The mode of entry decision reflects the level of commitment to and investment by the firm in international markets, as moving from licensing to foreign direct investment means a much greater investment in the market. The international firm may improve its marketing performance, therefore, by considering options

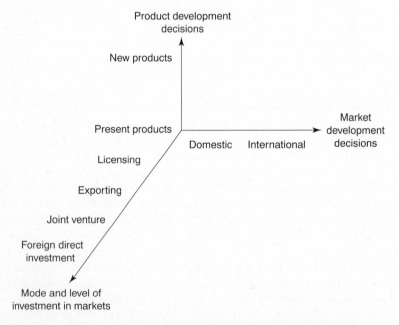

Figure 1.7 Product-market mode of entry decision for the international firm

regarding product development, marketing development and the means of entering new markets (Figure 1.7).

The firm in international markets attempts to improve performance through decisions on any of the above three dimensions, i.e. product, market and mode of market entry but improved performance means finding ways of achieving improved sales or improved profits or a combination of both (Figure 1.8). Four distinct ways of obtaining sales growth have been identified: market penetration; product development; market development; forward integration in the market. Market penetration would mean selling more products to existing customers in the domestic market. This may be difficult where the firm is already strong or where there are entrenched competitors with very large market shares. An aggressive strategy would be to take shares from competitors by attracting away their better customers. The nature of the industry may make it difficult for the firm to discourage competitors by raising the stakes. Big-brand companies frequently raise advertising stakes or use pre-emptive pricing and announcements of capacity additions to discourage competitors. With regard to new product development a firm might use its own people or consultants. Alternatively, it could license or joint venture from overseas where appropriate.

Market development strategies might mean identifying new segments not yet properly served in the domestic market or segments in nearby markets. Market integration would probably mean marketing agreements, taking over distributors or retail outlets, which may or may not be feasible. Very often successful international firms start by selling through agents, subsequently taking an equity position in those agents and, later still, acquiring the agency and its customer base to give the firm a strong competitive presence in the market. Firms sometimes integrate forward into the market by acquiring manufacturers who would assemble or produce locally.

The second way of improving marketing performance would be to improve profitability, which would mean increasing yield, reducing costs, integrating suppliers, reducing investment intensity or focusing on key segments (Figure 1.8). Yield increases may come about through an improvement in the sales mix, e.g. pushing the high-margin lines, increasing price or reducing margin. This last approach may not be possible for smaller, weaker firms in a highly competitive and fragmented market; many would, however, have room for manoeuvre with regard to the mix of items they sell. At the other extreme the firm may decide to rationalize its product line and to rationalize segments of the market served or distribution. Selective distribution and a clear customer focus in foreign markets may be an attractive option for some firms.

Clearly, any firm may pursue a number of the strategies outlined and it is important that those selected serve to promote the well-being of the company overall. In deciding the best way forward, the firm is constrained by the market, by growth in the market and by its competitors.

Successful companies invest in the market but they also invest in people to ensure that they are capable of managing in different cultures and under different political regimes. They must also invest heavily in adapting their products and services and in developing products and services specifically for international markets (Figure 1.9). Investing in people, products and markets allows the firm to strategically differentiate itself from its

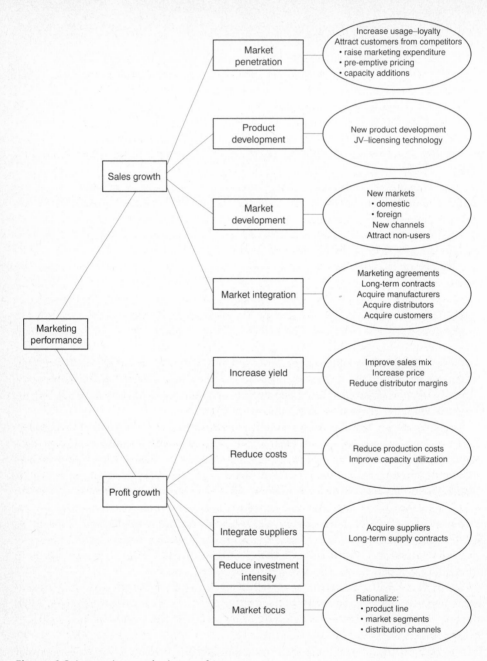

Figure 1.8 Improving marketing performance

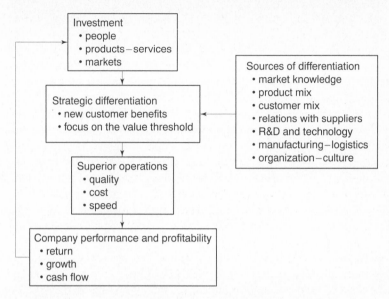

Figure 1.9 Company performance is related to strategic differentiation

competitors. Only by differentiating itself will the company succeed in international markets. Even successful commodity traders attempt to differentiate themselves by being different in some element of the marketing mix. Strategic differentiation means providing new customer benefits and focusing on customer value.

Company performance is related to strategic differentiation of customer benefits and the provision of value. Sources of differentiation include market knowledge, the product and customer mix and the relationships within the organization and with suppliers. By differentiating the product or service the company increases the value of its operations and, hence, improves performance which in turn leads to greater investment in the company, thereby allowing further differentiation.

Dynamics of the international firm

By slowly deepening its involvement in international markets the firm learns from mistakes and successes so that it can control its continued growth through internationalization. Learning by exporting means that the firm becomes familiar with the demand conditions in the eventual host country: the selling methods, distribution system or mode of transfer of products and services. By agency representation, the firm learns how to do business with a host country organization. Agencies also allow the firm to cope with legal and cultural constraints. In a sales subsidiary the firm learns how to control a foreign firm in the host country. It begins to coordinate its policies with the home firm and thereby obtains the experience of management at a distance. Only then does the internationalizing firm have to cope with the problem of organizing foreign production through foreign direct investment.

Many international firms shift slowly to foreign direct investment after first establishing a sales branch abroad, which in turn commonly precedes the establishment of a contractual relationship with a foreign sales agent. Agency contracts are frequently unsatisfactory, containing vague and difficult to enforce performance criteria. Attempts to support these by attempting to specify quantitative budgets for travelling, advertising, engineering and support, as well as certain inventory levels in the agent's premises, often prove unsatisfactory.

The transition from agency to branch sales office is facilitated by the manufacturer's gradual accumulation of information about the foreign market, acquired through monitoring its foreign agents and by expansion in sales volumes to levels which would support a facility of minimum economic size. The establishment of a sales branch also demonstrates to customers a more solid commitment on the part of the manufacturer to support the market in question.

Often triggered by the failure or termination of an agency, the establishment of a foreign sales subsidiary subsequently becomes the platform upon which a manufacturing investment may be made (Chandler, 1977, p. 369). Looking at the cost side of the equation the transition to manufacturing, however, depends on the relationship of production costs abroad to production costs at home in addition to tariffs and transportation, as well as control considerations.

The foreign direct investment process is stimulated by more than just economic incentives. An initiating force which galvanizes the firm into action is often required. The presence of a sales office also assists information collection and a better understanding of the market opportunities, thereby significantly lowering perceptions of uncertainty and raising the probability that the firm will engage in foreign direct investment if the underlying cost conditions permit.

Foreign direct investment stems from the possession by a firm of a competitive advantage or of certain unique assets. The ability to develop and protect the profits associated with these assets often requires the extension of some kind of control structure over productive assets which are distributed internationally. The implications of such control for the location of manufacturing facilities and the marketing of its output vary from time to time and may be unique to the firm in question.

Market innovation and profit growth

As noted in a preceding section, one of the principal determinants of market and sales growth is the extent to which the firm is able to diversify into new products and new markets. Many successful international firms are multiproduct organizations managing a portfolio of products for a variety of international markets. Any new product introduction must contain an innovation as perceived from the customer's viewpoint, and these customers are located in domestic and international markets. For successful innovations, sales of new products tend to rise quite rapidly since the firm meets customer needs competitively. In such circumstances the firm is rewarded with a valuable share of the product market and the successful introduction becomes a regular line within the firm.

Alternatively, sales growth may be achieved through market diversification. Such products follow the normal expected pattern of the life cycle framework. Eventually market share and growth will tend to stabilize, primarily because of imitation and greater competitive pressures. Afterwards, sales tend to grow only as fast as the overall market. The life cycle framework shows such sales growth as continuing but at a lower rate once market share has stabilized. Alternatively, for products which do not contain any significant innovation or are not perceived as innovative by customers, sales will initially rise as customers try the product and as a result of promotional efforts at the launch stage, but then fall off rapidly as potential customers become aware that the product is not sufficiently competitive or attractive. Such products are failures. In order to grow faster than the rate of growth in the market as a whole the firm must carry out further successful diversification. Sales growth is, therefore, related to the role of successful diversification achieved, whether this diversification is achieved through product or market diversification as was seen above. Given the preceding argument this relationship obtains even if the diversification results from objectives other than growth, e.g. the exploitation of higher profits in new foreign markets and the need to diversify into new foreign markets in order to provide more security against deterioration of business conditions in the domestic market.

The costs of company growth

The international expansion of the firm is not, however, costless. We recognize that significant costs are associated with successful diversification and these expansion costs reduce the firm's rate of return on capital. These factors are dominant in seeking growth through product or market diversification. First, larger expenditure on promotion generally results in a higher growth rate for a firm by making an increase in diversification more successful than otherwise. Second, greater expenditures on new product development would, by making products more appropriate and reliable, have a similar effect. Third, lowering price below that of other firms would normally also enhance growth by attracting more customers. These are costs of expansion and if they are regarded as capital costs then they result in a higher capital–output ratio. If they are regarded as current costs they result in a lower profit margin.

Fourth, there are limits to the organizational and decision-making capacity of managers. If managers attempt to carry out a high rate of diversification then fewer management resources can be devoted to each, which will result in the technical, financial, marketing and development aspects of each being less well researched or implemented so that the proportion of product-market failures may increase. When this occurs there will be excess capacity in the firm, thus raising the capital–output ratio. Recruiting new managers at a faster rate does not solve the problem since the additional managers lower the managerial efficiency of the firm. In such circumstances the rate of return on capital associated with faster diversification is lower.

Summary

This chapter examines the performance and growth of the firm as it diversifies into new international markets with particular emphasis on the role of competitive marketing strategies. In seeking to improve performance the firm must consider its options with regard to the development of products and markets and modes of entry to new markets in order to improve sales and/or profits. In attempting to improve the growth in sales the firm can pursue one or a combination of the following strategies: market penetration; product development; market integration to increase profits or reduce costs.

An important determinant of market and sales growth is the firm's capacity to diversify into new products and markets. Growth in a firm is essentially the creation of an internal market where none previously existed. This internalization by means of backward or forward integration or joint ventures or licensing gives the firm greater control of the market for inputs and services and reduces uncertainty. Costs of this process, however, include higher communication expenses and the need for skilled management. Firms internationalize to overcome competition and to exploit their competitive advantages in new markets. In order to succeed they must adopt multidimensional competitive strategies more suited to the complexities of the international marketing environment.

Innovative firms, having penetrated the domestic market, are keen to exploit their leads in foreign markets. Initially, this may be done through exporting. As demand grows in foreign markets the firm may increase its commitment progressively by moving through the spectrum of foreign sales subsidiaries, joint ventures or direct investments. In order to survive, however, firms must continue to innovate. Firms internationalizing through the use of a strong brand name must be aware that, while brand names endure, the ability to command a premium erodes over time.

With regard to strategy, most international firms operate with customized international strategies. The key issue for the firm is the gaining and retention of competitive advantage in the markets in which it operates. The firm must focus its strategic marketing efforts internationally on achieving the greatest possible match between its marketing efforts and customer requirements. To accomplish this it is necessary to focus closely on the customer and competitors.

Discussion questions

1. The improvement of marketing performance in the international firm can be visualized in terms of product decisions, market investment decisions and market development decisions. Discuss.

2. Explain the importance of research and development and innovation as determining factors in the choice of international market entry mode.

3. The predominance of large multiproduct firms in international markets suggests that there may not be any limit to the size of the firm. Would you agree?

4. What are the principal factors to consider when examining the growth of the firm through internationalization? Refer to market inefficiencies in your answer.

5. Identify and describe the nature of assets transferred in international marketing. What are the key characteristics of these assets and how do they affect their mode of transfer between one country and another?

6. Many factors affect the environment facing the international firm. Identify and describe the more important of these. How does the international firm cope with its environment?

7. What is the meaning of globalization for marketing and what are the principal arguments for and against it?

References

Boddewyn, J. J. (1981) 'Comparative marketing: the first twenty-five years', *Journal of International Business Studies*, **12** (1), 61–79.

Buckley, P. (1987) *The Theory of the Multinational Firm*, Acta Universitatis Upsaliensis, **26**, 64.

Chandler, A. (1977) *The Visible Hand*, Cambridge, MA: Harvard University Press.

Caves, R. E. (1996) *Multinational Enterprise and Economic Analysis*, 2nd edn, Cambridge: Cambridge University Press.

Craig, C. S., Douglas, S. P. and Grein, A. (1992) 'Patterns of convergence and divergence among industrialized nations: 1960–1988', *Journal of International Business Studies*, **23** (4), 773–87.

Douglas S. P. and Wind, Y. (1987) 'The myth of globalization', *Columbia Journal of World Business*, **22** (4), 19–29.

Enright, M. J. (1995) 'Creating national and regional strategies for competitive advantage', *The Island of Ireland Conference*, Irish Management Institute, Dublin, 13 December.

Hymer, S. (1970) 'The efficiency (contradictions) of multinational corporations', *American Economic Review*, **60**, 441–8.

Killing, P. J. (1982) 'Technology acquisition: license agreement or joint venture', *Columbia Journal of World Business*, **15** (3), 38–46.

Leeflang, P. S. H. and van Raaij, W. F. (1995) 'The changing consumer in the European Union; a "meta-analysis"', *International Journal of Research in Marketing*, **12**, 373–87.

Levitt, T. (1983) 'The globalization of markets', *Harvard Business Review*, **61** (May–June), 92–102.

Ohmae, K. (1989) 'Managing in a borderless world', *Harvard Business Review*, **67** (May–June), 152–61.

Ohmae, K. (1990) *The Borderless World*, New York, NY: Harper Business.

Porter, M. E. (1986) 'Changing patterns of international competition', *California Management Review*, **2**, 9–37.

Solberg, C. A. (1997) 'A framework for analysis of strategy development in globalizing markets', *Journal of International Marketing*, **5** (1), 9–30.

Teece, D. (1986) 'Firm boundaries, technological innovation and strategic management', in L. G. Thomas III (ed.), *The Economics of Strategic Planning: Essays in Honor of Joel Dean*, Lexington, MA: Lexington Books, pp. 197–9.

Vernon, R. and Wells, L. T. (1976) *Manager in the International Economy*, 3rd edn, Englewood Cliffs, NJ: Prentice Hall.

Wenke, M. (1994) 'Den typischen Euro-Verbraucher wird es auch auf absehbare Zeit nicht geben', *Handelsblatt*, **46** (7 March), 17.

Yip, G. S. (1992) *Total Global Strategy*, Englewood Cliffs, NJ: Prentice Hall.

2

Theories of the firm in international markets

To understand the role of international marketing in the firm it is necessary to consider decisions being made as part of a continuum and not as discrete components corresponding to the various modalities used to transfer assets internationally. It is limiting, therefore, to treat exporting behaviour as something very different from licensing, joint ventures or foreign direct investment through the establishment of an international firm. The literature is deficient in this regard since it is divided between that dealing with exporting decisions and that dealing with other modalities. This division of the literature is a reflection of the 'production–selling' versus 'marketing' syndrome evident among managers and scholars. A 'marketing' approach, as proposed here, is more comprehensive as it integrates all the international exchange modalities, as opposed to the 'production–selling' approach associated with separation of decisions into exporting and other exchange transaction modalities.

Recent interest in international marketing

Two sets of factors are thought to contribute to the recent interest in the discipline: the curriculum in business schools and the contributions made in the field of strategy. As a consequence of the first, there are now many textbooks with 'international marketing' in the title and many editors of established journals prepared to give more space to the subject. Indeed, interest has been so intense that journals devoted entirely to the subject have appeared.

Theory and practice in international marketing

Managers and firms have for a long time given explicit attention to the international marketing dimension of business and have recognized it as a separate field with regard to strategy formulation and the structural requirements resulting from internationalization. Academics have until recently ignored it as a field of study. A reason for the neglect according to Robock and Simmonds (1988) arises from the fact that earlier theories and generalizations, developed in response to the requirements of such large domestically oriented markets as that of the United States, were neither general nor universal. In contrast to purely domestic operations, marketing activities which take place across national boundaries require considerable familiarity with multiple marketing environments, international exchange rate determination and the various geopolitical pressures which affect the firm. The nature and significance of international marketing may be judged in the context of additional risk, conflict, environmental adjustments and the influences of socioeconomic change (Bradley, 1987).

Regarding the second set of factors alluded to above, the recent literature on strategy is of considerable importance (Chandler, 1977; Lawrence and Dyer, 1983; Porter, 1980; Prahalad and Doz, 1987; Yip, 1992). These authors have focused interest on examining the firm within its environment, its industry, technology, marketing and competitive positions and the role of government and public policy, dimensions which have a very powerful impact as the firm internationalizes.

Much of the literature on strategy has, however, ignored the marketing dimension. Because of the dependence by some scholars and managers on the simple matrix of some measure of firm advantage against a selected strategic customer group, Wind and Robertson (1983) argue that the outcomes ignore the fact that all markets are heterogeneous and thus a non-segmented strategy is inevitably suboptimal. A strategy for international marketing which assumes a non-differentiated approach is prevalent in this literature (Bartels, 1968; Buzzell, 1968; Levitt, 1983). These authors have argued that markets are global and that marketing strategies should also be global and, therefore, standardized and non-differentiated.

The underlying issues associated with these different views of the world stem from very different and somewhat myopic perspectives due to the origin of the work. While the recent thinking on strategy is very useful there is, nevertheless, a tendency to see problems as two dimensional, whereas by right they are multidimensional. The 'matrix models' have been weakest in predicting outcomes in complex, turbulent environments which characterize international marketing.

Trade theories of the firm in international markets

In this section we examine a number of theories which attempt to explain international business patterns. These patterns include the worldwide flow of imports and exports, the pattern of joint ventures and licensing arrangements and the location and direction of overseas investment.

Absolute advantage and the international firm

This theory is used as a framework for understanding and predicting international business patterns where trade between independent buyers and sellers in different countries is the predominant form of internation transactions. For economists, trade between countries arises because of the possession of an absolute or comparative advantage in the basis for trade. This explains trade between two countries, the first with an absolute advantage in the production of one product and the second in the production of a different product. Absolute advantage, the trade theory developed by Adam Smith, the eighteenth-century British economist, may arise because of differences in factors such as climate, quality of land, natural resource endowments, labour, capital, technology or entrepreneurship. According to this theory it is sensible for each country to specialize in the product in which it has an absolute advantage and to secure its needs of the products in which it has a disadvantage through foreign trade. The extent of benefit from specialization and trade will depend, of course, on the prices at which trading takes place. This brings in the concept of 'opportunity cost', meaning what a country will have to give up of one product in order to secure another. Like other trade theories this one assumes that a regime of 'free and fair' trade exists between countries, something much in dispute.

Comparative advantage and the international firm

If a country possesses an absolute advantage in the two products traded, however, there may not be any trade since the country with the absolute advantage in producing both products has nothing to gain. An alternative explanation may be sought in the possession of comparative advantage, the trade theory associated most closely with David Ricardo, the nineteenth-century British economist. With this theory, a country may have an absolute advantage in producing both products but, as long as the weaker country has a comparative advantage in the production of one of the products, trade will occur.

Consider two countries, Country A and Country B, with wine and soft drinks being the two products that these countries produce. The assumed output from one labour hour input for the two products in each country is shown in Table 2.1. Note that Country A has an absolute advantage in the production of both products, but comparative advantage lies predominantly in soft drinks. Country B has a comparative advantage in wine.

A company in Country A can only get 20 bottles of wine for 40 bottles of soft drinks at home. If the company brought the 40 bottles of soft drinks to Country B it could exchange them there for 27 bottles of wine (ratio of exchange in Country B is 1.5 bottles of soft drink = 1 wine ($40 \div 1.5 = 27$). The company would then take the 27 bottles of wine back to Country A and realize a profit equal to 7 bottles of wine.

If the Country B firm ships wine to Country A it would receive 32 soft drinks for it

Table 2.1 Absolute and comparative advantage contrasted – hypothetical example

Product group	Production per one hour labour	
	Country A	Country B
Wine	20	16
Soft drinks	40	24

(40 ÷ 20 = 2; 2 × 16 = 32) (compared with 24 at home). On return, the firm's profit would amount to 8 bottles of soft drinks. Both countries benefit, even though Country A can produce both products more efficiently.

Exchange rates and trade theory

It is necessary to introduce exchange rates to show that real cost differences in comparative advantage actually translate into monetary price differences (as was the basis for our simple trade model above). Assume that wage rates in Country B are 5 marks per hour and $10 per hour in Country A. Then, using the information in Table 2.1 it is possible to derive the cost of producing wine and soft drinks in both countries (Table 2.2).

Note again that the relative prices of the two products differ between countries. However, what about absolute prices? To see the effect of these we must introduce exchange rates. Assume that the $ exchanges for the mark at the exchange rate of $1 = 1.50 marks or 1 mark = $0.67. At the start of trade Country A soft drinks exporters would realize about $0.32 (0.21 marks × 1.50 = $0.32) from every bottle of soft drinks exported to Country B at a profit of $0.07 per bottle. Country B wine exporters would receive 0.33 marks ($0.50 ÷ 1.50 = 0.33 marks), thereby realizing a profit of 0.02 marks per bottle. At that exchange rate trade would occur just as shown under the barter situation above. Trade will continue until prices are equalized.

Suppose mark ÷ $ = $1.15, i.e. a considerable hardening of the mark or depreciation of the $; then at the start of trade Country A soft drink exporters would realize about $0.24 from every bottle exported (0.21 marks × 1.15 = $0.24) – a loss of $0.01 per bottle. However, the Country B exporter makes a relatively large profit – receiving 0.43 marks per bottle of wine exported ($0.50 ÷ 1.15 = 0.43 marks) and realizes a profit equal to 0.43 marks – 0.31 marks = 0.12 marks. There is unlikely to be any two-way trade for $ exchange rates greater than 1.61 marks or less than 1.19 marks. The lower limit break-even exchange rate is $1 = 1.19 marks (i.e. $0.21 × 1.19 = $0.25 = domestic price).

If trade is limited to wine and soft drinks then the $ value of Country A's soft drink exports must equal the $ value of Country A's imports and similarly for Country B in marks. This can only occur at exchange rates between the limits $1.00 = 1.19 marks and $1.00 = 1.61 marks, rates at which traders in both countries find it profitable to do business.

The comparative advantage concept, especially with exchange rates incorporated, is the less restrictive and more general. It also serves the useful purpose of demonstrating the

Table 2.2 Cost of production: wine and soft drinks compared – hypothetical example

| | Cost per bottle | |
	Country A $	Country B marks
Wine	0.50	0.31
Soft drinks	0.25	0.21

importance of exchange rate movements to the marketing strategies of the firm in inter-national markets. An adverse movement in exchange rates could easily wipe out the benefits of an otherwise excellent international marketing programme. Trade theories provide a first approximation of what might exist in a theoretical world but with government interference and changing political agencies they are unlikely to be found in practice. The comparative advantage concept, in particular, leads to a good first approximation in regard to exchange of goods and services between countries (Exhibit 2.1).

━━━ Exhibit 2.1 ━━━
The miracle of trade

It is mere common sense that if one country is very good at making hats, say, and another is very good at making shoes, then total output can be increased by arranging for the first country to concentrate on making hats and the second on making shoes. Then, through trade in both goods, more of each can be consumed in both places.

That is a tale of absolute advantage, such as Adam Smith might have told. Each country is better than the other at making a certain good, and so profits from specialization and trade. Comparative advantage is different: a country will have it despite being bad at the activity concerned. Indeed, it can have a comparative advantage in making a certain good even if it is worse at making that good than any other country. This is not economic theory, but a straightforward matter of definition: a country has a comparative advantage where its margin of superiority is greater, or its margin of inferiority smaller.

Accordingly, when people say of Africa, or Britain, or wherever, that it has no comparative advantage in anything, they are simply confusing absolute advantage (for which their claim may or may not be true) with comparative advantage (for which it is certainly false). Why does this confusion over terms matter? Because the case for free trade is often thought to depend on the existence of absolute advantage – and is therefore thought to collapse whenever absolute advantage is absent. But economics, thanks to David Ricardo not Adam Smith, shows that gains from trade follow, in fact, from comparative advantage. Since comparative advantage is never absent, this gives the theory far broader scope than most popular critics suppose.

In particular, it shows that even countries which are desperately bad at making everything can expect to gain from international competition. If countries specialise according to their comparative advantage, they can prosper through trade regardless of how inefficient, in absolute terms, they may be in their chosen speciality.

At first sight, this is an implausible, if not to say miraculous, finding. In economics, it stands apart. One distinguished practitioner has even called the principle of comparative advantage the only result in economic theory that is neither trivial nor false. That may be a little hard on the rest of economics, but it does suggest that the principle is worth the small effort required to understand it.

Source: adapted from *Economist*, 27 January 1996, p. 65.

The theory of comparative advantage provides important guidelines in the formulation of a theory appropriate to understanding the firm in international markets. As seen above, trade between countries is beneficial for all countries involved if each specializes in those products for which its factors of production, confined to land, labour and capital, make it, compared with other countries, more efficient. As also seen above, it need not have an absolute advantage in producing any product over all countries; it need only be relatively more efficient in producing some products than others.

Transactions costs in international markets

Since Hymer (1970), the internalization school has emerged which emphasizes the benefits and costs associated with internalizing business activity (Buckley and Casson, 1976; Rugman, 1981). The principal conclusion of this school is that:

> markets will tend to be relatively more efficient than firms in handling transactions between a large number of buyers and sellers. Markets will be at a comparative disadvantage when transactions are subject to a high degree of uncertainty and when they consist of long-term exchanges of complex and heterogeneous products between a relatively small number of traders.   (Buckley and Casson, 1976, pp. 167–8)

In order to provide unambiguous normative criteria useful to management and policy makers, the nature of the transactions which are being internalized must be examined. The unit of analysis is the transaction rather than the firm (Gannon, 1993; Williamson, 1979). A major assumption of this approach is that the purpose of business is to reduce business costs over time. It regards firms, markets and mixed modes as alternative control mechanisms. The selection of one or another mode of market depends on their efficiency properties. Transactions cost economics provides a framework for discriminating between those transactions which need to be internalized and those which do not (Teece, 1986).

Role of transaction costs

Practically every firm, by virtue of its history, possesses some kind of unique asset which is the potential source of a stream of profits to the owner. These assets may consist of a technological, marketing or managerial capability or a natural resource position not fully possessed by other firms.

Suppose that for any reason a firm cannot export; then it must sell its special assets or services – licensing in the case of know-how – to a foreign firm or it must establish a foreign affiliate. Suppose the source of the firm's competitive advantage is its technological know-how. If the regime of appropriability in which the firm operates permits only weak legal enforcement of rights over intellectual property, transactional problems will abound, and alternative control modes are likely to be preferred. (Teece, 1981). Know-how often cannot be codified since it has an important tacit component.

Even when it can, it is not always readily understood by the receiver, and it is extremely difficult to transfer without intimate personal contact involving teaching, demonstration and participation. Even when transaction difficulties are apparent, establishing a foreign subsidiary is an extreme response to the needs of a one-off transfer.

The above arrangements, although expressed in the context of assets which are based on technological know-how, extend to many different kinds of asset which are difficult to trade, e.g. managerial and organizational know-how, goodwill or brand loyalty. These represent types of assets for which markets may falter as effective exchange mechanisms. Accordingly, the existence of high transaction costs is one of the major issues which lies behind foreign direct investment, especially horizontal investment.

Limitations of trade theory and transaction cost explanations

There are a number of limitations in the trade theory interpretation of the firm in international markets, flowing in part from the simplifying assumptions of the model. Some key assumptions are that factors of production, land, labour and capital are immobile between countries, that perfect information exists as to international trade opportunities and that trading firms in different countries are independent entities. Also, the model assumes perfect competition and does not allow for oligopoly or monopoly. It does not explicitly recognize technology, know-how or management and marketing skills as significant factors of production which can be the basis for comparative advantage. Probably the most important limitation of trade theory is that it assumes that traditional importing and exporting is the only way of transferring products and services across borders. It does not recognize that the firm may supply foreign demand through, for example, licensing or foreign production.

It also misses the rationale behind the twentieth-century development of marketing by assuming that products sold in the international marketplace are standard, basic and transferable – wheat, cotton and wine, for example. Efforts are under way, however, by trade theorists to reconstruct international trade theory in order to allow for the implications of the firm in international markets.

The principal deficiency of international trade theory and transaction cost economics explanations is that while they contribute to our understanding of the greater wealth producing potential of countries on efficiency grounds they cannot explain differences in innovation or in the quality of products and services produced in different countries. Trade theory is based on an assumed homogeneity of firms as opposed to the diversity of firms observed (Hunt and Morgan, 1995, p. 5). These authors also argue that transaction cost economics can contribute to explaining firm diversity only by diverging from such neo-classical assumptions as homogeneous demand. In addition there is considerable difficulty in operationalizing transactions costs which limits the contribution of this aspect of the theory (Buckley and Casson, 1976). An alternative theory of competition which explains firm diversity by building on the concepts of comparative advantage and which can be applied to the international arena is required.

Comparative advantage theory of international competition

From the previous discussion there is considerable evidence that the traditional theory of comparative advantage must be modified to allow for significant resource heterogeneity and immobility among firms in an industry and between markets. In this context the firm gains a comparative advantage over other firms by making the best use of heterogeneous resources which are much more sophisticated than the traditional land, labour and capital assumed above. Intangible resources such as organizational culture, knowledge and competencies must also be included. These higher-order, complex resources are most important for modern companies and their countries, as attested to by Hong Kong, Japan and Singapore which have virtually no natural resources (Hunt and Morgan, 1995, p. 8). While these resources are not considered 'natural' endowments they form the most important resources that collectively constitute the competencies of the firm. This section is based on Hunt and Morgan (1995) who list nine premises which provide the basis of the theory of comparative advantage of the firm:

1. industry demand is heterogeneous and dynamic;
2. consumers have imperfect information;
3. people are motivated by constrained self-interest seeking;
4. the firm's primary objective is superior financial performance;
5. markets are never in equilibrium;
6. resources are the tangible and intangible assets which enable the firm to provide efficiently and/or effectively a product or service that is valued by some market or market segment;
7. resources are heterogeneous across firms and imperfectly mobile between firms and countries;
8. the role of management is to recognize and understand current strategies, to create new ones, to select those preferred, to implement or manage the strategies selected and to modify them through time;
9. environmental factors influence the conduct (strategies) and performance (profits) of firms; they do not determine them.

With regard to the first point it should be noted that consumer tastes within a generic product class not only differ greatly but they are always changing. Regarding information, consumers rarely have sufficient information on products or services that might match their tastes and preferences and obtaining such information is often costly in terms of time and money.

As consumers and managers, people are motivated by constrained self-interest seeking – people have two irreducible sources of valuation: pleasure and morality (Etzioni, 1988). People pursue pleasure and avoid pain but they are constrained in their self-interest seeking by considerations of what is right, proper, ethical, moral and appropriate. Different cultures and value systems directly influence the behaviour of consumers and managers in this regard and opportunistic behaviour is not assumed to prevail in all circumstances in different countries and cultures.

The primary objective of the firm is superior financial performance which it pursues under conditions of imperfect information about customers and competitors. Firms seek superior financial performance, which implies a level of financial performance which exceeds its referents, usually its closest competitors, rather than a maximum financial performance because they do not maximize profits because of the lack of information and because morality considerations constrain them from doing so. Superior financial performance is constrained by managers' view of morality, a factor which is highly influenced by culture. From time to time we note, however, that some firms are not constrained by morality considerations, as we see it, especially when they are operating outside their home base. In such circumstances there may be a clash of cultures which give rise to aberrant behaviour in one country.

The concept of long-run equilibrium in marketing is meaningless as markets are never in equilibrium (Dickson, 1992) and activities that produce turmoil in markets have positive benefits because they are the engine of economic growth (Hunt and Morgan, 1995, p. 6).

Firms have access, in varying degrees, to a multitude of potential resources which may be classified as financial, physical, legal (e.g. trademarks and licenses), human, organizational, informational (e.g. consumer and competitor intelligence) and relational (e.g. supplier and customer relationships). These resources are heterogeneous in that every firm possesses an assortment of resources that is in some way unique. Immobility implies that firm resources are not easily traded and so heterogeneity can persist through time despite attempts by firms to acquire the same resources as their successful competitors (Dierickx and Cool, 1989; Peteraf, 1993). When a firm possesses a unique or rare resource it has the potential for producing a comparative advantage for itself (Barney, 1991). According to Hunt and Morgan (1995, p. 7) a comparative advantage in resources exists when a firm's resource assortment enables it to produce a product or service that, relative to existing competitors, is perceived by some market segments to be of superior value and/or can be produced at lower cost. Comparative advantage translates into a competitive advantage if the resource cost–customer value ratio is better than that obtained by competitors. A comparative advantage in resources can translate into a position of competitive advantage in the marketplace and superior financial performance, but not necessarily.

Using the above resource cost – resource value framework Hunt and Morgan (1995) derive nine possible competitive positions (Figure 2.1). Ideally the firm would prefer to be in cell 3 where its comparative advantage in resources provides superior value at lower cost. The positions identified as cells 2 and 6 also give rise to competitive advantage and superior financial performance whereas cell 5, the parity position, provides average returns.

Firms in cells 1 and 9, although having a comparative advantage in either value or cost, may or may not have superior returns – it depends on circumstances and the competitive position is indeterminate. In cell 1 the advantage of lower relative resource cost may result from a sacrifice in relative value for consumers and so prices will generally be lower. Depending on the extent to which the discounts are less than, equal to or greater than their relative advantages in resource costs, these firms are at positions of competitive

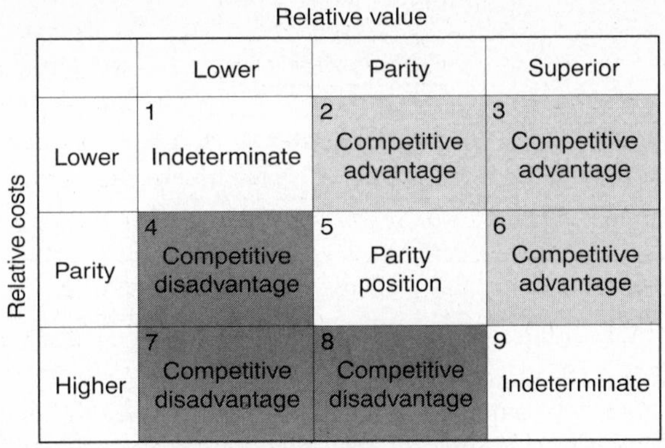

Relative value

	Lower	Parity	Superior
Lower	1 Indeterminate	2 Competitive advantage	3 Competitive advantage
Parity	4 Competitive disadvantage	5 Parity position	6 Competitive advantage
Higher	7 Competitive disadvantage	8 Competitive disadvantage	9 Indeterminate

Relative costs

Figure 2.1 Determining competitive position for the firm.
Source: adapted from Hunt, S. D. and Morgan, R. M. (1995): 'The competitive advantage theory of competition', *Journal of Marketing*, **59** (April), 7 (Reprinted with permission from the American Marketing Association.)

advantage, parity or competitive disadvantage respectively. The competitive position of firms in cell 9 is also indeterminate as it refers to the situation where the firm provides products or services at superior perceived value but at relatively high resource cost.

If no firm can produce a superior value for some particular market segment and no firm has a cost advantage, implying that all innovation has ceased, then the parity position represented by cell 5 applies. As Hunt and Morgan (1995, p. 7) point out, this is the marketplace situation addressed in part by perfect competition theory in economics but it is a degenerative case which is unlikely to persist in many markets through time.

With regard to the eighth point in the list above it should be noted that strategies that yield a comparative advantage and superior financial performance do so because they rely on those resources in which the firm has a comparative advantage over rivals. Sometimes it is a single resource, such as a trademark, but more usually it is an assortment of resources. For example, country-specific endowments create the environment in which companies are established and learn to compete effectively in certain areas and, as such, affect essential ingredients for achieving competitive success (Porter, 1990). Sustained, superior financial performance occurs, therefore, only when a firm's comparative advantage in resources continues to yield a position of competitive advantage despite the activities of competitors (Hunt and Morgan, 1995, p. 8).

Lastly, because environmental factors are presumed to influence strategy and performance, not to determine them, relative resource heterogeneity and immobility imply that strategic choices must be made and that these choices influence performance. Different resource assortments suggest targeting different market segments and/or competing against different companies, possibly in different country markets. According to Hunt and Morgan (1995) competition consists of a constant struggle among firms for a comparative advantage in resources which will yield a competitive advantage to them in the market and in turn, a superior financial performance (Figure 2.2). The same process produces superior quality in the goods and services in the country, greater efficiency in their production and innovation. Hence, comparative advantage in resources at the

Figure 2.2 Comparative advantage theory of competition
Source: adapted from Hunt, S. D. and Morgan, R. M. (1995) 'The competitive advantage theory of competition', *Journal of Marketing*, **59** (April), 9. (Reprinted with permission from the American Marketing Association.)

company level drives competitive advantage for the company in the market which in turn benefits the company itself and the economy at large.

International marketing theories

Marketing in the late 1980s and 1990s has taken on a strong strategic orientation reflected in a shift in the firm's focus away from the customer and the product to the external environment facing it. It has been argued that, to succeed, the firm must cater for its customers within the context of its environment (Hayes and Abernathy, 1980; Wind and Robertson, 1983). This environmental emphasis is important in the development of an incentive for business to cross national boundaries.

Marketing is the process of identifying and selecting customer values, providing, communicating and delivering ideas, goods and services to create exchanges and relationships that satisfy individual and organizational objectives. These mutually beneficial exchanges apply to single-person companies and to complex international companies and reflect Glazer's (1989) view that marketing is the 'discipline responsible for understanding and coordinating the relations between the organization and its environment'. In doing so, the firm must understand its own strengths and weaknesses, changes in the environment and the broad class of market opportunities that are consistent with the firm's distinctive competence and with current and future environmental conditions. Observing these requirements led Barabba and Zaltman (1991, p. 61) to identify the three fundamental marketing objectives of any firm as follows:

1. to ensure that customers understand the basic concept behind a product;
2. to show customers the relevance of the firm's product to their needs;
3. to remove or reduce barriers to exchanges so that customers can participate in the exchange with minimum effort.

These objectives relate to the competitive advantages possessed by the international firm. They include a consideration of product development, product differentiation, production processes, managerial skills, economies of large-scale production and other

LEEDS METROPOLITAN UNIVERSITY LIBRARY

characteristics of the product, the firm or the industry. It should be remembered that these variables are also found in purely domestic markets. International marketing is a discipline containing a number of paradigms which draw on a number of theories. Theories are operationalized through the decisions taken by managers in dealing with the international environment. Identifying suitable paradigms is important since a paradigm indicates what a discipline should study, what questions it should ask and what rules should be followed in interpreting the answers obtained (Cateora, 1993).

Definitions in international marketing

Many writers have offered different suggestions as to what the discipline of international marketing should study. Cateora (1993) defines international marketing as the performance of business activities that direct the flow of a company's goods and services to consumers or users in more than one nation. For Cateora it is the complexity and diversity found in international marketing operations which distinguishes the discipline. Terpstra (1983) also stresses the complexity of international marketing. Keegan (1989) distinguishes between domestic and global marketing and states that the differences between the two derive entirely from differences in national environments, company organization and strategies in different national markets. For Kahler and Kramer (1977) international marketing is broader and consists of exporting or producing and marketing in more than one country without the goods crossing national borders. This definition begins to recognize the key role of the firm in international marketing.

Fayerweather (1982) recognizes the dominant factor in the international marketing process as the firm: it must be significantly involved in international business having permanent operations in two or more countries. This broad definition refers to marketing associated with business processes intersected in some way by national borders; these processes are identified by Fayerweather as (a) economic transactions, (b) cultural and sociopsychological interactions and (c) political interactions. An important aspect of Fayerweather's view is that the concept 'national borders' should be interpreted flexibly to include the multidimensional nature of internation contact as implied in the three business processes.

The discipline is, therefore, a broad one encompassing many aspects of management. Indeed, for many scholars of international marketing the discipline is perceived so broadly that they do not attempt a definition, claiming by implication that the discipline defies definition. This is poor guidance to scholar and manager alike. As an alternative working definition the following is offered:

> International marketing processes and decisions require the firm to identify needs and wants of customers, to produce assets to give a differential marketing advantage, to communicate information about these assets and to distribute and exchange them internationally through one or a combination of exchange transaction modalities.

The correspondence between this definition of international marketing processes and decisions and well-known definitions of marketing is intended (Ohio State University Marketing Staff, 1965; Sweeney, 1972). Following Carman (1980), this study is called the discipline of international marketing which contains a number of paradigms, each paradigm drawing on a number of theories. Clearly, therefore, international marketing is not a single theory but, rather, a discipline containing a number of theories which when applied become the operating technologies of practitioners engaged in the international marketing process (Carman, 1980).

Search for an international marketing paradigm

There are a number of paradigms in current use in the international marketing which have received attention by researchers in the field. The geobusiness paradigm, most closely associated with research initiated at Uppsala University and the Stockholm School of Economics in particular, but developed and added to by others with widespread affiliation, serves as a useful paradigm in which to understand the literature on international marketing and the decision-making processes adopted by firms attempting to cope with the difficulties of internationalization. These researchers recognize that the individual firm is 'the motive force and that international business patterns are shaped by the adjustments of specific enterprises, operating competitively over a range of national environments to survive and grow' (Robock and Simmonds, 1988, p. 50). These authors propose the geobusiness model which suggests a paradigm based on a set of conditioning, motivation and control variables which allows for most of the decision areas faced by the firm in international markets (Figure 2.3).

Because they are also interested in how the overall system is governed, Robock and Simmonds include as constructs a set of control variables, some of which are country specific. Central to the work of many of the writers working within the geobusiness paradigm is the role of key conditioning and motivation variables in the growth of the firm through stages of internationalization (Bilkey, 1978; Bilkey and Tesar, 1977; Cavusgil and Nevin, 1981; Johanson and Vahlne, 1977; Reid, 1981; Wiedersheim-Paul et al., 1978). The kinds of issues examined at length by these authors include items which are country specific such as differences in the economic, technological, cultural and political environments. Motivation variables examined are those which are firm specific and classified as internal determinants of the firm's internationalization behaviour. Other variables, such as its competitive position in the international arena, are classified as external determinants.

A managerial theory of international marketing in the business system

Traditionally, marketing in the business system was viewed as a way of producing products and services and then selling them to myriad interested customers. Modern marketing thought, however, means having a customer focus: identifying values desired by customers, providing them in some way, communicating these values to customer

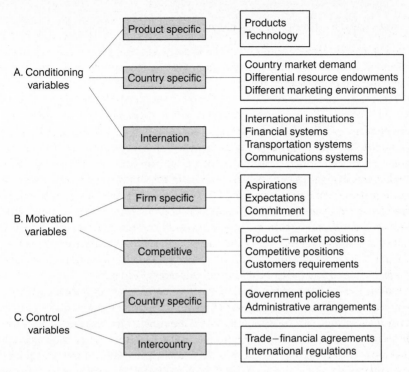

Figure 2.3 Constructs of the geobusiness paradigm
Source: adapted from Robock, S. H. and Simmonds, H. (1998), *International Business and Multinational Enterprises*, 4th edn, Homewood, IL: Irwin.

groups and delivering the value. Values mean benefits focused on solving customer problems and not merely on the products and services which serve as the vehicle of the solution. The focus is on the customer and on solving problems faced by the customer.

Seeking value from the customer's perspective means building a long-term mutually profitable relationship with customers instead of trying to maximize profits on each transaction. An emphasis on relationships rather than individual transactions focuses on the customer as the profit centre, not the product. This approach views marketing as a continuous relationship with customers (Dyer *et al.*, 1987) in contrast to the more traditional view which is transactional, short term, dyadic, virtually adversarial and focused on immediate sales response.

Marketing is concerned with customer relations arising from exchanges, especially long-term relationships (Gummesson, 1987). With a strong continuing relationship the customer becomes more profitable. In many situations, particularly in industrial markets, there are several parties involved in the relationship. Buyers and sellers operate in a network of suppliers, customers, financial institutions and governments. The whole network becomes part of the relationship (Håkansson, 1982). Within the network companies adopt different orientations, which affects the value created in the business system.

Role of marketing in the business system

In creating value companies recognize that customer needs change dramatically from one period to another depending on personal circumstances, changes in the environment and in the economy, and changes in outlook. Value in marketing means delivering on a whole range of promises to the customer. Products and services that customers perceive have a superior value compared with those of competitors are demanded while others are not, hence, the importance of the concept of 'value added'.

The fundamental management issue in marketing is to understand the customer's perception of value and to determine a superior value position from this perspective and to ensure that, by developing a consensus throughout the company, that value is provided and communicated to the customer group. Choosing the value position is one of the most important strategic decisions facing the company. In doing so, it is critical to understand that customer value is the result and not the conduit. Once chosen, it is the task of management to ensure that everyone in the company directly contributes to delivering the chosen value. This is the corporate marketing viewpoint, a real marketing orientation, which contrasts with many of the other viewpoints expressed earlier.

The modern value orientation views marketing as a series of four delivery processes whereby the business system is designed in such a way that value is delivered by the company to the customer through a number of discrete stages. In this view of marketing, it is first necessary to identify society and customer values to be promoted by the company. The company selects the value most appropriate for the market of interest, taking into account the special needs of customers and the activities of competitors. In the second stage, the company attempts to provide the value identified. It does this in a number of ways. The emphasis is on the provision of value, not its manufacture or delivery process. This is the key to an understanding of marketing. The third stage in the process is to communicate the value to customers and potential customers through advertising, public relations and personal selling. In the last stage the company attempts to deliver the value to customers, which is done through distribution and logistics, direct marketing and sales promotion.

In many companies more attention is given to some of these stages than to others. For example, technical companies often give considerable attention to the earlier stages, especially the first two: identifying, selecting and providing value. In industries where product innovation is quickly imitated or surpassed competitive strength may be more sustainable by seeking advantage in communicating and delivering the value to customers.

At present, many service companies attempt to provide customized personal services which are quickly imitated. Banks and other financial institutions, for example, have used new technology to provide better branch services and improved cash delivery systems. By providing integrated financial information and sophisticated management of personal and corporate finance, however, some banks build longer-term relationships which create imitation barriers, thereby giving them a more sustainable competitive advantage than would be available from the use of technology, such as automated teller machines, alone. In these cases success stems not just from selecting a value position but from the innovative and thorough attention to detail involved in the delivery of the value to customers.

Marketing is the integrated, long-term process of planning and implementing the design, development, pricing, promotion and distribution of goods, services and ideas in the context of a business system to create relationships and exchanges that satisfy individual and organizational objectives. This is as true for small firms as it is for complex multi-nationals.

All company activities, including product and service concepts, must be derived from the company's mission and be consistent with it. It is, therefore, misleading to think that only the marketing function in the company affects marketing outcomes. This narrow viewpoint has been called the new marketing myopia. It is important for the company to recognize that value emanates from the business system in which the company operates and that the company may leverage other actors in the system (customers, suppliers and particularly others who complement the firm in what it provides) in creating that value. While it may be recognized that everyone is in marketing it is also important to act on it and to practice it as well. There are many others within the company and within the business system who can affect the success of the firm's marketing.

Orientation of the company

Some companies, however, adopt a short-term focus. Short-run financial controls such as the quarterly rate of return on investment, for example, may cause firms to miss the real lesson of the marketing concept: to recognize the fundamental and enduring nature of customer needs (Levitt, 1960) while acknowledging that the technology of want satisfaction is transitory (Anderson, 1982, p. 23). A long-term marketing focus enables firms to compete for the future. Competing for the future means creating and dominating emerging opportunities (Hamel and Prahalad, 1994). For a variety of reasons, therefore, the company may be oriented in different ways. It is possible to classify firms or organizations depending on whether they are supplier-production oriented, customer-sales oriented, competitor oriented or marketing oriented.

Supplier-production-oriented firms emphasize how well they perform some function which they believe customers require. While the company's product may be technically the best, competing products or services may meet customer needs in a simpler or cheaper way. These companies focus on suppliers with the objective of reducing costs or improving productivity. It is a cost and production view. Some companies easily fall into the trap of believing in their own technical superiority while more customer-focused competitors, who recognize customer needs, develop more attractive and more relevant value-laden products and services.

A customer-sales orientation means focusing exclusively on customers as the way to achieve long-run profits. It means directly appealing to customers by offering a better match of products or services to customer needs. It is assumed that customers carry out intensive searches to find the product or service which meets their needs and that once found loyal patronage follows; these are questionable assumptions (Oxenfeldt and Moore, 1978, p. 44). An unbalanced customer focus reflects the situation where the product category or brand manager devotes attention only to customers and pays less attention to others in the business system. Too great a focus on customers can lead to rapid pseudo-product innovation and differentiation, short product life cycles and emphasis on small-batch production of specialized products and services which may be responses to wish lists rather than to real customer needs. In such circumstances it is necessary to take account of trends in the environment and the activities of suppliers and competitors. Taking account of the activities of competitors should help the company in deciding when it is overfocused on customer wants as opposed to real needs.

A particularly degenerative form of customer orientation arises when the firm produces products or services and through strong selling methods attempts to convince potential customers to patronize their company. The emphasis is on the immediate transaction and sales volume in the short run.

A competitor orientation views customers as the ultimate prize to be won at the expense of rivals. Sources of competitive advantages are well-developed distribution systems, preferential treatment by suppliers and lower costs. A competitor orientation implies that the firm attempts to capitalize on the weaknesses of vulnerable competitors to win market position and customers from them, which produces a high level of sales and long-run profits. At the same time, the firm attempts to remove its own weaknesses to defend market position and to minimize the loss of customers to competitors. A competitor orientation based on pursuing competitive advantage means accepting four propositions (Hunt *et al.*, 1981, p. 268):

- competition consists of a constant struggle of organizations to develop, maintain or increase their differential advantage over other companies;
- differential advantage is the principal source of marketing innovation;
- the foundations for differential advantage are market segmentation, selection of product and service appeals, product improvement, process improvement and product innovation;
- over time competitors attempt to neutralize the differential advantage of any new entrant to the market.

In traditional industrial economics texts, competition for customers is typically defined as arising from other firms in the industry which make products or provide services similar to those of the company from a manufacturing point of view. This industry perspective is irrelevant when the focus in marketing is on solving customer problems. Customers are interested in what they buy, not whether the provider belongs to a particular industry. Competitors should be determined, therefore, from the viewpoint of the customer. In this view of the business system, banks and software companies, although from separate traditional industries, could end up competing to supply customers with added value products and services such as e-money and smart cards. Similarly, banks and insurance companies provide competing financial services. Not long ago neither considered the other as competitors. Increasing industry convergence and the breakdown of traditional industry boundaries mean that the traditional view of competition is becoming less relevant (Hamel and Prahalad, 1994, p.45).

A similar situation arises on the supply side; firms compete with the company in attracting the resources of suppliers. Competition for suppliers frequently crosses traditional industry and international boundaries. Listening to and working with suppliers is just as important as listening to customers (Branderburger and Nalebuff, 1996). Many companies now recognize the importance of working with suppliers, acknowledging that they are equal partners in the creation of value within the business system. In this view of the business system, supplier relations are just as important as customer relations. Both share the common goal of increasing wealth. Both create value and provide access to markets, technology and information. In the traditional view of the business system the company serves customers and depends on suppliers for essential raw materials and other inputs.

The traditional view of the business system consisted of these four actors: the company, the customer, suppliers and competitors. The relationship among these actors can be cooperative but was frequently seen as adversarial, especially between the company and its competitors and suppliers. However, the system ignores a very important actor, the firm which serves in a complementory capacity (Brandenburger and Nalebuff, 1996). These are firms which complement the company and its suppliers, thereby increasing the value to customers. Complementors are most important in international markets: agents, distributors, joint venture partners, suppliers and other service organizations. By including such firms in the framework a much richer and more accurate view of the business system in which international marketing activity takes place is obtained.

Complementors, as the name suggests, provide complementary rather than competing products and services, e.g. faster computer hardware persuades people to upgrade to more powerful software and vice versa. A complementary relationship exists if customers value the company's product or service more when they have the other firm's product or service than when they have the first alone, e.g. a McDonald's Big Mac and Heinz ketchup. Many firms are both competitors and complementors with respect to their suppliers. British Airways and Singapore Airlines compete for passengers, landing slots and gates, but they are likely complementors with respect to the provision of the new Boeing 777 (Sabbagh, 1995). Any product or service which makes another more attractive complements it reciprocally.

As we move further into the knowledge-based economy, such complementary relationships on the supply side are likely to become standard practice. This is especially true where there is a large front end investment and where the variable costs are relatively modest. Practically all the costs in designing computer software are front end, so the larger the market, the greater the leverage and the more development costs can be spread. Note what happens when complements are missing, as they often are in developing and Eastern European countries. It becomes very difficult to carry out simple business functions without a range of complementary services. By focusing on a business system that gives place to the role of complementary products and services, we arrive at a new way of conceptualizing business – how wealth can be increased for all participants in the system – rather than focusing on obtaining a greater share of a fixed amount of wealth.

The value system emphasizes win–win outcomes and suggests win–lose outcomes may be a subset which occur in selected circumstances only. In win–lose circumstances, discussion focuses on market share, winner takes all, dominant players, etc., all of which suggest a fixed availability of wealth. The value interpretation of the business system, however, focuses on providing added values and new wealth.

Market orientation

A market-led company has a clear mission and understands who its customers are, how it should organize to serve them and how it should apply its resources to create value. It identifies customer needs, selects a target market, designs and packages a product to meet market requirements and ensures customer satisfaction by consulting with its customers regarding product dimensions which require improvement, i.e. listening to customers but not necessarily doing everything they suggest, understanding whether and where value can be delivered. Day (1994, p. 37) summarizes the principal features of a market orientation as a set of beliefs which place the customer's interest first and the ability of the organization to generate, disseminate and use superior knowledge about customers and competitors. For Hunt and Morgan (1995, p. 11) a market orientation refers to the systematic:

- gathering of information on customers and competitors both existing and potential,
- analysis of the information for the purpose of developing market knowledge and
- use of such knowledge to guide strategy recognition, understanding, creation, selection, implementation and modification.

Potential customers are included to protect against the dangers of companies being customer led (Hamel and Prahalad, 1994) whereby the focus is on the articulated needs , wants and desires of existing customers. Potential competitors are included to guard against the hazards of changing technology resulting in new competitors entering the market.

There are certain dangers in adopting too short a view in marketing. Customers may know what their needs and wants are but these needs and wants are often defined in terms of existing products and services. Unless the company can take the longer view it is likely to produce imitative products and services rather than innovative ones. Long-term customer relationships are central to marketing (Grönroos, 1987, p. 7). A short-term view predisposes companies toward developing products and services for existing markets. Marketing innovation is associated with creating new markets whereas imitation is concerned with increasing competition in existing markets. 'The real competitive threats to technologically active companies arise less from changes in ultimate consumer preferences than from abrupt shifts in component technologies, raw materials, or production processes' (Hayes and Abernathy, 1980, p. 73). There is a tendency in high-technology companies to believe that the technological superiority of a product is the determining variable of commercial success (Levitt, 1960; Davies and Brush, 1997).

Firms which respond to short-term pressures only 'simply delude themselves into believing that consumer surveys, techniques and product portfolio procedures automatically confer a marketing orientation on their adopters' (Anderson, 1982, p. 23). The fundamental insight of the marketing concept has little to do with the use of particular analytical techniques. Marketing is, therefore, a management concern and not just a specialist operational function within the organization. It is a concern for managing customer relationships within the business system.

Market-led companies operate in the longer term and examine long-run trends, threats and opportunities with a view to developing new products and identifying new markets for assured long-term survival and growth. A market orientation is also required for international markets which are turbulent and very competitive. Market turbulence and competitive intensity have been found to have a significant impact on the manager's attitude toward market orientation, which is the determinant of intention to adopt a market orientation (Powpaka 1998, p. 48).

A long-term marketing orientation, which draws together the supplier-production orientation, the customer-sales orientation and the competitor orientation, while recognizing the importance of complementors, creates value in the entire business system (Bradley, 1998). The business system as a whole produces value (Lanning and Michaels, 1988) within a set of dynamic relationships (Brandenburger and Nalebuff, 1996) among customers, suppliers, competitors and complementors with the company (Figure 2.4). Resources such as raw materials, labour and knowledge flow from suppliers to the firm. Products, services and ideas flow from the firm to its customers. Either of these parties is likely to be located in different countries and in different cultural systems. Payments flow in the reverse direction from customers to the firm and from the firm to suppliers. The business system succeeds if it produces value for its participants – otherwise it perishes. Each participant must add value, otherwise there is no reason to be there. An effective business system is a value system, where added value is the source of power in the business system. The question is one of determining the importance of the company to all other participants in the business system.

In a competitive world, it is difficult to create added value. Usually, added value arises by making better products, using resources more efficiently, listening to customers to determine how to make more attractive products and working with suppliers to discover more efficient ways of running the company's business, while being more effective for them. Companies which cannot produce an added value in the business system are not able to sustain a premium over cost, i.e. the company makes very little money.

Viewing the value in the business system as the result of a network of important relationships highlights two important facts. First, decisions made by one firm affect and are affected by decisions by other firms. Second, firms often make decisions that are

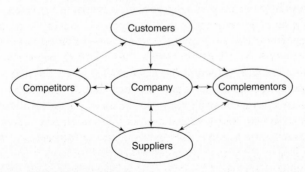

Figure 2.4 Value in the business system
Source: adapted from *Co-opetition* by Adam M. Brandenburger and Barry J. Nalebuff. Copyright © 1996 by Adam M. Brandenburger and Barry J. Nalebuff. Used by permission of Bantam Doubleday Dell Publishing Group, Inc.

normally associated with those of other actors in the system. Thus, the firm makes important decisions which affect suppliers, just as suppliers make important decisions which are normally thought of as being in the purview of the firm. Because so many decisions are part of a network in which a decision in one firm directly or indirectly influences decisions in other firms, major decisions must be consistent with the goals of participants in the network and their products. Herein lies the importance of the contribution of the market-as-networks paradigm discussed previously. Decisions must also complement each other to maximize their overall impact. These notions of consistency and complementarity, introduced by Barabba and Zaltman (1991, pp. 212–16) in the case of decisions within a single firm, are here extended to include the network of firms in the business system and are important elements of the analytical framework used which focuses on synergy among diverse firms. The firm in the business system is a member of a network in which added value and synergy is created.

Every activity within the business system must be consistent with the firm's overall objective or mission. Thus, if the objective of the firm is to be a pioneer in bringing value-added branded beverages to a wide range of customers in diverse markets, all the elements and choices of supplier, complementor, competitor and customer must be consistent with that objective. Similarly, all product values must be consistent with the goals of the firm. Hence, the importance of a well-defined mission within the firm to ensure that the desired product concept is properly imbedded in the customer's mind. The product concept or corporate mission is the essential idea that the customers should associate with the firm. All decisions regarding the business system must logically derive from the product concept or corporate mission. This is the test of consistency in the business system.

Second, all decisions within a network of decisions must reinforce each other positively. While marketing mix decisions regarding price, promotion and distribution channels may be consistent with a marketing objective, they themselves may not complement each other. The complementarity principle reduces the firm's options to a single set of actions that are more complementary to each other than is true for any other set of actions. The result is a set of actions that are supportive of a higher objective but also assist each other to be more effective in achieving the larger objective.

When decisions in the business system are made with the principles of consistency and complementarity in mind, synergy within the circle is enhanced. Collaboration and strategic thinking play a large part in whether the synergy is positive or negative. By being consistent in its actions in the business system and making decisions which complement each other so that the value added in the network is greater, the firm understands the difference between available action which is tactical and developing a longer-term position, which clearly conveys a corporate image or product concept, which is consistent with the firm's objectives and complements or reinforces other initiatives. Strategic thinking requires reflective action to maximize the value added in the network.

Using the value chain

Porter (1985, Chapter 2) has done much to narrow the gap between the strategy domain of marketing and marketing planning by introducing the powerful notion of the value chain. The notion of competitive strategy refers to a competitive battle of all aspects of a firm's operations. Porter's value chain stems from the idea of value being added progressively to a product as it passes through the stages of inbound logistics, operations, outbound logistics, marketing, sales and service. Value may also be added by the support activities of the firm's infrastructure, human resource management, technology development and procurement. At each stage of the value chain there exists an opportunity to contribute positively to the firm's competitive strategy, by performing some activity or process in a way that is better than competitors', and so providing some uniqueness or advantage. If a firm attains such a competitive advantage which is sustainable, defensible, profitable and valued by the market, then it may earn high rates of return even though the industry structure may be unfavourable and the average profitability of the industry modest.

The Porter framework of value creation is, however, essentially production driven with an emphasis on the margin accruing to the firm. A marketing viewpoint would focus on the customer and attempt to determine value from the consumer's perspective. An emphasis on customer satisfaction means attempting to determine the values required now and in the future by consumers, as well as the amount required, how it should be delivered and when it should be provided. Customer satisfaction also stems from attention to raw materials, engineering quality, design and innovation. The purpose of the firm in this value-added view is a never-ending search for continuous improvement in the cost base, through value analysis and value engineering. Collaboration is required among firms to provide this value and ensure customer satisfaction. Of course, adversarial competitive relationships also exist, but an emphasis on customer satisfaction in a re-defined value chain introduces a balance between the concepts of collaboration and competition.

Marketing strategies may be developed for all stages of the value-added chain. Understanding how best to apply marketing to the firm, irrespective of how many stages of the value-added chain are included within the scope of the firm or where in the chain the firm operates, is facilitated by understanding that firms have points of vulnerability and points of leverage (Figure 2.5). It may be argued, therefore, that achieving international competitive advantage may be obtained by isolating and unbundling selected elements of the business system for which the perceived value is not worth the delivered cost (Gilbert and Strebel, 1988).

Positioning the firm in the business system

The core of the concept of positioning the firm in the business system is that the firm should be viewed as competing within a value-added chain within a business system, not an industry. A productive activity is viewed as a chain of many parts ranging from design to use by the final consumer. The various parts of this chain can be ordered in terms of stages of perceived value added. The objective of a firm's process positioning is to organize the business system to achieve an increase in the level of perceived value added or a reduction in the price charged, so that the total perceived value to the customer exceeds the collective cost to the firm of performing the value activities embodied in the final product. Process positioning for competitive advantage is based on the company's ability

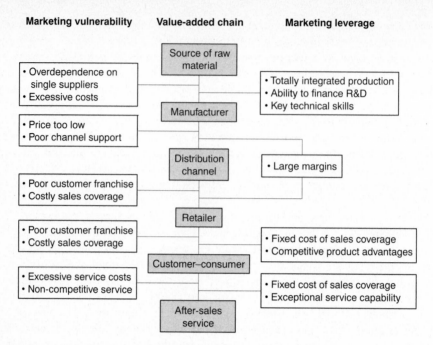

Figure 2.5 Marketing vulnerability and leverage in the value-added chain

to organize the business system to provide the final customer with the desired perceived value at the lowest delivered cost, which requires superior performance in at least one of the business system activities (Gilbert and Strebel, 1988).

High perceived value strategies are more appropriate in the emerging stages of the product life cycle when the manufacturing process is not a significant competitive factor. Technology is still evolving, the business system has not stabilized and competition tends to be confined to product innovation and development. High perceived value strategies tend to favour product markets with short life cycles. Low delivered cost strategies, however, are more appropriate at the standardization phase of the product life cycle which is characterized by rapid market development. Attention is focused on the production process and resources are directed to the entire business system with process technology, market positioning and distribution efficiency becoming critical.

Application of the product-market and business system framework

In a study of 100 wholly Irish-owned successful manufacturing firms, where success was defined as having at least one-third of total company sales in each of the two previous years derived from export markets, Bradley and O'Reágáin (1994) found the following:

- The internationalization step is more likely to be successful if a highly concentrated approach is taken – focusing on a few markets and products.
- Success reflects an emphasis on quality rather than on price-related factors and these firms targeted a narrow range of customer groups – a strategy pursued by 68 per cent of the successful firms surveyed.
- Effective organization of the key activities of the business system contributes an important competitive edge in the pursuit of quality-based strategies.
- Contracting out of business system activities which are not critical to the quality of the final product facilitates international competitive advantage by allowing firms the flexibility to deliver a superior quality product more cost effectively.

These conclusions have a number of implications for the management of firms seeking to develop international markets for the first time and for those already in the early stages of internationalization:

- concentrate resources and effort on a small number of familiar markets and on products matching customer requirements in the selected market,
- identify those parts of the production process which contribute most to final product value for selected customer segments and concentrate efforts on these and
- explore the potential for providing more cheaply those elements of the product which cost the firm more to produce than their value to the customer.

The potential for contracting out these activities to specialist subsuppliers or complementors may be warranted. In these circumstances the international marketing strategy may involve careful resource allocation within the product-market and business system.

Summary

Interest in international marketing as a subdiscipline of marketing is a relatively recent phenomenon. It appears that practitioners of international marketing are much further advanced in their thinking than are researchers. Research in the area has built on theories and paradigms developed in other areas, especially international trade theory, industrial organization and strategic marketing. Valuable insights into the conditions under which international exchange of assets occurs may be gleaned from international trade theory, especially the effect of fluctuating exchange rates on marketing programmes. From industrial organization theory the role of the firm in the internationalization process, and especially the reasons for foreign direct investment, may be understood.

Because the firm in international markets must deal with relatively high transaction costs it is necessary to consider various ways of transferring assets abroad. The different modes of foreign market entry identified are exporting, competitive alliances based on licensing and joint ventures and foreign direct investment. It is necessary to examine each in the context of a theory or set of paradigms.

A number of marketing theories and paradigms were identified and discussed, many of which have components which are relevant to the firm in international markets. The interaction paradigm in the context of a systems-exchange framework appears to hold high promise, as with this it is possible to identify the transactions costs and to measure the attainment of other non-financial marketing objectives. The chapter ends with a section outlining the dominant position of the firm in international markets and the need for a managerial theory of international marketing within the business system. This approach is developed and identifies the key role of value added and its provision within a business system which is increasingly international in its activities and orientation. This dominance stems from its ability to complete the international marketing task in an effective way.

Discussion questions

1. Explain what is meant by a theory of international marketing. What is meant by a paradigm? Why is it important to have a suitable paradigm for the study of international marketing in the firm?

2. What is the significance of the systems-exchange paradigm as applied to the firm in international markets?

3. Describe and evaluate the principal constructs of the interaction and the geobusiness paradigms.

4. How relevant is the life-cycle model to the understanding of international marketing?

5. What are the principal contributions of international trade theory, if any, to the study of the firm in international markets?

6. Describe the international marketing task facing the firm and outline an approach to the study of international marketing.

References

Anderson, P. F. (1982) 'Marketing, strategic planning and the theory of the firm', *Journal of Marketing*, **46** (Spring), 15–26.

Barabba, V. P. and Zaltman, G. (1991) *Hearing the Voice of the Market*, Boston, MA: Harvard Business School Press.

Barney, J. B. (1991) 'Firm resources and sustained competitive advantage' *Journal of Management*, **17**, 99–120.

Bartels, R. (1968) 'Are domestic markets and international markets dissimilar?', *Journal of Marketing*, **32**, 56–61.

Bilkey, W. J. (1978) 'An attempted integration of the literature on the export behaviour of firms', *Journal of International Business Studies*, **9** (1), 33–46.

Bilkey, W. J. and Tesar, G. (1977) 'The export behaviour of smaller sized Wisconsin manufacturing firms', *Journal of International Business Studies*, **8** (1), 93–8.

Bradley, M. F. (1987) 'Nature and significance of international marketing: a review', *Journal of Business Research*, **15**, 205–19.

Bradley, F. (1998) 'From Clashmore Containers to value relationships in the business system', *Irish Marketing Review*, **X**, y–z.

Bradley, F. and O'Reágáin, S. (1994) 'Successful SME strategies for international markets', in

M. Lambkin and T. Meenaghan (eds), *Perspectives on Marketing Management in Ireland*, Dublin: Oak Tree Papers, pp. 409–34.

Brandenburger, A. M. and Nalebuff, B. J. (1996) *Co-opetition*, New York, NY: Currency-Doubleday.

Buckley, P. J. and Casson, M. (1976) *The Future of the Multinational Enterprise*, London: Holmes and Meier.

Buzzell, R. (1968) 'Can you standardize multinational marketing', *Harvard Business Review*, **46** (November–December), 103–13.

Carman, J. M. (1980) 'Paradigms for marketing theory', *Research in Marketing*, **3**, 1–36.

Cateora, P. R. (1993) *International Marketing*, 8th edn, Homewood, IL: Irwin.

Cavusgil, S. T. and Nevin, J. R. (1981) 'Internal determinants of export marketing behaviour: an empirical investigation', *Journal of Marketing Research*, **18**, 114–19.

Chandler, A. D. Jr (1977) *The Visible Hand*, Cambridge, MA: Harvard University Press.

Davies, W. and Brush, K. E. (1997) 'High-tech industry marketing: the elements of a sophisticated global strategy', *Industrial Marketing Management*, **26**, 1–13.

Day, G. (1994): 'The capabilities of market-driven organizations', *Journal of Marketing*, **58** (October), 37–52.

Dickson, P. R. (1992) 'Toward a general theory of competitive rationality', *Journal of Marketing*, **56** (January), 69–83.

Dierickx, I. and Cool, K. (1989) 'Asset stock accumulation and sustainability of competitive advantage', *Management Science*, **35** (December), 1504–11.

Dyer, R. F., Schurr, P. H. and Oh, S. (1987) 'Output sector munificence effects on the internal political economy of marketing channels', *Journal of Marketing Research*, **51** (April), 347–58.

Etzioni, A. (1988) *The Moral Dimension: Towards a new economics*, New York, NY: The Free Press.

Fayerweather, J. (1982) *International Business Strategy and Administration*, 2nd edn, Cambridge, MA: Ballinger.

Gannon, M. (1993) 'Towards a composite theory of foreign market entry mode choice: the role of marketing strategy variables', *Journal of Strategic Marketing*, **1**, 41–54.

Gilbert, X. and Strebel, P. (1988) 'Developing competitive advantage', in B. J. Quinn, H. Mintzberg and J. M. Robert (eds), *The Strategy Process*, Englewood Cliffs, NJ: Prentice Hall, pp. 70–9.

Glazer, R. (1989) *Marketing and the Changing Information Environment: Implications for strategy, structure, and the marketing mix*, Cambridge, MA: Marketing Science Institute.

Grönroos, C. (1987) 'Defining marketing: a market oriented approach', *Working Paper 170*, Helsinki: Swedish School of Economics.

Gummesson, E. (1987) 'The new marketing – developing long term interactive relationships', *Long Range Planning*, **20** (4), 10–24.

Håkansson, H. (1982) *International Marketing and Purchasing of Industrial Goods: An Interaction Approach*, New York, NY: Wiley.

Hamel, G. and Prahalad, C. K. (1994) *Competing for the Future*, Boston, MA: Harvard Business School Press.

Hayes, R. H. and Abernathy, W. J. (1980) 'Managing our way to economic decline', *Harvard Business Review*, **58**, 67–77.

Hunt, S. D. and Morgan, R. M. (1995) 'The comparative advantage theory of competition', *Journal of Marketing*, **59** (April), 1–15.

Hunt, S. D., Muncy, J. A. and Ray, N. M. (1981) 'Alderson's general theory of marketing: a formalisation', in B. M. Enis and K. J. Roering (eds), *Review of Marketing 1981*, Chicago, IL: American Marketing Association, pp. 267–72.

Hymer, S. (1970) 'The efficiency (contradictions) of multinational corporations', *American Economic Review*, **60**, 441–8.

Johanson, J. and Vahlne, J. E. (1977) 'The internationalization process of the firm: a model of knowledge development and increasing foreign market commitments', *Journal of International Business Studies*, **80** (1), 23–32.

Kahler, R. and Kramer, R. L. (1977) *International Marketing*, 4th edn, Cincinnatti, OH: Southwestern Publishing.

Keegan, W. J. (1989) *Global Marketing Management* , 4th edn, London: Prentice Hall International.

Lanning, M. J. and Michaels, E. G. (1988) 'A business is a value delivery system', *McKinsey Staff Paper*, **41**.

Lawrence, P. R. and Dyer, D. (1983) *Renewing American Industry*, New York, NY: The Free Press.

Levitt, T. (1960) 'Marketing myopia', *Harvard Business Review*, **38** (July–August), 24–47.

Levitt, T. (1983) 'The globalization of markets', *Harvard Business Review*, **61** (May–June), 92–102.

Ohio State University Marketing Staff (1965) 'A statement of marketing philosophy', *Journal of Marketing*, **29**, 43–4.

Oxenfeldt, A. R. and Moore, W. L. (1978) 'Customer or competitor: which guideline for marketing?', *Management Review* (August), **61** (8), 43–8.

Porter, M. E. (1980) *Competitive Strategy*, New York, NY: The Free Press.

Porter, M. E. (1985) *Competitive Advantage: Creating and Sustaining Superior Performance*, New York, NY: The Free Press.

Porter, M. E. (1990) *The Competitive Advantage of Nations*, New York, NY: The Free Press.

Powpaka, S. (1998) 'Factors affecting the adoption of market orientation: the case of Thailand', *Journal of International Marketing*, **6** (1), 33–55.

Prahalad C. K. and Doz, Y. L. (1987) *The Multinational Mission*, New York, NY: The Free Press.

Reid, S. D. (1981) 'The decision maker and export entry and expansion', *Journal of International Business Studies*, **12** (2), 101–12.

Robock, S. H. and Simmonds, K. (1988) *International Business and Multinational Enterprises*, 4th edn, Homewood, IL: Irwin.

Rugman, A. M. (1981) *Inside the Multinationals: The economics of internal markets*, London: Croom Helm.

Sabbagh, K. (1995) *21st Century Jet – The Making of the Boeing 777*, London: Pan.

Sweeney, D. J. (1972) 'Management technology or social process', *Journal of Marketing*, **36**, 3–10.

Teece, D. (1981) 'The market for know-how and the efficient international transfer of technology', *Annals of the American Academy of Political and Social Science*, **458**, 81–96.

Teece, D. (1986) 'Firm boundaries, technological innovation and strategic management', in L. G. Thomas (ed.), *The Economics of Strategic Planning: Essays in Honor of Joel Dean*, Lexington, MA: Lexington Books, pp. 187–99.

Terpstra, V. (1983) *International Marketing*, 3rd edn, Chicago, IL: The Dryden Press.

Wiedersheim-Paul, F., Olson, H. C. and Welch, L. S. (1978) 'Pre-export activity: the first step in internationalisation', *Journal of International Business Studies*, **9** (1), 47–58.

Williamson, O. E. (1979) 'Transactions cost economics: the governance of contractual relations', *Journal of Law and Economics*, **22**, 233–61.

Wind, Y. and Robertson, T. S. (1983) 'Marketing strategy: new directions for theory and research', *Journal of Marketing*, **47** (2), 12–25.

Yip, G. S. (1992) *Total Global Strategy*, Englewood Cliffs, NJ: Prentice Hall.

3
Resources and managerial capacity

It is essential that we understand why and how a firm attempts to internationalize. This chapter provides guidance to a resource audit or internal assessment of the firm. The chapter is divided into two parts. The first part examines the firm as an organization and deals with the products it makes and the firm's advantages. The second part focuses on the people in the firm, especially the characteristics of those people who make the strategic decisions in the firm – the management. By proceeding in this way we will have a better understanding of the firm as it adjusts to the international marketing environment. In Chapter 4 we look outwards from the firm to the strategic options available and the constraints imposed on the firm. Hence, these two chapters deal first with internal considerations and, second, with external influencing factors.

Resources and aspirations

A major incentive for internationalization arises when the firm possesses excess or unused resources. These may be physical resources such as money, excess capacity in production or special knowledge, highly specialized labour and machinery, byproducts from existing operations or financial resources. In moving into a new field, a firm may develop new strengths and find another set of underused production resources, which sets the stage for another round of expansion that may be in a domestic or international market.

Excess capacity in the firm

By excess capacity we mean any slack in any resource under the firm's control. It does not refer only to physical plant and equipment but can also refer, and often does, to underutilized organizational and managerial resources which could be used in assisting the firm to internationalize. Firms are endowed with different amounts and types of resources and competencies, which allow them to compete in different ways. Firms which are better endowed have lower average costs than competitors and can provide products and services at lower cost or provide greater customer satisfaction (Barney, 1991). Resources

c, and may be physical, such as unique supply source, production facilities,
.munications–television cabling system, or intangible, such as patents and
organizational, such as skills, routines, processes and culture.

se resources are difficult to transfer among firms because of transaction costs and
.use the assets may contain tacit knowledge (Teece *et al.*, 1996, p. 15). Such resources
.d core competencies of the firm, particularly those which involve collective learning
and are knowledge based, are enhanced as they are applied (Prahalad and Hamel, 1990).
Resources and competencies which are distinctive and superior, relative to those of rivals,
may become the basis for competitive advantage if they are matched appropriately to
market opportunities (Thompson and Strickland, 1996, pp. 94–5). These resources may,
therefore, provide both the basis and direction for the growth of the firm itself, i.e. there
may be a natural trajectory embedded in a firm's knowledge base (Peteraf, 1993, p. 182).

Identifying the firm's competitive advantages

For competitive advantage to exist, the firm must adopt a superior position in the market,
which would provide above-normal returns for the ability to predict a market need in the
absence of competition. Superior market positions depend on the firm's customer base,
relations with suppliers and complementors, relations with customers, e.g. brand equity,
facilities and systems, and the firm's own endowment of technology and complementary
property rights. These are the company's assets or resource endowments which the
company has accumulated over time. In addition, the company must possess certain
capabilities, the glue that binds the firm's assets together and enables them to be used to
advantage (Day, 1994, p. 38). Capabilities are so deeply embedded in the organization's
routines and practices that they cannot be traded or imitated (Dierickx and Cool, 1989).

The firm's advantages can be derived from the nature of the firm's products, markets,
technological orientation or resources (Table 3.1). Examples include competitively priced
products, technically superior products and technological intensity in the firm's production. Products produced at very competitive prices will often find success in international
markets because of the features they offer at low prices. Thus, high-quality calculators and
digital watches produced in huge numbers led to the rapid internationalization of many
Japanese companies.

Although these differential advantages 'are not sufficient, by themselves, to initiate
export marketing, these unique advantages are important in preparing the firm and in
providing initial motivation for management' (Cavusgil and Nevin, 1981, p. 114). Thus,
firms which produce competitively priced and technically superior products have clear
marketing advantages which can be exploited on international markets.

Role of knowledge in competitive advantage

In the 1990s, there has been a very substantial change in the way that we think of business
and the economy. Until the early 1990s, the mind set was conditioned by a scarcity
paradigm which emanated from the industrial age, where the focus was on managing and
allocating scarce resources, managing risk and seeking efficiencies. In the knowledge age

Table 3.1 Resources required for internationalization

Excess capacity

- financial
- physical
- knowledge

Competitive advantage

- products
- brand equity
- markets
- technological orientation
- resources
- knowledge

of the new millennium, the focus is on abundance, where considerations such as growth, adding value, creating wealth and exceeding customer expectations, not just meeting them, have become the mantra of managers. In a knowledge-driven economy, technology is the tangible manifestation of knowledge. It is knowledge which is the principal source of value and power. Technology raises returns on investment and living standards, while bypassing the laws of diminishing returns, the centrepiece of economic thinking.

If the firm's competitive advantage is insufficient or is short lived, so too will be the benefit for the firm. For this reason, firms attempt to reduce the possibility of substitution and imitation. Substitutions reduce profits by making the firm's demand curve more elastic, one of Porter's (1980) five forces. However, preventing imitation is perhaps a greater protection of benefits accruing to the firm. These include things such as property rights to scarce resources, marketing information and factors which impede imitative competition. Of particular interest here is the concept of causal ambiguity (Lippman and Rumelt, 1992), which refers to uncertainty regarding the causes of differences among firms. Causal ambiguity prevents would-be imitators from knowing exactly what to imitate or how to do it (Peteraf, 1993, p. 183). Such uncertainty arises from special product formulations, brand management competencies, internal company management routines and other processes which can be patented or copyrighted and limit imitation.

The greater the technological intensity of the firm's output, the greater the likelihood that the firm will distinguish itself on international markets. The possession of these advantages presupposes that the firm also has an abundance of another key resource: knowledge. Knowledge of opportunities or problems is assumed to initiate decisions. Furthermore, the evaluation of alternatives is based on some knowledge about relevant parts of the market environment and about performance of various activities (Johanson and Vahlne, 1977). By market knowledge these authors mean information about markets and operations which is somehow stored and reasonably retrievable, in the minds of individuals, in computer memories and in written reports. Knowledge is considered to be vested in the decision-making system which may be the firm or business unit (Johanson and Vahlne, 1977, p. 26).

Knowledge can be divided into two types: objective, which can be taught, and experience or experiential knowledge (Penrose, 1959). Objective knowledge refers to knowing the facts or being explicit whereas experiential knowledge refers to tacit knowledge or knowing how something is done. These two forms of knowledge underlie the firm's advantage. One important outcome of this is that there is a direct relation between knowledge and commitment to markets. Knowledge is a resource and, consequently, the better the knowledge about a market and the more it is controlled and managed, the more valuable are the resources and the stronger is the organizational commitment to the market.

The critical distinction is between knowledge which is explicit and capable of articulation and, therefore, transferable at low cost and knowledge which is tacit and manifested only in its application and not amenable to transfer. By distinguishing between these two forms of knowledge, it is easier to consider the issue of transferability across space and time and between individuals, especially when located in different countries and conditioned by different cultures. Explicit knowledge is revealed by its communication whereas tacit knowledge is revealed through its application. This distinction is important for the manner and mode of transfer of products, services and technology in international markets.

The transferability of knowledge also depends on the ability of the recipient to integrate the various elements of knowledge. Efficiency of knowledge integration is facilitated when it can be expressed in terms of a common language, particularly if it can be codified in such a way to take advantage of modern developments in communications technology. Examples of such knowledge would be a profile of consumers of a particular product in different markets around the world or the marketing strategy for a brand to be sold to consumer markets in diverse cultures. Much knowledge is, however, idiosyncratic and cannot easily be integrated. Such knowledge is specific to a particular situation and may require the transfer of people, or at least, extensive interaction between people in different countries.

In international marketing, explicit knowledge is transferred by means of finished products and services which are usually exported whereas tacit knowledge is transferred internationally by means of strategic alliances or foreign direct investment depending on the degree of application involved. Strategic alliances or foreign direct investment modes are used for tacit knowledge because individuals are the principal repositories of such knowledge and the movement of people is required.

In controlling and managing their knowledge base, firms attempt to establish property rights on values at least equal to those created by the resources used. The appropriability of knowledge depends on whether it is tacit or explicit. Tacit knowledge is not directly appropriable because it cannot be directly transferred. It can be appropriated only through its application in production. Explicit knowledge, because it is in the public domain, may be re-sold, by anyone who acquires it without losing it, i.e. it is what economists call a public good. Except for patents, brands and copyrights, where, in most countries, knowledge owners are protected by legally established property rights, knowledge is generally inappropriable by means of market transactions. Hence, the preponderance of brands, patents and copyrighted knowledge in international markets on the one hand, and intrafirm transfers such as joint ventures or foreign direct investment on the other.

The transferability and appropriability of knowledge together provide a reason for the dominance of the firm in international marketing. There is an asymmetry in the economics of knowledge: knowledge acquisition requires greater specialization than is needed for its utilization (Grant, 1996, p. 112). Knowledge production requires the coordinated efforts of individual specialists who possess many different types of knowledge, but markets are unable to coordinate this activity because of their failure to cope with the immobility of tacit knowledge and the risk of expropriation of explicit knowledge by a potential buyer. Firms exist, therefore, as institutions for providing goods, services and technology because they create conditions, e.g. propinquity, under which multiple individuals can integrate their specialist knowledge (Grant, 1996, p. 112).

Analyzing the firm's capability in terms of its knowledge base provides an understanding of the conditions under which competitive advantage is both built and sustained (Grant, 1991, p. 452). In many cases, competitive advantage depends on the firm's procedures for integrating knowledge. Most successful firms use complex sets of routines, attitudes and operations, supported by sophisticated communications technologies which are manifest in the firm's culture and management practices. For international marketing firms, the greater the span of knowledge being integrated, and the more sophisticated the procedures used, the more difficult it is for rivals to copy.

The dilemma for the international firm is to sustain competitive advantage by building barriers to imitation while effectively replicating that knowledge internally, but across markets. Building equity into brands, competitive alliances and foreign direct investments are alternative ways of addressing the dilemma in international markets.

Knowledge and the scale and scope of the firm

The scale and scope of the firm's international activities also depend on knowledge, especially explicit knowledge, which, once created, can be used in multiple applications at its marginal cost. Markets are, however, inefficient in transferring knowledge except where that knowledge is explicated in products.

If markets transfer products efficiently, but knowledge transfer is inefficient, vertically adjacent stages of production will be integrated within the same firm if production at one stage requires access to the knowledge used in the previous stage. If the output at a subsequent stage can be processed without the need to access the knowledge used in the previous stage, however, then efficiency would dictate two separate firms linked by the market (Demestz, 1991). Single-product firms tend to dominate most industries because of the difficulty of integrating the myriad types of specialized knowledge required in manufacturing. At the same time much knowledge can be used in different products and, hence, benefits from economies of scope. In such circumstances, efficient utilization of knowledge suggests the formation of multiproduct firms. There is a need for congruence between the firm's knowledge domain and its product domain (Grant, 1996, p. 120). For this reason, firms tend to form around product–knowledge constellations. An imperfect match between a firm's product and knowledge domains creates opportunities for a market for knowledge. Such knowledge markets are often realized as competitive alliances.

Firms with broad resource bases tend to pursue diversification (Penrose, 1959; Montgomery and Hariharen, 1991). These firms tend to enter new markets where the resource requirements match their resource capabilities. International market diversification is the result of excess capability in resources which have multiple uses and for which there is market failure. In order to utilize more fully its R&D or its new product development capability, competencies which are imperfectly mobile across markets and face high transaction costs, a firm might seek opportunities outside its original market. The more generalizable the resources, the wider the opportunities available. A firm in the commodity paper business with expertise in cost cutting and financial skills embodied in a management team operating with firm specific routines might be able to diversify quite widely into many international markets.

Inefficiency in the markets for knowledge and a recognition of economies of product and market scope encourage firms to diversify their product-market portfolios in order to exploit fully their knowledge resources. The issue faced in international marketing is that different types of knowledge are applicable to different sets of product-markets which makes it difficult to achieve congruence between the firm's knowledge domain and its product-market domain. (Grant, 1997, p. 453). Specialization and flexibility are two knowledge resources in seeming abundance among small firms in Italy which has allowed them to compete successfully in international markets (Exhibit 3.1).

In many cases this kind of knowledge cannot easily be acquired: at the time of entry to a market the knowledge may not even exist. It has to be acquired through a long learning process in connection with current business activities. This factor is an important reason why the internationalization process often proceeds so slowly.

▬▬▬ Exhibit 3.1 ▬▬▬
Italian Sorpresa

There is a network of medium-sized exporters in Italy that have been growing fast and are beginning to resemble a more flexible version of Germany's *Mittelstand*. In many northern Italian cities, it is easy to find a class of *media industria* that now have revenues of over 200 billion lire ($130m) and whose sales and profits are doubling every two or three years.

At first sight, it is a bewilderingly diverse collection of firms. On closer inspection, however, these firms nearly always share two common attributes: specialization and flexibility. Crespi has built up sales of 260 million lire by knowing how to adapt the new synthetic materials coming out of the world's big chemical companies to the ephemeral tastes of the fashion industry. The expertise need not be high-tech: La Doria's bright idea was to spot the export potential of own-label fruit and vegetables back in the 1970s (quite a feat in a country that is only now going through its own private-label revolution).

Natuzzi helped create the niche that it has come to dominate, by turning leather furniture into an affordable luxury. Part of its secret is a pricing system that allows it to set an exact cost in terms of labour and materials for each design. Natuzzi, which comes up with as many as 120 new models each year, segments its market tirelessly, exploiting every possible type of customer.

Neither Crespi nor Natuzzi could have achieved this without the flexibility for which Italian manufacturing is famous. Natuzzi can produce any of more than 1 million combinations of colour and design on a single assembly line. Another feature commonly associated with Italy's *Mittelstand* is a network of small suppliers. A classic example is Benetton, which built up its clothing chain by relying heavily on an intimate network of trusted clothing manufacturers.

Sceptics point out that Italy's entrepreneurial exporters have benefited mightily from tax evasion as well as from the plunging lira, but the cynics overlook two countervailing disadvantages of being a small business in Italy: a scarcity of capital and managerial talent and an abundance of government bureaucracy. There is good and bad news in all this. The good news is for entrepreneurs: Italy manages to create companies regardless of the fact that its state bureaucracy is just as unfavourable as theirs. The bad news is for governments. Italy shows that entrepreneurship is largely out of reach of government policy. Sensible ideas, such as keeping inflation low and stimulating competition, can help make things a little easier.

Source: adapted from *Economist*, 2 March 1996, pp. 63–4.

Characteristics and aspirations of the firm

According to the general management and marketing literature, sustainable success for most companies derives from profits, growth, market share, customer loyalty, image and positioning. Cash flow compared with sales is, however, a fundamental prerequisite for flexible action, especially in the face of the strategic uncertainty, which arises in international markets.

Criteria for success

In each of these performance indicators, successful companies tend to score much higher than the less successful ones. Successful companies have a special strength in cost, quality or speed to market, but they are better than the less successful companies on all three dimensions (Rommel *et al.*, 1995, p. 5). Superior results, according to these authors, are obtained by:

1. Vertical integration – the firm should capitalize on areas where it is strong, otherwise outsource, reduce the number of suppliers and integrate them better.
2. Product range and customer structure – need to concentrate on value segments and core products offering optimum customer value.

3. Product and service development – increase downstream development efficiency by reducing risk upstream and continuously innovate, in small rapid steps.

On the first point, when the result is operationally superior, the best companies produce a higher proportion of value added within the firm than their less successful rivals. Successful companies have fewer suppliers and often rely on a single supplier. A smaller number of suppliers enables closer cooperation with each, almost as if partners and certainly not as adversaries. Such a relationship places greater demands on suppliers and the customer in the business system, as indicated in Chapter 2. Each must work with and support the other, often providing advice and technical assistance. Hence, successful companies focus a great deal of attention on suppliers.

With regard to the second point, Rommel *et al.* (1995) conclude that limiting the variety of the product range and focusing on a narrow range of customers improves the company's return for sales. With regard to product and service development, successful companies systematically create products for selected market segments and consistently reject any suggestions to incorporate extra performance features which are not valued by the customer. It is particularly noted that, for successful companies, an understanding of customer needs is the most important source of new ideas, whereas less successful companies depend on observing competitors. Successful companies focus on customers rather than on competitors. Successful companies are also known to make frequent small incremental improvements in product value at varying intervals which produces an almost continuous stream of innovations, all perceptible to the customer (Rommel *et al.*, 1995, p. 20). Success comes by recognizing the value of small rapid steps reflecting the different life cycles of different product features. According to these authors, companies that attempt to achieve major advances in innovation over longer intervals are often too late in recognizing that a particular technology has become obsolete.

Success depends, therefore, on how well the firm exploits the value-added chain to provide products and services required by defined market segments while engaging in continuous innovation of its products and services. There are, however, a number of factors, including the firm's objectives and goals, its technology, its products, its location and its size, which are believed to influence the performance on international markets and the likelihood of success (Table 3.2).

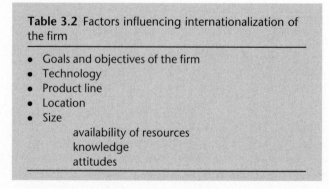

Table 3.2 Factors influencing internationalization of the firm

- Goals and objectives of the firm
- Technology
- Product line
- Location
- Size
    - availability of resources
    - knowledge
    - attitudes

Goals and objectives of the firm

Managers are concerned with the goals of the firm and the extent to which they are achieved. Avoiding undue instability in sales performance is related to a basic goal, i.e. security and survival. The more unpredictable the firm perceives variations in its sales performance to be, the more concerned it will be to find other sources of sales and growth in order to insulate it from potential disturbances. Two forms of diversification – creating and marketing a new product and selling internationally – provide the firm with a degree of insulation ensuring that if it suffers a loss in one market it is less likely to experience losses in all markets. Thus, where the basic security of the firm is threatened by market fluctuations, a powerful reason for international operations may be developed.

The strategies that the firm is capable of adopting will be constrained by its past behaviour and actions. The firm's history of previous investments and its operating routines constrain its future behaviour. The opportunities for expansion are influenced strongly by previous activities. A type of internationalization process or a similar process within the domestic market may have to be passed through before it is prepared for the international market.

The strategic decisions facing the firm in international marketing collapse into two groups – those related to products and those related to markets. The firm examines its existing product portfolio and decides whether new products are necessary. This new product decision has a profound impact on the success of the firm. At the same time the firm must decide whether to enter new markets. Entering new international markets also has a profound impact on the success of the firm (Figure 3.1). Initially, the firm provides a product or service for the domestic market. It may then decide to expand by providing additional products and services for the domestic market before expanding into international markets. Alternatively, it may decide to internationalize on the basis of a single successful product. There are many examples of companies following both routes to international markets. In attempting to expand internationally some firms first develop a portfolio of products with the ultimate objective of entering numerous international markets while other firms expand rapidly into many international markets first and only

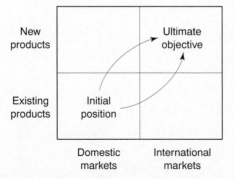

Figure 3.1 International product market portfolios

later do they develop a full portfolio of products. Both approaches ultimately serve the objective of being present in a portfolio of markets with a portfolio of products.

Product range in the firm

Another important factor is the type of product line produced by the firm. Products can be described in different dimensions: degree of standardization, complexity and the software–hardware relationship in sales. The most important dimension is the software–hardware relationship since it stresses that a product is, in effect, 'a package of services'. The higher the hardware content – given the degree of technical complexity – the smaller the information flow needed between seller and buyer and, therefore, the greater the chance for a potential seller of being exposed to export stimuli. Products which include a more comprehensive package of software demand a more extensive flow of information and closer contacts between seller and buyer. This tends to favour already-established business connections and consequently tends to decrease the possibility of an 'outside' firm getting an order.

Some firms have successfully internationalized their activities by concentrating on knowledge-based products for which demand is highly income elastic. Over time it may be possible for the firm to change its product portfolio in the direction of knowledge intensity while at the same time seeking product markets which are income elastic (Figure 3.2). During the 1960s Japanese firms followed this strategy quite successfully. By judging which product markets were likely to be income elastic and to require sophisticated technology they were able to produce consumer electronic products and others in high demand. Many Japanese firms moved from producing cheap low-quality products to producing income elastic knowledge based products such as camcorders and more recently highly sophisticated industrial and consumer electronic products.

Location of the firm

As a firm expands its operations into more distant regions, it is moving into less familiar territory – more 'foreign' markets. Communication is more difficult and costly than for

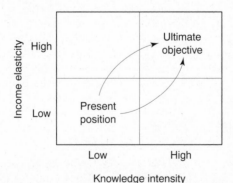

Figure 3.2 Product-market income elasticity and knowledge intensity

the local region. As these barriers are overcome, the relative 'foreignness' of distant markets is reduced. Also, the firm is likely to develop skills in marketing a product at a distance.

As the firm expands into additional regions in the domestic market, it will extend its communication network. From the extended network, there is a greater likelihood of exposure to attention-evoking factors – those influences which cause a firm to consider an international strategy, e.g. an overseas enquiry. This process is probably more likely to operate in a large country such as the United States or Australia than in a small country such as Belgium or New Zealand.

The location of the firm affects the transport costs of products and also, more importantly, information flows. One of the reasons given for the high efficiency in urban regions is that a large number of firms and places of work, concentrated in a small area, improves the conditions for production and creates a favourable 'enterprise environment'. This is especially true in the case of 'information production' that contains a high proportion of face-to-face contacts, since direct personal contacts are often more efficient than other means of contact. These are preferable when the exchange of information involves uncertainty or when it is impossible to foresee what will happen when the information transmitted creates new situations demanding a new exchange of information.

Size of the firm

When a firm's horizons are very limited, even if it has an excellent product, it will have little knowledge of the market. In general, small firms are:

- less aware of the potential of exporting;
- less confident of their ability to export;
- less knowledgeable about how to export or where to find the relevant information.

Many small businesses wrongly believe that only a large enterprise can handle the technical details of international markets but frequently find that the only significant difference between small and large firms concerns documentation. This is due to the fact that the small firm has less elaborate systems than the large firm and in most cases one person has multiple responsibilities. Large firms have the organization to handle all the extra form-filling and coordination work involved in dealing with overseas clients. Company size may, however, dictate the size of a business opportunity that can be undertaken. Thus small companies frequently find the risks too great and the financial demands too high to undertake very large research projects. There may, therefore, be three main considerations with respect to size, as follows:

1. resources;
2. lack of market knowledge;
3. perceived inability to survive in international markets.

The availability of resources such as managerial and foreign marketing know-how, adequate financing and research and development tend to be limited in the small firm, which has less spare resources to devote to internationalization activity. The larger firms' needs for financial assistance may be met by corporate funds and venture capital. Small firms do not have ready access to these sources. They usually have less money, therefore, for development of new products and production capacity. Furthermore, the small firm generally does not have adequate management personnel to devote to overseas markets; it also typically lacks expertise in market research and planning. Finally, the smaller firm is usually not as expert as a large firm in processing documentation, the complexity of which increases manifold in overseas dealings.

On the second point, the small firm will have less knowledge and information about markets than the larger firm with 'market scanning' ability. This may be alleviated slightly if the firm is positioned in a favourable enterprise environment. By interacting with neighbouring firms, information about markets and market needs may be easily assimilated. A major deterrent for internationalization is a belief by small firms that they are not capable of carrying out business overseas. Managers of small firms adopt generally conservative patterns of business behaviour and attitudes which undermine the effectiveness with which they can operate in a competitive environment.

Management of the firm

Three characteristics of management are responsible for stimulating internationalization behaviour: managerial aspirations; commitment by the firm to international market development; management expectations (Johanson and Vahlne, 1977). These factors interact with the firm, its resources and charcteristics and, taken together, produce a certain international marketing behaviour (Figure 3.3).

Managerial aspirations for internationalization

Aspiration levels are widely discussed in the literature on the theory of the firm as a determinant of risk-taking behaviour. The importance the decision maker places on the

Figure 3.3 Internal influences on international marketing behaviour
Source: adapted from Johanson, J. and Valhne, J. (1997) 'The internationalisation process of the firm – model of knowledge development and increasing foreign marketing commitments', *Journal of International Business Studies*, **8** (1), 22–30.

achievement of various business goals such as growth, profits and market development is believed to be a direct determinant of decision-making behaviour. Some empirical studies, like that of Simmonds and Smith (1968), support this assumption by revealing a positive relationship between export marketing behaviour and the decision maker's preference for business goals.

The reluctance of some firms to consider internationalizing may be attributable to senior management's lack of determination (Cavusgil and Nevin, 1981). A general willingness among the decision makers to devote adequate resources to international activities appears to be critical, because in carrying out the international marketing function many tasks are new to the firm and involve a commitment of financial and managerial resources.

Another aspect of managerial aspirations relates to the concept of international orientation which is specific to the individual manager (Reid, 1981); this appears to be important in regard to aspirations. Cunningham and Spigel (1971) report that successful exporters recognize that growth and long-term improvement in profitability are achievable only through the adoption of an international marketing outlook. Differences between individuals in international orientation may explain differences in behaviour. It is likely that an individual with a high degree of international orientation will have a higher probability both of being exposed to attention-evoking factors and of perceiving them.

The value system and past history of the principal decision maker are also important. The decision maker's international outlook, i.e. the extent to which he or she perceives and considers as interesting events occurring outside his or her own country, is of central importance (Wiedersheim-Paul *et al.*, 1978, p. 48). These authors suggest that it may be more relevant to distinguish between local and distant markets than between the domestic and the export markets.

Aspirations in international marketing are affected by many factors including the orientation of management. An accurate assessment of the firm's strengths and weaknesses and an assessment of how it should respond helps the firm to develop realistic aspirations for international markets.

Commitment to internationalization

The more specialized the resources are in respect of the specific international marketing endeavour, the greater is the firm's commitment to international marketing. The degree of commitment is higher the more the resources are integrated with other parts of the firm. Their value is derived from these integrated activities (Johanson and Vahlne, 1977). Furthermore, according to others (Penrose, 1959; Madhok, 1997) the development and integration of new knowledge with a unique application occurs incrementally within the firm. An incremental approach to knowledge acquisition enables management to form more realistic perceptions on how best to internationalize (Eriksson *et al.*, 1997). Incremental resource commitments lead to increased experiential knowledge which is stored in the procedures and routines of the firm which are directed at the internationalization process (van Ittersum and Candel 1998, p. 304). An example of resources which cannot easily be directed to another market or used for other purposes is a marketing organization which is specialized around the products of the firm and which has established an integrated system for maintaining good customer relations in various international markets.

The other aspect of organizational commitment to international marketing refers to the amount of resources committed. Here we refer to the size of the investment in the market including investment in marketing, organization, personnel and other functional areas. Included are the gathering of foreign market information, assessment of foreign market potential and formulation of basic policies towards international marketing and planning.

Managerial expectations and internationalization

Many factors influence management expectations about the effects of international markets on business goals. Expectations reflect the decision maker's present knowledge as well as perceptions of future events. Managers tend to form expectations or opinions about the profitability and riskiness of international marketing on the basis of their own knowledge and/or the experience of other firms. Environmental variables, e.g. unsolicited orders from foreign buyers or fluctuations in the exchange rate, play an important role in management's subjective assessment of the desirability of internationalization.

There is a degree of conflict regarding the role of profits from international markets as an influence on expectations. Classical economic theory implies that a firm's probability of entering international markets will vary directly with the profit its management expects. It is generally believed that the firm's attitudes towards international markets vary directly with the perceived profitability and inversely with the perceived intensity of domestic competition (Bilkey and Tesar, 1977). Experimental exporting seems to relate primarily to non-profit considerations (Bilkey, 1978). In an attempt to measure the firm's motivation to export, Bradley and Keogh (1981) draw on expectancy valence theory to develop a model of export motivation based on the following four assumptions:

1. Managers of firms have preferences among the various results which are potentially available if the firm decides to internationalize.
2. Managers have expectancies about the likelihood that an effort on their part to internationalize will lead to the intended international marketing behaviour and performance.
3. Managers have expectancies about the likelihood that certain results will follow their behaviour.
4. The decisions made are determined by the manager's expectancies and preferences in a given situation.

The expectancy valence theory of motivation is based on the idea that effort leads to performance and behaviour which in turn leads to certain results which may or may not be attractive to the growth and development of the firm (Figure 3.4).

The single most important determinant of a manager's expectations regarding the performance and behaviour of the firm for a certain level of effort committed to the internationalization process is the actual business situation facing the firm. As managers gain more experience of a given situation, they are better able to develop more accurate

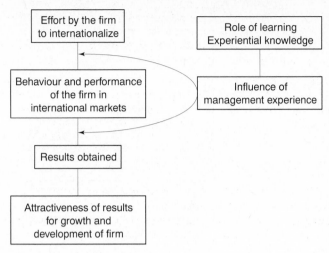

Figure 3.4 Motivation to internationalize

expectations regarding the behaviour and performance of the firm in international markets. Herein lies the role of experiential knowledge. Government sponsored programmes promoting experience of international markets are quite valuable in this regard.

The second aspect of the model, behaviour and performance leading to outcomes, shows that expectations about the consequence of performing a task also influence motivation. Since successful task performance can lead to a number of possible outcomes – various degrees of success or failure – this part of the model shows a number of expectations which reflect the manager's subjective probability regarding various results, which are strongly influenced by the actual business situation, the manager's previous experience and advice received.

They are, therefore, also experientially determined. The third aspect of the model concerns the attractiveness of the various possible results, which can be thought of as varying from very desirable to very undesirable. The model suggests, therefore, that a manager's motivation to perform or behave in a particular fashion will be influenced by his expectations of results and the attractiveness of the outcomes. This theory of motivation suggests that managerial behaviour is, to a considerable extent, a function of the interactive processes between the characteristics of the manager, such attitudes towards growth and personality traits such as cognitive style and the manager's perceived environment.

Attitude towards company growth

In this and the following sections we examine the relationships between attitudes to company growth, motivation to internationalize, the intellectual or cognitive style of managers and the stage reached in international markets (Figure 3.5). Attitudes towards the growth of the firm are determined largely by perceptions of senior management

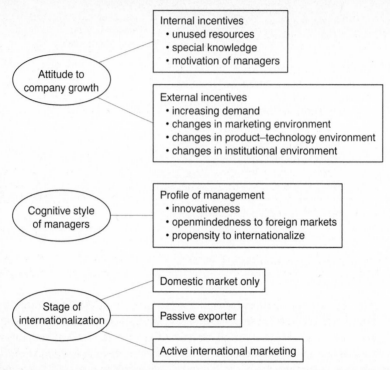

Figure 3.5 Relationship among attitude to company growth, cognitive style of managers and stage of internationalization

regarding opportunities and barriers to expansion. For instance, if it is accepted that the basic goal of the firm is security for its assets and survival, then the attitude towards growth through expansion into new products and new markets will be strongly influenced by the degree of variation perceived by managers in such variables as future sales and profits.

Where the degree of variation is high attitude towards growth will be positive, keeping in mind the insulation of the firm from potential disturbances (Wiedersheim-Paul *et al.*, 1978). Consequently, a strong motive for growth exists where the basic security of the firm is threatened by market fluctuations, and the manager's attitude becomes a powerful reason for developing diversified operations. Market changes, therefore, constitute a major force in forming attitudes towards growth of the firm.

At all times, the firm faces a variety of incentives to grow in one or more directions, but at the same time there are barriers to be overcome in implementing an expansion programme. The incentives to expand or grow may originate outside the firm or within it. External incentives to growth include increasing demand for a particular product or service, reflecting changes in the marketing environment and changes in the product technology environment which call for exploitation. External incentives in the institutional environment to grow internationally might include new or improved government-assisted business development schemes or favourable changes in tariffs and other policies designed to encourage international marketing activities.

Internal incentives to grow arise largely from the existence within the firm of a pool of unused productive services, resources and special knowledge. In many cases the firm will have a supply of these resources, but in others some resources may have to be acquired or somehow introduced. The presence of unused management services or their ready availability to the firm means that it can grow by increasing total investment. Clearly, then:

> Whenever a firm's management feels that the firm's capacity for growth is greater than that permitted by existing market and existing products, it will have an incentive to diversify. The possibility of producing new products and acquiring new markets frees the firm from the restrictions on its expansion imposed by the demand for its existing products, although not from the restrictions imposed by its existing resources.
>
> (Penrose, 1959, pp. 144–5)

Consequently, the critical restriction on growth is that imposed by existing resources, including management. It is important, therefore, to examine management attitudes toward growth of the firm in general separately.

Attitudes toward growth are also thought to be influenced by the dynamics of learning or experience and the motivation of management. The firm possesses the unique capacity to initiate its own growth: new staff may be hired, demand for the firm's products induced to expand and suppliers of capital persuaded to provide the necessary finance. 'Such growth must be based on past success and the rate is, therefore, subject to considerable dynamic restraint' (Marris, 1964, p. 114). It has been shown further that motivation and learning are two constructs which are precursors of management's attitude toward growth. The stronger the firm's motivation to grow, the greater will be the activity it generates, including search activity for new opportunities. In this connection Marris' dynamic restraint has been recognized by others: 'Over time the firm's attitude toward growth will be influenced by the type of feedback which it has received from past expansionary efforts' (Wiedersheim-Paul et al., 1978, p. 50). Consequently, attitudes toward growth are to a certain extent also determined by management perceptions of opportunities, and these opportunities are environmentally determined.

Cognitive style of managers

International outlook, foreign market orientation and dynamic firm management all refer to the same underlying aspect of management – a cognitive style which gives rise to an attitudinal propensity towards internationalization, reflecting the manager's innovative-ness and open-mindedness toward new foreign markets. The more open-minded the cognitive style of the manager, the more favourably will negative exporting outcomes be accepted (Welch and Wiedersheim-Paul, 1980). Bradley (1984) uses the term 'dogmatic' to refer to a closed cognitive style, the opposite of open-minded managers. Dogmatic managers display a closed cognitive style and are unlikely to adapt to a changing ill-structured international business environment. Firms with a high proportion of such managers are, therefore, less likely to export than their less dogmatic or more open-minded counterparts. In a study of the cognitive style of Canadian and Japanese managers, Abramson *et al.* (1993, pp. 584–5) conclude that the North American tendency to overlook relationship building is reflected in the finding that the Canadians displayed a cognitive style that reduced the importance of the human element in favour of analytical, impersonal, rational factors. These authors suggest that, in dealing with the Japanese, North American managers may benefit from special training in intercultural interaction skills.

Finally, environments, business frameworks and management tasks which are highly structured, as they are in a well-established domestic market, tend to be favoured by the highly dogmatic manager (Faschingbauer *et al.*, 1978). It is thus likely that they will not exhibit a high propensity to internationalize. International markets are demonstrably unstructured, involve considerable risk, require considerable innovation and adoption of new ideas and management processes and are characterized by the need for information and the assistance of external support agencies. It is expected, therefore, that active international companies will be much less dogmatic than their passive counterparts. The style of mangement of international companies has some of its roots in the cultural origins of the managers themselves but is also influenced by the way managers think and the way they have been trained to think (Exhibit 3.2).

Exhibit 3.2
Style of management in different countries

In-depth analysis of senior executives from more than 2,500 companies representing the U.K., Ireland, France, Sweden, Germany, Finland, Spain and Austria clearly highlight no common European management style but, instead, four distinct styles of strategic management.

- Directive leadership: Spanish, British, Finnish, and half of the Irish companies strongly displayed the characteristic of strong, bordering on autocratic, leadership. Qualities of determination and a passionate belief in the vision being pursued, coupled with a people orientation, characterise how strategies are formed and initiatives implemented.
- Consensus-driven: The senior managers of Swedish and the remaining Irish companies would go to considerable lengths to ensure clarity of communication and shared understanding of policies and operational concerns through considerable discussion and attention to detail. Talking is not enough.
- Striving for the common goal: Emphasis on professional skills coupled with a strong leadership drive and a discipline for effective follow-through helps clearly identified ends to be met. Not surprisingly, the top management of German and Austrian companies fall into this category. Surprising, however, is the degree of friction and poor personal relationships exhibited.

● Managing as élites: The French stood out – as the only ones who as a nation display a particular management style. Surprisingly, no other European companies showed similar characteristics. The predominant influences of the Grandes Écoles is obvious, as displays of autocracy, drive, debating qualities and considerable intellectual sophistication are linked to personal styles of being distant and 'communicating on a need to know' basis. Attention to detail and compliance with systems and procedures is evident. The discipline for 'follow through', however, is lacking.

The implications of such findings for mergers, acquisitions and the running of multi-nationals, are fundamental. Similar symptoms in one context could mean morale concerns and in another a misunderstanding of market circumstances. Getting the styles right is a serious business.   *Source:* adapted from A. Kakabadse, 'Performing in style', *The Independent*, 7 April 1993, p. 31.

Preventing internationalization failure

There are many factors which are believed to influence the pre-internationalization stage. These include managerial time and expense which must be devoted to sales, visiting foreign markets and collecting market information. As a result of these search and information gathering activities, the manager is more likely to develop a balanced positive attitude towards internationalization. The experience thus gained allows the manager to perceive problems as a series of small manageable issues that are more easily resolved.

The investment of managerial time is especially important for smaller firms. This initial stage in the internationalization process 'warrants careful study as it represents a key establishment phase in the process of international growth' (Welch and Wiedersheim-Paul, 1980, pp. 333–4).

The firm new to international marketing has, however, no previous experience or measure of performance in international markets on which to base a level of aspiration regarding the outcomes of this new activity. For this reason the objective criterion of successful feedback will vary widely from company to company and is likely to be highly related to the perception and expectations of the key decision makers in each instance (Welch and Wiedersheim-Paul, 1980, p. 338). If the manager has a well-developed international outlook on the environment, the negative aspects of feedback are likely to be accorded less importance than the positive elements (Wiedersheim-Paul *et al.*, 1978, pp. 48–9).

The likelihood of withdrawal from international markets as a result of perceived negative early experience of such markets is thought to be strongly related to the degree of commitment to the internationalization process. Many authors on the subject argue that psychological commitment as manifested through changes in attitude is more important than financial commitment. Lack of such commitment frequently shows itself as passive performance in international markets responding to unsolicited requests from foreign potential customers instead of actively seeking new foreign business. A passive disposition usually results in the firm eventually withdrawing from international markets.

Discussing exporting as a primary form of internationalization, Welch and Wieders-heim-Paul (1980, pp. 341–3) state 'firms displaying an active form of export marketing behaviour may fail as exporters for some period of time. Usually this comes about because of developments in the firm's external environment which are beyond its immediate control . . .' and the likelihood of success of the new venture 'is not assisted by the adoption of a relatively passive degree of export marketing activity in response to the initial involvement – failure almost becomes a self fullfilling exercise as the marketing effort is not sufficient to maintain or expand export sales'. In new ventures such as exporting, growth is not spontaneous or self-generating – it requires the coordination of decisions and actions to carry the firm beyond the stage of experimentation.

Motivation to internationalize

The way in which managers are motivated to internationalize their firm's activities was discussed above under management expectations. It is possible to measure motivation to internationalize by:

1. understanding the manager's attitude towards company growth,
2. identifying the manager's cognitive or intellectual style, and
3. determining how the manager is motivated to continue in business in stressful situations.

There appears to be no significant difference between passive and active exporters in regard to attitude towards company growth (Bradley, 1981). This study also concluded that there is a strong positive correlation between exporting experience and motivation to export. Potential exporters, having no experience, are least motivated to export, whereas the most experienced group were highly motivated. Active exporters are also much less dogmatic about their environment and their role in business than are potential exporters.

Strategic and opportunistic approaches to internationalization

A major difficulty facing many firms in attempting to internationalize is that they respond to the environment and international competition by trial and error or as a process of incrementalism based on an opportunistic response to market development. As a result, beneficial small changes are gradually adopted in a process of adapting to the existing situation, an evolutionary, expedient process. Because it is expedient and evolutionary it frequently produces meagre short-term results which are opportunistic and, therefore, not coupled with their long-run consequences. In contrast, the requirement for firms seeking to survive in international markets is to adopt a revolutionary or strategic perspective on international competition. Strategic competition is comprehensive in its commitment; it involves the dedication of the whole firm (Mitchell and Bradley, 1986).

Strategic approach to international markets

For firms new to competing in international markets the reluctance to compete on strategic terms rather than on the basis of increments is understandable for two reasons. First, strategic failure can be as widespread in its consequences as strategic success (Welch and Wiedersheim-Paul, 1980). Second, incumbents in foreign markets frequently possess a competitive advantage over new entrants. Strategic success frequently depends on the culture, perceptions and attributes of the firm and its competitors. The basic elements of strategic competition refer to the firm's ability to understand competitive interaction as a dynamic system that includes the activities of competitors, customers, finance and the resources of the firm itself (Bradley, 1985). It also includes the ability to use this understanding to predict the consequences of a given intervention in that system.

Strategic competition also means that there are uncommitted resources which may be dedicated permanently to uses which have a long-term payoff (Penrose, 1959). It also implies that management has the training and skill to predict risk and return with sufficient accuracy and confidence to justify the commitment of such resources. Finally, it means that firms must be willing to act deliberately to make the commitment to invest in marketing and markets (Johanson and Mattsson, 1984).

It is this lack of commitment to developing marketing resources within the firm and to developing markets which has recently come to be recognized as a central management concern. To counteract some of the problems which arise firms spend considerable sums of money developing staff. Recently there has been a trend towards internationalizing the staff of the firms themselves.

International market experience

Much of the literature on export marketing refers to the activity just described as a process of internationalization by which firms gradually increase their international involvement (Johanson and Vahlne, 1977). The incrementalism of this process has been stressed. In this section we suggest that management behaviour differs from one stage to another. This suggests a learning process whereby experiential knowledge is obtained through the firm's international experiences which, through its effect on perceptions, knowledge and confidence, results in either increased or decreased commitment to the internationalization process (Yaprak, 1985). The essence of these arguments is that the firm evolves through sequential phases of commitment. Firms further along the path are likely to have greater knowledge and are likely to possess more sophisticated management skills than domestic and passive firms.

Lack of knowledge in respect of foreign markets and operations is an important obstacle in the development of international operations. Objective market knowledge from which it is possible to formulate theoretical foreign market opportunities and experiential knowledge which allows the manager to perceive concrete export marketing opportunities are both necessary (Johanson and Vahlne, 1977, p. 26). The internationalization process through which the firm proceeds depends, therefore, on obtaining experiential knowledge, and thus the firm moves through a process of increasing foreign market commitment. The identification of an internationalization process in international market development has encouraged the formulation and testing of the concept of stages in international market development.

Various 'stages models' of internationalization have been proposed (Bilkey, 1978; Cannon and Dawson, 1977). Their similarities outweigh their differences. A three-groups framework which includes firms which are entirely domestically oriented and have no record or knowledge of international markets and have never received an export order, passive exporters or firms which respond to unsolicited inquiries and active international marketing companies which exhibit a continuous pattern of winning foreign business is sufficient for the present discussion.

For firms to move through the first stage, they require the influence and direction of senior management and perhaps a change in their orientation and perception of the attractiveness of international markets *per se*. The second group, passive exporters, are those who have some experience of international markets, having responded in the past to unsolicited export orders. Critical to this stage is the receipt of an unsolicited export order (Bilkey, 1978, p. 42). While passive exporters have some history of meeting export orders, they do not devote any direct sales or marketing effort to winning international business. These firms are still experimenting with the internationalization process. The third group includes experienced international marketing firms. Management expectations in regard to the effect of international marketing on profits, company growth and objectives are the most important determinants of international marketing behaviour among these firms. This three-groups model has been used in a number of circumstances and is believed to be particularly appropriate in analysing the internationalization behaviour of smaller firms (Bradley, 1981; Bradley and Keogh, 1981). In recent years there has been some criticism of the stages model as many firms do not seem to follow its predictions, especially firms in high technology industries with short product life cycles. Nevertheless, the stages model does provide a useful categorization of the kinds of problems faced by the firm at various stages of evolution to becoming an international firm.

Commitment to internationalization

Commitment to international markets requires that the firm devotes financial and human resources, as well as management attention, to carrying out tasks that are new to it and for building the infrastructure required for export marketing. Commitment to international market development means devoting resources to understanding and to developing the market. The firm's resources and characteristics are interwoven and influence the level of commitment, aspirations and expectations which among them determine how the firm behaves in international markets.

Commitment is also related to risk and uncertainty perceptions, where instability or a decline in the domestic market may increase the firm's search for diversification possibilities, thus decreasing the risk previously associated with exports. This, therefore, results in a more favourable attitude and probably increased commitment.

Firms classified as 'committed exporters' exhibit a higher propensity to engage in certain planning activities than do non-committed or passive exporters (Cavusgil, 1984). These activities include budgeting, the statement of specific export goals and the creation of a distinct structure or responsibility centre for export management. However, empirical tests have produced disappointing results, even for companies regarded as aggressive exporters (Tesar and Tarleton, 1982). There is little evidence to support the hypothesis that all stages of the exporting process result from a carefully developed strategy devised to achieve the maximization of specified goals. Given the way in which firms commit resources to international marketing, it is reasonable to conclude that for some stages in the process, at least, international marketing activity tends to be unplanned, reactive and opportunistic.

Measuring commitment to international markets

While commitment is not directly measurable, certain proxies can be used to indicate commitment (Daniels and Robles, 1982). The first is determination of whether firms are engaged in exporting. Many firms decide not to export even when unsolicited orders come to them (Simpson and Kujawa, 1974). Export activity therefore, however slight, marks an important decision in the commitment process. The second proxy, length of export experience, is based on the theory that exporting is a development and learning process. Even if firms have commenced exporting, however, and have some involvement over a prolonged period of time, there is no assurance of high commitment.

Sales may be so small, cyclical or treated passively that management does not incorporate foreign market conditions into its overall strategy. For this reason a third proxy, export volume as a percentage of total production, is sometimes used as the basis of the premise that a greater dependence on exports indicates a greater commitment.

Similarly, other proxies such as visits to foreign markets, time spent abroad in a given year, attendance of trade fairs, purchase of reports, foreign communications and other similar measures may be used as indicators of export commitment.

The firm in international markets is mainly motivated by internal factors such as a desire to increase profit, to achieve company growth, gain experience and to spread risk (Mitchell and Bradley, 1986). These motivations did not, however, seem to shift dramatically over the stages of the exporting process described but were rather stable.

Regarding expected profitability, optimism tended to increase by stage of internationalization. This probably shows the role of experience and its effect on the perceived risk of the firm during the process. Statistical tests showed that this optimism and decreased risk perception translated into greater commitment, as hypothesized. On the basis of this finding there is strong support for a determining relationship among exporting motives, expectations and aspirations and subsequent commitment to exporting activities.

International marketing motives when filtered through the organization and mediated by management are likely to result in certain expectations and aspirations which in turn translate into positive or negative commitment to international marketing.

Resources and management: an integrated view

Resources and capabilities determine the firm's long-run strategy and are the primary source of profit. In an environment which is changing rapidly and where consumer tastes and preferences are volatile and myriad, as found in international markets, a definition of the business in terms of what the firm is capable of doing may offer a more durable basis for strategy than a traditional definition, based on needs and wants of consumers. Defining markets too broadly is of little help to the firm that cannot easily develop the capabilities to serve such a broad market.

The firm's ability to earn profits depends on two factors: the success of the firm in establishing competitive advantage over rivals and the attractiveness of the industry in which the firm competes. As was seen above, the two sources of competitive advantage are the ability of the firm to reduce costs and its ability to differentiate itself in ways that are important to customers. The ability to establish a cost advantage requires the possession of scale-efficient plants, access to low cost raw materials or labour and superior process technology. Differentiation advantages derive from brand reputation, proprietary and patented technology and an extensive marketing network covering distribution, sales and services.

The attractiveness of an industry depends on the power the firm can exert over customers, rivals and others in the business system, which derives from the existence of market entry barriers. Market entry barriers are based on brands, patents, price and the power of competitive retaliation. These are resources which are accumulated slowly over time and a new entrant can only obtain at disproportionate expense (Grant, 1991, p. 115). Other sources of market power such as price-setting abilities depend on market share which is a consequence of cost efficiency, firm size and financial resources. Grant (1991) has integrated these ideas in a way which serves as a very convenient summary of this discussion (Figure 3.6). An important aspect of the framework for international marketing is that the resources which confer market power may be owned individually by firms or by independent firms located in different countries.

Summary

This chapter focuses attention on the resources and managerial capacity required for successful internationalization. Resources are linked to aspirations in the firm and also determine the extent of its competitive advantage in international markets. The characteristics of the firm in terms of objectives, technology, product location and size influence the aspirations of managers and hence the success of the firm. The principal resource available to the firm is open-minded management which seeks to develop the firm in international markets. By committing resources in a strategic way the firm can succeed in international markets. There are, however, many kinds of firm, many of which never succeed abroad. Only a small proportion of firms successfully internationalize.

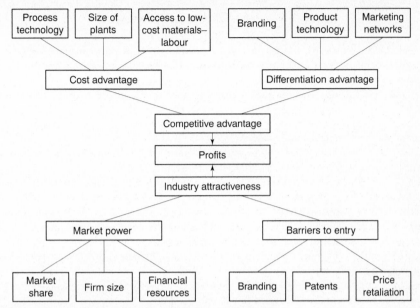

Figure 3.6 Resources determine profitability in the firm
Source: adapted from Grant, R. M. (1991) 'The resource-based theory of competitive advantage: implications for strategy formulation', *California Management Review*, Spring 1991, p. 118. Copyright © 1991 by the Regents of the University of California. Reprinted by permission of the Regents.

Discussion questions

1. A major prerequisite for success in international markets is possession by the firm of a competitive advantage. Identify and discuss the most common sources of competitive advantage found in international firms.

2. While most firms pay close attention to the importance of external factors as they internationalize, many firms fail to consider internal factors adequately. What are these internal factors and how important are they to the firm in international markets?

3. Is it necessary to adopt a specific business outlook for success in international markets? Is such an outlook a prerequisite for the motivation in firms to internationalize?

4. Many commentators have suggested that firm size and motivation to succeed in international markets are closely correlated. Discuss. Is there a possible conflict in this relationship?

5. The process of internationalizing the firm can be seen as a sequential process of increasing knowledge and foreign market commitment. Discuss.

6. Distinguish clearly between opportunistic and strategic international marketing. Is there a relationship between opportunistic international marketing behaviour and a commitment to compete in international markets?

References

Abramson, N. R., Whane, H., Nagai, H. and Takagi, H. (1993) 'A comparison of Canadian and Japanese cognitive styles: implications for management interaction', *Journal of International Business Studies*, **24** (3), 575–83.

Barney, J. B. (1991) 'Firm resources and sustained competitive advantage', *Journal of Management*, **17**, 99–120.

Bilkey, W. J. (1978) 'An attempted integration of the literature on the export behaviour of firms', *Journal of International Business Studies*, **9** (1), 33–46.

Bilkey, W. J. and Tesar, G. (1977) 'The export behaviour of smaller-sized Wisconsin manufacturing firms', *Journal of International Business Studies*, **8** (1), 93–8.

Bradley, M. F. (1981) 'Attitudes to export marketing growth among small scale enterprises: a discriminant analysis', *Proceedings, Marketing Education Group, (United Kingdom), Annual Conference, St Patrick's College, Dublin, 7–9 July*.

Bradley, M. F. (1984) 'Effects of cognitive style, attitude toward growth and motivation on the internationalization of the firm', *Research in Marketing*, **7**, 237–60.

Bradley, M. F. (1985) 'Key factors influencing international competitiveness', *Journal of Irish Business and Administrative Research*, **7** (2), 3–14.

Bradley, M. F. and Keogh, P. (1981) 'Export management: motivated–openminded', *Journal of Irish Business and Administrative Research*, **3** (2), 29–40.

Cannon, T. and Dawson, G. (1977) 'Developing the export potential of small firms', *Industrial and Commercial Training*, **8** (7), 292–5.

Cavusgil, S. T. (1984) 'Organisational characteristics associated with export activity', *Journal of Management Studies*, **21** (1), 3–9.

Cavusgil, S. T. and Nevin, J. R. (1981) 'Internal determinants of export marketing behaviour: an empirical investigation', *Journal of Marketing Research*, **18**, 114–15.

Cunningham, M. T. and Spigel, R. I. (1971) 'A study in successful exporting', *British Journal of Marketing*, **5** (1), 2–12.

Daniels, J. D. and Robles, F. (1982) 'Choice of technology and export commitment: the Peruvian textile industry', *Journal of International Business Studies*, **13**, 67–87.

Day, G. (1994) 'The capabilities of market-driven organizations', *Journal of Marketing*, **58** (October), 37–52.

Demsetz, H. (1991) 'The theory of the firm re-visited' in O. E. Williamson and S. G. Winter (eds), *The Nature of the Firm*, New York, NY: Oxford University Press, pp.159–78.

Dierickx, I. and Cool, K. (1989) 'Asset stock accumulation and sustainability of competitive advantage', *Management Science*, **35** (December), 1504–11.

Eriksson, K. J., Johanson, J., Majkgard, A. and Sharma, D. (1997) 'Experiential knowledge and cost in the internationalization process', *Journal of International Business Studies*, **28** (2), 337–60.

Faschingbauer, T. R., Moore, C. D. and Stone, A. (1978) 'Cognitive style, dogmatism and creativity: some implications regarding cognitive development', *Psychological Reports*, **42**, 795–804.

Grant, R. M. (1991) 'The resource based theory of competitive advantage: implications for strategy formulation', *California Management Review* (Spring), 114–35.

Grant, R. M. (1996) 'Toward a knowledge-based theory of the firm', *Strategic Management Journal*, **17** (Winter Special Issue), 109–22.

Grant, R. M. (1997) 'The knowledge-based view of the firm: implications for management practice', *Long Range Planning*, **30** (3), 450–4.

Johanson, J. and Mattsson, L.-G. (1984) 'Marketing assets in networks', *Proceedings, Second International Marketing Strategy Seminar, University of Manchester Institute of Science and Technology, Manchester, 2–4 September.*

Johanson, J. and Vahlne, J.-E. (1977) 'The internationalisation process of the firm model of knowledge development and increasing foreign marketing commitments', *Journal of International Business Studies,* **8** (1), 23–30.

Lippman, S. A. and Rumelt, R. P. (1992) 'Uncertain imitability: an analysis of interfirm differences in efficiency under competition', *The Bell Journal of Economics,* **13**, 418–38.

Madhok, A. (1997) 'Cost, value and foreign market entry mode: the transaction and the firm', *Strategic Management Journal,* **18**, 39–61.

Marris, R. (1964) *The Economic Theory of Managerial Capitalization,* New York, NY: The Free Press of Glencoe.

Mitchell, O. and Bradley, F. (1986) 'Export commitment in the firm – strategic or opportunistic behaviour', *Journal of Irish Business and Administrative Research,* **8** (Part 2), 12–19.

Montgomery, C. A. and S. Hariharen (1991) 'Diversified expansion by larger established firms', *Journal of Economic Behaviour and Organization,* **12**, 71–89.

Penrose, E. (1959) *The Theory of the Growth of the Firm,* Oxford: Basil Blackwell.

Peteraf, M. A. (1993) 'The cornerstones of competitive advantage: a resource based view', *Strategic Management Journal,* **14**, 179–91.

Porter M. E. (1980) *Competitive Strategy: Techniques for analysing industries and competitors,* New York, NY: The Free Press.

Prahalad, C. K. and Hamel, G. (1990) 'The core competence of the corporation', *Harvard Business Review,* **68**, 79–91.

Reid, S. D. (1981) 'The decision maker and export entry and expansion', *Journal of International Business Studies,* **12** (2), 101–12.

Rommel, G., Kluge, J., Kempis, R.-D., Diederichs R. and Brück F. (1995) *Simplicity Wins,* Boston, MA: Harvard Business School Press.

Simmonds, K. and Smith, H. (1968) 'The first export order: a marketing innovation', *British Journal of Marketing,* **2** (Summer), 93–100.

Simpson, C. L. and Kujawa, D. (1974) 'The export-decision process: an empirical inquiry', *Journal of International Business Studies,* **5** (Spring), 107–17.

Teece, D. J., Pisano, G. and Shuen, A. (1996) 'Dynamic capabilities and strategic management', *University of California, Berkeley, Working Paper,* July, 53 pp.

Tesar, G. and Tarleton, J. S. (1982) 'Comparison of Wisconsin and Virginia small and medium sized exporters: aggressive and passive exporters', in M. R. Czinkota and G. Tesar (eds), *Export Management,* New York, NY: Praeger, pp. 85–112.

Thompson, A. A. Jr. and Strickland, A. J. III (1996) *Strategic Management,* 9th edn, Chicago, IL: Irwin.

van Ittersum, K. and Candel, M. J. J. M. (1998) 'Development of experiential knowledge in internationalization through customer–supplier relationships', in P. Andersson (ed.) *Track 6, Consumer Behaviour, Proceedings, 27th, EMAC Conference, Stockholm, 20–23 May,* pp. 297–308.

Wiedersheim-Paul, F., Olson, H. C. and Welch, L. (1978) 'Pre-export activity: the first step in internationalization', *Journal of International Business Studies,* **9** (1), 47–58.

Welch, L. and Wiedersheim-Paul, F. (1980) 'Initial exports – a marketing failure', *Journal of Management Studies,* **9** (October), 333–44.

Yaprak, A. (1985) 'An empirical study of the differences between small exporting and non-exporting US firms', *International Marketing Review,* **2** (Summer), 72–82.

4

Strategic options for the firm

In this chapter we outline a framework for analysing international marketing strategies and discuss a number of options open to the firm. The manager needs a framework to assist in making a selection among such strategies. The international competitive environment which directly affects the performance of firms in the various product markets is becoming increasingly complex and dynamic. Successful international firms first examine the competitive environment before determining the appropriate marketing response. In implementing such responses a clear indication of how to combine the various product-market options available with the appropriate means of foreign market entry is clearly desirable.

Marketing orientation in international competitive environment

A marketing orientation attempts to free the firm from the shackles of competition by identifying and developing a competitive advantage. Competitive advantage derives from the firm's orientation to its environment and the competition. A marketing orientation means starting with customer needs and focusing the firm's resources on these needs at a profit. It also means matching the firm's resources with the needs of the market. Marketing means identifying and managing the area of overlap between the company's resources and customer needs to ensure that the customer obtains:

- the benefits desired when and where wanted at an acceptable price, while
- producing a profit for the firm.

Frequently used marketing strategy options include:

- new products;
- new markets;
- more intensive and/or new distribution channels;
- better production facilities;

- increased marketing expenditures;
- price reductions;
- acquisition of other companies.

In this chapter we are concerned with developing and entering new foreign markets and the role of marketing strategy in assisting the firm in so doing. Developing foreign markets means treating the world market as a series of segments, each with different needs and wants. Successful market segmentation means careful selection of country markets, regions and customers. A related decision refers to market sequencing to acquire product experience and customer ranking, distribution penetration and market expansion (contiguous versus distant markets) as the firm develops its various product markets. Consideration of market flexibility involving variation in the mix across markets and by stage of development of product markets is, therefore, central to the growth of the firm.

Ideally, international market entry costs should be reasonable with the cost of error acceptable, and the industry structure should be favourable with little chance of competitive retaliation. This means entering the markets in the right manner which often involves product-market studies, new product features, less product at lower price, built-in quality and reliability, smaller versions of standard products, better customer relations or sequenced distribution and selective promotion.

New market entry should support other aspects of the firm's business. This means entering the right markets resulting from accurately targeted industries to accommodate company resources while recognizing the stage of product-market evolution. Consideration must also be given to scale effects on the marketing mix while accounting for the strength of competition.

Challenge of innovative companies

In recent years, we have witnessed a revolution in the way companies challenge customers and other competitors in international markets. Expensive branded products have been challenged by less expensive, high-quality substitutes. An increasing number of suppliers of superior products and services have joined the fray, thus widening the competitive cycle. New technologies have allowed cross-category competition, especially in services, but also in traditional materials industries. Low-cost information, outsourcing, reduced scale of manufacturing have contributed to lowering the barriers to entry. The internet and abundance of customer information has reduced switching costs. Frequently, newcomers to a market have easier access to capital and they may also have large cash flows from their home market which represents a formidable threat to incumbents, especially if they are inefficient, small and not very innovative.

Required international marketing response

Rising foreign competition, from the Far East in particular, turbulent financial markets and new technologies have created an era of rapid and painful change for many companies.

Many companies accustomed to operating in less volatile times with protected and virtually guaranteed markets under relatively fixed exchange rates, have faltered or closed.

For the firm new to international markets, there are a range of possible outcomes which are defined by a limited number of key variables, but the actual outcome may lie anywhere along a continuum, bounded by a range of possibilities, where it is difficult to identify any natural scenarios. Scenarios that identify the extreme points of the range of possible outcomes are relatively easy to develop (a worst-case scenario – a best-case scenario), but these rarely provide much guidance for strategic decisions (Courtney *et al.*, 1997, p. 72). When Guinness introduced its subsequently very successful Draught Guinness in a can to export markets, all that market research could identify for the UK market was a broad range of potential penetration rates ranging from 15 per cent to 40 per cent of the relevant segment. Such a broad range of estimates is, however, quite common when entering a foreign market with a completely new product or service. In such circumstances, it is difficult to determine the level of latent demand. Guinness would be very likely to follow a very different and more aggressive strategy if it knew for certain that its market penetration rates would be closer to 40 per cent than to 15 per cent.

In new international markets there are, therefore, unlikely to be discrete actionable scenarios for the company to follow, so that deciding which possible outcomes should be developed into alternative scenarios is as much an art as it is a science. Courtney *et al.* (1997, p. 72) offer some general rules:

1. develop only a limited number of scenarios – the complexity of juggling more than four or five tends to hinder decision making;
2. avoid developing redundant scenarios that have no unique implications for strategic decision making – ensure that each scenario presents a distinct profile of the industry – structure, conduct and performance;
3. develop a set of scenarios that collectively account for the probable range of future outcomes and not necessarily the entire possible range.

Once the company has identified the broad thrust of its development, it attempts to identify a number of strategic options. In general, firms attempt to design their strategic options to secure the large pay-offs of the best-case scenarios while minimizing losses in the worst-case scenarios. Most firms make modest initial investments in international markets that will allow them to increase or reduce the investment as the market evolves. Before the full-scale introduction of Draught Guinness into the UK, for example, Guinness conducted a number of market trials. Other companies enter into limited joint ventures for distribution to minimize the risk of entering a new market. Firms often licence an alternative technology on the chance that it might prove to be superior to existing technology.

At the same time, firms attempt to complement risky strategies with other initiatives to protect itself, e.g. cost reduction, gathering competitive marketing information or developing in-house skills.

Product-market development

In order to avoid opportunistic responses there are a number of things that successful firms do and a number they eschew. In a period of rapid change and discontinuity in the environment, the successful firm avoids knee-jerk reactions to difficulties in the market place. Successful product markets can only be developed with patience and careful planning. Longridge Winery in South Africa patiently built up its customer base and developed its products to suit particular market segments. Longridge wines are now well established and supported by a network of distributors in many countries (Exhibit 4.1). Firms should, therefore, avoid attempting to introduce instant new products. Only products or product attributes with a very short life cycle can be introduced at short notice and without due strategic thinking. Creating a permanent and successful challenge in most markets is very difficult. The most difficult task is to develop a new product which will permanently avoid the attention of direct competitors. Examples of many such successes may be cited:

- Polaroid instant camera;
- General Foods soluble decaffeinated coffee;
- Hewlett-Packard scientific calculators;
- Honda lightweight motorcycles;
- Baileys Original Irish Cream.

Eventually, competition may become direct as competitors imitate the strategy, e.g. Kodak, Nestlé, Texas Instruments, Kawasaki and Emmetts and the many other cream liqueur imitators. The current battle in the international market place between Fuji and Kodak also serves to illustrate this point. Successful companies also avoid attempting to develop instant new markets. In this context it should be realized that there are very few left and those that remain must be treated in a deliberate and strategic way. It is usually wrong to jump into markets; since they follow certain rhythms the company may miss the opportunity. A more powerful strategy is to get in ahead of the crowd and to enjoy the benefits of a developing marketing infrastructure. In this way the firm avoids the bandwagon effect when the costs of serving the market begin to increase and the market then declines or disappears.

   One way some companies have of beating the crowd is to use their products and services as platforms. This is a recognition that competition has moved firms beyond the business of supplying a product alone. Products and services have become platforms for information, additional technology and service. Indeed many products and services have changed from being a goal in themselves to being a means of establishing close, long-term, interactive customer relationships.

Technology, product and market decisions

The firm must also consider in which direction it should innovate when considering an internationalization strategy. The simplest move, as was seen above, is to sell existing products abroad. Rarely does such a simple strategy work. Usually the firm must adapt its products, and sometimes even its technology, when considering entry to new inter-national markets, thus innovating on three dimensions: product, technology and market (Figure 4.1). The origin in this diagram, Point 1, represents present circumstances and

━━━━━━ **Exhibit 4.1** ━━━━━━

Longridge Winery of Stellenbosch goes global

Longridge Winery in Stellenbosch, a relative newcomer to the ranks of Cape Wine Wholesalers in South Africa, has been quick to develop a reputation as négociant, importer, and a winery with strong links to Burgundy. From its inception in 1992, trading first as négociant Du Preez & Laubser (D&L), Longridge was earmarked as an international operation. The first order taken by co-founder Johann Laubser came from the UK. It now concentrates on producing its own wines, the winery's case-count has risen to nearly 200,000, some 80 per cent of which is exported.

Johann Laubser admits that they earned their stripes by supplying European Supermarkets with custom-made 'Buyers' Own Brands' (BOB), particularly in France and the Benelux countries. But, despite its on-going success in this field, Longridge is committed to shifting the emphasis to 'the development of good, strong own-brands' under its own labels. More than half of the 200,000-odd cases produced by and for Longridge from the 1997 vintage will be sold as own-brands, mainly Longridge and second-label Bay View.

Alex Dale, the company's oenological expert with a decade of experience in the Burgundy wine trade, explains the philosophy and aims of Longridge by reflecting on the role that independent producer wholesalers such as Penfolds, Lindemans and Rosemount have played in gaining international recognition and success for Australia as a producer of wine at the quality end of the scale. To support this strategy, Longridge has concentrated on establishing links with reputable international distribution companies such as Rèmy Martin, John E Fells & Sons (jointly owned by Symington Port and Spain's Torres families) and Moët-Hennessy (to cover the burgeoning Asian market).

The company hopes to build similarly lasting relationships at source. Leading private cellars supply special parcels, and Longridge also relies on half a dozen or so contracted growers, mostly on prime land in the Stellenbosch and Durbanville regions to provide some quality raw materials required to produce fine wines. 'We feel it's essential if we wish to be in control of our own destiny,' says Dale.

Source: adapted from *Wine (South Africa),* July 1997, pp. 50–3.

any distance in any of the three directions specified represents an innovation (Carroad and Carroad, 1982). Selling an existing product overseas without any change is represented by Point 2 which is itself an innovation since it involves a whole new marketing programme for a different market.

The firm might also innovate by developing a new product based on existing technology, Point 3. An example of this would be the introduction of a private label brand of whisky to position against brand leaders. The firm may reduce its production costs by introducing new technology. A change to computer process technology in the food industry, Point 4, could mean improved product and or lower product cost. Here the product is unchanged and so are the markets but the technology is modernized.

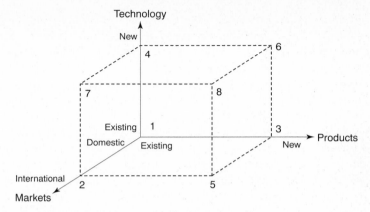

Figure 4.1 The technology–product–market decision
Source: adapted from Carroad, P. A. and Carroad, C. A. (1982) 'Strategic interfacing of R&D and marketing', *Research Management*, January, 28–33.

Frequently, firms develop new products for new international markets but based on present technology, Point 5. The introduction to Greece of branded regato cheese by the Irish Dairy Board under its Kerrygold brand would fit this situation. In this case product development was substantial but a large lucrative market in Greece was discovered and developed. The technology of regato cheese manufacture was known as the Irish Dairy Board had previously exported similar, but unbranded, cheeses to other European countries, especially Italy.

When Guinness developed its alcohol-free beer, Kaliber, it required a new technology to remove alcohol from the beer, which resulted in the development of a new product for an existing market, Point 6. Alcohol-free beers have successfully entered the beer market. For some beer consumers alcohol-free beers have replaced ordinary beers, especially under certain circumstances, e.g. before driving, after a long drinking session or for health and dietary reasons. Interactive video is an example of a new technology in an existing product which entered the new educational and training market, threatening traditional books and teaching methods in the process, Point 7. Finally, Baileys Original Irish Cream was a new product based on a new technology, aimed at a new market, Point 8. It was a new product in that it is made from whiskey and cream but with lower alcohol than products it was designed to replace. It was based on a new technology since it is difficult to mix spirits and cream successfully. The product was developed in Ireland but from the start it was developed for the large lucrative international markets throughout the world, especially the US. Clearly, any innovation which takes the firm along two or more of the dimensions discussed above requires considerable planning and company resources. Innovating on any one dimension requires considerable care. The difficulty arises when firms attempt to minimize the extent of the innovation when the customer requires innovation on more than one dimension and perhaps on all three dimensions.

Innovation provides unambiguous advantages to the customer and the innovator, especially if the innovation is also pioneering. There are a number of customer responses, the benefits of which accrue to the pioneer. When customers successfully use the first brand in a new product category or in a new market, they will tend to favour it over later entrants because they know with certainty that it provides desired values and works for them. The pioneer also influences how consumers evaluate attributes in the product category and the pioneer's product may become the standard for the category. For this reason, the pioneer may be able to 'lock in' consumers in categories that have high switching costs. This is especially true in industrial markets. Lastly, firms that enter international markets early and position themselves near the centre of the market can obtain higher profits. The pioneer also benefits more directly from the technology leadership which accrues from being first in the market. Technology enables pioneers consistently to have better products than competitors and, with a limited number of technology suppliers, long-term agreements may prevent late entrants from obtaining the technology.

There are, however, a number of disadvantages of being the innovator. Free rider effects are present when a late entrant is able to acquire the same technology at a lower cost. Late entrants may sometimes have access to cheaper or more productive labour or materials than the pioneer. The late entrant may also be able to 'leap-frog' the pioneer by acquiring new and better technology. Frequently, pioneers, especially if they are small under-resourced firms, may be unwilling or unable to commit sufficient resources to succeed in new markets.

Strategic corporate response: general considerations

In formulating a strategy, the company must distinguish between purpose, what it exists to do, and constraints, what it must do in order to survive. 'The answer to developing a good strategy . . . lies in the manager's understanding of the fundamental points: the benefits of having a well articulated, stable purpose, and the importance of discovering, understanding, documenting, and exploiting insights about how to create more value than other companies do' (Campbell and Alexander, 1997, p. 42).

The purpose limits the range of strategic choices that must be evaluated and, therefore, helps to simplify strategy development. The more focused and detailed the purpose is, the more likely it is that a company will be able to develop a winning strategy. The firm's purpose can define the product or technology, the market to be targeted, the type of positioning to be achieved and the values that must guide behaviour (Campbell and Alexander, 1997, p. 50). A well-defined company purpose gives long-term directional stability to the firm without forcing it into an unrealistic strategy.

In recent years we have witnessed a convergence of strategic responses to new international competition among companies. The convergence of strategies among market leaders is a good indication of maturity in a particular industry. Many of these responses relate to marketing while others relate to the modes of international market entry. Others refer to costs, finance and the need to restructure the firm to compete in international markets (Figure 4.2).

Two general considerations face the firm intent on developing an international marketing strategy. First, it is necessary to examine its cost structure, which may result in

Figure 4.2 Convergence of strategic responses

the need to reduce costs and/or restructure the firm. Second, it is necessary to determine the firm's position on the issue of growth and how that can be achieved in the circumstances of discontinuity which typifies international markets.

Managers of international firms face two challenges: (1) to ensure that strategy does not reflect the biases rooted in the company's successes in the domestic market; (2) once a viable strategy is discovered, that resources are allocated in a way that accurately reflects the strategy. The strategy should reflect the firm's environment and the resource allocation should reflect the strategy (Christensen, 1997, p. 142).

In providing guidance to the company about what it should do in international markets, it is first necessary to define the fundamental issues likely to be faced, then to formulate an appropriate strategy and, lastly, to prepare a plan to manage the myriad projects through which the strategy can be implemented. At the first stage, the company identifies the economic, technological, demographic and competitive factors in the firm's environment, which constitute threats or create opportunities. At the second stage, the firm becomes involved in three activities: discovering what needs to be done and identifying initiatives for each activity; ensuring that the initiatives are congruent with each other and with the company's overall mission; determining how every group in the firm will contribute to achieving the strategy. In the third stage, it is necessary to develop a plan that allocates money and people to implement the strategy (Christensen, 1997, p. 143). Too often there are barriers to implementation, ill-defined projects, lack of priorities, company politics and conflicts between short- and longer-term views of market needs. A strategy can only be implemented, however, if there is a deliberate mechanism in place to ensure that the resource allocation reflects the strategy.

Cost cutting and restructuring the firm

Cost cutting and restructuring the firm are not strategic responses to the market but reflect failure to develop the appropriate marketing response (Porter, 1987). Sometimes firms do not recognize this and engage in simple or serious cutbacks. Successful firms avoid cosmetic cutbacks. This type of response frequently focuses and occupies managers' minds and shifts them from the main thrust of the business. Successful firms also avoid the situation whereby very deep surgery is required: a last resort all too frequently used by a number of companies, in which significant parts of the firm are cut away and can damage its ability to perform in relation to its market. Situations arise whereby what remains of the firm becomes risk averse and resists any new ventures because of the fear of further deep surgery.

In these circumstances only a revival of the economy at large or the world economy can pull the firm back from collapse. This partly explains the weakness of many firms meeting the international marketing challenge and also explains some of the diversification activity of many having reorganized as holding companies.

Company growth and discontinuity

To be sustaining, growth and development must come from within the company. It cannot be foisted on companies directly through grants and favourable loan terms or other public policy initiatives. The environment facing companies in the new millenium will be completely different from that of the 1990s. Policy makers, working at the macro level, provide the necessary framework for competition in the late-1990s. The hardware of such support might consist of financial and other incentives. The software, the more attractive option, consists of, among other things, providing through the education system the right people to manage. Winners cannot be picked but must be developed (Storey *et al.*, 1987).

The question of overcoming these problems must be addressed. Successful firms, recognizing periods of discontinuity, may introduce a range of corporate changes; the basic philosophy of the firm is thereby questioned. Corporate change means introducing new strategic thinking with institutional support within the company for a new environment. This means a thorough review of the risks facing it, which begins to react to discontinuity by tightening its risk review process and developing or strengthening strategic thinking within the company. This should be a continuing process and should be quite specific.

Foundation for strategy development

Much interest has been shown recently by strategy and policy theorists in the whole area of strategy development, the formation of contingency theories and the categorization of companies into particular strategy archetypes. Much of this research has the objective of specifying and defining the relationship between variables under the firm's control, such as marketing, production and investment decisions, and those variables generally outside the firm's control, usually referred to as environmental. A strategic market as the smallest area within which it is possible to be a viable competitor (Kay, 1990, p.3). The strategic market is determined by the interaction of demand factors which influence the shape of the market with the supply factors which define the boundaries of the industry. Many strategy models have been developed which suggest a limited number of identifiable strategies, each of which involves a different pattern of competitive positioning objectives, investment strategies and competitive advantages in order to be successful.

It is apparent that strategy at a corporate level represents the cumulative direction of the organization given the nature of the industry, the competitive environment and internal factors related to production, finance, marketing and personnel. The firm may follow one of three options: to build, to hold, or to harvest (Buzzell *et al.*, 1975); it may be a performance maximizer, a sales maximizer or a cost minimizer (Utterback and Abernathy, 1975); it may manage its resources with one of six options in mind, i.e. to increase share, to grow, to produce profits, to encourage market concentration, to introduce a turnaround or to liquidate (Hofer and Schendel, 1978).

Strategies at this level of an organization have been described as 'master strategies' and the later functional or operational strategies as 'programme or substrategies' (Steiner and Miner, 1977). These would include plans for the specific use of resources, physical and intangible, formulated to achieve the overall purpose. The lines of demarcation are blurred; however, despite inevitable overlap it has continued to be standard practice that strategic alternatives at the programme level be detailed and analysed dependent on the overall strategy (Thompson and Strickland, 1996). Hence, at the corporate level, for example, management may decide that an aggressive growth strategy is required for which it will then be the responsibility of functional management to develop appropriate programmes. One such functional strategy may be marketing, where management attempts to formulate plans on how the organization should compete in given markets with a given technology in order to meet a given objective. Concern rests on developing a functional marketing strategy to compete in international markets.

Competitive strategies

The traditional management literature presents the case for two mutually exclusive types of competitive advantage that a firm may possess: low cost or differentiation. These result from a firm's ability to cope with the forces of the value chain better than its rivals. In seeking cost leadership a firm sets out to become the low-cost producer in its industry while the firm which seeks to be unique in its industry along some dimension widely valued by buyers follows a strategy of differentiation and obtains a premium price (Porter, 1980). In the first situation the firm depends on a broad scope, serves many industry segments and may operate in related industries while in the second situation the firm depends on uniqueness arising from product design, service, spare parts availability or a distributor network.

The view that a cost leadership strategy or differentiation strategy should be absolute and are incompatible is rejected by Phillips *et al.* (1983) who argue that a highly differentiated position is compatible with low costs. Other researchers have also provided evidence which shows a high-quality and low-cost position as compatible (Hayes and

Wheelwright, 1984). The research evidence of Phillips *et al.* (1983) is strong and refutes the traditional received wisdom that the attainment of a high-quality position would involve strategic trade-offs, such as higher relative direct costs or marketing expenditures.

Most industries compete with a range of factors. The European motor industry has identified five sets of factors believed to lead to competitive superiority: a competitive industry structure, improved assembly methods, meeting market needs, R&D and competing in international markets (*The Financial Times*, Thursday 8 December 1988). The recent spate of take-overs among French retailers seems to indicate that size and cost are two factors which dominate competition in international retailing (Exhibit 4.2).

━━━━━━━ **Exhibit 4.2** ━━━━━━━

Hypermarket cannibals

Daniel Bernard, chairman of Carrefour, the hypermarket group, has a word to describe the transformations taking place in French retailing: 'cannibalism'. Two supermarket groups – Franprix and Leader Price – have been acquired by a rival, Casino, for FFr3.5bn (£360m). Both Casino and a fourth retailer, Rallye, have in turn been the object of a FFr28bn hostile takeover bid by a fifth, Promodès.

Paul-Louis Halley, the chairman of Promodès, says: 'The most important reason behind our bid is the globalization of commerce. If you look at the size of the US and south-east Asian markets, and the speed at which they are developing, we would be much more competitive as a single group'. Daniel Bernard agrees. 'Size is very important, if France is to remain in the retailing race'. Why does size matter? Because, he emphasizes, it helps to increase your negotiating position with suppliers; it is also needed to mobilize enough investment to match your rivals.

For a long time, French retailers could expand organically, without acquisitions. In the 1960s and 1970s, they took an early lead in the development of hypermarkets, partly because the government was encouraging large suburban shopping centres with the idea of fighting inflation by intensifying competition between retailers and driving down prices. The heady expansion in hypermarkets has meant that the retailing business is becoming saturated.

There are other difficulties. In 1996, legislation against 'predatory pricing' was enacted to redress an imbalance of power between small and large suppliers. The larger companies have responded by launching ambitious international expansion programmes. Carrefour and Promodès, for example, have opened stores in southern Europe, South America and south-east Asia. Casino has identified a smaller number of markets where it believes there is strong growth potential, notably Poland and Taiwan. However, Mr Halley argues that it is important to have 'a strong home base' from which to make forays abroad.

Source: adapted from *Financial Times*, Weekend, 6–7 September 1997, p. 7.

Analysing competitor strategies

Every firm has a marketing programme used to attract and hold customers. The best competitors use their marketing skills to obtain advantage in the market by meeting customer requirements more efficiently than other firms. Some firms compete on the basis of product superiority, innovation, prices, availability, image and reputation, and service. Firms must identify these customer advantages as well as determine competitor weaknesses. In this regard there is a close relationship between the firm's competitors and their strategies. The more its strategy is similar to that of another firm, the more they compete. In many situations it is possible to separate competitors into groups that pursue different strategies. A group of firms in an industry following the same or similar strategy along key dimensions is known as a strategic group.

Investing in manufacturing and marketing

The attainment of any strategic position is not only a question of good analysis or commitment but also involves a number of specific investment decisions (Cook, 1983). The construction of efficient scale facilities and the vigorous pursuit of cost reduction through accumulated experience is associated with cost leadership. Research and design, quality control and customer service facilities are more important when differentiation is pursued. These discrete instruments are generally not mutually exclusive. A level of exclusivity will exist, however, in managerial coordinating capacity and the need to select a system of internal organization, evaluation and reward that will be designed for optimal pursuit of the chosen strategy. Different managerial talents and organizational measures of success will be needed depending on the strategy followed (Porter, 1985).

The essence of global competition is the management of international cash flows through the strategic coordination of manufacturing operations and marketing systems (Prahalad and Doz, 1987, Chapter 3). This statement applies equally to small and large firms irrespective of the extent to which the firm has expanded its marketing internationally and the extent to which it has located its production abroad. Managing cash flows emphasizes both costs and prices.

Managing costs and prices

In managing the cost side the successful competitor is concerned with factor costs, scale and technology effects and exchange rate fluctuations. Factor costs refer to the location specific advantages that accrue to a manufacturer, e.g. labour cost differentials, availability of cheap raw materials and components, access to low-cost capital and government-sponsored industrial promotion incentives. Size, location and technological sophistication of manufacturing plants in different countries can present the firm with significant cost advantages. This is most apparent in comparing a single-plant firm which exports to serve international markets and a multiplant firm serving a selected portfolio of markets. The portfolio of markets allows the firm to leverage differences in competitive market structures to exploit the resulting price differentials.

Exchange rate fluctuations can eliminate cost advantages or make certain locations more attractive. Successful competitors learn how to manage these three elements of cost: labour costs, manufacturing scale and technology and exchange rate fluctuations (Figure 4.3). The successful competitor does not attempt to reduce the impact of any one of these elements while ignoring the others. It is a question of seeking a balance among the three factors while maintaining flexibility. To do so the firm may have a portfolio of manufacturing locations that allows it to exploit both factor cost advantages and exchange rate differentials (Prahalad and Doz, 1987, pp. 43–4). With much of the world's trade denominated in US dollars, the EMU or other stable currencies this factor is less of a problem than it was. The portfolio of manufacturing locations, nevertheless, provides the firm with the opportunity of leveraging factor cost advantages with the objective of integrating them into a global network which would also consider exchange rate fluctuations. The infrastructure also permits the firm to pay constant attention to the need to seek improvements in technology and productivity.

On the price side the firm usually attempts to obtain the highest net price possible. A number of factors influence the ability of the firm to derive such prices: market structure; access to distribution channels; brand power; the product line. With regard to the first issue, the market in each country is unique in terms of its competitive structure; the intensity of competition determines the level of prices and is dependent on the number and type of competitors in the market. In order to exploit the resulting price differentials, especially when competitor costs are the same as those of the firm, it is valuable to be present in a portfolio of markets. Differential pricing in different international markets can give rise to problems, however, especially when parallel importing is encouraged. Access and command of distribution channels is also a well-known competitive advantage. Well-known brands with a quality image command a premium. Established reputations allow for a price premium. Control over the distribution channels due to a broad product line also gives rise to a premium which, according to Prahalad and Doz (1987, p. 46), suggests that in addition to being present in a portfolio of markets a firm should attempt to develop a brand and distribution presence in its key markets. Finally, a

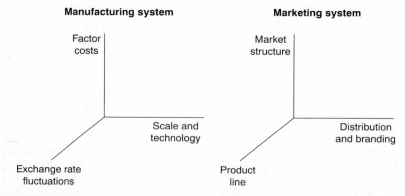

Figure 4.3 Managing the manufacturing and marketing systems for international competitiveness.   *Source*: adapted from Prahalad, C. K. and Doz, Y. L. (1987) *The Multinational Mission*, New York, NY: Free Press.

wide product line can be as effective in allowing the firm to compete on price as being present in many markets. The Swatch story is a good illustration of how the Swiss watch industry responded to Japanese competition by reorganizing, cutting costs and introducing new sophisticated technology to compete on price where the retaliation would produce the greatest damage. Just as a firm can use its portfolio of markets to cross-subsidize competitive battles, so it can cross-subsidize among products within a market. The choices open to Ben & Jerry's , the super premium ice-cream producer in the US, are not so obvious. Faced from below with a challenge from premium ice-creams in its local market the company considered international markets but there it faces Häagen-Dazs entrenched in its product category. Given the entire marketing strategy and focus of Ben & Jerry's a solution is not easy (Exhibit 4.3).

━━━━━ Exhibit 4.3 ━━━━━
Ben & Jerry's Raspberry Rebels

Today, Ben & Jerry's has 30% of the $261m American market for 'super-premium' ice-cream compared with 43% for Häagen-Dazs. At Ben & Jerry's, sales have risen only slowly in the past three years, and its profits and share have wavered. Tastes change: the sort of American who can afford to buy Ben & Jerry's is just the sort who has become worried about cholesterol. That has called for new products to compensate for flagging sales of the original ice-cream. However, the sheer intuition that got Ben & Jerry's started may be too unreliable to create a succession of star sorbets and funky frozen yoghurts.

Most of all, standing still is an open invitation to the company's competitors. Häagen-Dazs and Ben & Jerry's face encroachment from below by the much larger 'premium' ice-cream brands, which are made well, but with less cream and a less obsessive commitment to luxury than the super-premiums. The firm's marketing has since evolved – widespread radio advertisements and television advertisements to follow. However, even if the new approach is a success, it will take Ben & Jerry's only so far. Unless Americans so overcome their fear of fat that they start to indulge in flavours such as Chunky Monkey by the tubfull, Ben & Jerry's will find it hard to grow much faster than the stagnant American market for ice-cream. That suggests looking abroad, which could put still more pressure on the firm to step away from its roots.

One reason is that overseas expansion will not be easy. Häagen-Dazs is already present internationally. The brand has the advantage of the multinational marketing and distribution network of Grand Metropolitan. Häagen-Dazs is strong in several big markets outside America, including Japan, whose 640,000 tonnes of annual ice-cream consumption is the second largest in the world. Another difficulty with being international is that Ben & Jerry's idiosyncrasies risk translating badly in different parts of the world.

In Europe, strong advertising has established Häagen-Dazs in consumers' minds as a sophisticated, sexy luxury. Against this, Ben & Jerry's zaniness can look goofy. Some of the firm's other virtues will also be worth less and cost more to international customers. Messrs Cohen and Greenfield generously decided to support their neighbours on Vermont's dairy farms by buying milk and cream exclusively from them. It was also a sensible commercial decision: Vermont cream has a good, wholesome reputation. Proclaiming on tubs that the ingredients come from Vermont is a selling point in New England. But the assertion resonates less with Californians, let alone Bavarians; while the tie to one corner of America raises transport costs. Häagen-Dazs, by contrast, is made in two places in the United States, as well as in Canada, France and Japan.

Source: adapted from *Economist*, 6 September 1997, pp. 63–4.

International competitive strategies

The fact that a firm is an international competitor says very little about its international strategy except that it operates in several countries. Many of the strategic issues facing firms competing internationally are very much the same as those competing in domestic markets only.

In identifying an appropriate generic strategy for international markets, the firm has a choice between using the same strategy that is successful in the domestic market or developing a different strategy (Figure 4.4). Using the same strategy means transferring the skills, talents and assets and the mode of their use to new international markets. In general, such a strategy may be used when the firm has already achieved scale economies in the domestic market or has access to finance, labour and materials which give it a considerable cost advantage over competitors in the new market. Using the same strategy is also feasible for companies which have developed a strong brand name in the domestic market and can use it to differentiate itself in the foreign market. The reputation of the company and its brands encourages the use of the same strategy.

In many situations, a different strategy may be required. Sometimes, firms can avoid market entry barriers by changing the accepted business structure. This may mean offering competing products through different distribution channels, e.g. direct marketing and internet selling, thereby passing traditional intermediaries and challenging large local competitors. It may also be possible to build greater reliability and service into products, thus overcoming service network barriers, a strategy followed by Toyota in the early days in the US, when garages were not well disposed to Japanese cars. This approach provides the greatest benefits to the entering firm, because it is very difficult for the incumbent to retaliate. Avoiding entry barriers in this way is a strategy followed by the Aldi supermarket chain. Aldi supermarkets are small, sparsely furnished, located in deprived centre city areas and carrying about 600 non-perishable high-turnover products. Their approach is to limit spoilage and to rely on word-of-mouth communication and a strong market presence. Overheads are kept to a minimum and Aldi does not advertise. The company has expanded into many European markets, including France and the UK, while it challenges hypermarkets by building stores in poor regions, which have suffered from economic recession.

Figure 4.4 Deciding generic international marketing strategies

Alternatively, the company may attempt to avoid direct competition in developing its strategy. In entering a new foreign market, the firm may aim at a different, but contiguous, market which represents a flank attack on direct competitors. Such an approach poses two dangers for incumbents. First, it gives the new entrant a base to gain experience and credibility before entering the core market. Second, it may be possible that the peripheral position becomes the core market.

Using a different strategy may give the company an opportunity to add value and to respond to change in market needs and technology. An exaggerated commitment by local firms to large-scale, but obsolete, plant exacerbates the exposure to be exploited by the new entrants. Such opportunities arise when incumbents are unwilling or unable to adapt to changes which magnify the benefits offered by changing the dimensions of the product or service, thereby providing greater value. With regard to choosing a different strategy, two dimensions, geographic differentiation and global integration, are also critical to the type of strategy the company should pursue (Prahalad and Doz, 1987, pp. 157–8). The appropriateness of responding to local needs or the pressures for global integration is contingent upon the characteristics of the industry.

International marketing strategies

Generic market segmentation

Three generic market segmentation strategies have been identified which may be applied to international markets: an undifferentiated strategy, a differentiated strategy and a concentrated strategy. Companies sometimes make no effort to segment the market. The company does not recognize that the market is capable of being segmented. A firm following an undifferentiated strategy gives no recognition to market segments but rather focuses on what is common to all customers in the market. Products and services in such firms are designed and developed to suit the broadest possible customer appeals. The advantages of such a strategy are that it minimizes certain costs and helps to concentrate the attention of the competition in one or two areas of the market. This last point assumes that competitors will not attack across a broad front but will select points where they are strong and the company is vulnerable.

In certain circumstances it is inappropriate to attempt to segment the market (Young *et al.*, 1978). These authors identify three sets of circumstances when market segmentation is unlikely to provide any benefits:

- the market is so small that marketing to a portion of it is not profitable,
- heavy users constitute such a large proportion of sales volume that they are the only relevant target and
- the brand is the dominant brand in the market.

In relation to the market size, in some product categories the frequency of usage is so low that the market can only sustain one of the brands. Because such a brand must appeal to all segments decisions on product positioning, advertising, distribution and pricing must be based on an analysis of the entire market. When heavy users dominate the market for a product, conventional market segmentation is meaningless since most of the marketing effort will be directed at that group. If the heavy user group itself is large other segmentation criteria may, however, be applied. Lastly, when the brand is dominant it draws its customers from all segments. In such circumstances targeting a selection of segments may reduce instead of increase sales.

A differentiated strategy means operating in two or more segments using separate marketing strategies in each segment. A differentiated approach has the effect of enlarging the size of the total market but costs are increased.

A concentrated strategy means operating in one segment only. Companies following such a strategy often attempt to seek dominance through specialization. The key advantages of a concentrated strategy are that the company may be able to obtain specialization economies. The risks associated with such a strategy are usually greater.

Five important factors influence a company's segmentation strategy. Successful segmentation is related to company resources, the type of product, the stage in the life cycle, the degree of homogeneity among buyers and the strategies followed by competitors. The value of segmented markets increase if a number of conditions are present:

- the company possesses information on the particular buyer characteristic;
- marketing efforts can be effectively focused on the chosen segments; and
- segments are large, profitable and stable.

Market segmentation involves a trade-off. Applying too many of the various segmentation criteria which are available could result in too great a number of segments for the company to manage. In such circumstances the company attempts to aggregate customer dimensions into useful categories for the purpose of segmentation. Various analytical and quantitative techniques are available to assist the company in determining the optimum number of segments to derive a trade-off between comprehensiveness and practicality. Product-market and customer segmentation is discussed in detail in Chapter 9.

Cultural and geographic market segmentation

One of the simpler management approaches to market segmentation is to treat different cultural and geographic regions or countries as different market segments. This approach is very common in large market areas such as the US or Europe. At a very general level European markets may be treated as similar based on language, geographic proximity and level of development. This preliminary approach to segmentation has been suggested by Vandermerwe and L'Hullier (1989) who identify six market clusters for developed markets in Europe (Figure 4.5).

The value of this approach depends on the existence of regional disparities in tastes or usage or some other important criterion. Usually there is a market variation in consumption patterns but this is not always the case. In some markets, especially markets like the US, mass media, transportation and multiple production locations have substantially eroded many of these differences based on geographic factors. Many differences still remain, however, and the emergence of local differences based on ethnic and cultural factors has again presented the possibility of successful geographic segmentation.

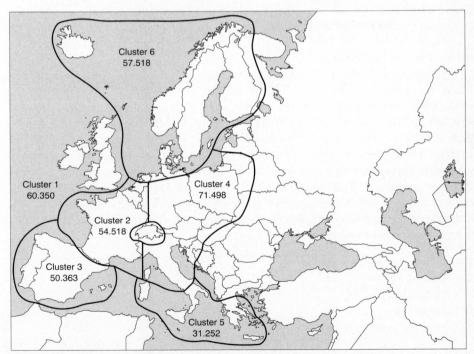

Figure 4.5 Six European market clusters (1000's people)
Source: Vandermerwe, S. and L'Huller, M. (1989) 'Euro consumers in 1992', *Business Horizons,* January–February, 34–40.

Standardized or customized international strategies

There is considerable debate in the marketing literature on the appropriateness of niche versus global strategies (Levitt, 1983; Quelch and Hoff, 1986). This is the old standardization debate in new clothes, which is not very different from the issue as debated in the late 1960s when the questions 'can you standardize multinational marketing?' and 'are domestic and international markets dissimiliar?' were raised (Bartels, 1968; Buzzell, 1968). Conceptualization of the problem is the key to understanding the behaviour of international firms but so too is their actual behaviour, which is often much further advanced than the prescriptions of theoreticians. Many firms expect to respond to these internationalization questions by developing a global image for their products and company, by customizing products for specific markets and by standardizing products for all major markets.

Many writers have argued for a standardized, instead of a differentiated, approach to international markets. According to these authors a standardized approach is desirable because sales may be higher owing to a consistent product image across different geographic markets. Furthermore, costs can be reduced by amalgamating production activities, moving to low-cost locations without sacrificing quality and obtaining the economies associated with formulating and implementing a single standardized marketing plan (Walters, 1986; Yip, 1989). The other school of thought, those who favour differentiation, argues that because few markets are exactly alike it is necessary to adapt the marketing mix to ensure that sufficient customization exists to satisfy buyer needs in each market (Quelch and Hoff, 1986; Wills *et al.*, 1991). In the recent literature there appears to be support for the former point of view.

Szymanski *et al.* (1993, p. 11) in an empirical study of the US, UK, Canadian and West European markets, mostly in the EU, discovered that the strength and form of the relationships between the various marketing mix, other competitive strategy, market structure and business performance factors are relatively similar across the four markets. Hence, these authors conclude that businesses may be better off standardizing their strategic resource mix to capture the benefits purported to be associated with a standardized approach to serving multiple national markets. Sometimes standardized brand strategies appear to succeed whereas, in other cases, they fail dismally. By examining 17 cases of international marketing standardization in nine US and European companies, Kashani (1989) discovered that nine were successes and eight were failures. He identified five reasons for lack of success:

1. insufficient research;
2. overstandardization;
3. poor follow-up;
4. narrow vision;
5. rigid implementation.

Nearly half the programmes examined had no formal research prior to starting – two-thirds of these failed. Of the remaining firms that did research the market, two-thirds succeeded. Even when a programme is standardized, it still needs local adaptation. Standardization usually involved one or two elements of the marketing mix, leaving the rest for local adaptation by country managers. With regard to follow-up, the failure to institute a regular communication system with subsidiaries to ensure enthusiastic commitment gave rise to considerable problems among the companies surveyed. A structure is required to coordinate and implement the strategy on a continuous basis. If this is too rigid and inflexible, however, it may be imposed without regard to local conditions. A very narrow vision by headquarters may lead to implementation difficulties. There needs to be a continuous involvement of the local subsidiary to calibrate the strategy. Standardization of strategy is a means to an end, not an end in itself – it should be flexible, therefore, to ensure continued commitment by local management.

The issues of standardization and differentiation or customization focus attention on the marketing mix or marketing programme. The issues of local responsiveness and global integration focus attention on process issues in the firm, whether activities should be centralized or decentralized. The company management process may enforce standardization or it may merely coordinate activities in various markets. Less centralized still are companies which attempt to persuade local endeavours to mimic the headquarters standard. For companies which insist only on cross-fertilization of ideas, information is the only activity centralized. A completely decentralized company ignores all central tendencies. The company should address programme and process issues to judge how they affect its international strategy (Figure 4.6). Within the business system, the marketing function tends to be the least centralized but, within the marketing programme, brand positioning is usually highly standardized. Baileys Original Irish Cream Liqueur follows the same positioning strategy in all markets. Distribution and pricing tend to be less standardized. It is also necessary to consider the type of product or service. Culture and scale economies have different effects, depending on product type. For example, consumer electronics have very high scale effects but very few culture effects, whereas food products have low scale effects but very high culture effects. The international marketing strategy should reflect these differences. Lastly, there is a country effect. Companies frequently standardize the marketing programme and centralize process issues for smaller markets, especially if sales are low and for new markets that require more support from the company.

Figure 4.6 Customizing international marketing strategies

Implications of standardizing international marketing strategies

In a literal sense choosing to use a standardized international marketing strategy involves offering identical product lines at identical prices through identical distribution systems, supported by identical promotional programmes, in several different countries. This would contrast strongly with completely 'localized' marketing strategies which contain no common elements whatsoever. These approaches are at extreme ends of a continuum and the firm may decide to avail itself of only some of the cost savings as a result of standardization. While Buzzell ultimately suggests that a balanced consideration of the benefits and costs of standardization is required, he favours a single marketing strategy. Levitt (1983) is even more hard hitting, suggesting that a new reality has emerged which consists of global markets. This is based on increasingly similar consumer desires through-out the world. Even more apparent is the presumed Europeanization of markets with one single internalized market which directly affects EU countries and indirectly affects neighbouring countries. Levitt points out that the firms that are prepared for the single internal EU market will benefit from enormous economies of scale in production, distribution, marketing and overall management, which will provide these firms with a cost competence and potential competitive advantage, thereby beating competitors that still live in the disabling grip of old country centred assumptions.

Indeed, the (formerly named) EC Commission viewed the strategy of focusing on country-centred needs as one of the enormous costs of a non-Europe (Commission of the European Communities, 1987). If this were to continue it would be to the advantage of Europe's competitors, Japan and the United States, who may carry out R&D work more economically, based on large home markets, and also produce for all markets in bulk. A failure by firms to follow a single European market outlook and use the collective resources of such a market will contribute to the uncompetitiveness of these firms, their low productivity and poor innovation record.

Not all companies are able to adopt a standardized strategy as its appropriateness varies from industry to industry. At one end of the spectrum, Porter (1986) suggests, are multi-domestic firms, in which competition in each country, or a small group of countries, is essentially independent of competition in other countries. In these industries a firm may enjoy a competitive advantage from a one-time transfer of know-how from its home base to foreign countries. The firm may adapt its intangible assets for each country, however, and, accordingly, the competitive advantage of the firm is largely specific to each country. Examples of industries operating in this mode would be retailing, distribution, insurance, and retail banking. At the other end of the spectrum are what are termed global industries. The term global, like the word strategy, has become overused and perhaps misunderstood; it should not be taken literally but, rather, should be applied to a collection or a region of markets. A global industry is one in which a firm's competitive position in one country is significantly influenced by its position in other countries. In these industries firms do not operate with a collection of individual markets but a series of linked markets in which rivals compete against each other across these markets.

A firm may choose to compete with a country-centred strategy, thus focusing on specific market segments or countries, when it can carve out a niche by responding to whatever local country differences are present. The firm that follows this approach does so at considerable risk to itself from competitors that follow a global strategy. It also misses opportunities for cost savings and scale economies. The purest global strategy would be to concentrate as many activities as possible in one country and to serve markets from this base with a tightly coordinated market offering. This is not only the domain of companies such as Toyota or Xerox, but smaller international firms could clearly also gain by coordinating their international marketing endeavours through joint ventures and other alliances. As a result of such a strategy, clear advantages may accrue in the rapid attainment of scale and learning thresholds, the sharing of development and commercialization costs and establishing significant if shared positions in international markets.

Product-market and business system resource allocation

Internationalization is often synonymous with achieving rapid company growth. In their study of fast-growth businesses in the UK, Storey *et al.* (1987) found that one of the main characteristics which distinguished growth companies was the importance of exports in their sales.

Concentration on strong products and markets and on critical cost areas of the business system may be the route to international market success, especially in small open economies. Concentration on strong products and markets is concerned with the company's marketing strategy, while concentrating on the critical cost areas of the business deals with the importance of the business system for competitive advantage in international markets. In this context the company must consider how to allocate its resources and concentrate its endeavours among the various market segments identified. It may wish to concentrate on one or a few segments or serve all segments with the same strategy. Similarly, the firm has to consider where in the business system to allocate its resources. It may wish to devote most of its resources to manufacturing, some to assembly and less to distribution and customers, depending on circumstances. A generic market-business system resource allocation strategy attempts to identify the key product markets and the key stages in the business system to concentrate resources in order to be successful (Figure 4.7).

Regarding product-market resource allocation the choice is between diversification and concentration (Ayal and Zif, 1979). The first implies fast penetration of a large number of product markets and diffusion of effort among them. The second is based on concentration of resources in a few product markets and general expansion into new areas. Product-market concentration appears to be a rewarding route to success in international markets, especially for the smaller firm because it allows attractive markets to be targeted and resources to be focused on these markets only. Using a market concentration strategy, the first international market then acts as a bridgehead both for diversification into other international markets and for launching other products internationally.

Underlying the second assumption is the view that the key success factor is to find a source of competitive advantage through reorganization of the business system. The objective of this reorganization is to achieve a superior cost–quality combination in a way which makes it difficult for competitors to emulate. The argument to be tested is that the

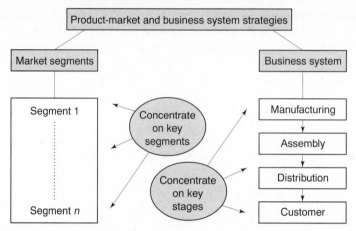

Figure 4.7 Generic product-market and business system strategies

key to success is to use the flexibility which the firm enjoys to unbundle the business system so as to focus on those elements of the value-added chain which yield the greatest return, while rearranging the provision of the other elements of the chain as cost effectively as possible.

Resource allocation in international markets

The resource allocation decision determines the distribution of the company's resources among specific countries and products, the 'basic strategies in international marketing' (Segler, 1987). Once the international market portfolio of the firm has been determined, additional markets may be chosen which are consistent with it. In deciding the scope of its desired international market coverage, two generic strategies are available: product-market concentration and diversification (Ayal and Zif, 1979).

Market concentration involves the purposeful selection of a small number of the most promising markets initially for more intensive development (Hirsch and Lev, 1973; Ayal and Zif, 1979; Piercy, 1982). It has been argued for a small firm that serving up to six markets is considered a concentration strategy while, for larger established firms, concentration suggests a maximum of ten markets (Piercy, 1982). For the smaller firm going international for the first time from a small home market, two or three markets would appear to constitute a reasonable span for a concentration strategy. A concentration strategy may be particularly attractive for the smaller firm as it requires a relatively low initial investment in marketing facilities, avoids the cost of dealing with small orders to less well-known markets, limits the span of managerial control and enables more visits to be made to each market. It also keeps the costs of international market research within the limits of the company's resources (Ryans, 1988). Market concentration may also provide a springboard for subsequent diversification and consequent stabilization of the firm's exports (Hirsch and Lev, 1973). The issues regarding product concentration may be developed in an analogous way.

Market diversification involves the simultaneous entry into as many markets as possible (Hirsch and Lev, 1973). A market diversification strategy normally implies more than 12 country markets with marketing resources divided equally (Piercy, 1982).

The objective of a market diversification strategy is to obtain a high rate of return through market development rather than market penetration, while maintaining a low level of resource commitment by selecting more accessible target markets. A market diversification strategy involves a greater risk for the firm since it requires a larger initial investment in markets. Greater risk attaches to market spreading but where it is successful it has been shown to be more profitable (Hirsch and Lev, 1973). In the longer term, this strategy is usually followed by a period of market consolidation in which the number of markets is reduced as less profitable ones are abandoned (Ayal and Zif, 1979).

In practice, a firm is unlikely to select a position at the extremities of the spreading–concentration spectrum but more probably will pursue a mixed strategy, selling to a relatively large number of markets while concentrating resources on a selection of these. The advantage of such a mixed strategy is that it allows a firm to focus its strategy on the most promising markets, while leaving sufficient flexibility to accept opportunistic business in others (Piercy, 1982). The issues regarding product diversification may be developed in a similar manner.

Investment in product markets usually occurs between the extremes of complete concentration and complete diversification. Product-market allocation strategies are closely interlinked; market allocations impose constraints on the range of feasible product allocation strategies if the firm is to sustain its competitive position.

For most companies that combine market and product diversification strategies it is unlikely that they would have sufficient resources to make the required marketing effort for all markets and products. This is the risk of underinvesting in markets, a problem which arises in rapid growth markets especially (Figure 4.8). The risk of overinvesting arises if the company serves only a few markets with a small range of products which may leave some important markets open to competitors. This difficulty is most likely to occur in companies with new innovative products for which it is important to be the first mover in international markets. To avoid the risk of under- or overinvesting it may be necessary

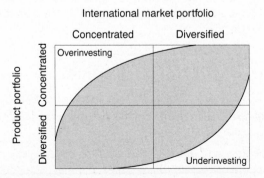

Figure 4.8 International market and product allocation strategies

to balance product and market allocation strategies by selecting a position in the shaded area of the figure.

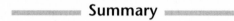

Summary

This chapter is concerned with the role of marketing strategy in assisting firms entering foreign markets successfully. When developing new products for a market it is necessary to emphasize that marketing is performed along three dimensions: technology, customer segment and customer function. As with domestic markets, foreign markets must be segmented and targeted to provide customer benefits in gaining a competitive advantage. The firm must innovate in a number of directions when entering international markets. General considerations of firms entering foreign markets are niche versus global strategies, cost cutting and company restructuring.

A number of different master and substrategies can be pursued as a basis for competition in international markets. It is important, however, to keep in mind that industries compete on a range of factors. It may be possible, therefore, to group competitors into strategic groups when analysing competitor strategies in an industry. There tends to be a close relationship between the firm's competitors and their strategies. The more similar the strategies the more they compete. Many firms compete on the basis of cost and non-cost factors.

Strategies pursued by firms also involve investment decisions such as managing the cash flow based on manufacturing and marketing decisions. Managing costs and prices is an important aspect of this decision area.

In developing an international marketing strategy the firm must consider the value of a standardized approach or a differentiated approach. Although there is much evidence to support a standardized approach for some elements of the firm's marketing strategy, it may be necessary to customize in a number of key areas to meet the needs of specific markets.

An increasingly important topic in developing an approach to international markets is how to exploit the value added in the business system. Successful firms decide the appropriateness of allocating marketing resources to specific areas. Developing a successful international marketing strategy means optimizing the product market and the business system resource allocation.

Discussion questions

1. The world market is really a series of market segments, each with different needs and wants. Successful international market segmentation requires a careful selection of country markets, regions and customers. Discuss.

2. What are the advantages and disadvantages of competing directly with strong rivals in international markets? When would you recommend a direct competitive response?

3. International market expansion usually means innovating in a number of directions

simultaneously. Discuss the value to the firm of the technology–product–market framework in deciding how to proceed.

4. The firm in international markets must manage manufacturing and marketing costs. What are these costs and how do they affect the fortunes of the firm?

5. An international marketing strategy is based on market considerations and competitive factors. How should the firm analyse and cope with these issues in formulating a strategy for international markets?

6. In developing an international marketing strategy how should marketing resources be allocated to product markets and the business system. How may synergy be obtained?

References

Ayal, I. and Zif, J. (1979) 'Market expansion strategies in multinational markets', *Journal of Marketing*, **43** (Spring), 84–94.

Bartels, R. (1968) 'Are domestic and international marketing dissimilar?', *Journal of Marketing*, **32**, 56–61.

Buzzell, R. D. (1968) 'Can you standardize multinational marketing?', *Harvard Business Review*, **46** (November–December), 102–13.

Buzzell, R. D., Gale, B. T. and Sultan, R. G. M. (1975) 'Market share: A key to profitability', *Harvard Business Review*, **53** (January–February), 97–106.

Campbell, A. and Alexander, M. (1997) 'What's wrong with strategy?', *Harvard Business Review*, **75** (November–December), 42–51.

Carroad, P. A. and Carroad, C. A. (1982) 'Strategic interfacing of R&D and marketing', *Research Management* (January), 28–33.

Christensen, C. M. (1997) 'Making strategy: learning by doing', *Harvard Business Review*, **75** (November–December), 141–56.

Commission of the European Communities (1987) *Europe Without Frontiers – Completing the Internal Market*.

Cook, V. J., Jr (1983) 'Marketing strategy and differential advantage', *Journal of Marketing*, **47**, 68–75.

Courtney, H., Kirkland, J. and Viguerie, P. (1997) 'Strategy under uncertainty', *Harvard Business Review*, **75** (November–December), 67–79.

Hayes, R. H. and Wheelwright, S. C. (1984) *Restoring Our Competitive Edge*, New York, NY: Wiley.

Hirsch, S. and Lev, B. (1973) 'Foreign marketing strategies – a note', *Management International Review*, **6**, 81–8.

Hofer, G. W. and Schendel, D. E. (1978) *Strategy formulation: analytical concepts*, St. Paul, MN: West Publishing.

Kashani, K. (1989), 'Beware the pitfalls of global marketing', *Harvard Business Review*, **67** (September–October), 91–8.

Kay, J. A. (1990), 'Identifying the strategic market', *Business Strategy Review*, **1** (Spring), 2–24.

Levitt, T. (1983) 'The globalization of markets', *Harvard Business Review*, **61** (May–June), 92–102.

Phillips, L., Chang, D. R. and Buzzell, R. D. (1983) 'Product quality, cost position and business performance: a test of some key hypotheses', *Journal of Marketing*, **47**, 26–43.

Piercy, N. (1982) *Export Strategy, Markets and Competition*, London: George Allen and Unwin.

Porter, M. E. (1980) *Competitive Strategy*, New York, NY: The Free Press.

Porter, M. E. (1985) *Competitive Advantage*, New York, NY: The Free Press.

Porter, M. E. (1986) 'Changing patterns of international competition', *California Management Review,* **28**, 9–37.

Porter, M. E. (1987) 'The state of strategic thinking', *The Economist* (23 May), 21–22.

Prahalad, C. K. and Doz, Y. L. (1987) *The Multinational Mission,* New York, NY: The Free Press.

Quelch, J. A. and Hoff, E. J. (1986) 'Customizing global marketing', *Harvard Business Review* **64** (May–June), 59–68.

Ryans, A. B. (1988) 'Strategic market entry factors and market share achievement in Japan', *Journal of International Business Studies,* **19** (Fall), 389–409.

Segler, K. G. (1987) 'The challenge of basic strategies', *European Journal of Marketing,* **21** (5), 76–89.

Steiner, G. A. and Miner, J. B. (1977) *Management Policy and Strategy,* New York, NY: Macmillan.

Storey, D., Keasey, K., Watson, R. and Wynarczyk, P. (1987) *The Performance of Small Firms,* London: Croom Helm.

Szymanski, D. M., Bharadwrj, S. G. and Varadarajan P. R. (1993) 'Standardization versus adaptation of international marketing strategy: an empirical investigation', *Journal of Marketing,* **57** (October), 1–17.

Thompson, A. A. and Strickland, A. J. III (1996) *Strategic Management: Concepts and Cases,* 9th edn, Homewood, IL: Irwin.

Utterback, J. M. and Abernathy, W. (1975) 'A dynamic model of process and product innovation', *OMEGA,* **3**, 639–56.

Vandermerwe, S. and L'Hullier, M. (1989) 'Euro consumers in 1992', *Business Horizons,* (January–February), 34–40.

Walters, P. G. (1986) 'International marketing policy: a discussion of the standardization construct and the relevance for corporate policy', *Journal of International Business Studies,* **17** (Summer), 55–69.

Wills, J., Samli, Coskun, A. and Jacobs, L. (1991) 'Developing global products and marketing strategies: a construct and research agenda', *Journal of Academy of Marketing Science,* **19** (Winter), 1–10.

Yip, G. S. (1989) 'Global strategy: in a world of nations?', *Sloan Management Review,* **31** (Fall), 29–41.

Young, S., Ott, L. and Feigin, B. (1978) 'Some practical considerations in market segmentation', *Journal of Marketing Research,* **15**, 405–12.

5

Global, regional and emerging markets

This chapter describes recent trends in world output and trade and relates these developments to the current interest in free trade, global, regional and emerging markets. The nature of trade and competition in industrial markets is reviewed as an introduction to a discussion of the flurry of trade agreements and market integration initiatives which have taken place in recent years, which have resulted in trade barriers and the cost of international business falling (Exhibit 5.1). The General Agreement on Tariffs and Trade (GATT) and the role of the World Trade Organization is discussed. The impact of the rise of trading blocs and other economic and political institutions such as the EU and NAFTA is also examined, and less developed agreements are discussed. Trade developments in the more important regions of the world are described and the importance of trade in economic development and particularly its role and the contribution of marketing to human development, especially in developing countries, are documented. An understanding of developments in global, regional and emerging markets provides the background to a deeper appreciation of the international marketing environment discussed in greater detail in the next three chapters.

══════ Exhibit 5.1 ══════
The Shrinking World

Contacts between the world's people are widening and deepening as natural and artificial barriers fall. Huge declines in transport and communication costs have reduced natural barriers. Shipping is much cheaper. Communication is also much easier and cheaper. In the 1980s, telecommunication traffic was expanding by 20 percent a year. The Internet, the take-off point for the information superhighway, is now used by 50 million people, with the number of subscribers tapping into it doubling every year.

Artificial barriers have been eased with the reduction in trade barriers (tariffs, quotas and so on) and exchange controls. In 1947, the average tariff on manufactured imports was 47 percent; with full implementation of the Uruguay Round, it should fall to three percent. Spurred by the fall of barriers, global trade is expected to grow six percent annually for the next 10 years. Some of the changes in international trade and finance reflect advances in technology. The lightning speed of transactions means that countries and companies now must respond rapidly if they are not to be left behind. Technological change is also affecting the nature of investment. Previously, high-technology production had been limited to rich countries with high wages. Today, technology is more easily transferred to developing countries, where sophisticated production can be combined with relatively low wages.

The increasing ease with which technology can accompany capital across borders threatens to break the links between high productivity, high technology and high wages. The availability of higher levels of technology all over the world is putting pressure on the wages and employment of low-skilled workers.

The international spread of cultures has been at least as important as the spread of economic processes. Today, a global culture is emerging. Through many media – from music to movies to books – international ideas and values are being mixed with, and superimposed on, national identities. The spread of ideas through television and video has seen revolutionary developments. There now are more than 1.2 billion TV sets around the world. The United States exports more than 120,000 hours of television programming a year to Europe alone, and the global trade in programming is growing by more than 15 percent a year.

Popular culture exerts more powerful pressure than ever before. From Manila to Managua, Beirut to Beijing, in the East, West, North and South, styles in dress (jeans, hair-dos, t-shirts), sports, music, eating habits, and social and cultural attitudes have become global trends. Even crimes – whether relating to drugs, abuse of women, embezzlement or corruption – transcend frontiers and have become similar every-where. In so many ways, the world has shrunk.

Source: adapted from *Human Development Report 1997*, published for
United Nations Development Programme (UNDP), Oxford University Press, New York, p. 83.

World output and trade

Since 1960 world trade and output exhibited varying levels of growth. In earlier decades growth rates were higher than experienced more recently. Throughout the period growth rates were higher in trade than in output. This is a clear indicator of the increased internationalization of economic activities and the greater mutual dependence existing in the global market place.

In recent years there has been a great deal of comment regarding trade and industrial activity in the triad economic powers, namely US, Europe and Japan. Between 1990 and 1996 trade between Europe and Asia increased from $238 billion to $430 billion and trade between North America and Asia increased from $316 billion to $520 billion (Figure 5.1). At the same time trade across the Atlantic between Europe and North America increased from $249 billion to $327 billion.

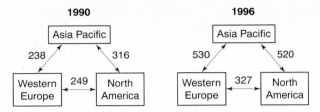

Figure 5.1 Triadic Trade Relations 1990 and 1996 (US$Billions)
Sources: OECD Foreign Trade, November 1991 and July 1992 and World Trade Organisation *Annual Report 1997,* Vol. 2.

By decomposing these trade patterns further it can be seen that in 1996 intra-European trade was worth $1,558 billion while intra-North American trade was worth $297 billion (Figure 5.2). Trade between Western Europe and the former Soviet Union showed the latter to be in deficit. Trade between Western Europe and Asia was roughly in balance. The same was true for Western Europe–Africa trade, North America–Latin America trade and North America–former Soviet Union trade, although at much lower levels. There was an approximate balance between Western Europe and Asia and between Western Europe and North America. There was, however, a large imbalance in trade between Asia and North America, the latter in deficit (Figure 5.2). It is the imbalances which have given rise to sharp debates in recent years, particularly in the United States. The argument has centred on issues such as 'free trade', the emotive 'fair trade' and the need to 'integrate and manage' regional markets in order to survive in the global economy.

Concept of free trade

Free trade is traditionally promoted by the world's most advanced economic power. It was Britain in the nineteenth century and the US after World War II. Now there is no clear leader. Instead we have a triad of economic powers: United States, Japan and Germany. The theoretical justification for free trade derives from the work of Ricardo in the last century who argued that free trade was beneficial based on the notion of comparative advantage; countries specialize in certain goods rather than aim for self-sufficiency. This applied even if a country could produce everything more cheaply than others, because there would be activities where this country would enjoy a relative cost advantage. This theory has applicability in a world where there are no transport costs and where productive factors are not mobile. Multinational companies use the opportunities of free trade to become the cheapest producers of goods. This search for absolute advantage keeps wage rates down, promotes unattractive working conditions and can be unfriendly to the environment. Competition becomes the key phrase in the argument.

In recent years unemployment has been increasing. European countries have not been able to compete with regard to labour costs with Thailand, Sri Lanka, Indonesia, Taiwan and Hong Kong. There is political pressure to protect jobs through trade measures and social provisions. The idea of free trade is also under attack by environmentalists, who see unrestrained growth through free trade as contrary to sustainable use of the world's resources in the future.

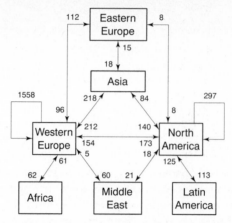

Figure 5.2 Trade flows between different regions of the world, 1996 (US$Billions)
Source: World Trade Organisation *Annual Report 1997*, Vol. 2 (Part 3, p. 23).

Developments in industrial markets

In recent years we have witnessed what amounts to a new competitive world economic order. The combination of open global competition and rapid technological change has eliminated jobs and prevented wages from rising in traditionally wealthy regions of the world. Economic recession in Europe and wage competition from the newly industrial-izing countries have added to the pressure for economic adjustment. Many industrialized countries are now seeing ways of reintroducing a low-wage economy in order to compete with Asian countries, who have gone in the opposite direction by combining a relatively low-wage system with a knowledge-intense industrial system.

The demise of the Cold War has meant that socialism in its extreme form is no longer fashionable. With these trends has come the integration of new capitalist countries and many developing countries into the global economy. Accompanying the demise of the Cold War has been the influx into Western Europe of products and people from Eastern Europe and the developing countries. This new competition has tended to keep prices down.

As a result there has been an increase in the number of industrial market companies which seek to locate abroad. They are also investing in labour-saving technology. Both of these are efforts to stay competitive. Many of these companies also locate abroad for marketing reasons. Rising incomes, especially in Asian countries, have presented oppor-tunities for US and European companies in these regions, which are avidly being taken. Rising demand for consumer products in these new markets and freer trade are likely to create more, not less, economic growth.

In responding to this changing marketing environment firms have put pressure on governments to establish economic and political structures which would allow business to revitalize and flourish. As a result there has been harmonization and convergence in the political, technical, legal and fiscal environments. This is especially true in Europe with the establishment of the Economic Union. Other regions of the world are following similar paths of development; in North America there is NAFTA, in Latin America there are a number of groups. Mercosur is perhaps the most significant at present. Behind these endeavours to integrate the economies of member countries is the assumption that a greater similarity is appearing among the markets of the various countries. Indeed, there is general acceptance of the view that market similarities are more pronounced with regard to customer behaviour and life styles now than at any time in the past. This may be a false assumption, however, even in developed regional markets such as the EU, where consumer tastes and preferences are highly fragmented.

Trade agreements and market integration

The world economy is now more integrated than it has been for many years as a result of the many trade agreements and market integration mechanisms (Exhibit 5.2). The success of trading blocs in the world economy depends on members having similar economic structures, being geographically close to each other, experiencing a political commitment and showing evidence of trade compatibility (Fieleke, 1992; Schott, 1991). The first criterion refers to the need to accommodate the redistribution of trade flows, employment and income which would necessarily arise from the integration of the economies. These are issues which pose major economic and political problems for member countries.

Many successful trade blocs exhibit geographic proximity. Rarely do we see free trade arrangements being formed between countries great distances apart. Generally, meeting the geographic criterion means having contiguous borders or non-contiguous borders separated only by water. For trade agreements to be successful they should create more trade than they divert.

Regarding political commitment, for success it is generally necessary to witness a convergence of national trade laws and polities and a commitment to establish regional institutions. Here the issue is the division of gains between less advanced countries joining highly developed economies. The durability of trading relationships is at stake. The belief of some countries that they are not sharing in the gains of the trade agreement, but are simply forced into buying high-cost manufactured goods from other members, limits the enthusiasm for market integration. As a consequence, it becomes necessary to establish national laws and policies and regional trade and political institutions among members to regulate the imbalance in gains and losses among members. The administration of such joint policies necessarily weakens national sovereignty in favour of a more equitable division of benefits among member countries.

Lastly, if there are significant comparative advantages among the member countries the economic benefits may be substantial. The central issue is not, however, whether countries are competitive or complementary but whether their cost structures are close to world cost levels. Only in such circumstances will complementarity lead to large trade creation and little trade diversion.

━━━━━ **Exhibit 5.2** ━━━━━

Deeper and broader integration of the global economy

The world economy is now more closely integrated than at any time in the post-war period. The principal difference between the process of globalisation at the beginning of the century and now is the scale and pace at which it is taking place. The liberalisation of trade and capital flows and reduced transportation and communication costs have greatly increased the speed at which markets are integrating.

Since 1985, the volume of world trade has expanded almost twice as fast as world output and the rapid liberalisation of financial markets has seen international transactions in bonds and equities in major advanced economies increase to well over 100 per cent of GDP compared with less than 10 per cent in 1980. Gross flows of portfolio and foreign direct investment have also more than trebled in the advanced economies in the last decade. As for the developing countries, their share world trade increased by over 26 per cent in the period 1985–1995. In addition, there are no indications that the process of global economic integration is slowing down. Failure to recognise this fact now and to adapt adequately and promptly will leave national economies and firms vulnerable to competitive pressures and unable to benefit from the opportunities that globalisation will present.

Source: adapted from a speech by Peter D. Sutherland, former Director General, UNCTAD–GATT, and Chairman, Goldman Sachs, to the University College Dublin Graduate School of Business Alumni Association President's Dinner, University College Dublin, 21 November 1997.

General Agreement on Tariffs and Trade

Two of the major aims of the Uruguay Round of trade talks under the auspices of the GATT completed in 1993 were to remove as many invisible trade barriers as possible while at the same time extending the GATT's competence and powers. Had the Uruguay Round of GATT talks foundered the system of free trade established as part of the post-war international settlement would have been under threat. Protectionism would have been back on the agenda of many countries, especially those faced with recession and high unemployment.

The removal of trade discrimination is the focus of GATT. Every country in GATT opens its markets to every other country. Once an agreement between two countries is achieved that benefit is automatically extended to every other country. Small countries enjoy better access to larger markets through GATT than they could ever have negotiated themselves.

The final act embodying the results of the Uruguay Round contains the results of the negotiations since the round of talks was launched in Uruguay in 1986. In addition to creating the World Trade Organization (WTO), the agreement contains crucial provisions in five principal areas (Table 5.1).

Table 5.1 Provisions of the GATT Uruguay Round of trade negotiations

1. Eliminate or significantly reduce:
   - tariff rates for most goods
   - technical standards as a barrier to trade

2. Phase out:
   - bilateral quota agreements on textiles (the Multifibre Agreement)
   - voluntary restraint agreements

3. Expand GATT coverage to include:
   - agreements on trade in services and cross-border investments
   - procurement policies for services and construction

4. Harmonize:
   - global protection of intellectual property
   - the application of sanitary measures for internationally traded goods
   - rules of origin
   - import licensing procedures

5. Create new standards–procedures:
   - for regulating government
   - for the revision of unfair trade laws
   - for settlement of disputes
   - for the activities of pre-shipment inspection companies
   - for the revision of standards for customs valuation
   - for market access and subsidies for agricultural products.

World Trade Organization

The WTO is a single institution comprising the GATT, as modified by the agreements under the Uruguay Round. Membership of the WTO entails accepting the agreements. The WTO is a legal entity and is accorded privileges and immunities similar to those accorded to the specialized agencies of the United Nations. The WTO is the principal institution responsible for international trade in goods and services. In many respects, it has the same status as the IMF or the World Bank. The WTO had 81 countries as founder members and 150 countries are expected to join eventually, including China and Russia. The new international trade framework under the WTO is expected to reduce the uncertainty associated with business activity and thereby to provide further security for international investors.

Approaches to market integration

European Union

The Single European Market, first agreed in the 1985 Single European Act (SEA), is a market without borders allowing free movement of people, goods, capital and services for the 350 million people in the EU's 12 member countries, in 1997 extended to include Austria, Finland and Sweden, bringing the total EU population to 374.32 million.

The Single European Market started on 1 January 1993. It allows mobility of goods, people, services and capital and fulfils the ambition set out in the Treaty of Rome 1957 of forming a genuine common market. The Single European Market is enshrined in the SEA, which came into effect in 1987. The primary objective of the SEA was to increase competition and to build a more homogeneous European business environment to counteract a perceived deterioration in international competitiveness relative to North America and Asia. The European Union has accomplished many community targets and faced down national interests in a number of areas. A number of key areas still remain to come under EU policy influence: energy, transport and telecommunications.

The process of harmonizing regulations and laws on products, trade and people has given the EU a strong position in the international economic and political community. Member countries recognize that a formal renunciation of sovereignty in important areas once held to be the sole prerogative of member countries and a combining of resources can maximize benefits to the community. The EU has recently come under attack for many reasons. In the eyes of many it has become an organization which does rather more for business than for people, is undemocratic, intrusive and unaccountable and which by hyperintensifying competition in European industry contributes to destroying rather than creating jobs (Gardner, 1993).

Since 1992 the European Business Survey has monitored the responses of a large sample of small and medium sized European companies throughout Europe to determine the impact on them of the European Union (Exhibit 5.3). Data from this survey are used in later chapters to illustrate the impact of changes in the EU on different aspects of business.

─────── Exhibit 5.3 ───────

European Business Survey of small- and medium-size businesses

Since the introduction of the Single European Market in 1992, the European Business climate has changed dramatically: the European Union (EU) has expanded from 12 to 15 nations (following the introduction of Sweden, Austria and Finland as members).

During this period, the European Business Survey, a comprehensive study of business confidence, attitudes and trends among European small and medium-sized enterprises (SMEs), sponsored by Grant Thornton International Business Strategies Ltd, has traced the changing climate in Europe. The 1997 Survey reports that SMEs in Europe have broadened their horizons, are now trading more widely and are increasingly planning to enter new markets.

All fifteen EU countries are covered, together with Malta, Norway, Switzerland and Turkey. Postal questionnaires were sent in the domestic language of each country, with companies in the Brussels region of Belgium being sent both Flemish and French language versions. In Switzerland, questionnaires used the languages appropriate to the cantons.

Almost 50,000 questionnaires were dispatched and over 4,900 replies received. This makes the Survey one of the most comprehensive to be carried out on a European scale. The main sample consisted of companies with turnover of between one million and 10 million ECU. In addition, some private companies with a turnover of between 10 million and 100 million ECU are included. More than a third of the responses were from companies with between one and 25 employees and only three per cent of the sample had more than 500 employees. This field work was carried out at the end of 1996.

Source: adapted from *European Business Survey* (1997), Grant Thornton International Business Strategies Ltd, London, May.

North American Free Trade Agreement

In August 1992 the United States, Canada and Mexico signed a free trade agreement to establish an open market throughout the North American continent. The key issues in this North American Free Trade Agreement (NAFTA) are:

ı staged elimination of customs barriers over 15 years;
ı includes intellectual property rights and services;
ı historical US–Mexico cultural links;
ı wage differentials may increase competitiveness where productivity allows;
ı weakness in infrastructure, especially transport and communications;
ı unlike EU political union not envisaged;
ı possible links to Central and Latin American free trade initiatives;
ı side agreements limiting low wage competition.

NAFTA forms the world's largest and richest trading bloc. Within the NAFTA area are 360 million people with a combined GNP of 6.5 billion. The United States is likely to benefit most from NAFTA since it produces about 80 per cent of the goods and services of the group. The agreement contains the possibility of eventually establishing a North American common market, but not a political union. The first of these objectives has been questioned by Sargent and Matthews (1997, p. 388) who argue that, instead of freeing trade, NAFTA has imposed further limitations so that 'it may be more useful for decision makers in organizations to conceptualize NAFTA as not representing free trade but instead another form of managed trade and investment'.

Asia–Pacific Rim

One of the striking features of Asian economies, particularly those on the Pacific Rim, is their lack of homogeneity. While Europe has pursued an industrial strategy of convergence and integration, Asian countries are content to remain heterogeneous. Hong Kong, for example, has pursued a free market approach to economic development while

South Korea has been interventionist in the extreme. There is as yet no evidence that the situation in Hong Kong has changed since the former UK colony was returned to China. At the same time, significant economic development has not occurred in other countries in the region. In the West the model for economic development has depended on deregulated markets and privatization; the Japanese approach, now being exported to other countries in the region, depends more on selective import protection and the use of subsidized credits as an instrument of industrial policy. Under a mildly interventionist regime governments attempt to do two things: maintain macro economic stability through conservative fiscal and monetary policies and invest in people through public education, training and healthcare programmes.

While there have been a number of endeavours in the Far East to form industrial development and trading blocs such as the ASEAN group, nothing similar to NAFTA emerged until Asia Pacific Economic Cooperation Group (APEC) was formed.

The development and growth of economies in this region has a direct impact on company development in other parts of the world. European and Japanese manufacturers of equipment and machinery, for example, have benefited from the industrialization process in East Asian countries. In 1995, for instance, German mechanical engineering firms exported 15 per cent of their output to the region, which absorbs 10 per cent of total German exports (Commerzbank, 1997). East Asia has been developing its own capital goods industry and firms in the region meet such exacting standards that they have become an important source of standard machines in the world market. Meanwhile, it is acknowledged that European firms are less successful with standard machines, but they excel in the design of sophisticated mechanical systems and customized solutions. The question which arises is: will this life cycle trait continue to such an extent that European firms become niche producers? This is hardly a strategy open to the large number of machinery manufacturers in Germany.

New markets in Latin America

Since the early 1980s Latin American countries have been actively reforming their economies. Trade liberalization through reducing import tariffs and removing import licences has been a central feature of the reform programme. In recent years these reforms have been extended to include trade agreements which represent a deeper international commitment which is more difficult to reverse than purely domestic policy changes. Despite their success in increasing trade, such agreements can lead to trade diversion from established patterns with the US and Europe in which case production is merely shifted to less efficient producers. The economic reforms in Latin America and rising incomes have encouraged many well-known international companies to provide products in Latin America designed specifically for local market conditions instead of merely exporting products which were designed for their domestic markets (Exhibit 5.4).

Although Latin America represents a large market for many categories of goods, its total economy is less than one-quarter of that of the United States. As countries in the region move to more open markets for goods and investment, they have formed a number of trade blocs. Furthermore, more than two dozen bilateral and multilateral trade

━━━━━ **Exhibit 5.4** ━━━━━
A car is born

Launching a new product is so fraught with difficulties that many companies prefer to do so in the safety of their own home markets rather than in strange or distant lands. That makes it easier for them to correct any early problems before transferring production overseas. However, it also leads too many firms to go into emerging markets with inappropriate products, designed with the wrong consumers in mind.

Nowhere is this truer than in the car industry. However, Fiat chose Brazil, rather than its native Italy, as the site for initial production and launch of the Palio, its new 'third-world car'. From the Palio's design through to its manufacture, it was different from Fiat's European cars.

So far, this approach seems to have been vindicated. In Brazil, at least, the Palio has been a stunning success. In the 12 months after the car's launch in April 1996, Brazilians bought nearly 250,000 Palios – more than twice the previous record for a new car in Brazil. Contrast that with the fate of Ford's tried and tested Fiesta, launched in Brazil just a month after the Palio. Ford invested $1.1 billion in a new assembly line at its factory in Sao Bernardo, a Sao Paulo suburb. Its aim was to produce exactly the same car, in exactly the same way, as it does in Western Europe.

Having decided on a new third-world car, Fiat soon began to refine its strategy. Fiat wanted a range of cars that would be modern, sufficiently flexible to suit local conditions and easy to build in large enough numbers.

This international group soon changed both the factory and the product. The Brazilians insisted that the new car should also have some non-European features. For a start, although the Palio is broadly similar to the Punto, it was designed to be slightly bigger, since it would serve as the sole family car for many Brazilian buyers. 'It's not a second car for Europeans', says Giovanni Razelli, who, in 1994, took charge of Fiat's international operations. The second big difference is that the Palio is stronger than the Punto, since it is designed for the rough roads of the Brazilian interior rather than the smooth motorways of Italy.

Having designed a car for emerging markets, Fiat's next challenge was to ensure that the firm could manufacture in such a market and still reach European standards of quality and cost control. However, will the Palio travel? A product closely tailored to consumer tastes, in a protected market, clever manufacturing techniques, a booming market and splashy publicity have all helped the Palio in Brazil. However, has Fiat fulfilled its aim of building a third-world-beating car? Mr Razelli insists that the Palio family was designed to be flexible. Details such as colour schemes and manufacturing techniques can be adjusted to suit local needs. Nevertheless, the Palio has passed its first test, demonstrating on the way the rewards that flow from relentless attention to detail when launching a product for emerging-market consumers.

Source: adapted from *Economist*, 13 September 1997, pp. 74–5.

agreements have been signed among nations in the regions. Most of the agreements contemplate the elimination of internal tariffs or quotas on many categories of goods as well as the eventual elimination of all internal tariffs and the observance of a common external tariff (Dominguez and Brenes, 1997, pp. 4–5).

In recent years there have been a number of initiatives to integrate some of the larger economies of Latin America. In 1991 Honduras, Guatemala, El Salvador, Panama and Costa Rica agreed to establish a new common market in Central America.

Less developed but showing some promise recently are agreements between Andean region countries under the Andean Pact, which endeavours to establish a common external tariff, and the Caribbean Basin Initiative (CBI) which provides duty free access for most CBI exports to the US in an effort to encourage economic development in Central America and the Caribbean.

Mercosur was established in 1991 by four Atlantic rim countries of South America: Argentina, Brazil, Paraguay and Uruguay. The principal objective of Mercosur (El Mercado Común del Sur) is the economic development of the region through the establishment of a single market among the four countries based on the free movement of goods and services, the establishment of a common external tariff and trade policy, the coordination of macro economic and sectoral policies and the harmonization of legislation in order to strengthen the process of integration (Perez del Castillo, 1993, p. 639). All tariffs and non-tariff restrictions on internal trade were expected to be eliminated by the end of 1994. The four member countries have a combined population of nearly 200 million. The area of the Mercosur countries is about 11 million square kilometres larger than the United States and Mexico combined; ultimately it is expected that if Mercosur succeeds it will seek a close economic relationship with NAFTA.

Investors and traders often make much of the political risk of doing business in Latin America but the new reforms in the region and particularly the formation of the various market integration initiatives have reduced the exposure. As a result, one of the principal sources of economic risk, export specialization, has been in decline. Increased diversification of exports 'enhances prospects of exchange rate stability and reduces the likelihood of economic and financial crises' (Amin Gutiérrez de Piñeres and Ferrantino, 1997, p. 476).

Central and Eastern European markets

With the fall of communism industrial firms in the west view Central and Eastern European countries as affording great opportunities in capital equipment replacement and in the provision of skills and advanced technology. Unlike most developing countries, Central and Eastern Europe is already highly industrialized, but most of its inefficient factories are still in government ownership and while wages are low labour productivity is also extremely low.

To date the flow of investment eastwards has been minimal. Potential investors in countries such as Poland, the Czech Republic, Slovakia, Hungary, Romania and Bulgaria have discovered that doing business there is bureaucratic, time consuming and frustrating even though these countries have between them a population of almost 100 million people. These six countries have embraced free markets and political pluralism. While change is slower in Slovakia, Romania and Bulgaria the leading reformers, Poland, the Czech Republic and Hungary, have freed most of their prices, introduced convertibility in their currencies, lowered trade barriers and welcomed foreign investors. With regard to trade with Central and Eastern Europe, the EU is by far the largest partner. In 1991 the EU exported $21.63 billion of goods to the region while $20.16 billion was imported. Broadly similar magnitudes are involved in imports from the former USSR. Exports, however, declined significantly between 1990 and 1991, reflecting the weak state of the economy there and political and social turmoil.

Special position of developing countries

There are clear economic reasons why most countries wish to share the benefits of international trade and investment. There are also very strong social and human reasons why open markets are desirable. The need to open markets and to develop economies recognizes that poverty in the world should be eliminated and that trade and marketing have a role to play in that process (Exhibit 5.5). Economic disparities are believed to give rise to political unrest and social disruption. Implementing the recommendations of the GATT may be seen as an endeavour to reduce economic disparities. In the early 1990s countries representing the richest fifth in the world were responsible for 85 per cent of the world's GNP, 84 per cent of world trade, 86 per cent of domestic savings and 85 per cent of domestic investment. The poorest fifth barely register on these scales (Figure 5.3). The recently endorsed Uruguay Round of the GATT talks are expected to reduce some of these disparities.

Many types of macro economic trade and policy can be prejudicial to the alleviation of poverty in developing countries which, if not removed, can make it very difficult for people there: trade policies which provide effective protection to import competing

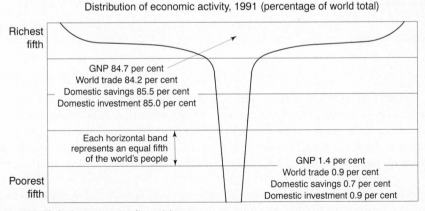

Figure 5.3 Global economic disparities
Source: United Nations Development Programme (1994), *Human Development Report*, Oxford: Oxford University Press, p. 63.

Exhibit 5.5
Consumer revolution in China

If you are ever in any doubt that China is in the throes of a consumer revolution, take a walk down Nanjing Road. Shanghai's premier shopping street has been carved in two by Pepsi and Coca-Cola, who have commandeered every lamppost to hang neon advertisements for their soft drinks. 'It is a chaotic outdoor media environment. Essentially, everything, everywhere is for sale,' says Soames Hines, former managing director of J Walter Thompson in Shanghai, the largest advertising agency in China.

Nevertheless, Hines puts advertising in its place. Most international companies in China 'are pushing packaged goods when their first concern should be getting a decent distribution system in place,' he says. Pricing, too, is critical. Customers, generally on monthly incomes of around $100 (£59), remain highly price sensitive.

Nor is the nature of the advertisement the determining factor, in Hines' judgement: 'Everyone likes to think that there is some mystique about China, but the Chinese consumer actually behaves much like any other. The key to getting it right is the advertising strategy, not the execution of the advertising.' By this, he means primarily understanding the needs of the market, and cites the example of S C Johnson's Toilet Duck.

Toilet Duck, with its hooked neck, designed to reach beneath the toilet's rim, positions itself in developed markets as a more convenient way to clean parts other products cannot reach. It was planned to launch in China with a Hong Kong advertisement that stressed these benefits.

However, even those Chinese who have modern toilets tend to use washing up water to clean them, and so, the Toilet Duck proposition would have been wasted. S C Johnson did some market research and 'avoided a very expensive mistake'. Hines has been 'consistently amazed' at how companies fail to spend time and money to understand the market before launching inappropriate products.

Source: adapted from *Financial Times*, Monday, 14 July 1997, p. 12.

manufacturing; overvaluation of exchange rates which lowers returns to agricultural exports; making imported food cheaper relative to domestic substitutes; high margins to government-sponsored commodity boards. At the same time subsidies for inputs and other non-price measures are often not sufficient to offset taxation and low product prices. Such policies tend to reduce or stop the flow of resources and to discourage investments in the developing countries. The trade and marketing developments which have occurred in the developed world and continue to expand have virtually bypassed countries in the developing world. The poverty and neglect thus created may well jeopardize some of the benefits accruing to the more developed world.

Closer trade links between developing and developed countries are expected to produce benefits for developed countries at two levels. First, there are gains from efficiency and specialization which arise from the traditional comparative advantages of trading part-ners. These include the benefits of the availability of greater variety of goods and possible benefits from scale economies and increased competition. Second, the benefits of efficiency and specialization themselves create more wealth for investment leading to greater growth rates. This endogenous growth may arise from the possibility of spreading product research and development costs over a larger market, thus reducing unit costs and encouraging more innovation and technical progress.

There is, however, a view that the emergence of new producers and new markets damages the economies of the developed world, that jobs are lost and that entire indust-ries wither away. Trade with developing countries has certainly affected the structure of manufacturing in developed countries. However, it is the contraction of some activities and the expansion of others that represent the very means by which gains from trade are realized.

The secondary round of benefits can lead to substantial gains for developed countries. With endogenous growth, it is estimated that the initial increase in output and income resulting from the Uruguay Round of trade liberalization would lead to an increase of 0.1 percentage point in the growth rate of developed countries. Expressed as discounted income, this could amount to a second-round increase in output of about 3.2 per cent of developed country GDP (Ghosh, 1996, p. 40). The gains from overall growth in trade integration with developing countries would be much higher.

Vicious circle of poverty

Any policy developed to improve the circumstances of the developing countries must take account of the interrelationship between economic and social factors and market situ-ations, which impose severe constraints on such communities as they attempt to expand production and marketing activities. Market imperfections lead to a vicious circle of low efficiency in production and marketing, leading to underemployed people and a mis-allocation of resources. In attempting to improve the marketing system it is necessary to consider a number of elements of the vicious circle (Figure 5.4).

The result of a weak economic structure and an inadequate social structure is a series of market imperfections which means that prices vary greatly for homogeneous products and are inflexible, markets are not cleared and participants in the markets lack knowledge concerning actual transactions and lack free access to markets. In addition, there are often price and quantity restrictions and individuals control the market, thereby exerting undue power. The final outcome of such a situation is underused resources, unemployment and poverty.

Market imperfections in turn lead to the vicious circle of low productivity leading to low real incomes, leading to low investment through low savings, low demand and finally, a weak or inadequate capital structure, which contributes further to market imperfections thereby ensuring that poverty continues. Intervention to promote development means breaking this vicious circle in a number of places to reduce market imperfections. By changing the demand constraint through the introduction of foreign buying power emanating from international markets, investment in local productive enterprise may

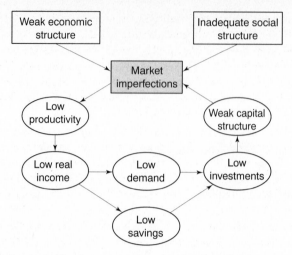

Figure 5.4 Marketing imperfections – vicious circle of poverty

arise, thereby improving the weak capital structure and so alleviating the poverty cycle. It is not a simple matter, however, as policy issues related to the weak economic and inadequate social structure also need to be addressed.

An institutional approach to marketing systems for developing countries means departing from purely economic solutions based on the transformation of existing production systems. It also means that it is not possible to depend solely on the modern sector but on a complete change of focus to developing value-added products in the community and changing policy to encourage such development. Communities in developing countries usually require special:

1 access to resources and markets;
1 access to credit and business services;
1 access to export markets;
1 access for women in the least developed countries, especially to resources and markets and the freedom to make independent decisions.

Relevance of marketing in developing countries

The relevance of basic marketing principles to developing countries is in dispute. Two opposing views may be presented. The first suggests that environmental factors prevent the straight transfer of marketing principles and concepts. Conditions of a strong market, increasing competition based on innovative products and services, better education and consumerism, all of which led to the acceptance of the marketing concept in the advanced world, are usually missing in developing countries. In addition, state planning frequently means that supply and demand are centrally controlled, which interferes with free market forces. It is often suggested that cultural factors also prevent application of the marketing concept.

The second view accepts that the marketing concept should be modified to take account of different environmental conditions but the principles and concepts should, nevertheless, be applied in developing country markets. While the marketing sophistication found in developed country markets may not be required, the basic functions and objectives of marketing remain relevant. The process is the same but there may be qualitative and quantitative differences, e.g. fewer products moving through the system, different kinds of products and a smaller variety.

Role of marketing in economic development

Because of both its functions and its philosophy, marketing can lead and encourage development. The marketing multiplier may be demonstrated as follows. Information is developed in marketing research which allows better utilization of resources. Efficient distribution enhances the productivity of the entire economic system. Better transportation and storage result in distribution economies, expanded markets and increased production. Better living standards can be diffused throughout the community simply by establishing retail outlets in strategic locations. In addition to promoting entrepreneurial initiatives and providing jobs, marketing also stimulates wants: people are presented with wider range of products. A higher level of production and a wider range of products follow.

In economic models of development marketing has no place, being considered as a part of the production system. The solution to the vicious circle of poverty means introducing capital on the supply side of the equation which increases productivity and creates disposable income (Figure 5.4). If the roles were reversed and production were seen as part of marketing, latent demand would first be identified. The role for marketing would be then to convert this latent demand to effective demand as it pushes producers to develop marketable products and improve distribution systems to ensure that products reach the market without perishing or damage on the way. Consequently, marketing effectively links developing countries with international markets which are essential for development.

Phenomenon of emerging markets

Developing country markets are different from those in the developed world, often because of poor access to information. In the former, buyers and sellers do not have the same access to information for three reasons (Khanna and Palepu, 1997, p. 42):

1 the communications infrastructure is not sufficiently developed;
1 there are no mechanisms to corroborate the claims made by sellers;
1 consumers have no redress mechanisms if a product does not deliver on its promise.

In developed markets, and increasingly in new emerging markets, information is often part of a product's brand equity. A company with a reputation for quality products and services may use its brand name to enter new international product markets. In many instances, successful brand companies can diversify into unrelated business using the company brand. Samsung has used its name for a range of products from televisions to microwave ovens. Where information is not accessible, companies face much greater costs in building credible brands than do companies in developed markets.

Radical changes are, however, taking place in the forces which influence the formation of consumer tastes and preferences, their information seeking and purchase behaviour and the diffusion of new products and ideas. Douglas and Craig (1997, p. 380) believe the reasons for these changes may be attributed to two factors:

1. massive waves of migration which are taking place, as consumers from emerging markets economies are moving to industrialized economies – the diaspora of Chinese spreading throughout Asia, the United States and Europe is cited as an example;
1. consumers are becoming more mobile and travelling more both for pleasure and for business and as a result are becoming more exposed to products, lifestyles and behaviour patterns of consumers in other countries.

These authors argue that these patterns have generated an increasingly complex pattern of consumer behaviour in which countries and countries can no longer be viewed as a set of distinctive value systems. Rather, a complex collage of culture and context is emerging in which no clear demarcation line identifies where one culture begins and another ends, and influences from one country or culture are constantly permeating others while at the same time cultural influences are becoming all pervasive adding to the necessity of under-standing how they affect consumption (Douglas and Craig 1997, pp. 380–1).

Recognizing mutual dependence

The developed markets are increasingly dependent on emerging markets in the developing world. The continued expansion of developed economies depends on investment in and trade with the developing world. Emerging developing country markets are responsible for an increasing proportion of the exports from developed countries. The ability to increase exports to new markets is also important because these countries are selling so much to the developed world. The enhanced competitiveness of emerging markets derives from the economic reforms, low wage rates and increased productivity (Garten, 1997, p. 47). Two additional reasons for mutual dependence between developed and developing markets exist. First, changing market conditions and ageing demographic profiles in developed markets have made developing markets attractive. Second, any decline in the size or growth of developing country markets would lead to more severe rivalry among developed country governments as they attempt to protect their economies.

First-mover and long-term advantage in emerging markets

In a study of the investment decisions of 15 Western multinational companies in various industry sectors in the Ukraine, Bridgewater (1995) concluded that they made little use of traditional marketing planning techniques and were not interested in the precise nature of uncertainty in the market. According to Bridgewater (1995, p. 794), the process of assisting market attractiveness was less influenced by rational assessment of the risks and opportunities of the market, than by the actions of oligopolistic rivals. The risk of entry into an uncertain market was offset by the benefits of gaining first-mover advantage for such a time as the market situation improves.

In new emerging markets, larger companies take a long-term view, especially for infra-structural projects and industrial products. Indeed, many firms attempt to be present in a portfolio of markets so that if a project is delayed or, for some economic or political reason, cancelled the company can rely on other markets. For example, the 1987 stock market crash and Mexico's peso crisis posed severe problems for General Electric. More recently, General Electric has experienced a cancellation of a number of projects in Asia. Another large company, Asea Brown Boveri (ABB) lost the contract for the Bakun Dam in Malaysia. ABB recognizes, however, that its presence in Asia is not just for a single project and that the benefits of exporting from a low-cost area could more than offset the expected temporary decline from within the market (Exhibit 5.6). It may also be noted that infrastructure projects cannot be postponed indefinitely, as they are essential to economic development. Lastly, though some companies depend on Asian markets for a large part of their sales, most large companies, particularly, still sell most of their output in developed country markets.

═══ Exhibit 5.6 ═══
ABB axe swings into action

ABB, the Swiss-Swedish engineering group, has never made a secret of the fact that its strategy of expanding production in emerging economies requires steady job cuts in its established manufacturing centres in Europe.

In cutting 10,000 jobs in Europe and North America, ABB has moved faster than it had intended because of economic turmoil in south-east Asia, which includes some of its most important markets. The axe is to fall mainly in Germany, Italy, Spain, Sweden, Switzerland and the US. The principal cuts and closures will be concentrated in power generation, which accounts for about a quarter of ABB's business. The indefinite postponement of the $5 billion Bakun hydro-electric project in Malaysia was a particular blow, for which ABB is taking a separate charge of $100 million.

Göran Lindahl, ABB's Chief Executive, decided that the economic slowdown in south-east Asia, compounded by the decline of currencies in the region, has made it necessary to accelerate east Asian expansion. He also says that current weakness makes south-east Asia a more attractive export base for ABB. Mr Lindahl remains confident that the Bakun dam project, the biggest contract in ABB's history, will go ahead within the next two or three years.

Mr Lindahl describes the proposed cuts as 'an aggressive move which was ahead of the market'. But analysts say it looks more like a reaction to south-east Asia's problems. Freddie Hasslauer, of Sal. Oppenheim, the Zurich broker, says it highlights the fact that, although developing country growth rates are higher than in OECD nations, so are the risks.

Source: adapted from *Financial Times*, Wednesday, 22 October 1997, p. 28.

Marketing stages and levels of economic development

The role of international marketing in the development of a country may be seen in a simple stages model of marketing. By relating different approaches to marketing and the different levels of economic development experienced, different international marketing outcomes are derived (Figure 5.5).

In poor stagnant countries, exchange, where it occurs, is usually through barter. Marketing activities are limited in such self-sufficient economies. In the second stage of development the economy is emerging and beginning to develop and the emphasis is on distribution, storage and transport, the appearance of trade specialists and other inter-mediaries. Barter is replaced by money. The emphasis is still, however, very production oriented. By this stage local producers sell to expanded markets nearby. The third stage, referred to here as industrializing, arises when modern technology extends to most areas of economic activity. Trade with other countries may occur as production and distribu-tion are now well established and marketing shifts from an institutional focus to a more sophisticated form of consumer satisfaction, based on extended products and brands. The final stage of mass consumption arises when advanced technology spreads to all economic activity. The society has considerable discretionary income and manufacturing capacity strains the distribution system, which increases the level of competition. Trade with numerous foreign countries is now essential for continued growth and prosperity.

By relating these factors the United Nations Development Programme (1997) was able to portray the relationship between income levels and human development in a number of countries, a selection of which are shown in Figure 5.6. In the figure three pairs of countries with similar income levels are compared: Trinidad and Tobago with Gabon; Ecuador with Papua New Guinea; Honduras with Senegal. In all pairs, even though income levels are the same, life expectancy, adult literacy rates and the human develop-ment index are very different. Other factors clearly influence the outcome. The corres-

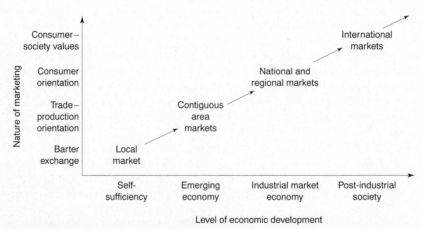

Figure 5.5 Marketing and economic development

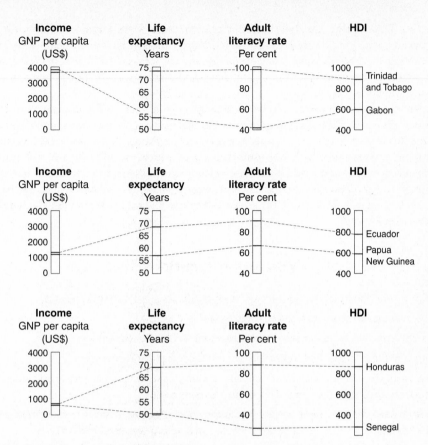

Figure 5.6 Similar income, different human development, 1994
Source: United Nations Development Programme 1997, *Human Development Report*, Oxford: Oxford University Press, p. 46.

pondence between income and the human development index is more obvious in the case of the Latin American and Caribbean countries than it is for the African countries and Papua New Guinea.

To the extent that the relationship between international marketing and income levels can be maintained and the subsequent correlation between income levels and human development supported, it is obvious why international organizations such as the United Nations, GATT, the EU and other bodies take such a direct interest in international marketing and trade related matters.

Summary

World output and trade have increased significantly in recent decades, trade at a faster rate than output. The increase in trade has internationalized the economies of many countries. Traditional models of economic growth based on mercantilism and protected markets do not give the desired result, especially to businesses that see the benefits of open international markets. Because business benefits and consumers also benefit from cheaper, more available goods and services there has been a great deal of political interest in reducing these barriers to trade.

Open international markets are encouraged by the various GATT agreements and by the establishment and strengthening of international bodies and organizations such as the EU, the WTO and NAFTA and other regional trade groups. Many other trading blocs have come into existence with the result that a large part of world trade now takes place within and between these trade blocs. The developing countries, unfortunately, have not been included in these developments. It is argued that international marketing has a strong role to play in developing these economies and integrating them with countries in the developed world.

Discussion questions

1. Why in your opinion, is world trade growing at a faster rate than world output?
2. How realistic is the concept of free trade today?
3. Describe the linkage between market integration and trade agreements.
4. What are the principal features of the world's major trade agreements?
5. Does your town or region benefit from your country's participation in a trade agreement or economic–political union such as may be found in the EU?
6. Describe the vicious circle of poverty found in developing countries; how may open markets alleviate some of the problems associated with underdevelopment?
7. Is international marketing relevant to developing countries?

References

Amin Gutiérrez de Piñeres, S. and Ferrantino, M. (1997) 'Export diversification trends: some comparisons for Latin America', *International Executive*, **39** (4), 465–77.

Bridgewater, S. (1995) 'Assessing the attractiveness of turbulent markets: the Ukrainian experience', *Journal of Marketing Management*, **11**, 785–96.

Commerzbank (1997) 'Europe challenged by Asia's rise in engineering', *Viewpoint in Harvard Business Review*, **75** (July–August) 4.

Dominguez, L. V. and Brenes, E. R. (1997) 'The Internationalization of Latin American enterprises and market liberalization in the Americas: a vital linkage', *Journal of Business Research*, **38**, 3–16.

Douglas, S. P. and Craig, C. S. (1997): 'The changing dynamic of consumer behavior: implications for cross-cultural research', *International Journal of Research in Marketing*, **14**, 379–95.

Fieleke, N. S. (1992) 'One trading world or many: the issue of regional trading blocs', *New England Economic Review*, (May–June), 3–20.

Gardner, M. (1993) 'Survey of the European Single Market: citizens sceptical about their prospects', *Financial Times* (19 January).

Garten, J. E. (1997), 'Troubles ahead in emerging markets', *Harvard Business Review*, **75** (3), 38–50.

Ghosh S. R. (1996) 'Reverse linkages: the growing importance of developing countries', *Finance & Development*, (March), 38–41.

Khanna, T. and Palepu, K. (1997) 'Why focused strategies may be wrong for emerging markets', *Harvard Business Review*, **75** (July–August), 41–51.

Perez del Castillo, S. (1993) 'Mercosur: history and aims', *International Labour Review*, **132** (5–6), 639–53.

Sargent, J. and Matthews, L. (1997) 'NAFTA, the financial crisis, and multinational manaagement in Mexico', *International Executive*, **39** (3), 375–92.

Schott, J. J. (1991) 'Trading blocs and the world trading system', *World Economy*, **14**, 1–17.

United Nations Development Programme (1997) *Human Development Report*, Oxford: Oxford University Press.

6
The sociocultural environment

International business has always been recognized as an activity involving investment decisions or the exchange of products and services across national boundaries. It is only in recent years, however, that sociocultural influences have been identified as critical determinants of international management behaviour. International business, and especially international marketing, is seen as a cultural as well as an economic phenomenon. The growing use of anthropology, sociology and psychology is an explicit recognition of the non-economic bases of international marketing behaviour.

Meaning of culture in international marketing

The analysis of the sociocultural environment with the help of anthropological, sociological and psychological frameworks is increasing in importance for the firm in international markets. This sociocultural environment involves the following:

1 the learned behavioural features shared by people of the same culture;
1 real physical attributes or appearances;
1 physical idealized traits, i.e. advertisement stereotypes;
1 demographic characteristics such as population size, age distribution, etc. which when related to given income levels can help in defining the market potential.

Culture is a complex concept which includes specific knowledge, beliefs, morals, laws and customs shared by a society (Exhibit 6.1). Culture is broadly based on the following three elements:

1. norms, which are hierarchical rules specifying behavioural and thinking patterns according to varying situations,
2. ideology, which involves beliefs, physical and empirical knowledge, and
3. material culture, which covers all buildings, tools, machinery, etc. created and used.

With regard to the first point a distinction must be made at this stage between ideal norms to which people give verbal allegiance and real norms with which people actually comply. Ideology also includes cognitive and aesthetic ideas, aesthetic forms of expression and evaluative ideas which help define standards and judgements about oneself and others. Cultural interpretation for the international firm in the sense that it is a learned process differs in essence from instinct. There are two main ways, as follows, to develop cultural norms and values:

1. socialization, referring both to life experiences and the influences of institutions such as family, religion and education systems;
2. acculturation, which refers to a voluntary process of learning.

It is important to note that cultural elements are all interrelated and adaptive and therefore subject to change. Some cultural elements are more fundamental and are less susceptible to change than others.

Many writers claim that modern communications and rising income levels promote a common culture worldwide. If there were a common culture the international marketing task would be much easier. While there are many branded products and services which are available throughout the world this does not mean that these brands have the same meaning in different cultures. Brands such as Coca Cola, Sony, McDonalds, British Airways and Singapore Airlines are available worldwide but do they have the same meaning in different countries? The fact of their ubiquitous availability 'only tells us that there are some novel products that can be sold on a universal message. It does not tell us what they mean in the different cultures where they are visible' (Hoecklin, 1995, p.2). When people write about a convergence of cultures the evidence cited is usually taken from peoples' behaviour and practices with regard to the products they wear and the food they eat. However, these 'rather superficial manifestations of culture are sometimes mistaken for all there is; the deeper, underlying level of values, which moreover determine the meaning for people of their practices, is overlooked' (Hofstede, 1991, p. 181).

It is accepted, for example, that it is not enough to say that consumption of a product is a function of income; it is also a function of many other cultural factors. Furthermore, only non-economic factors can explain the different patterns of consumption of two different countries with identical per capita incomes. Culture is so pervasive yet complex that it is difficult to define: each scholar seems to have a separate definition. Culture has been called 'the integrated sum total of learned behavioral traits that are manifest and shared by members of a society' (Hoebel, 1960, p. 168). For present purposes culture may be considered the man-made part of our environment, or the distinctive life style of a people. Culture is not biologically transmitted; any given culture or way of life is learned behaviour which depends on the environment and not on hereditary factors (Terpstra, 1978, p. 87).

In the present context, therefore, the term 'sociocultural environment' is used to refer to all those factors behind a country's international marketing prowess which are of a learned nature. This makes it a rather omnibus term, covering attitudes, sociology, behaviour, psychology and cultural development of, and within, the country as a whole, and the various subpopulations which go to make up that country. Just as there is more to

Japan's prowess in international marketing than the strict application of the techniques identified in some textbook or manual so, too, is there for other countries with different cultural backgrounds.

==== Exhibit 6.1 ====

Cross-cultural competence: the tool of the future

Cross-cultural research has shown that culture plays a crucial role in human behaviour. First, culture is how we behave. There is a pattern that all people belonging to the same group share. We all know the rules even if we cannot verbalise them. We have learned these rules by watching and copying the behaviours of other group members.

Second, culture is the values we all share. We face values that often develop out of critical incidents. We discuss critical incidents with each other and through discussion, we draw conclusions. If the critical incident is something most group members react to, there will be a shared conclusion. This will be the very base for the development of future values to be shared by all members of the culture.

Third, culture is a 'filter' through which we all perceive reality. As human beings, we cannot grasp everything that happens around us. We need to focus our perception. This filter can easily be shown by the diversity of how different occupational groups perceive the same situation. For example, if construction workers and medical doctors are seated in the same room at the same time, the construction workers might focus on the construction of the room, whereas the doctors are more likely to focus on the people.

Why do we develop culture? One function is to help the group members identify themselves to other members. This is what lies behind the experience most people have while traveling in other countries. Another function is to give us identity. By telling you which groups I belong to, I give you a fairly good idea of who I am. On a deeper level, culture provides the rules, the morality, the values, and the ethics of the group; what binds people together. Without it, we could not stay together. This meets the need to belong.

Managers require a great deal of knowledge to work within their own cultural context. In the future, they will also need to be able to work with a culturally diverse population which also asks for more and different managerial competence. Managers who know how to bridge cultural gaps save their organizations money.

How do you bridge cultural gaps? To bridge cultural gaps, you need to respect others, even those who are different from yourself. What we know today is that individuals with a higher degree of self-esteem bridge cultural gaps more easily. All of us need basic trust in our lives. This is usually a balance between the stability of knowing and relying on your surroundings, and knowing and relying on your own self-esteem.

Source: adapted from *Global Management*, 1997, pp. 109–12.

Sociocultural environment

The sociocultural environment consists of those physical, demographic and behavioural variables which influence business activities in a given country (Figure 6.1).

Among human variations, the most noticeable are physical attributes or appearance. While most differences in appearance are readily apparent, there are a host of subtle variations that, although important to people within a given society, may be easily overlooked by non-discriminating outsiders. Size of individuals would seem to be one of the most noticeable differences, but many firms make mistakes in this respect. For example, a well known UK retailer, Marks and Spencer, attempted to sell men's suits in China based on UK patterns for tailoring, only to realize that they fitted few Chinese men because of their narrower hips and shoulders.

Not only must actual physical differences be taken into account, so also must traits that a country has idealized. Various populations have created wishful stereotypes of themselves that must be considered when creating imagery. For this reason, advertisements in the United States typically depict individuals who are somewhat younger and thinner than the majority of the people toward whom the product is aimed. In Germany there has been an idealization of the tall Nordic type, who is actually no taller than the average Pole, Frenchman or Dutchman.

Demographic changes also influence the international firm. Certain population characteristics are important to the international firm. For many products, population size may be used as a broad preliminary indicator of market potential. However, population size

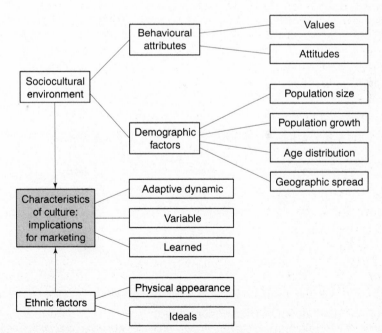

Figure 6.1 The sociocultural environment and marketing implications

should only be used in conjunction with income levels and other measures, as a large population may represent little potential where income levels are quite low.

It is important to study population growth rates: low population growth rates are more typical of countries generally regarded as more highly developed economically. This arises from an historical tendency of both birth and death rates to decrease following, rather than preceding, economic development. In most developing countries in recent years, the death rate has fallen markedly because of medical advances while the birth rate has remained high. This has caused an unprecedented population explosion that has hampered efforts to raise living standards.

Not only is the world's population growing rapidly, but the population density is shifting from the industrial countries of the North to the developing countries of the South. By the year 2050, population in the developed world is expected to increase by somewhat less than 200 million, whereas the developing areas of Africa, Asia and Latin America are expected to increase by two billion. The World Bank predicts that over four-fifths of the world's population will be concentrated in developing countries.

Age distribution in a foreign country is yet another factor which affects both sales and investment opportunities. A country with a larger proportion of people in the older age brackets would have a smaller market for items such as maternity and infant goods, and school equipment. Conversely, a more elderly population would represent a larger market for healthcare products. Hence, it is important to understand the impact of the age distribution in different international markets. The age distribution of selected populations is shown in Figure 6.2.

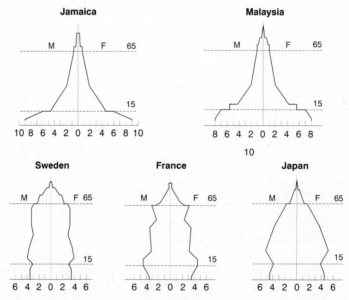

Figure 6.2 Age distributions of selected populations
Source: fashioned after Hornby, W. F. (1980), *An Introduction to Population Geography*, Cambridge: Cambridge University Press.

The age distribution of the population has important consequences for the size of the labour force and its productivity. If a population has a higher than normal proportion of very old or very young people, as may be found in France, Germany, parts of the US, and many developing countries, then fewer people, proportionally, will be available to do productive work. This may lead to a shortage of skilled or manual labour and greatly increased wage rates.

Overall, country data obscure differences that exist within individual nations. Within developing countries there are, typically, fairly substantial groups that have the characteristics of advanced countries. Of course, it is also possible to find backward areas or groups within the most developed countries. It is important to note, however, that the sociocultural environment varies greatly from country to country.

Interpreting culture for the international firm

Culture may be described as the ways of living built up by a group of human beings transmitted from one generation to another. Culture includes both conscious and unconscious values, ideas, attitudes and symbols which shape human behaviour and are transmitted from one generation to the next (Terpstra, 1978). 'Culture is a mental map which guides us in our relations to our surroundings and to other people' (Downs, 1971, p. 35).

In this sense culture does not refer to the instinctive responses of people, nor does it include one-time solutions to unique problems. Hall (1960) has stated that

> culture is man's medium; there is not one aspect of human life that is not touched and altered by culture. This means personalities, how people express themselves (including shows of emotion), the way they think, how they move, how problems are solved, how their cities are planned and laid out, how transportation systems function and are organized, as well as how economic and government systems are put together and function.

An alternative view of culture is that it 'is a way of habitual acting , feeling and thinking, channelled by a society out of an infinite number of variety of potential ways of living' (Kroebar, 1951, p.19).

That which gives humans their identity no matter where they were born is their culture – the total communication framework of words, actions, posture, gestures, tones of voice, facial expressions, the way they handle time, space and materials and the way they work, play, make love and defend themselves and their property (Hall, 1960). All human actions are modified by learning. Once learned, habitual responses and ways of interacting gradually sink below the surface of the mind and operate from the unconscious. Culture encompasses the knowledge, language, values, customs and material objects that are passed from person to person and from generation to generation (Funakawa, 1997, p. 15).

It is important to remember that some managerial functions are more sensitive to culture than others. Sensitivity of a particular function to cultural influence depends on the importance of direct exchange between that function and the cultural environment. Functions such as marketing and public relations generally demand more interaction with local culture than, for example, the functions of finance or production. The firm's competence in dealing with managerial issues across markets is based on three different but related abilities (Langhoff, 1977, p. 159):

ι to cope with cultural heterogeneity across different international markets,
ι to harmonize it products and services and their marketing with the symbolic meaning which target markets in different cultures assign them, and
ι to identify and exploit new opportunities in foreign cultural contexts in expectation of long-lasting competitive advantages.

Characteristics of culture

There are two ways in which a person develops norms and values (Engel, *et al.*, 1983). The first is learning by socialization, in which a person learns a culture when he or she is very young. Two different forces operate here. The first source of values is referred to as the institutional triad – families and religious and educational institutions. The second source is early lifetime experiences which may include war, social disturbances and family upheavals. Values and norms formed at this stage will lead to differences between the generations, when the population as a whole is being considered.

The second process is termed learning by acculturation and is the process of learning a culture of which one is not native. For example, if a firm wishes to invest in, or to sell to, another country, it must learn the culture of that country. For the firm in international markets the characteristics of culture are learned, interrelated and adaptive. These operate at times as subcultures involving language, religion, values, attitudes and other aspects of social organization (Table 6.1). Patterns which govern behaviour and perception come into consciousness only when there is a deviation from the learned pattern, as can happen in intercultural encounters which may lead to cultural bias.

To transcend this bias managers of firms in international markets must achieve awareness of the structure of their own system by interacting with others who do not share that system. This awareness may be achieved through the acquisition of the relevant language and of its associated conceptual frameworks.

In attempting to understand the impact of culture on the firm it is important to recognize that parts of culture are interrelated and that culture is adaptive and may change rapidly or slowly. The various parts of culture are interrelated. Cultural systems have a unity which, as a result of the interaction among the parts, is different from a simple sum of the parts. To achieve understanding of any culture, one must not only understand the content, but also how the system is put together and how its parts are interrelated. Culture is also adaptive, through either a discontinuous or an evolutionary process (Engel *et al.*, 1993). Culture responds to the physical and social environment in which it operates and has contact. It is especially important for the firm in international markets to monitor the change in the physical and social environment as such changes can in a relatively short period result in either positive or negative effects on the demand for the company's products.

Table 6.1 Characteristics and elements of culture

1. Learned
   ⌐ socialization
   ⌐ acculturation

2. Interrelated

3. Adaptive
   ⌐ discontinuity
   ⌐ evolutionary

4. Subcultures
   ⌐ nationality
   ⌐ religion
   ⌐ age
   ⌐ occupation

Elements of culture

⌐ Language
⌐ Religion
⌐ Values and attitudes
⌐ Social organization
⌐ Education
⌐ Technology and material culture

A very sharp discontinuity occurs in the pattern of cultural change when the value system of a culture becomes associated with the gratification of only one class. Other classes reject the logic of the value system and replace it with a new value system. In an evolutionary process change comes but is a process of modification and adaptation. The adaptive nature of culture is an important consideration in developing an understanding of behaviour in that culture. In the past cultural change was usually slow and gradual. The accelerated technological changes that characterize contemporary society, together with rapid changes in the institutional triad mentioned above, have created a situation where change is quicker and more unpredictable.

Most cultures are also characterized by a series of sub-cultures which involve sets of learned beliefs, values, attitudes, habits and forms of behaviour which are shared by subjects of a society and are transmitted from generation to generation within each subset (Bennett and Kassarjan, 1972). Members of subcultures typically conform to many of the norms of the dominant culture and deviate from others which are not compatible with the norms of their subculture.

There are a number of variables on which subcultures are based. Some are based on nationality, such as the Turkish immigrants in Germany, who represent about four per cent of the total population. In the United States race is an important base of subculture, while religion is often the base for subcultures, such as the Catholic minority in Northern Ireland. Indeed, the influence of religion on business through company regulations and restraints on consumer behaviour in some societies is all pervasive. Age can also represent an important basis for recognizing subcultures with, for example, teenagers and older age groups exhibiting quite different patterns of consumption. Often the values of a sub-culture are passed on to the dominant culture. For example, denim jeans, originally designed for miners in the American West, soon became popular among farm people and ranchers and decades later began to be worn by the youth subculture, are now worn by all age groups.

Elements of culture in international markets

Language is perhaps the most obvious difference between cultures and has been described as a cultural mirror which reflects the content and nature of the culture it represents. Language is human behaviour, not just a collection of words and sounds. It is the spoken and not the written language which most accurately describes and reflects the contempory behaviour and values of members of a culture. Some countries are linguistically homo-geneous while others are heterogeneous. Based on the 103 countries examined by Banks and Textar (1963) there is a preponderance of linguistically heterogeneous countries in Asia and Africa. Europe and the Middle East are about evenly balanced, while Latin America is almost homogeneous linguistically (Table 6.2). In addition to differences in official languages, nations also differ in the number of languages used within their boundaries. Looking at national official languages alone can give a misleading picture of the linguistic uniformity within countries. There are only about 100 official languages for all countries in the world, whereas there are at least 3,000 languages currently spoken throughout the world. Well under half of the countries of the world are linguistically homogeneous in the sense that 85 per cent or more of the population speaks the same native tongue. The degree of linguistic heterogeneity varies greatly between countries. Some countries are almost 'pure' linguistically, with nearly all the citizens speaking the same native tongue. A complicating factor in most countries, which is not easily resolved, is the issue of dialects. In countries where more than one language is spoken widely the issue of dialects is, of course, much more complicated. Switzerland is a good example of a small country in which there are a number of official languages but a range of dialects based on these languages.

Importance of values

Much of human behaviour depends on values and attitudes. Schwartz (1994) attempts to answer questions such as: 'how are the value priorities of individuals affected by their social experience and how do the value priorities held by individuals affect their behavioural orientations and choices'. Our values and attitudes help to determine what we think is right and wrong, what is important and what is desirable. A value is an enduring prescriptive or prospective belief that a specific mode of behaviour is preferred to an opposite mode of behaviour – this belief transcends attitudes towards objects and situations (Rokeach, 1968, p. 25). Using the work of Rokeach (1968), Schwartz and Bilsky

Table 6.2 Linguistic characteristics of selected regions of the world

Region	Countries examined	Linguistically homogenous	Linguistically heterogeneous
	(number)	(number)	(number)
Asia	17	3	14
Africa	24	3	21
Europe	27	18	9
North America	2	0	2
Latin America	19	15	4
Middle East	12	6	6
Oceania	2	2	0
Total	103	47	56

Source: based on data in Banks, A. S. and Textar, R. B. (1963) *A Cross-Polity Survey*, Boston, MA: MIT Press, pp. 72–5.

(1987, p. 551) derive seven distinct value domains which are predicated on three universal human needs: the biological needs of the individual, the individual's social interaction needs and the individual's social institutional needs. Some of the Schwartz and Bilsky (1987), and Schwartz (1990) value domains are highly culture bound while others are universal values:

Security: physical survival, mental well-being and threat avoidance. Relevant values focus on inner harmony, family security, national security and world peace.

Enjoyment: physiological satisfaction, pleasure, sensuousness, emotional gratification. Relevant values focus on pleasure, a comfortable life and happiness.

Restrictive conformity: restriction of behaviour which impedes others. Relevant values focus on preventing harm to others, being obedient, polite, clean, self-controlled.

Self-direction: reliance on capacity for independent thought and action. Relevant values focus on imagination, logical thought, independence and intellect.

Achievement: skills and competences to allow personal growth and improvement. Relevant values focus on ambition, capability and social recognition.

Prosocial: concern for welfare of others to ensure group survival. Relevant values focus on being helpful, forgiving and loving and on equality.

Maturity: appreciate, understand and accept oneself, other people, and the world. Relevant values focus on wisdom, open-mindedness, a world of beauty and courage.

As was seen in Chapter 2, people are motivated by constrained self-interest seeking. They are hedonistic, which drives them to seek pleasure, but at the same time they are constrained by restrictive conformity and morality (Etzioni, 1988). People pursue pleasure and avoid pain but they are constrained by considerations of what is right, proper, ethical, moral and appropriate which derive from the latent value systems of different cultures. Different cultures and value systems are, therefore, presumed to influence directly the behaviour of consumers and managers.

Values and religious beliefs are interrelated; each supports the other. Understanding religion and values in society means examining our deepest convictions. For Terpstra (1978) religion is a mainspring of culture. A person's religious beliefs influence consumption behaviour, social behaviour, manner of dress, ways of doing business, general societal values and harmony and conflict in society. Religion also affects our attitudes toward time, wealth, change and risk. All these factors are fundamental to marketing and understanding of consumer and buyer behaviour.

Not only does religion establish taboos and moral standards within a culture affecting behaviour, it also reflects the principal values of a people. Social mobility and the achievement ethic in the West are supported by Christian values of self-determination and the importance of work. The Hindu religion emphasizes reaching Nirvana through a combination of inherited status and a contemplative life. Where religion is important in a society, the religious institutions usually play an important role in either promoting or discouraging change.

It is important, therefore, to understand the direct influence of values and their indirect influence through attitudes and beliefs, on all aspects of commercial life.

Consumption and business behaviour may be directly related to values. For instance, achievement and success are regarded as being very important in some countries which can act as a justification for the acquisition of material wealth.

The recent economic turmoil in the economies of some Asian markets has been attributed to a neglect of old-fashioned values which had helped to create the economic prowess that allowed them to compete successfully with the West (Exhibit 6.2).

Attitudes towards time express important values in society, for example, and they are also culturally distinctive. Attitudes to time vary from culture to culture and occasionally within the same culture. In some countries, for instance, an executive knows what is meant when a client lets a month go by before replying to a business proposal. In other societies this would not be acceptable.

In Arab countries time does not generally include schedules as they are known and used in Western countries. The time required to get something accomplished depends upon relationships. In Latin America, to be kept waiting does not necessarily mean a lack of attention. Even in neighbouring European countries attitudes to time can be very different, causing conflict in management relations. In international marketing it is very important that we understand attitudes to time in different cultures. Attitudes to time are a manifestation of the latent values of society.

Language and communication in international marketing

In international marketing, language both facilitates and impedes effective communication. Unifying markets or operating units of the same company located in different countries and cultures is a major and challenging management task. The issue is how best to communicate across the company's functional and national boundaries (Marschan, *et al.*, 1997, p. 593). These authors argue that 'An important first step might be to include

Exhibit 6.2
The Value of Values

As you ponder the litany of 'I-told-you-so' prescriptions for East Asia's economic malaise, spare a thought for good old Asian values. The effort to get economies back into shape has to include a return to the values that made them world-beating. Take frugal living and the aversion to debt, credited for the region's high savings rates, not to mention its billion-dollar fortunes. Over the past decade, however, more and more of the rich have sought to impress with wasteful displays of wealth.

Hard work and learning are values which have slipped out of fashion a bit. Producing quality, affordable goods and services used to be the main ticket to wealth, but a growing number of Hong Kong students now dream of instant riches from poverty and stock trading. Japan got into the game early: in the bubble years, industrial firms relied on *zaiteku* or financial trading for a big chunk of their profits. Many lost their corporate shirts.

As for learning, Thailand's relative neglect of its schools has held back its climb up the industrial ladder, with science and engineering graduates falling short of industry needs by a third. Public and private spending on education amounts to a mere 4% of GNP, the lowest in the region.

Clearly, tons of money and radical policy shifts are needed to heal sick economies, but they won't work without the right values guiding people. Those old principles will, of course, have to be modernized. In anticipating adversity, for instance, the prudent can use futures to hedge against unfavourable market swings. If a firm maintains a safe debt-to-equity ratio, credit can speed up growth. And there may be reason to discourage certain Asian ways of doing business. Cronyism and corruption, in particular, rob people of opportunities for enterprise, add to business costs, and create rapacious monopolies. Letting market forces decide which enterprise wins or loses, would do much to promote fair competition as well as prudence, frugality and industry. Inevitably, no pain, no gain; recovery for both economies and values will be a long, difficult struggle. That too will help teach another wealth-creating principle lost on many of the boom's children: patience.

Source: adapted from *Asiaweek*, 5 September 1997, pp. 14–15.

language aspects at the highest level of strategic planning and implementation' (p. 596). For these authors, international marketing companies 'cannot allow language to become peripheral, given that it permeates virtually every aspect of their operations' (p. 597).

Language is a primary way of separating cultural groups (Griffin and Pustay, 1996). It establishes the categories on which our perceptions of the world are organized. Language has been described as the mirror of culture (Czinkota and Ronkainen, 1995). Our perceptions of the world depend on how language influences the way we think: thus 'speakers of any two languages will not perceive reality in exactly the same way; language is not merely a mechanism for communicating ideas, but also a shaper of ideas' (Ueltschy and Ryans, 1997, p. 482). In a study of the possibility of standardizing advertising in the US and in Mexico, these authors state that any advertising campaign using an emotional appeal may be difficult to standardize, since the success of an emotional appeal depends on viewers bringing similar cultural values to the situation (p. 491), but where advertisements are cognitively based the possibility of standardization exists but viewers prefer customized advertisements.

Language, as the primary means of communication among civilized peoples, is perhaps the most important single cultural input. Language is the medium we all use to make meaning from environmental stimuli. Clumsy or careless language use may result in inaccurate communication (Cundiff and Tharp Higler, 1984). The nuances of meaning for particular words may vary from language to language, and a literal translation may change the entire meaning. Poor translation and the misuse of language are among the common traps of international marketing, but no aspect of international marketing is insulated from the problems associated with the management of cultural issues (Ricks, 1983).

Managers who find it necessary to communicate in a foreign language should make use of a truly bilingual interpreter who will make certain that the meaning is not lost in translation. It can be dangerous for people with an elementary knowledge of a foreign language to act as their own interpreter. They can miss subtle meanings in written correspondence that may affect interest in a product, or even a possible sales contract. The same kinds of traps exist in oral communication, of which examples abound. The international manager should therefore be aware of the more obvious differences in languages and general behaviour as well as the more subtle influence it has on thinking and cultural identities.

A facility in foreign languages helps but it is not the answer to the issue of effective communications in international markets. It is essential to be sensitive to the business cultures found in the target market. Sensitivity to national business cultures has been found to enhance communication and to reduce conflict, which in turn leads to better relationship performance. Given the abundance of information on diverse cultures, factual knowledge about a foreign culture is easily attainable but adaptation to that culture requires practice and a willingness to change one's behaviour (LaBahn and Harich, 1997, p. 44). The implications are clear: cultural understanding and adaptation are important (Francis, 1991). Not much, however, is known about the process of becoming culturally sensitive. In an attempt to address the issue companies frequently hire locals as managers or managers who have demonstrated cultural sensitivity having worked in other countries. Unfortunately this may merely shift any misunderstanding which arises to another location abroad and down another management layer. This is an issue which is examined further in Chapter 19.

Social organization and education

Social organization concerns the way in which people relate to one another and organize their activities in order to live in harmony with one another. Social classes, the family, positions of men and women, group behaviour and age groups are interpreted differently within different cultures (Table 6.3).

Table 6.3 Social organization and class culture

Social class
Upper classes in different countries more similar to each other than to the rest of their society
Middle classes more apt to 'cultural borrowing'
Lower class more culture bound
Role of the family
Role of women

Social classes tend to have quite different consumption patterns which affect, among other things, the purchase of housing and home furnishings, food and alcoholic beverages. The degree of social mobility is also an important dimension of class structure, as is the relative size and number of distinct classes within a society. Figure 6.3 illustrates five different societies in terms of the relative sizes of different social classes; the top rectangle shows the size of the upper class relative to middle and lower classes. In some societies only a small number of distinct social classes can be identified, whereas in others, such as the United States or India, many different social classes exist side by side, each with its own particular needs and wants.

Upper classes in almost all countries seem to be more similar to each other than they are to the rest of their own society. Lower classes tend to be more culture bound, i.e. they are less aware of other cultures, whereas middle classes are more apt to participate in cultural 'borrowing'. Therefore, the larger the upper and middle classes, the more likely a market is to buy products and services that are not culturally bound.

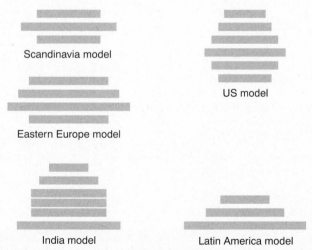

Figure 6.3 Relative importance of social class structure in different societies
Source: Cundiff, E. W. and Sharp Higler, M. E. (1984) *Marketing in the International Environment,* Englewood Cliffs, NJ: Prentice Hall.

The role of the family may also vary among cultures. In primitive and rural societies the family is the all-important social focal point, providing food, clothing, shelter, education, acculturation and a social centre.

In some of the more sophisticated urban societies the family may provide little more than food and basic acculturation. All other activities are partially or totally transferred to other groups, especially peers and educational institutions.

The role of women varies widely from society to society. In many societies women do not enjoy parity with men as participants in the economy. The extent to which they participate affects their role as consumers, consumption influencers and workers in the money economy.

In the industrialized world the educational system is synonymous with schools and these play a major role in passing on cultural values to the individual. In many developing countries, however, elders and oral historians play a greater role in the transmission of cultural traditions and values to young people. Formal education through schools has a strong relationship to literacy levels within a society. In those countries where schools are provided for the broadest possible group, literacy levels tend to be highest. Well-educated people tend to want more sophisticated information about products and tend to use more sources of information when making purchase decisions. It is important, therefore, for the international firm to understand the nature of the formal educational system, to whom it is available, and its relative importance in transmitting cultural values compared with other institutions.

Technology and material culture

Technology includes the techniques used in the creation of material goods; it is the educational and technical know-how possessed by the people of a society (Table 6.4). Material culture affects the level of demand, the quality and types of products demanded and their functional features, as well as the means of production of these goods and their distribution (Cateora, 1993). The marketing implications of the material culture of a country are many. Electrical toothbrushes, for example, which are acceptable in the West,

---

Table 6.4 Technology and material culture

The techniques used in the creation of material goods, the technical know-how possessed by the people of a society which affects:

1. level of demand
1. quality and types of products demanded
1. means of producing goods
1. means of distributing

and is related to:
1. aesthetic values or preferences in the arts, music or design

would be considered a waste of money in countries where income could be better spent on clothing or food.

Closely related to a country's material culture are its aesthetic values or preferences in the arts, music and design. For example, Americans often feel that Japanese homes are barren while the Japanese comment on the sterility of the American home. Similarly Hoover, the large washing machine manufacturer, found that the generally accepted ideas about what constitutes good design were different in the French and German markets. The German homemaker preferred a design that was larger and more sturdy in appearance, that gave a feeling of sound engineering and durability. The French homemaker preferred a smaller, lighter machine that did not overly dominate a small kitchen. No single compromise design would allow maximum penetration in both markets.

In the same way a visual advertising appeal that may seem attractive to potential buyers in some countries, may seem dull or incomprehensible in others. Guinness, when advertising in Germany, used the same advertising copy as in Ireland and Britain. The commercial consisted of a small humorous story involving Guinness. It was not successful because Germans do not read the small print in advertising, considering it as a waste of time.

Analysis of culture influence

Our own culture always interferes with our understanding of another culture because we must understand the other culture in terms of how it is similar to or different from our own. This is called the self-reference criterion (Lee, 1966). The firm must also acknowledge that cultural differences tend to stand out more than similarities, yet it is the similarities that may be more important. Similarities may be analysed across factors referred to as cultural universals (Table 6.5). While these phenomena are found in most cultures and are considered as universals, a similar mode of behaviour existing in all countries should not be presumed. For example, humour is not something that travels well even though joking is a universal phenomenon. Companies pursuing a global strategy for their products attempt to discover cultural universals since 'universal aspects of the cultural environment represent opportunities for global marketers to standardize some or all of the marketing programme' (Keegan and Green, 1997, p. 84). Analyses of business structure and behaviour should include, therefore, consideration of institutions, ideas and beliefs but they should be treated with caution since it is too easy to attempt to draw causal links between culture and modern business practice (Wilkinson, 1996, p. 442). A cultural study for international marketing decisions may be carried out on macro and micro levels (Figure 6.4). This section draws heavily on Cundiff and Tharp Higler (1984) and Terpstra (1978). The purpose of the macro study is to identify the general sociological climate towards business in a country, its attitudes towards foreigners and new products. The micro study is concerned with interpreting culture's impact upon a specific group of people in a country (Cundiff and Tharp Higler, 1984). Both levels of cross-cultural analysis are concerned with a search for cultural 'universals'. To the extent that aspects of the cultural environment are universal as opposed to unique, it is possible for the international firm to standardize some aspects of marketing the programme such as product design and communications, which are two of the major elements (Keegan, 1989).

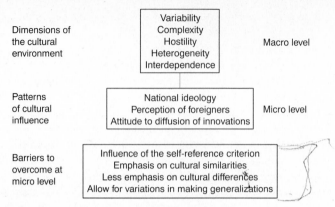

Fig. 6.4 Macro and micro analysis of cultural influence.

Table 6.5 Analysing similarities and differences using cultural universals

Phenomena found in most cultures and considered as universals:

athletic sports	games	modesty
cleanliness	gestures	mourning
courtship	gift giving	music/dancing
decorative arts	greeting	personal names
education	hair styles	property rights
ethics	hospitality	religious rituals
etiquette	joking	status
folklore	marriage	trade
food taboos	medicine	visiting

Source: Murdock, G. P. (1945) 'The common denominator of cultures', in R. Linton (ed.), *The Science of Man in the World Crises*, New York, NY: Columbia University Press, pp. 123–42.

Macro analysis of the cultural environment

The elements of a macro analysis of the cultural environment include an examination of variability, complexity, cultural hostility, heterogeneity and interdependence (Terpstra, 1978). By proceeding in this way the key influences within cultures and among cultures are identified (Figure 6.5). Within cultures variability refers to the degree to which conditions within a culture are changing at a low or high rate or are constant. As cultural environments become more turbulent, i.e. more variable, the unpredictability of operations increases. Facing unpredictability, the organization needs to become more receptive to change. Internal structures and processes need to be altered in order to cope with change. Open channels of communication, decentralized decision making and predominance of local expertise should help improve the firm's capacity for perceiving and adjusting to rapid change.

Cultural complexity refers to the degree to which understanding of conditions within a culture is dependent on the possession of background data which place it in its proper context. Cultures, according to Hall (1960), differ widely in the extent to which

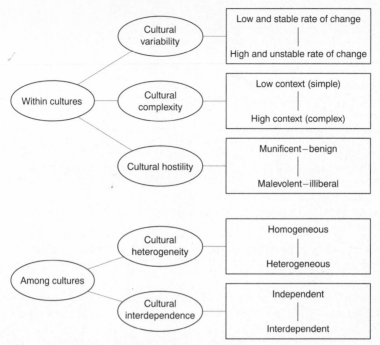

Figure 6.5 Key influences within and among cultures
Source: adapted from Terpstra, V. (1978) *The Cultural Environment of International Business,* Southwestern.

unspoken, unformulated, and unexplicit rules govern how information is handled and how people interact and relate to each other. In 'high-context' cultures much of human behaviour is covert or implicit, whereas in 'low-context' cultures much is overt or explicit. For a foreigner, ease of understanding and communication in a culture is inversely related to the importance that culture places on 'silent language' and 'hidden dimensions'. The amount of contexting required therefore extends from low in some cultures to high in others (Table 6.6). Hall places the former West Germany, Switzerland, Scandinavia and the United States at the lower end of the continuum, France in the middle and China and Japan at the high end of the scale.

Cultural hostility refers to the degree to which conditions in a culture are threatening to company goals. The extent of hostility depends on the perceived acceptability and legitimacy of the firm. Hostility means that the firm is less able to acquire raw materials, capital, personnel, information, goodwill, political favours and other resources. Hostility may also reduce the firm's ability to sell its products and services.

Among cultures heterogeneity refers to the degree to which separate cultures are similar or dissimilar. The cultures in which a firm operates can range from relatively homogeneous to extremely heterogeneous. Increasing heterogeneity means that there is greater variety which the firm must take into consideration in decision making.

Cultural interdependence refers to the degree to which conditions in one culture are sensitive to developments in other cultures. Interdependence of cultures operates by way

Table 6.6 Characteristics and context of culture

Low-context cultures

1 much information contained in coded, explicit, transmitted messages
1 fragile bonds and low involvement between people
1 fewer distinctions made between insiders and outsiders
1 change easy and rapid
1 examples: Germany, Switzerland, Scandinavia, United States

High-context cultures

1 much information implicit in the physical context or internalized within people
1 strong bonds and high involvement between people
1 greater distinctions between insiders and outsiders
1 cultural patterns long lived and slow to change
1 examples: China, France, Japan

Source: Hall, E. T. (1960) 'The silent language of overseas business', *Harvard Business Review*, (May–June), 88–96.

of contact. Advances in communication and transportation, growth or cross-border economic exchange, expansion of regional and international institutions and the emergence of transcultural interest groups all serve to increase the volume of transactions between different cultures. Given increasing cultural interdependence, the actions of the firm in one culture are likely to be exposed to the scrutiny of governments and interested groups in others. For example, in cases as diverse as bribery, sale of powdered infant milk in developing countries and ecological destruction, international firms have been faced with transcultural interest groups and demands. Each of the above factors is best interpreted as part of a continuum from low to high. Within and among cultures it is possible to find high and low expressions of each of the dimensions of culture discussed above.

Micro analysis of the cultural environment

We now turn to an examination of the patterns of cultural influence at the micro level in the market. National ideology represents the way the citizens of a particular country think about and react to various stimuli (Table 6.7). Frequently we wish to predict how the typical French, Italian or Portuguese person will act in certain situations. Even though all three of these countries are predominantly of the same religion, the Portuguese is likely to react more strongly to infringements of its rules than the French or Italians. The French have a much stronger sense of national pride and unity than the Italians or the Portuguese. As a consequence they tend to be less willing to substitute a foreign-made product for a French product, at least in areas that reflect national expertise. Sometimes such stereotyping is valuable; sometimes it is a great hindrance to understanding the micro cultural environment.

Economic philosophy is an important element in national ideology. Sweden had a strong national commitment to socialism and for several decades permitted extensive government involvement in business and economic affairs. This contrasts with the United

Table 6.7 National ideology and attitude towards foreigners

National ideology:

1   attitudes
1   economic philosophy
1   length of cultural identity

Attitude towards foreigners:

1   foreign products may be perceived as different and/or inferior, interesting and/or of high quality

States and other countries operating under a capitalistic ideology, where massive government involvement in economic affairs has been strongly resisted.

National ideology is strongest and most consistent in countries that have a long cultural identity. For example, there is a strong, easily identifiable national ideology in a country such as Egypt which, even though it has not consistently had political independence in recent centuries, possesses a long and consistent cultural history. However, some of the newer black nations in Africa have not had separate identities long enough to have developed strong national ideologies. Instead, different subgroups within these nations reflect the ideologies of the subgroups or tribes from which they descend. However, even in countries with strong national ideologies, these ideologies represent a general cross-section or average. Not all individuals fit the pattern. Nevertheless, it is important for the international firm to know the general national ideology so that it can fit the product and its marketing strategy into the local environment.

Allied to the preceding point is the observation that people may view that which is foreign as different and potentially threatening to existing patterns of action and behaviour. In some countries this reaction toward foreign peoples and ways is reflected in a fear of contamination or change from outside. An extreme example of this fear was the policy of the Chinese government in early years when foreigners and foreign products were not welcome. Yet even when foreigners and foreign products are not perceived as a threat to the local economy, they may still be perceived as different and/or inferior. It is for this reason that international firms often play down their foreignness and try to blend in with the local scene.

Not all attitudes towards foreigners and foreign products are negative, however. Highly sophisticated and talented individuals may be perceived as interesting rather than just 'different' by nationals of other countries. Foreign products of high quality are often viewed in the same light. Belgian lace, French wine, Japanese cameras and German microscopes are all viewed as distinctive and of extra high quality in world markets. In these instances, the foreign identification actually provides an advantage in the market place. Success in a foreign market, then, may depend on the firm's ability to blend in with the local scene and to develop a domestic identity, or it may depend on the firm's ability to convince local buyers that foreign means better.

Attitudes toward innovation diffusion influence the success or otherwise of the international firm (Table 6.8). Frequently when a foreign firm enters a market, it is introducing

Table 6.8 Influences on diffusion of innovations

Rate of adoption is influenced by:

ɩ resistance to change
ɩ perceived superiority of product
ɩ extent to which the product be 'tried' or 'explained'
ɩ cost of product
ɩ product compatibility with cultural values and tradition

a product or service that represents an 'innovation' in that market. If a product is sufficiently different from others in a market, local consumers may see it as something entirely new. Hence, the firm must try to anticipate how consumers in that market will react to change. If local people show a strong resistance to change, some other less resistant market may prove to be more promising. Even where the introduction of a new product seems promising, it is important to understand the process through which changes are introduced and accepted. Many well-known international brand companies such as McDonald's fail to appreciate the significance of this lesson (Exhibit 6.3)

Exhibit 6.3
Spice with everything

McDonald's, which now has seven restaurants in India, was launched there a year ago. It has had to deal with a market that is 40% vegetarian; with the aversion to either beef or pork among meat-eaters; with a hostility to frozen meat and fish; with the general Indian fondness for spice with everything. To satisfy such tastes, McDonald's has discovered that it needs to do more than provide the right burgers. Customers buying vegetarian burgers want to be sure that these are cooked in a separate area in the kitchen using separate utensils. Sauces like McMasala and McImli are on offer to satisfy the Indian taste for spice. McDonald's promises to introduce a spiced version of its fries soon.

McDonald's Indian experience has not yet been greeted with rejoicing. Yet, at least the firm has avoided the disasters of some other big American names. A few years back, violent protests in Bangalore in southern India over the quality of its food temporarily closed KFC, which sells fried chicken. Three years ago, Kellogg made a splash pitching breakfast cereals as a healthier alternative to the heavy Indian breakfast. Indians were unimpressed. Kellogg, facing mounting losses, is now selling to a westernised niche market instead.

Foreign companies have got three things wrong in India. They overestimated the size and disposable income of the much-touted Indian middle class. They underestimated the strength of local products in the markets they were entering. And they over-estimated the value of their reputation. Indian consumers seem unimpressed by the glamour of the western brands; food companies are scaling down their plans accordingly.

Source: adapted from *Economist*, 22 November 1997, p. 87.

A consumer's perception of an innovation may have a strong impact on how quickly it is adopted. An innovation that consumers see as being clearly superior to other ways of meeting their needs will be adopted faster than those products or services which do not have such relative advantages. If it is easy for consumers to understand the functions of an innovation and it can be 'tried' or 'explained', this product or service will also be adopted quickly. It follows that products or services that are less costly and more compatible with cultural values and traditional ways of doing things will be adopted faster than others. International firms need to be aware that they must communicate these qualities to markets when the product or service is seen as new.

Sociocultural distance as a barrier to internationalization

Normally, distance is thought of as the spatial difference between two or more points. Distance in this sense, which takes account only of physical or geographic characteristics, is a unidimensional concept and limiting when attempting to understand the internationalization process of business. In the present context, distance is also taken to include economic and sociocultural distance. It is possible to measure the separation of countries in terms of all three distance concepts to derive a separation of markets based on what is referred to in the literature as business distance (Luostarinen, 1980, pp. 124–52). Consequently, it is important to examine the effects of economic and sociocultural distance on the internationalization process in addition to purely physical considerations.

The importance of distance may be gauged by observing that companies tend to be more knowledgeable and to have more information about foreign markets which are culturally near to them than for more distant markets. The implication of this statement is that companies tend to favour markets which are culturally close and which are known to them. Companies new to exporting or contemplating the internationalization process tend to avoid those markets which are unfamiliar. So far the discussion has only considered the flow of information or knowledge. The same argument holds for the movement of products and people. For all three flows, therefore, cultural distance is an impediment and restricting force which predisposes the company to closer markets (Goodnow and Hansz, 1972).

An analysis based on sociocultural distance normally suggests that experience in international marketing, tourism, education and television and increases in the number of foreign-owned companies constitute the principal explanatory factors in encouraging an openness of attitudes towards international business. In a direct business context, of course, international marketing and tourism are probably the most directly effective. In terms of analysis of the sociocultural environment it may be concluded that, while it is difficult without proper historical data to observe any improvement in openness of attitudes to other nations, it is possible that experience in dealing with foreign nationals has a major impact on bringing about such an improvement. In a business context, this means international marketing, including service marketing activities such as tourism.

Cultural influences on the international firm – norms and behaviour patterns

Norms are standards shared by a society to which members are expected to conform. They are rules that specify appropriate and inappropriate behaviour. For the international firm it is important to note that some norms are more important than others. Some norms in a society are considered by its members as not being extremely important and, therefore, may be violated without severe punishment. These are referred to as 'folkways' and may be the target for innovative marketing on the part of the international firm. For example, Sunday opening of shopping centres in a traditionalist society may contravene folkways but be welcomed by a growing number of families where both partners share work and family responsibilities and find that Sunday is the only time they can shop.

Other norms of society, referred to as mores, are those which are seen as extremely important to the welfare of society and whose violation reaps severe punishment. A marketing practice which contravenes the mores of a society would be met by product failure, withdrawal from the market and even forced closure. An understanding of the distinction for each international market between its folkways and mores is an important managerial responsibility for the international firm.

A behaviour pattern is a uniformity of acting and thinking that regularly recurs among a plurality of people. The behaviour pattern, besides being a form of conduct, is also a norm of conduct. The international firm must make a distinction here; this time between ideal norms, those to which people give their verbal allegiance, and real norms, those with which people comply. Many people consider themselves to belong to a particular religion but do not follow its practices or dictates.

The manager of the international firm must realize that ideal norms are what the individual says or believes he would like to do which may coincide with the real norms, but which may at times have only an indirect and remote relationship to actual behaviour. Even when ideal norms do not coincide with real norms, they provide guides to behaviour in the sense of being remote goals which are to be reached indirectly.

Cultural ideology and the international firm

By a rather general consensus a society arrives at a body of meanings and beliefs that every 'right thinking' member is supposed to hold. This body of meanings constitutes the principles of thought in society. Social scientists refer to these principles of thought as the ideology of a society, which derives from ideas which are classified as cognitive, expressive and evaluative (Chinoy, 1967). For Chinoy, cognitive thought

> includes the beliefs men hold about themselves and the social, biological and physical world in which they live, and about their relations to one another, to society and nature and to such other beings and forces as they may discover, accept or conjure up. It embraces the whole vast body of ideas by which men account for their observation and experience.

Cognitive ideas include knowledge, skills and practical know-how. Knowledge comprises all we know about humans and reality from the social and natural sciences including theories and hypotheses yet to be proved. Language is probably the most important of all human skills since it is by means of language that humans are able to exchange ideas which makes organized social life possible.

In this context language and perception are intimately intertwined. Culture influences what we perceive: we never really see the physical world around us. The world we perceive is a product of the interaction between the physical aspects of the universe and what we have learned from previous experience.

These factors (language, ideology and intellectual styles in particular) affect the way people think and behave and also determine the disposition of managers in the international firm. Unfortunately, how we see ourselves and how others see us may be very different due to different cultural backgrounds. Frequently, too, we do not have full information about others, especially if they come from a distant country. In such circumstances we rely on what others tell us or on limited information which may produce a stereotype rather than a true interpretation of the situation. However, it is very dangerous to use stereotypes in international marketing even though they are often used as inoffensive short-hand ways of summarizing the basic national characteristics of a country (Exhibit 6.4). A deeper cultural analysis is required if the differences in underlying cultural values are to be discerned.

Material culture and the international firm

By material culture is meant those material things which humans create and use, e.g. buildings, works of art, tools, machinery and transportation equipment. These things constitute a human-created environment interposed between people and the material environment and greatly influence human behaviour. By considering the importance to

---

═══ Exhibit 6.4 ═══
Stereotyping national characteristics

It can be useful to bear national characteristics in mind. (After all, they have a basic impression of us 'Rosbifs', as the French call us). The Germans are characterised by a Teutonic thoroughness and attention to detail: business is taken very seriously. To the French, Paris is the hub of the universe – even provincial Frenchmen grudgingly acknowledge this. They also tend to use the word 'impossible' when something is inconvenient. Italians have great flair and innovativeness, but need watching on schedules. Scandinavians are known for their politeness, thoroughness and tendency to take things seriously. They have a greater degree of egalitarianism than most other European countries (and are also more highly taxed). The Iberians are catching up fast technologically, but relationships tend to be rather formal. As for the Benelux countries, the Dutch are a bit like us, with a similar sense of humour, while the Belgians (who are the butt of the French) are again known for their thoroughness and have a phlegmatic approach.

Source: adapted from *Packaging Week (UK),* 12 June 1992, p. 37.

international business of the improvements in transportation and logistics which have occurred in the past 10–30 years we obtain a good measure of the effect of material culture on the international firm.

Summary

The elements which go to make up culture in the international marketing environment include the following:

ı language, the 'cultural mirror';
ı religion, which deals with intimate convictions;
ı varying attitudes towards time, wealth acquisition and risk taking;
ı technology and material culture development in general;
ı aesthetic values.

Through the analysis of cultural influences, an attempt has been made to determine international modes of behaviour. At the macro level the elements of the cultural environment involve the following:

ı cultural variability, which is a function of the rapidity of change and stability in a given environment;
ı cultural complexity, in the broad sense the sum of implicit rules;
ı cultural hostility, the attitude of specific markets towards the firm;
ı cultural heterogeneity, the multiplication of subcultures;
ı cultural interdependence, the related sensitivity of a specific culture to the development of others.

At the micro level, the main patterns of specific cultural attitudes include the following:

ı national pride;
ı economic philosophy;
ı national identity and fear of foreign influences;
ı attitudes towards innovation.

Sociocultural distance as a barrier to internationalization involves the notion of business distance which is multidimensional in nature. It takes into account not only the geographical distance and physical characteristics but also economic and sociocultural differences. The greater the business distance and subsequent lesser information flow from the market, the fewer the movements of products and people. This business distance has to a certain extent been diminished in recent years as a result of increased use of the media as a means of communication and increased travel.

Cultural analysis can, however, only be made in reference to one's own situation and thus tends to be subjective in nature. Despite these restrictions it is essential for a firm to understand fully the sociocultural environment in which it operates in order for it to succeed.

Discussion questions

1. What is culture? Why is an understanding of culture important in international marketing?
2. Outline and discuss the principal elements of culture as they affect the behaviour of the international firm.
3. The scope of culture is very broad and covers many aspects of behaviour within a country or culture. Describe the implications of this observation for the firm in international markets.
4. It is not possible to understand how markets evolve and how buyers react to marketing programmes developed by the firm without accepting that markets are based on individual and group behaviour determined by cultural conditioning. Discuss.
5. What role has the firm in international markets as an agent of cultural change? Is the role different in different countries?

References

Banks, A. S. and Textar, R. B. (1963) *A Cross-Polity Survey*, Boston, MA: MIT Press.

Bennett, P. and Kassarjan, H. (1972) *Consumer Behaviour*, Englewood Cliffs, NJ: Prentice Hall.

Cateora, P. R. (1993) *International Marketing*, 8th edn, Homewood, IL: Irwin.

Chinoy, E. (1967) *Society – An Introduction to Sociology*, 2nd edn, New York, NY: Random House.

Cundiff, E. A. and Sharp Higler, M. E. (1984) *Marketing in the International Environment*, Englewood Cliffs, NJ: Prentice Hall.

Czinkota, M. R. and Ronkainen, I. (1995) *International Marketing*, 4th edn, Fort Worth, TX: Dryden Press.

Downs, J. F. (1971) *Cultures in Crisis*, Beverly Hills, CA: Glencoe Press.

Engel, J., Warshaw, M. and Kinnear, T. (1983) *Promotional Strategy*, 5th edn, Homewood, IL: Irwin.

Engel, J. F., Blackwell, R. D. and Miniard, P. W. (1993) *Consumer Behaviour*, 7th edn, New York, NY: Dryden Press.

Etzioni, A. (1988) *The Moral Dimension: Towards a New Economics*, New York, NY: The Free Press.

Francis, J. N. P. (1991): 'When in Rome? The effects of cultural adaptation on intercultural business negotiations', *Journal of International Business Studies*, **22** (Third Quarter), 402–28.

Funakawa, A. (1997), *Transcultural Management*, San Francisco, CA: Jossey-Bass.

Goodnow, J. D. and Hansz, J. E. (1972) 'Environmental determinants of overseas market entry strategies', *Journal of Business Studies*, **3**, 33–50.

Griffin, R. W. and Pustay, M. W. (1996) *International Business*, Reading, MA: Addison-Wesley.

Hall, E. T. (1960) 'The silent language of overseas business', *Harvard Business Review*, **38** (May–June), 88–96.

Hoebel, A. (1960) *Man, Culture and Society*, New York, NY: Oxford University Press.

Hoecklin, L. (1995), *Managing Cultural Differences*, Wokingham: Addison-Wesley.

Hofstede, G. (1991), *Culture and Organizations: Software of the Mind*, Maidenhead: McGraw Hill.

Hornby, W. F. (1980) *An Introduction to Population Geography*, Cambridge: Cambridge University Press.

Keegan, W. (1989) *Global Marketing Management*, 4th edn, New York, NY: Prentice Hall.

Keegan, W. J. and Green, M. C. (1997) *Principles of Global Marketing*, Upper Saddle River, NJ: Prentice Hall.

Kroebar, A. L. (1951) 'The nature of culture', in A. L. Kroebar, *The Ancient Oikoumené,as a Historic Cultural Aggregate (a compendium of essays by A. L. Kroebar 1909–1951)*, Chicago, IL: University of Chicago Press.

La Bahn, D. W. and Harich, K. R. (1997) 'Sensitivity to national business culture: effects on US–Mexican Channel Relationship performance', *Journal of International Marketing*, **5** (4), 29–51.

Langhoff, T. (1997) 'The influence of cultural differences on internationalization processes of firms' in I. Björkman and M. Forsgren (eds), *The Nature of the International Firm*, pp. 135–64, Copenhagen: Handelshøjskolens Forlag.

Lee, J. A. (1966) 'Cultural analysis in overseas operations', *Harvard Business Review*, **44** (March–April), 106–14.

Luostarinen, R. (1980) *Internationalization of the Firm, Acta Academiae Series A*, Vol. 30, p. 260, Helsinki: The Helsinki School of Economics.

Marschan, R., Welch, D. and Welch, L. (1997) 'Language: the forgotten factor in multinational management', *European Management Journal*, **15** (5), 591–8.

Murdock, G. P. (1945) 'The common denominator of cultures', in R. Linton (ed.) *The Science of Man in the World Crises*, pp. 123–42, New York, NY: Columbia University Press.

Ricks, D. A. (1983) *Big Business Blunders*, Homewood, IL: Dow Jones–Irwin.

Robock, S., Simmonds, K. and Zwick, J. (1989) *International Business & Multinational Enterprise*, 4th edn, Homewood, IL; Irwin.

Rokeach, M. (1968) *Beliefs, Attitudes and Values*, San Francisco, CA: Jossey-Bass.

Schwartz, S. H. (1990), 'Individualism–collectivism; critique and proposed refinements', *Journal of Cross Cultural Psychology*, **21**, 139–57.

Schwartz, S. H. (1994), 'Beyond individualism/collectivism new cultural dimension of values', in U. Kim, H. C. Triandis, C. Kagitcibasi, S. Choi and J. Yoon (eds), *Individualism and Collectivism – Theory, Methods and Applications*, Cross Cultural Research and Methodology series, **18**, pp. 85–119, Sage Publications.

Schwartz, S. H. and Bilsky, W. (1987), 'Towards a psychological structure of human values', *Journal of Personality and Social Psychology*, **53**, 550–62.

Terpstra, V. (1978) *The Cultural Environment of International Business*, South-Western Publishing Company.

Ueltschy, L. C. and Ryans, J. K. Jr. (1997) 'Employing standardised promotion strategies in Mexico: the impact of language and cultural differences', *International Executive*, **39** (4), 479–95.

Wilkinson, B. (1996) 'Culture, institutions and business in East Asia', *Organization Studies*, **17** (3), 421–47.

7

Public policy environment

In this chapter we discuss the political environment facing the international firm. Political policies are manifested through public policy laws and regulations which affect the flows of products, services, people, technology, investment and money. The management issues which arise are examined from the points of view of the firm in the source country involved in the transfer and the recipient firm in the host country. Circumstances arise occasionally in which firms in international marketing find themselves in dispute over some aspect of marketing. In such situations arbitration is frequently used but the law is referred to quite frequently. For this reason the legal framework in which disputes may be settled is also examined.

Political environment of international marketing

A crucial aspect of doing business in a foreign country is that permission to conduct business is controlled by the government of the host country. The host government controls and restricts a foreign company's activities by encouraging and offering support or by discouraging and banning its activities, depending upon the interests of the host. Reflected in its policies and attitudes towards foreign business are a government's ideas of how best to promote the national interest considering its own resources and political philosophy. An analysis of the political environment should include a number of factors: the type of government in the host country; its philosophy; its stability over time; its disposition to international business.

The type of government (democracy; dictatorship; monarchy; socialist or communist) gives an insight into the business–political environment. The type of government is determined by the procedure through which the citizens form and express their will and the extent to which their will controls the composition and policy of government. Under parliamentary government the people are consulted from time to time to ascertain the majority will and, therefore, policies of the government theoretically reflect the majority opinion of the population. Under absolutist governments (monarchies and dictatorships), the ruling regime determines government policy without specifically consulting the needs and wants of the people. Although the absolutist form of government is uncommon, it may be found in some countries in the Middle and Far East and in some developing countries.

The philosophy of the government towards business in general and foreign business in particular should also be taken into account. Conservative governments usually promote a broad role for private business with a minimum of restrictions. Socialist governments, on the other hand, may encourage public ownership of business with an emphasis on restrictions and a more comprehensive regulatory environment.

Because of different political viewpoints, international firms are often treated in a very different way to local businesses. In some countries the prevailing philosophy is that imports are to be discouraged but foreign investment in manufacturing encouraged, e.g. Greece. In other countries, only joint ventures find government support. The international firm must discover the perceived role for foreign business activity in a country.

Risk and uncertainty in international markets

Risk refers to general environmental risk, industry risk and firm-specific risks (Miller, 1992). The first refers to those variables that are constant across all industries within a given country, e.g. political risk, government policy uncertainty, economic, social or physical environmental uncertainty. Industry uncertainty refers to risks associated with differences in industry-specific variables, e.g. materials or labour supply, quality and availability. These uncertainties would also include product-market uncertainties, such as changes in consumer tastes and the availability of substitutes and complements. Competitive uncertainty would also be part of industry risk and refers to the firm's ability to predict accurately the amount and type of goods available in the market, which varies owing to competitive rivalries among firms, entrance of new firms and technological change. Firm-specific risk arises from such things as product liability issues, credit uncertainties, behavioural uncertainty among employees and customers, and R&D uncertainty. International markets exacerbate these uncertainties because the firm must perform these functions in different cultures and because international operations are, by their nature, difficult to control and manage (Brouthers, 1995, p. 10).

Firms in international markets face all three types of risk, environmental, industry and firm-specific risks, simultaneously, so decisions in one risk area affect the magnitude of risks and decisions in other risk areas. Management must be cognisant of the overall risk management package, as studies that look at only one international risk variable, e.g. political risk or financial risk, may lead to incorrect entry mode decisions because other related risks, such as social or product-market uncertainties, have been ignored (Brouthers, 1995, p. 10). Assessing and quantifying political risk in international markets, it must be emphasized, is especially difficult.

Common political risks

The risks an international firm faces from the political environment can be significant (Figure 7.1). A range of political risks exist depending on the countries in question, the

Figure 7.1 Analysing political stability in host country: risks, harassment and nationalism

firm and the nature of its business. At one extreme it may lose all control, ownership of assets and market access; at the other extreme, it may simply face customs delays or problems in obtaining working visas for headquarters staff.

A firm can lose ownership of foreign assets in one of four ways: confiscation; expropriation; nationalism; domestication. Confiscation requires nothing more than a government decision to take control of a foreign firm's assets in its country: no payment is made to compensate the firm for its loss. Expropriation differs only in that compensation is given for the firm's assets; very few feel satisfied with the compensation given when their assets are expropriated. In most cases the payment is not negotiable but, even when a government is willing to discuss compensation, there is likely to be disagreement on the basis for valuing the firm's assets. Confiscation and expropriation usually arise because of the development role of international firms in a country. Both forms of risk are higher in resource-based industries such as oil exploration and refining and in the extractive industries.

Nationalization is the process whereby a government decides to take over ownership of an industry for its own control. Both local and foreign-owned firms may be affected. Government ownership and management of an industry may give it more control over the country's economic life and are usually tied to issues of economic sovereignty, national defence or control of strategic industries.

Domestication represents a variety of pressures that can be placed on a foreign-owned firm to transfer ownership and/or control to local citizens. At one extreme, a foreign investor may be forced to sell shares of stock to local investors at a predetermined price. Alternatively, the firm may be asked to develop a plant for sale to locals over a certain time period, but the business is allowed to determine how the transfer of ownership will occur. Other examples of domestication policies include pressure to employ nationals at top decision-making levels, permits required for importing equipment, parts, personnel or technology.

Political harassment can take many forms and can affect all areas of business operations, from labour relations to customer relations, product design or pricing. The foreign firm may be singled out for harassment, or an entire industry may be the target of new, restrictive regulations.

A government's power to license may be used to harass. A licence may be required to establish a business, acquire foreign exchange, purchase imports, change prices, hire or fire personnel or sell to government agencies. Changes in tax policy can also be used to capture more revenue and penalize businesses.

Another form of harassment for the foreign firm is social unrest. Political terrorists in Europe, Latin America and the Middle East have increasingly used kidnappings of business executives to publicize their demands and to fund their causes. Damage to property from riots and insurrections can also be significant.

Nationalism can have similar effects to those discussed above. Citizens of every nation typically have some sense of national identity, which manifests itself in national feelings, pride and attitudes towards foreign firms and products: patriotism. The excessive form of this is chauvinism. Today, nationalism is considered a divisive force, hindering regional and international cooperation.

Firms attempt to reduce political risks by identifying points of political vulnerability, establishing positive political–business interaction and promoting among government officials the need to regulate international transfers of various resources and assets. Governments attempt to regulate the political environment within a legal framework which forms the basis of control (Table 7.1).

Table 7.1 The political environment of international business

Political environment

- Analysis of political environment
- Identifying political vulnerability
- Establishing a positive political–business interaction

Regulation and control of international transfers

- Rationale for regulation
- Transfer of products and services
- Transfer of money
- Transfer of persons
- Transfer of technology

International legal framework

- Existing international law
- Major world legal systems
- Minimizing international legal problems
- European Union law

Role of government

In recent years, there has been a revitalized discussion on the appropriate role for government in business and in international business in particular. Too much government is not considered a good thing, yet too little government perhaps even less so:

> good government is not a luxury but a vital necessity. Without an effective state, sustainable development, both economic and social, is impossible . . . [and] . . . effective states clearly do have some common features. One is the way government has set rules underpinning private transactions, and civil society more broadly. Another is the way government has played by the rules itself, acting reliably and predictably and controlling corruption (World Development Report, 1997, foreword)

According to this report, there are five crucial functions for governments:

1. to establish a legal foundation in society;
2. to maintain an effective non-distortionary and stable macro-economic policy environment;
3. to invest in basic social services and infrastructure;
4. to protect vulnerable members of society;
5. to protect the environment.

Governments cannot provide growth, but they can provide an institutional framework to support the markets that are concerned with growth. For speedy growth and development governments cannot afford to be capricious. The application of predictable rules and policies reflects how credible the state is as a source of exports or as an attraction for investors. Poor state credibility results in lower investment and growth and undermines development. In preparing the World Development Report (1997) 3,600 entrepreneurs in 69 countries were surveyed who reported that many countries perform their core function poorly: they fail to ensure law and order, they fail to protect property and they fail to apply rules and policies predictably. These countries are not considered politically credible and tend to be eschewed by investors and businesses. Companies were asked to rank each of several indicators which, when averaged, provided a composite indicator of the reliability of the institutional framework. The results of this survey, normalized to the high-income OECD countries, yield a political credibility index for the countries involved (Figure 7.2).

The report shows a direct correlation between the level of political credibility and growth of GDP per capita and gross investment as a proportion of GDP. When markets are underdeveloped, the government can sometimes reduce coordination problems and information gaps to encourage growth. Many industrial economies in their early stages of development use various mechanisms to promote market growth. Interventions range from the highly elaborate strategic use of subsidies to the less intrusive export promotion and special infrastructure incentives. The ability to choose wisely among these interventions and to use them effectively is critical. Countries that have pursued an active industrial policy successfully could not have done so without strong institutional capability (World Development Report, 1997, p. 6).

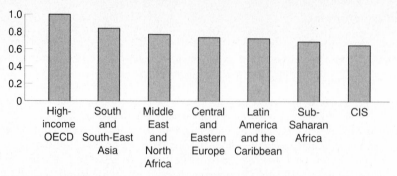

Figure 7.2 Political credibility index (credibility index high-income OECD = 1)
Source: World Development Report 1997, New York, NY: Oxford University Press, p. 5.

Although it is by no means a recent phenomenon, there are now many multinational companies which command more wealth and economic power than some states. Indeed, of the world's 100 largest companies, 50 are megacorporations; the 350 largest companies account for 40 per cent of global trade (*Human Development Report 1997*, p. 92). The turnover of many of these companies exceeds the GDP of many countries. The size of some states and the corporate power wielded by well-known international companies may be judged by comparing turnover and GDP (Table 7.2), although it might be argued that a comparison of net worth and GDP might be more relevant.

With increased international competition between companies and industries, there are likely to be winners and losers, especially in the short and medium term. Many sectors of society thrive and grow in a world of dynamic growth, but others suffer. The challenge for governments is to take advantage of international business growth, while ensuring that vulnerable groups are not marginalized. Three sources of tension exist between economic growth and social stability (Rodrick, 1997):

1. lower trade barriers mean greater freedom to move capital and skills;
2. diffusion of technology and skills places people in different countries as competitive adversaries;
3. social insurance and other protection schemes come under threat owing to funding difficulties.

With regard to the first point, people at the upper end of the skills spectrum are more mobile. People at the lower end, in contrast, are less mobile, so their jobs can be outsourced to international workers, who are cheaper, more mobile or more flexible. With regard to the second point, technology transfer may have an adverse effect on the relationships between countries which have very different sets of values and norms. Competition can lead to a weakening of these values in individual countries. Pension benefits in Europe, for example, are affected by the requirements of the Maastricht Treaty. With regard to the last point, because capital is mobile, it is difficult to tax, so taxes fall disproportionately on income which adversely affects the less mobile and the poorer in society.

Table 7.2 State and corporate power, 1994

Country or corporation	Total GDP or corporate sales
	US$billions
Indonesia	174.6
General Motors	168.8
Turkey	149.8
Denmark	146.1
Ford	137.1
South Africa	123.3
Toyota	111.1
Exxon	110.0
Royal Dutch–Shell	109.8
Norway	109.6
Poland	92.8
Portugal	91.6
IBM	72.0
Malaysia	68.5
Venezuela	59.0
Pakistan	57.1
Unilever	49.7
Nestlé	47.8
Sony	47.6
Egypt	43.9
Nigeria	30.4
Top five corporations	871.4
Least developed countries	76.5
South Asia	451.3
Sub-Saharan Africa	246.8

Source: adapted from *Human Development Report 1997*, New York, NY: Oxford University Press, p. 92.

Importance of political stability

Stable governments are more likely to ensure continuity in government policy as it affects business. Stable systems allow firms to plan their affairs with some degree of certainty. Political instability arises from political risks of doing business in a foreign market, political harassment and excessive nationalism. Change is the main source of political risk, and radical change causes the most difficulty for business adjustment. Because change in a government or its political philosophy can lead to unknown consequences for business, it is more disruptive than other business constraints. The situation in developing countries may be somewhat less predictable owing to extra constraints. Nevertheless, a cabinet reshuffle or a change in policy can seriously affect the business environment facing the international firm. The international firm should become aware of the processes whereby policy changes are instituted.

Political risk in international business exists when discontinuities occur in the business environment, when they are difficult to anticipate and when they result from political change (Robock, 1971, p. 7). To constitute a risk, these changes in the business environment must be capable of adversely affecting the profits or other goals of a particular firm. There are several sources that the international firm can use to measure political instability; the most common simple mechanism is to use one or more of the stability indices developed by political scientists. A good example of a political instability index is that developed by Political Risk Services (PRS), formerly Frost and Sullivan, which provides assessments of political risk based on a grading system reflecting:

1. restrictions on repatriation of profits or capital or exchange controls,
2. payment delays facing exporters,
3. policy related to fiscal and monetary expansion and
4. foreign borrowing by the government.

Countries are rated on a numerical score for each risk category and then rated on a four letter scale from A for the least risky to D for the most risky. PRS provides the following description for each category:

A **countries**: no exchange controls, no repatriation restrictions or other barriers to financial transfer and little likelihood that controls will increase in the forecast period.

B **countries**: modest or occasional delays in financial transfers; a reasonable chance that delays will be high in the forecast period.

C **countries**: modest to long delays and even stops on financial transfer; a reasonable chance that the barriers will increase and little chance that they will decrease in the forecast period.

D **countries**: heavy exchange controls and long delays on the transfer of currency; little chance that conditions will improve within the forecast period.

Analysis of political environment

Some products appear to be more politically vulnerable than others. Favourable political attention can mean protection, reduced tax rates, exemption from quotas, control of competition and other concessions. Political vulnerability, however, can also lead to labour agitation, public regulations, price fixing, quotas and other forms of government harassment if, for any reason, the product is considered to be undesirable.

A change in attitudes towards politically vulnerable products does not always come from obvious instability in the political system. Even an orderly change of government, or a change in existing government attitudes, can lead to a drastic change in public policy towards certain products.

The safest long-term strategy for minimizing political risk is to acknowledge the importance of positive interaction with host governments. Some firms implement this by reminding personnel that they are 'guests' in foreign markets and that continued permission to operate is contingent on showing the benefits brought to host countries. Benefits arise in four ways: resource or product transfer; balance of payments effects; employment or income contributions; social or cultural benefits.

International firms use a variety of techniques to ensure a supportive political environment. For example, in many developing countries large importers from developed countries have designed programmes to assist local industry. In spite of efforts at being a 'good citizen', different modes of entry or investment which render the venture less risky may be the only long-run solution to hostile political environments, e.g. joint ventures and licensing where the technology used is unique and the risk is high.

Another approach towards establishing a positive political–business interaction may be the political payoff or bribe. The political payoff has been used in many countries to avoid confiscatory taxes or expulsion, to ensure agent acceptance of sales contracts and to provide monetary encouragement to an assortment of people whose actions can affect the effectiveness of a company's programmes. The definition of bribery can range from the relatively innocuous payment of a small sum of money to minor officials or business managers to expedite the processing of papers or the loading of a truck to the extreme of paying large sums to top-ranking government officials to ensure that the company receives preferential treatment. It is not always clear when bribery actually does occur; bribery is very much an ethical issue, being dependent on the country and circumstances in question. Nevertheless, there are various forms of payents made which in the minds of many people constitute a form of bribery and are considered corrupt.

Regulating international transfers

The issue of international transfers covers the physical transfer of products through importing and exporting, financial flows, the transfer of people, the transfer of technology and cross-border data flows. The question arises as to why, in view of the widely espoused benefits of free trade, countries sometimes attempt to control such international transfers. There are numerous reasons for this (Table 7.3).

It is more convenient to classify these political controls under four headings: attempts to control the transfer of products and services; the transfer of money; the transfer of people; the transfer of technology.

Table 7.3 Reasons for controlling international transfers

ı Revenue goals
ı Employment protection
ı Development goals
ı Balance of payments objectives
ı Sectoral adjustment policies
ı Health and safety protection
ı National security
ı International political goals

Regulating transfers of products and services

The most common type of trade control is the tariff or duty, a government tax levied on goods shipped internationally, most commonly in the form of an import tariff, but there are numerous others which can be equally effective (Table 7.4). Import duties serve primarily as a means of raising the price of imported products so that domestic products gain a relative price advantage. A duty may be classified as protective in nature even though there is no domestic production in direct competition. For example, if a country wishes to reduce foreign expenditure because of balance of payments problems, the government may impose a tariff in order to curtail consumption. In many developing countries tariffs are a major source of government revenue and in other countries they are an important source.

Sometimes a country holds the value of its currency so that it buys less of a foreign currency than might be the case in a free market. This is referred to as exchange rate manipulation. In such circumstances, its products will have a relative cost advantage. There is much evidence that artificially maintained exchange rates have been major influences on world trade in the last few years. US Government officials and business commentators frequently accuse Japan of manipulating the exchange rate.

The most common form of quantity control is the quota. With regard to imports, a quota most frequently sets a limit on the quantitative amount of a product allowed to be imported in a given year but it may also apply to monetary values or market share. The amount frequently reflects a guarantee that domestic producers will have access to a certain percentage of the domestic market. Export quotas may be established in order to ensure that domestic consumers have sufficient supplies at a low price to prevent depletion of natural resources or to attempt to raise an export price by restricting supply in foreign markets, e.g. OPEC restrictions on oil output. Quotas can produce inefficiencies and the allocation of quotas is often quite arbitrary and open to abuse since they are based on an administrative rather than a market system.

'Buy local' legislation may restrict purchases by government agencies to local suppliers or ensure that a certain percentage of the product for governmental purchase must be sourced locally. Aside from direct legislation, campaigns are sometimes conducted by governments to persuade their nationals to buy locally made products and services rather than those of foreign origin. Indeed, in some countries government agencies have been established to promote such campaigns, many of which are increasingly being questioned at international level. In recent years the EU Commission has taken a keen interest in such campaigns and seeks to limit their application.

Table 7.4 Mechanisms used to restrict international transfer of products and services

1 Tariffs on imports
1 Exchange rate manipulation
1 Quantity controls – quotas
1 Buy local legislation, standards and licences
1 Restrictions on services

It has not been uncommon for countries to set classifications, labelling and testing standards in such a manner as to allow the sale of domestic products but to inhibit the sale of foreign-made products. These are sometimes ostensibly for the purpose of protecting the safety and health of domestic consumers; however, imports have often been tested under more onerous conditions than have domestic products. Under EU legislation such practices are being eliminated for the 15 member countries.

Internationally traded services have not been exempt from restrictions. There are reported incidents of widespread discrimination by countries which favour their own firms. Among the complaints have been that Japanese Airlines obtain cargo clearance more quickly in Tokyo than do foreign airlines, that Argentina requires car imports to be insured with Argentine firms and that Germany requires models for advertisements in German magazines to be hired through a German agency, even if the advertisement is made abroad. Similarly, extensive industry regulation in Australia prevents international advertising agencies growing in that market.

Regulating money transfers

Countries influence international transfers of money through foreign exchange controls, capital controls, policies of tied aid, supervision of the foreign operations of domestic banks and other financial institutions and taxation.

Taxation laws are used in many ways to influence international financial transfers. Taxation levied on remittances of profits, for example, encourages re-investment and discourages remittance back to the tax jurisdiction. In both the United States and the United Kingdom, the policy is shifting from taxation on remittances towards taxation on income, whether or not remitted. Taxation laws are also being created to discourage tax deferral through transfer of funds to corporations owned and registered in different tax jurisdictions.

Control over funds granted for foreign aid has at times been attempted through tied aid or tied loans. The granting country sometimes requires that funds be utilized in purchasing goods or services from the granting country, hoping to avoid balance of payments problems from the outflow of funds. An increasing number of countries are beginning to tie their aid in this fashion.

Regulating people transfers

National policies controlling the entry and exit of people from a country are generally not motivated primarily by international business considerations. Broader political, economic and social considerations invariably underlie such policies, which generally distinguish between people entering a country for a temporary stay, such as tourists, and, at the other end of the spectrum, people who want to enter a country on a permanent basis. Passports and visas are the basic means of controlling this form of international movement.

Most countries, anxious to expand their tourist industry, impose minimum restrictions on the entry of persons on temporary visits. The most restrictive policies are applied to persons who wish to seek employment in a foreign country or to become permanent residents. The general world pattern in the early 1990s, apart from free internal movement within the EU and the Arab states, has become one of selected and limited immigration. For most countries the basis for admitting immigrants has increasingly favoured those professionally trained or highly skilled, with resources and able to join the workforce so that they do not create a burden on social welfare systems. For the under-privileged of any country, the opportunity to gain admission to another country is steadily decreasing.

Regulating technology transfers

The concept of technology encompasses technical and managerial know-how that is embodied in physical and human capital and in published documents and is transmitted across national boundaries in various ways. In recent years governments, especially those in developing countries, have encouraged inflows of technology as a major means of achieving national development goals.

In industrially advanced countries few controls exist over the international transfer of technology or even the price received for such transfers. This is so even when the international sale of technology can produce major social costs in the shape of unemployment and redundant production facilities. Even taxation authorities have little say on transfer prices as long as they are determined at arm's length. If there is an infringement of patents or if fees and other legitimate royalties are not paid the hurt party in the transaction may seek damages or other redress. However, attitudes in the developing countries differ markedly. They are predominantly buyers rather than sellers of technology. The objectives of the developing countries are ambitious. They want to ensure that imported technology is appropriate to their needs, which generally means smaller-scale and labour-intensive technology, and that it will actually be transferred to local nationals.

Importance of exchange rate stability

A country's export dependency may be seen as a competitive weakness or as a strength. It seems to depend on the macroeconomic environment and the effectiveness of public policy, especially with regard to exchange rates. Government policies that positively affect the environment are thought to have contributed to the strong export-led economies of the ASEAN region. In recent years, the export success of Irish firms is thought to be influenced by positive macroeconomic policies, but especially the maintenance of exchange rate conditions, which were attractive to steady trade. Floating exchange rates discourage trade, while the incentive to do nothing is greater the more volatile are the exchange rates (Krugman, 1989). Companies tend to be risk averse, especially with regard to international markets, which means that exchange rate instability tends to lead to lower levels of exports (Viaene and Vries, 1992). For the past few years the currency stability provided by the European Monetary System (EMS) has contributed to higher levels of intra-EU trade (Vona and Bini-Smaghi, 1990). It is expected that the new European Monetary Union (EMU), when fully operational, will provide a still greater incentive for such trade.

The EMU, which comes into force on 1 January 1999, represents the advent of a culture of stability in Europe that is essential in promoting a stable and efficiently managed economic framework for the region. Many of the fundamental arguments put forward in the past few years for and against EMU were political. The economic arguments for and against EMU were finely balanced between those in favour and those against. Supporters of EMU suggested that membership of a thriving monetary union which would create a market as large and as wealthy as the US would provide Europe with greater influence in world affairs. Opponents objected that membership of EMU would require too much discipline on members and would involve greater cooperation and centralization of decision making within the political process. This group also had argued that other issues such as enlargement and reform of institutional processes should have been a priority.

The EMU is now a reality and the new currency, the euro, is the most visible proof yet that people of Europe are part of a wider European Union. Of the EU's 15 member states 11 joined the EMU and use the euro; Britain, Denmark and Sweden have remained outside the system by choice while Greece did not meet the entry criteria set down in the Maastricht Treaty of 1992. Until 1 January 2002 there will be a transition period during which national currencies will continue to exist but as elements of the euro.

One of the major benefits of EMU is to arrive at an optimum currency area for the EU as it is argued that there are benefits from sharing a currency across national borders. These benefits include more transparent prices, lower transaction costs, reduced uncertainty for investors and greater competition. The European Commission in Brussels has stated that these gains represent about 0.5 per cent of the GDP of the EU. Additional benefits of the euro include the end of exchange rate fluctuations between EMU members and the consequent price stability as EU monetary policy is maintained by an independent European Central Bank.

There are, however, some costs of moving to the euro and a single monetary policy. Members of EMU can exercise an independent monetary policy no longer nor can they modify the exchange rate. The only major policy instrument in this area left to national governments is the cost of labour and its productivity which are affected by labour mobility and the flexibility of wages.

With prices in the EU denominated in euros instead of francs or pounds or pesetas, price comparisons will be immediate and retail and wholesale competition will increase. For the past three or four years the big consumer products industries such as cars and pharmaceuticals have been cutting costs and forming strategic alliances in preparation for a regime of greater competition and lower margins. Improved competition within the EU is preparing many firms for the global marketplace.

Consumers stand to gain from this competition provided that industries do not concentrate in particular locations within the EU. Countries on the periphery, especially, fear that the single currency may have such an effect since it encourages specialization, which may result in concentration of certain industries near the centre of the enlarged single market.

National governments have expressed concern that much of the industrial restructuring that the euro is producing will deliver benefits only if industry can reduce its labour force. Rigid European labour laws indicate that labour cost savings may not so easily be found. Labour productivity is, however, recognized as the key economic variable at country level now that the EMU is in place.

International legal framework

One of the interesting observations that can be made about the international economy is that there is nothing equivalent to national legislation ensuring an equitable taxation system, environmental management and labour rights, and protection against large monopolies. Efforts have been made to regulate the global economy, but with little effect.

The legal environment for international business consists principally of the laws and courts of the individual nation states. Increasingly, international firms, especially high-technology firms, are going to court or using political influence to resolve claimed infringement of patents and other similar intellectual property. Since no single international commercial legal system exists, the international firm is confronted with as many legal environments as there are countries. The national systems differ significantly in philosophy and practice, and each nation-state maintains its own set of courts in complete independence of every other nation. The closest approximation to an international legal framework is a patchwork system of treaties, codes and agreements among certain nations that apply to selected areas of international business activity.

What is normally called international law is more accurately described as international public law or the law of nations. It consists of a body of rules and principles that nation-states consider legally binding. It can be enforced through the International Court of Justice, international arbitration or the internal courts of the nation-states. It is mainly concerned with the relationship between states, the delimitation of their jurisdictions and control of war. In recent years, international law has also emphasized the protection of individual human rights, even against the individual's own state.

Apart from EU institutions, the only international court is the International Court of Justice at The Hague. It is the principal legal organ of the UN, and all members of the UN are parties to the statute establishing the court. The function of the court is to pass judgement on disputes between states. Private individuals or corporations do not have direct access to the International Court.

From the standpoint of international business, the most important approximation to international law is the growing number of treaties and conventions covering commercial and economic matters. The more important international agreements are referred to as treaties. Those of lesser importance are called conventions, agreements, protocols or acts. All these forms are agreements between two or more nation states which normally become legally enforceable through the municipal courts of the participating countries and an international court is not essential. Very frequently such agreements, enshrined in the laws of one of the countries, are bilateral and result from political pressure.

Since there is no 'international law' covering commercial transactions, where necessary the international firm must have recourse to the laws of the countries concerned. A first step here would be to understand the world's major legal systems. It is also important to understand how the international firm can minimize legal problems. It has become increasingly important to understand the interplay of national law and international law, particularly EU law.

EU laws and directives

Business is subject to the requirements of the law whether in the domestic market or in the foreign market. For most businesses it is a relatively easy matter to comply with the law because of familiarity and a homogeneous culture. In dealing in foreign markets, however, different local laws apply. In the EU a process of ensuring commonality in the application of laws is already at an advanced stage. From a series of national laws, all different in many respects, there is now agreement that a common law should apply throughout the EU.

The most significant EU laws which affect the firm international markets are the rules governing competition. While most firms are too small in an EU context to be affected by these laws it is, nevertheless, as well to know that they exist and to understand what is implied. EU competition laws prohibit, under heavy penalties, any agreements between companies which may affect trade between member states of the EU by preventing or distorting competition. Such agreements might be those fixing prices, or offering unequal conditions between equivalent customers or limiting markets by preventing a distributor to sell in response to unsolicited enquiries from outside an allotted territory. It is important, therefore, that any agreements the company makes with agents or distributors are not anti-competitive, especially where there is any element of resale price control or exclusivity in sales territories.

In many EU countries there are local competition rules in addition to the EU laws. Many of these refer to the prohibition of resale price maintenance and in most cases the authorities have the power to impose maximum prices. In many cases, however, they refer to sales territories and the possible loss of competition (Exhibit 7.1). The protection of copyright, patents, trade marks and designs varies from country to country and it is important to ascertain before entering the market whether the enforcement of the company's rights in these matters is likely to be a problem in the target country market.

Exhibit 7.1

Export bans apply outside EU

The EU's competition rules apply to export bans relating to territory outside the EU where the effect of the ban is the prevention, distortion or restriction of competition within the EU and the ban is liable to affect inter-state trade, the European Court of Justice ruled recently. The judgement arose in the context of a dispute between Yves St Laurent Parfums and Javico International, its distributor for Ukraine, Russia and Slovenia.

Under the distribution contracts Javico International agreed that the products were solely for sale in the three countries and could not be sold elsewhere. Shortly after entering into the agreements, Yves St Laurent discovered products supplied to Javico were being sold in the UK, Belgium and the Netherlands. Yves St Laurent terminated the contracts and sued for compensation and damages in French courts where the action was successful. Javico appealed, arguing the distribution contracts were void for breach of the EU competition rules.

The matter was referred to the European Court which looked first at the impact of the competition rules on an export ban on the distribution of goods outside the EU. It said the impact depended on whether the aim or effect of the ban was to restrict competition to an appreciable extent within the common market and whether it would affect trade between member states. The Court said the aim of the restriction was to be construed not as being intended to exclude parallel imports within the EU, but rather as being designed to enable the producer to penetrate markets outside the EU. Thus, the contracts could not be regarded as having the aim of appreciably restricting competition contrary to article 85 of the Treaty of Rome. However, it said it was for the national court to determine whether such contracts had the effect of appreciably restricting competition.

In the present case the national court would have to determine whether the structure of the EU market in the relevant products was oligopolistic, allowing only limited competition within the EU network for distribution of the products. The national court would then have to establish whether there was an appreciable difference in the prices charged within and outside the EU. The effect of inter-state trade was to be appraised by reference to the position of the parties on the market for the products concerned. Thus, even a contract which imposed absolute territorial protection could escape article 85 if it affected the market insignificantly.

Intra-EU trade could not be appreciably affected if the products intended for markets outside the EU accounted for only a very small percentage of the total market for the products within the EU. The Court was asked whether the fact that Yves St Laurent's distribution system within the EU had received an exemption under the competition rules was relevant to the legality of the ban. The Court said the exemption applied only to agreements within the EU. The same was true for the EU's selective distribution block exemption. Thus, the Javico contracts could not benefit from either exemption.

Source: adapted from *Financial Times*, Tuesday, 12 May 1998, p. 15.

Major world legal systems

Two major structures have guided the development of legal systems in most countries of the world (Table 7.5). Common law is the basis of law in countries that have been at some time under British influence. Common law countries do not attempt to anticipate all areas in the application of a law by writing it to cover every foreseeable situation. Instead, cases in common law countries are decided on the basis of tradition, common practice and interpretation of statutes. Civil or code law countries have as their premise the writing of codes of conduct that are inclusive of all foreseeable applications of law. Codes of law are then developed for commercial, civil and criminal applications. Precedents are important in understanding common law as it is or has been interpreted. The laws themselves are the key to understanding the legal environment in civil or code law countries.

Even in common law countries there are often codes of law. The Uniform Commercial Code in the United States is a good example of this governing business activity. However,

Table 7.5 Major world legal systems

Common Law

ı countries at one time under British influence, or former colonies of Britain
ı law not written to cover all foreseeable situations
ı cases decided on basis of tradition, common practice, and interpretation of statutes
ı precedents important in understanding common law

Code Law

ı codes of conduct inclusive of all foreseeable applications of law
ı codes developed for commercial, civil and criminal applications
ı laws themselves important factor in understanding code law

common law does not differentiate between civil, criminal and commercial activities, and thus a business may be liable under any of these laws. Code law countries separate the three types of activity, but there are always areas where codes are not sufficiently specific and must be interpreted by the courts. Hence, most countries use common or code law as the basis for their legal system, but they rely on a combination of the two in applying the legal system to actual disputes.

Perhaps the best example of how common and code law differ is in the recognition of industrial property rights. These include trademarks, logos, brand names, production processes, patents, even managerial know-how. In common law countries, ownership of industrial property rights comes from use. In code or civil law countries, ownership comes from registering the name or process. The implications of this difference are obvious; a company may find itself in litigation in a code law country to gain the rights to use its own names or logos, and it may not win. The EU Commission is taking a keen interest in developing directives regarding such property rights which will have applicability throughout the community and will also affect firms outside the EU.

Intellectual property rights in international markets

A very large proportion of world business is now regulated by intellectual property rights. Counterfeiting, copying and 'piracy' are now very common and present obstacles to fair trade and a fair return to the owners of the intellectual property. The industries worst hit are chemicals and pharmaceuticals, books, software and music. To this list must be added the appropriation of brand names. The offending parties are usually companies in developing countries, where such practices are not illegal. To add insult to injury, the poor quality of the 'copy-product' damages the distribution and reputation of the genuine articles.

As a result of these trends, intellectual property rights were included within the Uruguay Round of GATT negotiations and there has been a considerable strengthening of those property rights in the following areas:

- stronger protection of trademarks, especially with regard to EU brands;
- industrial designs receive greater protection, especially for textiles and clothing;
- patent protection for pharmaceuticals and chemicals is being introduced in all countries who are members of the WTO;
- the EU semiconductor design protection to be extended internationally;
- future appropriation and misuse of geographic 'appellations' for food and beverages to be prohibited.

Legal aspects of marketing claims

Promotion is the area of marketing strategy where the impact of varying legal rules is particularly obvious. In Germany, for example, advertisements cannot claim that the firm's products are the 'best', since that is interpreted as violating a law that forbids disparaging competitors, whereas such practice has been quite common in the United States but is now on the wane. In Austria, premium offers to consumers come under the discount law which prohibits any cash reductions that give preferential treatment to different groups of customers. In France it is illegal to offer a customer a gift or premium conditional on the purchase of another product. Furthermore, a manufacturer or retailer cannot offer products that are different from the kind regularly offered. For example, a detergent manufacturer cannot offer clothing or cooking utensils. The typical premiums or prizes offered by cereal manufacturers would be completely illegal under this law.

The development and introduction of new products must conform to laws that regulate units of measurement, quality or ingredient requirements, safety or pollution restrictions and industry standards. This may force the firm to modify its products in every national market in order to meet varying legal rules. Labelling and branding also face many laws regulating their use. Product liability is yet another area of concern; the differences in interpreting implied and explicit warranties and product returns are special areas of concern to the international firm.

The use of specific terms which are not bound to one culture is most important for the international firm when writing a contract for business in a foreign market. Consider the problems that might be caused by terms such as 'premium', 'first rate quality' and 'commercial grade' when a different country's cultural and legal perspectives are used to interpret such terms.

Conflicts can also arise when units of measurement such as weight and length are not sufficiently clear. Standard contracts used in domestic markets are often inadequate in international marketing because they make too many assumptions about the interpretation of terminology, e.g. garment sizes as small, medium or large. Another example which caused considerable difficulty for a food exporter to the United States was liquid measure instructions based on the Imperial measure of the pint; in Europe a pint contains 20 fluid ounces of liquid, whereas in the United States it contains 16 fluid ounces. As the US pint is smaller, instructions to add a certain quantity of liquid based on the Imperial pint measure caused havoc in food preparation.

Summary

In this chapter concern has rested on analysing the political environment as it affects the firm in international markets. The key questions examined were the importance of political stability in providing a basis for international marketing activities, irrespective of the mode of entry used. The political risks of operating abroad are much greater than those of operating in the familiar domestic market: political philosophies, cultures and laws are different, which affects the way business is done. Attitudes to property and contracts are therefore also very different.

In some markets the political–business interface is quite strong and positive, whereas in other countries business is seen as a basis for taxation and control. For these reasons some markets are more open and dynamic than others. Governments in all countries, however, attempt to regulate cross-border flows of products, services, people, money and other assets. Furthermore, the regulation of technology transfers is of increasing interest in recent years. Regulations provide a source of anxiety to some firms, especially those seeking open markets and freer competition. To other firms regulation is seen as a source of protection and monopoly power.

Countries, separately and together, attempt to coordinate regulation and controls through a legal framework. To date, the legal framework which applies to business transactions tends to vary from country to country. The code of law which applies in an individual country can complicate matters. Increasingly, transnational bodies, including the EU, are taking a greater interest in providing a coordinated legal framework within which the firm in international markets can operate. Because of cost and the time factor involved, international firms prefer arbitration as a means of settling disputes.

Discussion questions

1. What aspects of international marketing are most affected by political instability in a country?

2. How can you measure political instability? Is political instability also a matter of perception?

3. Some countries have been more successful than others in developing a positive political–business interaction. Discuss. Evaluate the situation in your own country.

4. Regulation of international transfers of any kind is invidious and should be banned by the recognized international authorities. Discuss.

5. The manager of the international firm can cope with regulations once they are clear and unambiguous. Do you agree?

6. Regulations which remove restrictive business practices in major world markets should be favoured. Discuss.

7. How do firms minimize international legal problems?

8. European-based firms are increasingly faced with EU directives, laws and regulations. How will this affect the role of national law and how will it affect the marketing of products and services in Europe? What effect will it have on firms outside the EU?

References

Brouthers, K. D. (1995) 'The influence of international risk on entry mode strategy in the computer software industry, *Management International Review*, **35** (1) 7–28.

Human Development Report 1997, New York, NY: Oxford University Press.

Krugman, P. R. (1989) *Exchange Rate Instability*, Cambridge, MA: MIT Press.

Miller, K. D. (1992) 'A framework for integrated risk management in international business', *Journal of International Business Studies*, **23** (Second Quarter), 311–31.

Robock, S. H. (1971) 'Political risk: identification and assessment', *Columbia Journal of World Business*, (July–August), 6–20.

Rodrick, D. (1997), 'Has globalization gone too far?', *California Management Review*, **39** (3), 29–53.

Viaene, J. M. and Vries, C. G. (1992) 'International trade and exchange rate volatility', *European Economic Review*, **36**, 1311–21.

Vona, S. and Bini-Smaghi, L. (1990) 'Economic growth and exchange rates in the EMS: their trade effects in a changing external environment', in F. Giavazzi, S. Micossi and M. Miller (eds), *The European Monetary System*, 2nd edn, London: Cambridge University Press.

World Development Report (1997) *The State in a Changing World*, Oxford: Oxford University Press.

8
Creating competitive advantage

There have been very many changes in the international competitive environment in recent years. Competition for US, European and other Western countries now comes from resource-poor countries especially Japan, Hong Kong, Singapore and many other countries in South East Asia. These countries have consistently achieved more rapid increases in productivity, output and exports than the more established countries by deepening their knowledge base and concentrating on advanced and sophisticated products. Such changes have forced the older competitors to question their approach to competing internationally and to examine the role of advanced technology developed through creative industrial and commercial policies. The critical element of the response by older countries has been to seek effective participation by national governments in shaping the business environments in which their companies compete.

Marketing challenge of open markets

Among the more significant responses by successful companies worldwide to the removal of protective barriers and globalization of markets has been the almost frenetic search for new ways of entering and staying in foreign markets. The strategic concern lies in seeking ways of establishing effective equity and non-equity ways of entering and developing foreign markets through exporting, foreign direct investment and corporate alliances based on joint ventures and licensing. For many firms, some or all of these approaches to competing in international markets represent new challenges and opportunities.

The challenge in a competitive environment is corporate survival and the opportunity is growth through internationalization. The question facing managers is to what extent they are preventing the development and growth of their firms by adhering to the delusion of protected markets instead of adapting to a changing world which has become increasingly international. The firm in international markets must deal with a changing environment in the context of a public policy which is both national and international. The international marketing environment requires it to make decisions in the context of a number of issues which affect its well-being (Figure 8.1). Two major forces are at play in

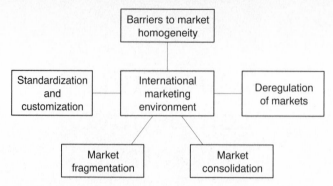

Figure 8.1 International marketing environment

the international marketing environment. Markets are fragmenting with the participation of a greater number of smaller countries in the international marketing activities and the growing importance of regional markets. Regional markets are a relatively new feature of what were once large homogeneous markets such as the US and China where local tastes dominate and a national approach to marketing of products is on the wane. Simultaneously, the big-brand companies have been investing heavily to consolidate markets behind heavily advertised products in the EU, the Far East and in the developing world. These two forces are subject to numerous pressures, market deregulation, standardization and customization and other barriers to homogeneity of markets.

Created assets in international marketing

By creating a comparative resource advantage in production and trade governments seek to promote a competitive advantage among firms in their jurisdiction. Usually governments attempt to create an assortment of resources. For example, country-specific endowments in areas such as electronic design skills, design and weaving skills for the fashion industry and other 'economic cluster' benefits help to create an environment in which companies are established and learn to compete effectively in certain areas and, as such, provide the essential ingredients for achieving international competitive success. Creating competitive advantage at firm level in this way raises productivity and the incomes of people and allows a higher standard of living for people through international marketing and trade with other countries. The process of creating and sustaining competitive advantage in one where history matters as the base of already established industries, institutions and values affects the process of industrial development (Porter, 1998, p. 175). According to Porter (1998, p. 19) differences in national economic structures, values, cultures and institutions also contribute profoundly to competitive success

Most countries and governments actively support the creation of competitive advantage for enterprises located within their borders. Some do it explicitly: Japan, Korea, Taiwan, Singapore, Ireland and Portugal are examples. In many other countries the support is less explicit but, nevertheless, effective: the United Kingdom, Germany and the United States. This chapter examines the ways and means of actively creating a competitive advantage in international marketing.

Comparative advantage and competitive advantage

A fundamental economic principle is that any country's standard of living depends almost entirely on its own domestic economic performance and not on how it performs relative to other countries. Failing to appreciate this principle leads to trade wars. Indeed, in terms of the model outline in Figure 2.4, countries are competitors, customers and complementors. While they sell products that compete with each other, they are also each other's principal export markets and suppliers of useful imports.

Frequently, there are politicians who state that a country should be more productive to compete internationally. The reason a country should try to be more productive is to produce more and thereby to raise the standard of living. A country that is not productive will have a low standard of living but, as seen in Chapter 2, it still has the option of exporting to superior rivals those products that it does not make too badly and import from them the things which are made badly. Doing so delivers a somewhat higher standard of living than a country with a very low domestic productivity might enjoy. This is why economists focus on imports – the purpose of international trade is to import products and services the country wants. Exports are the price paid for the imports in demand by the citizens of a country.

Countries do not compete with each other in the same way that Toyota competes with Renault. Trade between countries can be win–win, whereas companies such as Toyota and Renault are almost pure rivals – the success of one tends to be at the other's expense. A country, is therefore, not the same as a large company.

The distinction made above raises the need to separate two important concepts which are often confused – comparative advantage, which deals with countries and competitive advantage, which deals with companies. France and Japan would experience certain comparative advantages, whereas Renault and Toyota seek competitive advantages. By concentrating on improving productivity in a country and providing R&D and other assistance, the country lowers the price of imports which may indirectly feed into the competitive advantage of companies. Comparative advantage focuses on efficiency of national production, whereas competitive advantage emphasizes effectiveness of the company. While comparative advantage concentrates on lower costs and prices, competitive advantage stresses superior management polices aimed at providing consumers with products and services required (Samli and Jacobs, 1995, p. 24). The critical issue for society is that it is necessary to seek congruence between the international trade and investment policies of the governments and the strategies of firms and industries.

Country and company competitiveness

Competitiveness for the firm refers to its ability to increase earnings by expanding sales and/or profit margins in the market in which it competes so that it defends market position in a subsequent round of competition as products and processes evolve. Competitiveness in this sense is almost synonymous with the firm's long-run profit performance relative to its rivals. An analogue exists at the national level, but it is much more complicated (Cohen *et al.*, 1984). A country's competitiveness is the degree to which it can produce goods and services that meet the test of international markets while simultaneously expanding the real incomes of its people.

International competitiveness at national level is based on superior productivity performance and the economy's ability to shift to high-productivity activities, which in turn can generate high levels of real wages. Competitiveness is associated with rising living standards, wealth, expanding employment opportunities and the ability of a country to maintain its international obligations. It is the country's ability to stay ahead techno-logically and commercially in those product markets likely to constitute a larger share of world consumption and value added in the future and not just the ability to sell abroad to maintain a trade equilibrium (Cohen *et al.*, 1984).

To understand the issues, the dynamics of competition in international markets must be clarified. Three different competitive situations are encountered (Cohen *et al.*, 1984). The newly industrializing countries (NICs) have entered European markets by combining, in varied formulas, low-cost labour, government promotion and standard mature technologies. European firms have responded in three ways to such competition: off-shore production to match foreign labour costs; speciality products to move competition away from price; innovative automation to reduce the labour content in manufacturing to become low-cost producers. The second competitive situation arises in industries where product quality and costs depend on dominating complex manufacturing processes; success depends on factors such as the quality and speed of product design, the organi-zation of production and services, e.g. cars and TVs. Competition in such industries tends to be concentrated among the advanced industrial countries of Europe, North America and Japan.

In the third situation are high-technology industries where advances in product perfor-mance based on research and development are critical. As advanced products are copied, however, holding markets in high-technology competition depends on sophisticated manufacturing and marketing skills since the pace of imitation is faster. Competitors are closer to the same technology frontier and design processes can be accelerated.

The common feature of these three forms of competition is the importance of manufacturing and marketing systems in retaining industrial competitiveness and the ability of firms to understand and cope with the interaction between them. Even in the so-called haven of high technology, long-run competitiveness rests on the firm's ability to translate product advantage into enduring market position through the application of sophisticated marketing expertise. It is the position of the firm relative to its competitors that is important.

Location of competitive advantage: industry and region

There is a debate in the literature with regard to the location of international compe-titive advantage. Researchers at Morgan Stanley have attempted to determine where competitive strengths lie. Their research indicates that, in agricultural industries, competitive advantage is spread evenly between developed and developing countries (Table 8.1). In commodities such as paper, consumer non-durables and textiles, developing countries have a disproportionate share of the competitive advantage. In complex industries, such as chemicals, pharmaceuticals, motor vehicles and technology, however, competitive advantage favours the developed countries.

Importance of labour productivity

Because most countries produce most of their goods and services for domestic consumption it is not necessary that the country be internationally competitive: an uncompetitive country, unless it is very small and open, continues regardless. The standard of living of its people falls; however, when countries compete the gain can benefit all owing to the law of comparative advantage, irrespective of their ability to compete. Eventually an uncom-

Table 8.1 Industry and regional analysis of international competitiveness

	Countries with revealed advantage	Comments
Resource based industry:		
Food	18	Agriculture evenly divided, developed and developing worlds
Tobacco	19	Developing world has the edge
Beverages	14	Developed countries 2/3 of the advantage
Metals	15	Equal split between developing and industrial countries
Chemicals	8	US, Japan, Europe – no developing countries
Paper	9	Canada, New Zealand, Scandinavia, Malaysia, Indonesia, Brazil, Chile
Energy	12	Developing World
Advanced processing industry:		
Apparel and textiles	16	All but four in developing world
Pharmaceuticals	10	US and Europe lead, but China and India improving
Other consumer	13	Nine in developing world (Asian Tigers) – non-durables toys, sporting goods, perfumes
Motor vehicles	11	Japan, Germany, Belgium and Sweden lead; also South Korea, Mexico and Brazil
Capital Goods	12	Japan the powerhouse; Germany, Denmark, France and Switzerland have the balance
Technology	13	Japan and Asia lead; Switzerland, Finland, Belgium, and Sweden also qualify

Source: *Competitive Edge 1996*, Morgan Stanley, p. 30.

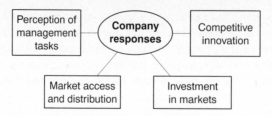

Figure 8.2 Company responses to international trends

petitive country must lower its costs to restore competitiveness. This may occur as a result of low inflation or depreciation of the currency. For a country what matters therefore is productivity, not competition, since productivity is directly related to economic performance. Internationally productivity growth rates serve as a competitive benchmark.

Productivity growth means higher living standards. The faster the rate of productivity growth the faster the country can grow without inflation. Changes in relative productivity growth affect a country's standard of living. A country which lags in productivity will also lag in incomes and eventually become a low-wage economy, which will tend to shift the pattern of comparative advantage away from capital-intensive to labour-intensive businesses.

Challenge facing the international firm

The successful firm caters for its customers within the context of the firm's competitive environment, which has become increasingly international. The competitive milieu consists of domestic and international customers and competition, and national and public policies and regulations. It is influenced by social, cultural and educational trends throughout the world. The international marketing environment influences the strategic options open to the firm (Bradley, 1987). The company copes with this environment in a number of ways, some of which relate to how it perceives its task while others involve investment in products, markets and marketing (Figure 8.2). Successful companies perceive their task as developing an international orientation in all of their activities which translates into innovative products and services aimed at international markets. They also invest heavily in international markets by establishing a presence there through sales subsidiaries, assembly plants and even production facilities. Often the key factor is to discover how best to reach customers. Access and distribution issues often dominate the competitive advantage of firms.

Industrial and commercial policy environment

Industrial and commercial policies may be regarded as tools which are used to affect the speed of the process of resource allocation among and within industrial sectors. This implies that, for a variety of reasons, public authorities may not accept the way the market allocates resources and achieves major structural changes (Bradley, 1985). According to the goals pursued by public policy, the process of reallocation may be retarded or accelerated, facilitated or impeded. For example, the national security argument might justify the maintenance of otherwise uneconomical production facilities, e.g. small, inefficient oil refineries. Employment measures may be needed because labour markets are imperfect. Manpower policies can also reduce the costs of adjustment, hence increasing the speed of reallocating human resources. Similarly, growth-oriented science and technological policies can ensure a socially sufficient flow of resources. There may also be a case for subsidizing R&D in high-technology industries affected by large fixed costs. Hence, industrial policy may be regarded as a positive response to the imperfections of modern markets – whether capital, labour or product markets. National governments, international policy-making bodies such as the EU and other similar institutions intervene in a variety of ways to influence how companies in their jurisdiction perform (Figure 8.3). These interventions take many forms. A popular theme at present is the need to deregulate key service markets such as airlines and telecommunications. Deregulation of airlines in the US allowed low-cost operators to enter the market and now many such competitors are challenging flag carriers in Europe and elsewhere (Exhibit 8.1). The provision of finance at attractive rates to new high-technology ventures and the actual sponsorship of a new industry such as aircraft construction are other examples. Governments improve competitive advantage by encouraging the introduction of new technologies and the demise of old ones.

Industrial and commercial policy may deal with such issues as the continued rise in the cost of economic adjustment and social resistance to it and in some countries it frequently addresses the necessity of simultaneously safeguarding social peace, especially in a society deeply divided by class. Industrial policy may be used to shift resources out of activities which have become uncompetitive owing to the pressure of international economic forces. Finally, it is increasingly being recognized by governments that, for a wide range of manufacturers, competitive advantage may be relatively malleable instead of rigidly predetermined by national endowments of resources. At present the last argument is critical as there are several economic and political reasons for an industrial and commercial policy which reflects the need to help domestic industries to respond to the

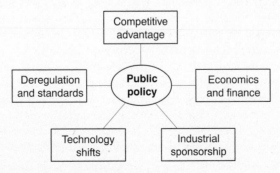

Figure 8.3 Public policy in international marketing

challenge of international competition. Contrasting with traditional trade theory, which treats national factor endowments and national technological developments as in some way determined outside the system, it is argued that, in many sectors, comparative advantage rests on relative capital endowments, which result from accumulated investment. Government policies can alter the process of physical and human capital accumulation over time to improve the country's strategic position in international competition.

The determinants of national advantage are a dynamic system which holds the key to up-grading and sustaining competitive advantage where the influence and reinforcement of these determinants leads to the phenomenon of clustering of industries and to the prevalence and importance of geographic concentration (Porter, 1998, p. 174). According to Enright (1995, p. 2),

> The key to developing competitive advantage in modern economic competition, in individual industries or across the economy, is to have an environment that creates processes, market incentives and capabilities to innovate and to improve, present in the local environment. All three are often necessary. Pressures and incentives result in competitive failures. Incentives and capabilities without pressure result in inefficiencies. Pressures and capabilities without incentives result in emigration.

▬▬ Exhibit 8.1 ▬▬
The new airline competitors

While the strongest carriers have been taking the path towards globalisation, a new breed of airline, led by visionary entrepreneurs, has evolved. So-called mavericks, such as SouthWest in the US, RyanAir in Europe, and Virgin Atlantic on long-haul routes have created new bases of competition. RyanAir operates in time slots others may consider 'useless', SouthWest operates out of the 'wrong' airports, while Virgin targets a product proposition at the 'wrong' price point. Several of these unconventional competitors have demonstrated that they can grow the market in their own right. RyanAir, for instance, has developed and extended the Dublin to London market. More than niche players, each of these 'mavericks' has become a significant force in the market in which it has chosen to compete. It will be fascinating to see how similar entrepreneurs in other parts of the world, such as Southeast Asia, develop these markets.

Importantly, both the strongest and the weaker airlines have been affected most by the success of these new competitors. The national flag carriers, in particular, with their legacy of uncommercial cultures, inappropriate route structures and turbulent industrial relations, are most jeopardised. Not only do they face a massive management challenge in bringing themselves up to more commercial standards but, as the regulators permit more competition, their position will weaken further.

Source: adapted from K. L. Brennan, 'A view to the future' *First Quarterly*, **2** (1), 82–3.

Nature and formation of industrial and commercial policy

Under the various international trade and investment agreements and under the auspices of the WTO, there is a general acceptance by governments in forming industrial and commercial policies that an effective national participation in the world economy is essential for economic security and growth. It is also believed that there is a close correspondence between performance in the domestic market and participation in international markets. As a result, the role of government is changing. It has less opportunity to focus attention on domestic markets only, as it must be fully involved in acquiring and developing technologies that transform and modernize the productive capacity of the economy. Governments are also active in attempting to create conditions to attract 'technology carriers' into the economy. These firms are attracted to countries that have coherent knowledge acquisition strategies and are advocates of international trade and investment.

Industrial policy may be applied at three levels: macro economic policy, sectoral policy or company-level policy (Defraigne, 1984). Macro economic policy is the least interventionist and leaves the functioning of industries and firms to the market mechanism to improve the general framework within which producer activities and consumer choices take place and to facilitate an automatic process of industrial adjust-ment. This type of policy is closest to the 'invisible hand' policy in vogue in the United Kingdom and the United States in the l980s and early 1990s.

Sectoral policies aimed at certain industries are justified when market imperfections, or 'market failure', affect specific industries. Such policies attempt to provide non-market mechanisms that improve the response given by the market forces existing in the relevant industry. Much of the work of the WTO and the GATT deals with sectoral policies and trade barriers that affect sectoral development in many countries. Because of the impact that open markets might have on key industrial sectors, governments frequently oppose the liberalization of trade in key products and commodities.

Public policy is increasingly designed to produce various forms of actions directed towards specific companies or industrial groups. Such micro level policies are now common in Europe, east and west, and particularly in the newly industrialized countries. Policies aimed at attracting foreign firms or developing small indigenous businesses are a clear illustration of this type of industrial policy. There are many instances of direct intervention by governments in the operational and strategic affairs of specific firms. Government policies of this type are found throughout the EU, particularly in France, Spain, Greece, Ireland, Scotland, Wales and other regions where large-scale industry never took hold. In recent years the Commission of the EU has attempted to wean the governments of member countries off state aid to industry. Instead of declining, state aid has been increasing and the offenders are the large countries such as France and Germany (Exhibit 8.2).

Government export promotion has a price attached to it which is rarely publicized. Governments emphasize the benefits of ministerial trade missions and encourage trade agreements with government financial support but, frequently, there are subsidies and other supports involved. Those who benefit from such promotion are the buyers and the politicians whose stock among the electorate rises because of jobs and exports. In general, governments rely on export subsidies, tied aid, R&D support and export credit guarantees to promote exports. Direct subsidies of exports are now banned by the rules of the World Trade Organization. Tied aid is often given for foreign policy reasons in addition to commercial reasons, but these have a danger of being confused. To address this matter, the OECD in 1996 adopted new guidelines on tied aid, aimed at ensuring that it be given only to projects that cannot be commercially financed.

With regard to R&D subsidies under World Trade Organization rules, governments may finance up to 75 per cent of a firm's industrial research costs or half the cost of product development. The argument for such support is that the firm undertaking the R&D may not obtain all the benefits from it – these can accrue to everyone. However, the difficulty arises in selecting good projects. Lastly, export credit guarantees insure exporters against the risk of default by their customers. Governments have used these to subsidize exporters by guaranteeing loans at below market interest rates. Many European countries, however, have encouraged private sector involvement in short-term export credit operations. With encouragement from OECD and the WTO, governments have not been using these ways of subsidizing exports as much as before.

There are a number of types of export promotion which can, however, be beneficial. Government-sponsored export promotion devoted to the general marketing of a country, but separated from any particular business deal or company, which would include publicity, information gathering and dissemination, would be beneficial. Governments also have a longer-term role of reassuring others of the stability of macroeconomic policies and the regulatory environment.

━━━━━ Exhibit 8.2 ━━━━━
State aid – the addicts in Europe

Until a few years ago, subsidies – state aids, in EU jargon, seemed to be declining. But they have since started to creep up again. Across Europe, firms received 44 billion ECUs ($52 billion) of aid in 1994. Nor have the most spendthrift been in the EU's poorer regions. Countries such as Spain, Greece and Portugal have increasingly accepted that they cannot afford subsidies and that their industries derive little benefit from them. In fact, some 90% of subsidies in Europe are now paid in richer central areas. The worst offenders are France and Germany, where state aids are still rising. Van Miert likens them to drug addicts that cannot kick their habit.

Mr Van Miert also points out that the bulk of such subsidies go not to new industries with a future, but to ailing giants in industries such as shipbuilding, coal-mining and cars; and that there is no evidence of lasting protection for jobs – rather the reverse, in fact. In 1994, subsidies to industry took up over 5% of all German public spending. By no means all of this was for the former East Germany; subsidies to coalmines, mostly in the west, amount to over 50,000 ECUs per miner every year. There is a continuing guerrilla war with France over aid to its biggest bank, Crédit Lyonnais. And France is alone in the EU in opposing further moves to trim subsidies to shipbuilding.

The addiction of the big two matters: given their political power, the commission has an uphill struggle overturning their state aids. That makes it harder to deal with others. No wonder Mr Van Miert dreads the day when he has to grapple with state aid in the EU's new members from Eastern Europe. The ultimate cure for the state-aid addicts has to come from Bonn and Paris, when the German and French governments lose their enthusiasm for aid. Fortunately, the single currency may soon persuade them.

The Euro will bolster the single market and through its linked stability pact, constrain public spending. Budgetary rigour, year in, year out, will eventually force France and Germany to choose between the welfare of their citizens and that of their industries. The choice should be obvious.

State aid to industry as a percentage of government spending 1992–94

Germany	5.4	Portugal	2.6
Italy	4.1	Greece	3.5
France	2.5	Denmark	1.7
Spain	2.4	Ireland	3.6
UK	1.0	Luxembourg	4.0
Belgium	3.5	Netherlands	1.4

Source: adapted from *Economist*, 22 November 1997, p. 81.

Strategies for development: countries and communities

As may be seen in later sections of this chapter, a national strategy consists of goals, a view regarding the attainment of these goals in a competitive environment and a set of policies and institutions to implement the approaches adopted. It is argued that the similarity between firms and countries is even stronger (Scott, 1985, pp. 71–2). Just as some firms are growth oriented, with a low dividend payout to permit a maximum level of re-investment in the business, so too are some countries. Similarly, some countries are growth oriented with strong incentives to promote savings and investment and thereby to reduce short-term consumption in favour of greater future returns. Other firms may have more modest growth aspirations and a higher payout of earnings. In the same vein, there are countries which give a high priority to short-term consumer benefits and choose to promote consumption rather than savings. Indeed, just as there are companies which change their behaviour without much regard for a strategic position, so too are there countries which switch from one set of industrial and commercial policies to a contrasting set, often on the whim of the government in office.

It is more important, however, to consider the broad thrust of government policies over the longer term than to worry about internal consistency in policies in the short term.

Using this criterion, as seen in preceding chapters, there are two very different types of country strategy: the invisible hand and the strongly interventionist. An alternative view of country strategies may be found in the degree to which countries are resource oriented rather than marketing opportunity oriented. Countries which are resource oriented tend to see markets and competition guided by the invisible hand as the most effective way to develop those resources. Governments in such countries are expected to play the role of benign regulators and observers, entering the fray only when state security or the national currency is threatened. In contrast, countries that are market led acknowledge a role for the visible hand of government in supplementing market forces. Such countries provide incentives to promote savings and investment in certain kinds of industries. They discourage consumption through heavy sales taxes, promote the mobility of resources and alter the risk–reward relationships. Many such countries actively promote the establishment of new industries and the attraction of foreign-owned industry through well-funded inward investment agencies.

Trends in comparative advantage

In the past 20–30 years a number of countries have improved their comparative advantage through a process of upgrading their industrial product portfolio. It is possible to classify trade between countries and trading blocs using a variety of schemes.

While there is no precise way of measuring comparative advantage, trade data allow us to observe revealed comparative advantage. By observing the ratio of exports to imports for a number of industries in different countries over time, it is possible to observe shifts in comparative advantage. In Table 8.2, ratios greater than one indicate that exports exceed imports for the product category and may be taken to indicate the existence of a revealed comparative advantage.

Table 8.2 Revealed comparative advantage – industries and countries

Industry sector	United States		Europe		Japan		Other Asia		Latin America	
	1980	1994	1980	1994	1980	1994	1980	1994	1980	1994
Food	2.05	1.45	0.70	0.87	0.09	0.04	1.40	1.27	3.49	2.11
Beverages	0.10	0.28	1.59	1.60	0.41	0.04	0.53	0.78	1.22	1.14
Chemicals	2.08	1.42	1.13	1.13	1.03	1.27	0.56	0.55	0.37	0.39
Paper	1.00	0.91	0.90	0.99	0.13	0.15	1.10	0.93	0.91	0.89
Apparel & Textiles	0.67	0.26	0.93	0.80	1.07	0.32	2.61	2.17	2.42	0.93
Pharmaceuticals	2.54	1.30	1.65	1.40	0.27	0.37	0.74	0.80	0.29	0.26
Motor vehicles	0.95	0.74	1.13	1.22	15.2	7.04	0.28	0.61	0.55	0.87
Capital goods	1.91	0.98	1.55	1.37	5.56	5.25	0.29	0.65	0.37	0.52
Technology	1.42	0.70	1.00	0.86	6.86	3.67	0.92	1.45	0.44	0.59
Total	0.87	0.74	0.90	1.05	0.92	1.44	0.88	0.97	1.18	0.93

Source: adapted from *The Competitive Edge 1997*, Morgan Stanley, p. 33.

From Table 8.2, it is clear that, between 1980 and 1994, the United States improved its position in beverages but lost it in motor vehicles, reflecting competition from Japan and Korea. The US has also lost out in food, chemicals, pharmaceuticals, capital equipment and technology.

In the same period, Japan has moved from being in deficit to having a strong surplus. Improvements have occurred in the high value added businesses such as chemicals and pharmaceuticals while at the same time a decline in the low value added industries such as food, beverages and textiles has been experienced. This fits with the implied policy recommendation outlined in Chapter 3, shifting production from low income – low knowledge intensive products to high income elastic – high knowledge intensive products (Figure 3.2).

Dynamic comparative advantage

Some of the successful Far Eastern countries such as Taiwan, South Korea, Singapore and Hong Kong have operated on the principle of dynamic comparative advantage. Instead of focusing on static factor endowments and rising short-run costs these economies have focused on factor mobility and the possibility of declining long-run costs based on the learning curve and scale economies. This is a dynamic theory of comparative advantage which focuses on the opportunities for change through time.

To place the issue of dynamic comparative advantage in context let us assume that we are dealing with a small open country such as New Zealand or Denmark or called Country X for illustration. In terms of Chapter 2, the short-run advantage for Country X might arise from specializing in producing commodity foods; the long-run advantage might arise from making a success of industrial electronics, a high-technology, high-growth rapidly changing industry. If Country X follows the theory of comparative advantage it sacrifices long-term growth for short-term gains and implicitly accepts a lower standard of living than its neighbours. Concluding otherwise implies that for some reason Country X is unable to compete in industrial electronics, a proposition much like the once popular notion that it was not possible to sell coals to Newcastle, the centre of the UK coal industry, whereas it is. A world of static comparative advantage and free trade favours the rich and the strong. It also favours those with natural resources and high levels of productivity in major growth industries.

In a world of technological change, differential rates of growth in volume and productivity across industries and declining costs, the rational choice for a small country such as Country X is to select growth industries and to use public policy to supplement market forces in order to organize the resources necessary for entry and successful participation in the international marketplace. Country X needs to think in terms of acquiring or creating strength in promising sectors rather than simply attempting to exploit the short-run comparative advantage as efficiently as possible. The relevance of the labour productivity argument outlined above should now be apparent.

Following this line of reasoning we are led to the conclusion that Country X should specialize in industrial electronics, not commodity foods, regardless of whether their costs are lower or higher than those prevailing in its rich neighbouring countries. Following the dictates of the dynamic theory of comparative advantage Country X, or any other growing economy, has a considerable measure of freedom to create the comparative advantages it wishes, provided that it has the will and ingenuity to create or borrow the necessary mix of policies and institutions to achieve the cost and quality positions required for success.

The criterion used by the Japanese in selecting which industries to promote is often described as higher value added. However, as Scott (1985) suggests, their selection criteria appear to have been more subtle and less mechanical and above all appear to require sophisticated judgements about the future. In this respect MITI has relied on two basic criteria: an income elasticity criterion and a comparative technical progress criterion. The income elasticity criterion suggests that industries with comparatively high demand elasticities with respect to world real income should be developed as export industries. The comparative technical progress criterion attempts to ensure that technical progress in the future of the selected industry is guaranteed, even though this may mean relatively high investment costs (Shinohara, 1982, pp. 24–5).

Growth and productivity strategies

It is possible to identify five different public policy initiatives which governments use to promote growth and productivity in their countries (Figure 8.4). Macro economic policies can contribute to long-term economic growth in a variety of ways. One approach is to maintain an undervalued exchange rate, which makes exports cheaper on world markets and boosts profit margins, investment and productivity. Undervalued exchange rates were part of the success of Japan and Germany in the 1950s–1970s. Using tax policy to promote savings and investment is a well-known alternative way of increasing supply. Tax-free savings accounts are an example of promoting individual savings, and accelerated depreciation is a way of promoting both savings and investment by companies.

Familiar sectoral approaches to promoting productivity and growth include the development of infrastructure: airports, seaports and roads, the educational system and active promotion of R&D. Centralizing and modernizing the European air traffic control system is an improvement in the infrastructure demanded by airlines for many years but yet to be provided. Public policy can also promote mobility in capital markets, labour markets and product markets. A high capital gains tax retards the mobility of capital by exacting a high penalty from those who would move their capital from one successful investment in search of another. Sometimes countries promote capital mobility by taxing real gains, not nominal gains which may be artificially high owing to inflation. Financial guarantees, implicit or explicit, are a means of reducing risk, reducing cost and increasing the mobility of capital. In some countries there are administrative as well as market criteria for the allocation of credit. There may, therefore, be aspects of administrative credit rationing in the system which is part of a national development plan, the effect of which is to promote capital mobility on administrative terms.

Public policy is frequently and extensively used in European countries to promote labour mobility with regard to up-grading of skills and to better paid employment. Government-approved employment agencies and training programmes are familiar elements of

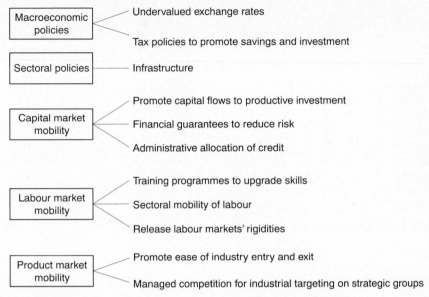

Figure 8.4 Public policy initiatives to promote growth and productivity

such policies. It may be argued, however, that within Europe in particular the very high unemployment payments have provided income security, which in turn has had the effect of reducing labour mobility.

The above policy matters have their principal effect outside the realm of marketing. Mobility in product markets can be assisted by promoting ease of entry and exit. Deregulation of airlines in the United States and Europe has brought new, low-price entries into the industry which in turn have provided a wider, better and cheaper service to customers. The same is beginning to happen in other industries, e.g. insurance, banking, telecommunications and road transport. The effect is to add new competitors and to change the nature of competition.

Public policy can contribute to or retard country competitiveness. In some countries there is very clear evidence of government interference in business which retards the growth of competitiveness. In other circumstances public policies on investment, trade and measures to improve labour productivity can make a country an attractive location for mobile international business. Such policies also assist indigenous business to develop and compete internationally.

Country competitiveness league tables appear from to time in the business press which rank countries on various criteria. The International Institute of Management Development in Switzerland uses 259 criteria to rank 46 industrialized countries on their competitiveness. The criteria include measures on the domestic economy, internationalization, government, finance, infrastructure, management, science and technology, and people. The rankings are intended to identify those countries which are best at creating competitive advantage and thereby provide conditions for business to be competitive internationally (Table 8.3).

Table 8.3 The world's 20 most competitive countries

Country	1997 rank	1998 rank	Country	1997 rank	1998 rank
United States	1	1	Ireland	15	11
Singapore	2	2	Britain	11	12
Hong Kong	3	3	New Zealand	13	13
Netherlands	6	4	Germany	14	14
Finland	4	5	Australia	18	15
Norway	5	6	Taiwan	23	16
Switzerland	7	7	Sweden	16	17
Denmark	8	8	Japan	9	18
Luxembourg	12	9	Iceland	21	19
Canada	10	10	Malaysia	17	20

Source: International Institute of Management Development, 1998.

Managed regional markets

Governments and integrated regional markets, such as the EU, sometimes encourage managed competition instead of promoting maximum competition. In a regime of managed competition, a firm might be encouraged to give up marginal products or product lines to concentrate on what it does best, while other domestic firms in the same industry would be encouraged to make similar concessions. The result is a narrower line for all firms, permitting a higher level of resource commitment behind each remaining product market. Managed competition requires the government or, in the case of a common market such as the EU, the EU Commission, to play a role in mediating decisions about who would give up what, and compliance would be monitored by the public body or an industry association. Restructuring policies in countries such as Japan are good examples of the industrial targeting of strategic sectors using managed competition as a guiding principle. Successful management of competitive forces brings to mind the relative success of countries such as France in telecommunications and rail transport, Brazil in aircraft and motor vehicles and Scotland and Ireland in electronics.

Successful intervention by governments does not depend on how refined plans are or how knowledgeable executives in the government-sponsored industrial development agencies are but rather on the broad strategy that is implemented. Public policy provides the framework within which business operates. It cannot pick winners.

Industrial policy, growth and welfare

According to Scott (1985) countries may be divided into two groups; those that emphasize productivity and growth and those which are concerned with the allocation of wealth by redistributing income through transfer payments. In the latter countries there has been a shift of responsibility away from the individual, the family and the firm and toward the government.

Over time an inordinate concern for income distribution appears to lead a country not only away from a concern for productivity but toward an increased dependency on the state to provide a living for a growing segment of the population. The typical roles and institutional responsibilities adopted by income redistributive and development-oriented countries have been specified by Scott (1985). A public policy based on income or wealth distribution emphasizes national economic security and entitlements in which the government takes responsibility for full employment among all members of society. Government policies focus on providing full employment and are complemented by unemployment compensation programmes, the liability for which is passed on to the tax payer. Such a policy emphasizes income redistribution and short-term consumer benefits. In contrast, a public policy based on industrial development emphasizes work, saving and investment job security in which the government takes responsibility for the stability and growth of the firm. Policies in such countries are complemented by programmes which support retirement and health care needs. Not all society members would benefit as by right under such policies. Performance in the economic arena would be the principal criterion for obtaining any benefits which arise. The costs of any support programmes are usually funded by the beneficiaries through their contributions. The impact of public policy on income distribution and savings in society is also important. A public policy based on income or wealth distribution emphasizes high minimum wages, transfer payments, taxes and borrowings. Savings policies are dominated by subsidized borrowing and situations where saving is actually penalized. The responsibility for income and savings policies rests with the government, and all members of society benefit. In contrast, a public policy based on development emphasizes a market clearing minimum wage, salary and profit sharing and corporate earnings. Savings policies are dominated by subsidized savings and restrictions on borrowings.

Over time these two extreme approaches to public policy produce very different results. Under a public policy based on income and wealth distribution savings will tend to be low, wages rigid, labour mobility low, greater dependence on the state and political priorities focused on due process. In contrast, under a public policy based on industrial development savings will be high, wages flexible, labour mobility high, responsibility for income levels retained by the family or firm and political priorities focused on performance.

Classifying country development strategies

The basic priorities of major national competitors may be compared by placing public policy as a vehicle for redistribution on one axis of a single diagram and public policy as an agency for development on the other. In this framework it would be possible for a country to have balanced priorities either in the upper left quadrant or in the lower right, or unbalanced strategies in the other two quadrants (Figure 8.5). Using this framework, Scott (1985, pp. 125–7) places the major western OECD countries in the lower left quadrant, indicating a low priority to the role of public policy in promoting industrial development and a high priority to a more direct role in income distribution. The reverse appears to be the case for Japan and other countries in the Far East.

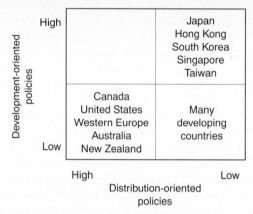

Figure 8.5 Classification of country development strategies
Source: adapted from Scott, B. R. and G. C. Lodge (eds) (1985) 'National strategies: key to international competition', in B. R. Scott *US Competitiveness in the World Economy*, Boston, MA: Harvard Business School Press.

There is evidence that this approach to industrial policy is rapidly changing in many western countries, especially in the EU. It still remains strong, however, in the United States and other developed countries such as Australia and Canada. Many developing countries are to be found in the low–low quadrant, a situation in which public policy regarding saving and investment is designed to create job security through an export competitive society.

In theory, the case for industrial targeting or a sector-selective industrial policy is simple and compelling. Industrial targeting has been successful on a sustained basis only when it has been a part of a productivity-oriented development strategy. Each country needs to turn its attention to comparing its strategy with those of its most successful competitors and to think comprehensively about reforms that are necessary to put its house in order. Excessive concern with the targeting issue is likely to lead policy makers to focus their attention on retaliating against other countries for unfair trade practices or to create a social welfare programme introduced as a courageous new way for public policy to help to build competitiveness. It should not require financial or technical wizardry to recognize that, in an increasingly interdependent world, the economy of each country cannot meet its various commitments unless there are significant changes in political priorities, i.e. a new emphasis on growth and productivity rather than on redistributing existing wealth.

Future of industrial and commercial policies

International competition in the preceding 30 years has been envisioned as competition among firms, with governments establishing the rules and enforcement processes. International competition was based on the concept of free markets, the invisible hand and a limited role for the state as the framework for domestic competition. This peculiarly Anglo-Saxon and American view of the world derived from Adam Smith has been challenged by a group of competitors that has found a positive role for the visible hand of government in creating comparative advantages and in promoting mobility of capital and labour in exploiting these advantages. Indeed, the whole thrust of the concept of dynamic comparative advantage is

> that the competitive challenge comes from well-managed companies based in countries characterized by developmentally oriented national strategies. How one views this challenge frequently tends to be influenced by whether one is positioned with the challengers or the challenged. (Scott, 1985, p. 138)

International competition is now influenced by national strategies as well as by the strategies of firms. A developmental strategy based on mobilizing the resources of a country to create comparative advantage in growth industries and industries in which technological change is rapid has been shown to yield higher growth over the medium term than simply accepting advantages as 'given'. The implications of this analysis for international competition according to Scott (1985, p. 140) are threefold:

1. the welfare states might realign their priorities and become much more competitive
2. the development-oriented countries might become increasingly security oriented, and somewhat less competitive, thereby progressing into the upper left quadrant (Figure 8.5), and
3. the welfare states might take the lead in restricting access to their markets, thereby reducing the competitive threat by restricting the roles of the most competitive players.

The evidence to date seems to suggest that countries emphasizing welfare considerations are developing competitive strategies and the development-oriented countries such as Japan are beginning to show signs of becoming more distribution conscious. Evidence on the third factor, as was seen in Chapter 5, points toward continuation of pressure to keep markets open, opening them further and avoiding a regression to closed economies. The only stable, mutually beneficial and supportive outcome would seem to require that the major competitors find broadly similar strategies in the upper left quadrant, the one area that is now almost empty. This would require that the leading developmental countries take on more distributional responsibilities as direct government functions and that the distributional countries make many changes to achieve more balanced strategies.

Policies for international competition in the EU

The pressures from each of the forms of competition described previously are moulded by the concerted strategies of such governments as Japan, Korea, Brazil and the United States, through its Department of Defense, to promote national industrial development and to enhance the competitive position of their firms. The Japanese government's systematic policies have helped to move the economy from labour-intensive manufacturing such as textiles to income-elastic products such as televisions, motor vehicles, computers and aircraft. Similar competitive pressures are present in countries such as Brazil, which has managed to penetrate the US steel and light aircraft industries. Clearly, therefore, comparative advantage is dynamic and can be created, and it is the belief in such creation that has encouraged many countries to play an active role in the development of local firms.

Increasingly battered by competition from the United States and Japan, European companies have been preoccupied with achieving the critical mass that will give them R&D strength, economies of scale and marketing strength to meet the challenge. The EU still does not, however, have the catalytic influence on industrial development that is exerted by the public authorities in the United States, Japan or the NICs. In these situations governments have the power to sponsor business development. The EU has only a fraction of the leverage over industrial R&D enjoyed by the government departments in the United States, especially the US Department of Defense. Also, the EU does not possess the scope for industrial targeting coupled with a systematic cooperation between all the economic actors needed to achieve such targeting, which is the hallmark of Japan's MITI. Cooperation with business seems to be the foundation of Japan's industrial strategy. Cooperation and sponsorship appear to be the key policy issues of the late 1980s and 1990s.

Underscoring the EU's role is the need to integrate policies on trade, industry, competition and R&D, at present pursued separately, into a welded single competitive strategy designed to improve the performance of European business. Progress on such matters often seems to be very slow. At the same time relocation of industry is a feature of company decisions and the debate is centred on whether it is better to locate in the centre of the EU or on the periphery. Costs, especially labour costs, seem to be the determining factor. Such relocation can cause industrial disruption and hardship.

The turbulent change in the environment implied by the completion of the internal market in the EU has brought with it very dramatic consequences for the unprepared. Because of the magnitude involved, the start of the new millenium must be viewed as a period of marketing discontinuity whereby it will be very difficult, if not impossible, to predict environmental change. Hence, it is likely that governments will continue to intervene in the system to support the growth and development of firms in their jurisdiction.

Summary

The international competitive environment has changed enormously over the past decades. Consequently, both government and firms have had to adapt their policies so as to ensure survival and growth through internationalization. National competitiveness is essential to enable the firm to stay ahead both technologically and commercially in important market segments.

Three competitive situations are evident in the world today: (1) newly industrialized countries which focus on low-cost labour, government promotion and standard mature technologies; (2) advanced industrial countries which rely on complex manufacturing processes to increase quality and reduce costs; (3) high-technology industries which concentrate on R&D in order to achieve advances in product performance. Essential to competitiveness in the firm in all three situations is a strong emphasis on manufacturing and marketing systems and on the ability to grasp the interaction between them.

It is not the marketing environment *per se* which is so important but, rather, the firm's ability to cope with it as it directly influences its strategic options. It is imperative to adopt an international orientation and multidimensional strategies.

Industrial and commercial policies are used to influence the allocation of resources in industrial sectors so as to achieve structural changes in capital, labour and product markets and to help domestic industries to respond to international challenges by addressing economic and political issues. Industrial policies may be applied at three levels: macro economic policy; sectoral policy; company-level policy.

This chapter describes how governments and public sector organizations apply both industrial and commercial policies to promote the well-being of enterprises. Similarities of behaviour between firms in relation to their growth orientation and incentives for saving and investment were discussed briefly. Different government policies were also examined, i.e. invisible hand versus heavy interventionist role of government. In the former approach governments play the role of benign regulators and observers; in the latter the government supplements market forces. Trends in comparative advantage were examined using a classification that ranks products traded by R&D intensity. Three trading regions were analysed: the EU, the United States and Japan. The analysis concluded that the three regions face key industrial development and corporate strategy decisions as their enterprises face the 1990s.

Three outcomes are likely for the future. Welfare states may realign their priorities and become more competitive. The development-oriented countries may become more security oriented and less competitive. The welfare states might take the lead in restricting access to their markets. Evidence to date supports these outcomes, e.g. the Japanese are showing signs of being more distribution conscious, while the Europeans are beginning to become more developmental in thinking and practice.

Comparative advantage is dynamic and can be created. Belief in such creation has encouraged many countries to play an active role in the development of local firms. The EU does not yet have a major influence on industrial development as is exerted by public authorities in the United States, Japan or the NICs.

Discussion questions

1. What is meant by international competitiveness? Distinguish between country-level competitiveness and company-level competitiveness.

2. The text describes industrial and commercial policies in international markets as falling into one of four categories. Describe and evaluate each approach and discuss the relevance of each to your country.

3. Industrial and commercial policies can provide the framework in which the firm in international markets operates. Public policies cannot be used to pick winners. Discuss.

4. Judging from the success of the Japanese economy and the recent take-off of the Tiger Economies there is much to recommend in a policy of industrial targeting. What would be your advice to policy makers in your own country?

5. An essential prerequisite for a firm attempting to succeed in international markets is that it should be market oriented and aware of competitors. If such a firm is located in a resource-oriented country, however, public policy is likely to take the form of the invisible hand strategy, with government providing little support to supplement market forces. Discuss.

6. In the chapter OECD statistics were used to compute the revealed comparative advantage of the EU, Japan and the United States. From these data each region was seen to face key industrial development and corporate strategic issues in the 1990s. Comment on these claims and say whether you accept the framework and analysis. If a similar framework were applied to data for your country what would the outcome be?

7. Now that the EU is beginning to formulate and implement industrial policies which affect the firm in international markets is there any value in individual EU countries pursuing their own individual country policies?

References

Bradley, M. F. (1985) 'Key factors influencing international competitiveness', *Journal of Irish Business and Administrative Research*, **7** (2), 3–14.

Bradley, M. F. (1987) 'Nature and significance of international marketing: a review', *Journal of Business Research*, **15**, 205–19.

Cohen, S., Teece, D. J., Tyson, L. and Zysman, J. (1984) 'Global competition: the new reality', *Working Paper of the President's Commission on Industrial Competitiveness*, Vol. 3.

Defraigne, P. (1984) 'Towards concerted industrial policies in the EC', in A. Jacquemin (ed.), *European Industry: Public policy and corporate strategy*, Oxford: Clarendon, pp. 368–77.

Enright, M. J. (1995) 'Creating national and regional strategies for competitive advantage', *The Island of Ireland Conference*, Irish Management Institute, Dublin, 13 December.

Porter, M. E. (1998) *The Competitive Advantage of Nations*, Basingstoke: Macmillan.

Samli, A. C. and Jacobs, L. (1995) 'Achieving congruence between macro and micro generic strategies: a framework to create international competitive advantage', *Journal of Macromarketing*, **19** (Fall), 23–32.

Scott, B. R. (1985) 'National strategies: key to international competition', in B. R. Scott and G. C. Lodge (eds), *US Competitiveness in the World Economy*, Boston, MA: Harvard Business School Press, pp. 71–143.

Shinohara, M. (1982) *Industrial Growth, Trade and Dynamic Patterns in the Japanese Economy*, Tokyo: University of Tokyo Press.

PART III

How the firm enters international markets

9

International markets and customers

This chapter describes the various factors the firm must consider when selecting international markets to enter for the first time. A process approach is adopted in the context of trial and error to assist in making decisions at various stages in that process. Two approaches are discussed: the opportunistic approach and the systematic approach. It is also shown how some firms start in the opportunistic mode and gradually shift to a more systematic approach. Five major influences or constraints on the market selection process are examined and an integrated view of the entire process is provided.

International market selection process

Success in selecting international markets influences not only the firm's growth potential but in many instances its ability to survive. The aim of the company must be to become part of each customer's buying process. This is especially difficult in international markets. Understanding the process is only the first step. Each customer must be treated as an individual. Increasingly, successful companies have discovered that technology enables customization of products and delivery systems. These are tasks which are difficult enough to do in stable domestic markets but in markets characterized by large discontinuities and rapid environmental changes, as found in international marketing, they are particularly difficult. Any attempt to understand customers and markets must take place in the context of rapid change which is often unpredictable.

Importance of international market selection

The wrong choice of market is a frequent source of two types of cost: the actual cost of unsuccessfully attempting to enter the wrong market and the associated opportunity costs, i.e. the missed opportunity of entering markets where the product might have been successful. Choosing the right markets and the right sequence of entry is an integral part of competitive strategy. Many foreign firms now compete in terms of operating a balanced portfolio of markets, grouping markets according to their similarity, having a deliberate policy of concentrating or diversifying marketing efforts and sequencing market entry to ensure optimum international competitive advantage. In designing the portfolio of markets a multicriteria approach to screening, identifying and selecting potential international markets may be necessary (Kumar *et al.*, 1994).

A careful approach to international market selection is essential because of the vast diversity that exists in international markets. Within a given country, it may be assumed that a reasonable degree of intersegment cohesiveness exists. At the international level, however, there are enormous differences in income, culture and politics. Discovering meaningful similarities between markets can help to standardize strategies, to reduce costs and to allow maximum advantage from common experience. It is not easy to do, however.

Approaching international market selection in an intuitive rather than a methodical manner can cause many problems of coordination owing to country differences. The decision to internationalize is a major commitment to enter a new field of business and should clearly be taken in a systematic way (Tookey, 1975). This involves the acquisition of information, its analysis and the generation of alternative courses of action.

It is important that the firm consciously selects international markets as opposed to reacting to short-term opportunities (Attiyeh and Wenner, 1981). These authors identify hidden cost 'traps' in the opportunistic approach: providing excessive production capacity for opportunistic business; agreeing initial design and engineering costs to obtain the first order; the additional costs stemming from low initial production efficiency, and repeat orders which do not materialize; the cost of unsuccessful bidding for opportunistic business and the dissipation of the company's efforts that may result from constantly pursuing opportunistic business abroad. For these reasons it is generally advisable to avoid such an opportunistic approach to the selection of international markets.

Competitive characteristics of the market

The kind of market in which the firm operates is an important determinant of success. When entering new international markets for the first time it is essential that firms take care in making their choice; economists have developed a useful way of classifying markets which may serve as a starting point in their investigations. Markets are purely competitive when there is a very large number of competing suppliers of undifferentiated products in markets with no entry barriers where information flows are very rapid and accurate. Examples of purely competitive markets include commodity trading and the financial markets.

Sometimes firms operate in monopolistic markets. In such markets there are many suppliers of slightly different products facing few entry barriers where information flows are imperfect. Examples of monopolistic markets include machine tool manufacturing and unbranded clothing companies. Companies which have successfully branded their products and services or which have otherwise differentiated themselves from the competition in the eyes of customers operate in oligopolistic markets, where there are usually suppliers of significantly different products facing some entry barriers and imperfect information flows. Examples of oligopolistic markets include detergents, fuel and oil, tobacco and, increasingly, other packaged consumer products.

Finally, some firms operate in monopoly markets where there is only one supplier of a totally differentiated product in a market with very high entry barriers and perfect information flows. An example of a monopoly market would be a utility, e.g. gas or electricity. Sometimes products classified as 'non-traded' have a certain amount of monopoly protection within a market. It is significant, however, that all markets experience competition; the issue is to determine the source and strength of the competition. With the removal of protection, deregulation of industries and opening of markets, few firms can rely on monopoly protection.

Mechanics of international market selection

In the absence of an incentive to internationalize, it is unlikely that the company will respond favourably to foreign market opportunities, and without a strong incentive it is unlikely that a conscious decision will be made to expand internationally. The market selection decision can, therefore, be traced back to the incentive to internationalize. Six major incentives to internationalize may be identified (Table 9.1).

The incentive to internationalize is not enough in itself, however; it must be coupled with an awareness of specific market opportunities. This awareness may arise in two ways (Figure 9.1). The first situation arises where certain stimuli bring a foreign market opportunity to the attention of the firm and it responds by entering the market; it may be said to choose its market opportunistically. The search and market identification are random or casual. The second situation arises when awareness of specific market opportunities results from a systematic comparison of prospective markets and the firm expands by entering the market; this approach to market selection would be termed 'systematic'. Frequently companies start with an opportunistic approach which on refinement and testing evolves into a systematic approach.

Opportunistic selection of international markets

If a firm is expanding internationally on an opportunistic basis, certain stimuli are required to bring market opportunities to its attention. The receipt of an unsolicited order or enquiry for product, price or distribution information from a potential customer may result from advertising in trade journals, by observation of competitors' activities in a particular market and through information obtained from magazines, newspapers, TV or

---

Table 9.1 Incentives to internationalize

- Compensate for lack of growth in saturated domestic market
- Reduce dependence on domestic market, especially if it is in decline
- Use excess capacity and/or spread overheads over greater volume
- Dispose of products no longer attractive on the domestic market
- Exploit unique competence in the firm
- Match domestic competitors entering foreign markets

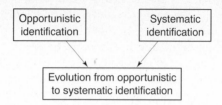

Figure 9.1 Identification of international market opportunities

radio. Sometimes governments supply information on export opportunities. In such circumstances this function would be mainly performed by a government-sponsored export promotions board.

The firm's response to an international market opportunity will be governed by a number of factors. The degree to which the company is affected by foreign country legislation, tariff and non-tariff barriers (NTBs), health regulations or industrial standards is likely to influence its reaction. These barriers are beginning to fall, however, under pressure from the WTO. The extent to which a company is sensitive to competitive pressure may influence its reaction to foreign market opportunities that come to its attention. Because of fear of foreign competition many firms may ignore promising opportunities and take a 'walled city' approach, concentrating on home markets or culturally close markets with a defensive intent (Ayal and Zif, 1979). An example here would be Norwegian companies exporting predominantly to Sweden and Finland or US companies concentrating on the US market or perhaps also selling to Canada or Mexico, depending on location.

The value to the company of adequate distribution in a foreign market may also influence its reaction to market opportunities. A company may be required to adapt its product to different tastes in each foreign market. In this regard it is quite possible that the company will react more favourably to market opportunities which need a minimal degree of product adaptation (Jaffe, 1974). Alternatively they may show a tendency to enter markets which are as similar as possible to those with which they are already familiar (Carlson, 1975). Finally, the reaction to a market opportunity which has arisen may be influenced by the business distance phenomenon examined at length in Chapter 6. Recall that the concept of 'psychic distance' comprises all those factors which weaken internationalization incentives. These factors may be seen as an amalgam of the physical distance, language and cultural differences between any two countries (Vahlne and Wiedersheim-Paul, 1977; Hallen and Wiedersheim-Paul, 1982). The concept of 'geocultural distance' is quite similar and is defined as 'barriers created by geographical separation, cultural disparities between countries, and problems of communication resulting from differences in social perspectives, attitudes and language' (Goodnow and Hansz, 1972). According to these two concepts, a company should react more favourably to opportunities with a shorter psychic or geocultural distance from the home market.

Systematic selection of international markets

Instead of merely responding to foreign market opportunities as they arise, the company may adopt a logical procedure for market selection (Figure 9.2). In principle, this is

concerned with establishing criteria for selection, researching markets potential, classifying them according to the agreed criteria and selecting those which should be addressed
first and those suitable for later development (Tookey, 1975).

We first examine what happens at Stage 1, during which preliminary screening of the
market is carried out. According to Root (1982) the purpose of preliminary screening is to
identify country markets whose size warrant further investigation. Root believes that
preliminary screening tries to minimize two errors: that of ignoring countries that offer
good prospects for the firm's product type and that of spending too much time investigating countries that are poor prospects. Preliminary screening thus requires a 'quick fix'
on the market potential facing the candidate product in many countries. The criteria used
in preliminary screening would, therefore, tend to be quite broad in their nature and
include quantitative economic and social statistics, which should be readily available for
most countries and be comparable across countries. These economic and social statistics
cover areas such as GNP, GNP growth, income per capita, private consumption and
population in each foreign market. These data are sometimes provided for regions and
areas within countries, which is very useful.

The criteria that should be applied to preliminary screening may be found under three
major headings (Figure 9.3). First, physical and geographical features, including the
physical distance of each market from the home country and the climate in each market,
are taken into account. Quantitative economic and social statistics, including GNP,

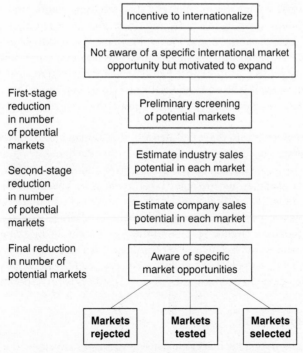

Figure 9.2 Systematic approach to international market selection

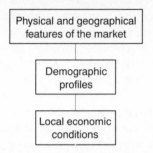

Figure 9.3 Preliminary screening of international markets
Source: based on Deschampsneufs, H. (1967), *Marketing Overseas*, Oxford: Pergamon.

income per capita, private consumption and similar measures, would be used. Second, population statistics including total population figures, geographical concentration and distribution by age group, the number of people of different sexes and level of literacy may be used to indicate the quality, concentration, current responsiveness of the market and its future growth potential. Third, local economic conditions must be considered. A large population may represent little potential if income per capita is extremely low. Aside from income per capita, Deschampsneufs (1967) suggests other measures of the wealth and purchasing power of potential foreign markets. These measures may be obtained in many ways, such as by finding out the number of cars owned per family and the number of homes with telephones, washing machines and other consumer durables.

Also related to local economic conditions is the financial economy of a country and the consequent adverse movements in exchange rates. This may be an overriding factor when considering its possibilities as an export market since if the country cannot pay for its imports then business cannot be done under normal circumstances. Other modes of entry such as foreign direct investment, licensing or countertrade may have to be considered if entry is desirable.

Exchange rate fluctuations have influenced the demand for consumer goods in international markets in important ways. With the declining yen, many Japanese consumers who used to visit Hong Kong, Bangkok and Singapore to buy imported European branded products and designer label items more cheaply than they could at home are leaving on holiday with less money to spend. Other consumer product markets also suffer in a downturn in the economy. The alcoholic beverage industry is particularly susceptible to an economic decline because of the way that the alcoholic beverage market works. When demand grows by 20 per cent, shipments from distillers increase by 30 per cent because new bars are opened which have to be stocked (*The Economist*, 6 December 1997, p. 68). When demand declines, the effect on distillers is correspondingly worse.

Industry market potential

The next stage of the systematic market selection process is to examine the total potential for the product category in each promising market. This may be defined as the 'industry market potential' and involves an examination of the most probable total sales of a product by all sellers in a designated country over a strategic planning period (Root, 1982). The markets with the most promising industry market potential should be examined to see whether the firm could gain a share of that potential in each case. This fine distinction is important, as it is clearly a waste of time and money for the firm to investigate how it will gain access to a market if there is no market for its product category in the first instance.

There are several criteria by which the industry market potential may be examined: imports of the product category; apparent consumption (local production added to imports less exports); actual sales figures. In forecasting sales the firm must also take account of social habits, local tastes and preferences and consumer trends in the market. Because of a possible historical bias, it is important when using sales or apparent consumption data that managers estimate their likely values in the future or make the necessary adjustments for foreseeable changes in the quantities (Root, 1982). Two approaches may be used here: the so-called naive model which involves a simple projection of historical sales data into the future; or a causal model. The latter involves the construction of product sales forecasts for each prospective market on the basis of certain variables which have a known relationship with product sales.

Social habits play an equally important part in determining the total sales potential of a product in each market. For example, in Italy the potential for DIY car maintenance products tends to be limited because the idea of asking a garage to care for the family car is firmly entrenched in the Italian mind. However, one should realize that such local tastes and preferences may be either short or long term because markets change continually.

Another aspect of examining industry market potential is the study of consumer trends. For example, in many countries the leisure market is a growing one and anything which is designed to increase the profitable use of leisure time may have worthwhile potential.

Consumer habits are, of course, becoming rapidly more international and individual markets tend to show fewer national differences, except in so far as there is a gulf between those markets where industry is sufficiently far advanced to create a demand for particular raw materials and industrial equipment and those where it is not. With regard to consumer markets it has been argued that a significant degree of convergence has occurred in tastes and preferences in the EU, but strategies formed on the basis of homogeneous markets in Europe may yet be a little premature.

Having identified countries with greatest total sales potential for the product category, the firm is then in a position to consider its own ability to gain a share of that potential in each case.

Company sales potential

During the third stage it is necessary to estimate the firm's sales potential. 'Company sales potential' is defined as the most probable sales that the firm's product in a designated country can attain over a strategic planning period. Company sales potential may also be viewed as its most probable share of a country's industry market potential (Root, 1982). When investigating this, the company examines a number of factors. Local import legislation, which may take several forms such as prohibition on importing certain products, the imposition of high tariffs or legislation affecting the composition of a product, is among the more important.

Competition in prospective markets is also a major concern. First, the firm must examine its own product in relation to those of its competitors in each market and decide whether it offers any real advantage. It is of little use trying to sell in a foreign market if the firm cannot offer the consumer something which has some edge on the competition. Approaches to analysing competitors are discussed in Chapter 10.

Distribution channel structure in each market also influences the company's sales potential. Here the company should concentrate on its ability to obtain adequate distribution in each foreign market and the degree to which it can match the distribution of the market leaders. The terms of distribution are also important, since it may be possible to improve them. If this is so, considerable success may be achieved.

Although it may have been considered initially in preliminary screening, the physical distance of each high industry market potential country from the home country may again be evaluated, albeit in greater detail. Here the firm may attempt to calculate transportation and other logistical costs to move the product from the home country to each of the foreign countries in question.

Language and cultural differences between the home country and each of the foreign markets may also be considered at this stage. For example, it may not be feasible for a telecommunications systems manufacturer to enter a small foreign market if all technical literature has to be translated specifically for that market, although in many such instances English is increasingly accepted. Cultural differences have great implications for the consumer products manufacturer.

At this stage of the process, the firm should be able to estimate its sales potential with some accuracy in a number of the most promising foreign markets. It should then be possible to place the most favoured markets in order of priority. The next set of questions is how many of these markets should be addressed, how to enter them and whether to do so simultaneously or in sequence.

Role of information sources

Systematic market selection is essentially an evaluative process. It is now appropriate to consider the information sources which may be used in applying these criteria. The principal information sources available may be found under six headings (Table 9.2).

The use of management knowledge and experience accumulated within the firm is very much dependent on the product category and on the individuals involved in the market selection process, but it can be important if the product category is specialized. Greater emphasis may be placed on management knowledge and experience in market evaluations where there is a lack of information from other sources. This emphasis, however, is influenced by the amount of experience and knowledge actually possessed by company managers, the length of time they have worked in the product area, their education and training, and degree of international exposure. Some firms maintain extensive internal company databases relevant to key export markets; these may be found in firms which have previously carried out investigations into prospective new markets or where they

Table 9.2 Information sources used in international market selection

Internal
- Knowledge and experience within the firm
- Company data

External
- Published reference materials
- Trade journals, magazines, newspapers
- Government or industry advisers and support services
- Trade associations, business clubs, consultants, market research agencies and market intelligence

have established an internal international market information system for the product category. The existence of such data tends to vary greatly. Many firms have access to commercially available computer-maintained databases which may be used as required.

Externally published reference publications on foreign markets are also available. The sources of information, such as status reports and trade intelligence, include central and commercial banks, chambers of commerce, embassies and consulates, trade associations and research institutes. It would be expected that although externally published reference sources would play a role in preliminary screening and in the estimation of industry market potential, they would be of less importance in the firm's estimation of its own potential in each market.

It is quite possible that valuable articles aiding systematic market selection may appear in trade journals, magazines or newspapers, but such articles are likely to play a greater role in the opportunistic identification of export markets. In recent years, however, the business pages of well-known business and financial journals publish in-depth market and industry analyses and profiles and provide information on country markets which may be used successfully by the exporting firm.

Services provided by government- and industry-sponsored promotion agencies which are related to systematic market selection may be grouped under two headings: advice and facilities; support services. Under the first heading the agency may provide a firm with information and advice on many aspects of foreign markets, such as market size, patterns of demand, costs and prices, local standards, servicing requirements, purchasing and distribution methods, competition from domestic and other imported products and choice of representatives.

Under the second heading the firm would be provided with market reports and surveys, profiles of foreign countries and other library facilities. Such support services would, therefore, have more in common with externally published reference sources than with direct contact with advisers.

Once management has satisfied itself that a relatively attractive demand exists for the company's products, that the firm can cope with the competitive conditions in the market and that the marketing costs are manageable, the next step is an on-the-spot survey. Various approaches for on-site market surveys have been used (Table 9.3).

Table 9.3 Research in international markets: approach to market surveys

- Measuring responses to exhibitions at local trade fairs, professional meetings and world trade centres
- Sampling of customer response by questioning (mailed, telephoned, or face to face)
- Pre-testing the market via free samples
- Consulting local anthropologists and sociologists familiar with the area

---

Evolution from opportunistic to systematic market selection

In some situations market awareness initially involves an opportunistic approach to market selection. Rather than solely evaluating the specific market opportunity, however, the firm compares the opportunity to other markets not already entered. This comparison may resemble the systematic selection procedure already discussed (Figure 9.2). By following this approach the company which starts with an opportunistic approach may discover that it eventually evolves into a systematic evaluation procedure.

Influences on selection of markets

A number of influences may affect the market selection process; they can hinder but they can also facilitate, stimulate and expand the process. Influences on the market selection decision may be discussed under five headings.

Company size and market selection

Because of a greater resource base, it is possible that a larger company may prefer to use more comprehensive market selection procedures than its smaller counterpart. The possible interconnection between firm size and quality of management may also result in the 'higher-quality' management of larger companies showing a greater tendency to engage in systematic market selection (Bilkey, 1978). There is no evidence that 'higher-quality' management is the prerogative of all large firms. Indeed, many smaller high-technology firms possess excellent managers with relevant international experience. It is necessary that the smaller firm develops a framework that allows specific and relevant questions to be asked, i.e. questions which are not too generic or simplistic (Papadopoulos, 1987, p. 155).

Influence of export sales

A company which exports a greater proportion of annual sales tends to be more dependent on international markets as a source of profitability and stability. Such a company may exercise greater care in market selection, as opposed to a company which exports a smaller proportion of total sales.

Companies which only export, say, 5 per cent of total sales are unlikely to give much attention to the method of selection of markets unless they see a strategic opportunity in their development.

Corporate goals and market selection

Many, if not most, influences on organizational decisions that define acceptable activities are associated with an organizational goal (Table 9.4). Corporate goals for exporting may cover non-maximizing behaviour and non-profit aims as seen in early literature on the subject (Tookey, 1964; Hunt *et al.*, 1967). These goals include the disposal of surplus production as opposed to profit objectives. Where these non-maximizing goals exist it is unlikely that the firm would use a systematic export market selection procedure with a view to identifying optimal opportunities.

In the more recent literature, however, more emphasis is placed on growth in turnover and profitability as goals for international sales. In a survey of UK firms, Piercy (1980) found that the vast majority of companies pursued the same goals in the domestic and export markets, where domestic business involves the pursuit of profits and exporting the pursuit of volume. Other goals discussed in the literature include the following: desire for sales stability with growth (Wiedersheim-Paul *et al.*, 1978); growth in profit from export sales; percentage profit on export sales, i.e. profit from sales in each market after deducting all costs; growth in export sales turnover; growth in share of each export market. The importance the firm places on the achievement of certain goals may also influence the market selection process. For example, Japanese strategic behaviour in the United States and many world markets suggests the following three goals (Kotler *et al.*, 1985):

1. Build market share over a long time period.
2. Disregard profits as market share is being obtained.
3. When a significant market position is established challenge US and other foreign competitors head-on in their principal product markets.

The aim is to build market position and then to worry about profitability. This will lead to quite different criteria for evaluating international markets, compared with those employed by US and European firms which focus on maintaining profitability levels or other goals where short-term financial returns dominate.

Table 9.4 Influence of company goals on international market selection

Corporate goals for international markets include the following:
- non-maximizing behaviour and non-profit aims, e.g. disposal of surplus production
- desire for sales stability with growth
- growth in profit from international sales
- percentage profit on international sales
- growth in international sales turnover
- growth in share in each international market

Influence of company strategy

Three possible strategic influences on market selection should be considered: market concentration, market segmentation and the timing and sequencing of entry to different markets.

The strategy of market concentration is examined first. A company may have a deliberate policy of concentrating its sales efforts on certain key markets. Such a strategy will provide an important guiding influence on both the systematic and the opportunistic approach towards market selection. A company which selects markets on an opportunistic basis may decide to concentrate on a limited number of the market opportunities which have come to its attention. In the process of deciding whether or not to pursue a market opportunity, a concentration strategy would lead the company to consider carefully its ability to obtain a minimum penetration level in the market in question.

With regard to concentration strategy and the systematic selection process, the degree to which each market facilitates a concentrated selling effort by the firm is emphasized throughout the selection procedure. Hence, they may place more emphasis on evaluating marketing costs, competition, distribution channel availability and 'depth' of prospective markets. From the point of view of market concentration, for example, many Belgian companies find France a more attractive proposition than Far Eastern countries.

In general, a policy of market concentration would tend to result in a more critical evaluation of prospective markets, while dissipation of effort may lead to less background research prior to market entry.

Value of market information

The systematic, and to some extent the opportunistic, approach towards market selection is dependent on the availability of sufficient information on international markets. The information required for evaluating foreign markets may be classified as country- or market-level or company- or product-level information. Country-level information consists of broad cross-comparable statistics, as would be used in preliminary screening or some stages of estimating industry market potential. Product specific information, on the other hand, is concerned with a detailed profile of individual markets and would be required in estimating company sales potential or in deciding whether or not to pursue an export opportunity which has come to the attention of the company.

With regard to country or market information, the services of international organizations, e.g. UN, WTO, OECD, EU, coupled with computerization and the information explosion, make it possible to collect reasonably comparable data where none existed before. By using UN publications, OECD Economic Reports, the Reports of the WTO, Eurostat, and the publications and other databases provided by commercial organizations, the firm should be able to obtain a comparable view of countries at the country or market level.

Unfortunately, the collection of company- or product-specific information is far more difficult. Apart from selective reports from organizations such as EIU, Predicast or Mintel, and Dialog, international reports on specific industries may be non-existent. As stated by

Papadopoulos (1983), however, there is a surprising amount of secondary data which provide product-specific information. This ranges from the purchase or consumption patterns of larger purchase items, e.g. cars, TVs or white goods, usually available through national statistical bureaux, to information on industrial or consumer small purchase items, e.g. soft drinks and detergents, which can be purchased from private research agencies. Hence, by examining the market for similar products, the company may estimate sales potential for its own category.

As information on prospective markets is required in more detail, it may be necessary to secure primary data on the product category. Therefore, executives of the firm may research overseas markets under consideration themselves, or they may commission the services of a market research agency. Information on prices, especially for consumer goods, is often relatively easy to obtain. It is also necessary to have information on a host of other factors such as trade margins, taxes and tariffs, marketing and distribution costs and other hidden costs which often arise when entering foreign markets.

Segmenting international markets

Strategic approaches to grouping international markets raise a different set of problems. Arranging things in classes according to some system allows the firm to generalize about problems rather than to face the endless or impossible task of dealing with each one on an individual basis (Liander *et al.*, 1967). An appropriate system of classifying or grouping markets can therefore be an important element in clarifying a firm's understanding of its international operations.

The grouping principle may also direct the selection of markets. Prior to a discussion of the possible relationship between market groups and market selection, it is necessary to consider the various techniques for classifying or grouping countries.

There are three reasons why it is important to identify appropriate macro variables to segment international markets:

- international markets vary from each other with regard to the degree of sophistication required,
- separating countries into different categories allows the firm to customize its marketing strategies and
- a consistent umbrella strategy or positioning can be used across a number of markets.

To the experienced manager market segments are easily identified using criteria common in the industry. Ways of identifying market segments tend to be based on buyer demographic and socioeconomic criteria, the size of the purchase, the motivation for the purchase and the manner of the purchase. This last is particularly relevant in industrial markets where tendering and other forms of doing business different from buying at list price are common. Some of these approaches may not be relevant to the circumstances facing the company in international markets and a number of them may not be practical.

Many companies question the relevance of the approaches just described and are prepared to challenge the traditional wisdom thereby expressed. Other ways of segmenting markets reflecting life cycles, family cycles and innovation cycles may be more appropriate. The company attempts to find approaches to segmentation which have a strong management orientation and are thus focused on management problems. The universal appeal of an innovative product adaptation can overcome some of these difficulties especially when a customized approach to positioning the product in the minds of consumers is followed (Exhibit 9.1).

━━━━━ Exhibit 9.1 ━━━━━
Market segmentation: same product different positioning in international markets

In the early eighties Pierre Marchand, director of the French publishing company, Gallimard Publishers, thought of compiling a new kind of encyclopedia. Traditional encyclopaedia are usually targeted at highly educated people who have been taught the need for learning by themselves. Marchand wanted to reinvent the concept of encyclopedia, making it a 'living book' not just something that you buy out of pure social obligation and that you put on the shelves for ever. He developed the idea of little pocket-sized (18 ×12 cm) paperback fact books which would treat a wide array of subjects such as history, literature, arts, music, and technology. The first titles included 'In search of lost Egypt', 'Lives and deaths of the whales', 'The Space Saga', 'Picasso: sane and the foolish'.

   First targeted at children, the books rapidly were seen to appeal to the general public. In January 1994, 194 titles had been published in France and the collection was classified into 16 series at six price levels ranging from 46FF to 38FF. The collection was very successful in France and was exported to other countries on a co-publishing basis in every country with Gallimard partners. In each country the collection was renamed:

   1989: 'Aguilar Universale' in Spain
   1990: 'Knowledge and Wisdom' in Japan, 'Standaard Ontdekkingen' in
          Belgium, 'Anakalipsis Delithanassis' in Greece, 'Pharos' in the Netherlands,
          'Horizont' in Norway.
   1991: 'Kréta konivek' in Hungary, 'Découvertes' in Portugal, 'Universale' in Italy.
   1992: 'New Horizons' in the United Kingdom, 'Discoveries' in the United States.
   1993: 'Découvertes' in Denmark.

This concept appeared to appeal to a wide range of people, and thus avoided a close segmentation of the market. The market positioning varied by country. In France the positioning strategy – 'On n'a jamais vu autant de choses entre la première et la dernière page d'un livre.' – stresses the amount of information provided by different sources in each book. In Italy – 'la prima biblioteca tascabile illustrata' – the emphasis is put on the pocket-sized aspect and the power of the illustrations. In the U.K. – the series for the 21st century – available now – stress as the newness and the innovativeness of the concept presenting it as a breakthrough. A medium priced strategy was also adapted to each country: a range of six prices in France from 43F to 86F but usually a single price in the other countries: £6.95 in England, L18,000 in Italy. Each book was translated and published with identical texts and illustrations from the French version. The cover and the testimonials were adapted depending on the culture, the history and traditions of each country.

Source: adapted from Catalog *New Horizons from Thames and Hudson, Découvertes Gallimard, Universale Electrea/Gallimard*; Featherstone, M. (1991) *Consumer culture and postmodernism*, London: Sage. Cova, B. and Svanfeldt, C. (1993) 'Societal innovations and the postmodern aestheticization of everyday life', *International Journal of Research in Marketing*, **10**, 297–310.

Market segmentation means dividing the market into customer groups who might merit separate marketing mixes reflecting different product benefits. Segmentation is based on identifying buyer characteristics which are related in some deterministic fashion to the likelihood that the company's products, services or ideas will be purchased. Usually market segments refer to contiguous but separate groups. Examples include purchasers of beer versus spirits and original purchasers of electronic components versus replacement purchasers. All are in the market for alcoholic beverages or electronic components but will buy different product benefits for different reasons. Decisions regarding three factors assist in the segmentation process: those which relate to the technology embodied in the product, the customer segment served and the function performed (Figure 9.4).

Market segmentation is the strategic marketing process of 'dividing a potential market into distinct sub-sets of consumers and selecting one or more segments as a market target to be reached with a distinct marketing mix' (Schiffman and Kanuk, 1978). International markets are typified by groups of buyers who require different products and services and respond in different ways to marketing efforts on the part of the company.

Consumer market segmentation

There are many techniques which may be used in segmenting consumer markets. Most depend on understanding underlying needs and wants and quantifying the responses of

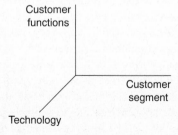

Figure 9.4 Marketing performed in three dimensions

different customer groups regarding the way in which desired benefits are related to price sensitivity. The methods used are usually based on one or a combination of demographic, socioeconomic and family characteristics, behavioural and psychographic factors, and benefit associated with the product or service.

Demographic features may be used to segment markets. For some products in most societies consumption is positively related to age: older customers tend to buy more than younger people; men and women buy different products and have different needs; the family life cycle may also be relevant to the purchase of consumer durables. This, of course, may vary by country. In such circumstances companies may attempt to segment markets by age groups, by income, ethnic origin and lifestyle. Similarly, older people may be divided into age groups.

Socioeconomic variables are frequently used in market segmentation. Occupational and income factors are mostly used to determine a person's social class. Social class and income have been used extensively as segmentation variable as they are thought to influence consumer behaviour. How appropriate the use of such factors is in many different markets is an issue to be faced by management.

Lifestyle segmentation methods classify people into different groups characterized by their opinions, activities and interests. It begins with people, their lifestyles and motivations, and then determines how various marketing factors fit into their living (Plummer, 1974, p. 37). Lifestyle has been used as the suggested basis for segmentation in a number of studies. One such approach identifies three groups which are presumed to be homogeneous across different European markets (Martin, 1988, p. 57; Kossof, 1988, pp. 43–4):

Group 1:   young people with homogeneous tastes in music, sport and culture.
Group 2:   socialites and trend setters who value independence, are wealthy, well educated, value exclusivity and reject stereotyping.
Group 3:   business people who travel abroad regularly, have a taste for luxury, are rich and almost entirely male.

Psychographic segmentation is performed by dividing the market into sections according to lifestyles or personality factors.

In previous chapters product benefits were emphasized, not the product itself. People buy products for their perceived benefits. Different product attributes provide different customer benefits. The benefits demanded by customers vary by country, by culture and by market segment. Companies attempt to provide differentiated products and services for different market segments, each with its own distinctive or unique customer benefit.

The objectives of market segmentation may also be to compete with substitute products available in the market. Segmenting the market for competitive substitutability is a strategy frequently used by large companies with resources to develop numerous brands aimed at different market segments. The R & Bailey and Company Ltd launched 'Baileys Light' for the weight-conscious US market and 'Baileys Gold', based on 12 year old whiskey and exclusive packaging, for the Japanese market to complement their world brand leader in the category 'Baileys Original Irish Cream Liqueur'. In a similar fashion Bacardi launched five specific brands of rum each aimed at a different segment of the market for alcoholic spirits:

- 'Silver Rum' to compete with vodka and gin;
- 'Amber Rum' to compete with American Whiskey;
- 'Gold Reserve' to compete with brandies;
- '983' to compete with Scotch whisky;
- '151 Proof Rum' to compete in the mixed drinks and cooking segments.

China is a market which has changed dramatically in the previous decade. Up to the mid-1980s, there were very few products and brands in China and consumers had to take what was produced and not what they wanted. Today, however, Chinese consumers have a vast array of choices, so producers must attempt to satisfy them. China's potential consumer market is enormous, but it is not as rich as some imagine and it is difficult to reach (Exhibit 9.2). To understand the modern Chinese consumer requires market segmentation. Using data collected and reports written by Gallup China and Coopers and Lybrand, Schmitt (1997) suggests that it may be possible to segment the Chinese market using traditional geographic and demographic characteristics. With regard to geographic segmentation, Schmitt (1997, p. 192) reports differences between urban and rural consumers and uses age, sex, income, education and occupation as demographic variables to segment the market. A summary of his findings shows that geographic and demographic variables may be used to segment customers within a large market like China:

Geographic segmentation:

- urban consumers are more likely to study advertisements before buying a consumer durable;
- they would pay higher prices for high quality products;
- they would buy a leading brand regardless of price;
- brand name recognition of foreign brands is higher among urban dwellers;
- they spend a higher percentage of income on food (37 per cent : 33 per cent);
- subsegments in urban, but especially in rural, areas are important, but little is known about them.

Demographic segmentation:
Age and sex:

- women in the 30–45 year age group appreciate value and convenience;
- men in the same group are utility shoppers, buying what they need or are asked to buy;
- younger people buy 'aspirational' products and are interested in ownership and leisure;
- young women are least concerned about price – they spend all their spare income on cosmetics and fashion.

Income, education and occupation:

- more affluent and better educated people are more likely to try new products;
- this group is also more likely to try products admired by others – a desire to conform to the norms of the reference group;
- entrepreneurs and people working in the private sector are more likely to try new products.

━━━━━ Exhibit 9.2 ━━━━━
How not to sell 1.2 billion tubes of toothpaste

China's potential consumer market is enormous, but it is not as rich as some imagine – and it is devilishly difficult to reach. Peter Perkins, regional manager of the research firm, DRI/McGraw Hill, breaks down China's consumer market into three main areas:

- Imported luxury goods, such as high-price spirits, designer watches and certain cosmetics, could find a market of 5 million people. This would represent the richest one per cent of those living in urban areas, but only the top 0.2 per cent of those in the countryside.
- Imported 'middle-class' products, such as jeans and cheap training shoes, could sell to around 20 million people: the top 2.5 per cent in cities and the top one per cent in rural areas.
- Locally made 'middle-class' goods, such as cheap electrical appliances, would have a potential market of 65 million people: the top 10 per cent in urban areas and the top 4 per cent in rural areas. This would also include most 'fast-moving consumer goods' (FMCGs), such as detergents and packaged foods.

The variety of China's consumers has already affected both branding and distribution. If any FMCG companies ever thought that the western brands would sweep all before them, they have abandoned that illusion. Instead, they are adapting to the reality of a segmented market. Both of the western soap kings, Procter & Gamble and Unilever, have entered the market through joint ventures with local companies. They are using local detergent brands, such as Lonkey and Panda, to build up their position, and are gradually adding international brands, such as Unilever's Omo and P&G's Ariel, for the premium end of the market.

In toothpaste, Unilever has a stake in two important local brands (Zhongua and Maxam) through a joint venture with the Shanghai Toothpaste Factory. Alexander Kemner, Unilever's board director for Asia-Pacific, says the company will introduce better packaging and greater manufacturing efficiency to these brands, and advertise them for the first time, while maintaining their price level; it will also add international toothpaste brands at the top of the market. Switzerland's Nestlé, like Unilever a master at succeeding in developing markets, is producing both cheap, powdered milk as well as more expensive ice-cream and instant coffee.

Source: adapted from *Economist*, 3 December 1994, pp. 63–4.

Segmenting Industrial Markets

In industrial markets the benefits sought are derived from the benefits of the product in use. Industrial buyers need different products for different purposes. Product benefits are relevant in segmenting industrial markets. Criteria used in industrial buying include guaranteed product quality, preferred supply status, immediate and reliable delivery, technical support and price. Market segmentation is appropriate in industrial markets under three sets of circumstances (Johnson and Flodhammer, 1980, p. 203), when:

- products and services are heterogeneous,
- products are used in a variety of industries and
- heterogeneous customers have different profitability requirements, buying structures and supplier requirements.

With regard to the first point some products and services are technologically complex and require highly technical sales, research and other support. Other products are less complex and less expensive and can be sold on a more conventional basis as might be found in consumer markets.

When industrial products are used in a variety of industries it may be possible to segment the market to a greater extent than if only a few applications exist. Frequently in industrial marketing the same product or a slightly modified one has different uses which indicate the value of dividing the market into segments, For example, the same or slightly modified compressor can be used in road engineering works and on building sites, two very different market segments. With regard to the third point, end-users have different needs and expectations which give rise to opportunities to segment the market.

By identifying customer benefits and differentiating products to serve the associated segments the firm attempts to position itself competitively against its rivals in its served product markets. To do so successfully it must develop products to produce customer benefits desired by different market segments. Benefit segmentation and differentiating products mean obtaining answers to a number of questions. How important is each benefit to each segment? How much better than competitors does the firm provide those benefits for each segment? This is the marketing task referred to as 'positioning', which involves market segmentation and product differentiation analyses to determine the degree of fit between the two. To position the firm and its products successfully it is necessary to examine its technology, its products and the international markets being considered.

Market segmentation: geography and zones of influence and business distance

An approach based on geographical groups and the groupings of countries on the basis of trading patterns has a number of attractions. Trading pattern groups would include the former Eastern Bloc countries, the EU, the dollar markets of North America and the Pacific and the pound sterling areas. Such an approach leads to the concept of zones of influence and the marketing consequences which arise as a result of such groups. Liander *et al.* (1967) advocates an alternative approach based on a geographical form of grouping, but dependent on:

- the levels of economic development,
- political and sociocultural factors,
- size of the firm's business in a country,
- the firm's ownership or distribution pattern in a country,

- sales growth potential in the country, or
- the stage of development of the target market.

Differences due to sociocultural and business distance reduce the level of commitment firms display to distant markets (Gatignon and Anderson, 1986). The more distant the market in terms of business distance the more likely is the firm to adopt an exporting mode of market entry and the less likely it is to invest in these markets. Risk and lack of knowledge of such markets help to augment the business distance involved. Countries or markets which are of close business distance are those which are politically stable, economically well developed, culturally homogeneous and similar and provide many market opportunities but have few legal and trade barriers. Such markets are typically close geographically and the cultural disparities and problems of communication resulting from differences in social perspectives, attitudes and language do not constitute impediments to business.

Key country segmentation variables

Country characteristics are frequently used as a basis for segmenting international markets. The guiding principle in choosing from among such variables is their performance as measures of effective demand in various countries. The factors which appear to have the strongest effect on demand are cultural and social structure, level of economic development and degree of technical sophistication. Culture is acknowledged as a latent determinant of consumer behaviour in different countries but, because it is difficult to define and measure cultural characteristics, it is not considered a useful basis for segmentation. To overcome this difficulty, many proxy variables are used – as was seen in Chapter 6 – social structure of the society, education, living standards. Measures of economic progress or development are associated with rising incomes, industrialization, changing trade patterns and the accumulation of physical and human capital.

Given the wide range of possible variables which are used to segment international markets, it is difficult for the manager to choose which are the more appropriate. As a result, a large set of variables are often used in an attempt to avoid making mistakes. Nachum's (1994) research attempted to find a small set of variables which would be more efficient while serving as an appropriate basis for segmentation of countries. Nachum's (1994, pp. 62–3) results show that there is no need to use a large set of variables – in most cases, a smaller set can be used, thus simplifying and reducing the costs of data collection. Using GNP for industrial products and population for consumer products proved ineffective, but trade data, energy consumption and production, and monetary variables have a strong explanatory power in measuring import demand for industrial goods. Different measures of income and stability of the currency were most important in explaining the import demand for consumer products.

Using affluence and convenience to segment international markets

A convenience orientation, the value placed on and active search for products and services that provide personal comfort and/or save time in performing various activities, may be used to segment country markets (Brown, 1989, 1990). A convenience-oriented consumption is not restricted to the purchase of only low-risk or low-involvement products but may involve a range of such goods – from frozen foods to microwave ovens, the use of shopping modes and delivery services. Luqmani *et al.* (1994) advocate the use of convenience-oriented consumption as a way of segmenting international markets, since 'comparing consumers cross culturally on the basis of their convenience-oriented consumption can lead to a useful differentiation among buying preferences and aid in selecting target markets' (p. 31). Based on their analysis, Luqmani *et al.* (1994), using ability to pay or affluence as the second variable, developed a portfolio matrix of markets (Figure 9.5).

The Innovators are high in demand for convenience and ability to pay and, therefore, provide the most immediate and significant market opportunities. These markets may be studied to judge how consumption and demand patterns may change as a result of increased pressure for convenience. The Utopians enjoy high affluence but, at present, they have a relatively low convenience orientation. According to the authors, people in these countries are attempting to re-define their values, lifestyles and concept of time, and its proper use. In such societies, there may be a movement toward more time-consuming, but environmentally less harmful, activities. The Traditionalists are low on both convenience orientation and affluence and present only limited market opportunities. The Emulators are high on convenience orientation but low on ability to pay. Their desire for the convenient products available in innovator countries may be influenced by international media and a ready acceptance of a Western solution to saving time and enhancing comfort, leading to opportunities for product re-design (Luqmani *et al.*, 1994, p. 32).

Linking market segmentation to market selection

The link between market grouping and market selection is clearly indicated by Liander *et al.* (1967). These authors discuss two main approaches towards developing country clusters and investigate the impact of each approach on market selection: the develop-

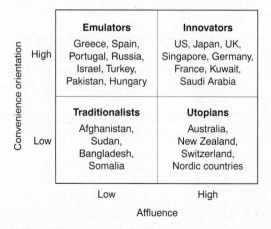

Figure 9.5 Convenience–affluence portfolio
Source: adapted from Luqmani, M., Yavas, U. and Quraeshi, Z. A. (1994) 'A convenience-oriented approach to country segmentation', *Journal of Consumer Marketing*, 11 (4), 32.

mental approach through cluster analysis and the regional typological approach. The first classifies countries into groups depending on their level of development. The technique emphasizes the degree of similarity between markets based on the number of attributes they share. In using this approach, a company would proceed to select markets as follows:

1. Assess the 'fit' between its products and each of the clusters and select the most promising cluster.
2. Select the most promising country from that cluster and, assuming favourable results from on-site research, introduce the product.
3. In deciding to enter additional countries, select from the same cluster before moving on to another.

The regional typological approach is similar to the first, except that countries are grouped by geographic location instead of by degree of development. The underlying assumption in this case is that countries of the same region display similar characteristics, e.g. culture, religion. As with the preceding approach, a company proceeds by selecting a region, then a development level and then a country within it. In future market entries, the firm would first consider those within the same development level as the preceding country and then those at different levels of development within the same region.

Other classification approaches have a similar impact on market selection; a company which groups markets on the basis of trading patterns may initially choose the more favourable trading pattern areas, and then enter the most promising markets in those areas in order of priority. The company may subsequently develop several marketing approaches, each tailored to the characteristics of the respective group. This matching of the marketing approach to group characteristics greatly reduces problems of coordination and control and may produce economies in production and reduce marketing costs (Sorenson and Wiechmann, 1975).

Systematic selection of customers

The most attractive customers within markets depend on the firm's position. A low-cost firm can sell successfully to powerful, price-sensitive buyers. A firm without cost advantage or product differentiation must be very selective in the selection of customers. In responding to these basic principles successful firms attempt to develop attractive buyers by building up switching costs, increasing value added and redefining the buyer's way of thinking about the product or service on offer. These firms are quick to eliminate high-cost buyers, especially marginal customers, in the growth phase of industry and product life cycles.

In these circumstances successful firms choose their customers with care. It is necessary to match the company's resources and capabilities with customer requirements. Convergent customer needs and company competences permit greater product differentiation and lower costs in servicing such buyers. Changes in demographic profiles and quantities purchased influence the growth potential in consumer markets while industry-related factors influence industrial markets. Buyers are not passive actors: they frequently spread purchases, qualify alternative sources, avoid switching costs, promote standardization, threaten backward integration or use tapered integration through contracts and other commitments. Some buyers have little intrinsic buying power while others are not very price sensitive. The cost of serving buyers can also vary greatly. Hence, it is important to evaluate each customer market thoroughly before committing resources to its development.

In evaluating alternative markets and customer segments within these markets the firm must assess its own strengths and weaknesses relative to those of its competitors, and it must also consider market developments. Following the broad framework provided above, this analysis will lead the firm to the selection of target countries and to an evaluation of segments within these countries. A systematic way of proceeding further emphasizing such evaluation and business strengths, segment by segment within each target country, is needed. By using the basic principles of segmentation analysis it is possible to proceed from country selection to customer selection.

Rationalization of product markets and customer segments

Segmenting markets may also be useful in another arena – managing the product-market portfolio. Concentration on special segments may be a desirable strategy in particular circumstances. Whether because of resource constraints, company size or strategic focus, such concentration may result in a reduction of product-market variety and management complexity. In developing international markets, successful companies frequently discover that they must provide a wide variety of products and product options to maintain a customer base. At the same time, companies tend to expand into numerous markets over time or, at least, to accumulate a large number of customers. It may be necessary to manage this variety, both on the product side and with regard to the customers. One way of managing variety is to perform an ABC analysis of products and markets, so that products are classified into three categories (Figure 9.6).

'A' products are those with a high turnover and high material value and usually are responsible for about 80 per cent of sales or profits but only 20 per cent of the company's products. 'B' products have a promising future and the prospects of eventually achieving A product status. These products are stars. Lastly, 'C' products are low-cost, low-turnover products and have a questionable future and are unlikely to grow.

In a similar way, it is possible to identify 'A' customers, those which are indispensable to the company, 'B' customers, which are likely to contribute large profits in the future, and 'C' customers which, for whatever reason, are never likely to be important to the company.

A study by Rommel et al. (1995) has revealed that successful machinery and component manufacturers use the ABC analysis. Most companies discover that they rarely recover full costs of supplying C customers. It is a different matter, however, if C customers can be served with the same products as A customers. In this way, it is possible to keep the negative effects of the added complexity due to excess product and customer or market variety within manageable limits. By limiting customer variety the company will also benefit from the leaner product range which also arises. This is achieved not by reducing the number of products and introducing the risk of losing key customers but by

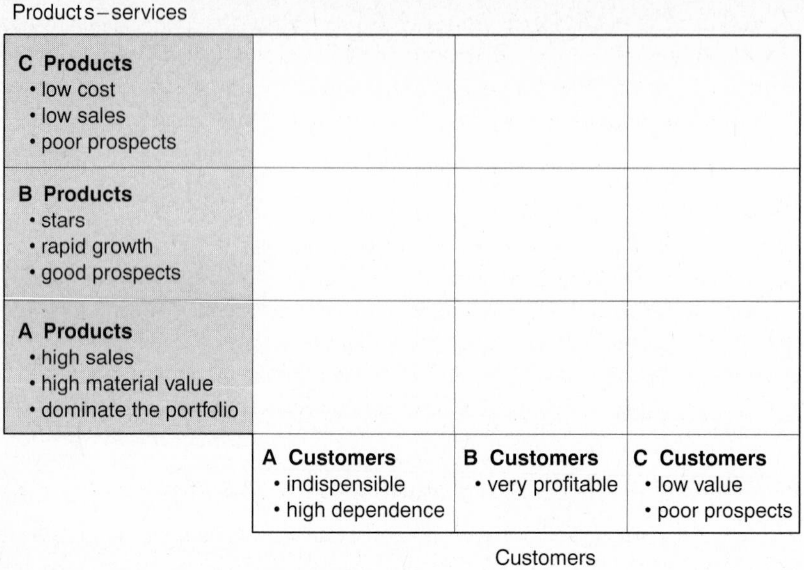

Products–services

	A Customers · indispensible · high dependence	B Customers · very profitable	C Customers · low value · poor prospects
C Products · low cost · low sales · poor prospects			
B Products · stars · rapid growth · good prospects			
A Products · high sales · high material value · dominate the portfolio			

Customers

Figure 9.6 ABC analysis of products and customers

concentrating on A customers. The company supplies A customers with the products that are important to them, even if some of them are clearly C products for the supplier.

The ABC analysis allows the company to judge the product market or customer mix that will maximize its return. In some cases, it may have to streamline its product-markets or even to discontinue some products or to relinquish some customers.

═══ Summary ═══

The objective of this chapter has been to provide an understanding of the dynamics of international market selection. A simple trial and error approach was developed to provide a benchmark against which to measure the selection of international markets. The market selection model begins with the incentive to internationalize. The essence of the international market selection approach involves the company becoming aware of market opportunities. It is suggested that this awareness may arise in three ways, as follows:

1. Opportunistically – where certain sources would bring market opportunities to the firm's attention. A number of factors would be taken into account in deciding whether or not to pursue these opportunities.
2. Systematically – where the company would become aware of certain opportunities as a result of exploring and evaluating many alternative markets.
3. A third option allowed for a combined opportunistic and systematic approach.

Emphasis was placed on the role of certain information sources throughout the above evaluative procedures. The possible influence of certain constraints on the selection process was also discussed. These include company size, proportion of sales exported, export goals, certain strategic considerations and the availability of international market information. In selecting international markets the firm must have access to various kinds of information. There are numerous sources, as follows:

- management knowledge and experience;
- internal company data;
- publications, trade journals and magazines;
- government- and industry-sponsored information agencies and marketing consultants.

There are several influences on the selection process, some of which hinder and others which facilitate selection:

- Larger firms are more likely to be systematic in their selection of international markets.
- Companies dependent on international markets for a large proportion of their revenues are more likely to adopt a systematic approach.
- Company goals and the relative importance placed on them may influence selection by concentrating on a limited number of options.
- A systematic approach places emphasis on evaluating costs, competition, distribution and customer needs in prospective markets.
- Availability of information influences market selection.

The firm is also faced with the decision of segmenting chosen international markets. Two general approaches are used: geographic areas or regions and zones of cultural influence and a selection of markets based on business distance. Market choices may be linked or embedded in each other, which introduces the notion of sequencing the selection of international markets. There are two principal forms of market sequence: market diversification by which the firm carries out fast penetration into a number of markets and allocates limited resources to each; market concentration by which the firm concentrates on a few markets and gradually expands. In the latter approach resources are allocated to a small number of markets initially.

Discussion questions

1. What are the advantages and disadvantages of an opportunistic selection of international markets?
2. Before the firm can take a decision to enter a specific foreign market there must be an awareness of opportunities in that market. How does the firm become aware of such opportunities?
3. How is it possible to obtain the relevant information to carry out a systematic analysis of markets prior to selection?
4. Outline and discuss the factors which influence the international market selection process.
5. Discuss the most common forms of international market expansion strategies. What are the key variables used in deciding between the two?

6. Identify an appropriate set of criteria to be used in evaluating and comparing country markets in terms of opportunities.

References

Attiyeh, R. J. and Wenner, D. L. (1981) 'Critical mass: key to export profits', *McKinsey Quarterly*, (Winter), 73–88.

Ayal, I. and Zif, J. (1979) 'Market expansion strategies in multinational marketing', *Columbia Journal of World Business*, **14** (Spring), 84–94.

Bilkey, W. J. (1978) 'An attempted integration of the literature on the export behaviour of firms', *Journal of International Business Studies*, **9** (1), 33–46.

Brown, L. G. (1989) 'The strategic and tactical implications of convenience in consumer product marketing', *Journal of Consumer Marketing*, **6** (Summer), 13–19.

Brown, L. G. (1990) 'Convenience in services marketing', *Journal of Services Marketing*, **4** (Winter), 53–9.

Carlson, S. (1975) 'How foreign is foreign trade?', *Acta Universitatis Upsaliensis, Studia Oceonomiae Negotiorum*, Bulletin No. 15.

Cateora, P. R. (1993) *International Marketing*, 8th edn, Homewood, IL: Irwin.

Deschampsneufs, H. (1967) *Marketing Overseas*, Oxford: Pergamon.

Gatignon, H. and Anderson, E. (1986) 'Modes of entry: a transactions cost analysis and propositions', *Journal of International Business Studies*, **17** (Fall), 1–26.

Goodnow, J. D. and Hansz, J. E. (1972) 'Environmental determinants of overseas market entry strategies', *Journal of International Business Studies*, **3**, 33–50.

Hallen, L. and Wiedersheim-Paul, F. (1982) 'The evolution of psychic distance in international business relationships', *Working Paper 1982/83*, Department of Business Studies, University of Uppsala.

Hunt, H. G., Froggatt, J. D. and Hovell, P. J. (1967) 'The management of export marketing in engineering industries', *British Journal of Marketing*, **1** (Spring), 10–24.

Jaffe, E. D. (1974) *Grouping: A strategy for international marketing*, New York, NY: American Management Association.

Johnson, H. G. and Flodhammer, Å. (1980) 'Some factors in industrial market segmentation' *Industrial Marketing Mangement*, **9**, 201–5.

Kossof, J. (1988), 'Europe: up for sale', *New Statesman and Society*, **1** (8), 43–4.

Kotler, P. (1997) *Marketing Management: Analysis planning and control*, 9th edn, Englewood Cliffs, NJ: Prentice Hall.

Kotler, P., Fahey, L. and Jatusripitak, S. (1985) *The New Competition* , Englewood Cliffs, NJ: Prentice Hall.

Kumar, V., Stam, A. and Joachinsthaler, E. A. (1994) 'An integrative multicriteria approach to identifying potential foreign markets', *Journal of International Marketing*, **2** (1), 29–52.

Liander, B., Terpstra, V., Yoshino, M. Y. and Sherbini, A. A. (1967) *Comparative Analysis for International Marketing*, Boston, MA: Allyn and Bacon.

Luqmani, M., Yavas, U. and Quraeshi, Z. A. (1994) 'A convenience-oriented approach to country segmentation', *Journal of Consumer Marketing*, **11** (4), 29–40.

Martin, J. (1988), 'Beyond 1992: lifestyle is key', *Advertising Age*, **11** (July), 57.

Nachum, L. (1994) 'The choice of variables for segmentation of the international market', *International Marketing Review*, **11** (3), 54–67.

Papadopoulos, N. G. (1983) 'Assessing new product opportunities in international markets', *Proceedings, ESOMAR Seminar on New Product Development*, Athens, 2–5 November 1983, pp. 69–88.

Papadopoulos, N. (1987) 'Approaches to international market selection for small and medium-sized enterprises' in P. J. Rossan and S. D. Reid (eds), *Managing Export Entry and Expansion*, New York, NY: Praeger.

Piercy, N. (1980) 'Export marketing management in medium sized British firms', *European Journal of Marketing*, **17** (1), 48–67.

Plummer, J. T. (1974): 'The concept and application of lifestyle segmentation', *Journal of Marketing*, **38** (January), 33–7.

Rommel, G., Kluge, J., Kempis, R.-D., Diedrichs, R. and Brück, F. (1995) *Simplicity Wins*, Boston, MA: Harvard Business School Press.

Root, R.F. (1982) *Foreign Market Entry Strategy*, New York, NY: Amacom.

Schiffman, L. and Kanuk, L. (1978) *Consumer Behaviour*, Englewood Cliffs, NJ: Prentice Hall.

Schmitt, B. (1997): 'Who is the Chinese consumer?, *European Marketing Journal*, **15** (2), 191–4.

Sorenson, R. Z. and Wiechmann, U. E. (1975) 'How multinationals view marketing standardization', *Harvard Business Review*, **53**, 38–56.

Tookey, D. A. (1964) 'Factors associated with success in exporting', *Journal of Management Studies*, **1**, 48–66.

Tookey, D. A. (1975) *Export Marketing Decisions*, Harmondsworth: Penguin.

Vahlne, J.E. and Wiedersheim-Paul, F. (1977) 'Psychic distance: an inhibiting factor in international trade', *Working Paper 1977/2*, Department of Business Administration, University of Uppsala.

Wiedersheim-Paul, F., Olsen, S. C. and Welch, L. S. (1978) 'Pre-export activity – the first step in internationalization', *Journal of International Business Studies*, **9** (1), 47–58.

10
Analysis of international competitors

The firm in international markets must deal with competitors in its own domestic market and in each international market it enters. Some of these competitors will be the same while others will be different and encountered for the first time. In order to prepare itself for such competition the firm must understand the behaviour of its competitors. The number, size, quality and origin of competitors affect the firm's ability to enter and compete profitably in a particular market. Indeed, the fortunes of the firm are determined by an interplay of what the firm itself does, what its customers want and what competitors do. It is not just a matter of only one or two of these elements.

In general it is more difficult to determine the competitive structure of international markets than it is to obtain information on market opportunities and environmental factors – topics discussed in preceding chapters. In the situation where the firm faces the same competitors in many markets it is clear that strategy must be integrated in some way, as a certain response in one market may have competitive repercussions in several. Where the firm meets several different competitors it is important to understand how each behaves so that initiatives and responses may be made.

Meaning of competition

Preceding chapters have examined environmental considerations and the ability of the firm to compete internationally. In Chapters 3 and 4 we saw that to be capable of competing in international markets the firm needs to have a complex mix of skills and accumulated knowledge which is mediated to customer groups through organizational processes to enable the firm to exploit its competitive advantage. The choice of which capability to nurture and where to commit resources must be guided by a shared understanding of the industry structure, the needs of customers, the positional advantages being sought and the trends in the environment (Day, 1994, p. 49). A general framework, developed by Day (1984), may be used to link the analysis of competitors in the context of the company's market position (Figure 10.1). Some markets are attractive; this depends on the firm's competitive position. Attractiveness is influenced by market factors, such as

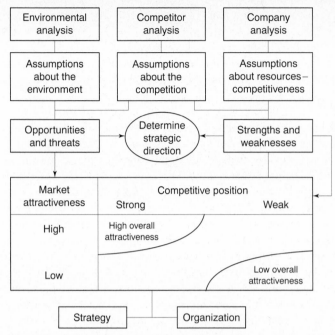

Figure 10.1 Linking competitor analysis to market planning
Source: adapted from Day, G. (1984) *Strategic Market Planning*, St. Paul, MN: West.

size and growth in the market and customer bargaining power; by economic and techno-logical factors, such as the nature and intensity of investment, the technology used and mobility barriers, by competitive factors, such as the structure of competition and substitutes, and by perceived differentiation and environmental factors such as social acceptance and regulations. The firm is competitive in international markets if it can sell its products and services and make a profit. Competitiveness has been defined as:

> the immediate and future ability of, and opportunities for, entrepreneurs to design, produce and market goods within their respective environments whose price and non-price qualities form a more attractive package than those of competitors abroad or in domestic markets   (European Management Forum, 1984)

In the economics literature firms in a fully competitive market can achieve only 'normal' returns, i.e. the risk-free rate in addition to some appropriate adjustment to allow for risk in the business. That may be what companies and investors actually receive through a rigid application of market forces but it is not what they set out to achieve. When firms plan new ventures they seek significantly higher returns and that almost always means achieving some degree of monopoly power in economic terms either over resources or markets. In a sense, business, and marketing in particular, is about a search for monopoly. Modern companies make monopoly acceptable by providing goods and services desired by so many people as to make their production profitable. The creation of brands and the control of access to customers confer on companies a limited form of monopoly power. In recent years to the power of branding and the control of distribution channels must be added the impact of continuous innovation and product differentiation and other technological advantages which add to the power of certain companies.

Many marketing companies are known for the standards of performance they set for their competitors and the guarantees of quality they provide for their customers. These companies, by setting performance and quality standards achieve market influence. By continuously innovating their core products they preserve their dominance of the relevant product category and by controlling branding and distribution they protect themselves against potential rivals. The success of R & A Bailey and Company Ltd is due almost entirely to the way it manages the Baileys brand through unique positioning and control of distribution in all major markets. Nestlé's success may be attributed to its powerful branding and competitive advertising while Procter & Gamble's success stems from continuously innovating mostly non-glamorous consumer products which perform better in areas of concern to consumers than competing products. Successful competitors therefore rely on, among other factors, branding, continuous product innovation and development and excellent customer relations through closely guarded channels of distribution.

The firm's competitive position is influenced by its market position – share, differentiation, product range and image, by its economic and technological position – cost structure, capacity and patents, and capability – management and marketing strengths, channel power and its relationships with labour and government.

Nature of competition among firms

The argument in this chapter is not that the firm should only focus on the competition; in the preceding chapter it was shown how important it is to focus on the customer as well. Indeed, a balance between the two is desirable. As was seen in earlier chapters some firms focus on the product only and exclude consideration of customers and competitors. A firm focused on customers pays great attention to customer issues in the development of strategy. In contrast, a competitor-oriented firm reacts to the behaviour of competitors. Both approaches have advantages.

A customer-oriented approach is better when the objective is to identify new opportunities, whereas the competitor-oriented approach is preferred when it is important to monitor strengths and weaknesses in other firm's endeavours. A market-oriented approach combines both approaches (Figure 10.2). Furthermore, the firm in international markets must also consider the international repercussions of the way it treats customers and responds to competition – an international market focus.

Establishing competitive positions of international markets

The success of any marketing strategy depends on the strength of the competitive analysis on which it is based (Henderson, 1983). Porter (1980) has developed a formal industry structure model for such analysis which consists of a review of all key industry players, new entrants, suppliers, substitutes, buyers and industry competitors themselves. Henderson outlines a number of competition principles drawn from biological theory and

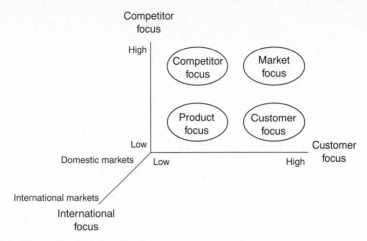

Figure 10.2 Changing focus of the firm

sets out to show that business is equally a question of the 'survival of the fittest'. Henderson makes the observation, drawn from Darwin's *The Origin of Species*, that the more similar competitors are to each other, the more intense their competition will be. This serves to underline the need for competitive analysis and advantage. Characteristic by characteristic, Henderson proposes that competitors should be compared in order to identify the unique advantage that sets a company apart and allows it to win in the competitive marketplace. The rules of good market competitive positioning are for the firm to attempt to create long-term sustainable positions. The distinction between contestable and sustainable is a matter of degree but, clearly, sustainability will be greatest where the advantage is based on a number of factors, where the advantage is large and when few environmental threats to it exist. In this context Ghemawat (1986) makes two suggestions for the firm. First it should not ignore contestable advantages, and small moves can be made if they avoid creating a competitive disadvantage. Second, as sustainability is also a function of management and organization resource commitment, the firm must decide to what extent it wishes to compete in a particular way and invest accordingly while maintaining the flexibility to compete effectively in other ways.

Hierarchy of competition

There is a hierarchy of competition facing the firm depending on the substitutability of products. Products which are close substitutes have a high cross-elasticity of demand. Products which are not so close as substitutes would have a low cross-elasticity of demand. The hierarchy of substitutability is shown in Figure 10.3.

In addition to the concept of product substitution it is important to understand the nature of the dynamics of the industry. To understand these the firm must understand the conditions underlying supply and demand. These factors influence industry structure, which in turn influences the behaviour of firms in the industry. The behaviour of firms with regard to product development, pricing, advertising and distribution determines

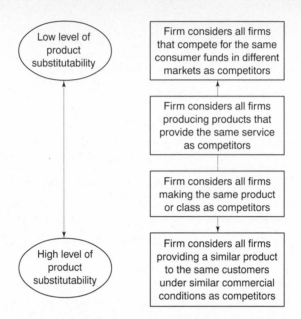

Figure 10.3 Identifying competitors by product substitution criteria

industry performance such as the efficiency, growth and profitability of firms. Competitors also have to be studied carefully from the point of view of their share of the market, their size and resources and pricing policies. This helps to indicate what opportunities there are for the firm's product and what sales may be possible. Another element of competitor analysis is an appraisal of market structure. Here one should investigate the degree of monopoly in the market and whether competition is rigorous or loose. Market structure bears directly upon ease of entry for a newcomer. Some country markets have strong associations of local producers who lend their collective efforts to keeping foreign firms out; others are dominated by a few large firms with a host of small followers; still others have no dominant firms and a loose competitive structure which facilitates entry. A framework based on these concepts, known in the economics literature as the study of structure, conduct and performance, allows the firm to examine the nature and source of competition in an industry (Figure 10.4).

An examination of the structure of the industry gives the firm much of the information it requires to understand the conduct or behaviour of its competitors. There are a number of points to consider. First, it is necessary to specify the number of firms in the industry and whether the product is standardized or highly differentiated. Second, firms desire to enter industries that offer attractive profits. Some are easier to enter than others. The major barriers to entry are brand strength, access to distribution, large capital requirements and scale economies, and international agreements. Some of these barriers are intrinsic to certain industries such as petroleum, coffee and tin, while others are established by the actions of firms already in the industry, e.g. the branded consumer products firms. Third, in an ideal world firms should be able to exit an industry freely but frequently

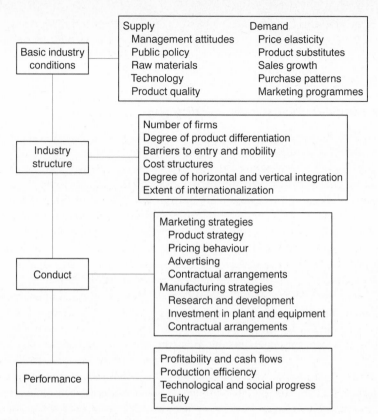

Figure 10.4 Analysis of industry competition
Source: adapted from Scherer, F. M. (1980), *Industry Market Structure and Economic Performance*, Chicago, IL: Rand McNally, p. 4.

there are barriers to exit, such as obligations to customers and employees, government restrictions and lack of alternatives.

When it is in the interests of firms they can be induced to lower the exit barriers for others, e.g. taking over the provision of employment in a town or taking responsibility for serving an established customer base.

The fourth consideration refers to cost structures which determine the strategic behaviour of firms in the industry. Firms with heavy manufacturing and raw materials costs behave differently from firms with heavy distribution and marketing costs. Firms tend to focus on activities associated with their greatest cost, which gives rise to competitive opportunities. Fifth, the ability to integrate backwards, forwards or horizontally can lower costs and provide more control of the market and the value-added chain. In industries which are thus integrated, firms may be found which manipulate their prices and costs in different segments of their business to earn profits where taxes are lowest. Transfer pricing to exploit the incentives provided by governments to attract foreign direct investment is an example of such behaviour. Firms that cannot integrate operate at a disadvantage. Finally, the extent to which the industry has internationalized affects structure and competition in the industry. Some firms compete only in the domestic market while others have the choice of competing in many markets which affect the nature and extent of competition in the industry.

Impact of competition on market and firm

Competition has positive and negative effects which must be considered. It also affects the market and the firm itself but if carefully monitored and managed can be to the firm's benefit. The product-market innovator has a lonely and expensive time in the market since it must educate consumers and other users of the value of the new product. Competition in this case can expand market opportunities for all firms in the industry which serve the market. The marketing programmes of all competitors when taken together usually help customers gain a better understanding of the product or service and encourage more people to enter the market. The world market for cream liqueurs is a good example. Competition also has a negative side for the firm which arises when competitors seek greater shares of the market. In this situation each tries to persuade customers to buy its product, service or brand rather than the offerings of competitors. In unregulated markets, as found for most products and services in Western-style economies, competition is essential to ensure that customers receive the best on offer. It is not altogether certain that consumers benefit from the spate of competitive alliances being formed between airlines in order to compete. At the same time it may be strategically necessary for some airlines to form alliances with others because it gives the consumer a complete travel package not possible otherwise. The result of such alliances is often aggressive competition between business systems which benefit both the consumer and the airline (Exhibit 10.1).

─────────── **Exhibit 10.1** ───────────
Alliances for competition in airline industry

The 'Friendly Skies' have never been friendlier aboard United Airlines. Not only is their flight as 'Smooth as Silk', it 'Arrives on Time'. Relations are just as cosy across the airport terminal where the Singapore Girl has struck up an association with Cathay Pacific and the 'World's Favourite Airline'.

Alliances are in the air these days and the new Star Alliance of United, Lufthansa, SAS, AirCanada, Thai Airways and Varig – recently launched in Hong Kong – underlies a trend dramatically changing airlines. Individual airlines have begun forming teams to share costs and these arrangements are set to revolutionise air travel. Rather than being confronted with 30 or 40 check-in counters at Kai Tak, passengers boarding at Chek Lap Kok will one day only have to choose between half-a-dozen. The same goes for business lounges.

> As Swissair president Philippe Bruggisser told *World Airline News* recently: 'Competition between companies is over'. The future is going to be competition between systems and I can see five to seven big systems emerging on the world market'. Familiar branding, such as the 'Friendly Skies' message that United invested in over the years to encourage passenger loyalty, has become much more expensive. Star Alliance partners insist, however, they will retain their own individual identities.
>
> Bob Pinkerton, Asian general manager for AirCanada, was adamant: 'Many people are wondering what will happen to the 'Friendly Skies', whether Lufthansa will still 'Arrive on Time', if Thai will still be 'Smooth as Silk', or whether the stripes of SAS or the AirCanada maple leaf logo will disappear'. 'The answer is no. Each airline will retain its own identity and culture', he said. Now those partnerships have become 'multilateral not bilateral', said Jurgen Thomsen, the local general manager for Lufthansa.
>
> In Asia, this seems to indicate competition is narrowing to a battle between the 'Big Two' partnerships – Star Alliance versus the Passages team of Cathay Pacific, Malaysia Airlines, Singapore Airlines, British Airways, Swissair, Austrian Air and SilkAir.
>
> *Source:* adapted from *Sunday Morning Post*, (Singapore), 14 September 1997, p. 1.

Benefits of competition

Successful firms recognize the value of competitors in the market for additional reasons. In general, the presence of competitors benefits the firm in three ways: they contribute to increase the firm's competitive advantage, they improve the structure of the industry and they help to develop the market (Porter, 1985, Chapter 6). The presence of competitors allows the firm to increase its competitive advantage in a number of ways. First, fluctuations in market demand can be shared, thus avoiding the necessity of providing enough capacity for peak demand. Second, product and service differentiation are easier where there is a credible competitor to provide a benchmark for measuring relative performance. Third, a high-cost competitor may provide a cost umbrella which allows a low-cost firm to enter international markets or increase profits if already there. Finally, a viable competitor may be an important motivator to reduce costs, to improve products and to keep abreast of technological and environmental change.

Competitors also help to improve industry structure in a number of ways. First, they can help to expand overall industry demand. This benefit frequently accrues to the innovator who is first in the market with a new product, especially in situations where the firm's sales are related to total industry advertising. To survive and grow in international markets a dimension often neglected is speed to market; to obtain a first mover advantage may be especially valuable (Exhibit 10.2). At the growth stage of the life cycle followers frequently spend disproportionately on advertising which tends to benefit the innovator, who is better able to service the market. Second, buyers, especially industrial buyers, seek a second and third source in an endeavour to reduce the risk of interruption to supply. This is especially true in industries such as the motor components industry. Third,

competitors may contribute to an attractive industry structure. A competitor that emphasizes product quality, durability and service in industrial product markets may help to
reduce buyer price sensitivity and to mitigate price competition in the industry. In
consumer product markets a competitor who spends a lot on advertising may hasten the
evolution of the industry into one with a few strong brands and high entry barriers
(Porter, 1985, p. 208).

The cost of developing new markets, especially for radically new products and where
product and process technology is still evolving, can be prohibitive for many firms. There
are three considerations: competitors can help by sharing the cost, reducing buyer risk and
standardizing the technology (Porter, 1985, p. 209). First, market development frequently
involves the cost of market testing, legal and technical compliance and perhaps providing
repair and service facilities in a market. Competitors can lower these costs, especially if the
market development efforts are in areas that deal with problems common to all firms in the
industry. Second, competitors lend credibility to an innovator's product. Buyers are
frequently reluctant to purchase a new product where only a single source exists, since the
buyer could be adversely affected if that supplier failed to provide the product or service or
if the supplier went out of business. Third, having competitors that use the same technology
as the firm can accelerate the process by which the technology becomes the standard.

Exhibit 10.2
A first mover competitive advantage for Sheridan's liqueur

In October 1992 R & A Bailey & Company, a subsidiary of IDV, in turn a major Grand
Met subsidiary, launched the 'Sheridan' liqueur brand. The liqueur was an innovation,
consisting of two separate spirits presented in a unique twin compartment bottle.
Because of the intense competition within the spirits sector, Sheridan's was launched
before the product and mix were perfected, so as to preempt competitive reaction.
Indeed, no consumer research was carried out prior to launch. Initially, the product was
launched in Ireland before being launched in Europe, North America and parts of South
East Asia. In each market the company used a consistent consumer proposition. This was
especially important as Sheridan's received a simultaneous world-wide Duty Free listing.

The product continues to be perfected, and the company is currently in the process
of changing the pouring system – arguing that consumers will drink Sheridan's more
regularly if it is easier to use. The fact that R & A Bailey and Company has been first to
market with this innovation and has the backing of a major international group to
leverage its first-mover advantage on a global scale, has meant that Sheridan's will have
the time to evolve and establish itself and to link emotional values to the brand – thereby
giving it an inherent advantage over later entrants.

Source: adapted from Mullane, S. (1994) 'The influence of first mover advantage on the firm's
choice of foreign market entry mode', *Research Paper*, Centre for International Marketing Studies,
Graduate School of Business, University College Dublin, Ireland.

Determinants of competitiveness in international markets

Competitiveness for the firm means its ability to increase earnings by expanding sales and/ or profit margins in the market in which it competes. This implies the ability to defend market position as competition in products and production processes evolve. The extent to which a firm proves successful in defending its position will clearly be dependent on its ability and the competitive strategy it chooses to follow. Where the markets involved are international in scope, then so also is the concept of competitiveness.

One great myth which must be dispelled, regarding competition in international markets, is that price explains all differences in competitiveness. While price is an important element in marketing strategy it is of course not the only element, as competitive advantage may be gained in price, speed of delivery, design or service provided and brands developed, to name the more obvious.

A tendency to place too much emphasis on the importance of costs, inflation and exchange rates in international markets is tantamount to recognizing no other form of competition than price. While costs and price factors have an important role to play, other factors influence the purchase decision, and this applies no less in international markets than at home.

In the European Business Survey of small and medium size business (see Exhibit 5.3), costs and competitiveness play a very different part depending on the country in question. With regard to costs, small and medium-sized firms in the UK and Turkey 'were most affected by increases resulting from changes in the membership and organization of the EU in the past five years' (Table 10.1). At the same time, changes in the EU have increased the competitive pressure on smaller companies in all countries surveyed. The increase in competition is particularly acute in Greece and less so in Luxembourg, but has been felt least in Norway, Malta and Switzerland – all non-EU countries. Swedish and UK companies did not experience much competitive pressure either.

Measuring competitiveness in the firm

While conventional economics recognizes the importance of non-price factors, the abundance of economic data which facilitate the measurement of price factors has created a not unexpected bias toward price variables. Price competitiveness may be measured by relative export prices and cost competitiveness by such indices as labour costs relative to a weighted average of the principal international competitors.

To assess the relative competitiveness of a firm Buzzell *et al.* (1975) have identified six factors (Figure 10.5), the most powerful of which have been shown to be relative product quality, level of innovation and marketing expenditure. Relative product quality refers to product attributes which are superior to those of competitors and innovation refers to the number of products introduced in the preceding three years as a proportion of current sales.

Marketing effort refers to marketing expenditures as a proportion of market sales. Relative service quality refers to the possession of superior or inferior attributes compared with competitors. Research and development is measured as a proportion of sales, and product availability refers to finished products inventory as a proportion of sales.

Table 10.1 Cost and competition changes in the EU

Country	Impact of costs (per cent)			EU changes on competition (per cent)		
	Reduced	Increased	No change	Easier	Difficult	No change
Austria	24	26	36	2	69	20
Belgium	19	24	34	1	59	26
Denmark	8	26	46	1	39	43
Finland	18	11	57	1	39	48
France	13	17	38	1	52	26
Germany	9	23	37	1	50	28
Greece	38	16	22	1	81	9
Ireland	19	25	37	0	57	29
Italy	6	19	45	1	40	34
Luxembourg	16	25	33	0	80	12
Netherlands	10	22	43	2	55	25
Portugal	11	27	38	0	72	16
Spain	28	14	37	3	53	25
Sweden	7	20	47	0	30	48
United Kingdom	6	36	38	1	33	48
EU average	14	22	39	1	49	30
Malta	0	20	17	0	23	15
Norway	0	12	48	1	18	45
Switzerland	7	15	31	2	29	25
Turkey	10	36	17	4	53	11
Survey average	14	22	38	1	48	30

Source: *European Business Survey* (1997), London: Grant Thornton International Business Strategies Ltd, May, pp. 34–5.

Day and Wensley (1988) suggest that two methods of evaluating a firm's competitive superiority are available: competitor-centred methods and customer-focused methods. The former relies on a comparison of the firm's key resources against those of its major competitors, and evaluations of the success factors attributed to those competitors that hold winning positions in the market. In this situation competitors are viewed as part of the same strategic group pursuing a strategy identical or similar to that being pursued by the firm and having basically the same resource configuration. The differences by which strategic groups are identified depend on circumstances and include the stage of the product life cycle, whether firms are consolidating or growing, the distribution channels used, their position on quality and the technology used.

The identification of the most competitive groups will depend on a few key variables, and it may be strategically important to know the relative importance of these variables. Although Kodak still dominated in all Western markets, outside Japan, in the early 1980s and its products were recognized by the majority of the world's photographers as being of

Figure 10.5 Evaluative factors in assessing company competitiveness
Source: adapted from Buzzell, R. D., Gale, B. T., and Sultan, R. G. M. (1975) 'Market share: a key to profitability', *Harvard Business Review*, January–February, 97–106.

the highest quality, the growing competition from Fuji and Konica was beginning to hurt. The real shock for Kodak came in 1984 when Fuji entered the US company's home ground and captured the sponsorship for the Los Angeles Olympic Games. From that point, Kodak very quickly decided it had to retaliate, and part of that retaliation involved taking on Fuji seriously in Japan. In doing so the company decided that it had to shed its American image and become more like a Japanese company. It began putting Japanese messages on its film packaging, sponsoring local fairs and flying a publicity blimp designed to look like a carp, a fish close to the hearts of the Japanese people. Such changes in its image and a strong emphasis on its commitment to the local market were considered necessary steps in a country where close business relationships are often crucial to success and loyalties are much stronger than in the West.

Customer-focused methods use customer comparison models whereby the firm is compared with its competitors. They also use customer satisfaction surveys and loyalty measures. In many cases direct competitors in international markets are highly visible or easily identifiable. Most firms know who their competitors are, but not always. For example, R & A Bailey and Company should be able to identify sets of products, alcoholic and non-alcoholic, with which its brand Baileys Original Irish Cream competes. It is likely that the brand competes in the overall beverage market. Substitute products can range from wine to beer. Because of consumption patterns, in Germany coffee may be a possible substitute, whereas in the United States soft drinks have a greater possibility of being a substitute. Also, within the alcohol beverage market itself, Baileys is competing with beer, spirits and wines. Again, 'beer culture' countries would have more of a tendency to substitute beer whereas 'wine culture' countries would tend to substitute wine. The products competing with Baileys Original Irish Cream could therefore be visualized as soft drinks, coffee and tea at one level, beers, wines and spirits at another level and liqueurs at a third, more focused, level.

Two lessons emerge from these observations (Aaker, 1988, p. 71). In nearly all industries the competitors can be usefully portrayed in terms of how intensely they compete with the business that is motivating the analysis. There are usually several very direct competitors, others that compete less intensely and still others that compete indirectly but are still relevant. A knowledge of this pattern can lead to a deeper understanding of the market structure. Those groups that compete most intensely may merit the most in-depth study, but others may still require analysis.

Understanding competitors in international markets

There are two sets of reasons why a firm should attempt to understand its competitors. Understanding current and likely future strategies of competitors and their strengths and weaknesses may suggest opportunities and threats for the firm which allow it to identify a strategic position which might be adopted. From Porter (1980) and Aaker (1988) it is possible to identify a set of six groups of factors, an analysis of which allows the firm to understand its competitors (Figure 10.6).

Competitor objectives, future goals and assumptions

Successful firms attempt to identify and understand objectives that competitors set for themselves and the assumptions they make about the future. Some firms, especially those in the United States, frequently operate on short-run financial objectives, whereas their Japanese competitors are known to operate on longer-term objectives. This also affects the market share objectives that a firm can set and how they are likely to respond when entering markets for the first time or when threatened by a competitor in an established market. Where the competitor is part of a larger organization it may also be important to understand the objectives held by the parent. The competitor may be seen by the parent as a growth unit or it may be expected to produce a cash flow to fund other areas of the business.

The competitor may have assumptions about itself or its industry which may or may not be true but which can still influence its strategy. For example, the competitor may

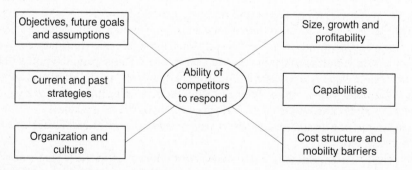

Figure 10.6 Understanding competitors
Source: adapted from Aaker, D. A. (1988), *Strategic Market Management*, 2nd edn, New York, NY: Wiley, p. 77; and Porter, M. E. (1980), *Competitive Strategy*, New York, NY: The Free Press.

perceive itself as having a high-quality premium product which might lead it to ignore a price cut by competitors, or it may be overly optimistic about the competition in the industry and make decisions accordingly.

Review of competitor strategies

In general the firm will wish to monitor, at a minimum, competitors' approaches to new product development and the basis for competition. In particular an analysis of strategies which work and do not work in particular circumstances would seem valuable.

Competitor organization and corporate culture

An understanding of the way in which managers in competing firms think and work together provides valuable information for the probable future activities of such firms. The choice of manager for a particular position can tell a great deal about the strategic thinking in the competitor firm. In addition, the way the firm organizes itself can give good clues as to its probable competitive behaviour and strategy.

A cost-oriented, highly structured organization that relies on tight controls to achieve objectives and to motivate employees may have difficulty innovating or shifting into an aggressive marketing-oriented strategy. A loose, flat organization that emphasizes innovation and risk taking may similarly have difficulty in pursuing disciplined product-refinement and cost-execution programmes. These two systems contrast markedly with a consensus-oriented system where the company senior managers are leaders of a closely knit team that they coach by asking questions rather than dictating answers. In this way people feel they have taken part in the decisions themselves, while management maintains a rein on the decision process. The organization culture, which is influenced by national cultures, tends to influence the approach taken. An approach which works in Japan may not work in the United States; an approach which works in the Nordic countries may not serve in Latin countries.

Size, growth and profitability of competitors

If there are many competitors in a market, it is usually necessary to identify the few most significant firms or strategic groups. One measure is their size and associated market share, both domestically and in each of the foreign markets under consideration. Firms that have achieved a recent and substantial increase in market share are also of interest even if they are relatively small. Growth rates, in addition to reflecting the success or failure of strategy, can suggest the possibility of organizational or financial strains that could affect future strategies.

Profitability rates associated with competitors may be relevant. A profitable firm will generally have access to capital for investment. Profits, however, may not lead to increased investment in situations where a subsidiary is expected to produce profits to be transferred to a parent.

Evaluating competitive strengths

Knowledge of a competitor's strengths and weaknesses can provide insights into how capable it is in pursuing various types of strategies. It also forms an important input into the process of identifying and selecting strategic alternatives (Aaker, 1988, pp. 80–5). One approach is to attempt to exploit a competitor's weakness in an area where the firm has an existing or developing strength. The desired pattern is to pit a strength against a competitor's weakness. Conversely, a knowledge of the competitor's strength is important so that it can be bypassed or neutralized. British Airways competes on service and a presence in all major markets. In terms of international market presence a number of US airline companies are attempting to catch up, especially American Airlines and Delta Airlines, which recently embarked on aggressive overseas campaigns with an emphasis on Europe.

What does it take to compete internationally and be successful? That is a question that Morgan Stanley (1997) have attempted to answer in a detailed analysis of global companies for a range of industries. They identified a wide range of factors which accorded firms sufficient competitive advantage necessary for international competition. Many of these factors such as low cost, differentiation and branding are common to quite a number of industries while others are different (Table 10.2).

Cost structure and mobility barriers

A knowledge of a competitor's cost structure, especially for a competitor that is relying on a low-cost strategy, can provide an indication of its probable future pricing strategy and its staying power (Aaker, 1988, p. 79). The goal should be to obtain information on both direct costs and fixed costs which will determine break-even levels. In some circumstances a great level of detail is required: labour and material costs, investment levels, and sales. In other circumstances, especially for international labour cost comparisons, it may not be necessary to carry out such an exhaustive analysis for many countries. Because of economies of scale, superior technology and lower wage rates, the cost advantages of certain countries, e.g. Japan, South Korea, and Taiwan, may be quite evident. High mobility barriers, especially if they are exit barriers, experienced in a few countries tend to increase competitive pressures within an industry. These barriers include specialized assets, fixed costs such as labour agreements and leases, relationships to other parts of the firm due to shared facilities, distribution channels or the sales force, government policies and managerial pride.

Identifying potential competitors

In addition to current competitors the firm should assess the potential of competitors who are likely to enter the market. Potential market entrants are motivated to enter a new international market for three reasons: product-market expansion, market integration and the possibility of exploiting unique competences in international markets.

Table 10.2 Global industries and competitive advantage

Industry type	Low cost	Global sourcing and distribution	Strong branding/ differentiation	Quality	Access to capital	Other competitive advantages
Automobiles	✔	✔	✔			
Capital goods	✔	✔		✔		Dominance in narrow niche; technological leadership
Technology		✔			✔	Labour skills; scale economies
Health care						Research; marketing skills
Consumer products		✔	✔			Financial strength
Media		✔	✔			Market share
Apparel & textiles	✔		✔			Service; management skills
Retail			✔		✔	Strong infrastructure; prime location
Hotels			✔		✔	Prime location
Chemicals	✔					Scale; raw materials
Paper– forest products	✔		✔			Well-timed investment
Transport				✔		Strategic alliances; infrastructure
Financial services	✔					Client relationships
Telecommunications			✔	✔	✔	Capital and labour efficiency; technological innovation

Source: Morgan Stanley (1996), *The Competitive Edge*, London.

A checklist which may serve to assist in the analysis of competitors and their positions would cover the principal areas of marketing (Table 10.3). The firm still needs to analyse its industry structure and competitors, to understand its buyers and sources of buyer value, to diagnose its relative market position and to seek to establish a sustainable competitive advantage with a broad or industry segment scope. However, there are questions peculiar to international competition which can affect the success of an international competitive strategy profoundly.

Table 10.3 Analysing competitors and positions

Who are the firm's competitors?
- current competitors
- potential entrants

What is their position in the market?
- segments served
- benefits offered
- strategy followed

What is the principal competitive advantage/weakness of each competitor in each position?

How are competing products positioned relative to
- each other
- customers' needs?

Product-market expansion

There are many examples of firms which seek to expand through the introduction of new products. With regard to market expansion there is much evidence of firms moving into new foreign markets. An example here would be the Finnish company Nokia which manufactures mobile telephones, computers, TVs and satellite TV reception dishes. Nokia considers itself to be too big for Finland and other Nordic countries and believes that the rest of the world is its market.

The restructuring of Nokia has involved weaning the group away from erratic Comecon markets and giving it a new international orientation skewed more towards high-tech trade with the West. Like many of its oriental competitors, Nokia has shown a long-term commitment to growth at the expense of short-term profit and shareholders' gratification. Such a company represents a major competitive threat to firms with similar products selling to western Europe or other markets at present.

Market integration

Customers and suppliers are potential competitors. In Europe, as for many years in the United States, General Motors, a major customer for components, absorbed many auto component manufacturers to ensure that delivery and quality standards of vital components were met. Suppliers are also potential competitors. Texas Instruments began making watches, calculators and computers that use its components. Suppliers, feeling they have the critical ingredients to succeed in a market, may be attracted by the margins and control that come from integrating forward. For example, having established the Virgin record company in the United Kingdom in the early 1970s, the Virgin retail empire expanded rapidly both in the United Kingdom and abroad.

Motives associated with unique competences

An existing small or insignificant competitor with critical strategic weaknesses can turn into a major entrant if it is purchased by a firm that can eliminate those weaknesses. For example, the Electrolux take-over of the debt-ridden Zanussi company promised a new lease of life to the Italian appliance manufacturer by injecting fresh capital and managerial resources. Hence European competitors such as Siemens-Bosch, AEG-Telefunken, Philips-Bauknecht, Thomson-Brandt and Thorn had to re-evaluate seriously the competitive threat from Zanussi. Similarly Freightliner, a Daimler-Benz company, used its technology prowess and its ability to reduce delivery times in serving the premium sector of the trucking market in the US.

All companies that compete successfully in international markets rely on some combination of competencies. Such capability may be related to the unique way that the company integrates the market which means integrating customer tastes, developing customers in numerous markets and building global brands to obtain scale and scope benefits, all to develop an effective competitive posture in the international markets served. Besides being able to integrate markets, the company must also be an innovator which means converting new product ideas into profit, establishing and maintaining facilitating mechanisms in the company and obtaining senior management commitment and leadership for the endeavour. Lastly, it is necessary to customize the company's endeavours for different customer tastes, to select the most appropriate distribution channels and to cope with market regulations and protection so that country or segment market programmes may be developed.

Information on international competitors

Sources of information on international competitors can be divided into field data and published data. Field data sources include feedback from the company's own sales force and engineering staff, distribution channel members, personnel hired from competitors and security analysts. Meanwhile, published sources include articles in newspapers, trade journals and magazines, advertisements for management positions, promotional materials, annual reports and advertising. Competitors may also be examined from the point of view of what they say about themselves and what others say about them (Table 10.4).

It is unlikely that data to support a full competitor analysis could be compiled in one massive effort. Data on competitors usually come in small flows and must be put together over a period of time to yield a comprehensive picture of the competitor's situation.

Compiling the data for a sophisticated competitor analysis needs an organized mechanism and a competitor intelligence system to ensure that the process is efficient. Data obtained in the market and published data are the two sources of general information about competitors (Figure 10.7). A small firm may not have the resources or staff to attempt some of the more sophisticated approaches, whereas a company with a large stake in monitoring key competitors should probably be following each approach.

In recent years, research companies and investment analysts have been evaluating the competitive capability of international companies. In the study already referred to

Table 10.4 Specific sources of information for evaluation of competitors

Public	*Source of information* Trade professionals	Government	Investors
What competitors say about themselves			
Advertising	Manuals	SEC reports	Annual meetings
Promotional materials	Technical papers	FIC	Annual reports
Press releases	Licences	Testimony	Prospectuses
Speeches	Patents	Lawsuits	Stock–bond issues
Books	Courses	Antitrust	
Articles	Seminars		
Personnel changes			
Want ads			
What others say about them			
Books	Suppliers–vendors	Lawsuits	Security analyst reports
Articles	Trade press	Anti-trust	Industry studies
Case studies	Industry study	State–federal agencies	Credit reports
Consultants	Customers	National plans	
Newspaper reporters	Subcontractors	Government programs	
Environmental groups			
Consumer groups			
Trades unions			
'Who's Who'			
Recruiting firms			

Source: Rothschild, W. E. (1979) 'Competitor analysis: the missing link in strategy', *Management Review*, **68** (7), 22.

Morgan Stanley identified a long list of companies which, based on a range of criteria, possess a global competitive advantage. A subset of these companies is reproduced here for illustrative purposes (Table 10.5). Many of the companies identified are clearly world leaders in their field and possess clear sustainable advantage, while others, although leaders, have an advantage which is sustainable for a much shorter period, but for at least four years. The other significant feature of these companies is the portfolio effect on their revenues. At the same time, the importance of a strong position in the domestic market is noted.

It is estimated the Asea Brown Boveri's (ABB's) competitive advantage depends primarily on its strong position in Asia and that it is one of the top three industrial equipment manufacturers (Table 10.5). It is also noteworthy that it obtains its revenues from around the world, principally in Europe but also in Asia and North America. ABB's current competitive advantage is likely to last between 5 and 10 years. In contrast General

Table 10.5 Competitive stability in selected companies

Company	Description of global competitive advantage	Sustainability of advantage
Asea Brown Boveri ABB (Sweden/Switzerland)	One of top three industrial equipment manufacturers with strong presence in fast-growing, low-cost Asia	5–10 years
BMW (Germany)	Positioning permits global growth and has more stable returns than competitors	10 years
British Airways (United Kingdom)	World's most international franchise airline with high-quality, consistent service	10 years
Citicorp (United States)	Premium provider of financial services in US and emerging markets with global brand name potential	10 years
Coca-Cola (United States)	World's best selling soft drink with best brand name	20+ years
Federal Express (United States)	Global distribution strength and growth opportunities in logistics management and internet	5 years
General Electric (United States)	A strong management track record with a history of success in a diverse product portfolio	10–30 years
Gillette (United States)	One of the strongest and most powerful brand franchises in the world. Has just acquired Duracell	20+ years
Intel (United States)	Leading manufacturer of microprocessors with unsurpassed technological and manufacturing skill	4–6 years
Microsoft (United States)	World's leading software provider with the strongest customer base	4–6 years
Procter & Gamble (United States)	One of the best known consumer products companies with strong marketing, management, brands and R & D	20+ years
Samsung (Korea)	Largest producer of DRAM chips. Well positioned to exploit the next surge in the DRAM cycle	3–4 years
Sony (Japan)	World's most recognized brand name in consumer electronics	4–5 years
Unilever Plc (Netherlands)	One of the world's best consumer products companies	10 years

Source: *The Competitive Edge*, Morgan Stanley and Company Inc, 25 October 1996 (and updates through 15 July 1997).

Electric's competitive advantage is expected to last between 10 and 30 years. For other companies such as Samsung or Federal Express the competitive advantage is sustainable for five years or less while for big-brand companies such as Coca-Cola the period is much longer (Table 10.5).

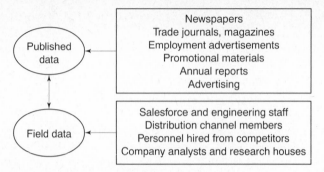

Figure 10.7 General sources of information on competitors

Company competitive capability

By way of summary, the company's competitive capability is determined by its ability to innovate, to integrate and to customize (Figure 10.8). Innovation refers to the ability of the firm to convert new ideas into profits, i.e. to commercialize them. This means establishing in-company mechanisms to facilitate innovation which must involve the commitment and leadership of senior managers.

By integration is meant the ability to understand and integrate customer tastes, to cope with global branding if it is a feature of the market and to serve customers who may be located in diverse countries and influenced by diverse cultures. It also means attempting to gain marketing and manufacturing scale benefits if they exist while defining the scope of the firm to compete effectively.

Customization refers to the ability of the firm to understand:

- customer tastes in different markets,
- new and evolving international distribution channels,
- market regulations and consumer protection legislation and
- how to design and implement a marketing programme in different national markets while allowing for spill-over effects, especially if the markets served are contiguous.

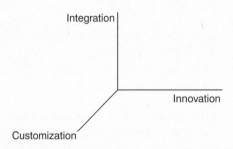

Figure 10.8 Company competitive capability

Strategic control for competition

The assumption that firms in different countries behave in the same way and operate with the same set of values is delusory in the extreme. At a minimum, firms in different parts of the world operate on different value systems and have different views regarding the time horizon of their investments, as has already been noted. Not all firms emphasize short-run earnings. A concentration on quick returns may sacrifice the future for the present.

The television industry is a good illustration of how different approaches to competition have resulted in the fragmentation of the European consumer electronics industry, the virtual disappearance of that industry in the United States and the emergence of Japan as a most formidable competitor in world markets. Alliances and rationalization through interfirm sales of consumer electronics business units are now seen as part of the response by European and US companies to the Japanese onslaught.

Many firms have recently reorganized themselves into small flexible business units to respond to a changing world market. Such changes recognize the necessity for strategic control and not just bureaucratic control in the firm. Firms differ with regard to how they view the need for strategic direction, rapid decisions and good communications. For some firms, especially older firms in more traditional industries, strategic control tends to be diffuse and unfocused. In consequence, such firms are slow to adapt and are very bureaucratic. Many European and US firms in particular have turned strategic control into tactical control, which allows headquarters to understand the market and the competition, but it severely inhibits initiative and decision making. This is a special problem for the firm operating in several markets, where central management attempts to impose direction on all details of the firm's endeavours to compete. The result is bureaucratic control, inflexibility and a limitation on the firm's ability to compete.

Many more firms have recognized this torpor recently and have changed; newer firms are being established with flexibility and strategic positions central to their thinking. Strategic strength also derives from a consensus within the firm regarding its mission and strategy which are manifested as a strong corporate culture.

These lessons have been learned by many firms in Europe and the United States. Their fruits are beginning to be seen in the competitive behaviour of the smaller high-technology firms and the reorganized large electronics firms, especially. Such a process results in a deep understanding across all organizational levels which makes close tactical control unnecessary. Firms operating in this culture become a strong competitive force.

Large bureaucratic firms which once dominated many markets are no longer protected. Three elements have changed the situation: the proliferation of small firms, increased competition and rapidly changing technology. The low cost of entry to some markets and the declining advantages of scale give rise to need for rapid responses, integrated decisions and specialist managers in all areas of activity. Low cost of entry and ability to produce small batches at low cost show that for some industries size is not important. In such circumstances it becomes very difficult to differentiate products. The firm with the strongest position will be the one able to develop flexibility and from that a successful competitive strategy.

Rapid changes in technology have meant shorter life cycles and numerous product changes within the life cycle. For this reason firms which traditionally depended on patents now find that the value of patenting is severely limited. Furthermore, many countries now produce their own patents, causing some overlap since inventions are frequently discovered simultaneously. There is also the difficulty of enforcing patent rights: in some markets there is an ideological objection to the payment for intangible benefits.

Competing on quality

International competitors are successful because they compete through quality focused on the needs of customers. Customer orientation is an attitude fostered as corporate culture and not a series of discrete responses to customer enquiries or complaints. At the heart of competing on quality is a serious commitment to the production of quality products augmented with quality service, sometimes through a heavy brand-marketing programme. In this context it is important to realize that when a company offers a product in a foreign market without the same level of after-sales service as in the domestic market in reality the company is offering a product of inferior quality (Asugman *et al.*, 1997, p.12). Successful firms are dedicated to ensuring long-term customer loyalty through products and brands which may be produced and priced to serve a wide market but which also have an appropriate level of after-sales service. The degree to which an emphasis on quality results in competitive advantage is a function of how well the various activities within the firm and between the firm and its customers work together.

For many businesses success arises from a series of small steps rather than being dependent on a few very large developments (Figure 10.9). Both approaches to competing are found in practice. Some firms follow the route of strategic leaps, making a few major steps forward at critical points in the development of the product market. These leaps may take a number of forms: product redesign; new product development; entering a new international market; an alliance or joint venture with another firm to compete internationally; a change in technology; the acquisition of a supplier. At the opposite end of the continuum the firm could develop itself through a series of relatively small steps with the same cumulative effect. This would mean a constant effort to strengthen the firm's competitive position through an incremental approach: improved products, better delivery, reduction of rejects and better order processing.

Few firms choose such extreme positions as those outlined but, rather, choose positions along the continuum. Among international competitors, however, it is generally believed that German and Japanese firms seek incremental improvements within an existing technology, whereas US, and to a lesser extent UK, firms adopt approaches which are more strategic in nature.

The risk of the incremental approach is that the firm will be leapfrogged and left behind by a competitor who abandons its traditional technology, moves to a new lower-cost manufacturing location or develops a new more successful market strategy. Conversely, the risk of the strategic leap approach is that the new expected breakthrough may not be available exactly when required. A response to this predicament is to adopt an incremental approach until a breakthrough comes. However, firms following these different approaches are usually organizationally very different and firms which operate

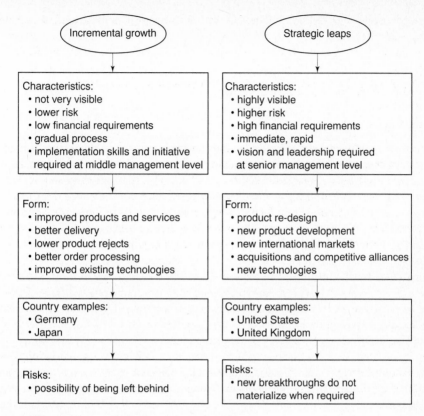

Figure 10.9 Incremental growth or strategic leaps

on the expectation of repeated breakthroughs cannot easily change. Firms which adopt the incremental approach, however, can eventually accommodate themselves to profound changes, i.e. the ability to progress through incremental change does not preclude the ability to master a major change (Hayes and Wheelwright, 1984). These authors further suggest that developing the capability to make regular incremental improvements may enhance a firm's ability to make occasional leaps.

Competing through manufacturing

Manufacturing strategy for international competition may be evaluated in terms of the emphasis given to product specific factors or a reduction of inventories through the adoption of just-in-time philosophy and the standardization of components. Such a manufacturing strategy provides:

- an emphasis on activities that facilitate, encourage and reward the effective interface between manufacturing and marketing as well as between manufacturing and design,

- an interaction of product and process technology to meet customer needs in a competitive environment, and
- an exclusive focus on factors that are essential to the long-term success of a business.

Competing through flexibility and price

In some businesses, particularly those with a high fashion content such as apparel, there is a very clear trade-off between lower labour costs which can be obtained in some Far East countries and the need for faster turnarounds and deliveries to respond to the changing whims of fashion. For many years clothing makers in the United States and Germany, in particular, relied on cheap manufacturing in Asia. The time lag between order and delivery has forced these firms to bring production back to, or near, the domestic base. Indeed, there is evidence of some companies from traditionally low-wage countries in Asia, particularly Taiwan and South Korea, moving their production to the United States and Europe to avoid rising costs and quotas and to get closer to their customers to avoid obsolescence.

Until recently US and European apparel companies were locating abroad since they could afford to make incorrect predictions about the market and still win because labour in the Far East was very cheap and customers were less demanding. Now labour costs in the Far East are rising and computer-aided design systems can lay out patterns with minimal waste which are sent directly to automated cutting machines. Consumers have become more demanding regarding fashion and many retailers have found that they must discount heavily to move older merchandise. Items made closer to the market in smaller lots for faster delivery allow quicker reaction to fashion and reduce the effect of the markdown.

In recent years there have many opportunities for air travellers to shop around for low-priced alternatives. Many low-cost, no-frills, flexible airline services have been introduced to compete with the traditional high-cost service provided by flag carriers (Exhibit 10.3).

▬▬▬ Exhibit 10.3 ▬▬▬
A ticket to fly without the thrills or frills

Air travellers in Europe are being weaned from a sweet and sour diet of air-miles, spartan lounges, smart(ish) uniforms and high prices. Nearly 10m a year are swallowing the no-food, no-frills offering of Europe's latest breed of entrepreneurs: founders of low-cost airlines. But how do they do it? And how long do the likes of Virgin Express, Debonair, Ryanair and EasyJet have before the leading operators start to fight back?

Low-cost airlines are, predictably enough, all about squeezing costs. As EasyJet's founder, Stelios Haji-Ioannou, is fond of reminding his customers: 'If you want to have a meal, go to a restaurant.' By flying out of secondary airports, the airlines also save significant costs from landing charges and obtain take-off and landing slots that are unavailable at more prestigious airports. Landing charges can account for up to 10 per cent of an airline's cost base.

The other secret of these airlines' success is picking the right flights. Some carriers, such as Ryanair, have avoided direct competition with any large airlines. Many of its routes from Dublin to UK cities such as Glasgow, Leeds, Cardiff, and Bournemouth were underdeveloped before Ryanair took them on. Morgan Stanley analyst Matthew Stainer says Ryanair has created more of a market than it has taken away from the traditional airlines.

When the low-cost airlines do go head-on, they go for the fat underbelly of Europe's most unwieldy airlines. Virgin Express has gone for Sabena, the Belgian carrier. Sabena responded by cutting a deal with Virgin Express whereby the latter flies Sabena customers into London, using Sabena's access to scarce slots at Heathrow. 'It's competition by running away,' said one analyst caustically.

Source: adapted from *Financial Times*, Wednesday, 22 October 1997, p. 25.

Organizational change for competition

Many successful firms reorganize themselves when changing their competitive stance on world markets. In recent years such reorganization for large firms has taken the form of shifting from rigid, centralized management structures towards smaller, independent business units. Such firms find that more bureaucratic structures are quite adequate for national and even regional markets but flexible organic structures are required for global competition. In this respect, in 1988 Siemens launched the largest reorganization in its history, the first stage of which was to cut central operations, to remove two management layers and to reassign 9,000 staff at headquarters. The second stage was designed to divide Siemens' seven very large operating divisions into fifteen smaller, more flexible business units with separate decentralized sales and marketing staffs. In preparing the reorganization Siemens realized that it was overly dependent on its domestic and regional markets; only 50 per cent of overall sales come from outside Germany and only 10 per cent from the United States. Siemens began to place greater emphasis on international competition, especially in the microelectronics sector, where, compared with its major competitors worldwide, it invested heavily in R & D to compete with the Japanese in microchips and computer memories.

Siemens is stronger in some of its divisions than others, which enables it to be a world competitor. In the very competitive medical imaging business, Siemens is No. 1 in Europe, No. 2 in the United States after General Electric and No. 4 in Japan. The medical equipment business developed its flexibility long before the present reorganization. Cut-throat price competition, short product cycles and the necessity of targeting global markets to sustain high levels of R&D have for decades demanded a different corporate culture. Seventy-five per cent of Siemens' medical products are less than five years old compared with 50 per cent for the company as a whole. This is a good example of how a firm can successfully develop a competitive posture by studying one of its own divisions and transfer the lessons to other parts of the organization.

Summary

This chapter is divided into four parts. In the first part the meaning of competition was discussed from the point of view of the firm attempting to compete in international markets. We noted that success depends on good analysis of the competitive environment and a recognition that firms adapt positions in order to compete. It is important that the firm acknowledges that a hierarchy exists in the levels at which competition takes place. Some firms deliberately select positions in the hierarchy in order to compete while ignoring others. Competition brings with it certain key benefits in terms of developing the market and industry structure and allowing the firm to improve its own competitive advantage by focusing on strong and weak points. Many factors contribute to competitiveness in firms; costs and prices but also the other elements of the marketing programme including product quality, delivery and reputation. A number of ways of measuring competitiveness for the firm in international markets were identified and discussed. The next two sections were devoted to examining how the firm can understand its competitors. Various criteria were identified including size, competitor objectives, strategies, organization, cost structure and general capability. In examining potential competitors it is important to understand motives for product-market expansion, motives among competitors for integration with suppliers and customers, and their ability to compete. The final section deals with the need to establish strategic controls for competition in international markets. This means deciding on ways of competing in a structured and controlled fashion in such areas as quality, manufacturing, flexible systems, innovation and organization. Examples of successful international firms are recounted to illustrate the key points.

Discussion questions

1. What are the principal influences on a firm's competitive position? Do they differ between domestic and international markets?

2. Identify the factors which must be examined in detail in order to give the firm an understanding of the structure of the industry in which it operates. Explain why each factor identified merits attention.

3. Sometimes the presence of competitors in the market can have favourable consequences for the international firm. Discuss.

4. Discuss how you would evaluate competitiveness in a market. Distinguish between price competitiveness and cost competitiveness. What other variables are used to compete?

5. In order to understand thoroughly competitors in international markets, the firm must understand current and future strategies of existing competitors and also their strengths and weaknesses. The firm must also examine potential competitors. Outline an approach to such an analysis.

References

Aaker, D. A. (1988) *Strategic Market Management*, 2nd edn, New York, NY: Wiley.

Asugman, G., Johnson, J. J. and McCullough, J. (1997) 'The role of after-sales service in international marketing', *Journal of International Marketing*, **5** (4), 11–28.

Buzzell, R. D., Gale, B. T. and Sultan, R. G. M. (1975) 'Market share: a key to profitability', *Harvard Business Review*, **53** (January–February), 97–106.

Day, G. S. (1984) *Strategic Market Planning*, St Paul, MN: West.

Day, G. (1994) 'The capabilities of market-driven organizations', *Journal of Marketing*, **58** (October), 37–52.

Day, G. S., and Wensley, R. (1988) 'Assessing advantage: a framework for diagnosing competitive superiority', *Journal of Marketing*, **52**, 1–20.

European Management Forum (1984) *Report on International Industrial Competitiveness*, Geneva.

Ghemawat, P. (1986) 'Sustainable advantage', *Harvard Business Review*, **5** (64), 53–8.

Grant Thornton International (1997) *European Business Survey*, London.

Hayes, R. H. and Wheelwright, S. C. (1984) *Restoring Our Competitive Edge*, New York, NY: Wiley.

Henderson, B. D. (1983) 'The anatomy of competition', *Journal of Marketing*, **47**, 7–11.

Morgan Stanley (1997) *The Competitive Edge*, London.

Porter, M. E. (1980) *Competitive Strategy*, New York, NY: The Free Press.

Porter, M. E. (1985) *Competitive Advantage*, New York, NY: The Free Press.

Rothschild, W. E. (1979) 'Competitor analysis: the missing link in strategy', *Management Review*, **68** (7), 42–54.

Scherer, F. M. (1980) *Industry Market Structure and Economic Performance*, Chicago, IL: Rand McNally, p. 4.

11
Entering international markets

One of the most significant developments in business practice in recent years has been the rapid growth of international activities – exporting, strategic alliances, foreign direct investment and sourcing of products and components abroad have expanded dramatically. In such circumstances many firms enter new international markets to source components more competitively and to enter new growing product markets holding more promise than the domestic market. For example, Heineken Brewery typically first enters a new international market through exporting; then it licenses a local brewer to produce its beer and eventually it acquires the same brewer or another as a way of establishing a full investment commitment in the market.

In this chapter the strategic aspects of the market entry decision as it applies to international marketing are examined. Various means of market entry are related to the firm's choice of market strategy. The relationship between market strategy, complexity of international markets and market entry is considered in some detail. A series of approaches is discussed and an attempt is made to integrate them into a form which enables the firm to make an optimum choice of entry strategy.

International market entry and competition

Firms are established and grow with increases in the spatial distribution of business transactions, increases in the similarity of these transactions and increases in the likelihood of changes in prices and costs of the assets being transferred (Coase, 1937). All three conditions are much more likely to occur in international markets than in purely domestic operations. Spatial distribution of exchange transactions is usually greater for international marketing. As the volume of transactions rises with the development of international business and as a determined move by the firm away from opportunistic exporting occurs, the second condition comes into play. With differential interest rate regimes, different inflation rates and fluctuating exchange rates, which typify international markets, the third condition comes into play.

Interest by the scholar and manager in the behaviour of the firm in international markets arises when the firm transfers assets internationally, where an asset is defined as something that is owned by a specified person or firm on which it confers a competitive advantage which may or may not be capable of being objectively valued. Successful firms possess one or more assets which may be tangible, such as finished products. In such cases the international transfer modality is usually through exporting. Where the assets are intangible, i.e. where the asset represents technological know-how, marketing know-how or brand loyalty, the transfer is normally performed through one of the other exchange modalities. Observing these differences enabled Levitt to coin the phrases 'high-tech' for the intangible assets and 'high-touch' for the product categories (Levitt, 1983). Consequently, it is possible to conceive of the international firm as exchanging a firm specific rent yielding asset giving the firm its competitive advantage which may be found somewhere on a scale from high-touch to high-tech.

A well-known strong brand in the domestic market may not be sufficient when going international. A domestic identity may have little impact abroad. One way of addressing this issue is to attach the company's corporate identity to a well-known and respected company or brand in the target market. When FedEx wanted to increase its recognition in Europe, it joined with Benetton – FedEx sponsored one of Benetton's Formula 1 Racing Cars in Europe. According to Karen Rodgers, Managing Director of Key Customer Relations at FedEx, 'In dual sponsorships companies need to align themselves with an overseas partner that has a common objective. We aligned with Benetton's racing team because their image aligned with our brand, which connotes the image of speed and high tech' (Del Prete, 1997, p. 2).

Foreign market entry mode

Possession of a firm specific rent yielding asset of the kind described may provide the *raison d'être* for international marketing operations (Teece, 1983). Furthermore, it is possible to specify the international exchange transaction modality by determining the extent to which the knowledge or know-how embedded in the asset being transferred is explicated. The greater the codification or explication of the knowledge and know-how associated with the asset being transferred the more likely will the transfer be through exporting. When knowledge and know-how in the asset is tacit and difficult to codify, organizational and marketing factors raise the transaction costs associated with exporting and thereby promotes the use of other forms of exchange. These pressures are shown as a movement in transfer modality from exporting through licensing and joint ventures to the establishment of a full international firm (Figure 11.1). Again, the modality dimension is also perceived as a continuum parallelling the market asset continuum already described. By their very nature commodities, mature products and innovative products are high-touch, easy to define and separate from the firm (Levitt, 1983). In contrast, technical inventions, product coordination competences, technical skills and strategic marketing skills are to be found more toward the high-tech end of the continuum. Firms whose competitive advantage or uniqueness derives from technical skills, product coordination skills or marketing skills seldom resort to exporting activities, joint ventures or licenses since product bundles and constantly changing marketing strategies are difficult to contract out and hence are likely to be performed within the firm.

Figure 11.1 Competitive advantage in international markets: exchange of assets

Concept of market entry

The concept of market entry relates to the ease or difficulty with which a firm can become a member of a group of competing firms by producing a close substitute for the products they are offering. The firm must develop a set of products, assets and management activities for new markets entered (Yip, 1982). Concern here rests with new international markets. Successful entry depends on a number of factors. It depends on how the firm:

1. uses information about opportunities for profitable market entry,
2. accesses productive resources,
3. accesses markets and
4. overcomes market entry barriers.

Successful international firms usually perform better than local firms on all four of the above factors. Foreign market entry is characterized by one or a combination of the following situations:

1. the entrant's competitive advantage on cost, selling strategy or product appeal enables the firm to take most of the market from a weak local firm,
2. the entrant can obtain sizeable amounts of business from several local firms for reasons of competitive advantages which they cannot match, or
3. the firm enters the market as part of a strategy of interfirm relationships involving markets for other products.

Successful foreign market entry requires a superior performance on all aspects of marketing: 'Entry is one of the supreme tests of competitive ability. No longer is the company proving itself on familiar ground, instead it has to expose its competencies in a new area' (Yip, 1982, p. 85). In deciding the appropriate mode of entry to foreign markets, the firm must answer two questions: (a) what level of resource commitment are they willing to make and (b) what level of control over the operation do they desire? These two questions can only be evaluated in the context of the risk that management believes it may encounter in the country being considered for entry (Brouthers, 1995, p. 10). In high-risk countries, firms may not be willing to commit resources. In countries they perceive as low risk, they may desire control over the operation assuming that they are as capable of managing the foreign operation as the domestic. Risk perception, therefore, shapes the evolution of the two questions which in turn leads to entry mode choice. The challenge of entering new international markets is formidable and successful companies use varying modes of market entry.

Market entry decision framework

A market entry decision framework, which identifies four sets of factors thought to be critical to the entry mode choice decisions, has been proposed by Gannon (1993, p. 47). These four sets of factors refer to marketing strategy variables, organization-specific variables, target country variables and industry-specific variables (Figure 11.2). Gannon subsumed into his framework the myriad entry mode variables identified by researchers over a period of half a century. A comprehensive examination of the entry mode choice is necessary given an environment characterized by shortened life cycles, rising R&D costs and the commercialization of innovative products and processes, the reduced lead time between the launch of innovative products and the arrival of imitative ones and radical political charge (Gannon, 1993, p. 51).

Generic market strategies for international competition

The firm in international markets, however, faces two generic market entry strategies (Ayal and Zif, 1979): a market concentration strategy, i.e. concentrating in a few select markets, or a market diversification strategy, i.e. spreading over a large number of markets (Figure 11.3).

The objective of a market diversification strategy is to obtain a high rate of return while maintaining a low level of resource commitment. The firm following this strategy selects the more easily available market targets while minimizing risk and investment. As will be shown below, the method of market entry will frequently be some form of exporting or licensing. The success of the strategy depends very much on the choice of agents, distributors or licensees. The responsibility for marketing and distribution falls to the partner abroad. Product modification is unlikely to be more than that required to meet standards and general market preferences. The firm will attempt to charge high prices to produce high margins.

Market or concentration has been described as the purposeful selection of relatively

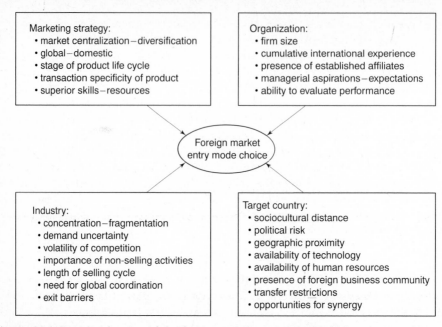

Figure 11.2 Decision framework for foreign market entry mode choice
Source: adapted from Gannon, M. (1993) 'Towards a composite theory of foreign market entry mode choice: the role of marketing strategy variables', *Journal of Strategic Marketing*, **1**, 48.

few markets for more intensive development. Such a strategy will be characterized by a slow and gradual rate of growth in the number of markets served. Its advantages, by no means universal to all industries, include specialization, scale economies and growth by penetration (Piercy, 1982; Hirsch and Lev, 1973).

A market concentration strategy is based on a longer-term view of opportunities in international markets. In this case the firm supports its entry to the market with a heavy commitment of resources in pursuit of longer-term profitability through market penetration. For some firms this may mean direct investment in local manufacturing facilities or local acquisition of an operating firm. Longer-term marketing relationships are established to ensure that the firm's products and reputation are well known and accepted. Strong contacts with customers, suppliers, distribution outlets and the government are cultivated. Prices are determined with an objective of sales growth. Short-term profits may be sacrificed. The firm adapts its products and services to the precise needs of each international market. A market concentration strategy recognizes that there may be direct competition with local firms and other international firms.

Market diversification involves a relatively equal spread of resources across many markets. The relative advantages of such an approach include flexibility, a reduced concentration and a way to capitalize rapidly on some significant competitive advantage. Of course, the firm may pursue a mixed strategy in which it follows neither a pure concentration nor a pure spreading strategy but, instead, sells to a large number of markets while concentrating its resources on a selection of these. It is easy to see how such

Figure 11.3 Market, segment, and competitive positioning
Source: adapted from Ayal, I. and Zif, J. (1979) 'Market expansion strategies in multinational marketing', *Journal of Marketing*, **43**, 84–94, and Piercy, N. (1982) *Export Strategy: Markets and Competition*, London: George Allen and Unwin.

a situation could arise as firms often receive what is referred to as opportunistic business, outside the geographic markets in which they are concentrating.

As firms move further away culturally from the home market, however, barriers become more important. Experience in close markets is necessary before venturing further away (Shoham and Albaum, 1995, pp. 99–100). According to these authors, for firms considering an initial entry into international markets, the implication is that operating in close markets is superior to operating in distant markets, and that they can assume that operating in such markets is less difficult than what they may have expected.

Neither market concentration nor market diversification is a universal remedy for the expansion problems facing the firm. Each strategy has its own strengths and weaknesses which requires the decision maker to find a match between the firm's situation and a possible strategy. In the longer term a strategy of diversification will frequently lead to a reduction in the number of markets, according to Ayal and Zif (1979). This is a result of consolidation and abandonment of less profitable markets. With limited budgets and managerial resources, the level of resources allocated to each market under a strategy of diversification will be lower than with concentration.

Market strategy and competitive strategy

The two strategies of market concentration and market diversification should lead to the selection of different levels of marketing effort and different marketing approaches in each market. Firms have reasonably fixed financial and managerial resources and thus the level of resources allocated to each market in a strategy of market diversification is likely to be lower than under a strategy of concentrating in fewer markets. Specifically, a lower level of marketing effort implies less promotional expenditure, more dependence on agents and a stronger tendency for price skimming. On the other hand, it is argued, concentration involves substantial investment in market share and using an aggressive competitive strategy based on heavy penetration pricing.

That the competitive strategy should vary at all is rejected by Piercy (1982), who takes the view that price or non-price competition may be combined successfully with market concentration or market spreading. However, it varies according to the situation for each firm, its objectives, its strategic capability and the market characteristics.

The strategic choices facing the firm suggest, therefore, taking account of segment strategies within countries (Figure 11.3). A country and segment concentration strategy means concentrating on specific market segments or niches in a few countries and on a gradual increase in the number of markets served. In this case competition on the basis of non-price factors tends to be very prevalent owing to the need to specialize to serve the needs of the segments.

A country concentration and segment diversification strategy means concentrating on markets but spreading the firm's product appeal across a number of different segments within those markets. One would still expect competition on non-price factors but the firm seeks a price advantage by capitalizing on economies of scale in promotion.

A country diversification and segment concentration strategy means concentrating on segments or niches while spreading across many country markets. Firms following such a strategy would be expected to seek a price or cost advantage by economies in promotion or production. Non-price factors, however, would still play a significant role owing to the segment specialization. Finally, a country and segment diversification strategy is based on a dual spreading in both segments and markets. This aggressive strategy is sometimes followed by firms with a product line appealing to many segments. Price factors play an important role in the competitive strategy as the firm seeks a fast entry into the market. This strategy may also be applied by smaller organizations by the engagement of commission agents or by a superficial coverage of the markets.

Linking market strategy, complexity and entry

One of the hallmarks of successful market entry is the ability to be flexible. Because of the complexity of international markets it may be necessary for the firm to shape its entry strategy to accommodate the specific needs of the market place. By complexity is meant the difficulties which arise in dealing with customers, competition, intermediaries and governments. The added dimension of different cultural and competitive situations adds to the difficulty of interpreting signals from such an environment. This issue is referred to by Lawrence and Dyer (1983) as information complexity.

Processing of market signals from diverse situations can be quite difficult, especially for firms new to international marketing. Market complexity forces the firm to choose its entry mode from a wide range of available options which involve varying degrees of commitment: from exporting through strategic alliances to foreign direct investment.

Market complexity must be examined in the context of marketing strategy. Three possibilities are identified. In situations where market complexity is low the firm intent on market diversification might choose to export. In situations of high market complexity it may be advisable to acquire a local firm or to invest directly in the market in circumstances where a market concentration strategy is being followed. The firm may form strategic alliances such as joint ventures or marketing cooperation agreements with partners in

Market strategy	Market skimming	Export	Strategic alliances
	Market penetration	Strategic alliances	Acquisitions and direct investment
		Low	High
		Market complexity	

Figure 11.4 Market strategy, complexity and entry

circumstances where market diversification is the strategy. Similarly, a strategic alliance such as licensing and franchising may be appropriate where market complexity is low and market concentration is the objective (Figure 11.4).

The degree of complexity existing in the market is likely to affect the choice of entry mode. A highly complex market might favour a direct investment mode, whereas a situation of low marketing complexity might favour exporting as a means of entering international markets. Strategic alliances fall somewhere between the two extremes. The firm facing a relatively complex marketing environment may form a joint venture or other alliance with a partner firm abroad to reduce the complexity factor. In this regard many firms considering entry to the Chinese or Japanese markets seek local partners, since the local culture is so strange to them that they need somebody with similar interests to mediate between themselves and local customers, employees and government agencies.

A strategic alliance can, however, increase marketing complexity for the firm in certain circumstances. A major cause of failure in joint ventures is inability on the part of one of the partners to understand the external environmental factors: cultural differences; government rules and regulations; the market; sources of supply; competition; currency movements. Complexity may also be increased by a failure to understand the decision-making process. In many oriental countries firms place a heavy emphasis on a consensus decision-making process, whereas in the West the emphasis is on the outcome or decision itself.

One of the difficulties of using a strategic alliance to enter international markets arises when firms fail to agree on objectives regarding market strategy. In forming an alliance both partners should clearly and systematically communicate to each other their goals and expectations. Senior executives with responsibility for the alliance must in turn communicate these to other members of the joint venture. Disagreements over basic objectives spread into disagreements over other issues, such as differences in opinion about dividend pay-out policies, debt–equity ratio, marketing policies and quality control methods.

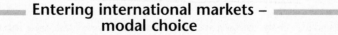

Entering international markets – modal choice

Entry into foreign markets usually represents a diversification strategy which is expected to provide the firm with a source of profitable growth. Typically, the company going abroad for the first time or entering additional foreign markets does so with a low share of the market having selected rapidly growing markets. Such markets require strong cash flows to finance development. The firm contemplating an internationalization strategy faces two decisions:

1. which markets to enter, the market choice question, and
2. how the firm should enter the markets chosen, the market entry question.

Entering new foreign markets may be achieved in a variety of ways, e.g. exporting and its various derivatives, strategic alliances in their various forms including marketing co-operation agreements, licences, franchising and joint ventures, and foreign direct investment and acquisition. Each of these ways of entering the foreign market places its own unique demands on the firm in terms of organizational and financial resources. Very often, entering international markets is not a matter of choice but of necessity to stay competitive in new and established markets.

Business development: new product markets

As was seen in Chapter 4, the choice of international strategy revolves around the position that the firm takes regarding the markets it enters and the products and technologies employed. The firm may choose to grow and develop by adapting its strategies to new international markets, developing or adapting products for such markets or a combination of such strategies. The requirements for success may be well known and understood or they may be unfamiliar to the firm. Newness of a technology, process or service embodied in the product to be sold abroad refers to the degree to which that technology, process or service has not been used already in the company's products. Some products require considerable adaptation and modification before they can be sold in most foreign markets.

Newness of a market refers to the degree to which the products of the firm have not been sold in a particular foreign market. This is very much a matter of business distance. The US market for cream liqueurs in 1978 was very new, when Baileys Original Irish Cream was the first such cream liqueur to be launched there. Familiarity with the technology or process refers to the extent to which knowledge of the technology or process and its application in differing market circumstances exists within the company. This experience may not already have been incorporated in the firm's products. Familiarity with the market refers to the extent that the characteristics and mores of the market are understood within the company, but not necessarily as a result of participating in the market. Here we are referring, for example, to the knowledge that the management of the R&A Bailey Company had of the workings of the US market before the Bailey brand was launched there.

In order to classify the opportunities available to the internationalizing firm it is necessary to draw up a framework. If the domestic market business is referred to as its existing business, then competitive market factors associated with internationalization may be characterized as existing, similar or distant in the sense of business distance. A similar classification can be applied to products and underlying technologies: existing products, similar products and new products.

A checklist developed by Roberts and Berry (1985) helps to distinguish between familiar and unfamiliar technologies, processes, products and services and between familiar and unfamiliar markets which may be used to determine the precise nature of the product market being considered (Figure 11.5).

By applying the tests described above, it is possible to classify new international marketing opportunities in a 3 × 3 new business development matrix (Figure 11.6). Positions in this matrix may be further classified into those which are more or less

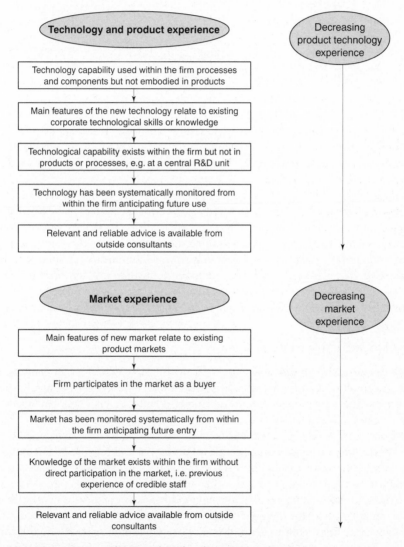

Figure 11.5 Measuring product-market development constraints
Source: adapted from Roberts, E. B. and Berry, C. A. (1985) 'Entering new business: selecting strategies for success', *Sloan Management Review*, Spring, 5–6.

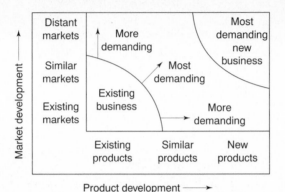

Figure 11.6 New business development: markets and products

demanding on the resources of the firm. In the bottom left-hand corner there is no extra pressure on the firm as this cell represents existing business, i.e. serving existing markets with existing products. As the firm moves away from this point in any direction the strategies become more demanding. The most demanding is to develop totally new products to serve distant markets.

The literature supports the view that familiarity of the firm with its products and familiarity with the market being considered are the critical variables that explain much of the success or failure in approaches to internationalization. Related expansion strategies, i.e. strategies similar to those used in the domestic or existing markets, tend to perform better than other forms of international strategies, which frequently result in lower returns for unrelated diversifications abroad and highest profitability for related strategies. Successful international companies typically do not attempt to exploit potentially attractive new opportunities which require skills that they do not possess.

Foreign market entry strategies

A wide range of options are available to the firm wishing to enter foreign markets. In this section the principal means of entry are discussed briefly: exporting, strategic alliances, international direct investments and acquisitions (Figure 11.7). These entry modes are part of a continuum of increasing commitment to international markets by the firm and are discussed at length in later chapters.

By exporting to a foreign market the firm operates in a selling mode and exploits the internal marketing resources of the firm. Typically, exporting works where an equity participation in the foreign market is either not feasible or not desirable. At the early stages of new market development exporting may be the only feasible way of determining whether a market exists for the product, particularly when it faces entrenched competition. Many companies export first and seek a deeper commitment if initial efforts are successful. Heineken used an innovative marketing approach based on the 'perceived popularity' of the brand in their initial exporting efforts in Hong Kong (Exhibit 11.1). There are also various forms of competitive alliance which the firm might develop, the

Figure 11.7 Generic foreign market entry strategies

═════════ **Exhibit 11.1** ═════════

Heineken exploits perceived popularity to enter Hong Kong market

In some Asian markets and in particular product categories, there are examples of major shifts in market shares, often taking place over only a few years. One example is the big change in Hong Kong in beer brand consumption patterns in recent years, which suggest that brand loyalties are perhaps not as fixed as once thought. About five years ago, San Miguel and Carlsberg in Hong Kong together accounted for 70 per cent of the total beer market. Today, they only account for about 45 per cent of total volume. How could such big brands lose market share, especially given the loyalty for such historically entrenched brands? Obviously, companies like Heineken which have gone from a 5 per cent share to over 20 per cent have been doing something right.

The Heineken brewer did not achieve these remarkable share gains directly. It was the local distributor which truly understood the cultural drivers of the Hong Kong beer market. The company knew that they were coming from behind against brands with huge market shares and large and very effective advertising budgets. To spend millions of advertising dollars to achieve anything against two major and entrenched brands was considered unrealistic. The distributor basically tapped a key Asian value – make people truly believe the beer is popular.

What the Heineken beer distributor in Hong Kong did was to push the product first in aspirational, on-premises outlets where it might develop an up-market niche; also, perhaps most importantly, they asked on-premises staff to leave the bottles on the table, either by not pouring full beers or by not collecting the empties. Suddenly, the little green bottles were seen everywhere, being drunk by white collar, up-market types in expensive, trendy outlets. This evolved until suddenly more and more people were drinking the beer and it eventually took on its own momentum.

This general approach is really the only way to beat the entrenched brand loyalty phenomenon. As marketers this is the biggest key to marketing to Asians – *perceived popularity*. If you can convince Asians that many of their colleagues are buying your brand and you can make it highly visible, you may have a winner.

Source: adapted from Robinson, C. (1996) 'Asian culture – the marketing consequences', *Journal of the Marketing Research Society*, **38** (1), 58–9.

principal ones being licensing and joint ventures. Licensing avoids the risks of product and market development by exploiting the experience of firms who have already developed and marketed the product (Killing, 1980). With very significant international marketing opportunities and expensive technology, the cost of failure becomes too large to be borne by one firm alone. In such circumstances, joint ventures become an increasingly attractive means of entering foreign markets (Killing, 1982).

In some circumstances the firm will prefer to acquire an existing company or to invest abroad. In such cases they may consider building a new plant and developing an entire manufacturing and marketing establishment abroad, referred to in the literature as foreign direct investment. Alternatively, they may choose to buy into a firm or to acquire the entire assets of a foreign firm which will allow it very rapid entry to new markets.

Determining optimum entry strategies

Entry strategies which require high corporate involvement should be reserved for new businesses with similar market characteristics and product requirements. Entry mechanisms requiring low corporate input seem best for unfamiliar sectors (Roberts and Berry, 1985, p. l0). Large-scale entry decisions outside the sphere of the firm's familiarity are liable to miss important characteristics of the product market, thereby reducing the probability of success.

This suggests a two-stage approach when a firm desires to enter unfamiliar new foreign product markets. The first stage should be devoted to building corporate familiarity with the new area. Once that is done the firm can then decide whether to allocate more substantial resources to the opportunity and, if appropriate, select a mechanism for developing the business. Active nurturing of a minority investment in a foreign company allows the firm to monitor new technologies and markets. Over time, active involvement with the new investment can help the firm to move into the not-so-demanding similar product-market positions of Figure 11.5, from which it may be easier to exercise judgement on the commitment of more substantial resources.

Acquisitions of small, high-technology, rapidly growing firms may provide a more transparent window on a new product or market which can assist the transition towards higher familiarity. Before the firm reaches this stage of maturity in international marketing it will normally consider strategies involving less commitment.

In dealing with market entry to existing and similar product markets, the firm is presumed to be fully equipped to undertake all aspects of new business development. The market entry framework used in this section is based on an adaptation of Roberts and Berry (1985). The firm has a number of choices available to it (Figure 11.8). First it may decide to develop existing product markets, the least demanding option. Usually this is done by improving the marketing programme to encourage a greater penetration of the existing markets served by the firm, which could choose to develop a range of similar products for sale in existing markets, an option slightly more demanding in terms of product development issues. This product development strategy is quite common among firms, especially those in large competitive markets. Alternatively the firm may decide to develop new markets nearby which are similar in terms of business distance to those

Distant markets	Strategic alliance	Acquisition – foreign direct investment	Acquisition – foreign direct investment
Similar markets	Export	Strategic alliance	Acquisition – foreign direct investment
Existing markets	Develop existing product markets	Develop new products	Strategic alliance
Markets Products	Existing products	Similar products	New products

Market development →

Product development →

Figure 11.8 Market entry modes: product–market evolution
Source: adapted from Roberts, E. B. and Berry, C. A. (1985) 'Entering new business: selecting strategies for success', *Sloan Management Review*, Spring, 5–6.

already served, an option slightly more demanding in terms of market development. The firm would normally enter such markets by exporting.

A more demanding strategy in developing business would be to develop a range of similar products for entry into similar international markets. In such circumstances a strategic alliance may be worth considering: licensing may be a useful alternative since it offers rapid access to proven products. A joint venture may also work since it gives access to a new market for a range of jointly manufactured products which may be similar to the firm's existing range.

A strategic alliance in the form of a joint venture may be an attractive proposition for the firm seeking to enter distant markets with an existing set of products. In this case the firm understands the product technology very well but seeks assistance in a distant market which would normally require a very different approach, which could be supplied more readily by a local firm.

A strategic alliance in the form of a licence may be attractive for the firm seeking to develop new products for an existing market which has become more competitive (Figure 11.8). In such circumstances, joint ventures between large firms providing access to markets and small firms providing the technological capability may also be particularly appropriate (Hlavacek *et al.*, 1977). Finally, for the firm attempting to develop a range of similar products for distant markets, the entry method would favour acquisition or foreign direct investment (FDI). The same is true for the firm attempting to develop entirely new products for markets which are similar. The most demanding business development strategy also calls for a heavy commitment by the firm. Acquisition or direct investment seems appropriate for new products in distant markets (Figure 11.8).

From the preceding discussion it is clear that there is no unique combination of product-market situation and entry strategy. Indeed, managers recognize that in choosing modes of entry it is necessary to recognize considerable interaction among them (Agarwal and Ramaswani, 1992). There are a number of circumstances where the firm must seek additional support before making a selection of entry strategy.

No one strategy is ideal for all new businesses. Within familiar markets virtually any strategy may be adopted and exporting or acquisition is probably most appropriate. In unfamiliar areas, however, these two high-involvement approaches are risky and greater familiarity should be established before they are attempted. Small-scale investments and small selective acquisitions constitute ideal vehicles for building familiarity and are often the preferred entry strategies in unfamiliar situations.

Sequencing international market entry

Strategic sequencing of international market entry raises a different set of problems which must be considered. As a result of long-term objectives, market choices may be linked and embedded in each other. For firms with little international experience, the frequently quoted sequential route to international markets appeals on grounds of risk aversion, reversibility and learning but to the seasoned international firm intent on the maximization of net present values the sequential route is far from logical.

> Within a model of bounded rationality, we would expect the international firm to seek net present value maximization . . . subject to a series of constraints – risk aversion, experience in the host country, psychic or cultural distance, information quality [and] external constraints which would include legal requirement and so on
>
> (Buckley and Tse 1996, p. 312)

Two broad and contrasting approaches to the sequencing of entry into foreign markets have received favour in the literature; the first relies on the concept of the product cycle and the second is an combination of approaches, here referred to as strategic sequencing of foreign market entry.

Product life cycles and sequenced market entry

The product cycle framework suggests that firms innovate new products at home for the home market and as the market matures the product is sequentially introduced in new less developed markets (Figure 11.9). Using such a life cycle model, Vernon and Wells (1976) offer an explanation of trade and production patterns for manufactured products in the United States. According to these authors the United States is more likely than other countries to initiate the production of certain types of items – those that appeal to high-income consumers or those that are labour saving. Initially, domestic market needs are satisfied.

Soon, however, foreign markets demand the new product and exports from the US begin. As foreign incomes grow, as lower-income consumers abroad begin to buy the older product and as prices begin to fall, US exports increase. However, at some point the market abroad is large enough for manufacturing to begin there. At this stage, US exports to that market cease to grow as rapidly as before; they may even decline. They continue, however, to go to markets where production has not yet begun.

The effect of the eventual movement of efficient production facilities from the United States to less developed countries is shown in Figure 11.9. Initially, manufacture will take place in another advanced country such as the United Kingdom or Germany because, in

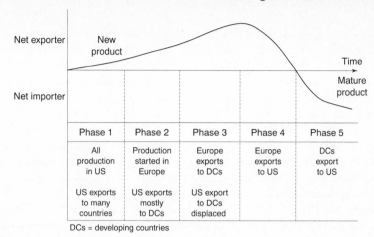

Net exporter

Net importer

New product

Time

Mature product

Phase 1	Phase 2	Phase 3	Phase 4	Phase 5
All production in US	Production started in Europe	Europe exports to DCs	Europe exports to US	DCs export to US
US exports to many countries	US exports mostly to DCs	US export to DCs displaced		

DCs = developing countries

Figure 11.9 The product lifecycle framework applied to international markets: a US perspective
Source: adapted from Vernon, R. and Wells, L. T. (1976) *Manager in the International Economy*, 3rd edn, Englewood Cliffs, NJ: Prentice Hall.

the early stages, the US firm is under little pressure to reduce costs by using cheaper foreign labour. Also, the innovator decides to manufacture close to the market at the early stage of a product's life so that market information can quickly and easily be translated into rapid product changes.

In the third phase of the cycle, US exports to non-producing countries begin to be displaced by exports from other countries. In the fourth phase, foreign production in some countries reaches a sufficient scale that costs are low enough to overcome the transportation and any tariff protection the US manufacturer possesses. The United States becomes a net importer of the product. A further stage has been hypothesized in which the less developed countries become exporters of the mature product.

While the product life cycle model has some intuitive appeal and provides a useful framework for explaining early post World War II foreign manufacturing investment by US companies, its explanatory power has waned with changes in the international environment, especially the rise of Japanese competition and innovation. Vernon (1979) has recognized these limitations, noting that many international companies have developed global networks of subsidiaries and a global scanning capability. Furthermore, the US market is recognized as being no longer unique among national markets in either size or factor cost configuration. Also, initial production does not necessarily occur in the market which inspired the innovation. Production may be located wherever costs and other factor availability are advantageous. The life cycle framework fails to recognize that many new products are launched simultaneously in numerous markets; global roll-outs are a common feature in many product markets. An alternative explanation is necessary.

Strategic sequencing of market entry

In examining the strategic sequencing of foreign market entry the work of Ayal and Zif (1979), referred to above, suggested a hierarchical approach producing a slow sequence of entries to different markets depending on their receptivity. This approach has been dubbed the waterfall model (Ohmae, 1989) to depict the situation where innovations trickle down in a slow-moving cascade from the most to the least technologically advanced country (Kalish *et al.*, 1995, p. 106). According to this approach, after a successful domestic launch of a new product, the company introduces it into other advanced countries and then into less developed countries. This is the old Vernon and Wells life cycle model in new clothes. Despite the anecdotal and other evidence available (Davidson and Harrigan, 1977), alternative approaches have been advocated. The sprinkler diffusion strategy which means simultaneously entering all relevant markets has been recommended by Ohmae (1985), who argued that, with increased global competition, the sprinkler strategy in all markets is the only viable choice.

According to Kalish *et al.* (1995), who examined the two approaches, global competition does not always force a firm to introduce a new product simultaneously in all its markets. The determining factors appear to be the nature of the product, the market cost conditions and competition. A firm prefers the waterfall strategy according to Kalish *et al.* (1995, p. 115) when:

- the product has a long life cycle;
- the foreign market is small relative to the domestic market;
- the foreign market is not innovative and growth is slow;
- there are weak competitors in the foreign market and they collude;
- the entering firm enjoys a monopoly position in the foreign market.

The rapidly changing marketing environment, the integration of regional markets, the rapid diffusion of technology and the world-wide access to communications and information technologies would indicate that most of the above conditions do not hold for the majority of companies active in international markets. Market conditions would, therefore, seem to advocate the adoption of a sprinkler rather than a waterfall strategy (Kalish *et al.*, 1995, p. 115).

A market sequencing strategy based on concentration or diversification is widely discussed in the literature (Hirsch and Lev, 1973; Ayal and Zif, 1979; Sizer, 1983). As was seen above two generic strategies may be used:

1. Enter a small number of the most promising markets initially; only after a 'presence' is established in these markets and the potential of the product proved are new and less lucrative markets entered.
2. Enter simultaneously as many potential markets as possible; initial wide diversification is followed by a period of consolidation where less profitable markets are abandoned.

These two approaches to market sequencing have implications for different elements of the marketing programme, especially pricing.

Ayal and Zif (1979) suggest that, after a number of years, both strategies may result in the firm operating in the same number of markets. The alternative expansion routes may generate totally different consequences in terms of sales, market shares and profits over time. A rapid rate of market expansion is usually accomplished by devoting limited resources and time to a careful study of each market prior to entry. With this approach the firm may make more mistakes and may be more likely to enter unprofitable markets.

The strategy chosen usually depends on the nature and extent of the resources that the firm is able and willing to invest in the markets examined. It also depends on the relative attractiveness of its domestic market, in particular its size and growth rate.

An alternative approach is to develop a strategy based on sequencing and market groups. As illustrated earlier, the sequence of market entry may be dependent on the firm's policy of grouping foreign markets. Hence, the sequence of entry might be as follows:

- clusters of countries selected on the basis of common criteria;
- select the most promising cluster of countries and then select the most promising country from that cluster;
- in deciding to enter additional countries, select from the same cluster before moving on to others.

Market groups may also influence the entry sequence in other ways. Many firms find that they need more than one foreign market to provide sufficient volume of sales to justify the modifications to products and production methods involved and to allow these to be made economically. The firm may, therefore, group markets with similar characteristics, and a product for a group of markets having been adapted, all markets in that group may be entered simultaneously or at least rapidly in sequence depending on other characteristics. There are many examples of this approach, as may be observed in firms which manufacture products customized for linguistically homogeneous markets.

Summary

The chapter is divided into three sections. In the first section we examined the issue of international market entry from the point of the firm attempting to internationalize. The concept of entry to international markets was discussed in the context of how the firm uses information about opportunities in foreign markets; how it acquires resources, accesses the markets and overcomes entry barriers.

Generic market entry strategy is the subject of the second section. Two generic market entry strategies may be used by the firm in international markets – a market penetration strategy by which the firm concentrates in a select number of markets, and a market skimming strategy by which it enters a large number of markets simultaneously or in rapid succession. These strategic alternatives apply to country markets and to segments within each country market. The greater the range of choice the more complex the decision.

In the third section, the choice of entry method is discussed. Entering foreign markets may be achieved in a variety of ways: exporting and its various derivatives; strategic alliances, especially joint ventures, licensing, acquisitions and foreign direct investment. A framework based on market familiarity and product technology familiarity is used to help the firm to decide its optimum choice.

In the last section the important topic of sequencing is examined. The choice of one market may be linked to the choice of another. For this reason it may be important to examine a combination of entry methods involving a sequence of decisions over time for related markets. Two alternatives are discussed – the possibility of entering a small number of promising markets initially or simultaneously entering as many markets as possible. Sequencing may be seen as a generic long-run strategy for the firm in international markets. A range of possible options, as found in the literature, is discussed for their relevance to the firm.

Discussion questions

1. Why does the international firm often have to combine different levels of market entry to reach world markets effectively?

2. It has been argued that technology is a major determinant of the mode of entry to international markets. Give your reasons why you agree or disagree.

3. What are the strengths and weaknesses of each mode of market entry for a medium-size firm selling a patented sophisticated electronic component? The firm at present is working close to full capacity and demand for the component is doubling every two years. An immediate decision is required.

4. Discuss the commonly held belief that there is no single market entry strategy which is appropriate in all circumstances.

5. Describe the market entry decision framework based on market and product familiarity developed in the chapter.

References

Agarwal, S. and Ramaswani, S. N. (1992) 'Choice of foreign market entry mode: impact of owership, location and internationalization factors', *Journal of International Business Studies*, **23**, 1–27.

Ayal, I. and Zif, J. (1979) 'Market expansion strategies in multinational marketing', *Journal of Marketing*, **43**, 84–94.

Brouthers, K. D. (1995) 'The influence of international risk on entry mode strategy in the computer software industry', *Management International Review*, **35** (1), 7–28.

Buckley, A. and Tse, K. (1996) 'Real operating options and foreign direct investment: a synthetic approach', *European Management Journal*, **14** (3), June, 304–14.

Coase, R. H. (1937) 'The nature of the firm', *Economica*, **4** (New Series) (16), 386–405.

Davidson, W. H. and Harrigan, R. (1977), 'Key decisions in international marketing: introducing new products abroad', *Columbia Journal of World Business*, **12** (Winter), 15–23.

Del Prete, J. L. (1997), 'Winning strategies lead to global marketing success' *Marketing News*, **31** (17), 1–2.

Gannon, M. (1993) 'Towards a composite theory of foreign market entry mode choice: the role of marketing strategy variables', *Journal of Strategic Marketing*, **1**, 41–54.

Hirsch, S. and Lev, B. (1973) 'Foreign marketing strategies – a note', *Management International Review*, **6** (73), 81–8.

Hlavacek, J. D., Dovey, B. H. and Biordo, J. J. (1977) 'Tie small business technology to marketing power', *Harvard Business Review*, **55** (January–February), 106–16.

Kalish, S., Mahajan, V. and Muller, E. (1995), 'Waterfall and sprinkler new-product strategies in competitive global markets', *International Journal of Research in Marketing*, **12**, 105–19.

Killing, P. (1980) 'Technology acquisition: license agreement on joint venture' *Columbia Journal of World Business*, **15** (Fall), 38–46.

Killing, J. P. (1982) 'How to make global joint ventures work', *Harvard Business Review*, **60** (May–June), 120–7.

Lawrence, P. R. and Dyer, D. (1983) *Renewing American Industry*, New York, NY: The Free Press.

Levitt, T. (1983) 'The globalization of markets', *Harvard Business Review*, **61** (May–June), 92–102.

Ohmae, K. (1985), 'The triad world view', *Journal of Business Strategy*, **7** (Spring), 8–19.

Ohmae, K. (1989), 'Managing in a borderless world', *Harvard Business Review*, **67** (May–June), **152**–61.

Piercy, N. (1982) *Export Strategy: Markets and competition*, London: George Allen and Unwin.

Roberts, E. B. and Berry, C. A. (1985) 'Entering new businesses: selecting strategies for success', *Sloan Management Review*, **26** (Spring), 3–17.

Robinson, C. (1996) 'Asian culture: the marketing consequences', *Journal of the Marketing Research Society*, **38** (1), 58–9

Shoham, A. and Albaum, G. S. (1995) 'Reducing the impact of barriers to exporting: a managerial perspective', *Journal of International Marketing*, **3** (4), 85–105.

Sizer, J. (1983) 'Export market analysis and price strategies', *Management Accounting* (January), 30–3.

Teece, D. J. (1983) 'Technological and organizational factors in the theory of the multinational enterprise', in M. Casson (ed.), *The Growth of International Business*, London: Allen and Unwin, pp. 51–62.

Vernon, R. (1979) 'The product cycle hypothesis in a new international environment', *Oxford Bulletin of Economics and Statistics*, **41** (4), 255–67.

Vernon, R. and Wells, L. T. (1976) *Manager in the International Economy*, 3rd edn, Englewood Cliffs, NJ: Prentice Hall.

Yip, G. S. (1982) 'Gateways to entry', *Harvard Business Review*, **60** (September–October), 85–92.

12

Exporting

Exporting is one of the quickest ways to enter a foreign market. For some firms it is also a very successful way of internationalizing. Many firms, however, attempt to enter foreign markets through exporting but fail. Failure in international markets can be costly in terms of managerial and financial resources and the opportunities forgone. For these reasons, exporting as an entry strategy must be approached with care.

Because of the impact on the balance of payments national policies in many countries focus on encouraging the export of products and services. Very often government-sponsored export promotion agencies encourage firms to export before they are ready for competition on international markets. Herein lies the potential for conflict between the macroeconomic policies of export-led growth at national level and the policies at the level of the firm in respect of company growth and development in a managed way.

Determinants of export behaviour

The determinants of export behaviour are considered to emanate from three sets of influences on the firm: experience and uncertainty effects; behavioural and firm specific influences; strategic influences. Before discussing each of these it is necessary to outline the meaning of exporting as a means of entering international markets.

Entering foreign markets through exporting

Exporting is the simplest way of entering a foreign market. The level of risk and commitment is minimized since investment in terms of managerial and financial resources is relatively low. Exporting is often chosen as a means of entry when the following prevail:

1. The firm is small and lacks the resources required for foreign joint ventures or international direct investment.
2. Substantial commitment is inadvisable owing to political risk, or uncertain or otherwise unattractive markets.

3. There is no political or economic pressure to manufacture abroad.

From a macroeconomic viewpoint, exporting provides countries with foreign exchange, employment, opportunities for vertical integration of businesses and, with the resources obtained in international markets, a higher standard of living (Czinkota *et al.*, 1992). At the level of the firm itself, exporting may provide a competitive advantage, improve its financial position, increase the use of plant and equipment and improve the technology base in the firm (Terpstra and Sarathy, 1994). Generally, firms export for a number of reasons. Objectives frequently include those associated with geographic expansion, lowering unit costs because of increased volumes and the selling or disposing of surplus production abroad. Food products and commodities often fall into the last group.

Apart from the disposal objective, firms which become involved in exporting must consider the question of product adaptation. This subject is treated at length in Chapters 15 and 16. The exporter will have to examine production facilities to judge whether they are sufficient to meet increased demand and to provide prompt delivery. Occasionally it may be necessary to alter designs, which raises issues of technical and design features of the product, packaging, legal requirements, approval and certification and the cost of any modifications required. Finally, the firm must be concerned with sales and technical literature which may have to be made available in a number of languages, in metric and or Imperial measure, and aimed at the needs of local markets.

When Derwent Valley Foods, a UK food company started in 1982 by people who believed in the concept of 'adult snacks' and owners of the Phileas Fogg brand began to produce innovative, high-quality products and later to export them, it discovered the need for adaptation packaging was an area where Derwent has had to make an effort. It began by having UK packaging with a second language stuck on top but found that each market must have dedicated packaging. For the Dutch market, for example, dedicated packs meant getting the Dutch written in an old style of the language which in turn meant that the preparation work had to be done in Holland. In the UK the package used was the pillow pack, but in Europe the block bottom pack works better for both storage and display (*Food Processing*, May 1992, pp. 37–38).

Market potential is a major determinant of the extent to which exporting is used as an effective mode of entry. Successful firms constantly monitor current and potential further demand in export markets. The firm's position, with regard to the suitability of its products against the competition and customer requirements, is also assessed. Here the firm will be concerned with product and service innovation and new product development. A matter of increasing concern to exporters is the availability of distribution and sales outlets for their products in export markets. Finally, the firm must consider standards and regulations, factors which develop into non-tariff barriers, and the possibility of patent infringements. Consequently, the firm considering exporting as a means of entering foreign markets must prepare itself thoroughly if it is to succeed.

Exporting, as noted already, is part of a continuum of increasing commitment to internationalization. Being a very versatile mode of foreign market entry, firms frequently use it in conjunction with other entry modes (Figure 12.1). The greater the commitment the higher the risk but also the more control the firm has over its international operations.

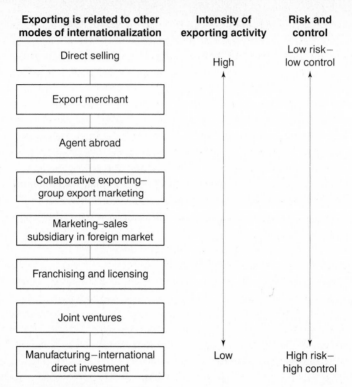

Figure 12.1 Exporting is part of a continuum

Exporting may be found at the initial stages of internationalization and again at the more committed stages where the firm, having taken an equity position in a foreign market, decides to export from there to other third markets.

Experience and uncertainty effects

There are various schools of thought regarding the way in which the firm begins to internationalize its operations. Many approaches are related to learning and knowledge of markets and marketing. One of the earliest studies declares that lack of knowledge with respect to foreign markets and operations is an important obstacle to the development of international operations and that the necessary knowledge can be acquired mainly through operating abroad (Johanson and Vahlne, 1977, p. 23). However, these authors state that:

> By market knowledge we mean information about markets and operations in these markets, which is somehow stored and reasonably retrievable – in the minds of individuals, in computer memories, and in written reports. In our model we consider knowledge to be vested in the decision making system: we do not deal directly with the individual decision maker
>
> (Johanson and Vahlne, 1977, p. 26)

Knowledge and learning with regard to exporting is possessed by the firm and accumulated by it over time so that some become established exporters, while others with less knowledge of foreign markets have further to go in terms of learning.

The key role of experience in export decision making arises from observing that the firm's involvement in international markets is frequently a gradual process. This behaviour suggests a learning process as it adopts successively more complex export structures and as it enters markets of greater business distance over time. Indeed, exporting may be seen as a stage before foreign production in the firm's internationalization.

One of the most frequently quoted studies of increasing export involvement is Johanson and Wiedersheim-Paul's (1974) study of the foreign operations of four large Swedish firms, Volvo, Atlas Copco, Sandvik and Facit. At the outset four different stages in the development of operations were distinguished in the study:

1. no regular export;
2. export via independent representatives or agents;
3. sales subsidiaries;
4. production or manufacturing plants.

This stages model reflects successively larger managerial and financial resource commitments as well as a more active involvement. The first stage means that the firm makes no resource commitment to the market, while the fourth stage implies a much larger resource commitment than the other three.

In examining the historical international development of the four firms, the study looked not only for evidence of a stages chain but also at the choice of foreign market. Two variables were considered important in this choice: size of market and business distance between the home and foreign markets. In general the study found that the stages chain accurately described the behaviour of the four firms.

The study supports the hypothesis that a firm's involvement in individual foreign markets is a gradual process. To a lesser extent it supports the hypothesis that a firm's choice of foreign market is influenced by business distance. Similar results were found in other Swedish studies (Johanson and Vahlne, 1977).

The gradual process of involvement in individual markets abroad can be understood as a response by firms to the greater uncertainty and ignorance which are associated with international business: 'Foreign operations are different from domestic and the difference is very much related to the problems of knowledge and the cost of information' (Carlson, 1975, p. 20). A firm beginning to export to a foreign market is not only likely to be ignorant of the market itself but is also likely to encounter what Carlson has termed 'frontier problems', which include potential problems involving both official procedures related to selling in a foreign market, e.g. customs regulations, and also foreign trade technicalities (Carlson, 1975, p. 7). The level of uncertainty and ignorance concerning these elements will tend to increase the greater the business distance between the markets.

During the early stages of exporting, firms exhibit a more concentrated foreign market focus, while increased involvement in foreign markets encourages diversification to a wider range of markets (Dalli, 1994; Naidu and Prasad, 1994). Many factors may explain this behaviour. With expansion, the firm's resource base may increase (Naidu and Prasad, 1994) while diversifying minimizes risks and exploits opportunities better than a concentrated strategy (Dalli, 1994). Also, the number of problems of managing a business in different foreign markets diminish as the firm gains more export expertise. With increased experience of the foreign market the firm begins to commit more resources to the endeavour. Eventually this may mean establishing a special unit within the company to organise and manage exporting activities (Exhibit 12.1).

Exhibit 12.1
Roll out the barrel

Exports are now a crucial element in the Guinness Ireland Group (GIG) success story, accounting for about 35% of the company's total output. After experiencing double digit growth in Europe in the early 1990s, GIG is now enjoying similar success in the North American market. To cope with the large expansion of exports, GIG set up a separate Export Business Unit in 1996. The main task of the unit was to co-ordinate all exports from the group's five breweries in Ireland into one channel and offer a one-stop-shop service in terms of customer service, including logistics, technical backup and pricing.

A key element in this growth has been the promotion of draught products shipped directly from Ireland. In turn, this has created a huge import business through the return of empty kegs to Ireland. While a lot of the growth in Europe has been due to the company's highly-successful development of the 'Irish Pub' concept, GIG is now making major inroads into the biggest market of all – North America – which has made the company Ireland's largest exporter by volume to the US. GIG ships 70 forty-foot containers of draught product from Dublin to the US every week – the equivalent of about 22,500 kegs. Exports to the US have grown by almost 25% for the past two years and are likely to maintain that trend for the foreseeable future.

The task of ensuring that this amount of product is shipped to order lies with Noel O'Rourke, Export Manager of GIG. From the brewery at St James's Gate, he coordinates the movement of kegged, packaged and bulk Guinness products form the five breweries to markets throughout the globe. South America remains as the 'final frontier', but this market is already being targeted.

The market breakdown is 40% Europe, 40% North America and 20% the rest of the world. Because of the size of the market and its distance from the production base, North America poses the greatest challenge, but also has enormous potential for further growth. 'As our volume has grown we have become increasingly conscious of the standards of customer service we provide and the standard which the customer expects', says Noel O'Rourke.

Source: Adapted from *Exporting Today*, (Ireland), January–February 1998.

Acquiring knowledge of export markets

As a firm's knowledge of an export market increases, the uncertainty factor diminishes. The key type of knowledge required here, however, appears to be experiential knowledge, i.e. knowledge obtained through operating in the market or 'learning by doing' (Carlson, 1975, p. 8; Olson, 1975). It is this type of knowledge which, according to Johanson and Vahlne (1977, p. 28) gives a decision maker a feel for the market and which allows the identification of concrete opportunities, as distinct from theoretical opportunities which may be apparent from objective or codifiable knowledge. The nature of objective knowledge is such that it can normally be acquired by, or transferred between, individuals relatively easily, e.g. operating manuals, but the acquisition of experiential knowledge is, by definition, a more gradual process.

Carlson has argued that the acquisition of knowledge of foreign operations follows a learning curve: 'At first this is a slow and difficult process. But as sales orders start to come in, the rate of accumulation of knowledge will increase, until at a certain point it reaches a peak. Later it will level off' (Carlson, 1975, p. 8).

This gradual acquisition of international experience suggests an explanation for the gradual involvement in foreign markets described above. Johanson and Vahlne (1977) developed the link between these two processes at a theoretical level: the level of involvement and the nature of the involvement. They then linked these dimensions with the gradual acquisition of experience. First, increases in the level of financial or resource commitment to the market are likely to be gradual. As uncertainty is gradually reduced through experience the firm may be more willing to increase the level of its commitment. Uncertainty affects risk, which affects the level of investment. A firm is therefore likely to be inhibited initially from committing large sums to a foreign market. As it acquires more market experience its inhibitions concerning investment expenditure are likely to weaken. In most countries government assistance of some form or another is available, which helps to reduce the uncertainty and to remove the risk of exporting.

Second, the nature of a firm's involvement will be gradual in the sense that it is likely to be an extension of the firm's existing activities in the market. According to Johanson and Vahlne (1977, p. 29), decisions to commit resources to foreign operations are made in response to perceived problems and opportunities in the market. Despite the theoretical development of the area and notwithstanding the Swedish findings on evolving export structures the precise dynamics of the export learning process is extremely vague.

Behavioural and firm-specific influences

In general, traditional economic theories of trade have given way to more behaviourally oriented theories as explanations of export behaviour (Bilkey, 1978). Trade theories, while having a function at the national level of analysis, are inadequate at the individual firm level. More recent theories of exporting are strongly influenced by the behavioural theory of the firm, which stresses decision-maker characteristics, organizational dynamics and constraints and ignorance and uncertainty as key variables in decision making.

Exporting has been described as a developmental process based on a learning sequence involving stages (Bilkey and Tesar, 1977). Six learning stages are assumed by these authors (Table 12.1). The Bilkey and Tesar research is one of the few empirical attempts to take account of experience effects and other behavioural influences. Their conclusions are based on an empirical study of 423 Wisconsin manufacturers. The probability of the firm moving from one stage to the next depends on the firm's international orientation, on its perception of the attractiveness of exporting and on management's confidence of competing successfully abroad (Bilkey, 1978). Increasing competition in world markets coupled with an inability to offer competitive prices abroad are the two most serious perceived barriers to exporting (Leonidou, 1995, p. 21). The limited availability of market information also constitutes a major impediment. Leonidou also reports that organizational inhibitors also exist – the firm's export experience, its size and the number of years in business. In this framework unsolicited export orders are critical to the firm becoming an experimental exporter. The movement between stages also depends on the quality and dynamism of management. For the experienced exporter at Stage 5, the proportion of output sold abroad depends on the firm's expectations with respect to the expected effect of the export operations on the profits and growth of the firm. In a study of Canadian firms Katsikeas *et al.* (1997, p. 67) discovered major differences between exporting stages:

- experimental and active exporters consider environmental munificence to play a more important role in influencing successful exporting than do committed exporters;
- committed exporters view export competence as a more important factor leading to success than do experimental exporters;
- export market accessibility is more important to the attainment of successful exporting activity among experimental exporters compared with active and committed exporters.

Despite the intuitive plausibility of the conclusions, the findings themselves are at best suggestive. Besides the dubious nature of some of the results (export experience was, for example, inversely related to the measure of quality of management), there are clearly methodological limitations in attempting to determine the effects of export experience by measuring large sample responses at a point in time. The stages models of export

---

Table 12.1 Stages in internationalization

Stage 1: Firm is not interested in exporting; ignores unsolicited business
Stage 2: Firm supplies unsolicited business; does not examine feasibility of active exporting
Stage 3: Firm actively examines the feasibility of importing
Stage 4: Firm exports on experimental basis to country of close business distance
Stage 5: Firm becomes an experienced exporter to that country
Stage 6: Firm explores feasibility of exporting to additional countries of greater business distance

Source: adapted from Bilkey, W. J. and Tesar, G. (1977) 'The export behaviour of smaller Wisconsin manufacturing firms', *Journal of International Business Studies*, **8** (2), 93–8.

development have recently come under attack on the grounds that they lack explanatory power and it is unclear how to predict movement from one stage to the next (Andersen, 1993, pp. 227–8).

A number of more recent export behaviour studies have suggested that direct stimuli, such as economic incentives and unsolicited orders, may be less important than internal behavioural influences. Cavusgil and Nevin (1981), for instance, concluded that four groups of variables internal to the firm explain whether firms engage in exporting:

1. managerial expectations about the effects of exporting on a firm's growth;
2. the extent to which management systematically explores exporting possibilities and plans for exporting;
3. the presence of differential firm advantages (including firm size);
4. the strength of managerial aspirations towards growth and market security.

These authors argue that it is management's predisposition to exporting which determines how a firm responds to export stimuli.

Managerial influences on exporting behaviour

In a similar vein Simpson and Kujawa (1974) found that active exporters tended to have higher profit perceptions concerning the effects of exporting and lower risk and cost perceptions than non-exporters. Again, the implication is that any direct stimulus, i.e. economic benefit, to exploit an export opportunity is likely to draw a different response from firms depending on their perceptions of exporting effects. Czinkota and Johnston (1983) and Abdel-Malek (1978) examined the relationship between firm size and attitudes to exporting and perceived problems in exporting. Both concluded that size was not a significant influence using samples of small- to medium-sized firms. The results of other earlier studies on the effect of size on a firm's propensity to export have been mixed, however (Bilkey 1978, p. 36). Rynning and Andersen (1993, p. 25) conclude, however, that government support should be made available only if the firm is large enough to allow for a division of labour and it should be present in markets outside its immediate area. Most companies attach limited importance, however, to export stimuli relating to aspects of national export policy but the receipt of unsolicited orders from customers abroad is an important factor in stimulating export decisions (Katsikeas, 1996, p. 14).

Background influences identified in other studies include personality factors, which are believed to affect the international orientation of small firms: 'A closed cognitive style reflected in the extent to which a manager is dogmatic about the international environment would seem to explain why potential exporters do not get started and are therefore not motivated to export.' (Bradley, 1984, p. 253).

The studies considered so far suggest that there are a large number of variables which potentially influence the initial export decision. Some of these may be regarded as more immediate in the causal process than others.

It is important to know whether the various influences discussed above are active at later stages of the internationalization process. There is some evidence to suggest that they are. Bilkey and Tesar (1977) provide one possible answer: it is possible that the relative strength of different influences changes as a firm becomes more experienced. It is possible, for example, that purely economic influences become relatively more important at the later stage, when exporters are more experienced.

Strategic influences on exporting

For many years there has been a debate in the literature concerning the degree to which a firm's international marketing activities can be standardized between countries (Levitt, 1983; Buzzell, 1968). Buzzell has argued against what he considers is an overemphasis on the need to adapt to individual markets. As support for his argument he points both to the success of certain multinationals having a high degree of standardization in their international strategies, e.g. Pepsi-Cola, and to the Italian household appliance industry. He also emphasizes the cost economies of standardization. At the same time he concedes that differences between markets may compel a firm to adapt. Market characteristics which he identifies as key influencing factors include stage of economic development, stage of product life cycle, marketing institutions and legal restrictions in the market.

Whether firms are actually influenced by environmental factors in deciding on the degree of adaptation is another question. Weinrauch and Rao (1974) found that over half of the exporters sampled adapted at least some elements of the marketing mix when selling abroad. Again, however, non-strategic reasons were behind many of these adaptations. Prices were increased because of the need to cover 'additional export costs', or products were adapted because of legal requirements in the foreign markets. Many small Italian firms limit their international commitment to exporting through agents and representatives and base their strategy on product quality, innovation flexibility and adaptation to individual customer needs (Bonaccorsi, 1993, p. 68). These studies suggest that environmental factors may not influence export decisions significantly in a strategic marketing sense. Finally, in formulating an international marketing plan, as in choosing a foreign market or a foreign market entry mode, most writers suggest that firms should engage in a detailed market analysis as a necessary step (Thorelli and Becker, 1980; Root, 1982). Root, for instance, suggests that before committing itself to a foreign market a firm should carry out a competitive audit of that market.

The findings discussed earlier in which firms tend to choose psychologically close markets initially suggests, however, that exporters may encounter difficulties in accumulating and evaluating the type of information required for competitive audits. Instead of choosing rationally between competing markets in the somewhat formal manner suggested by Root, firms may instead be constrained to pick those markets with which they feel most comfortable.

The export strategy that a firm develops has been shown to be closely linked to the export performance the firm achieves (Cooper et al., 1985). It appears, therefore, that a strategic approach to exporting is strongly related to marketing orientation among managers of firms who also have a strong international marketing orientation.

It is also likely to be related to the firm's strategy in the domestic market. Leonidou and Katsikeas (1996, p. 543) argue for an investigation of the export development process in conjunction with developments in the firm's domestic business strategy and environment, e.g. the introduction of new products in the market, changes in competitive structure and intensity and alterations in economic and political conditions.

Export decision process

Preparing for export markets

A firm's pre-export activities have been identified as an influence on the initial export decision. Wiedersheim-Paul *et al.* (1978) suggest that a firm's domestic expansion pattern, i.e. whether the firm expanded interregionally or not, affects its likelihood of exporting. Firms which expand activities into regions outside their immediate region in the domestic market are more likely to export than firms which confine themselves to their home region.

It is suggested that interregional expansion forces firms to develop skills in coping with uncertainty and in 'marketing a product at a distance' (Wiedersheim-Paul *et al.*, 1978, p. 51). The acquisition of these skills is more likely to predispose a firm towards exporting. A complex mix and interaction among these factors produces a certain level of commitment to exporting.

According to Welch (1982), four groups of factors influence export commitment. A simplified version of Welch's model identifies these as pre-export activities, direct export stimuli, latent influences on the firm and the role of the decision maker (Figure 12.2). The pre-export activities of information search, questioning of customers and others with knowledge of the process and tentative experimentation such as attending trade fairs or visiting the market are believed to have a pronounced effect on subsequent exporting behaviour. Direct export stimuli may come from within the company itself as a result of evaluations carried out by management or they may derive externally from the market.

Latent influences on the process include the history of the firm and its background and experience. Firm characteristics such as its ability to innovate, its flexibility and its record for customer service are other important latent influences. The firm's actual and potential base can determine the company's commitment to entering new foreign markets. Similarly, the external environment must be considered. The importance of exchange rates, economic growth in the target market and accessibility must be considered.

The role of the decision maker must be assessed. Decision makers are people with different personalities who operate in different value systems, have formed different attitudes to international markets, have different cognitive styles and have different experiences on which to base their evolutions. Each of these elements influences the decision maker in terms of commitment.

Within this system, there are a number of important feedback loops which must also be considered. The decision maker influences the pre-export activities carried out. The direct export stimuli also influence the decision maker and there is an interaction between export stimuli and the latent influences on the firm.

These include aspirations of management for goals such as growth, profits and market

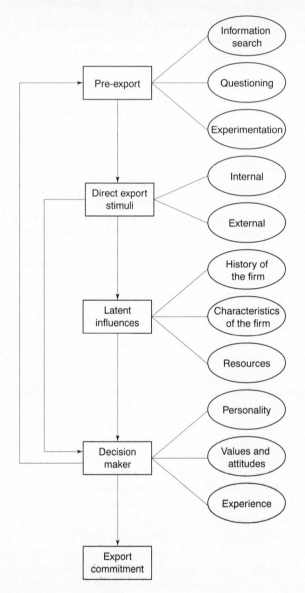

Figure 12.2 Commitment to exporting
Source: adapted from Welsh, L. (1982) 'Decision-making in the international context' in *Proceedings of the Seminar on Management Decision-making*, European Institute for Advanced Studies in Management, Oslo, June 1996, p. 96.

development. Aspiration levels are widely discussed in the theory of the firm literature as a determinant of risk-taking behaviour. The importance that the decision maker places on the achievement of the firm's business objectives is believed to be a direct determinant. Empirical studies support this expectation by revealing a positive relationship between export marketing behaviour and the decision maker's preference for certain business goals (Simmonds and Smith, 1968). Definite psychological motivational barriers to the internationalization process exist, which may be attributed to the absence of appropriate managerial aspirations.

Learning to export

Many small- and medium-sized enterprises wishing to become internationally traded companies seem to stall at the experimental exporter stage – Stage 4 (Table 12.1). Thus it would appear that anything which lowers the perception of risk for the individual company and provides more favourable expectations of profit would encourage these firms. Usually elements of encouragement are treated as independent of one another and subsumed under the rubric of motivation, whereas there is good reason to believe that more complex interactions are involved. Some researchers have sought to demonstrate that a certain cognitive style or international orientation is a necessary prerequisite for the motivation to internationalize. In this context Bradley (1984) maintains that the emphasis in the recent literature on motivation alone is misplaced.

He argues that attitudes to firm growth and motivation to internationalize both determine the level of internationalization reached by the firm (Figure 12.3). Attitude to company growth is influenced by the marketing environment technology and the institutional environment. Attitudes are also influenced by the way managers think or by their cognitive styles, whether they are closed minded or open minded.

The cognitive style of managers also influences the experience the firm has when it does venture abroad. Open-minded managers are more likely to report a positive experience from tentative internationalization steps whereas, for closed-minded managers, the experience is more likely to be negative. The outcome of these experiences influences the firm's motivation to internationalize, which may be low or high.

Many firms rely on third parties to take the initiative in developing export markets, which tends to lead to low expectations and passive behaviour. The experience of international markets thus gained by the firm becomes an important determinant of international marketing behaviour. Presumably, successful experience has a positive effect on the internationalization process, whereas a poor performance has a negative effect (Bradley, 1987).

A highly motivated firm with a positive attitude to growth is more likely to move from being a potential exporter to being a passive one to eventually being an active exporter, whereas a firm with low motivation and an indifferent attitude to company growth is likely to remain as a potential exporter or stall at the passive stage.

Size of firm and exporting activity

In many countries export-led growth is expected to come from the small-firm sector. The key issue becomes one of determining the extent to which the smaller firms possess the critical mass, will and commitment required to enter and compete successfully in export markets. Research on small exporting companies in many countries shows this sector to be

Figure 12.3 Influences on the internationalization process: a summary

highly unstable. Only a fraction of small exporters become established. Many treat international markets opportunistically and many are soon forced out by competitive pressures. Small firms face the danger of too much, or not enough, success and they frequently overextend themselves. They also spread their managerial and financial resources too thinly across markets. Other small exporters remain in foreign markets without success and finally resign themselves to inevitable failure before withdrawing.

Advances in all forms of communication help the smaller firm. Improvements in telecommunications and international airfreight services permit them to internationalize much more easily than could happen in the past. Indeed, the role of the internet has allowed many small firms access to customers in distant markets, once thought to be the preserve of large competitors. Furthermore, small high-technology companies have been very successful in international markets. Specialized firms serving niche markets do not need to be big. Their strengths are built on knowledge, technology and customer service, not size.

Many factors appear to influence the decision to export and subsequent exporting activity. Size of firm may be an influencing factor in some circumstances but is not the only factor, nor even the dominant influence in some situations.

Export marketing groups

There are many reasons why firms come together to form export marketing groups (Bradley, 1985). Frequently, firms form groups to counteract a common external threat such as increased import competition, entry by a new competitor or new public policy. Group marketing schemes are frequently found among small-scale firms attempting to enter export markets for the first time. Many such firms do not achieve sufficient scale economies in manufacturing or marketing because of the size of the local market or the inadequacy of the management resources available (Figure 12.4). The characteristics are typical of traditional, mature, highly fragmented industries such as furniture, textiles, clothing and footwear.

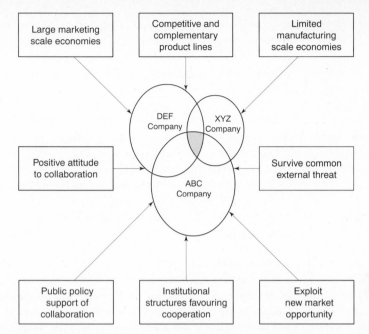

Figure 12.4 Forming export marketing groups: collaborative pressures and areas of common interest
Source: adapted from Bradley, M. F. (1985) 'Market and internal organisation in exporting for SMEs', *Developing Markets for New Products and Services Through Joint Exporting by Innovative SMEs Seminar*, Commission of the European Communities, Luxembourg, 6–7 March.

There are good behavioural reasons for collaboration among such firms. It is known that small and medium enterprises working together learn a great deal about international markets, and the experience obtained serves to confirm these firms as established exporters. Collaborative endeavours may need support from public policy in order to ensure that the benefits accrue to the small firms. Increasingly, small and medium enterprises become positively disposed towards export marketing groups when the benefits of such collaboration are apparent.

Of increasing importance in the formation of export marketing groups is the pervasive role of public policy in the management affairs of small firms. The increasing burden of dealing with the government forces smaller firms to seek new ways of accommodating these demands. In many countries state agencies are established with the objective of assisting small firms to export.

Other factors influencing the firm to join with others in such a group are the opportunities of effectively marketing a complementary product line, the presence of a positive attitude toward collaboration and the possibility of exploiting a new market opportunity. In forming groups firms try, as far as possible, to avoid competitive challenges arising within the group.

Finally, and perhaps the central issue to be discussed in forming export marketing groups, is the matter of common or shared interest among the participating firms. Firms

usually have different motivations for joining with others. Sometimes they wish to participate in groups to promote their range of products abroad, or to attend trade fairs or to sell
to particularly difficult markets. Others seek more sophisticated participation whereby the
product range of all the firms, e.g. a range of furniture, would be manufactured to an agreed
design by the different members of the group and distributed using the same marketing
programme in the same foreign markets. Frequently, firms have conflicting views as to
what the group should do and the area of common interest is thereby reduced. The size of
the oval shapes in Figure 12.4 attempts to indicate the extent of desire for three firms to
participate in an export marketing group. In this situation the area of common interest,
where the ovals overlap, is smaller, indicating restricted scope for the formation of a group.

In general, export marketing groups tend to be successful in situations where firms are
already marketing oriented, financially strong and fully appreciate the benefits and limitations of the group structure (Bradley, 1985). Some of the problems associated with
traditional export marketing groups may be avoided through the establishment of a
jointly owned and managed sales company to serve the export markets of interest. Such a
sales company, which would be owned in equal parts by a group of cooperating firms with
complementary (but not competitive) products and services, would be established as an
independent operation with profit-centre status. One of the major tasks of this company
would be to balance the interests of the other stakeholders and adjudicate on contentious
issues. From a study of successful consortia a number of guidelines for the creation and
operation of a jointly owned sales company are as follows:

1. Participant's products must be complementary upstream and downstream if total
   packages are being offered and horizontally if a 'full-line' range is to be made available
   (for example, in menswear: suits, overcoats, ties, socks and underwear).
2. Products or services must be compatible in quality and technology: low-technology
   equipment, for instance, is unlikely to fit comfortably in a range of high-technology
   products.
3. For horizontally linked products, customer firms and, ideally, individual buyers should
   be the same for all stakeholders.
4. Each participating member should have one nominee on the jointly owned sales
   company board holding a single vote.
5. The coordinators's (a member of the consortium) appointee makes the most effective
   chairman.

The essential ingredient is compatibility of corporate culture and, even more important,
of the chemistry of the individuals on the sales company board.

Assessing export competitiveness

Cost of exporting

Many firms new to exporting fail to realize that the cost of reaching the market can be
formidable. Sometimes it is advisable for the firm which does not have adequate funds to
seek new outlets in the domestic market rather than to enter a foreign market.

Many costs arise in exporting. A number of these are difficult to quantify but are nevertheless important. These include the cost of product modification and any packaging or labelling changes which have to be made and also the cost of researching the foreign market. The cost of obtaining customer and competitor information can be substantial and must be considered.

For the firm new to exporting it is important to realize that it is investing in its development and growth. Cash will be required for the initial research and for visits to the market selected; these tend to rise as the firm becomes more committed to the export market. Other costs also increase. Extra raw material for the increased demand will cost more money. Finally, the foreign customer may take a long time to pay. All these factors place a severe strain on the firm's cash flow. These are general considerations.

At a more specific level the firm must estimate the cost of sending a consignment of a product to a foreign buyer. First there are the costs of extra people, e.g. an export executive or manager. It would be necessary to add the cost of travel based on a number of visits to the market in a year. Second, one or two sales staff might be required to support the export manager. Third, it is necessary to allow for the cost of custom documentation, labels, samples and promotion. For some product groups these costs tend to be relatively high. Food marketing costs tend to be relatively high in foreign markets because of the cost of label changes, of complying with health regulations and of launching, including promotion through in-store testings and promotions.

By far the more important costs are those associated with the services provided by intermediaries such as distributors, wholesalers and retailers and agencies such as transport and insurance companies. Some of these costs are borne by the exporter while others are absorbed by the intermediaries and covered by their margins. A study of the cost of exporting Australian wine to the United Kingdom illustrates many of these points (McDougall, 1989). McDougall estimates that the retail price of a case of Australian wine in the United Kingdom was \$A180.41 while the price received by the winery was \$A56, less than one-third of the retail price (Table 12.2). The single largest element in the cost of a case of wine in these circumstances was the retail margin.

This example illustrates well the cost components that the exporting firm must consider. The information is based on a cost plus approach to the market, i.e. the final retail price is estimated based on identifying each cost element and accumulating them to find an estimated price at retail.

For most businesses cost is the only basis for establishing export pricing policies. This is understandable as individual cost elements for materials, labour and overheads can be measured and sometimes compared with those of competitors. Misunderstandings can occur between the company's accountants and salesforce in the interpretation and application of these cost elements. The two most common cost-oriented approaches to pricing are full absorption costing and marginal costing. Manufacturing costs are the basis for most pricing decisions because the elements which make up these costs can be sourced from within the company itself and are readily understood by everybody in the company. Having determined the costs of materials, direct labour overheads and a margin to allow for fixed costs and profit, these are added together to establish an appropriate price.

Absorption costing aims to recover or absorb the fixed costs of the exporting business.

Table 12.2 Estimated retail price in 1988 of a case of Australian wine in the United Kingdom

Cost factors	Per cent	$A	Remarks
Barossa Winery price	31.0	56.00	Assume selling price of $56 per case
Transport to Port Adelaide		0.35	Cost $347 to ship a container from Barossa Valley to Port Adelaide. On average, a container will hold 1,000 cases
Port Adelaide to			
United Kingdom	1.2	2.20	Adelaide–UK is $2,000/container
Landed cost			
United Kingdom	32.5	58.55	
Import duties and			
excise tax	12.1	21.90	As of June, 1988, import duties per litre of $0.20 and excise taxes of $2.2/litre or $21.87/case (assume $21.90 VAT)
Landed with duties and			
taxes	44.6	80.45	
Value added tax is 15 per cent	6.7	12.07	
Total landed cost	51.3	92.52	
Importer margin	15.4	27.75	An importer or distributor in the United Kingdom will charge between 25 and 40 per cent margin (assumed 30 per cent)
Wholesale price	66.7	120.27	
Retail margin	33.3	60.14	Retailer margins are approximately 50 per cent
Retail price	100.0	180.41	Equivalent to $15.03/bottle (750ml)

Notes:
1. The cost to ship a container from Port Adelaide to either the United States or Canada was about $2,500.
2. Importers in the United States will probably take a 40% margin.
3. In Canada, agents might be used at a commission of 10% of landed cost.

Source: McDougall, G. (1989) 'Barossa Winery: penetrating the international market', *International Marketing Review*, **6** (2), 18–33.

Costs are estimated and each unit sold is expected to carry or recover its share of variable and fixed costs. With regard to variable costs this approach is correct. The difficulty arises with regard to the allocation of fixed costs and in particular the use of an unchanged recovery rate for all subsequent pricing decisions made in the planning period. The firm usually decides the recovery rate for fixed costs at the beginning of the planning period based on a forecast of the number of units expected to be sold. Accountants usually advise a price based on full cost at normal capacity but where the actual number of units sold deviates from plan the overhead recovery rate used to calculate cost and fix price will be incorrect. If actual sales volumes fall below expectations the price charged will be insufficient to recover fixed overheads and losses may ensue. If sales exceed plan fixed overheads will be recovered and leave a surplus. In such circumstances it may be possible to reduce price without adversely affecting profit targets.

While in the long term all fixed costs must be recovered, otherwise the company goes out of business, the use of absorption costing is not especially helpful in making short-term price decisions. This is where marginal pricing may be used. Despite these difficulties absorption costing rather than marginal costing is the most common system found in industry. Absorption costing is usually used to establish the prices of new products where:

- specified sales levels are expected to be achieved and a separate production facility is planned – this is the conventional situation where the company plans to recover all costs;
- the company aims to recover its investment quickly thereby enabling a reduction in price at a later stage – this may encourage competitors to match the product offer at a lower price;
- the company adopts a price skimming strategy with a progressive reduction in price over the longer term – the reverse of this, a low price to penetrate the market quickly, and then to increase price progressively, is generally not feasible.

Marginal costs are those which, at a given level of output, are incurred when one additional unit is produced. Whereas absorption costing is used in primary pricing decisions for standard products, marginal costing is often used in what might be described as secondary pricing decisions, e.g. export orders, unusual quantities, once-off deals or subcontracting. Marginal analysis helps to answer the question: what happens to total profits if the selling price is changed? In this way marginal costing is future oriented; all past costs are sunk costs. With marginal pricing the company attempts to establish prices in order to maximize the total contribution to fixed costs and profit. Marginal cost pricing is useful when surplus manufacturing capacity is available to produce additional sales without any increase in fixed costs. This is usually a short-term phenomenon as in the longer term fixed costs must be recovered. Many companies in highly competitive industries work below full capacity and are able, in the short term at least, to increase output by more intensive utilization of the plant or the introduction of overtime working. Using marginal cost pricing may be attractive in the following circumstances:

- a low launch price generates a high rate of acceptance resulting in greater sales accompanied by positive experience curve effects;
- a secondary pricing decision is involved;
- surplus capacity exists owing to recession or slack demand;
- a short product life cycle is expected because of expected new technology;
- limited production runs or prototype production is involved;
- there is already a range of products generating sufficient contribution to meet fixed costs.

A major limitation of all cost-oriented pricing systems is that they do not take into account what the customer is prepared to pay for the product. This is the topic of the next section.

Pricing in export markets

The cost plus approach should be complemented by examining retail prices in the market and working backwards. It is necessary, therefore, to examine the market, the customer's needs and the effect these are likely to have on price. The successful firm attempts to maintain flexibility and discretion in price decisions; i.e. too much concentration on the cost side of the equation gives rise to an extremely jaundiced view of the scope available. The market and its potential should be the starting point and costs should be used to determine whether what is desired by the market can be produced at a profit.

One approach to this is to attempt to determine the effect of a market opportunity on profits or contribution by working backward from the established or accepted range of market prices and simultaneously working forward from the cost side. The gap that remains, if there is one, presents the firm with an estimate of profits or contribution to overheads. Where there is no gap remaining the firm should examine its costs more carefully or examine the potential of other market segments or different markets.

An illustration of the procedure demonstrates its value to the exporting firm. Assume that the firm has been asked by a potential customer in Germany to quote in DM for a quantity of the firm's Deluxe Honeyspread product. Furthermore, let us assume that initial market research in Germany indicated that the price bracket for a 12-jar carton of the product was DM60. There are two things the firm will want to know: will there be a profit or will there at least be a contribution to the overheads? Table 12.3 shows how it is possible to price from both ends, the demand side and the cost side, to see what profits or contribution can be made.

It is worth noting that there are many charges or costs which at first sight may not be obvious. Local wholesaler and retailer mark-ups, here assumed to be 25 per cent, and duties, here assumed not to apply because the business is being conducted entirely within the EU, are perhaps the two most important. From the CIF price thus derived it is necessary to allow for freight and insurance to arrive at the FOB price. Other deductions include dock handling charges in the exporter's country and the allowances to cover the direct export costs. Two sets of costs are assumed, direct manufacturing costs and an allocation for overheads. All figures are in DM to facilitate the discussion of the two approaches. By following this procedure two sets of residuals are computed: profits or contribution to overheads depending on circumstances. Many firms find that when this kind of analysis is performed the profit area disappears and the area of contribution may not be substantial. The example illustrates the importance of performing a detailed cost and price analysis before deciding whether to export to a particular market.

Successful firms in international markets frequently use both costs and prices in determining their competitive position. An overemphasis on one or other can lead to trouble. IKEA, the Swedish self-assembly furniture firm, recognized the market opening in many countries for entry-level furniture systems which were priced relatively low. By producing self-assembly kits and retailing them through catalogues and retail outlets on the outskirts of large cities IKEA has successfully entered many markets.

In the United States, Japanese, UK and German firms are perceived to compete in very different ways with regard to price. Two aspects of price were seen as important to buyers

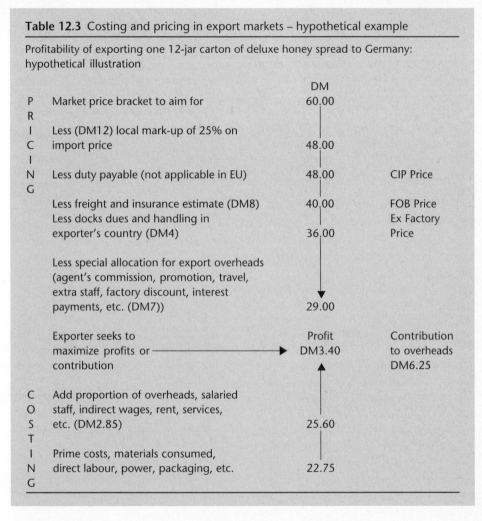

Table 12.3 Costing and pricing in export markets – hypothetical example

Profitability of exporting one 12-jar carton of deluxe honey spread to Germany: hypothetical illustration

		DM	
P	Market price bracket to aim for	60.00	
R			
I	Less (DM12) local mark-up of 25% on		
C	import price	48.00	
I			
N	Less duty payable (not applicable in EU)	48.00	CIP Price
G			
	Less freight and insurance estimate (DM8)	40.00	FOB Price
	Less docks dues and handling in		Ex Factory
	exporter's country (DM4)	36.00	Price
	Less special allocation for export overheads		
	(agent's commission, promotion, travel,		
	extra staff, factory discount, interest		
	payments, etc. (DM7))	29.00	
	Exporter seeks to	Profit	Contribution
	maximize profits or	DM3.40	to overheads
	contribution		DM6.25
C	Add proportion of overheads, salaried		
O	staff, indirect wages, rent, services,		
S	etc. (DM2.85)	25.60	
T			
I	Prime costs, materials consumed,		
N	direct labour, power, packaging, etc.	22.75	
G			

in the United States in a study by Williamson (1991): price volatility and relative price levels. The Japanese were perceived to have the lowest price volatility and lowest relative price for comparable products and were rewarded with the largest market share, represented by the size of the circle (Figure 12.5). Prices of German products were perceived to be high and somewhat volatile while UK products were perceived to be priced higher than the Japanese but lower than the German. They were perceived, however, as being very volatile and suffered in terms of market share. Even though the data on which Williamson based his study are almost 10 years old the message is still the same. A low-price–low price volatility strategy is more attractive than a high-price strategy where prices are volatile owing to fluctuating exchange rates. The £ sterling–US $ exchange rates were fluctuating considerably at the time of the study. Exporting companies seek the comfort of stable exchange rates and stable prices but it is up to them

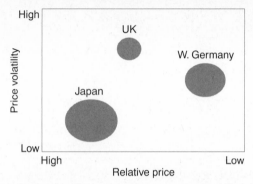

Figure 12.5 Export strategy and export performance in the US market
Source: adapted from Williamson, P. (1991), 'Successful strategies for export', *Long Range Planning*, 24 (1), 57–63.

to provide value in their products and services. The move toward a more benign exchange rate environment addresses the first issue; the second is a matter for companies themselves.

Coping with exchange rate movements

Exchange rate movements against the company's national currency can be favourable or unfavourable. These currency movements are important for exporters because they directly affect the 'bottom line'. Depending on the length of time and the volume of trade involved the consequences may be critical for the exporter. The situation is less serious where a large proportion of raw materials is also sourced from the same export market. Under the European Monetary System (EMS) 11 members of the EU now have the protection of the euro which removes the adverse effects of exchange rate movements. Much of international trade not denominated in the euro is carried out in US dollars and, hence, provides a similar protection against unexpected exchange movements.

For trade outside either of these currency systems companies may attempt to minimize the currency risk associated with export marketing by diversifying the range of export markets. Another way is to negotiate with the foreign buyer for payments to be made in the company's own currency. A further option, increasingly used by exporters, is to hedge against future exchange rate losses or gains by entering into forward foreign exchange contracts to protect against fluctuations. Many banks offer forward foreign exchange contracts for all major traded currencies. Such contracts are referred to as fixed or option where the former is used when the exact date of payment is known and the latter when the exporter is unsure of the actual date. The objective of such hedging is to protect the exporter's receipts from exchange rate movements over a period of time, usually ranging from three weeks to two years. Funds do not change hands until the contract completion date. The cost of the contract reflects the difference in interest rates between the domestic and the foreign currencies on the amount for the specified period. The principal advantages for exporters of contracting forward are:

- the elimination of uncertainty regarding the value of foreign payments;
- accurate cash flow budgeting of foreign receipts;

- a recognition that most companies do not wish to enter into currency speculation, preferring to concentrate on their core business activities.

Pricing for export competitiveness

While the management of costs is very important for success in international markets it is not the only consideration. The firm must also consider other factors. Costs serve as a bottom line and indicate how successful the firm is in serving the needs of particular customer groups. They do not indicate how that satisfaction might be achieved.

The successful firm usually competes on a number of marketing-related factors such as the product and associated services, quality, design, uniqueness, delivery reliability, business relationships and price. Buyers have many suppliers to choose from in most situations. In large country markets in particular, buyers can choose from among myriad suppliers located in many foreign countries.

Competitive success in export markets derives, however, not just from objective managerial characteristics but also from behavioural related aspects, such as attitudes, values and norms (Holzmüller and Stöttinger, 1996, p. 48). According to these authors, there are aspects of corporate culture which have a positive impact on export performance. Companies that are less power oriented, more flexible, organized, goal driven and consensus oriented tend to be more successful exporters (Holzmüller and Stöttinger, 1996, p. 48). Export competitiveness is influenced by both managerial and marketing issues and behavioural and attitudinal factors.

The reality of export marketing is that many factors must be considered in establishing export prices:

- the company's export marketing objectives – is the firm attempting to penetrate or skim the market?
- the position of the product in the market and in the life cycle;
- the activities of competitors;
- other elements of the marketing mix;
- the company's financial and marketing strength and the characteristics of the export market.

Even acknowledging the relevance of all of the above factors the firm is still faced with making a decision on what price to charge. Unfortunately there is no way of determining what the best price should be. Prices can range from the low suggested by marginal cost pricing to a price higher than the competition on the assumption that the product can carry a premium for quality or some other benefit. For new products which are innovative a price skimming strategy may be used. Marginal cost pricing can be used to set the minimum prices to be charged. Successful companies use absorption costs to set long-term prices. It is also essential to consider competitor products and prices when setting prices. Finally, for exporters the financial stability of the respective currencies of buyers and seller must be considered. Taking all these factors together suggests that a range of prices from the low of marginal cost price to the high upper price limit which represents a premium for product quality over competitor prices must be considered (Figure 12.6).

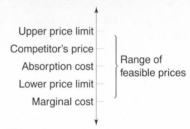

Upper price limit
Competitor's price
Absorption cost   } Range of
Lower price limit   feasible prices
Marginal cost

Figure 12.6 A range of feasible prices

Payments and finance for exports

Methods of payment

There are four basic methods of payment for exports. In order of security for the exporter they are advance payment, payment by cheque, payment by bank draft and payment by telegraphic transfer. The chosen method will depend on the respective standing of buyer and seller, competitive pressures and the degree of security required by each party. Regardless of payment method, it is important to obtain a credit reference on the customer from a credit reference agency.

Advance payment means that the importer pays the exporter at some agreed stage prior to despatch of the goods. Although full payment in advance is obviously most desirable for the exporter, it is only obtainable when there is a seller's market, or occasionally when such terms are customary in a particular trade. It is more common for a sale contract to require partial payments in advance; for example, the contract could stipulate 20 per cent payment on signing with the remaining 80 per cent due after despatch of the goods under one of the other methods of payment. When exporting on advance payment terms or 'open account terms' payment is usually by cheque, bank draft or telegraphic transfer.

It is very common for exporters to despatch goods and to request payment by return cheque or in accordance with agreed credit terms. Although this is the simplest method for the exporter, receiving payment by cheque from another country has a number of disadvantages. First of all, postal delays can cause problems. It may be more accurate to state that the post is too often blamed for late payment.

Second, there is always the possibility that the cheque will bounce. Because of the time and distance involved, it is always more difficult to resolve such problems. When a cheque in foreign currency is returned unpaid to the company's account, the bank will debit the company using the current rate on the date of receipt of the cheque. This rate could be worse than that used to lodge the cheque so the company also faces potential loss on exchange in addition to bank charges. The third disadvantage is that the bank rate quoted to convert currency may not be as favourable as that for currency received by telegraphic transfer. The reason is that the bank has to wait until the cheque clears the banking system before it is reimbursed.

Payment by bank draft is a much more secure way to settle outstanding invoices. One bank draws a cheque on another and the exporter receives a fully negotiable draft. Payment can normally be obtained immediately and drafts can be issued in local or foreign currency. If the bank wants to verify the signatures on the draft, this can involve a short delay. Postal and other delays apply in the same way to the draft as for the cheque and the rate of exchange may be less favourable than payment by telegraphic transfer.

Payment by telegraphic transfer is the best way to transmit funds from the point of view of speed, security and invoice details. Most telegraphic transfers are made through SWIFT, a computerized payment system used by most international banks. To help the customer to pay by SWIFT, the company should supply its bank details, i.e. account number, bank address and other relevant details.

Next to advance payment, the most secure method of payment is formally to request a letter of credit, also known as documentary credit. This is a written undertaking given by a bank on behalf of the buyer to pay the seller an amount of money within a specific time, provided that the seller presents documents strictly in accordance with the terms laid down in the letter of credit. The procedure begins by the importer agreeing to pay the exporter by means of an irrevocable letter of credit, the benefit of which is that the exporter has a bank payment commitment before despatch of the goods.

The exporter should note that this is conditional on documents being presented which comply strictly with the terms and conditions of the letter of credit. If the exporter does not comp   cumentation, the bank's commitm   the buyer authorizing payment   uctions.

It is ver   orrect or do not comply with the   lost as a result of such discrepan   tract, but on the basis of document   t.

There a   nt types of international trade. Ho   r 'revocable'. Letters of credit are   he parties to the credit cannot be   otection for exporters. Revocable   led by the importer and accordingl   e letter of credit clearly states it is   oreign issuing bank will usually ins   porter that the letter of credit has l   itions. Unless the credit is confirme   on the foreign issuing bank's und   ts are presented. When the advising bank adds its confirmation, it guarantees that, provided that all terms and conditions of the credit are strictly complied with, payment will be made irrespective of what may happen to the issuing bank or the importer abroad.

The importer will need documents under the letter of credit with evidence of the shipment of the goods. The documents most often required are commercial invoices, complete sets of bills of lading or other transport documents, insurance certificates, certificates of origin and certificates of inspection. If for any reason the company cannot comply with the terms of a letter of credit, it should immediately contact the buyer and request that an amendment be issued by the buyer's bank.

The Headingley Library
Leeds Metropolitan University

Borrowed

Customer   Zhou, Mi

Due Date

1 International marke   27/9/2007,23:59
1702215488

07.09.2007 21:12:54

For renewals telephone (0113) 812 6161
Thank you and see you soon

When the company is able to comply with the terms of the credit, it can despatch its goods and present the documents to the bank where the credit is available. If the bank finds them in order, it will effect payment or acceptance in accordance with the credit terms. When letters of credit are available by payment, the exporter is paid shortly after presentation of correctly tendered documents. When credits are available by acceptance, the exporter receives an undertaking to pay on a future date with an accepted bill of exchange. This can usually be converted into cash by discounting it.

The rules governing letters of credit are issued and revised from time to time by the International Chamber of Commerce (ICC) and are adhered to by banks virtually worldwide. There are many different forms of letter of credit to suit most export transactions.

A documentary collection is a collection order with shipping documents attached. A bill of exchange may also be included. The documents, including a transport document, go to the exporter's bank, which then sends them to a bank in the buyer's country. The overseas buyer is then notified of their arrival and the terms on which they will be released.

If an exporter is dealing with a first-class buyer with a long and successful business relationship, business is often conducted on an open account basis. Competitive pressures may also make this a necessity. The exporter despatches the goods and sends the documents directly to the buyer. Immediately, or in accordance with agreed credit terms, the buyer makes payment by cheque, bank draft or telegraphic transfer.

The risks of non-payment need careful consideration as legal procedures to enforce payment under open account are more complicated than for a bill of exchange. When trading on open account, an exporter should consider how cash flow and banking facilities are affected if, as is common, payment is delayed. These delays have to be funded from some source, the firm's own cash resources or bank facilities. For the importer, open account is very attractive, as payment can be made cheaply and with minimum formality.

Invoicing in domestic currency is a simple approach for the exporter but, unfortunately, not a strategy to increase business or expand into new markets. The exporter has no exchange risk, passing the risk to the importer abroad. Invoicing in euro within the EU is now essential for business in the EU.

Currency hold accounts are very similar to commercial current accounts but are maintained in foreign currency. They are ideal for traders who have a two-way currency flow. Currency receipts for exports are held on account to meet payments in that currency. They are very flexible and payments can be made by cheque, bank draft or telegraphic transfer. Interest may also be earned on cleared credit balances with currency accounts in many cases.

Forward contracts are the traditional way to remove foreign exchange risk. These remove the fluctuation risk and help the company to calculate export prices as it calculates invoice values on an exchange rate fixed well in advance of receiving payment. The bank fixes a rate for a payment due on a specified date. Regardless of what happens to currency markets in the meantime, the forward contract rate applies to the transaction. Both the bank and the customer are obliged to fulfil the contract. The only problem is that, if the currency does not materialize as expected, the company could suffer a foreign exchange loss.

The option forward contract is a variation of the fixed forward contract, outlined above, and is very useful to the exporter who is confident of payment, but not sure when it will appear. It is like a standard forward contract but, instead of one maturity date, provides a period between specified dates for delivery of currency. In simple terms, this is a much more flexible form of forward contract.

Another way to manage currency risk is to borrow foreign currency. Exporters who are confident of receiving payment in foreign currency can approach the bank to negotiate a foreign currency loan. If the bank lends the currency, it can be converted to local currency on the day the loan is drawn down. The loan remains in foreign currency and should be repaid when the currency payment arrives. From the date the loan proceeds are drawn down, currency risk is eliminated. The exporter may also benefit from a low rate of interest, depending on the currency involved.

Finance for exports

A traditional source of funds to business people and exporters is the use of overdraft limits. A borrowing limit is agreed on a current account and is reviewed by the bank from time to time. Overdrafts are technically repayable on demand with interest charged rates on the day to day balance. Overdrafts are a fluctuating borrowing and the account is normally expected to revert to credit for fixed periods each year, a policy which would be set by local banking institutions.

Loans are a more formal and less flexible way of borrowing than overdrafts. They are granted for a specific purpose with agreed regular reductions taking place over the life of the loan. The interest rate depends on market rates, the duration of the loan and the credit standing of the borrower. Provided that the borrower complies with the terms, the bank cannot ask for repayment sooner than the agreed period.

Invoice discounting is a flexible source of finance linked to sales performance. As sales grow, so does the funding based on the approved debts. The service is designed for substantial business with a good financial record, effective credit control and administration.

Since finance available is based on the fluctuating debtor balance, businesses enjoy higher funding than is normally available through loans or overdrafts. This eliminates the need for frequent negotiation with bankers for extended facilities. Generally, the rates of interest for advances are slightly above normal overdraft interest rates. There is also an administration fee for the service. Finance is normally 'with recourse', which means the finance house could look to the firm for repayment or reduce the funding in the event of default by the customer. Companies with good profit margins and growing sales derive the best benefits from invoice discounting facilities. Having an export credit insurance policy can facilitate obtaining finance and have a favourable effect on the interest rate charged.

A bill of exchange is an unconditional written order from the seller, requesting the buyer to pay on demand, or on a specified future date, a certain amount of money. The person to whom the bill of exchange is addressed signs the bill, signifying acknowledgement of the debt and the intention to make payment.

Depending on the method of payment used, bills may be accepted by importers or banks for payment in the future. On acceptance, the company may be able to convert the bill into cash by discounting it with its bank. The credit rating of the acceptor of the bill will be a major factor for a bank providing discount finance. When bills are drawn under letters of credit, there is little formality subject to complying with the letter of credit document requirements.

Summary

Exporting is the simplest way of entering a foreign market, requiring a low level of investment in terms of managerial and financial resources and consequently a low level of corporate commitment and risk. This makes it an ideal first step to internationalization for many firms and a useful strategy for firms in risky and uncertain markets. The export decision is influenced by three sets of influences on the firm: (a) experience and uncertainty effects; (b) behavioural and firm specific influences; (c) strategic influences on exporting. The firm's activities at the pre-export stage have an important influence on the firm's initial export direction. Several factors affect the firm's decision to internationalize: degree of international orientation; previous experience; perceptions of risk and return. Government-sponsored export stimulation measures, product characteristics and unsolicited export orders also play an important role at this stage. Opinion among researchers and managers is divided on the issue of the relationship between firm size and export success. The importance of a positive managerial attitude to exporting and the necessity of committing managerial and financial resources to the internationalization process is emphasized, however, irrespective of the size of the firm. The costs associated with exporting – market research, product adaptation, market visits, shipping and agency fees – have a strong influence on a firm's export activity and it is in this area that a large firm may have an advantage over a small one. In assessing the cost of exporting and competitiveness the areas of service, quality, design and product uniqueness are very important. The exporting firm succeeds by being cost competitive and also by being competitive in other areas of marketing.

Discussion questions

1. Why is exporting frequently considered the simplest way of entering foreign markets and favoured by smaller firms?

2. Three sets of factors are believed to influence the firm's decision to export. Identify these factors and discuss their relative importance.

3. The behaviour and activity of the firm prior to exporting is thought to have a very great effect on the degree of success of the firm. Discuss.

4. Size of firm is often cited as a barrier to successful exporting. It is argued that the firm must be large to succeed. Do you agree?

5. What is meant by export competitiveness? How might the firm determine its overall competitiveness in export markets?

References

Abdel-Malek, T. (1978) 'Export marketing orientation in small firms', *American Journal of Small Business*, **3**, 24–35.

Andersen, O. (1993) 'On the internationalization process of firms: a critical analysis', *Journal of International Business Studies*, **24** (2), 209–231.

Bilkey, W. J. (1978) 'An attempted integration of the literature on the export behaviour of firms', *Journal of International Business Studies*, **9** (1), 33–46.

Bilkey, W. J. and Tesar, G. (1977) 'The export behaviour of smaller Wisconsin manufacturing firms', *Journal of International Business Studies*, **8** (2), 93–8.

Bonaccorsi, A. (1993) 'What do we know about exporting by small Italian manufacturing firms? *Journal of International Marketing*, **1** (3), 49–75.

Bradley, M. F. (1984) 'Effect of cognitive style, and attitude toward growth and motivation on the internationalization of the firm', in J. Sheth (ed.), *Research in Marketing*, Vol. 7, Greenwich, CT: JAI Press, pp. 237–59.

Bradley, M. F. (1985) 'Market and internal organization in exporting for SMEs', *Developing Markets for New Products and Services Through Joint Exporting by Innovative SMEs Seminar*, Commission of the European Communities, Luxembourg, 6–7 March.

Bradley, M. F. (1987) 'Nature and significance of international marketing: a review', *Journal of Business Research*, **15**, 205–19.

Buzzell, R. D. (1968) 'Can you standardize multinational marketing', *Harvard Business Review*, **46** (November–December), 102–13.

Carlson, S. (1975) 'How foreign is foreign trade?', *Acta Universitatis Upsaliensis, Studia Oeconomiae Negotiorum II*, Uppsala, Sweden, Bulletin No. 15.

Cavusgil, S. T. and Nevin, J. R. (1981) 'Internal determinants of export marketing behaviour – an empirical investigation', *Journal of Marketing Research*, **18**, 114–19.

Cooper, R., Elko, G. and Kleinschmidt, J. (1985) 'The import of export strategy on export sales performance', *Journal of International Business Studies*, **16** (Spring), 37–55.

Czinkota, M. and Johnston, W. J. (1983) 'Exporting: does sales volume make a difference?' *Journal of International Business Studies*, **14** (1), 147–53.

Czinkota, M. R., Rivoli, P. and Ronkainen, I. A. (1992) *International Business*, 2nd edn, Fort Worth, TX: Dryden.

Dalli, D. (1994) 'The exporting process: the evolution of small- and medium-sized firms toward internationalization' in C. N Axinn (ed.) *Advances in international Marketing*, Vol. 6, Greenwich, CT: JAI Press, pp. 85–110.

Holzmüller, H. and Stöttinger, B. (1996) 'Structural modeling of success factors in exporting: cross-validation and further development of an export performance model', *Journal of International Marketing*, **4** (2), 29–55.

Johanson, J. and Vahlne, E. (1977) 'The internationalization process of the firm – a model of knowledge development and increasing foreign market commitments', *Journal of International Business Studies*, **8** (1), 23–32.

Johanson, J. and Wiedersheim-Paul, F. (1974) 'The internationalisation of the firm – four Swedish cases', *Journal of Management Studies*, **3**, 305–22.

Katsikeas, C. S. (1996) 'Ongoing export motivation: differences between regular and sporadic exporters', *International Marketing Review*, 13 (2), 4–19.

Katsikeas, C. S., Deng, S. L. and Wortzel, L. H. (1997) 'Perceived export success factors of small and medium-sized Canadian firms', *Journal of International Marketing*, **5** (4), 53–72.

Leonidou, L. C. (1995) 'Export barriers: non-exporters' perceptions', *International Marketing Review*, **12** (1), 4–25.

Leonidou, L. C. and Katsikeas, C. S. (1996) 'The export development process: an integrative review of empirical models', *Journal of International Business Studies*, **27** (Third Quarter), 517–51.

Levitt, T. (1983) 'The globalization of markets', *Harvard Business Review*, **61** (May–June), 92–102.

McDougall, G. (1989) 'Barossa Winery: penetrating the international market', *International Marketing*, **6** (2), 18–33.

Naidu, G. M. and Prasad, V. K. (1994) 'Predictors of export strategy and performance of small- and medium-sized firms', *Journal of Business Research*, **27**, 85–101.

Olson, H. C. (1975) 'Studies in export promotion. Attempts to evaluate export measures for the Swedish textile and clothing industries', *Research Paper*, University of Uppsala.

Root, F. R. (1982) *Foreign Market Entry Strategies*, New York, NY: Amacom.

Rynning, M.-R. and Andersen, O. (1993) 'Structural and behavioural predictors of export adoption: a Norwegian study', *Journal of International Marketing*, **2** (1), 73–89.

Simmonds, K. and Smith, H. (1968) 'The first export order: a marketing innovation', *British Journal of Marketing*, **2**, 93–100.

Simpson, C. and Kujawa, D. (1974) 'The export decision process: an empirical enquiry', *Journal of International Business Studies*, **5**, 107–17.

Terpstra, V. and Sarathy, R. (1994) *International Marketing*, 6th edn, Fort Worth, TX: Dryden.

Thorelli, H. B. and Becker, H. (1980) *International Marketing Strategy*, Oxford: Pergamon Press.

Weinrauch, J. D. and Rao, C. (1974) 'The export marketing mix: an examination of company experiences and perceptions', *The Journal of Business Research*, **2** (4), 447–52.

Welch, L. (1982) 'Decision-making in the international context', in *Proceedings of the Seminar on Management Decision-Making*, Oslo: European Institute for Advanced Studies in Management, June.

Wiedersheim-Paul, F., Olson, H. C. and Welch, L. S. (1978) 'Pre-export activity: the first step in internationalization', *Journal of International Business Studies*, **9** (1), 47–58.

Williamson, P. (1991) 'Successful strategies for export', *Long Range Planning*, **24** (1), 57–63.

13

Strategic alliances

In this chapter we examine various types of interfirm alliances formed to enter and compete in international markets. In particular, we examine the nature of strategic alliances and how they form part of the continuum of entry methods. The next section examines marketing partnership agreements, followed by sections on licensing, franchising and joint ventures. The last section examines ways of evaluation and controlling strategic alliances in international markets.

Nature of strategic alliances

Competitive alliances allow firms to procure assets, competencies, or capabilities that are not readily available in competitive factor markets, particularly specialised expertise. A joint venture to gain access to complex technological or product development capabilities would be an example. Tangible assets, such as reputation, would also be included. For example, a global alliance formed with a local host to enhance the firm's reputation in the local market (Oliver, 1997, p. 707)

For British Airways strategic alliances are necessary to serve their customers wherever in the world they wish to fly (Exhibit 13.1).

Exhibit 13.1
Staying ahead of the pack in British Airways

British Airways must be a global business, capable of serving our customers' needs wherever in the world they wish to fly, according to Robert Ayling, Chief Executive. 'To help achieve this, we have already formed alliances with a number of other like minded airlines in parts of the world where our own presence is not as prominent – Qantas, one of the top pacific carriers; Deutsche BA, Germany's number two airline; and TAT and Air

Liberaté, France's leading independents. In the UK, we have reached franchise agreement with a range of regional carriers, taking the British Airways brand to communities and routes which we cannot serve directly ourselves'.

'Last summer, we announced plans for a new alliance with the leading US carrier, American Airlines. The alliance does not involve any exchange of equity or other forms of cross-ownership. Both airlines will retain their own identities, brands, and nationalities, and will continue to operate their own services across the Atlantic and elsewhere with their own craft and crew, and offering their own distinctive styles of service. You will still be able to choose to fly on British Airways or American Airlines'.

'Co-ordinating our schedules will also mean we can offer you the widest choice of departure times between the UK and the USA. Transfers between British Airways and American Airlines flights will be as simple as possible, so your travel is as hassle free as we can make it'.

'Our alliance depends on approval by the competition authorities on both sides of the Atlantic. This is expected to hinge on the UK and the US governments ending their current restrictions on flights between the two countries. With many other airlines already queuing up to take advantage of this, it will mean more competition and choice for consumers, and that will result in more downward pressure on fares and more upward pressure on service standards'.

Source: adapted from *First Quarterly*, 1997, **2** (1), 87.

Access to technology and markets

Strategic alliances may be used by firms to obtain increased access to a technology they do not possess or to a market they would like to enter. Licensing is seen as a low-risk, low-reward way of entering these markets that the firm is not really interested in developing or believes to be very complicated and risky. This option is frequently taken as a 'better than nothing' strategy. Synergistic new-style joint ventures in which large companies join small ones to create a new entry in the market are increasingly in evidence. The small company provides the products and technology while the large one provides access to the market (Hlavacek *et al.*, 1977). Technology is defined as know-how relevant to the solution of manufacturing and marketing problems. It is necessary to distinguish between process technology, which relates to functions within the firm such as purchasing, production or marketing, and product technology, which relates to product and services manufacturing. For many firms independent technological development would result in inferior products and low-entry barriers.

A frequent response of firms attempting to enter protected market or markets manifesting the neo-protectionism sometimes provided by governments or accorded to favoured incumbents, is to establish manufacturing operations behind these barriers. Critical to success in these circumstances is access to local distribution.

Basis for a strategic alliance

Firms may form an alliance to compete in international markets based on the exchange of a range of assets. The possession of product-market knowledge is such an asset. Access to markets and distribution channels are assets possessed by some firms and sought by others, thereby giving rise to the possibility of a strategic alliance. Similarly, product and process know-how, spare manufacturing capacity, scarce raw materials and unique management resources may form the basis of a strategic alliance in the markets (Table 13.1).

The strategic alliance may take many forms. It may range from a simple contractual agreement to cross-distribute products to production agreements where the production stages of a product are shared. There are many types of marketing and production agreements, forming the basis of strategic alliances. A partnership which reflects greater commitment may be found under franchising, licensing and joint ventures. These various forms of alliance represent a continuum of increasing commitment to the partnership.

Table 13.1 Immediate complementarity in strategic alliances

Nature of alliances		Nature of asset
Marketing partnership	Partner A	Product-market knowledge; market access–distribution
	Partner B	product know-how
Production agreements	Partner A	Process know-how; manufacturing capability; raw materials; management
	Partner B	Product and process know-how
Franchising	Partner A	Market access–distribution; manufacturing capability; management
	Partner B	Product-market knowledge; market access–distribution; product and process know-how; raw materials; management
Licensing	Partner A	Product-market knowledge; market access–distribution; manufacturing capability; raw materials; management
	Partner B	Process know-how;
Joint ventures	Partner A	Market access–distribution; product know-how; manufacturing capability; raw materials; management
	Partner B	Product-market knowledge; product and process know-how; raw materials; management

The commitment in agreements may refer to one product market for a limited period, whereas the joint venture usually involves the commitment of financial, managerial and technological resources for a considerable time (Table 13.1).

In all strategic alliances there is a reciprocal arrangement in the exchange. This reciprocity may be complementary in the short term and of immediate benefit to the partner firms.

As strategic alliances are nurtured and grow over time the partner firms may form closer alliances or bonds. With experience and a better understanding of each other's capabilities and objectives the form of the alliance may evolve toward a situation where the partners work together to gain access to new third markets and raw technologies. Sometimes firms begin to develop and manufacture new products jointly. This dynamic convergence of resources, capabilities and business objectives may occur quite rapidly but is usually an evolutionary process taking a number of years. The final point in the convergence stage arises when the firms decide to form a functional merger (Table 13.2). Evolutionary complementarity reflects the strengths of each partner in the key assets to be exchanged. Note the complete matching of resources and capabilities under each heading: each firm possesses strengths of a complementary nature which form the basis of the alliance.

Table 13.2 Evolutionary complementarity in strategic alliances

Nature of alliance or agreement	Nature of asset possessed by Partner A and Partner B
Market access	Market access–distribution
Raw material access	Raw materials; management
New product development	Product-market knowledge; product and process know-how
Manufacturing	Manufacturing capacity; management
Financial merger	Product-market knowledge; market access–distribution; product and process know-how; manufacturing capacity; raw materials; management

Marketing partnership agreements

For firms with significant sales and physical distribution systems established in a large market such as the United Kingdom or Germany, there may be opportunities to market the products of, say, US firms suitably adapted for the market through the existing channels of distribution. For the smaller firm particularly, organic internal growth or acquisition may not be an option. A partnership on a complementary basis may be less risky and potentially more rewarding. Looked at from the opposite perspective there are many small- to medium-sized exporters in the United States who are not active in international markets but who provide a ready made pool of well-equipped, technically sophisticated but internationally inexperienced firms who could serve as partners to European firms with guaranteed market access.

In services there has been considerable activity in establishing partnerships to compete in the global marketplace. Airlines, especially the smaller ones, have discovered that partnership agreement, possibly leading to full mergers, may be the only way to survive in global markets. Indeed, the larger airlines have recognized that none of them on their own is capable of serving the global needs of customers and many have formed marketing partnership agreements to provide a relatively seamless service to customers. Many such large alliances now exist which compete as business systems one with the other with the objective of gaining and holding market share of a growing business (Exhibit 13.2).

=== Exhibit 13.2 ===
Airlines follow alliance trends

Singapore Airlines (SIA) was due to sign an agreement with Ansett Australia and its 50% shareholder Air New Zealand at the end of June. The deal will tie all three into a major regional – and ultimately global – airline alliance. The alliance will initially give Singapore Airlines greater access to Australia, from where it derives 20% of its business, and will open the door to Europe for Ansett. The alliance will mean joint services between Australasia and Europe via Singapore, joint pricing by the airlines, and revenue sharing.

An alliance between SIA and Ansett would give the carrier a better chance of tapping the revenue produced by services which allow airlines to carry passengers to multiple destinations. For all three airlines, the importance of the agreement is that in the new era of global alliances, the linchpin of competition is the strength of a link-up's regional hubs, especially those that enable carriers to dominate major flows of international passenger traffic. This latest alliance will establish the Lion City as a superhub.

Singapore Airlines has previously steered away from full-blown alliances, although it has continued to show interest in Australia after losing out to British Airways (BA) in the 1992 Qantas sale. An attempt to buy into Melbourne-based Ansett in 1993–94 foundered because SIA baulked at News Corp's asking price for its half share. SIA, despite being one of the world's two most profitable airlines (along with British Airways), was in danger of becoming isolated as the leading carriers continue to forge global alliances.

For Ansett, Air New Zealand and to some extent, Singapore Airlines, it was a case of join a club, or be sidelined from the global dogfight in the skies.

Source: adapted from *Asian Business*, July 1997, p. 68.

Licensing in international markets

Licensing avoids the risks of product and/or market development by exploiting the experience of firms that have already developed and marketed the product. It also provides a useful vehicle for the internationalization of small firms that might not have the capital or foreign experience to establish a joint venture or a wholly owned subsidiary (Carstairs and Welch, 1983). It possesses the advantage of reducing a firm's exposure to financial risk, as fixed asset investment is minimized owing to the utilization of another firm's existing investment.

The cost of transferring technology is frequently cited as an impediment to such developments. Williamson (1975) and Teece (1981) suggest that criteria based on minimizing transaction costs should be the determinant of the control structures chosen for the transfer of know-how. The greater the possibility of transferring technology in coded or blue-print form the lower the cost of transfer. Uncodified or tacit knowledge requires face-to-face communication for successful transmission and is therefore slow and expensive to transfer. Herein lies a major value of licensing; the costs of knowledge transfer are relatively low.

Nature of international licensing

Licensing is the purchase or sale by contract of product or process technology, design and marketing expertise. It involves the market contracting of knowledge and know-how, which is a 'sleeping asset – it lies hidden in people's heads, their desk drawers and filing cabinets – a potential source of income waiting to be packaged' (Millman, 1983, p. 3).

International licensing arises when a firm provides for a fee or royalty technology needed by another firm to operate its business in a foreign market. Licensing of this form involves one or a combination of the following: a brand name; operations expertise; manufacturing process technology; access to patents and trade secrets. The licensor firm gains access to a foreign market with very low investment and frequently obtains the investment and market knowledge of a competent local firm. The licensee firm gains access to a foreign technology with very low investment.

International licensing may be a preferred strategy in some circumstances. It may be attractive in situations where host countries restrict imports and/or foreign direct investments, where the foreign market is small, where the prospects of technology feedback are high, where technological change is so rapid that the licensor remains technologically superior and where opportunities exist for licensing auxiliary processes without having to license basic product technologies (Contractor, 1981, p. 74).

License agreements generally fall into two categories: a current technology license, giving the licensee access to the technology which the licenser possesses at the time of the agreement; a current and future technology license, giving access to technology developed by the licensor in a specified product area during the life of the agreement. License agreements vary depending on circumstances but normally contain aspects of a technical, commercial and organizational nature in addition to the patented technology being transferred.

Increasingly, firms in different parts of the world share the development of new technology. Many Japanese, European and American firms have united to exploit technological advances in addition to marketing and manufacturing capabilities. They have done so by licensing arrangements involving cross-regional alliances with firms which operate outside their domestic markets. Managers of Australian licensee firms are more likely to be internationally oriented, to have a greater awareness of successful inward licensing activities of other firms and to have lower perceptions of the costs of inward licensing (Atuahene-Gima, 1992, p. 83). These firms also perceive higher general market competition than do non-licensee firms.

Benefits of licensing

There are several reasons why a company might wish to acquire technology or know-how through licensing. The firm in a high-technology industry which lacks resources required for research and development may have no alternative but to license. In an industry where technology is changing rapidly it may also be wise for some firms to consider licensing. Licensing is especially important in diversification strategies where new markets can be entered by buying not only product technology but also marketing and production know-how. There are numerous very clear benefits to licensing in international markets (Table 13.3); there are also a number of disadvantages.

Licensing can improve the cash flow position of the licensee. Because technology licensing allows the firms to have products on the market sooner than otherwise, the firm benefits from an earlier positive cash flow. In addition, licensing means lower development costs. As Lowe and Crawford (1984) show, however, licensing can mean less profits in the longer term. The immediate benefits of quick access to new technology, lower development costs and a relatively early cash flow are attractive benefits of licensing (Figure 13.1).

Table 13.3 Advantages and disadvantages of licensing in international markets

Advantages of licensing

- Access to difficult markets
- Low capital risk and low commitment of resources
- Information on product performance and competitor activities in different markets at little cost
- Improved delivery and service levels in local markets

Disadvantages of licensing

- Disclosure of accumulated competitive knowledge and experience
- Creates possible future competitors
- Lack of control over licensee operations
- Passive interaction with the market
- Exclusion of some export markets
- Organizing licensing operations: cost of adaptation, transfer and controlling

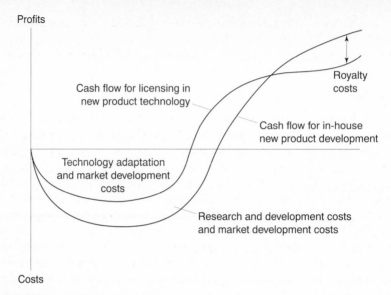

Figure 13.1 Life cycle benefits of licensing
Source: adapted from Lowe, J. and Crawford, N. (1984) *Technology Licensing and the Small Firm*, England: Gower.

There are several technological reasons why a firm would consider licensing to enter a foreign market. For bulky or heavy products of low value, transport costs may be so high as to make exporting prohibitively expensive. Sometimes a local manufacturer with product knowledge is required, especially when the product requires installation and service support. In such circumstances it is unlikely that an agent could provide the necessary back-up.

Frequently a complementary arrangement may be developed whereby the licensor exports a high-technology component and the licensee provides the less critical assemblies, harnesses, mountings and cabinets. This arrangement is more like a joint production agreement.

There are also territorial reasons why licensing could be an attractive means of entering foreign markets. Few firms have the salesforce necessary to cover wide geographic markets in many different countries, nor do they have sufficient manufacturing capacity to service such large markets. Thus, where the potential market is large, licensing partners can be an attractive development.

In addition, developing country governments frequently restrict imports or give preference to local firms, both of which encourage local production. In such circumstances, licensing may be the appropriate means of entering the market.

Financial considerations may be an important determinant for the smaller firm in possession of advanced technology. Licensing in such circumstances may open foreign markets that might otherwise be beyond its reach. Small- and medium-sized firms attempting to expand and grow frequently experience cash flow and liquidity problems.

Since licensing income is largely pure profit involving little extra investment, licensing for such firms may speed up the cash flow from new foreign markets. When successful, licensing in many international product markets may be relatively painless and profitable.

Prerequisites of successful licensing

There are a number of prerequisites for successful licensing. The licensor must have exclusive and easily transferable property rights to the product or process technology being licensed. It must also be possible to identify benefits associated with the license, including the value of the license to the partner firm. The licensing firm should be in a position to control the operation, including the geographic market area in which the license is to apply. At the same time the licensee should have developed a level of technical competence sufficient to cope with the application of the technology in production and marketing.

Sometimes firms are opposed to licensing their technology or, as often claimed, their birthright. Opposition to licensing is usually centred on reluctance to divulge accumulated knowledge and experience that has been hard to develop; this fear stems from the situation where a company may find cheaper or improved versions of its own products competing against it at a later date. Other reasons for the decision not to pursue licensing include lack of real control over licensee operations, blocking off export areas, doubts about the suitability and transferability of technology and difficulties of organizing licensing operations in traditional manufacturing-oriented companies.

The major prerequisite of successful licensing is an organizational climate conducive to international business. A separate licensing section under a licensing executive is often preferred, no matter how small, so that it can be clearly seen that the activity carries status by people within the licensor and licensee firms.

The license package

Most licensing packages consist of proprietary know-how and patented products or processes specified in great detail. Proprietary know-how relies mainly on secrecy within the licensor company and as a contractual obligation of the licensee. Patented products and processes enjoy a measure of additional legal protection and limited monopoly rights. License packages generally contain elements of the following:

- patents, designs, trademarks, copyrights;
- product and process specifications;
- quality control procedures;
- manufacturing layout drawings and instruction manuals;
- commissioning to achieve a performance guarantee;
- technical and commercial training programmes;
- product literature and other sales support material.

It is difficult to police licenses. The difficulty begins during the pre-signing period when a balance is required between whetting the prospective licensee's appetite and not divulging too much information, in the event of the negotiation falling through. Some technologies are very concise and the whole license may depend on disclosure of some novel design or process: a problem of information disclosure which can sometimes support the formation of a new international firm (Williamson, 1975).

The form of the license transaction is fairly well established and involves some combination of the following elements:

- a down payment on release of the written-up part of the technology;
- progress payments leading up to commissioning one or more products to the licensor's performance specification;
- minimum royalty – a guarantee that at least some annual income will be received by the licensor;
- running royalty – normally expressed as a percentage of normal selling price or as a fixed sum of money for units of output.

Other methods of payment include lump sums with no deferred payment related to output, a conversion of royalties into equity, management and technical fees and complex systems of counterpurchase, often found in licensing arrangements with Eastern European and developing countries. If the foreign market carries high political risk, then it will be wise for the licensor to seek high 'initial' payments and perhaps compress the timescale of the agreement. Alternatively, if the market is relatively risk free and the licensee is well placed to develop a strong market share, then payment terms will be somewhat relaxed and probably influenced by other licensors competing for the agreement.

Barriers to international licensing

There are a number of limitations in using licenses internationally. The market for licenses is imperfect. The buyer has a weak basis for bidding, especially for undisclosed technology, until it has been supplied. It is also very difficult to communicate subtle and complex technologies successfully from one firm to another, especially across cultures. There are heavy costs of knowledge transfer.

It is difficult for the licensor to ensure that licensees maintain adequate quality control in production: a serious problem when the licensor's brand or trade name is used. It is difficult and expensive to police other clauses in the agreement, e.g. territorial limits. For these reasons technology leaders are often forced towards an equity involvement to protect their assets. Such pressure may ultimately force them to consider foreign direct investment. In recent years the EU has recognized the need to protect licensing from the adverse effects of competition policy.

Licensing arrangements generally prohibit or inhibit the flexibility of later expansion into a sophisticated marketing operation or manufacturing. Licensing contains another risk; if the business is extremely successful the profit potential will be limited by the licensing arrangements. There is also the danger of commitment to an incompetent local firm. Termination clauses rarely prevent a great loss of time and resources.

============ **Franchising to enter international markets** ============

Nature of franchising

Despite the recent escalation of publicity, franchising is not by any means a new phenomenon. It is frequently seen as a recent 'import' into Europe, particularly from the United States. The real pioneers of modern franchising, however, were almost certainly the British brewers of the eighteenth century who created a system of tied house agreements with their publicans which remains widespread to this day (Stern and Stanworth, 1988). Franchising, a derivative of *francorum rex* or 'freedom from servitude' is now a very significant organizational arrangement in the US economy accounting for approximately 34 per cent of all retail sales and 10 per cent of gross national product in 1988. In contrast the figures for retail sales in Europe are between two and three per cent and in the United Kingdom three per cent (Ayling, 1987). The significance drawn from this by Ayling is that it 'highlights the potential for franchising' in Europe. There is considerable interest in the literature in franchising as part of the firm's competitive strategy and internationalization process (Huszagh *et al.*, 1992; Eroglu, 1992).

There are various forms of franchises, job franchises, investment franchises and business format franchises being the most common (Brandenburg, 1986). Business format franchising is the most common form found in international markets (Table 13.4).

Table 13.4 Forms of franchising

Job franchising

- Wholesaler–retailer
   Spar, Londis, VG, Service Master

Investment franchise

- Manufacturer–retailer
   Petrol service stations
- Manufacturer–wholesaler
   Pepsi-Cola, 7UP
- Other
   Holiday Inns, Avis Rent-a-Car, Coca-Cola

Business format franchise

- Trade marks, trade names
   KFC (Kentucky Fried Chicken), Prontaprint
- Licensor–retailer
   McDonald's, Wimpey International

Sources: adapted from Brandenburg, M. (1986) 'Free yourself from servitude', *Accountancy*, **98** (1118), 82–6, Stern, P. and Stanworth, J. (1988) 'The development of franchising in Britain', *National Westminster Quarterly Review*, (May), 38–48, Vaugh, C. L. (1979) *Franchising*, 2nd edn, Lexington, MA: Lexington Books.

The launching of the Body Shop and Prontaprint on the UK's USM, on the NYSE and the Tokyo Stock Exchange is a powerful indication of what can be achieved with a properly executed franchising strategy. One of the best known examples of international franchising is Benetton. Benetton franchisees arrange all their own finance, but they pay no fees or royalties. Their obligations are to carry only Benetton clothes, to achieve certain minimum sales levels, to follow guidelines for price mark-ups and to adopt one of the standard shops layouts. The locations are chosen by the company or one of its agents. Benetton devised a technique of clustering several of its shops in the same area, sometimes as many as three or four on the same street. With more than 100 designs in each collection, different items are usually on display in each shop. Thus, the failure of a single store is offset by the success of the others, and valuable comparisons and a degree of internal competition are provided as well. This is often a cause of grievance among licensees who seek a degree of exclusivity. Franchising offers a unique organizational approach to decisions on distribution arrangements and the choices surrounding vertical integration (Norton, 1988a) by providing more control than market exchange (Rubin, 1978) while avoiding some of the negative features of full integration (Harrigan, 1986).

Franchising is a particular form of licensing of intellectual property rights (Adams and Mendelsohn, 1986). Trademarks, trade names, copyright, designs, patents, trade secrets and know-how may all be involved in different mixtures in the 'package' to be licensed. Franchising is a form of marketing and distribution in which the franchisor grants an individual or small company, the franchisee, the right to do business in a prescribed manner over a certain period of time, in a specified place (Ayling, 1987). A more formal legal definition is provided by Adams and Mendelsohn (1986) who view franchising as a marketing method with four distinct characteristics, as follows:

1. A contractual relationship in which the franchisor licenses the franchisee to carry out business under a name owned by or associated with the franchisor and in accordance with a business format established by the franchisor.
2. Control by the franchisor over the way in which the franchisee carries on the business.
3. Provision of assistance to the franchisee by the franchisor in running the business both prior to commencement and throughout the period of the contract.
4. The franchisee owns his/her business which is a separate entity from that of the franchisor; the franchisee provides and risks his own capital.

Another good example of the value of franchising is that of the Swedish furniture manufacturer IKEA which franchises its ideas throughout the Western world, especially in Europe and North America.

Reasons for growth in franchising

A number of factors have contributed to the rapid growth rate of franchising (Stern and Stanworth, 1988). First, the general worldwide decline of traditional manufacturing industry and its replacement by service-sector activities has encouraged franchising, which is especially well suited to service and people-intensive economic activities, particularly where these require a large number of geographically dispersed outlets serving local markets. Second, the growth in popularity of self-employment is also a contributory factor to the growth of franchising (Ayling, 1987). Government policies of many countries have improved the climate for small business as a means of stimulating employment.

As franchising becomes increasingly well known and understood, the chances are that it will appeal to a growing number of people. As a consequence, it can be expected that there will be a corresponding increase in the number of franchise opportunities. Further, there is an increasing shift by large companies towards divestment from centralized control of an increasing proportion of their business activities. Third, the law surrounding franchising permits its rapid growth. Around the world, particularly in North America, Australia and the EU, franchising has been more or less exempt from legislation concerning competition laws. Finally, the involvement of major clearing banks has lent stability to the franchise industry and has also improved the image of the franchising business significantly. This is especially true in the United Kingdom.

Advantages of franchising

The major advantage of franchising as a means of rapidly entering a number of international markets is that it is a method of expanding business activity over a wider area more quickly than is possible if done internally. This occurs because in franchising a business format is sold to someone who will operate it in the manner which has proved to be successful, using the energies of a self-employed person with local knowledge. The franchising formula enables this expansion with minimum capital outlay. It creates additional income to the franchisor in the form of fees and royalty payments. A promising franchise will attract highly motivated operators.

The franchisor's small central organization, consisting of a few skilled experts, does not constitute a heavy overhead (Ayling, 1987). The franchisor is unburdened by day-to-day details which would arise in the case of many wholly owned outlets. In addition, Rubin (1978) highlights the following four specific advantages from a franchise as opposed to operating an independent business:

1. The trademark of a franchise and the product sold is valuable and the franchisee is willing to pay something to sell these products or services.
2. The franchisor often gives managerial advice to the franchisee.
3. The franchisor often makes capital available to the franchisee in some form, e.g. co-signing a bank loan or buying the plant and leasing it to the franchisee.
4. To the extent that franchisees are closer to being employees than entrepreneurs, they may simply lack the requisite human capital to open a business without the substantial assistance of franchisors.

Using a battery of tests, Falbe and Welch (1998) conclude that the three most important factors contributing to the success of franchise arrangements within the NAFTA region were quality of the business format system itself, the brand name associated with it and the level of economic activity and business environment in the country where the franchise would operate. These authors discovered, however, that there were significant differences between countries on the perceived extent of success or failure. The two variables which gave rise to differences in perception were country location and franchise strategy. Failure stemmed from franchisor and franchise activities.

Disadvantages of franchising

Franchisees are owner-managers who typically bear the residual risk of a local operation, because their wealth is largely determined by the difference between the revenue inflows to the operation and the promised payments to the franchisor and other factors (Norton, 1988b). From the point of view of the franchisor, the major risk is the effect the franchise will have on brand names.

Companies involved in franchising generally have identifiable brand names which are an assurance of uniform product quality. The vital importance of this quality assurance in the case of businesses dealing with non-repeat customers has already been noted. A major problem facing companies with valuable brand names is controlling the action of agents throughout the organization to assure the continued value of the trademark.

Legal aspects of franchising

The market for franchise operations is competitive, with the only monopoly element being the trademark. Hence, Rubin (1978) has difficulty in understanding why courts would want to interfere at all in the franchisor–franchisee relationship. Rubin speculates that perhaps part of the justification for anti-trust intervention in the United States may be that, once the contract is signed, the franchisor is in a monopoly position relative to the franchisee, but warns that this argument rests on the misinterpretation of the nature of the relationship between the two parties. Legally, the franchisee is a firm dealing with another firm – the franchisor. What Rubin does not recognize is that the economics of the situation is such that the franchisee is far closer to being an employee of the franchisor than an independent entrepreneur. The bargaining power in the relationship clearly rests with the holder of the master licence. Pizza franchiser Kay Ainsely of Domino's has sold master licences in more than 25 countries.

> Pizza is a universal food [she says] and wherever we go in the world there's a long list of prospective buyers. However, we're never in a hurry to sell a master licence. We look for a substantial investor who will work within our proven operating methods, but who is also capable of helping us adapt our product to local needs.

Domino's is one of America's most successful home-delivery pizza chains (*International Herald Tribune*, 19 February 1992, p. 11).

In Europe, the Commission of the EU published a new draft of a block exemption regulation in 1988. This was designed to allow franchising exemption from competition laws. The EU's landmark judgement in this area came in the 1986 case of Pronuptia et Paris GmbH, in which franchising was deemed exempt from Community competition restrictions. The 1988 draft initiative allows franchisors to grant franchisees territorial immunity.

======= **Joint ventures to enter international markets** =======

A joint venture is formed when two or more firms form a third to carry out a productive economic activity (Harrigan, 1985). A joint venture has also been seen in wider terms: 'an equity arrangement between two or more independent firms' (Gullander, 1976, p. 104). The latter definition includes equity alliances between firms to organize production and marketing on a regional rather than a country level, e.g. AT&T's 25 per cent stake in Olivetti. Joint ventures have increased in the variety and form they take and have become strategic rather than tactical in nature (Harrigan, 1985). To complicate matters further, Root (1988) categorizes joint ventures not only by their core characteristics along the value-added chain but also by geographic scope and dominant mission, i.e. strategic orientation. In a study of joint ventures among Spanish firms Valdés Llaneza and García-Canal (1998, p. 62) report that, while in domestic joint ventures the partners may want to seek collusive practices, access to the technological know-how of others or to penetrate new sectors, international joint ventures are usually motivated by the desire of at least one of the partners to use the agreement as a means of international expansion.

Various forms of joint venture are found in practice (Table 13.5). Sometimes firms participate in a spider's-web strategy consisting of many firms. Two dangers are associated with this strategy: (a) indirectly forming a link with a competitor; (b) the possibility of a take-over. Frequently, firms will cooperate for a period of time and then separate. In contrast, other firms find their bonds with joint venture partners becoming tighter. In these circumstances, full integration may result. An intricate and complex spider's-web joint venture network is shown for the automotive industry in Figure 13.2 which illustrates the point.

Siemens now expects competitors in different supply fields to joint venture with each other to single supply the best and leading high-technology solutions for Siemens to be at the leading edge of their product developments (Byrne, 1998, p. 37).

Table 13.5 Alternative joint venture strategies and objectives

Spider's-web strategy
- Establishing a joint venture with a large competitor
- Avoid absorption through joint venture's with others in network

Go-together then split strategy
- Cooperating over extended period
- Separate
- Suitable for limited projects (construction)

Successive integration strategy
- Starts with weak inter-firm linkages
- Develops towards interdependence
- Ends with take-over or merger

Source: Gullander, S. (1976) 'Joint ventures and corporate strategy', *Columbia Journal of World Business*, **11** (1), 104–14.

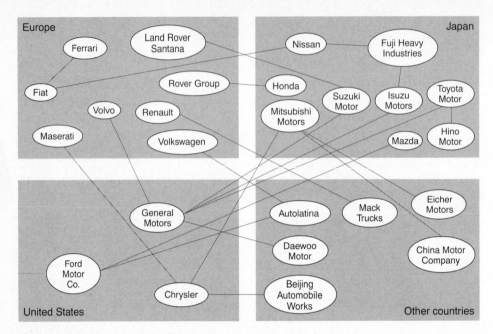

Figure 13.2 Spider's web joint ventures in automotive industry
Source: Devlin, G. and Blackley, M. (1988) 'Strategic alliances: guidelines for success', *Long Range Planning*, (October), 14–23.

Benefits of international joint ventures

A joint venture may be considered a mode of interfirm cooperation lying between the extremes of complete vertical integration of business activities within one firm and the opposite case where stages of production and distribution are owned by separate companies, which contract with each other through conventional market mechanisms.

Four major advantages for joint ventures may be identified in the literature: (a) avoidance of interfirm contracting, transactions and negotiations costs (Williamson, 1975); (b) reduction in costs, or economies of scale from combining common administrative, transport and marketing expenses in two or more stages of production or distribution; (c) internalization of technological or administrative secrets within a firm which minimizes the risk of dissipation of competitive advantage arising from these secrets (Teece, 1981; Rugman, 1981); (d) the ability to implement technological changes more quickly and over more stages of production (Contractor and Lorange, 1988)

The formation of joint ventures is frequently cited as a way of reducing risk to the partners. A joint venture may be attractive in a project involving a large investment. It may also be beneficial in diversifying the portfolio of investments of one or all partners. In this context it has been noted that joint ventures make it possible to access the marketing knowledge of the partner firm active in the market immediately rather than waiting for the internal development of such skills.

Joint ventures facilitate faster market entry and payback. This is of particular significance in such industries as pharmaceuticals where the certification process consumes a great deal of time. It is often possible in joint ventures to combine slack facilities and expertise in the partner firms. In such circumstances the cost of the joint venture to the partnership may be less than it would be to each partner operating independently. Finally, a joint venture may enable a partial containment of the political risk associated with forming an alliance with a local partner. In such circumstances, the local partner would ensure that negative public policy interference was minimized while meeting host country industrial policy. The benefits of joint ventures are summarized in Table 13.6.

Access to new resources

Many firms turn to joint ventures as a way of diversifying activities and for company growth. The small company frequently provides entrepreneurial enthusiasm, vigour, flexibility and advanced technology while the large company provides capital, worldwide channels of marketing, distribution and service. This combination allows for the rapid diffusion of technology-based product innovation into large international markets. The synthesis implied can create a significant competitive advantage.

Access to valued and scarce human resources with appropriate education and cultural background is a key factor in joint venture formation. One of the critical reasons why European and American companies enter joint ventures in Japan is the inability of companies 'going it alone' to attract local management as a result of their 'outsider' status (Abegglen and Stalk, 1985). This is supported by Cateora (1993) who states that numerous joint ventures have been formed with the express intention of acquiring nationals with managerial ability. The local partner's participation in the development of the joint venture imposes less of a burden on its managerial capabilities than would a wholly owned or controlled subsidiary (Killing, 1982).

Access to capital is another resource frequently sought when firms enter a joint venture. Capital markets are characterized by significant transaction costs and credit markets are likely to be imperfect for young firms with little or no track record or experience and for investments in risky projects with no collateral such as research and development (Hennart, 1988). Technology-based firms frequently encounter severe opposition in securing funds for expansion. O'Donoghue (1986) found that 50 per cent of outgoing joint ventures considered access to capital to be important.

Access to distribution channels is also an important motivating factor. Strategic advantages under this heading include an existing marketing establishment, links with buyers, knowledge of the local market and culture, a recognizable brand name and market access. Joint ventures also enable the other partner to reduce its average distribution costs as there is a greater volume throughput (Ohmae, 1989). Equity positions in a partner company can be acquired strategically to strengthen marketing agreements such as Olivetti's agreement to market AT&T products in Europe, where AT&T had relatively little market experience.

Stopford and Wells (1972) found that general knowledge of the local economy was ranked as the most important contribution that a local partner could make to an international firm seeking entry to the market. Anderson and Coughlan (1987) support

Table 13.6 Benefits of joint ventures

Facilitates technology transfer
- codification–public knowledge
- converting head knowledge to production
- impact of technology on marketing relationships
- discovery of price of technology

Access to resources
- rapid product diversification strategies as means of corporate growth favours joint ventures
- provide funds and access to local capital markets
- each partner concentrates resources on an area of greatest advantage
- avoids necessity of developing international management skills
- access to knowledge of local environment and markets
- may reach critical mass for internationalization
- more efficient competitive position

Political pressures
- meets host country pressure for local participation
- provides local control of job creation and technology transfer
- preferential treatment (remittance of royalties)
- may avoid local tariffs and non-tariff barriers

Access to markets
- quick and efficient access to distribution
- by-pass trade barriers
- image–attitude to local company

Other reasons
- good public relations
- curbs potential competition
- provides temporary relief for weak product portfolio

this view by saying that some form of quasi-integration is likely to occur if the markets under consideration are outside Europe or the United States. In such circumstances a form of internal uncertainty is created by the business distance involved (Anderson and Gatignon, 1986). Uncertainty due to business distance may cause some firms to under-value foreign investments (Root, 1983), thereby resulting in a lower form of commitment. Cultural similarity between partners is, however, a critical antecedent for success in international joint ventures (Lin and Germain 1998, p. 189). These authors also discovered that the longer a joint venture has lasted the better its overall performance. Cultural differences may be at least partly responsible for the failure of some strategic alliance. In studying the failure of the Volvo–Renault alliance Bruner and Speckman (1998, p. 149) report that 'one is struck by how much of it is explained at the interfaces of human behaviour: nation, cultures, allies, owners versus managers, and senior managers versus operating managers'.

Joint ventures and host country policies   *Different approach*

Foreign firms sometimes express reservations over host government ownership restrictions. Imposing a joint venture on a reluctant international firm may curb its contribution to the new company, thereby reducing the venture's productivity. While joint ventures may have narrower product lines, smaller scale and less input of the investor's technology they are especially useful in obtaining access to difficult markets, such as Eastern European markets.

Eastern European countries, and more recently the People's Republic of China (PRC), have forged economic and financial relationships with Western capitalist firms. Companies such as Procter & Gamble, which has argued that this entry mode is inconsistent with its company strategy, have entered into such arrangements in China and other former socialist countries in Eastern Europe. The growth potential of these markets provides the incentive to overcome accepted company philosophies. Governments of countries such as India, Mexico, China and even France try to encourage joint ventures with local partners through a variety of means. The mechanisms through which joint ventures are encouraged may be quite direct or subtle, such as in France where preferential procurement may occur for joint ventures (Gomes-Casseres, 1989). Saudi Arabia has a policy of encouraging joint ventures which transfer sophisticated technology, not something you can go and buy in the open market. In these command or semi-command economies the governments control the ownership of the trading and industrial enterprises; they also control the country's resources and distribution channels and are important customers for imported goods and technologies (Child and Markoczy, 1993).

Western companies, in particular European companies, frequently use joint ventures to enter new markets in Eastern Europe (Hood and Young, 1994). In Eastern Europe the government, often represented by a privatization board, is the key stakeholder in such joint ventures in that they control critical resources (Brouthers and Bamossy, 1997, p. 286). These authors report that in strategically important industries such as oil and gas and telecommunications the key stakeholder appears to provide frequent and extensive influence in all stages of the negotiation of a joint venture including, most importantly, in the post-negotiation stage. In consumer non-essential products such as tea, coffee, milk and beer, key stakeholder influence appears to be very low, in both extent and frequency (Brouthers and Bamossy, 1997, p. 304). In Eastern Europe, governments as key stakeholders dominate the relationship in establishing and managing joint ventures with international companies.

Strategic alliances have also been used extensively in China; most of the investments in China in terms of number and value continue to be joint ventures, but the business press has recently being reporting difficulties for western firms. The value of *guanxi* or personal and corporate networks established as a result of the alliances, however, provides a fertile soil for sales force marketing and credit liberalization and binds literally millions of Chinese firms into an extensive network of relations that can be invaluable in expanding market share (Luo, 1996, p. 542). Nevertheless, with regard to most cases of international joint ventures in China foreign managers are generally dissatisfied with their performance (Vanhonaker and Pan, 1997, p. 11). The key problem areas for foreign managers were quality of local sourcing, the recruitment of skilled Chinese managers and the lack of clarity in laws and regulations. The least difficult areas were in exporting and financing (working capital) and foreign exchange. These operational concerns were noted irrespective of the national culture of the foreign partner, the geographical location of the joint venture in China or its business scope.

Joint ventures are useful in any country which restricts market entry by exporting through tariff or non-tariff barriers. The Piper Aircraft Company was forced to enter a joint venture with Embraer, the Brazilian aircraft manufacturer, as the Brazilian government increased tariffs on imported planes from 7 per cent to 50 per cent, thereby effectively prohibiting imports (Moxon, 1987).

Cost of joint ventures

Joint ventures may be criticized because they are unstable for a variety of reasons, because they may be instrumental in creating a competitor and because the costs of control become too high. Taking the instability issue first, many studies have highlighted the high break-up rate of joint ventures (Killing, 1982). Seventy per cent of the partnerships in studies by McKinsey and Coopers & Lybrand eventually broke up as well as half of those in Harrigan's (1988) sample. In recent years many of the once lauded joint ventures between Western firms and firms in China have ceased. International joint ventures are believed to be inherently unstable and to be 'marriages of convenience'. International joint venture instability is, however, not necessarily an indication of failure as is often assumed. The fact that many are short lived may be attributed in part to their very nature and the strategic intent their parents bring to cross-border collaboration (Reuer, 1998, p. 167). Parents may select international joint ventures as a temporary gap-filling mechanism, as a means of taking an option on an emerging technology or market, as a structured choice suited to the features of exchange at the time of market entry or as a response to legal and political conditions in the host country.

The characterization of joint ventures as inherently unstable has been questioned, therefore, as such characterization fails to recognize that the joint venture might have been intended as a transitional structure (Harrigan, 1988). Multinational firms are more likely to buy out their partners when they already control a majority of the shares of a company and are more likely to divest when they hold a minority shareholding. In this sense, joint ventures may be viewed as 'instruments providing firms with flexibility in responding to trends that are difficult to predict' (Gomes-Casseres, 1989, p. 99). Finally, this author found that the change from joint ownership to wholly owned subsidiary is likely to occur in countries with which the international firm is already familiar. Stopford and Wells (1972) believe that firms tend to reserve proprietary knowledge for modes of entry that they control completely.

Sometimes joint ventures create competitors unnecessarily. According to Lasserre (1984), there exists the possibility for long-term opportunistic behaviour from the technology buyer when the technology supplier is no longer needed. This viewpoint may be criticized, however, on a number of grounds. First, the pace of technical change has resulted in shorter product life cycles which means that this risk is minimized by a constantly changing environment. Second, the technology supplier will probably be constantly updating and improving existing products in order to maintain its competitive edge. Third, joint ventures can be dangerous for the technology buyer, particularly when the recipient uses the alliance to avoid investment to design and innovate. This short-term orientation can result in a dependency spiral as the technology buyer contributes fewer and fewer distinctive skills. This may force the buyer to reveal more of its internal operations to keep the other partner interested.

Alliances with Japanese companies have resulted in American companies failing to develop essential manufacturing skills, thus preventing them from moving down the experience curve. This failure stems from US firms taking a short-term orientation and ignoring organizational learning opportunities that a joint venture affords them. Fourth, the tension between cooperative and competitive strategies varies according to the type of activity. The risks of disclosure are higher for some activities than for others. Government regulation and interlocking directorates carry higher risks of disclosure than do mergers.

On a more general level the difficulties associated with joint ventures may be summarized under three major headings (Table 13.7). As the network of joint ventures becomes larger there is increased possibility of conflict of interest among the partners. The cost of controlling the joint venture becomes significant. The need for control strengthens the argument for unambiguous control within a single firm, as found in foreign direct investment and acquisition modes of entry.

A number of conditions have been identified under which it is easier to operate international joint ventures. These conditions have been classified into dominant and shared partnership arrangements (Killing, 1980). The circumstances under which each works best are as follows:

1. Dominant partnership:
   - the international partner should be dominant when it is important to have long-term control of know-how; the local partner should be passive and outside the industry;
   - the local partner should be dominant when the international partner's skills are needed only temporarily and can easily be transferred.

2. Shared partnership works if the skills of both partners are required over time:
   - choose a partner with complementary skills;
   - give the joint venture autonomy;
   - allow partners to buy out for a change in conditions.

In a study of international joint ventures involving Chinese firms Ding (1997, p. 43) concludes that dominant managerial control exercised by foreign partners is significantly and positively related to performance and conflicts between partners significantly hinder performance. This author proposes that international managers should recognize that the extent of managerial control they are able to exercise over a joint venture's activities will increase the likelihood of meeting their expectations. He also suggests that that it is necessary to formulate an effective conflict management strategy to resolve problems which generally arise in regard to quality control, export and import arrangements, wages and labour policy, and administration. These conflicts arise from divergent objectives,

Table 13.7 Difficulties with joint ventures

Loss of control over foreign operations
- large investment of financial, technical, or managerial resources favours greater control than is possible in a joint venture

Joint ventures are difficult to coordinate
- lack adequate procedures for protecting proprietary information
- shared decisions affect global marketing arrangements

Loss of flexibility and confidentiality
- change in product-market mission may make joint venture a liability
- unease about sharing technology
- one partner may form alliance with other partner's competitor
- managerial dependency between joint venture and one of partners

disparate expectations and priorities, incompatible business and management practices of the two partners and social and cultural differences between the home and host country. Four strategic tasks are particularly critical for effective international joint venture performance in China (Osland and Cavusgil, 1996, pp. 124–5):

- gaining decision-making control of critical business functions,
- developing an effective sales force,
- retaining trained international joint venture managers and
- influencing government officials.

Gaining decision-making control of critical business functions enables one side of the joint venture to be able to coordinate and implement its strategies. Clearly these are matters which should be attended to at the initiation stage of the joint venture.

The performance of joint ventures is also influenced by the context in which they exist. In an examination of successful US–China joint ventures Lin and Germain (1998, pp. 189–90) discovered that cultural similarity between partners is a critical antecedent for joint venture success – the greater the cultural similarity the better the performance. These authors also discovered that only in limited circumstances is relative power an influence on performance. The greater the partner's relative power, however, the more likely it is to force its preferred solution when disagreement occurs. Lastly, Lin and Germain (1998) report that the longer a joint venture has lasted the better its performance. Obviously, selection is occurring in that only successful joint ventures are allowed to continue. Clearly, joint venture age breeds familiarity which translates into an open style of problem solving to the mutual satisfaction of the partners.

While many companies have experience of joint ventures, circumstances never remain the same. What begins as a relatively straightforward plan can change for many reasons. The benefits and risks associated with some joint ventures can be very high for both partners, especially where the investment involved is high and the venture involves new technologies and new markets.

===== **Evaluation of strategic alliances** =====

Like enterprise in general, many risks are associated with strategic alliances. The issue for the firm is how it can obtain as much value as possible while maintaining control of its assets and how it can select a partner to attain this objective. Root (1988) classifies risks associated with collaborative agreements on the basis of whether they are fiduciary or environmental. Fiduciary risk refers to the probability that the partner will fail to honour elements of the agreement. Environmental risk is the amount of the firm's assets which would be directly affected by changes in the political, economic or competitive environment. According to Root, there is a trade-off between the two types of risk; the acquisition of control is often at the expense of increased exposure to environmental risk.

Obtaining value and control in strategic alliances

The issue of obtaining value and control in competitive alliances is especially important for the international firm. A useful framework, on which this section is based, has been developed by Lorange (1985) which allows these issues to be examined. Marketing cooperation agreements tend to be focused on a specific narrow set of objectives and limited in time. Assume two partners to the agreement: Partner A, the local firm, and Partner B, the international firm. The strategic value of such agreements tends to be high for both partners (Table 13.8). Time may be critical and so a rapid entry may be essential for success. It may be too expensive and too time consuming for Partner A to attain such objectives by itself. Similarly for Partner A, access to the new product may be critical for success. Many such firms have identified gaps in the market and do not possess products in

Table 13.8 Value and control in strategic alliances

Nature of alliance	Strategic value	Desired control
Cooperation agreements	Partner A: high Partner B: high	Partner A: high Partner B: low
Licensing	Partner A: high Partner B: low	Partner A: high Partner B: high
Franchising	Partner A: high Partner B: high	Partner A: high Partner B: high
Joint Ventures	Partner A: high Partner B: low	Partner A: high Partner B: low

Note: Partner A is the local firm in the foreign country; Partner B is the firm in the home country.

Source: adapted from Lorange, P. (1985) 'Co-operative ventures in multinational settings: a framework', *Second Open International IMP Research Seminar on International Marketing*, University of Uppsala, 4–6 September.

this portfolio to serve the new requirements. A marketing agreement with Partner B may bring temporary respite. While Partner B would wish for as much control as possible, from a practical point of view much of this control may be given to local firms (Table 13.8). Because Partner A – the local firm – is closer to the customer, it will tend to exercise greater control.

The strategic value and desired control are high for both partners in a franchising arrangement. For the international firm, Partner B – the franchisor – the strategy is to develop and invest in a franchising concept and package. The local firm, Partner A – the franchisee – develops a business in the local market based on the franchise package. The local firm invests funds and time to develop a local market position.

For the franchisor the degree of desired control over strategic resources tends to be high because of the importance of the contract for the implementation of that firm's internationalization strategy. For that reason the franchisor retains control over the franchising package. For the franchisee the strategic value is also high and so the franchisee retains control over its local organization and the market. Unlike joint ventures, there is no common organization in terms of people. Informed contact between the partners ensures that the value creation process works smoothly. Franchising as an organizational form may be stable and mutually beneficial, as it allows both partners to obtain their strategic needs in terms of control and value.

The strategic value of licensing tends to be different for licensor and licensee. For Partner B – the international licensor – the alliance is likely to have a relatively low strategic value. The licensor is typically more interested in its own domestic market; its major business interests lie there and not in dealing with foreign firms. The licence agreement is often seen as marginal for Partner B – the licensor. The licensor should acknowledge, however, that through licensing it can obtain rapid diffusion of know-how and obtain relatively painless pay-offs. For the licensee – Partner A – the strategic value tends to be high. The licensee frequently stakes its own business on obtaining a unique know-how which gives the licensee a competitive advantage in the local market.

The level of control tends to be high for the licensor since it controls the know-how as well as the support organization. Control is also high for the licensee since it controls the commercialization of the know-how, which is typically a small component in developing the business.

Finally, joint ventures pose a different set of problems for examination. For the sake of argument, assume that Partner B – the international partner – is the majority owner in the joint venture. For this firm the strategic value of the joint venture tends to be high. The international partner possesses the unique know-how, technology or marketing and often acquires missing dimensions in the value-creating chain that it does not already possess and offers the minority partner participation in the business in this way (Lorange, 1985, p. 31). The joint venture is strategically critical to Partner B. For Partner A, the local firm, the strategic value tends to be smaller; its position in the joint venture is typically not essential to the implementation of its overall strategy.

For Partner B, control over resources tends to be high. By ensuring a high degree of control over the joint venture, Partner B can exercise control over its own resources and know-how so that they do not leak to Partner A. Partner A has little strategic control over its strategic resources once they have been committed to the joint venture. The ability of the different forms of competitive alliance to cope with environmental change is a key consideration with regard to developing relationships with firms in international markets. These relationships arise from contact with partner companies. Sometimes such contacts are very much at arm's length but frequently they involve the exchange of personnel for considerable periods of time. In joint ventures it is usual that training would mean the exchange of staff, and the development of joint ventures would need an extended two-way flow of key people between the partners. For these reasons it is important to examine how a particular form of competitive alliance responds to changes in the environment and how the partners in the alliance maintain contact (Table 13.9).

Marketing partnership agreements are frequently established for a particular product market and have a relatively short time scale. Usually an annual contract forms the basis of such a relationship with the option of extension where mutually agreed. In many situations, however, at least one party will not disclose full intentions regarding the longer-term development of the relationship and will reserve position to observe how the arrangement evolves. Sometimes firms see such relationships as a temporary measure until a more permanent arrangement can be found, e.g. a new product developed locally. In such circumstances the relationship may have only a temporary life. The continuation of the relationship depends very much on the two partners to ensure the performance of a specific task. Marketing partnership agreements are usually not equipped, therefore, with significant adaptive or environmental coping mechanisms and it is difficult to develop new business relationships within such partnerships.

In contrast, franchising arrangements have the potential for being stable and mutually beneficial for both partners since they permit both to achieve their respective strategic values. Furthermore, both partners gain from the relationship. The extent of the links between the partners required to attain their respective objectives is low. One of the potential weaknesses of this form of relationship is the relatively low ability of franchising to cope with major environmental changes.

Like franchising, the level of day-to-day contact in licensing required between the licensor and licensee tends to be low. The license agreement forms the basis of the contact and may require an initial period of training but, once the operation is running smoothly,

Table 13.9 Environmental change and organizational links in strategic alliances

Ability to cope with environmental change	Continuous organizational links between partners	
	High	Low
Low	Marketing partnership agreements	Franchising
High	Joint ventures	Licensing

Source: adapted from Lorange, P. (1985) 'Co-operative ventures in multinational settings: a framework', *Second Open International IMP Seminar on International Marketing*, University of Uppsala, 4–6 September.

there is little need for extensive further contact between the partners. Because the licensee has obtained a unique know-how which gives a competitive advantage in the local market the licensing arrangement tends to be highly adaptable to changing environmental circumstances. The licensing contract is easily modified to accommodate changes in the environment (Lorange, 1985, p. 25).

Joint ventures between two independent partners tend to be able to cope with environmental change as a matter of course. A well-designed joint venture can be well equipped to adapt to a changing environment, particularly if established initially with such flexibility as an objective. A joint venture can sometimes be much more flexible than its parents, while at the same time involving extensive continuous organizational links with the partners. Nevertheless, firms sometimes prefer a licensing arrangement for many reasons. In the early 1980s, Atlas Copco was negotiating an entry into the People's Republic of China and faced a choice between a joint venture and a licensing arrangement. To facilitate the decision, Atlas Copco developed a list of 13 decision criteria (Table 13.10). Having evaluated the situation, Atlas Copco decided to license only. Between October 1983 and May 1985 six licensee agreements were negotiated and signed. One agreement was negotiated but left unsigned.

Selecting a partner for a strategic alliance

The key to forging mutually satisfactory joint ventures is a realistic assessment of the firm's strengths and weaknesses in the proposed venture (Harrigan, 1985). It is also necessary to assess the commitment of potential partners to the success of the venture and their willingness to contribute resources or to provide a market for the products in a manner that accommodates their partners' needs. In searching for an appropriate partner for the strategic alliance the company faces four dilemmas: how to find local firms, how to determine an operational fit with the prospective partner, how to assess compatibility and how to specify and detail the project in the alliance (Smith and Reney, 1997, p. 180). Search costs are high as major companies do not as a rule wish to sell their technology and smaller companies are more difficult to locate since they do not generally advertise their position (Killing, 1980). It may be necessary to look beyond the obvious candidates engaged in the same business to companies with marketing and manufacturing capabilities in related or complementary product or service areas.

In some cases the process of partner selection is not performed thoroughly. The first candidate, generally discovered through contacts established by mail or arranged by a banker or a business colleague already established in the country is often the one with whom the company undertakes discussions. Little or no screening is done, nor is there an in-depth investigation of the motives and capabilities of the candidate. This situation is changing rapidly, however, as firms have become wiser in the ways of international markets and the pitfalls that may be encountered if a strategic approach is not followed.

In more favourable cases, where the firm is already engaged in business in the country, the selected partner may be the agent who is already working for the company. For the foreign partner, there is the advantage of entering into an agreement with someone who is already familiar with the company's products and the parent company. However, the fact

Table 13.10 Deciding between a joint venture and a license agreement in the People's Republic of China: Atlas Copco

Decision criteria	Joint ventures	License
1. Equity contributions of capital or equipment	Yes	No
2. Management responsibility	Yes	No
3. Administrative and production responsibility	Yes	No
4. Responsibility for adapting technology	Yes	No
5. Responsibility for final product	Yes	No
6. Dependent on local infrastructure	Yes	No
7. Buy back agreements	Yes	No
8. Component deliveries	Yes	No
9. Final customer contacts (exports)	Yes	Yes
10. Training and other technical assistance	Yes	Yes
11. Initial fee	Yes	Yes
	Export	No export
12. Royalty	Yes	Yes
	Export	No export
13. Dividend	Yes	No
	Export	

Source: Sandberg, H. (1986) 'Atlas Copco – licence agreements', *Chinese Culture and Management Conference*, Economist Intelligence Unit, Intercontinental Hotel, Paris, 23–24 January.

that a local company proves to be a good distributor does not guarantee that it will be as good in a joint venture involving manufacturing activities (Lasserre, 1984). To overcome this problem Lasserre proposes a method of assessing a partner based on analyses of the strategic fit and the resources fit of the firms involved. This approach has been adapted to accommodate an international firm and a local partner (Figure 13.3).

It is proposed first that potential partners examine their own resources through a detailed resource audit involving the firm's technology, financial and human resources and experience. Second, the potential partners should then carry out a detailed product-market audit of their respective operations. A comparison of these two sets of audits presents the potential partners with a resources fit and a product-market fit. The next step is to determine the strategic direction for the alliance, if there is to be one. The alliance might take the form of a marketing partnership agreement, a license, a franchise or a joint venture.

Lasserre maintains that this detailed approach to assessing a potential partner for an alliance is rarely implemented since it requires time, effort and investment in data gathering. A minimum period of one to two years of prior contacts and long-term missions by the foreign company to familiarize itself with the country culture and the business practices of the local company would seem to be required in most circumstances, especially for alliances requiring greater commitment, such as joint ventures.

Because both partners have similar expectations with regard to strategic value and the

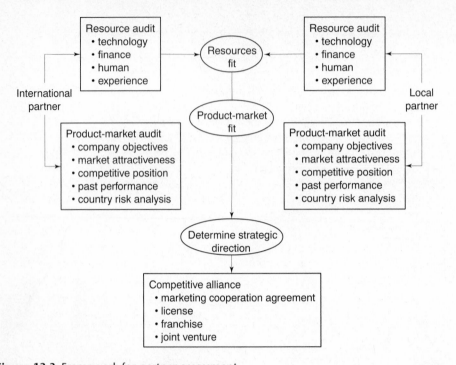

Figure 13.3 Framework for partner assessment
Source: adapted from Lasserre, P. (1984), 'Selecting a foreign partner for technology transfer', *Long Range Planning*, **17** (December), 43–9.

need for control, it is likely that franchising and joint ventures would produce a better resource and strategic fit than would marketing partnership agreements and licensing. The match in terms of resources and strategy for the latter two is frequently not as harmonious. Circumstances often arise where only one of the partners achieves the objectives established. For these reasons, marketing partnership agreements and licensing arrangements tend to degenerate over time and ultimately dissolve for partners who actively seek to attain their strategic objectives.

Summary

This chapter examines the various forms of strategic alliance found among firms in international markets. Four distinct forms of strategic alliance are discussed: marketing partnership agreements; licensing; franchising; joint ventures. Each involves the need to work closely with a firm located in a different market and culture. Greatest commitment to international markets is usually found among equity joint ventures established to transfer product or marketing technology.

14

Foreign direct investment

In the preceding chapter the discussion ended with a description and evaluation of joint ventures, the form of competitive alliance involving greatest investment and commitment by the firm. In Chapter 12 we discussed exporting as the mode of entry to foreign markets, which is based on organic growth by the firm. In this chapter foreign direct investment, which refers to the acquisition of foreign-based firms and the financing and management of new ventures abroad, is examined. Within the analytical framework adopted, expansion by the firm into international markets through acquisition and new venture investment represents the greatest degree of commitment and requires a greater investment of resources than the other modes of market entry.

Locational advantage in international markets

In classical economic theory the firm is assumed to have perfect and costless knowledge of, and to be prepared to take advantage of, attractive opportunities wherever they exist. The firm is usually born with a geographical horizon limited to a locality, a region or a home country, but these horizons change. The change may be a result of internal forces such as senior management, the development of a new technology or product, observed need for a larger market and so on, or it may be the result of external forces such as customers, governments, the foreign expansion of a competitor or a dramatic event such as the formation or enlargement of a trade bloc such as the EU or the opening of new markets such as those of Eastern Europe.

To operate successfully abroad, the firm must have certain compensating advantages that more than offset the innate advantages of local firms. Local firms generally possess an intimate knowledge of the local economic, social, legal and public policy environment, and they do not face foreign exchange risks and misunderstandings which often arise in cross-cultural operations.

Firms engage in both horizontal and vertical investments. The objective of horizontal investments are to produce in foreign locations the same products manufactured in the home market. Vertical investments are supply oriented, intended to produce abroad raw materials or other production inputs which are then supplied to the firm at home or to other subsidiaries. The foreign firm may have privileged access to raw materials or minerals because of firm-specific advantages such as an established marketing system, managerial capacity, control over transportation or access to capital. Increasingly it is not a product embodied asset which drives firms abroad but the implicit contracts between suppliers and large customers located abroad, reflecting the international firm's ability to manage the logistics of continuous supply and adaptation to customer needs (Caves, 1998, p.10).

Firms sometimes internationalize to create an internal market whenever transactions can be carried out at a lower cost within the firm. The creation of an internal market permits the firm to transform an intangible piece of research or understanding of the market into a valuable property specific to itself. The firm can exploit its advantage in all available markets and still keep the use of the information internal in order to recoup its initial expenditures on research and knowledge generation.

The propensity of a particular enterprise to engage in foreign production also depends on the locational attractions of its home country's endowments compared with those offered by other countries, including financial and other inducements to locate there (Dunning and McQueen, 1981). Differentials in the supply–demand relationship of resources among countries generate basic economic pressures for the international flow of resources and create opportunities open to the multinational firm (Fayerweather, 1982).

Motives for foreign direct investment

Market-based motives for foreign direct investment (FDI) usually refer to the foreign market being attractive or conducive for the expansion of the firm's activities. These motives are based on access to raw materials, technology, intermediate goods and final products. Dunning (1998) has identified four reasons for foreign direct investment:

Resource seeking: upgrading quality of resources and availability of local partners to jointly promote knowledge and/or capital-intensive resource use.

Market seeking: increased need for presence close to users in knowledge-intensive sectors and growing importance of promotional activities by regional and local development agencies.

Efficiency seeking: increased role of governments in removing obstacles to restructuring economic activity and facilitating the upgrading of human resources; availability of specialized industrial clusters (science parks); an entrepreneurial environment and enhanced competitiveness and cooperation among firms.

Strategic asset seeking: opportunities offered for exchange of localized tacit knowledge, ideas and interactive learning; access to different cultures, institutions and systems and different consumer demands and preferences.

This typology is useful for dealing with widely different markets and reflects much of the factor cost arguments within international trade in that markets at a lower level of development might be expected to attract a greater level of supply-based FDI than more developed countries.

A further approach to FDI arises in the internationalization of the firm studies where foreign direct investment is a strategic alternative adopted when firms have gained market knowledge and experience through previous forms of participation (Chapters 4 and 11–13). The particular value of this framework arises in the view of FDI as a stage which is reached by firms, governed by an incremental knowledge of host markets and progressive experience of foreign market environments. This approach, in placing emphasis on firm knowledge, experience and commitment and on the *psychic distance* between home and host markets is potentially useful in considering how foreign firms gain understanding and interact with the host environments through foreign direct investment.

Nature of FDI

Investment in foreign markets may take several forms. An important distinction is made between portfolio investment and FDI. Portfolio investment refers to the purchase of a shareholding in companies, usually through various stock exchanges, with the purpose of obtaining a return on the funds invested. Since it is not directly concerned with the control and management of the foreign enterprise we are not immediately concerned with it here. Foreign direct investment refers to participation in management and effective control of the enterprise in addition. It also means the establishment of international operations by a firm or the expansion of existing operations. Usually there is a heavy financial commitment involved. More important, perhaps, is the transfer of technology, management skills, production processes, manufacturing and marketing, and other resources.

The choice between foreign direct investment and exporting the knowledge or know-how depends on the additional costs of doing business in the foreign market and on the cost and feasibility of selling the knowledge and know-how.

Classical investment theory suggests that the reason for foreign direct investment is profit maximization, i.e. the factors of production move to where the highest rate of return can be earned; it is concerned with mobile factors of production. Behind classical investment theory is classical trade theory: the former is an extension of the latter; capital-rich countries tend to export capital intensive products and to invest capital abroad. Labour-rich countries tend to export labour intensive products and experience a migration of workers to better-off countries. Classical investment theory is a macroeconomic theory which does little to explain the investment decisions of individual firms.

The firm which invests abroad transmits equity capital, entrepreneurship, technology or other productive knowledge in the context of an industry-specific package. In most investments abroad where the firm replicates what it does well in one market, the importance of some unique asset or competitive advantage in the firm is recognized in another. It may be a potential invention or a differentiated product which is in demand in the target market. For the possession of some special asset to encourage the firm to invest abroad two conditions must exist: (a) the asset must be a public good within the firm, e.g. knowledge fundamental to the production of a profitable product, and (b) the return attainable must depend, at least partially, on local production (Caves, 1971, pp. 4–5). The essential feature of an asset conducive to foreign direct investment is not that its opportunity cost should be zero but that it should be low relative to the return available through foreign direct investment.

The traditional market imperfections view that states that FDI occurs when its expected net present value is both positive and greater than those of alternative modes of foreign market entry and production. This is a narrow view since it does not take account of uncertainty in international markets and the lack of information which may force the firm to postpone entry through FDI because of the size of the investment and risk involved in favour of a mode of entry with less commitment. The timing of market entry through FDI may become an issue.

The firm investing abroad must also consider factors other than the net present value. Otherwise it may forgo valuable opportunities. Investments in overseas markets should also be viewed as options that buy the firm rights to later investments, rights to flexibility or the right to enter new markets. An FDI options-driven strategy assumes that an investment today may derive its value from the future choices it makes possible; it serves as a valuable platform for future investments (Rivoli and Salorio, 1996, p. 337).

Managerial motives for FDI

Many firms that internationalize through the direct investment mode do so to gain better access to scarce raw materials or intermediate products. Many, particularly those that use commodities such as oil, bauxite or timber, integrate backwards to ensure an adequate supply of raw materials. Sometimes the reason for foreign direct investment is to develop foreign sources of components. More common is the situation where the firm's intention is to assemble final products for sale in local foreign markets.

Investment of this form is often chosen as an alternative to exporting for several reasons, many of them related to market imperfections (Exhibit 14.1). First, investment in the foreign market may improve the firm's ability to serve that market and nearby markets. By designing products for local conditions the firm provides a better service to distributors and customers. Second, the firm may be forced to establish in a local market to defend it from competitors. Local production may lower the final cost of the product through lower production and distribution costs. Third, local production may be unavoidable where government policies and trade barriers are such as to make exporting unattractive.

Foreign direct investment also occurs where competitive alliances make certain objectives unattainable. Sometimes firms are not in a position to control the use and exploitation of their technology by licences or joint ventures; those that depend for their competitive advantage on patents and similar forms of protection fall into this category. Foreign direct investment may provide the opportunity for a more efficient utilization of the technology and greater profits. The situation may be very different in services. Erramilli (1990) argues that customized services are likely to use integrated market entry modes that give the firm control over international marketing operations whereas entry for hard services such as software and engineering appear to be similar to that found in the manufacturing sector.

Exhibit 14.1
Creatures of imperfection – multinationals are not even global

Multinationals are not exploiters of purity but rather creatures of market imperfections, or failures. The best way to understand their behaviour is to understand those imperfections and how they are developing. Broadly, two sorts of imperfections are relevant. One is the structural imperfection, which may be natural (transport costs, for example) or man-made. The other sort of imperfection is inherent in transactions and markets themselves and has not, on balance, been disappearing. Examples are the uncertainty that a supplier will deliver on his promise; the volatility of exchange rates; the difficulty that customers face in evaluating unfamiliar products; the costs of negotiating deals; economies of scale in production, purchasing, research and development, distribution or marketing, which give advantages to existing firms and impose barriers against newcomers; concerns about infringements of intellectual property rights; uncertainty about competitors' actions; the opportunity to spread risks through diversification.

The modern multinational is thus a creature of imperfection, organising itself to adjust to market flaws and, indeed, to create such flaws. And if proof is still needed, consider this: multinationals are not even global.

Source: Adapted from *The Economist*, 27 March 1993.

There are a number of managerial reasons for entry to foreign markets through foreign direct investment. Many firms capable of investing in foreign markets possess a number of advantages not available to local firms. The foreign firm can sometimes gain a significant share of a local market when local firms do not have adequate management or marketing skills or when the local market has operated on the basis of administered prices. Foreign firms frequently have access to proprietary technology, which gives them an advantage. They may also possess scale economies which allow them to compete aggressively.

FDI and operating efficiency

The specific reasons behind a firm's decision to invest abroad are operating efficiency, risk reduction, market development and host government policy (Figure 14.1). It is frequently possible to manufacture products more efficiently outside the domestic market. A firm increases the efficiency of the production process if it locates where the factors of production are cheapest. For example, in the early 1980s, a number of German clothing manufacturers established production facilities in the Far East because German labour is relatively expensive.

At the end of the 1990s other locations, especially in Eastern Europe, have begun to

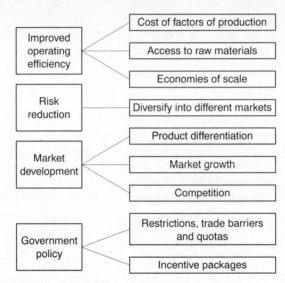

Figure 14.1 Reasons for foreign direct investment

feature. Efficiency gains may also be possible if operations are closer to the source of raw materials, e.g. oil, ores and timber. Similarly, efficiency gains are possible when the firm produces closer to the market. It is essential for most service industries to locate in the market. This explains the location of many US firms in Europe and Japanese firms in Europe and the United States. German motor manufacturers are now locating in the US and other countries both for cost and market reasons. In a study of five Chinese companies, McDermott and Huang (1996, p. 13) discovered that they internationalize their operations because they have absorbed and improved the technologies and equipment imported from developed countries and thus created their own competitive advantage through technological development. According to these authors, despite their quality improvements, costs and thus prices, remain their main competitive advantage abroad.

Sometimes firms internationalize through investment to guarantee access to raw materials or cheaper labour. In the latter situation firms are known to twin plants in their network, e.g. a capital-intensive factory in one country twinned with a labour-intensive one in another. Firms, especially those in services, internationalize by acquisition, especially to protect the domestic market and to hold on to customers there. Advertising agencies frequently follow their clients abroad to protect their domestic operations. Finally, a shortage or restriction on foreign exchange may encourage a firm to locate abroad to protect its profits and sales.

FDI and risk reduction

Firms sometimes internationalize through the investment mode to reduce risk. Risk reduction is further enhanced through diversification since it is unlikely that all the firm's investment will perform at the same level of profitability. Because expansions and contractions in different countries do not occur at the same time, the firm should be able to stabilize its earnings by locating in several foreign countries.

A second cost-related factor is economies of scale. Scale economies arise in several areas of the firm's operations, most often associated with production as occurs, for example in car manufacturing in Europe where different components are produced in different countries. European and even global manufacturing networks are frequently more cost effective than concentrating the production process in one location. Scale economies also occur in financing and marketing. Financial economies of scale may be obtained by a firm with international operations when the firm gains access to several capital markets. Marketing scale economies are evident in many products and services, especially franchised fast foods, soft drinks and clothing.

FDI and market development

Foreign direct investment may also be explained by the firm's desire to exploit the market. Some firms possess certain advantages in the design and development of products and services. The source of these advantages lies in the ability of the firm to differentiate its products and services. Product differentiation is a strong motive for foreign direct investment (Hymer, 1976). Investment abroad allows such firms to internationalize product differentiation advantage to other countries where profitable. Because advantages stem from specialized knowledge, technology and patent protection, foreign-based firms are usually not in a position to compete, hence the reason for foreign direct investment among such firms.

Sometimes foreign markets grow faster than domestic markets, or better prices are available because of less competition. There are many markets throughout the world where only a few well-known brands share the market. Freightliner was clearly motivated by market development reasons when it began an aggressive internationalization strategy (Exhibit 14.2). Foreign markets may also open up to foreign competition due to income growth, population growth or the reduction of ownership barriers.

Exhibit 14.2
Freightliner speeds product changes and looks overseas

With the US heavy-duty truck industry running out of gas this year, Freightliner Corp is trying to build new roads to profitability. Considered the king of heavy-duty truck makers in the US, Freightliners, a Portland, Oregon-based unit of Germany's Daimler-Benz AG, is revving up diversification plans in a bid to insulate itself from the industry's first downturn in years. The truck maker is now seeking to build a name for itself overseas.

The company will begin producing heavy-duty trucks in Saudi Arabia, South Africa and Israel. Jim Hebe, Freightliner's President, says those countries are only beginning to develop appetites for American-style trucks. In addition, Freightliner 'is very close' to establishing manufacturing operations in Asia, most likely China, Jim Hebe says. Freightliner, which sells its vehicles in 23 countries, also has production facilities in Australia and Mexico.

The international moves by Freightliner are part of a broader strategy by Daimler to increase its world-wide truck business. 'We're looking for markets and special niches where we can achieve a dominant position and a competitive advantage without making significant capital investments,' Jim Hebe says.

Source:Adapted from *The Wall Street Journal*, Monday, 22 July 1996, p. B4.

FDI and government policy

Governments frequently impose tariffs and quotas which force a firm to locate behind the barrier. In such circumstances foreign direct investment may be the only way for the firm to gain access to a market. Japanese car manufacturers have located in Europe and the United States to avoid import quota restrictions in these markets. Furthermore, as discussed in an earlier chapter, governments frequently provide attractive incentive packages to firms considering foreign direct investment as a mode of entry to international markets. With the operation of the WTO it is increasingly difficult to use tariffs and quotas but non-tariff barriers such as blocked channels are still a problem. It is unlikely that exchange rate movements are the dominant factor in foreign direct investment decisions, at least in the short term. Such decisions are typically made in response to long-term market strategy considerations and cannot be implemented so rapidly as to accommodate short-term exchange rate fluctuations. A decision to invest abroad requires several years to come to fruition and it is difficult, in the short term, to reverse such decisions. The possibility of exchange rate changes may, however, be a motivating factor to make or enlarge foreign investments. By locating production in several currency areas the firm can shift some of its production among locations and thus avoid potential exchange rate losses.

The basic motives for foreign direct investment are thus numerous. For some firms they include securing market positions in foreign markets, overcoming tariff and non-tariff barriers to trade, exploiting new markets, benefiting from government financial incentives, securing supplies and low-wage labour. In addition, firms engage in foreign direct investment because they have superior marketing skills. Firm-specific competitive advantages frequently reside in their excellent marketing skills, their network of distributors and their well-established relationships with customers.

Determinants of location for FDI

In manufacturing foreign direct investment five sets of factors are thought to be important determinants. First, the size of the market in the host country is likely to have a positive effect on the inflow of foreign direct investment. Since such investment is a commitment of resources in uncertain or unfamiliar markets, firms tend to invest in countries with larger markets to compensate for the risks involved.

Second, proximity of the host country measured on a business distance scale results in a general lowering of costs of managing foreign subsidiaries which would have a positive effect on the inflow of foreign direct investment. Production costs are a primary motivator of foreign direct investment. A number of US-based international companies employ either a joint venture or mostly a foreign direct investment strategy to enter India and are taking a longer-term view regarding the market and its opportunities (Chandrasekaran and Ryans, 1996, p. 611). Several of these firms are relying on their Indian operations as a source of engineering and R&D talent and as a base for developing global strategies. The preference for foreign direct investment suggests a desire to maximize manufacturing economies, a commitment to the market and a vote of confidence in the Indian economy and plans for its development.

Third, the size of the firm is correlated with foreign direct investment. Firm size is frequently taken as a proxy for a number of ownership-specific advantages possessed by the firm. Foreign direct investment requires significant funds to establish abroad. Larger firms seem to be more able to cope with the costs and risks involved. Fourth, experience gained through various forms of international operations has a positive effect on foreign direct investment. Previous investments or marketing experience gained in one country assists the firm when investing in another.

The greater the international experience possessed by the firm the greater the learning. Finally, firms in oligopolistic industries tend to mimic each other's foreign direct investment decisions in order to maintain a competitive equilibrium. Such oligopolistic reaction contributes positively to foreign direct investment.

As the subsidiaries of multinational companies become more embedded in host countries it is likely to lead to a deepening of their value chains and a propensity for them to engage in higher-order or more innovative activities. This is most certainly the case in Ireland where government policy has promoted higher-order activities among the mobile multinational companies which have flocked there to capitalize on the spatial industrial clusters and other locational advantages. These developments are well documented in various studies on the location of FDI (Papanastassiou and Pearce, 1997; Shan and Song, 1997). Commenting on these and other findings, Dunning (1998, pp. 59–60) concludes that, with the gradual dispersion of created assets and as firms become more multinational by deepening or widening their cross-border value chains then, from both the viewpoint of harnessing new competitive advantages and more efficiently using their home-based assets, the structure and content of the location portfolio of firms becomes more critical to their global competitive positions.

Trends in foreign direct investment

One of the major reasons for the growth in foreign direct investment since the 1960s is the increased differentiation in the marketing of products and services abroad. Other reasons are costs and technology transfers and access to new markets. In 1980 foreign direct investment was dominated by the United States. Japan subsequently entered the scene, particularly to reduce costs. With the integration of the EU market, the triad of the US, EU and Japan dominates world inward and outward foreign direct investment. The EU is the world's largest foreign direct investor, representing about a half of OECD outward investments since 1980, almost three-quarters of which goes to the United States (Thomsen and Woolcock, 1993, pp. 10–11). When EFTA countries are included foreign direct investment from Europe accounted for almost two-thirds of OECD foreign direct investment in 1991.

Role of marketing and differentiated products

The lack of a good marketing infrastructure in many countries in earlier years meant that the distribution of differentiated products through agents and other intermediaries was not managed as well as that of standardized commodities. For most differentiated products it is necessary to invest heavily to identify and cultivate customers and to learn how to price the product, to display it and to demonstrate and advertise it. Most agents or small intermediaries in foreign markets are reluctant to make such heavy investments. There is always the danger that if they are too successful they will be bypassed by the foreign manufacturer or local retailer. Local distributors or agents will only invest in distribution if they control the supply sources or markets through equity participation. Manufacturers or retailers of products which require considerable demonstration and service or require specialized facilities must frequently integrate forward or backward into distribution.

Cross-foreign direct investment

The very large multinational firms have been involved in cross-direct investments in each other's countries for many years. Firms in the United States continue to invest heavily in Canada, Europe and Japan. Recently they have begun to invest heavily in South East Asia and Eastern Europe. Similarly, European firms have become quite aggressive in Japan and the United States. Japanese firms have been very active in foreign direct investment in the United Kingdom and using the United Kingdom as a base from which to bound into continental European markets. German, Japanese and UK firms have been very active in the US market using foreign direct investment as the means of entry (Williamson, 1991). The form of the investment, however, varies considerably. While most German and UK investment is in manufacturing, Japanese investment is predominantly in wholesale distribution (Figure 14.2). In this way the Japanese are guaranteeing distribution for products exported to the United States as well as manufactured there. There are three reasons for such cross-investments. First, some multinational firms are in a position to enjoy economies of scale by operating production facilities in different countries, while still using an integrated system of strategic planning to monitor and control production for different markets throughout the world. The Ford Motor Company follows such a strategy in the production of certain models of car in designated centres for supply to widespread markets. Second, opportunities for product-market differentiation are increased since it is

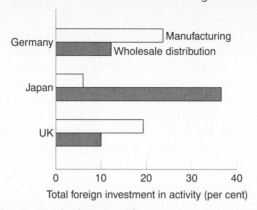

Figure 14.2 Foreign investment in the US market
Source: Williamson, P. (1991) 'Successful strategies for export', *Long Range Planning*, **24** (1), 57–63.

possible for the firm to target specific market niches in different countries while supplying them efficiently by coordinated centralized operations. Third, the convergence of consumer tastes in certain product markets allows the firm to design and produce products and services for global markets. These three sets of factors encourage firms that have the resources to build a presence in each market area. This is usually done by establishing a fully controlled, wholly owned subsidiary.

Cross-border or Community-based foreign direct investment in the EU has grown faster than inward investment from outside the EU (Eurostat, 1996). By 1989 Community-based foreign direct investment had overtaken foreign direct investment from outside the EU. The increase in foreign direct investment within the EU may be attributed to the effects of the Single Market. Most of the increase in foreign direct investment is in services foreign direct investment. The Single Market encouraged the growth of services, especially financial services, through rights of establishment within the territory of another member state. The Single Market did not, however, promote cross-border servicing of customers by financial institutions, hence the great interest in foreign direct investment in financial services. More recently, especially since 1990, there has been a large increase in foreign direct investment into Germany, contrary to the normal pattern. This reflects an increase in inward investment by firms seeking access to the post-unified German market and access through the former East Germany to nearby former socialist countries such as the Czech Republic, Poland, Slovakia and Hungary.

Conditions for success in foreign direct investment

For the firm to be successful in foreign direct investment it must possess a strategic competitive advantage that more than offsets the cost of operating in foreign markets. The competitive advantages must reflect certain characteristics. First, the firm should be able to transfer assets abroad at a low incremental cost without adversely affecting revenues or profits at home. Second, the sale or lease of these assets to an independent firm must involve substantial transaction costs so that the best way of guaranteeing that the benefits accrue to the firm is by internalizing them in a subsidiary, rather than by selling or leasing

(Buckley and Casson, 1976; Dunning, 1981; Teece, 1981). The assets in question are intangible, e.g. knowledge and know-how, which may apply to new products and production processes, to the design and implementation of marketing programmes and to the general management of international operations. Such knowledge and know-how is very mobile internationally, with the result that arm's length transactions in such assets tend to be subject to high transaction costs and to a high degree of uncertainty. The firm possessing these assets may decide to internalize them within a subsidiary and to use them more profitably in foreign markets when relative factor costs, tariffs, transport costs and market size allow.

International market entry by acquisition

As noted in the preceding chapter on competitive alliances, acquisitions can be beneficial in situations where firms experience asymmetric access to information or require specific market assets or other resources. In such circumstances one firm may acquire another which possesses information, assets, brands, distribution networks or skilled management which can be used to improve the performance of the first firm.

There are many reasons for foreign market entry by acquisition. The most important are to be found in the areas of rationalization of production across different locations, restructuring of industry and achieving complementarity of operations. A second set of motives are market driven – market expansion and strengthening of market position are also very important.

Relying on the market might take a long time, be more expensive or be impossible. The lower transaction costs involved mean that acquisitions can be a better alternative to competitive alliances or organic growth through exporting. UPM-Kymmene, the Finnish forestry group, decided on a series of worldwide acquisitions to achieve the economies of scale necessary to serve customers with global needs (Exhibit 14.3). Deciding to enter foreign markets through an acquisition investment mode is akin to the big decision in the 'build or buy' alternatives facing firms as they expand.

Acquiring an established firm in the foreign market presents it with an established means of entry with institutional support and a working network of suppliers, intermediaries and customers. It is a quick way of entering the market as it bypasses all the planning and negotiation stages which are necessary in building a complete new production facility.

It may, of course, be much more expensive to enter the market in this way and other dangers of foreign acquisitions may be encountered (*Business Week*, 30 October 1995, p. 66):

- Foreign acquirers usually pay more for targets than a domestic buyer would, often with inflated hopes of future synergies.
- Differences of language and culture aggravate integration of two management teams.
- Misperceptions about the target's home market can lead to marketing mistakes.
- Vertical integration is much harder in cross-border deals than in intracountry deals.
- Employees tend to be even more frightened of new management if bosses are from another country.

================ Exhibit 14.3 ================
Paper-maker unwraps global aims

UPM-Kymmene, Europe's largest forestry group is one of the few genuinely trans-continental producers in a traditionally fragmented industry. A joint venture with Asia Pacific Resources International of Singapore created the world's biggest alliance for the production of fine paper, used for printing, copying and writing. Shortly afterwards the $650m acquisition of the US paper-making subsidiary of New Zealand's Fletcher Challenge gave UPM-Kymmene a production base in the North American market, where it had already had substantial export sales.

The company, now the world's largest pulp and paper producer after International Paper of the US, is setting a cross-border consolidation trend. According to Juha Niemelä, UPM-Kymmene Chief Executive, 'We have satisfied our strategic intent. We saw we needed to be a worldwide producer, not just a worldwide seller . . . having achieved this in the US and in Asia, I am content with our position today'.

Since 1996, he has slimmed group operations, narrowing the company's focus in paper production to just three grades: magazine paper, newsprint and fine paper. It has spun off non-core interests. Producers, Mr Niemelä says, need to achieve economies of scale to serve customers with increasingly global needs. This means having to focus on fewer segments. Bigger machines facilitate specialization. 'Producing some kind of all-round grade is no longer a winning concept', Mr Niemelä says.

Source: adapted from *Financial Times*, Tuesday, 6 January 1998, p. 16.

The high cost of entry is frequently offset against the market potential which is presumed to exist. In recent years a number of large European firms have acquired US firms, since a strong presence in the growing US market is seen by these firms as an essential ingredient of their worldwide strategy. A similar pattern has also appeared in Europe, especially in food industries and branded business. Acquisitions frequently have as a central objective the ownership and management of well-known brands. Scarce shelf space in supermarkets and market power resting with supermarket chains has meant that customers have focused more attention on one or two brands in the market, which have become highly valued assets in take-over attempts.

The major attraction of entry by acquisition to a foreign market is that it is very much quicker than entry through fixed investment in new facilities and internal development of assets. Acquisition has two major advantages. First, the firm obtains assets that are already in use so the return is quicker than from fixed asset investment. Second, acquisition provides the firm with immediate market share without any increase in capacity. Speed may be an important consideration to allow the firm to enter new foreign product markets quickly and thereby to exploit first-mover advantage.

Expansion by acquisition can take two general forms. At one extreme are acquisitions which are a complete legal integration of two or more firms. At the other extreme are acquisitions involving only changes in the ownerships of the firms involved. In the first case the assets and liabilities of two or more firms are transferred into a single firm, existing or new. This form of entry by acquisition involves major reorganization, from changes in the membership of the board to changes in products sold. Generally, legal acquisitions involve integration of the constituent parts of companies, a process which is not easily reversible. One of the major difficulties of this form of acquisition is that integration of management functions and determination of joint strategies may be a long and difficult task.

In the second situation, where a change of ownership allows an acquisition to occur, the take-over of one company by another is the most common form. Here both firms continue to exist as separate legal entities. This form of acquisition is performed by a purchase of shares or a public take-over bid. Acquisition in this way unifies the businesses while still maintaining a considerable degree of decentralization between the members of the new entity.

A complicated network of acquisitions of this form can result in a complicated structure, even involving subsidiaries large enough to make their own acquisitions. Although complex, they can be stable and profitable. Success in such firms is frequently due to flexibility and the decentralized management structure which continues.

A network of independent firms, although owned centrally through shareholding arrangements, is likely to be able to adjust better to changing social, political and business considerations in international product markets than are firms which are single legal entities. Decentralized management allows the firm to back out of difficult situations. A change of strategy is easier to implement through the sale of shares than by selling off fixed assets. In decentralized management situations, as occurs, for example, in subsidiaries, managers may have a keener sense of their roles than would occur, for example, in a divisionalized or branch structure. A combination of the advantages of concentration of physical and intangible assets and of a decentralization of management and responsibility which permits flexibility occurs in acquisitions involving ownership changes only (Jacquemin *et al.*, 1989). Expansion into international markets by this form of acquisition suffers from problems arising in the area of human resources. Sometimes working relationships deteriorate to such an extent that managements clash and redundancies and reorganizations occur. The uncertainty thus created can prevent the success of the acquisition.

Success factors in acquisitions

Very few firms deliberately set out to acquire firms that will result in failure. In a study by Coley and Reinton (1988), successful acquisitions had a number of common features. Typically, after acquisition the firms were reorganized to offset the high cost of purchase. The operations of the acquired firms were strengthened by adding new management and sometimes new capital. Most important, the new owners systematically identified and assessed the value created by the acquisition and carefully managed the integration process.

Successful acquisitions normally involve strategies to limit risk, to identify and assess elements of synergy, to achieve scale economies, to acquire sequentially and to maintain constant leadership from senior management (Figure 14.3). Somewhat curiously, given

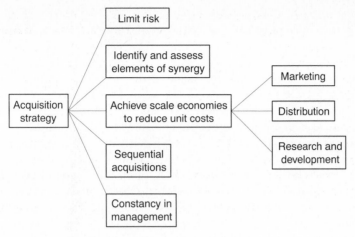

Figure 14.3 Components of successful acquisition strategy

that cultural similarity is important for joint ventures (Chapter 13), according to Morosini *et al.* (1998, pp. 153–4) acquisitions are more likely to be successful the greater the cultural distance between the countries of the firms involved. The reason given by these authors is that cross-border acquisitions in more culturally distant countries are likely to provide a mechanism for international companies to access diverse repertoires of innovation, entrepreneurship and decision-making practices which have the potential to enhance the combined firm's performance over time

A key influence in acquisition strategies is the possibility of reduced unit costs arising from better marketing and distribution arrangements and research and development work as applied to manufacturing. Centrally coordinated, such arrangements can produce scale economies. Marketing effectiveness is increased if a standardized approach to positioning can be adopted. Similarly, distribution economies can be realized by integrating several minor distribution networks and increasing the number of product lines through an existing network. A higher degree of research and development specialization can be achieved through the consolidation of several similar research areas which may lead to shorter development time and quicker commercialization.

A sequenced acquisition strategy can produce dominance in an industry sector or market. By targeting firms for acquisition in a clearly defined sequence a firm can become the dominant player in a region, or even in the world. In the early 1970s Electrolux was just one of several firms with a share in the appliance sector of the electrical products industry. By the end of the 1980s, with more than 250 acquisitions behind it, Electrolux was the dominant player in this sector. The firm also maintains a low profile in the industry in that it retains the brand names of the companies it acquires. Electrolux follows a planned acquisition strategy in the five steps illustrated below (Eng and Forsman, 1989):

1. A specific geographic market is targeted.
2. A critical mass in the market is created by buying firms with established brand names.

3. Production is rationalized while taking account of the firm's capacity in other countries. Weak product lines are eliminated in favour of large-volume production lines.
4. Financial management is centralized and country marketing services are coordinated.
5. All viable brands are supported to maintain customer loyalty in different markets and to hold shelf and floor space.

Acquiring firms sequentially to enter and dominate industry sectors across many international markets requires a stability of leadership policy in the firm. A mission to develop corporate and marketing strategies through internationalization by acquisition is a long-term strategy achievable only over many years. It is not a short-term strategy: dominance of market position is achieved only with patience, strategic thinking and a constancy of leadership in senior management. Sometimes the marketing logic is enough to overcome any organizational difficulties which would need to be faced. The marketing and manufacturing complementarity which existed between Electrolux and Zanussi was a large factor in facilitating that acquisition in the early 1980s.

Success and failure in UK and US acquisitions

In evaluating ways of entering international markets it is worth noting that many, if not most, acquisitions fail if success is defined as adding value above the total cost of analyzing, executing and implementing the acquisition strategy. The reasons for such failure may be attributed to acquisition strategies which are unfocused and insufficient analysis of the targeted industry and company. Furthermore, many firms rely too much on the potential for financial engineering, scale economies and synergy. Finally, a lack of clear strategy for the acquisition and lack of a thoroughly prepared implementation framework are also contributory factors in failure.

In order to examine the success or failure of acquisition as a corporate growth strategy, McKinsey and Company studied the performance of the 'Fortune 250' companies and the top 150 companies in *The Financial Times* 500 which had used acquisitions to enter new markets (Coley and Reinton, 1988; *Economist*, 1988, p. 113). McKinsey studied 116 mergers and found that 16 per cent could not be judged a success or failure. Success was measured as the firm's ability to earn back its cost of capital or better on the funds invested in the merger. By this standard, 23 per cent were successful and 61 per cent were not. The larger the acquisitions and the greater the diversification the smaller was the likelihood of success (Table 14.1). The major reason for failure was companies paying too much for acquisitions and an inability to introduce operating or financial changes sufficient to offset the premiums (*Economist*, 1988, p. 113). In this context it is interesting to note that companies frequently have multiple objectives in making acquisitions. International acquisitions do, however, create value for the shareholders of the acquiring companies. The argument that international acquisitions enable firms to exploit their firm-specific intangible assets in other countries and thus to increase the value of their firms has received strong empirical in a study of 236 acquisitions by US firms in Canada, the United Kingdom and in other European countries (Markides and Oyon, 1998, pp. 132–3).

Table 14.1 Success in UK and US acquisitions

Size of firm acquired		Degree of diversification	
		Low	High
Small	Firms in category:	20	16
	Success rate:	45 per cent	38 per cent
Large	Firms in category:	26	35
	Success rate:	27 per cent	14 per cent
No. of acquisitions	*Success*	*Failure*	*Unknown*
116	23 per cent	61 per cent	16 per cent

Source: adapted from Coley, S. and Reinton, S. (1988) 'The hunt for value', *The McKinsey Quarterly*, Spring.

In general, the owners of firms which are of potential strategic importance to another firm are aware that they possess valuable assets so they attempt to ensure that a premium is paid for the firm. It is not unusual to witness firms with mediocre performance records and poor prospects commanding price–earnings multiples of over 20. In such circumstances the acquiring firm must use all its skill to structure and negotiate the offer package so that the risk of failure is minimized. The acquisition of Chrysler by Daimler Benz announced on 7 May 1998 raises the question of whether the two companies can work together. While the companies appear to be successful and complementary in terms of product range market coverage and distribution (Exhibit 14.4) they will have two bosses in two headquarters operating to very different manufacturing standards under different work cultures. Daimler Benz may be inclined to impose its methods on Chrysler but this may be short sighted given the manufacturing skills in Chrysler and the differences in the demand for cars in the US and Europe. The merged company, Daimler–Chrysler, has very poor market penetration in Latin America and Asia and Daimler Benz's other businesses such as aerospace may have to be sold off as the core business of the new venture is cars.

Firms accept a price premium where elements of synergy and scale economies warrant it. A well-planned acquisition can ensure production and marketing synergy. One of the principal elements in the merger of ASEA of Sweden and Brown Boveri of Switzerland was that the new company, ABB, should have the resources to become the low-cost producers in all its businesses, while being the most technologically advanced in the market with sufficient capacity and financial resources to commercialize new technical innovations rapidly.

Public policy and cross-border acquisitions

Cross-border acquisitions are likely to continue growing and in general to be welcomed by policy makers, as in most cases they do not adversely affect competition and the consumer should benefit. Unless the resulting market share held by the new corporate

Exhibit 14.4
Daimler Benz–Chrysler merger

Daimler-Benz AG, Germany's luxury auto maker and biggest industrial firm, and Chrysler Corp, the No. 3 auto maker in the US, announced one of the biggest corporate mergers of all time, which will capitalise the new merged entity at $92 billion. This will be the biggest industrial merger of all time.

The transaction is set to reshape the industry, particularly as car makers struggle with a worldwide glut of capacity. Never before has such a large US corporation been essentially sold or merged into a foreign company. Although a European industrial company has never made an acquisition on this scale, the most striking feature of the deal itself is not the size, but its unique structure spanning two continents. Never has one of America's prime industrial companies – let alone one of the Big Three car manufacturers – been run at least partly form abroad, as DaimlerChrysler will be. Altogether, the combined company will have an estimated £130 billion in annual revenues. By comparison, Ford Motors' 1997 revenues were about $154 billion, General Motors' about $178 billion, Toyota's about $99 billion and VW's $63 billion. It will become the world's fifth largest maker of cars and light trucks, ahead of Nissan with $54 billion revenues (Table).

Chrysler hopes that Mercedes will provide the international clout that it needs, and the expertise to revive its mass-markets range, which has been languishing for decades. For Chrysler, the deal will provide a much stronger base in Europe, where it is now a small player with only one percent of the Western European market in unit sales. GM and Ford each has about twelve percent of that market. For Daimler, the deal will represent a huge leap in the US. The north American sales of the company's Mercedes-Benz cars have grown sharply in recent years, but the company remains a niche player confined to the high-end market.

On the positive side, there is a sense that Daimler needs to expand beyond German borders. For Germans, the central issue is by now familiar, if paradoxical: to stay competitive in the evolving global market they know they must seek their fortune increasingly outside Germany. 'Daimler', said Michael Stürmer, a leading German historian, 'is pushing very consciously into globalization, and in that sense, Daimler-Benz is no longer a German company'. Many observers say a DaimlerChrysler alliance sounds like a dream team that would give both companies a greater global presence and force its smaller competitors to scramble for cover.

The combination of Daimler and Chrysler probably means that the days of the rest of Europe's regional car groups are numbered. The likes of Renault and Peugeot-Citroën, which are overly dependent on their home markets, must be quaking at this latest development. So too must Fiat, which is in the middle of an ambitious international expansion that does not include North America, the world's biggest car market. 'The issue that excites the market is the global reach', combined with an almost total lack of overlap says Stephen Reitman, European autos analyst at Merrill Lynch in London.

The new company would have an impressive range of models: Daimler's car-making division, Mercedes-Benz, produces the best luxury cars in the world, in addition to some innovative small ones just coming to market and several untried commercial ventures. Chrysler's saloon cars are outgunned in America by Ford and GM, but its average profit for each vehicle is the highest of the Big Three, thanks to its strength in minivans and Jeeps, where margins are fattest. Daimler has less than one percent market share in the US, and Chrysler's market share in Europe is equally minuscule. 'Daimler has seized the initiative with this move' Reitman says.

The planned merger raises the question whether the two companies can make this merger work. Maryann Kellyer, an American car analyst, accepts the logic of the merger, but fears that putting such different companies together will be difficult: 'When it comes to the cultures of these two companies, how they think and act and what drives their decisions, they're oil and water', she says. The firms are successful and complementary, and there will certainly be some savings, such as in joint distribution. But realising these savings will stretch the talents of Mercedes' managers, who will have to raise the standard of Chrysler's passenger cars. Big expensive cars which drive superbly on the *autobahn* are not the same as the big cheap cars that most Americans prefer to drive. Other differences could also prove hard to reconcile. DaimlerChrysler is to have two bosses – Mr Schrempp and Chrysler's Robert Eaton. Such arrangements are notoriously dodgy. And the group will be run from two headquarters, one in Stuttgart and one in Michigan. Chrysler is a lean North American producer, which buys 70 percent of its added-value from outside; Daimler is a fully integrated German maker of luxury cars, famed for its world-class design and engineering. Chrysler has come back from the brink of bankruptcy twice in recent years. It survives, thanks only to its distinctive and lean way of involving suppliers in its innermost thinking. Daimler will be tempted to impose its methods on Chrysler. But it has more to learn than it realises from Chrysler's manufacturing skills. If it fails to recognise this, it is in for trouble.

Companies in 1997	GM	Ford	Toyota	VW	Daimler Chrysler	Nissan
Employees	608,000	350,000	151,000	279,000	421,000	135,000
Revenue ($m)	178,174	153,627	98,740	62,914	130,064	53,700
Net income	6,698	6,920	3,112	756	4,567	627
Production						
Cars	5,474,000	n/a	3,100,000	3,942,000	1,590,000	2,172,000
Trucks	3,302,000	n/a	1,790,000	395,000	2,446,000	571,000
Total	8,776,000	6,943,000	4,890,000	4,337,000	4,036,000	2,743,000
Headquarters:	Daimler-Benz:	Stuttgart, Germany				
	Chrysler:	Auburn Hills, Michigan, U.S.				

Sources: adapted from *The Sunday Business Post* (Dublin), 10 May 1998, p. 15; *New York Times*, Saturday, 9 May 1998, p. D1; *Economist*, 9 May 1998, pp.69–70; *The European*, 11–17 May 1998, p. 9.

entity is substantial in the relevant market, such acquisitions and competitive alliances are more likely to benefit consumers. A case in point was the take-over battle in the UK confectionery industry. Both Nestlé and Jacob–Suchard had small shares of the UK market and a merger between either and Rowntree Mackintosh would not seriously reduce competition, whereas a merger with Cadbury and Rowntree Mackintosh would.

On purely commercial grounds a cross-border acquisition between either Nestlé or Jacob–Suchard and Rowntree Mackintosh made marketing sense. Rowntree, with world brands such as 'Kit Kat', 'Rolo' and 'After Eight' was a leader in the fastest-growing confectionery segment: chocolate coated treats that frequently contain caramel, biscuits or nuts.

In contrast Nestlé and Suchard were concentrated in the shrinking market for solid chocolate. This take-over activity in the United Kingdom reflected pressure to consolidate a fragmented European confectionery market. A number of other mergers are worth noting in this context. Cadbury Schweppes had acquired Poulain, a French chocolate manufacturer. Cadbury itself had been a target of a take-over from the General Cinema Corporation. In 1987, Suchard bought a Chicago company, EJ Brach and Sons, for $730 million. Suchard also bought Belgium's leading chocolatier, Cézote d'Or, and Nestlé agreed to pay $1.3 million for the Italian food company, Buitoni, which includes the chocolate maker Perugina (*Business Week*, 9 May, 1988).

The merger between Grand Metropolitan and Guinness in 1997 with a combined turnover of £13.7 billion allows the new entity to claim to be the world's largest spirit business. The two firms' portfolios of brands complement each other in Asia, where brandy and whiskey dominate, and in the US, where white spirits such as vodka are the tipple of preference. The merged company also expects to experience a decline in marketing and distribution costs.

Public policy interest in acquisition is frequently concerned with two issues: competition and efficiency. Governments view acquisitions as providing an opportunity for increased efficiency in industry. At the same time, however, they are concerned about any reduction in competition which might result from an acquisition. Situations where efficiency gains are large for a small reduction in competition are generally welcomed. In some cases small losses in competition would be traded for small gains in efficiency, depending on circumstances. In general, however, governments and public policy makers resist acquisitions which produce only small efficiency gains for large reductions in competition.

Industry in the EU has been examined to determine the extent of efficiency gains and reduction of competition which would arise if unbridled acquisition activity were to take place (Jacquemin *et al.*, 1989). These researchers have found that large efficiency gains for a small loss of competition would arise if acquisitions were to occur in high-technology industries such as advanced materials, chemicals, pharmaceuticals, computers, telecommunications and electronics, motor vehicles, aerospace and specialized instruments (Table 14.2). Only small efficiency gains but severe loss in competition would occur if acquisitions occurred in low-technology areas such as building materials, metals, paint, furniture, paper, rubber and tobacco.

Table 14.2 Impact of acquisitions on competition and efficiency

Reduction of competition	Potential efficiency gains	
	Small	Large
Small	Steel	Advanced materials
	Machinery	Chemicals–pharmaceuticals
	Leather and leather products	Computers, office automation
	Clothing and textiles	Telecommunications
	Pulp, paper and board	Electronics
	Jewellery, toys, musical	Aerospace
	instruments	Instruments
Large	Building materials	Boilermaking
	Metal products	Cables, heavy electrical plant
	Paints and varnishes	Railway equipment
	Furniture	Shipbuilding
	Paper products	Confectionery, chocolate
	Rubber products	Flour, pasta
	Tobacco	Beer

Source: adapted from Jacquemin, A., Buigues, P. and Ilzkovitz, F. (1989) 'Horizontal mergers and competition policy in the European Community', *European Economy*, **40**, 27–32.

Market entry through new ventures and acquisitions: an evaluation

Comparison of acquisitions and new ventures

New venture foreign direct investments are frequently less costly than acquisitions since the scale of the firm's involvement can be precisely controlled and the production facility can be expanded exactly in line with achieved market penetration. In general, smaller firms prefer the new venture approach because they lack the financial resources for a take-over; another reason is because the choice of location is open to the entrant and a least-cost site can be selected, which frequently comes with an attractive incentive package provided by the host government because of the employment potential of the new facility.

New venture foreign direct investments also avoid inheriting problems which may exist in established firms, while at the same time it is possible to introduce the most modern technology and equipment. For larger firms new venture foreign direct investment can be the best alternative market entry mode when suitable candidates for acquisition are not available. This was how Wal-Mart viewed its entry into Germany. With its unique retailing formula it was important that the company establish a new venture over which it would have full control of every aspect of retailing; location, merchandise mix, display, general management and corporate culture (Exhibit 14.5).

By acquiring a foreign-based firm, other advantages accrue to the firm. Generally the acquisition route means a quicker payback and cultural and difficult management

================= Exhibit 14.5 =================
Wal-Mart goes shopping in Europe

Wal-Mart Stores has conquered the US with its cut-price goods, becoming by far the country's biggest retailer. Now, it is Europe's turn. This week, Wal-Mart took its first step into the European retail market by buying the Wertkauf hypermarket company from Germany's Mann family. Its success in the US is attributable to many factors, but high on the list is a corporate culture that places heavy emphasis on customer service. Wal-Mart is also highly regarded for its advanced retail technology which enables it to have the right quantities of goods in the right place at the right time, while keeping costly inventories to the minimum.

Since starting its international expansion in 1991, Wal-Mart has already become the biggest retailer in Canada and Mexico. It has also dipped its toe into emerging markets, opening small numbers of stores in Argentina, Brazil, Indonesia and China. Yet retailing notoriously travels badly. Retailers that develop a successful concept in their home market usually find that they need to adjust the formula to suit local conditions overseas: yet in doing so, they risk undermining whatever it was that made them successful in the first place.

Previous US ventures into Europe have a mixed record. McDonald's and Toys牙'Us may be growing, but Woolworth sold its UK stores. Sears Roebuck pulled out of Spain, J. C. Penney sold its Sarma stores in Belgium and Safeway sold its UK outlets. If Wal-Mart's European venture is to succeed, then it will have to overcome the obstacles that have discouraged other US retailers; much higher costs for real estate, labour and distribution than in the US, plus tastes that differ widely from one country to another.

Still, European retail analysts say Wal-Mart has probably made the right decision by starting in Germany. Although competition is intense, the market is large, and in some ways, German retailing is not as advanced as it is in other countries. Nicholas Jones, an analyst at Goldman Sachs in London, says that the depth and breadth of assortments are inferior in German hypermarkets, as are store layouts and visual presentation. And relatively few German retailers are equipped with the systems and logistics that are among Wal-Mart's strengths.

Source: adapted from *Financial Times*, Weekend, 20–21 December 1997, p. 15.

problems may be avoided. The major advantage of the acquisition mode of entry is the purchase of critical assets, products, brand names, skills, technology and, above all, distribution networks. This last asset has been central to many of the recent large acquisitions and attempted acquisitions in Europe. Finally, acquisitions do not usually disturb the competitive framework in the host country and for that reason are often not hindered greatly by public policy.

There are a number of thorny problems, however, in pursuing the acquisition route. Firms frequently find it very difficult to value the assets being acquired, e.g. the value of brands. Furthermore, it is often very difficult to determine the degree of synergy that will exist between the firm's existing assets and the acquired assets. As noted above, there may be considerable costs associated with integrating a previously independent company into a larger group. Finally, the search costs to find a suitable firm to acquire can be substantial.

Foreign direct investments in the United States

There are many reasons why the United States is an attractive location for direct investment by companies located in other countries. The size and importance of the US market means that many large international companies with strong brands view it as central to their international activities. In this category are included many of the well-known Japanese companies such as Sony and Toyota. Similarly, European companies have discovered that the size and growth of the US market make it essential to be active there. Philips, Electrolux and many of the luxury producers of cars have established strong bases in the United States. The confidence of participating in world markets has encouraged these firms to compete with US firms in their home market. Foreign firms operating in the United States do not, however, appear to earn higher profits than randomly selected American-owned firms which tend to be less R&D intensive, and more advertising intensive, than foreign-owned firms (Kim and Lyn, 1990, p. 51).

A second major reason for the importance of the United States as a location is the intermittent fear that protectionism will take hold there. Behind trade barriers, foreign firms can continue to serve the market successfully. With the integration of world markets and the actions of the WTO this reason is less important now. Corporate restructuring in the United States has increased the number of US firms available for acquisition. When this is combined with a depreciated US dollar and strong growth in the US economy, the incentive to acquire firms in the United States becomes very attractive. A currency depreciation reduces the foreign currency cost of acquiring assets in the country in question and further protects local production since imports become more expensive. Strong growth improves the earnings of local firms making them more attractive acquisition targets. Finally, foreign investing companies have, in recent years, been attracted to the United States by financial and other incentives provided by state governments, by lower costs and to minimize the effects of exchange rate fluctuations. Under attack from Japanese competitors and burdened with heavy manufacturing costs, Germany's BMW set up an assembly plant in Spartanburg, South Carolina in 1992. Eberhard von Kuenheim, BMW's chairman, said an American factory was 'the next consistent step for BMW because it would help to minimize the effects of exchange-rate fluctuations [and] it also helps that production costs are 30 per cent lower in America than in Germany, and that the state of South Carolina was offering incentives, estimated by some to be worth up to $130 million' (*Economist*, 27 June 1992, p. 74).

Management view of foreign direct investment

From the point of view of the firm there are market entry advantages and disadvantages associated with the two forms of foreign direct investment. Each can be judged in terms of its effect on the firm's costs and on its product markets (Table 14.3). The cost advantages

Table 14.3 Advantages and disadvantages of acquisitions and new venture mode of entry into foreign markets

Key influencing factors	Advantages	Disadvantages
Cost factors	Reduced transport costs Scale economies Host government incentives Reduced packaging costs Elimination of duties Access to raw materials and labour	High initial capital investment High information and search costs Nationalization or expropriation
Product market	Management control Market access Effective marketing	Management constraint factors Loss of flexibility Increased marketing complexity

of foreign direct investment lie in the areas of reduced transport costs, unit production and marketing costs and access to materials and cheaper labour. The cost disadvantages arise from the high initial capital investment, high information and search costs and the threat of nationalization and expropriation. The product-market advantages of foreign direct investment as a mode of entry are threefold: greater management control; better access to markets; more effective marketing. Disadvantages arise because of increased marketing complexity from the need to coordinate subsidiary and headquarter marketing programmes.

Summary

Participating in international markets through foreign direct investment is often considered to be the most intense form of commitment to international markets. Foreign direct investment may take the form of acquisitions or new ventures. Acquisitions are by far the more popular of the two forms, since market entry is quick and can be very effective. It is an expensive option, however, especially if the acquired firm is already well established in the market through the possession of a well-known branded product.

Foreign direct investment through new ventures is favoured by smaller firms generally and by firms motivated as much by manufacturing reasons as by market reasons. Scale effects can be an important determinant of the new venture mode of entry to international markets.

Foreign direct investment through whichever form generally causes concern at the political level in either the source or host country. In recent years the benefits of foreign direct investment, particularly if motivated for marketing reasons, have been judged to outweigh the costs. Foreign direct investment, even cross-investment, is a feature of international business which is likely to remain with the more open markets in the new millennium.

The advantages for the firm in entering international markets through foreign direct investment may be found in reduced costs, more effective marketing and tighter control of manufacturing and marketing.

Discussion questions

1. Foreign direct investment is the most expensive option when considering ways of entering international markets. Discuss.

2. Foreign direct investment is more suited to industrial products firms than to consumer products firms. Discuss.

3. Explain the recent interest by large companies in acquiring branded consumer products firms abroad.

4. Classical investment and trade theory would suggest that foreign direct investment should be one-way. Explain why cross-investment occurs.

5. Some commentators argue that more open markets encourage foreign direct investment while others argue that it is protection which determines such investment. How can you reconcile these contrasting positions?

6. What are the advantages and disadvantages of acquisitions and new ventures as options within foreign direct investment?

7. By what criteria would you judge a particular foreign direct investment activity to have succeeded or failed? Illustrate your answer.

References

Buckley, P. J. and Casson, M. (1976) *The Future of the Multinational Enterprise*, New York, NY: Holmes and Meier.

Caves, R. E. (1971) 'Industrial corporation: the industrial economics of foreign investment', *Economica*, **38** (149), 1–27.

Caves R. E. (1998): 'Research on international business: problems and prospects', *Journal of International Business Studies*, **29** (1), 5–19.

Chandrasekaran, A. and Ryans, J. K. Jr. (1996) 'US foreign direct investment in India: emerging trends in MNC entry strategies', *The International Executive*, **38** (5), 599–612.

Coley, S. and Reinton, S. (1988) 'The hunt for value', *The McKinsey Quarterly*, (Spring), 93–100.

Dunning, J. H. (1981) *International Production and the Multinational Enterprise*, London: George Allen and Unwin.

Dunning, J. H (1998): 'Location and the multinational enterprise: a neglected factor?' *Journal of International Business Studies*, **29** (1), 45–66.

Dunning, J. and McQueen, M. (1981) 'The eclectic theory of international production: a case study of the international hotel industry', *Managerial and Decision Economics*, **2**, 197–210.

Economist (1988) *The World in 1988*, London.

Eng, E. and Forsman, A. (1989) 'Mergers and acquisitions – Swedish efforts to gain access to the Common Market', *International Marketing Seminar*, Department of Marketing, University College Dublin.

Erramilli, M. K. (1990) 'Entry mode choice in service industries', *International Marketing Review*, **7** (5), 50–62.

Eurostat (1996), *Eurostatistics*, Brussels.

Fayerweather, J. (1982) *International Business Strategy and Administration*, 2nd edn, Cambridge, MA: Ballinger.

Hymer, S. H. (1976) *The International Operations of National Firms: A study of direct foreign investment*, Cambridge, MA: MIT Press.

Jacquemin, A., Buigues, P. and Ilzkovitz, F. (1989) 'Horizontal mergers and competition policy in the European Community', *European Economy*, **40**, 13–39.

Kim, W. S. and Lyn, E. O. (1990) 'FDI theories and the performance of foreign multinationals operating in the US', *Journal of International Business Studies*, **21** (1), 41–54.

Markides, C. and Oyon, D. (1998) 'International acquisitions: do they create value for shareholders?', *European Management Journal*, **16** (2), 125–34.

McDermott, M. and Huang, C. H. (1996), 'Industrial state-owned multinationals from China: the embryonic years, 1985–92', *Asia Pacific Business Review*, **3** (1), 1–5.

Morosini, P., Shane, S. and Singh, H. (1998): 'National cultural distance and cross-border acquisition performance', *Journal of International Business Studies*, **29** (1), 137–58.

Papanastassiou, M. and Pearce, R. (1997) 'Technology sourcing and the strategic role of manufacturing subsidiaries in the UK: local competences and global competitiveness', *Management International Review*, **37** (1), 5–25.

Rivoli, P. and Salorio, E. (1996) 'Foreign direct investment and investment under uncertainty', *Journal of International Business Studies*, **27** (Second Quarter), 335–57.

Shan, W. and Song, J. (1997) 'Foreign direct investment and the sourcing of technological advantage: evidence from the biotechnology industry', *Journal of International Business Studies*, **28** (2), 267–84.

Teece, D. J. (1981) 'The multinational enterprise: market failure and market power considerations', *Sloan Management Review*, **22** (3), 3–17.

Thomsen, S. and Woolcock, S. (1993) *Direct Investment and European Integration*, London: Pinter.

Williamson, P. (1991) 'Successful strategies for export', *Long Range Planning*, **24** (1), 57–63.

15

The consumer products firm

In this chapter we examine consumer products and brands in international markets. The chapter is divided into four sections. The first section examines the factors which lead to fragmentation and consolidation in consumer markets. The next section examines how consumer products firms active in international markets respond to such trends. In the third section the ways in which firms implement their brand strategies are evaluated. Finally, ways of protecting the brand and the firm are discussed: brand protection from infringements in the market and protection for the consumer products firm from take-overs.

Consumer products in international markets

For centuries consumers have sought choice in the things they buy. The growth in consumer products markets which is much discussed in the literature and in the popular media is not simply a phenomenon of the late twentieth century. Exotic products were in demand in Europe from the time they were discovered as a result of endeavours by trading companies to expand their business empires.

The general increase in living standards fuelled the demand for choice. As more products were produced better, faster and in greater quantities, and as the consumer was willing to pay for them, this led to continuous growth in consumer demand, interrupted by the slumps of the 1920s, the 1930s, the 1940s and the 1970s and in some countries in the 1980s.

Consumer products are usually associated with developed countries. Food, clothing, toys, cars, beer and magazines are often cited as examples. Most developing countries also have a very high demand for the products mentioned, and the growth in many of these markets is faster than growth in developed country markets. Nevertheless, many consumer products are developed first in Western-style developed country markets and rapidly transferred to developing country markets. Large multinational companies are usually at the centre of such activity.

The concept of a deterministic international life cycle model as proposed by Wells

(1968) does not seem to have much to support it, however, in the 1990s. Japan is a leader in the production and international sale of electronic consumer products. It leads the world in the production and further development of calculators, TVs and watches. It has also developed products such as personal stereos and mini hi-fis: the United States and Europe are at present experiencing Japan's dominance in these product markets. This is a trend likely to continue for some time with the development of the Pacific Rim countries.

The extension of the EU market is also expected to give rise to growth in consumer choice as well as an increase in the penetration of consumer products from non-EU countries, as internal and external trade barriers fall and as distribution channels are opened and developed.

International consumer products are usually developed sequentially from market to market or region to region, leading to the same products and services being available in many countries and even worldwide. A good example of the development of a product over time and across different markets is laundry powder, which initially began as bar soap and is still used in that form to wash clothes in many developing countries. The introduction of soap powder was followed by non-biological soap powder. When this product reached maturity in Western Europe, liquid detergent was introduced. It is likely that this product will also spread throughout world markets. These product generations may be seen over time in a single market and at a given point in time in different markets (Figure 15.1).

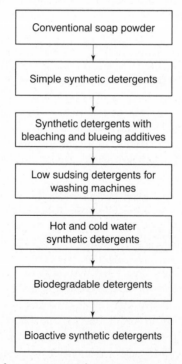

Figure 15.1 Generations of consumer products: some products such as laundry powder have been available for a long time in different countries and in different forms

The product innovation which has gone into something as basic as soap or laundry powder demonstrates how the manufacturer keeps changing the product to suit the needs of different markets at different times. Later we shall see how other firms use branding to represent key elements of constancy desired by consumers. For some consumer products companies being innovative and creative in new product development is not an easy task as Procter & Gamble discovers on a regular basis (Exhibit 15.1).

========== **Exhibit 15.1** ==========
Proctoids' new improved future

Polishing the image of the household products group is one thing; the real battle is for innovation and growth, but 'Oh, you'll like John Pepper', says a Procter & Gamble staffer at the company's headquarters in Cincinnati, Ohio. 'He's a real down-to-earth, friendly kinda guy'. Mr. Pepper does, however, seem to have changed P&G into a more people friendly organization. At the same time Pepper is on a mission to reinvigorate growth: he aims to double revenue in the next 10 years. If that sounds a lot for a company already so large, it is less than Coca-Cola and McDonald's have achieved in the past decade – thanks in large part to the opening up of vast new markets around the world.

But there is an important distinction between these companies. In the list of the world's top brands published by the Interbrand consultancy last year, McDonald's and Coca-Cola ranked first and second respectively. P&G's highest ranking brand was the recently acquired Tampax at number 21. In a sense Coca-Cola and McDonald's do not have to do anything very imaginative to increase revenues. Their colas and burgers are not necessarily the best – others score higher in taste tests – but they are the world's most wanted. So their basic strategy amounts to making sure as many people as possible can get their products.

P&G does not have the luxury of these universally sought-after brands. It has to battle for every extra dollar by inventing 'new improved' products – striving to make household goods that genuinely do the job better than those of its rivals , then charging a premium price for them. Unlike Coca-Cola, for example, which has hardly changed Coke's formula in more than a century, P&G has changed its Tide detergent 30 times in the past 50 years. 'we live or die by product innovation and technology', Mr Pepper says. 'We know that if we don't have it, we can't grow the business in North America. Nor can we succeed in China or Russia the way we need to'. Of course, P&G has always been an innovator. Its Dreft was the first laundry detergent, Crest the first fluoride toothpaste on the mass market. Pampers, the disposable nappies, and Head & Shoulders, the anti dandruff shampoo, were also mass-market firsts.

Still, Pepper says, P&G cannot afford to be complacent on innovation. 'There are a lot of areas where we have to accelerate it', he concedes. In particular, that means pushing hard to bring out more 'new to the world' products, creating whole new categories that did not previously exist. Three examples, already being test-marketed in the U.S., are Dryel, a product that allows people to dry clean their clothes at home in a tumble dryer; Febreze, a spray that gets rid of odours on clothes and home furnishings; and ThermaCare, a pain-relieving, heat-releasing pad that can be wrapped around aching muscles and joints. Significantly, says Mr Pepper, the last of these draws on the company's knowledge of paper, chemical and analgesic technologies. 'A focus today is on sharing technologies across our respective businesses to a level we have never done before. We're very diverse across food, healthcare, paper products and laundry, and seeking to see how we can carry technologies from one to another is proving very fruitful'.

In spite of his softer, kinder image, Mr Pepper gives no indication that P&G will become any less aggressive. 'I wouldn't express any objective we have as wanting to be a lovable company', he says. 'We want to be an admired company. But I want people to love our brands'.

Source: adapted from *Financial Times*, Thursday, 21 May 1998, p. 24.

Market fragmentation and consolidation

It has been argued that differences in tastes, languages, culture and technical standards are among the more serious obstacles to market consolidation. In international markets tariffs and non-tariff barriers force manufacturers to think locally. At the same time retailers are still very much national organizations focused on one country only, although this is changing. These two factors dictate, to a large extent, the nature of the consumer products market in many parts of the world. In the regime of international markets characterized by these barriers large firms are deprived of one of their favourite weapons, cost leadership stemming from manufacturing scale effects, while smaller firms proliferate and compete by serving speciality niches. Additional causes of market fragmentation in international markets are low industry entry costs and high exit costs. The absence of experience curve effects in some industries ensures that the industry remains fragmented. The strong determination of national governments to support the development of industries believed to be of strategic importance can also contribute to market fragmentation, which is especially true, but waning, in telecommunications and airlines and was true in consumer electronics in Europe.

In traditional consumer mass markets as found, for example, in the United States, population age structures, the increase in the number of women working away from the home and the recognition of a multilingual and multicultural society have forced many companies to cope with fragmented markets by developing niche strategies. Many of the same influences have always existed in Europe. At the same time the media are saturated with claims for standardized products, while consumers seek variety and supermarkets seek higher margins.

Many traditional marketing companies are beginning to exploit the new information technologies to identify customers and determine their motivation. Targeted media are being used to reach these emerging target segments: direct mail; cable TV; the internet;

advertisements displayed in areas frequented by the targeted customer segment. Retailers seek higher margins and control of shelf space so they rarely allow decisions in this area to be made without care. Large retailers dictate the amount and type of shelf space and display that a product receives.

These are among the more important factors which have influenced trends towards increased fragmentation in markets. They are more influential in some markets than others and the ability of firms to cope with them varies correspondingly. High culture bound items such as food, clothing and medicine are more likely to be sold in fragmented markets, whereas consumer electronics and music, especially music aimed at the youth market, will probably continue to serve a standardized consolidated market.

There are a number of ways in which firms attempt to counteract or offset the effects of fragmented markets. Successful international firms frequently introduce low-cost standardized products covering most market needs, thereby replacing many specialized products. In the 1970s Philips manufactured 90 TV models for 12 countries but in the 1980s it changed its policy and developed the Matchline Series, consisting of 25 models to be sold in 12 countries.

Some firms systematically try to raise marketing expenditures to a level where firms that are not well funded are forced out. This is a common strategy in the packaged foods business, tobacco, detergents and especially breakfast cereals. One strategy, already discussed in Chapter 14, involves the firm in acquiring its competitors and rationalizing production capacity. The Swedish firm Electrolux systematically acquired competitors to dominate the European white goods industry and to become a significant competitor through its acquisitions in the United States. Finally, firms sometimes invest heavily in capital equipment, which raises the minimum scale necessary to be an efficient operator. Companies use various combinations of the above approaches to consolidate markets.

Convergence of international consumer markets

According to Levitt (1983) consumer markets are converging to such an extent that products will serve world markets. He cites the trend toward a world youth culture fed on rock music, fast food and fashion. The standardization of international marketing practices for consumer products is predicated, according to Levitt, on an international equalization of relative income levels, increasing personal consumption, a convergence of ownership patterns of durable consumer products and increased and better communications.

Following the above line of discussion, companies observe that if they desire a position in the global market they need to brand their products or services. The strength of well-known brands in their respective market segments allows the firms behind them to dominate the market and to out-manoeuvre or out-spend potential rivals. The cost of a would-be usurper is considerable: a national advertising campaign would probably cost $100 million of the brand builder's money in the United States, $60 million in Japan and $50 million in the United Kingdom.

The interesting feature of consumer markets throughout the world is that products and services quickly transfer among markets and the time that products and services are left unchallenged in any market has shortened.

Parallel to these developments have been those in communications which also bring about a convergence in consumer markets throughout the world. The footprints of many European TV stations, in particular, extend well beyond national boundaries. Various European-wide channels have an impact on which products are sold, from where and to whom. One of the features of this communications explosion is the pressure it places on managers to consider European-wide advertising for European brands. In the United States the opposite trend is in evidence. The expense of national TV coverage in the United States, together with a recognition of valuable niche markets, has resulted in market fragmentation there. Worldwide brand standardization appears to be most easy to apply in 'hi-tech' products such as computers and software, cameras and other sophisticated equipment or in 'hi-touch' products such as perfumes and other luxury items which reflect underlying universal themes (Domzal and Unger, 1987). More culture-bound products are less susceptible to global branding. Of all the products advertised in a comparable publication in the United Kingdom and France only perfume and beauty products were standardizable (Whitelock and Chung, 1989). Standardized international branding offers greater market efficiency than localized branding (Onkvisit and Shaw, 1989, p. 26), by reducing advertising and inventory costs. Branding in Europe, however, does not appear to be converging on greater standardization (Boddewyn *et al.*, 1986). It has been estimated that only 45 'Eurobrands' are widely on sale in identical format in at least the four largest countries (Exhibit 15.2). Convergence appears still to be

====== Exhibit 15.2 ======

Eurobranding – whither the cross-border cornflake?

A recent survey conducted for the FT found that of the tens of thousands of products commonly sold in European supermarkets only 45 'Euro-brands' were widely on sale in identical format in at least the four largest countries. Nielsen, the market research company, found that Euro-brands were particularly common in personal-care products. Multinational companies such as Colgate-Palmolive, Gillette, L'Oréal and Unilever have done much to standardise their products and packaging sizes across borders. Snacks and some alcoholic drinks are also acquiring a more European flavour. Brands which span most countries include Kit-Kat, Toblerone and Twix chocolate bars, Johnnie Walker Red Label Whisky, Baileys Irish Original Cream, Heineken lager and Guinness.

In other types of food, Kellogg's cereals, Uncle Ben's rice, Heinz ketchup and Danone yogurt are sold Europe-wide. So are Whiskas, Sheeba and Pedigree petfoods made by Mars, which has been harmonising its European range. Yet if the tastes of European consumers are converging on these products, the prices still vary widely. Will prices converge as the single market develops? In theory they should since large differentials would be likely to encourage cross-border shopping and parallel import flows. However, the theory only applies if there are enough similar products.

Source: adapted from *Financial Times*, 4 January 1993.

a long way off. In deciding whether to promote Eurobrands or national brands Wolfe (1991) concluded that customer needs, production and distribution costs and legal constraints would have to be considered.

For developing countries the source of pressure for a world view on consumer products and markets stems from interest in these countries in attempting to raise living standards and modernize. A major contributory factor in this process is technology which has 'proletarianized communication, transport and travel. It has made isolated places and impoverished peoples eager for modernity's allurements' (Levitt, 1983, p. 92). According to Levitt, developing countries seek technology transfer to allow them to leapfrog to a better life.

A more concrete measure of convergence is to determine the similarity of purchasing power in different countries. Some years ago the United Nations devised the Purchase Power Parity (PPP) to indicate the different levels of spending power in different countries. The PPP comprises a comparison basket of items such as average incomes, interest rates, insurance, utilities, energy, mail, newspapers, taxes and other consumer expenses. The United States is taken as 100 and other countries are measured against it (Table 15.1). Using the PPP to assess consumer purchasing power we see that 20 Indians or two Spaniards equal the purchasing power of one US person.

Reasons for branding

If a consumer product is unbranded it may be difficult for the manufacturer to be independent and to succeed internationally on a long-term basis. Unbranded products can be successful for products of low perceived value or low involvement, e.g. jelly confectionery for children. Sometimes such products are sold under a private label brand on a regional or country basis. The role of the manufacturer or private label in the branding process demonstrates that branding is very important in consumer products markets as it gives the consumer a reference point throughout the purchasing process.

Table 15.1 Purchasing power parity (PPP) in different countries

Country	PPP	Country	PPP
United States	100	Chile	35
Germany	89	Mexico	31
Japan	86	Russia	26
France	82	Brazil	22
Sweden	77	Turkey	22
Australia	77	Poland	20
Singapore	77	South Africa	16
United Kingdom	72	Egypt	15
Israel	62	Indonesia	12
Spain	56	China	8
Saudi Arabia	42	Kenya	6
Argentina	37	India	5

Source: The Economist Pocket World in Figures 1997.

By allowing others to control the branding the firm relinquishes the opportunity of creating the desired consumer and channel image. The goodwill associated with the brand is outside the manufacturer's control. The firm that controls the brand usually dominates the marketing of the product. For many firms, small enterprises in particular, it is usually easier to manufacture and to pay less attention to the international marketing aspects. Such an approach may have a lucrative financial payoff in the short term but in the longer term the firm is exposed.

Consumer products or brands

A product is something with a fundamental purpose; a brand offers something in addition. All brands are products or services in that they serve a functional purpose. Not all products or services are brands, however. Many products provide functional benefits only which makes it difficult to brand them as something differentiated and carrying added values. Other products are used by different groups of people in different markets and often for different purposes which also makes branding difficult, if not impossible. For example, variations in consumer product applications in different countries may make branding difficult. Pain relievers, for example, are usually targeted at the housewife in the United States, at the busy executive in Germany and in a number of other countries at people with hangovers. In such circumstances it is difficult to adopt a universal marketing or branding approach in each of these product markets as the customer group and the purpose of use vary so greatly. Nevertheless, successful international marketing companies frequently attribute that success to the popularity and performance of their brand portfolio.

So what is the difference between a product and a brand? A brand is a product or service that provides functional benefits and added values that some consumers value sufficiently to buy. Brands also provide information as a sophisticated form of value added. The purpose of branding is, and always has been, to provide information. The form of that information varies from market to market and from time to time. Some products make a visible statement about their users' style, modernity or wealth – examples include clothes, cars and accessories. Others purport to convey reliability, say, or familiarity, or something else. Buyers crave information. Brands offer a route through the confusion. Compaq, an American computer maker, has been the most successful at exploiting its brand, combining aggressive cost and price cutting with massive advertising. That blend provides valuable information:

> if you buy a Compaq, you can feel reasonably sure you are not paying too much and that your friends and colleagues will not laugh at you for making an outlandish, outdated choice. . . . Do not be fooled into thinking [branding] is really about baked beans, soap powder or notebook computers. It is all about information. And it will continue for as long as buyers need and want that information.   (*Economist*, 2 July 1994, pp. 9–10)

Added values form the most important part of this description of branding.

Strong brands are balanced between motivating benefits and discriminating benefits. Motivating benefits are the functional benefits that prompt the consumer to use any brand in the product class, and discriminating benefits, i.e. those benefits that prompt the consumer to buy one brand rather than another (Jones, 1986, pp. 28–34). It is generally accepted that no brand can be all things to all consumers. Striving to cover too wide a field will result in a brand that is No. 2 or No. 3 over a wide range of attributes rather than No. 1 over a limited range. Most companies attempt to achieve one or a combination of three things in branding:

- they may confirm the legal protection afforded by the inventor's patent,
- they may guarantee quality and homogeneity in a period when buyers and sellers have lost face-to-face contact – the brand becomes a mark of assurance for a level of quality, and
- firms may try to differentiate their products and services in a competitive environment.

Companies attempt to differentiate their brands through some unique combination of the marketing variables at its disposal. Differentiation has traditionally attracted the attention of economists:

> . . . various brands of a certain article which in fact are almost exactly alike may be sold as different qualities under names and labels which will induce rich and snobbish buyers to divide themselves from poorer buyers.   (Robinson, 1933, pp. 180–1)

This view is supported by many consumer brand managers. Branding is believed to add values to products and services, which arise from the experience gained from using the brand (familiarity, reliability and risk reduction), from association with the kind of people who are known users of the brand – rich and snobbish, young and glamorous, and from the belief that the brand is effective – branding of some proprietary drugs is thought to affect the mind's influence over body processes. There is some evidence to support this contention '. . . branding works like an ingredient of its own interacting with the pharmacological active ingredients to produce something more powerful than an unbranded tablet' (Lannon and Cooper, 1983, p. 206).

There is considerable variation internationally in consumer attitudes to brands as the Henley Centre–Research International study discovered in a syndicated survey of 6,500 consumers in six European countries. The study noted that well-known brands offer reliable quality throughout most of the EU. The meaning of brands at a general level varies considerably depending on the country. Very high proportions of people in Spain, Italy and the former East Germany believe that brands guarantee quality, whereas people in the Netherlands are more sceptical (Table 15.2). Finally the added values which derive from the appearance of the brand are very strong. Herein lies the special role of packaging for consumer and industrial products.

Brands in international markets

Brands are a relatively new phenomenon in international marketing, but branding has existed in individual countries in a dominant form at least since the start of the present century. Because they are targeted at the mass consumer market, consumer product brands are better known than industrial product or service brands. By the late nineteenth century most countries had passed trademarks acts establishing the brand name as a

Table 15.2 Meaning of brands

| | Brands guarantee quality | |
	Agree (per cent)	Disagree (per cent)
France	58	20
Italy	74	19
Germany (East)	66	23
Germany (West)	55	28
Netherland	43	37
Spain	77	19

Source: Frontiers, The Henley Centre–Research International, 1991–2.

protectable asset. Brands such as Coca-Cola (US), Mercedes-Benz (Germany), Persil (Germany) and Cadbury (UK) existed before the passing of the trademark acts.

Brands are usually developed within a country and then introduced to foreign markets as they become accepted through advertising, word of mouth promotion by visitors, adaptation and strategic development by the company. Another force for international-ization arose from the ease with which colonies could be guaranteed as markets for brands. A more natural expansion path was among countries of the same language and similar culture.

The main growth in international brands occurred, however, after World War II. Troop movements, especially the US military, have been associated with the successful introductions of many US brands to Europe and the Far East. With the resultant expansion of US culture across much of the world and through US business acquisitions and invest-ments in Europe in the 1950s and 1960s, many US brands or US-owned brands became well known internationally: Ford; Opel; Pepsi; RCA. European brand names also began to spread during the 1950s and 1960s as a result of improved transportation and com-munications systems.

Japanese companies have also grown into highly developed brand-centred firms. Sony, Mitsubishi, Sanyo, Honda, Suzuki, Citizen, Seiko, Toyota, Suntory, Sharp, Casio and Pioneer are brands which are easily recognizable throughout the world. To date Japanese brands have been concentrated in the field of electronics, motor cars and heavy earth-moving equipment. This is changing, as a visit to Japan's neighbouring Far Eastern countries proves. Japanese branded foods, cosmetics (Shiseido) and clothing (Kenzo) are now widely distributed in the region and much sought after. They are also available in Western markets though they have not yet dominated their segments. If a brand is to establish itself as a strong contender in the international market it should build or maintain its market position through its presence in the market. Being a brand leader in a geographical market, e.g. the United Kingdom, could create valuable intangible assets for the same brand in other geographical markets, e.g. Germany. Confirming this view Kim and Chung (1997, p. 379) note that in considering 'the transfer of brand image or intangible assets across different regions, brand popularity (brand leadership) should be considered a key strategic variable for building long-term and global decisions for a brand'. These authors conclude that 'understanding the dynamics of intangible assets is critical in marketing strategy development for long-term success in a global market, where brands originate from various different countries that have different 'home bases' or different invisible resource endowments' (p. 381).

In recent years there have been a number of articles written on international branding and the globalization of markets (Buzzell, 1968; Hamel and Prahalad, 1985; Levitt, 1983; Martenson, 1987). These studies have, however, concentrated on a conceptualization of strategies for international markets but they provide little information on brand globalization itself. There has been little empirical work in determining the extent of international brand diffusion, the identification of markets served internationally and the extent to which brand standardization occurs among consumer products firms in international markets (Rosen et al., 1989). In a study of 651 US brands these authors report that about 80 per cent of sales were achieved in the United States itself with a high proportion of the remainder in Canada. 'This modest foreign distribution is not compensated for by foreign production or export of similar products under different names' (Rosen et al., 1989, p. 17). Timing and age of brands do not appear to be significant, either. According to these authors 'older brands are not more likely to be widely internationalized nor standardized than younger brands . . . it appears that brands do not necessarily grow up into standardized international brands over time' (Rosen et al., 1989, p. 17). In order to understand the issues better it will be necessary to carry out longitudinal studies of brand diffusion into many markets, originating in a number of countries.

The preponderance of pan-European brands among the 100 top UK brands in consumer non-durables was examined by Whitelock et al. (1995) who discovered that both the nationality of the parent company (predominantly US) and the market of origin of the brand (again, predominantly US) had a significant effect on whether brands were pan-European. These authors attribute these findings to the long-standing activity of US multinationals in Europe but noted that, within a short period, most of the new pan-European brands in the 100 top UK brands would be of UK origin, belong to UK companies and launched relatively recently (Whitelock et al., 1995, pp. 91–3).

In a study of the European strategies of UK confectionery companies, Littler and Schlieper (1995, p. 30) discovered that the domestic market was the key influence on future developments and that the rest of Europe would be included at some future point, but the rest of the world did not feature in the strategic thinking of the companies studied.

International brand strategies

Until recently branding was thought to have marketing value only. In particular, brands were considered to be psychological in nature and, therefore, not in any sense real. They were thought to be the material of advertising managers but not possessing financial worth. In addition, the accounting profession had difficulty with valuing brands. Accountants, and indeed the legal profession, prefer to deal with tangible assets such as factories, machinery and transport equipment. A market may be established for these items, their value can be assessed and their worth entered in the balance sheet. All this is changing with the spate of financial transactions involving brands. Brands are now seen as being among the firm's most valuable assets.

The brands debate started in earnest in 1987 with the successful bid by Nestlé for the UK chocolate maker Rowntree Mackintosh, the owner of brands such as 'After Eight', 'Kit Kat' and 'Rolo'. Brand values depend on how these intangible assets should be treated. Nestlé paid £Stg2.5 billion to acquire Rowntree when the book value was £Stg668 million. Much of that premium can be considered the unaccounted value of the brands. The debate raises the issue of the firm's balance sheet: a reflector of company value or a historical record of costs not yet written off against revenues. Nestlé, considers that the purchase was worthwhile and that by balancing familiarity and efficency it obtains value from its brands (Exhibit 15.3). There are many ways of valuing a brand. The method used by the Interbrand Group is based on brand information covering the previous 10 years and future projections where each brand is assigned points in seven different categories:

- market share and ranking;
- brand stability and track record;
- stability of product category;
- internationality;
- market trends;
- advertising and promotional support;
- legal protection.

Exhibit 15.3
Branding at Nestlé – striking a balance between familiarity and efficiency

At Nestlé, our corporate and product brands are our main assets and we have to make sure they are used in the best possible way, according to Peter Brabeck, Nestlé Chief Executive. At a functional level, considerable gains can be realised in purchasing, fine-tuning production processes and rationalising distribution once a brand has achieved critical mass. However, there is far more to successful brand leadership than maximising economies of scale – we also need to appeal to the individual consumer's emotional side. Our brands must project a familiar closeness and they cannot do so if they are not in tune with the ethnic, social and religious background of the people who purchase them.

Successful brands are not only big; they are also strong. Their strength comes from daily contact with consumers. Having established familiarity, the brand moves into a position of trust – the common attribute of all popular brands. At Nestlé we use two brands on one product. The local, more intimate product might only be familiar and appeal to a small group of consumers. But all of the product brands in a given range are federated under the roof of authoritative, corporate strategic brands such as Nestlé or Nescafé. So a difficult equilibrium needs to be found between consumer familiarity and marketing efficiency.

Source: adapted from *Financial Times*, Friday, 17 October 1997, p. 12.

Irrespective of how brands are valued in financial terms, most companies believe that branding is important because it influences customer decisions and ultimately, creates value for the customer. Court *et al.* (1996) have attempted to provide support for this contention by examining the importance of brands to customers during the purchase process. They examined a number of product categories based on over 5,000 interviews in the US, Europe and Asia (Table 15.3). These studies reveal that in both consumer and industrial markets branding was a key factor behind the decision to buy. On average, the brand was responsible for 18 per cent of the total purchase decision. The lowest brand importance was three per cent and the highest 39 per cent.

Branding the competitive advantage

Most luxury products have built their reputation on quality and performance. They have been able to sustain that advantage over their competitors by transferring customer goodwill to a brand name or logo. The ability to make this transfer in one market has

Table 15.3 Relative importance of the brand

Product category	Market brand	Importance (per cent)	Location
Computers	Consumer	39	Europe
Computers	Industrial	26	US
Telecom – International Calls	Industrial	21	US
Airlines	Industrial	21	US
Food – beverage	Consumer	20	US
Retail banking	Consumer	18	Europe
Telecommunications: fixed lines	Consumer	17	Asia
Telecommunications: mobile	Industrial	16	US
Telecommunications: fixed lines	Industrial	14	Asia
Mortgages	Consumer	13	Europe
Car	Consumer	12	Europe
Telecom munications: mobile	Industrial	7	Europe
Computers	Consumer	3	US

Source: Court, D., Feeling, A., Leiter, M. and Parsons, A. J. (1996), 'Uncovering the value of brands', *McKinsey Quarterly*, **4**, p. 176.

facilitated brand building across markets. The brand names Gucci, Louis Vuitton, Tessori, Bang & Olufsen, Giorgio, Simone and Hasselblad are readily identifiable throughout the world.

In attempting to build an international competitive advantage the firm first ensures that the featured attributes give a competitive advantage in every market. Luxury, country of origin and prestige are important factors in building the demand for many consumer brands in most markets. These factors are especially important in Japan. If the attributes featured are not desirable it may be a mistake to attempt to internationalize.

Over time, competitive advantage can dissipate as a result of competitor activity. Competitive activity is usually not benign. It is also necessary to monitor consumers who change, sometimes unpredictably. Such change often arises because of sudden changes in the environment as occurred in a number of Asian markets in late 1997 (Exhibit 15.4).

Exhibit 15.4
East runs out of promise for top brands

For the world's largest consumer products groups, the fast-growing Asian economies have presented a mouth-watering opportunity in recent years. Upwardly mobile consumers in countries such as Korea, Thailand and Malaysia, have embraced the trappings of wealthier societies, from Scotch whisky and American cigarettes to French luxury goods and Japanese electronics products. The economic turmoil has reminded most of these groups that their sales growth of recent years can not continue un-interrupted.

The luxury goods market appears to have been hit hardest. Japan has been one of the prime sources of growth for prestigious European brands such as Chanel, Hermès, and Giorgio Armani since the 1980s and sales rose sharply in other Asian countries, notably South Korea and Taiwan, during the mid-1990s. The first sign of trouble emerged last year, when Gucci, the Italian fashion house and one of the fastest growing luxury brands of the 1990s, warned that duty-free sales to Japanese tourists were depressed by the weak yen.

Trading conditions have since deteriorated, as sales have fallen in some Asian markets. Joyce Boutiques, the Hong Kong-based company which owns one of Asia's biggest chains of designer fashion shops, went into the red in the first half of the current financial year. A number of European Fashion designers, including Armani and Gianfranco Ferre, are reassessing plans to go public in the light of Asia's economic instability. They may postpone flotation until market conditions improve, or join with larger industrial concerns, as rival Valentino has done by selling control to the HPI Group.

Source: adapted from *Financial Times*, Wednesday, 28 January 1998, p. 28.

One of the best measures of international competitive advantage in consumer products is sustainable market share for the brand. The brand with the largest share is invariably the most profitable, generates the most cash flow and has more surplus to invest in R&D, advertising and new markets. The successful consumer products company in international markets draws its strength, therefore, from branding, financial strength, international distribution and management capability (Figure 15.2).

A strong brand name influences consumers and retailers. The strength of the brand depends on real differentiation and genuine innovation that meets consumer needs while providing value for money which usually means a reasonable price for a superior product. To be innovative means creating a stream of new products in new product categories using new technologies. Innovation is particularly important in mature markets, where product extensions are the norm and it is essential to stay ahead of retailer own brands. Paralleling the need to innovate is the need to provide effective advertising and promotional support. Media advertising aimed at the consumer is increasing steadily. Advertising supports brands, whereas consumer and trade promotions tend to debase them, hence the decline in recent years in the use of promotion and the growth in advertising to build brands. Lastly, many successful brand companies are one-brand companies, e.g. Baileys, Heineken, Kellogg and Fuji. This enables them to focus brand support and product innovation to greater effect. For consumer products companies that maintain a range of brands, careful attention is given to managing the portfolio to ensure that it remains loyal to the company's core business. Culling of unsuccessful brands is a feature of successful consumer products companies.

Many successful consumer products companies expand abroad through acquisitions because it is the quickest and most efficient way to internationalize. In such circumstances,

Figure 15.2 Sustainable brand market share

a strong financial position with healthy cash flows is essential. Dominant positions in a large domestic market like the United States, the United Kingdom, Germany or Japan are the source of a strong cash flow. Most of the world's best known brands emanate from one of these markets. There are, however, some exceptions to this rule, e.g. Baileys, Heineken and Nestlé. Baileys domestic market, Ireland, is tiny and yet the brand dominates its category worldwide, selling in excess of 30 million cases. The same is true for Heineken. The Dutch market is very small relative to the US market and yet Heineken has become the most international of brewers – far larger internationally than Guinness or Anheuser Busch. Nestlé began in Switzerland, one of the smallest European markets, yet it dominates many sectors of the food industry. In these three cases, a narrow domestic base forced companies to internationalize at an early stage. They obtained their critical mass internationally, giving them the requisite cash flow for brand building.

These smaller country brands needed distribution in order to succeed internationally. International distribution is essential if the brand is to reach the largest possible number of customers at the lowest possible cost. A well-organized distribution system, such as that provided by many large companies like International Distillers and Vintners (IDV), can also create barriers to market entry. This is especially true in emerging markets, where incumbents can often deny access to international competitors. This is why companies like IDV have invested so heavily in distribution channels. Wide-reaching distribution systems allow the successful consumer products company to gain access to most markets around the world. The international distribution networks of many beverage companies are so powerful that they are almost the only viable way of reaching consumers worldwide.

Lastly, management of consumer products companies must be sensitive to different cultures and countries. A culturally diverse management team provides the company with the local expertize and contacts necessary to work in markets with diverse consumer tastes and retailing structures. As was seen in Chapter 6, successful international companies pay considerable attention to cultural differences in their staffing policies, realizing the importance of the people dimension in international marketing.

Sustaining the competitive advantage

A brand competitive advantage is based on an attribute or combination of attributes of the product or service which the consumer values more than competing offers. Firms compete on the basis of very specific attributes. In the washing-up-liquid market, for example, supermarket own labels compete on price, whereas Fairy Liquid, the Unilever brand, competes on softness for the hands and the claim that it 'goes further'. Quix, a Procter & Gamble brand, competes on performance and a luxury smell, while other brands compete on a claim of being fully biodegradable and non-toxic.

Each company chooses a different approach in order to be competitive. The approach must be changed among markets as the brand name may not be acceptable or the product attributes may not sufficiently differentiate the product or for some other reason the product may not be desirable. Manufacturers attempt to promote their competitive advantage to retailers and consumers to highlight actual or perceived differences, whether that refers to the brand name itself, price, speed of delivery, convenience, product quality or effective advertising.

Building and sustaining competitive advantage for the firm's product are continuous tasks throughout the life cycle of the product as the environment and competitors change and as new markets are entered and developed.

Many brands have existed for years and have dominated domestic markets with impunity, but to what extent is past success a guarantee of the future? This is the question that Morgan Stanley (1996) researchers attempted to answer. The literature has many examples of firms with seemingly strong brands, healthy finances and diversified distribution, but which are vulnerable to well-organized competitors. In their study, Morgan Stanley conclude that competitive advantage is more sustainable, i.e. in excess of 20 years, in product categories where there is clear product differentiation, where the brand awareness and manufacturing and distribution scale effects have created high barriers or in unique market niches where there is little room for late entrants. The companies identified by Morgan Stanley own internationally recognized brand franchises with a sustainable competitive advantage and have the financial strength and distribution capability to be global contenders (Table 15.4). These 23 companies have the following features in common:

- they all generate at least 30 per cent of their sales outside their domestic market (North America, Europe, Japan) with the significant exception of PepsiCo and Fuji;
- they have at least one major international brand with sales in excess of $1 billion that dominates their category (exceptions are Sara Lee and Unilever owing to proliferation of brand names with different regional names);
- all have a market capitalization in excess of $5 billion and at least a Standard & Poor's A debt rating.

Building and communicating brand values

Companies attempt to differentiate their brands from competitors by providing superior product quality at an acceptable price and value for money. The company also identifies other brand values it attempts to communicate to its customers. Two concepts have been identified as essential for the long-term success of brands or firms in international markets – brand popularity and country image (Kim and Chung, 1997, p. 361). Two other important factors contribute to the brand value mix and, hence, the popularity of the brand – the ability of the company to recruit and retain customers and their level of consumption of the brand and frequency of consumption (Figure 15.3).

Many well-known brands have established their popularity in all international markets of significance: Coca-Cola, McDonald's, Kodak, Heineken, Guinness, Honda, Ford, BMW, to name but a few. Popular brands are those that are widely sought after and are bought by a large cross-section of society. Brand popularity is considered as the accumulation of market acceptance and brand goodwill over time. Once a brand has become popular, the popularity component brings a positive contribution to the brand's loyalty, image or equity, or sales (Aaker, 1991; Kim and Chung, 1997). Brand popularity positively

Table 15.4 Brand competitive advantage

Company	Country	Brand power	Financial strength	Foreign presence	Sustainable advantage	Composite score
North America						
Coca-Cola	US	5	5	5	5	20
Procter & Gamble	US	5	5	5	5	20
McDonald's	US	5	5	4	4	18
Philip Morris	US	5	3	5	5	18
Kellogg	US	5	4	5	3	17
Avon Products	US	3	4	5	4	16
Eastman Kodak	US	4	4	4	4	15
CPC International	US	5	2	4	3	14
Colgate-Palmolive	US	3	3	5	2	13
PepsiCo	US	4	3	2	4	13
Sara Lee	US	4	3	4	2	13
H J Heinz	US	4	2	4	2	12
Seagram	Can	4	2	4	2	12
Mattel	US	5	1	3	2	11
Anheuser Busch	US	3	3	1	2	10
Polaroid	US	3	1	4	2	10
Ralston Purina	US	3	1	4	2	10
Revlon	US	3	1	2	3	9
General Mills	US	3	2	1	2	8
Europe						
Nestlé	H	5	5	5	3	18
L'Oréal	F	4	5	5	3	17
Guinness	UK	4	3	5	4	16
Heineken	N	5	3	3	4	15
LVMH	F	5	3	4	3	15
Unilever	UK	3	5	5	2	15
Grand Met	UK	3	3	3	3	12
Cadbury Schweppes	UK	3	1	4	3	11
Danone	F	4	3	1	2	10
Remy Cointreau	F	4	1	2	3	10
Wella	D	3	1	4	2	10
Beiersdorf	D	4	1	2	2	9
Carlsberg	DK	4	1	1	3	9
Allied Domecq	UK	2	1	3	2	8
Rest of World						
Fuji	J	4	3	2	2	11

Notes:

- Financial strength is a combination of size, as measured by market capitalization, and financial strength, as measured by Standard & Poor's Rating.
- Foreign presence is measured by proportion of international sales. Note that, although Remy Cointreau is present all around the world, it scores only 2 for distribution because of its small size, and, despite their uneven global distribution, scores for Philip Morris, Procter & Gamble and L'Oréal have been raised to the maximum owing to their strong international presence.
- All scores measured on a 1–5 (high) scale. The composite score is a simple addition of the others; maximum = 20.

Source: The Competitive Edge (1996), Morgan Stanley and Company Inc.

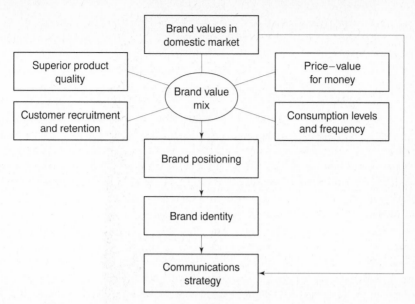

Figure 15.3 Building and communicating brand values in international marketing

influences brand performance not only directly in the short run but also indirectly in the long run by creating a favourable brand image. These factors, taken together, influence the brand value mix.

Once the brand value mix has been established the company positions the brand in the market taking account of customer needs and competing brands. The brand is given a clear identity in the marketplace and the company attempts to develop an effective communications strategy to ensure that having built up the brand its values are properly communicated.

Brands are perceived differently in different markets despite the product being the same. A Vauxhall in the United Kingdom, an Opel in Germany and General Motors in the United States may be exactly the same except for the branding in order to maximize the goodwill from the consumer in each market in terms of brand recognition, country of origin stereotyping, social status of the brand and perceived performance (Johansson and Thorelli, 1985). For these and related reasons brands originating in a particular country seem to create country-related intangible assets or liabilities that are shared by brands originating in the same country. Erickson *et al.* (1992) have argued that, since brands from the same country tend to be perceived as similar, consumer perceptions may not be purely brand specific but rather country specific. There is a need, therefore, to recognize that the brand values built up in the domestic market should be considered in developing the communications strategy for international markets. Successful companies may be able to build on the brand values created in the domestic market in the communication strategy used in foreign markets. By building on country-related intangible assets or country of origin images which are developed over long periods the company can make a positive contribution to sales and market share by influencing the effectiveness of marketing variables on sales.

Harmonizing brand strategy in different countries

At the present stage of development of the EU market it is difficult to know to what extent a company should attempt to harmonize its brand strategy. One side of the argument states that local differences will keep markets fragmented for many years. This is particularly true in culture-bound business such as food. In this case product innovation and brand development might continue to remain as a national phenomenon with little to do with other European or international markets. Developing a harmonized product and brand strategy may not be so easy in all circumstances.

The other side of the argument holds that many products would benefit from a European or international perspective in their development and management. In the food industry this would certainly apply to food ingredients but also to ready to eat frozen foods. The debate will continue for some time but to the extent that markets and consumer tastes converge there will be increased pressure for greater harmonization in product and brand development strategies. In recent years a number of companies in the DIY industry have adopted the position that the development of international and European brands is feasible.

One of the difficulties of branding is that the brand name chosen for one market may not work in another. This is a special problem in Europe as new opportunities appear and companies attempt to take brands across borders. Some brand names lose their impact in different markets. The decision facing the manufacturer or brand owner is whether to change the brand name when entering a new market.

Many manufacturers decide not to change brand names that are well established in different countries, recognizing that the country loyalty factor might be lost in any such attempt. The Unilever brand names for its main detergent in various countries, Omo, Persil, Presto, Via, Skip and All, have been maintained because to change them the company feared they would lose customers. Packaging was, however, standardized so that travellers from one country to another would recognize the familiar shape and colour and hopefully remain loyal. Mars, the US-owned confectionery manufacturer, did harmonize one of its brand names across markets with great success. The 'Snickers' confectionery bar once known as 'Marathon' in the UK was harmonized successfully by alerting customers well in advance of the change by using a 'flash' notice in the packaging stating that the product was soon to be called 'Snickers'. For a period after the name change the 'flash' changed to 'formerly known as Marathon'.

In some cases brand names translate so badly that they must be changed less they convey wrong meanings or cause offence. Selling 'Irish Mist Liqueur' or 'Body Mist' anti-perspirant products in Germany would be ill-advised since the word 'mist' in German means waste or manure. These pitfalls must be avoided but they have been so well noted in the popular trade press that they have become anecdotal and part of folklore so they need not detain us further.

Managing consumer brands in international markets

Implementing international brand strategies

In a general sense the company must make three related choices in developing and implementing an international brand strategy. First, it must decide which markets to serve, existing and new. This is an issue which has already been discussed. Second, the company must be concerned with product innovation. It may be necessary to develop new products and most likely it will be necessary to modify existing products if they are to be successful in international markets.

Third, perhaps the most difficult decision facing the company involves the issue of brand accessibility in international markets. Exclusive brands are demanded by people because of their uniqueness and exclusivity. Companies face an interesting trade-off – if they make the brand too widely available it may become debased whereas if too great a degree of exclusivity is maintained few people can avail of its benefits, which prevents brand growth. A degree of democratization in brand policy is necessary, therefore, to make the brand available and accessible to a wider consumer group. Brand accessibility through brand extensions or umbrella branding on a range of related products and brand availability in many international markets serves the objective of brand accessibility from the point of view of the company and the consumer. To ensure access to consumers for their brands large branded products companies attempt, where possible and legal, to own the entire distribution system for their brands, e.g. Coca-Cola in India, IBM in India and Brazil, International Distillers and Vintners, the beverages division of Grand Metropolitan, in all its principal markets. The company must, therefore, make decisions regarding these three aspects of its activities (Figure 15.4).

Establishing a brand platform internationally

Many features of the brand may be used in international marketing, the logotype and symbols, the name, positioning product features, packaging, advertising copy and other elements of the marketing mix to a lesser extent. In 1996, Electrolux reviewed the way

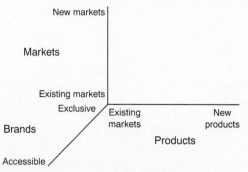

Figure 15.4 Markets, products, brands, global decisions

that they communicated the Electrolux brand throughout the world (Johansson, 1997). They decided it was important first to establish a brand platform which was a set of policies and guidelines for interacting with customers throughout the world in a purposeful and consistent manner (Figure 15.5). The company was attempting to develop a sharper focus for the brand, greater cost effectiveness and a cost leadership position. The basis of communications in Electrolux focused on corporate strategy, core values regional positions for the company and a set of common standards. The corporate strategy identified was based on the concept of the global appliance company: global, to maintain world leadership in the chosen field; appliance, to focus on household outdoor and commercial appliances; company, to ensure a common culture throughout the organization.

The core values of the company were based on caring for people – customers, employees, investors and suppliers. It also meant caring for the environment while focusing on customer needs. These values influenced the way the company manufactures and sells its products, the way it treats its customers and other stakeholders and the way it reduces the environmental impact of its products.

The communications also reflected regional positions in that local differences in market conditions cultures and attitudes were acknowledged. Lastly, it was agreed in the company that wide participation in the communications process was necessary to ensure the common standards of the company were met.

Recognizing differences and the domino effect

A firm may choose its competitive environment by changing its marketing programme in order to confront competitors directly in order to overtake and bypass them. The marketing programme can affect the product not only in the market where it was changed but

Figure 15.5 Communicating the Electrolux brand

also in other related markets where goodwill can be lost, even though the marketing programme has not been changed in those markets. This domino effect can be very damaging but it may also be exploited to promote the product or brand, especially in the fashion industry where success in New York, Paris, Milan, London or Munich can easily transform a domestic brand into an international one with the assistance of the media.

Sometimes the brand has to be changed when the firm enters a foreign market, even though all other aspects of the marketing programme, including the product, remain the same. In order to build a competitive advantage in a market, the firm must be aware of the differences between its home market and the foreign market. Adopting the 1960s US general management view that it is as possible to sell abroad as at home can quickly lead to new competitors entering the market or even to the collapse of the firm. A way of avoiding large-scale failures in foreign markets is to enter a smaller market first, one which is culturally and economically similar to the larger target market. French-, German- and Italian-speaking Switzerland could act as test markets for Germany, France and Italy, respectively, if care is taken in making the comparisons.

Competitive activity in the domestic market can force a firm to internationalize. Well-known brands such as Ford, Nissan and Sony were forced to internationalize because of insurmountable competition at home. All three companies pursued very aggressive market building strategies abroad in order to thwart and delay their principal domestic competitors, General Motors, Toyota and Matsushita, respectively. These firms built their competitive advantage abroad rather than at home and have managed to sustain their positions. Colgate-Palmolive also developed its competitive advantage abroad but varied the theme. It copied Procter & Gamble's products which were successful in the United States and pioneered them abroad. Colgate-Palmolive did not have a large R&D facility and always relied on Procter & Gamble ideas, although it was first to internationalize them. Colgate, the first fluoride toothpaste outside the United States, still dominates many world markets.

Developing competitive advantage may mean appreciating cultural differences and the different uses for products in different markets. Guinness is considered a mild aphrodisiac in the Caribbean, as an alternative drink with 'Green' associations in Germany, as a typical Irish drink in Ireland, Scotland and Wales but as a British drink in England. Consumers in each market consume Guinness for different reasons and the perceived benefits and images are also considered to be different.

Quality standards in brand strategy

Quality and standards are important issues in developing competitive advantage for consumer products. Quality leadership is considered essential if the firm wishes to assure itself of long-term product supremacy, at home and abroad. The Commission of the EU has harmonized many product standards across its member countries. It does this by setting minimum product safety standards which must be accepted by all member countries. In many cases these standards will become acceptable throughout the world. In such circumstances it is necessary to meet these minimum standards in order to compete. As these standards refer to minimum levels of attainment, competitive pressure is likely to push the market standard very much higher. Herein lies the risk for smaller consumer products firms. They could be trapped between the minimum and the competitive quality standards without any of the scale effects. This shake-out normally occurs when markets and industries begin to mature, as has happened recently in the personal computer industry. Many companies suddenly found themselves with products which were less advanced and less reliable than those of their competitors but did not have sufficient resources to overcome the disadvantage. Many withdrew from the market, leaving it to the now dominant brands such as Compaq, Dell, IBM and Apple.

To be competitive, adherence to normal product standards, i.e. conformance standards, is not enough. The firm must continuously monitor its operations in order to minimize costs and to increase quality. The firm in international markets uses quality management along with other elements of the marketing programme to create a total offering that is distinctive and has a competitive advantage in all markets entered. The task is easier if the firm faces the same competitors in each market, as the adjustments in the marketing programme are likely to be similar.

Understanding the customer's needs and their levels of satisfaction is central to the success of the international firm. In this context firms normally endeavour to operate with internationally compatible quality regulations and standards.

Brand extensions in international markets

In international marketing an effective way of leveraging product or corporate brands is through brand extensions. Brand extensions are new product introductions in which an existing corporate or brand name is applied to a new product category. Brand extensions allow the company to reduce the marketing communication costs involved in building new equity or images for their products.

A consumer product that is not targeted at a segmented market is unlikely to enjoy much success. A way of avoiding this, if the company or the product has a presence in the market, is to use the mechanism of brand extension. Letting a product benefit from the competitive advantage of an established product but using a variation of the marketing programme is a very popular approach for large consumer products companies. The car industry is a good example. Mercedes-Benz carries with it a very different connotation than Fiat or Toyota. Perhaps better known are the soft drinks umbrella brands used to include diet soft drinks. These products are priced and distributed in the same way as their ordinary counterparts but the product is changed. The image and promotion of the diet products are totally different from their non-diet counterparts. Some successful firms have used brand extensions to bring a range of new products to the market and to transfer the success from one market to another.

In brand extension strategies in international marketing a communication issue arises as to whether the company should focus on product-category factors or corporate factors. In the former the company focuses on the fit between the new product being launched abroad and existing products that are part of same brand whereas in the latter consumers' attention is drawn to characteristics of the company providing the new product. Both product and company driven strategies can be successful but there appear to be differences between countries.

When extending their brands abroad, US firms seem to rely primarily on the product-related benefits or images of their products whereas Japanese firms and other East Asian companies seem to focus on corporate equities (Han and Schmitt, 1997, p. 78). These authors give some examples of these differences: when extending established equity into new product categories, Procter and Gamble (P&G), a US company, does not use the P&G name but relies on the equity of, for example, its Tide and Crest brands, whereas Sony, a Japanese company, and Lucky Goldstar, a Korean company, offer a variety of products under their corporate names and introduce new products under the corporate name.

Clearly what works well with regard to brand extensions in the US may not succeed elsewhere and vice versa. The Japanese cosmetic manufacturer, Shiseido, provides a good illustration of the principle. Shiseido was successful with diapers in Japan but not in the US since Japanese consumers perceived the remote extension to be of high quality because it was done by a large well-known cosmetics firm while US consumers only considered the extension's low fit with cosmetics (Han and Schmitt, 1997, pp. 88–9). Companies thinking of using brand extensions in international markets should pay attention to the relative importance of product-related and company-related brand equity communication strategies in the foreign markets under consideration.

Pitfalls to avoid

There are many pitfalls in international markets for the unwary firm, especially in the area of consumer products and services. Packaging and labelling in foreign markets are particularly important decision areas, not only with regard to compliance with local regulations but also with regard to product enhancement, information and promotion. Some markets place greater value on packaging than others. Far Eastern markets value the decorative value of packaging a great deal and even industrial products are packaged to a much greater extent in Japan than in other Western-style markets. Besides changing the product, the R & A Bailey Company developed very sophisticated packaging for its extended brand 'Baileys Gold' for the Japanese market. Packaging is very important for consumer products because it provides the first impression which, if negative, can be very difficult to overcome later.

A related area which gives rise to many problems is that of language and instructions. Examples of poor instructions or no translation of instructions in packaged products abound. In these circumstances, the manufacturer is expecting too much and is also limiting the chances of success by not taking simple things, such as language, into consideration. On the other hand, attempting to enhance the product by providing meaningless information is pointless, as was demonstrated by Volvo in Germany and the United States, where the firm found that the projection of 'Swedishness' and Swedish engineering did not help sales as the claims did not mean much to consumers in these markets. The preparation of detailed copy to advertise a consumer product in Germany may be wasteful as Germans are believed not to be avid readers of advertising copy.

After-sales service is another minefield of traps for the unwary firm in international markets. A television or video player manufacturer, for example, causes severe dissatisfaction and even rejection among consumers if no provision is made for repair and replacement services in the target market. An otherwise good product is not likely to sell if the consumer becomes aware beforehand of the absence of such services. The consumer must have after-sales redress if required in order to feel assured of the quality of the product itself. The after-sales service function also enables the manufacturer to monitor the performance of the product in the foreign market, which allows the firm to rectify any damage that may occur to the product as a result, for example, of conditions in the physical environment. The manufacturer may also be able to change the marketing programme in response to a discrepancy between the real and perceived cultural and social circumstances in the target market. The after-sales service function for consumer durable products in particular is central to the success of the firm in international markets.

Long-term brand management

The life cycle concept applies to products and services and only through neglect by management does it apply to brands. It is the pressure of competition in the market which dictates the pace of innovation. There is nothing inevitable about it. This is not to deny that brands do not mature. Brands do reach maturity and maintain relatively constant permanent levels of market share in the face of competition. The decline stage of the brand life cycle is under management control. The life cycle, however, is a dangerous self-fulfilling concept. Successful brand companies do not ignore the life cycle concept; they manage it. In recent years Guinness' United Distillers Group has endeavoured to rationalize and strengthen its portfolio of whisky brands. Many brands were amalgamated, dropped or rejuvenated and new products introduced. Products become obsolete but brands can be adapted functionally to remain competitive. Many companies allow their brands to lose market share by the conscious transfer of resources from old to new.

For longer-term growth and development of the brand it is necessary to ensure continued and growing promotional support. The emphasis should be on those added values that have become the brand's unique property.

Protecting the firm and the brand

Counterfeiting and forgeries

Competitive advantage can easily be eroded in some international markets owing to counterfeits and forgeries. Counterfeiting means that another company uses the firm's competitive advantage to supply products to consumers at lower prices. It is a term frequently used generically to include a range of forged or faked products. The principal focuses of forgeries are luxury products such as branded shirts, suitcases, ladies handbags and watches. Counterfeits usually occur only where the trademark holder receives relatively high margins, where the brand is international and where the competitive advantage reflects a worldwide interest in acquiring the best in the market, irrespective of origin. In such circumstances brand logos are easily recognizable. The strength of the counterfeited brand logo rather than quality, which is usually inferior, carries the fake. The trademark owner attempts to ensure that the exclusivity of the brand is preserved because that element of the marketing programme is likely to have become the firm's principal competitive advantage, even superior to the product quality attribute.

Counterfeiting is big business and a serious problem for many countries, especially in the developed world, and for many brand companies in those countries. According to Michael Leathes, legal director of International Distillers and Vintners (IDV)

> A brand is costly to create and establish, but can be very easy and profitable to copy. Brands are our most important assets. Through them we communicate the quality of our products to consumers. They represent a huge investment of time, effort and money, that can be diluted, weakened, even destroyed by those who copy them.
>
> (*Financial Times*, 14 October 1993, p. 12)

The problem is far more costly than the mere market value of the bogus products. Counterfeits undermine legitimate business and obscure long-held legal distinctions about who owns ideas and inventions. Disputes caused by counterfeits create tensions between a number of highly regulated industrialized countries and some developing countries.

Familiar counterfeits include Gucci watches, Louis Vuitton bags, Cartier watches, Nike sports shoes and Sony consumer electronics. There are many others. Less familiar counterfeits include chemicals, computers, drugs, fertilizers, pesticides, medical devices, hardware and food. Most forgeries today come from the Far East, especially South East Asia. Many European distributors and retailers refuse to sell to these markets because they fear the potential emergence of fakes if their brands become successful there. On the other hand there are some products, such as Rubik's Cube, which it is claimed could not have been successful without forgery. Because of poor market development support for the original product other firms were left to develop the market. Although the product was successful the Rubik brand, in terms of sales and profits, was not.

Copying some aspect of an already successful brand is very popular among cosmetics, perfume and food producers. They sometimes attempt to copy specific aspects of the original product's competitive advantage. In food and beverages witness, for example, the worldwide proliferation of corn flakes, cream liqueurs and cola products, which clearly attempt to exploit some of the brand advantages built in the market by the brand leader. In early 1987 Giorgio, a perfume recently acquired by Avon, was selling for $135 an ounce while a copy, Parfums de Coeur Ltd, was selling a Giorgio imitation called Primo at $7.50 an ounce. Primo may be found in drug stores and discount outlets throughout the United States where the imitators mince no words: Parfums de Coeur declares on its packaging: 'If you like Giorgio, you'll love Primo' (*Business Week*, 1 June 1987). These direct references annoy the original designers who claim that the imitators are benefiting from their continued investment in the product and brand. Scents cannot be patented, however, so there is little they can do about it.

Furthermore, most imitators put disclaimers on their products: Lennox Laboratories Inc. sells an imitation of Giorgio called 'The Great Pretender' with the disclaimer 'Not

Genuine Giorgio' on the packaging (*Business Week*, 1 June 1987). Managers of designer brands report that the imitators damage moderately priced lines to a much greater extent than they harm those they imitate.

Brands in the grey market

The most common activity in the grey market arises when an individual or firm buys products from a foreign distributor where wholesale prices are low and then diverts them to the lucrative high-priced US or European markets, where domestic distributors who have paid a higher price are undersold. This issue of the grey market is intimately linked with attempts by firms to standardize some aspects of branding but to ignore or neglect others such as price and distribution policies, which creates opportunities for re-importers.

Currently, the grey market for cars in Europe causes concern for those in the trade but benefits the customer. Currency fluctuations produce significant price differentials on individual models from one country to another (Figure 15.6). The biggest source of grey market cars is Italy, where more than 10 per cent of the cars sold, or about 185,000 in 1995, end up in other countries (*Business Week*, 20 November 1995). Competition from grey market cars forces regular dealers to lower prices, which benefits customers. It also forces manufacturers to hold down prices to dealers in order to keep them competitive with the grey market. Because most of the re-importers are legitimate the car manufacturers' only hope of stopping them is to block the so-called renegade dealers from selling to the grey market. As the EU Commission welcomes the activity of re-importers, because they serve to integrate the European market and benefit customers, the manufacturers' only recourse is to remove the franchise if a contractual agreement prohibiting sales to re-importers has been broken.

Because wholesalers in different markets are treated differently, particularly for luxury goods and some expensive consumer goods and medicines, manufacturers sometimes deliberately encourage the grey market to develop temporarily. Publicly they argue that

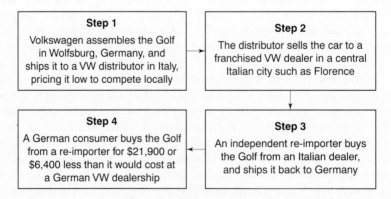

Figure 15.6 Driving a Golf through the grey-market
Source: adapted from *Business Week*, 20 November 1995, p. 21.

unauthorized imports of their products unfairly reduce their profits and damage their trademarks. Privately these companies may not sanction diversion but from time to time some of their sales people, in order to gain share or meet sales targets, will allow the grey market to develop.

Product diversion to grey markets occurs when manufacturers offer very different wholesale prices to different customers in different international markets. In such circumstances manufacturers can protect themselves by insisting that major wholesale customers sign contracts preventing them from selling their products outside agreed territories, though this may come under scrutiny from the Commission of the EU. Manufacturers design packaging for specific countries which runs counter to the advantages of standardization discussed above. Finally, they could also introduce regular audits of sales managers and distributors.

Summary

Underlying this chapter is the view that consumer markets throughout the world are at different stages of development. It is recognized that a particular consumer market may be very advanced in one product area but less advanced in others. The opposite may be the case in other markets. This causes a high degree of fragmentation in consumer markets. Two forces are, however, very influential in bringing about consolidation in some consumer markets – the pressure of convergence of consumer tastes and preferences and the benefits to companies of brand building as a means of entering and competing in many international markets simultaneously.

Because tastes and preferences are different in different markets the management of the brand across markets becomes a significant issue within the consumer products firm. The issue of standardization of the marketing programme across markets also becomes an issue and, frequently, companies accept the trade-off between scale economies and niche strategies. The firm must ensure that featured attributes present it with a competitive advantage in every market in which it operates. This becomes a constant struggle as such competitive advantage can erode as a result of competitor activity and poor brand management. Usually the firm must develop separate marketing programmes for its major international markets, although common elements may be found in a number of markets.

The management of international brands absorbs much management time and resources. Building and maintaining international brands represents a very heavy investment in marketing. Companies sometimes develop umbrella brands to be used in launching new products into markets.

There are many pitfalls in international marketing related to branded consumer products. In this chapter a number of problems associated with packaging, labelling and after-sales service were discussed. This chapter ended with a discussion on the need to protect the brand from counterfeits and forgeries and the developments of the grey market.

Discussion questions

1. Many consumer markets in the developed world are fragmented and consumer products firms develop programmes to consolidate these markets. It is argued that the natural convergence in these markets facilitates consolidation. Discuss.

2. What is branding and what are the key attributes of a good brand?

3. How do firms use brands to enter international markets?

4. Is there such a thing as a global brand? How would you recognize one? How do firms maintain such a brand?

5. Successful consumer products companies attempt to brand their competitive advantage. Discuss.

6. Protecting the brand from counterfeits and forgeries is becoming increasingly difficult as consumers throughout the world seek brands. Discuss.

7. How relevant is the concept of brand valuation? What are the implications for managers in the consumers products firm which has successfully developed an international brand? How would you determine the value of a consumer brand that you know?

References

Aaker, D. (1991) *Managing Brand Equity: Capitalizing on the Value of the Brand Name*, New York, NY: Free Press.

Boddewyn, J. J., Soehl, S. and Picard, J. (1986) 'Standardisation in international marketing: is Ted Levitt in fact right?' *Business Horizons*, **29** (November–December), 69–75.

Buzzell, R. D. (1968) 'Can you standardize multinational marketing', *Harvard Business Review*, **46** (November–December), 103–13.

Court, D., Freeling, A., Leiter, M. and Parsons, A. J. (1996), 'Uncovering the value of brands', *The McKinsey Quarterly*, **4**, 176–8.

Domzal, T. J. and Unger, L. S. (1987) 'Emerging positioning strategies in global marketing', *Journal of Consumer Marketing*, **4** (4), 23–40.

Erickson, G., Jacobson, R. and Johansson, J. (1992) 'Competition for market share in the presence of straegic invisible assets', *International Journal of Research in Marketing*, **9** (1), 23–37.

Hamel, G. and Prahalad, C. K. (1985) 'Do you really have a global strategy?' *Harvard Business Review*, **63** (July–August), 139–48.

Han, J. K. and Schmitt, B. H. (1997) 'Product-category dynamics and corporate identity in brand extensions: a comparison of Hong Kong and US consumers', *Journal of International Marketing*, **5** (1), 77–92.

Johansson, L. G. (1997) 'A perspective on global advertising', *Globalization at the Millennium: Opportunities and Imperatives, Marketing Science Institute Conference*, Le Meriden Hotel, Brussels, 16–17 June.

Johansson, J. K. and Thorelli, H. B. (1985) 'International product-positioning', *Journal of International Business Studies*, **16** (3), 57–75.

Jones, J. P. (1986) *What's in a Name*, Gower.

Kim, C. K. and Chung, J.Y. (1997) 'Brand popularity, country image and market share: an empirical; study', *Journal of International Business Studies*, **28** (2), 361–86.

Lannon, J. and Cooper, P. (1983) 'Humanistic advertising: a holistic cultural perspective', *International Journal of Advertising*, **2** (3), 195–213.

Levitt, T. (1983) 'The globalization of markets', *Harvard Business Review*, **61** (May–June), 92–102.

Littler, D. and Schlieper, K. (1995) 'The development of the Eurobrand', *International Marketing Review*, **12** (2), 22–37.

Martenson, R. (1987) 'Is standardization of marketing feasible in culture-bound industries? A European case study', *International Marketing Review*, **7** (3), 7–17.

Morgan Stanley (1996) *The Competitive Edge*, London: Morgan Stanley.

Onkvisit, S. and Shaw, J. J. (1989) 'The international dimension of branding: strategic consideration and decisions', *International Marketing Review*, **6** (3), 22–34.

Robinson, J. (1933) *The Economics of Imperfect Competition*, London: Macmillan.

Rosen, B. N., Boddewyn, J. J. and Louis, E. A. (1989) 'US brands abroad: an empirical study of global branding', *International Marketing Review*, **6** (1), 17–19.

Wells, L. T., Jr (1968) 'A product life cycle for international trade', *Journal of Marketing*, **32** (July) 1–6.

Whitelock, J. and Chung, D. (1989) 'Cross-cultural advertising', *International Journal of Advertising*, **8**, 291–310.

Whitelock, J., Roberts, C. and Blakeley, J. (1995), 'The reality of the Eurobrand: an empirical analysis', *Journal of International Marketing*, **3** (3), 77–95.

Wolfe, A. (1991) 'The single European Market: national or European brands', *International Journal of Advertising*, **10** (1), 49–58.

16

The industrial products firm

Industrial marketing is usually considered to be far more complex than consumer marketing because it involves a more intricate network of influences. There are usually many more people involved, each with a different background and perspective. Indeed, industrial buying in international markets may involve people drawn from different organizations in numerous countries. The technical nature of many of the products purchased adds to the complexity of industrial marketing. Generally the size of the purchase in money terms is greater and the buying relationship is more complex and long term. Relationships are often the focus of attention – individual transactions may be incidental. In consumer marketing, relationships between the company and the customer are usually established at arm's length through the medium of the brand. In industrial marketing myriad points of contact are a major feature.

In the marketing of industrial products technology is a more pervasive element, which frequently produces a technologically driven production orientation rather than a marketing orientation. This production orientation is due to the greater amount of inter-action and interdependence between marketing and other functional areas, especially manufacturing, R&D, inventory control and engineering. This interdependence may mean that the marketing function is mistakenly accorded a subservient role.

Industrial products firm in international markets

Most industrial products companies are highly 'customer bound' when it comes to internationalization. Suppliers are usually very closely bound to their customers, even for industrial components. The internationalization strategy of an industrial products company is co-determined with that of its customers. Since industrial marketing involves dedication to a small number of customers, the process of internationalization is likely to be a collaborative arrangement between customer and supplier. Internationalization of industrial products firms take place as part of the internationalization of a business system, so that one business system can more effectively compete with another in international

404

markets. The business system, comprising a set of independent firms, is held together through administrative arrangements, technical relationships and financial agreements. It is more appropriate, therefore, to examine the internationalization of the business system of which the industrial products firm is a member.

The role of industrial firms in international markets is growing for a number of reasons. In Chapter 4, the phenomenon of out-sourcing was referred to as firms seek others to provide elements of the value-added chain more cheaply than can be done within the firm itself. In this way, the firm can be more competitive if it concentrates on producing those elements of the final product which give the highest value added. Key words in the analysis of this situation are supply chain management, global sourcing, single sourcing and knowledge-based production. In recent years, for example, the growing importance of knowledge-intensive suppliers based on highly specialized and technological capabilities has been a phenomenon witnessed in the growth of systems suppliers which enables the buying firm to reduce the number of suppliers. Fewer suppliers facilitate decentralization of decision making and the reduction of coordination costs for large manufacturers in the car industry, for example.

Included in industrial marketing are component suppliers because of their contribution to the final product and because they contribute to the competitive strength of the business system through their efficiency and performance.

Other factors bind independent industrial firms together in the business system. The development of specific technical interfaces, logistical arrangements and the special tasks related to the development of new product generations are important ways in which supplier and customer firms are linked. For many industrial products firms it is necessary to complement the product offering with product maintenance, repair service and allied support activities (Czinkota and Johnston, 1981). In exploring the relationship in business-to-business markets between client satisfaction, product quality, services, and the role of the salesforce Chumpitaz (1998) concludes that product quality is the most significant variable followed by delivery service and that other important factors appear to be mediated by product quality. Product attributes in industrial markets appear to be very significant influences in the buying decision. Adapting to the specific product and service needs of customers increases the need for trust between the parties as switching costs rise. A number of reasons may be given for the higher cost of adapting to the preferences of industrial customers operating in different international markets: different business practices, different technical standards, logistical complexity of sending and receiving goods and different languages and culture. In addition, adapting industrial products for international markets frequently runs foul of the customer's or importer's requirements for design and style and detailed product specifications, quality levels and technical standards (Morgan and Katsikeas, 1998).

Nature of industrial markets

Industrial products are frequently classified according to their application, whereas consumer products are classified according to the manner in which they are purchased.

For example, industrial products have been classified as heavy equipment, light equipment, consumable supplies, component parts, raw materials, processed materials and industrial services (Haas, 1986). Jackson and Cooper (1988), however, criticize most classification schemes because of their inadequate handling of industrial services. They propose a classification which includes both goods and services and which divides them into three major groupings (Figure 16.1).

In this classification capital products have a long life span and involve a major capital outlay: land; buildings; major items of equipment. Operations products are products used in the operation of a business. These may be durable or non-durable. Finally, output products are absorbed by the products being manufactured in the firm.

Since an industrial product is purchased for business use and thus sought not for itself, but as part of a total process, buyers value service, dependability, quality, performance and cost, since the output of their own business is dependent to a large extent on the inputs used. Not all customers place the same importance on each dimension and therefore this marketing orientation which, typically, industrial firms have been accused of lacking is crucial in determining the product offering required by each customer.

The situation is further complicated when a firm operates in international markets where environmental factors differ. The level of economic development in a country is a major determinant of the demand for industrial products. The type of product needed and the level of demand are influenced by economic development (Day *et al.*, 1988). Culture has much less impact on industrial products than on consumer products. Culture, however, affects usage patterns, product features and product specifications.

Product quality includes both the physical product and the array of essential supporting services. The ultimate measure of high quality is customer satisfaction. Industrial marketing firms frequently misinterpret the concept of quality, which is not an absolute

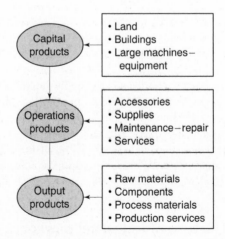

Figure 16.1 Classification of industrial products
Source: based on Jackson, R. W. and Cooper, P. D. (1988) 'Unique aspects of marketing industrial services', *Industrial Marketing Management*, **17** (2), 116.

measure but one relative to use patterns and standards. Since use patterns frequently differ from one country to another, standards will vary so that superior quality in one country may fall short of superior quality as determined by needs in another country.

The adequacy of a product must be considered in relation to the environment within which it is used rather than solely on the basis of technical efficiency. Equipment that requires a high degree of technical skill to operate, maintain or repair may be inadequate in a country that lacks a pool of technically skilled labour. This dilemma is particularly prominent in developing countries which demand the most up to date technology but lack the ability to absorb the high technology.

Markets as international networks

By observing that the industrial system in society comprises firms engaged in production, distribution and consumption, Swedish researchers concluded that the interaction which arises among firms in the system can be examined as a network of relationships (Johanson and Mattsson, 1986, pp. 242–3). Firms are seen as dependent on each other in the system, and their activities are coordinated through interaction; each firm in the network has relationships with customers, distributors and suppliers.

Industrial markets are highly interdependent and increasingly manifest a network of international relationships. Equipment, parts and component suppliers, for example, depend on the size and growth of the market for finished products. Demand in most industrial markets is, therefore, a derived demand, derived from further down the value-added chain or channel of distribution. Changes in demand or industry structure tend to have a knock-on effect back up the value-added chain and horizontally with other firms at the same level. Firms in the car components supply business, for example, have discovered this network effect as the merger, discussed in Chapter 14, between Daimler-Benz and Chrysler takes hold. According to Mr Woody Morcott, chairman of Dana, a car body parts supplier that works with both Daimler-Benz and Chrysler, 'The parts industry should be happy with this merger. Any time you have a good and healthy customer, that's a good company to do business with' (*Financial Times*, Thursday, 21 May 1998, p. 21). In an endeavour to speed up the product development process and to reduce costs Chrysler has resorted to outsourcing for much of its component requirements in what the company calls 'the extended enterprise system' which may benefit US component suppliers in the European markets and if applied in the merged group could also benefit some Daimler European suppliers in the US, but a shake-out is also quite likely (Exhibit 16.1).

Transactions between firms take place within a framework of established relationships. According to this view marketing activities in networks serve to establish, maintain, develop and sever relationships with the objectives of determining exchange conditions and expediting the exchange itself. In the markets-as-networks paradigm, the international firm establishes and develops positions relative to counterpart firms in foreign networks. Internationalization of the firm according to this view means integrating networks across national boundaries.

The markets-as-networks framework is an industry based view of the activities of numerous firms. Writers in this field refer to the context in which the firm operates. The

━━━━━━━ Exhibit 16.1 ━━━━━━━

Car components companies consolidate on both sides of the Atlantic

With components accounting for up to two-thirds of the cost of a vehicle, even a couple of cents off a part can amount to millions over the life of a model. With Chrysler and Daimler-Benz spending an estimated $60 billion on parts, the scope for savings is immense. The first savings could come by routing existing purchases through fewer suppliers prepared to lower their prices for bigger volumes. Later on, new jointly developed vehicles could be designed to share some components, increasing Daimler-Chrysler's leverage.

The chairman of Dana, a car components group in the US, Woody Morcott draws comfort from the fact that Chrysler has pioneered 'outsourcing'. The smallest of the 'Big Three' carmakers traditionally bought more from outside sources than its more vertically-integrated competitors. In recent years, Chrysler has made that a competitive advantage. Dubbing its approach 'extended enterprise', the company has turned to suppliers not just because of cheaper prices, but also because of their complementary talents. By devolving development and manufacturing work to suppliers, Chrysler has shortened its product development times and cut the costs of bringing new vehicles to market. Its approach, increasingly being copied by competitors, gives Mr Morcott confidence about the merger. 'Daimler has virtually admitted it hasn't developed outsourcing as well as Chrysler. That has to be good news for suppliers'.

Moreover, while North American suppliers may sense fresh opportunities in Europe, European rivals will be looking at the U.S. 'From the North American perspective, there's been a lot of quick enthusiasm . . . about opening the door to Daimler. But the opposite's also true', says David Andrea, analyst at Detroit based Roney & Co. Companies such as Valeo, Siemens Automotive or Robert Bosch – all big Daimler suppliers with sizeable bases in Motown – are expected to 'look increasingly to North America to balance out their sales'. What no one disputes is that the merger is likely to accelerate consolidation on the supply side as component companies seek to service carmakers on both sides of the Atlantic.

Source: adapted from *Financial Times*, Thursday, 21 May 1998, p. 21.

context refers to the interaction of cognitive, social and technological factors (Håkansson and Snehota, 1989, p. 12), thereby providing a much richer perspective than available in the industrial organization approach associated with Porter (1980, 1985). The social context of industrial marketing is important because it defines the characteristics of the social exchanges among firms rather than the characteristics of the firms themselves (Easton and Aruajo, 1994). The cognitive dimension captures the notion that the exchange context is a subjective enacted reality influenced by perception and experiences of the managers in the transacting firms.

The context in which the firm operates also determines how firms interact competitively with others in the network. Competition in the network view treats relationships among competitors as mediated through customers as well as suppliers of resources (Jüttner and Schlange, 1996, p. 481). For this reason, networks are characterized by a cooperation–competition mix (Axelsson, 1993) and firm behaviour among firms ranges from competition to collusion and change over time (Easton, 1990) and may be situation specific.

The inappropriateness of focusing solely on single dyadic relationships has led to the realization that firms are embedded in a range of relationships (De Burca, 1994, pp. 4–5). Business in any given relationship is often conditioned by relationships with third parties, such as the customer's customers, the supplier's suppliers, consultants, competitors, supplementary suppliers and middlemen, as well as public or semipublic agencies (Forsgren and Johanson, 1992). The markets for most industrial products and services depend on the efficiency of networks of relationships. The concept of a relationship and the longevity of interfirm dealings is the key to understanding industrial products marketing in the international arena.

Homogeneity in market networks

The more technical the product the more homogeneous the marketing system facing the industrial products company. In many industrial markets companies and countries are networked in tight relationships because of the large amounts of capital and technical expertise required to service the market. The United States, Japan and Europe are intimately linked in production and use of polyacrylonitrile (PAN) based carbon fibers (Figure 16.2). There are many joint ventures in this advanced composites industry, which allow companies such as Union Carbide, Celanese and Hercules in the United States access to a source of precursor materials, fibers and other fabricated materials in other parts of the world (Cammerota, 1984, p. 78), The network of relationships among PAN fiber manufacturers demonstrates the complexity of industrial marketing for technical products, but also indicates the importance of maintaining good marketing relationships within the system. The network of relationships is indicative of the market benefits these firms obtain from dealing with each other. Presumably because of the nature of the products long-term marketing relationships characterize the network of transactions.

Product development and international standards

For firms serving global markets, important decisions need to be made regarding the amount and management of resources used in product development. The most important competitive weapon may prove to be the skilful management and deployment of technical resources rather than the resources themselves. A Booz-Allen Hamilton survey quoted in Perrino and Tipping (1989) produced the following findings concerning industrial product development:

1. Markets are global but technology development is not. Technological developments occur in 'pockets of innovation' around the world.

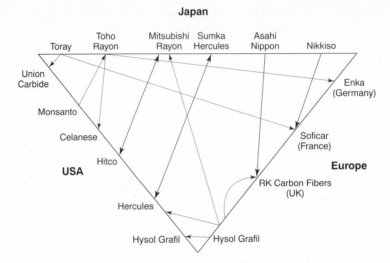

Figure 16.2 Fiber organizations – worldwide relationships.
Source: adapted from Cammerota, D. A. (1984) 'Developing trade patterns for advanced materials',
Proceedings of the International Research Seminar on Industrial Marketing, Stockholm School of
Economics, 28–31 August, p. 78.

2. There is a 'critical mass' necessary for technology development, mainly because of
   dramatically rising costs and the need for interdisciplinary teams and specialized
   equipment.
3. External relationships, i.e. joint ventures, research consortia or technology acquisition
   programmes, are becoming more important and more widespread than ever in an
   attempt to spread costs and risks.
4. Higher levels of R&D do not guarantee success in global markets. Companies can get
   more out of their research by linking it more closely to market needs and customer
   needs.
5. The use of the global network of technology core groups in each major market and
   coordinated is advocated.

A lack of universal standards is a problem in the international sale of industrial products.
Within Europe the problem is likely to disappear or become less critical with the harmonization of standards. However, between the United States and Europe there is a lack of
common standards for highly specialized equipment manufacturing such as machine
tools, and also the use of the Imperial system of measurement in the United States
compared with the metric system in Europe.

Efforts at universal standardization are being made through international organizations dedicated to the creation of international standards. The development of world
standards is also the focus of attention of the International Organization of Standardization. In the newer industries such as electronics, especially information and

communications industries standards in the traditional sense are not an issue. Proprietary standards, once a feature of these industries, are now very much a thing of the past as open standards allow numerous firms to participate in the development of new technologies and new applications as is happening now in attempts by leading companies to integrate mobile telecommunications with computing technologies (Exhibit 16.2).

Exhibit 16.2
Wirelessly connected, hopelessly stranded

Five leading high-tech companies introduced a technology that promises to accelerate the convergence of mobile communications and computing by allowing the wireless transfer of voice and data among mobile phones, laptop computers and other portable devices. The technology, which the companies call Bluetooth, uses short range radio signals to connect mobile devices within a range of 10 metres. It will enable a laptop user to browse the Internet through a wireless connection to a mobile phone left in a handbag or jacket pocket, for example. The Bluetooth device transmits information at a rate of one million bits per second, a speed fast enough to accommodate World Wide Web browsing, the companies said.

The technology is based on an open standard developed by L M Ericsson AB, International Business Machines Corp., Intel Corp., Nokia AB, and Toshiba Corp. Several other major companies have agreed to join the initiative, increasing the prospect that the technology will quickly become a global standard. 'What we're all looking for is plug and play', says Johan Siberg, president of Ericsson Mobile Communications. 'We need to be simple'. The first products incorporating the new technology are expected to hit the market in the second half of 1999, Mr Siberg said. All branches of the information technology industry believe connectivity holds the key to future growth.

Source: adapted from *International Herald Tribune*, Thursday, 21 May 1998, pp. 1 and 10.

Organization for buying

Industrial buying process

The industrial product purchasing process is one of the foundations on which the marketing strategy in industrial firms is based. The other is an understanding of competitive behaviour. Research on the industrial buying process has focused on multiphased decision making, the decision-making unit, the different purchasing situations and the degree of risk involved (Smith and Taylor, 1985). The buying process for industrial products is often conceptualized as a sequential process. Many classifications have been proposed. Ozanne and Churchill (1971) propose a five-stage model, while Wind (1978) prefers a twelve-stage model. Perhaps the most widely quoted classification, however, is the Robinson *et al.* (1967) buy stages model: awareness of the problem; deciding the appropriate product to solve the problem; searching for qualified suppliers; accepting offers; placing the order; evaluating the outcome.

Classifications such as these suggest that the industrial marketing firm should be able to identify the type of decision and the decision stage and hence the key people to influence at a particular time. Before this can be done one needs to consider the make-up of the decision-making group as well as the differences that exist between purchasing situations.

One method of determining the make-up of a decision-making unit (DMU), or buying centre, is to consider the roles that members fill. Roles have been classified in various ways: users, influencers, deciders and gatekeepers (Webster and Wind, 1972). The importance of different organizational roles varies with the phase of the buying process. The make-up of a DMU in terms of members and the roles fulfilled changes depending on organizational factors, the organization size and the buying situation (Wind, 1978). Industrial buying, however, is best considered as a set of interrelated variables cascading down from the environment to the transaction (Figure 16.3).

Both domestic and international factors have a large impact both on the composition of the buying centre and on the manner in which the product is purchased. The business area

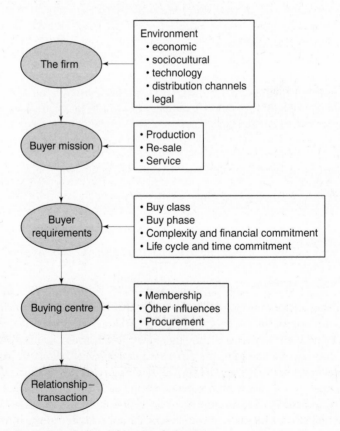

Figure 16.3 Influences in industrial buying behaviour

in which the firm operates determines the importance of the purchasing function. Without an understanding of the customer's mission, other knowledge may be fruitless. Determining the mission is the first step in determining who in the buying firm will be interested in the decision-making process.

The issues that relate specifically to purchasing are how the product will be used, how the product benefits the buyer, the stage of the purchase decision, the buying process, the size of the purchase and the duration of any contractual commitments. Suppliers must know the range of potential uses of the product and priorities in the buying firm.

The buyclass and buyphase variables are used by Robinson *et al.* (1967) to determine the relative influence of purchasing managers in the buying process. Regardless of the industry or buyphase of the purchase, the decision-making process is shared for all but the smallest, most routine decisions. The firm in industrial markets must search for the individual who has the most influence at each stage, rather than for the sole decision maker.

For Mattsson (1988) the money value of the purchase is relative across industries and firms. Money value is defined as the perceived impact of the purchase on organizational profitability and productivity (McQuiston, 1989). Purchasing departments use money values as a management intensity criterion. In very small companies the purchasing manager has little influence in most purchases because the amount is relatively large, thus involving senior management. In medium-sized firms more authority is delegated to the purchasing manager as the relative size of each purchase gets smaller. Larger firms usually establish criteria and guidelines for individuals and departments, even for small purchases; therefore individuals have less flexibility.

Decision makers in industrial buying

Because demand in industrial markets is derived it is the life cycle of customer firms that should receive emphasis. The strategic changes of the buying firms during the life cycle of their products must be the focus of attention in an organizational buying model.

The buyclass variable suggests that the level of management involvement should decrease as products progress from a new task purchase class to a straight rebuy, but during both the design and the product maturity stages, purchasing involvement tends to be high (Fox and Rink, 1978).

Time has two effects on the organization for industrial purchasing decisions that need to be measured. First, as the time horizon increases, interactions can be made routine and delegated down the managerial hierarchy. Second, as they become routine, decisions may start to exceed the time allocated for such activities.

The buying centre includes all members of the buying firm who are actively and significantly involved in the purchase decision process. Membership is fluid depending on product and buyphases. Five general areas in the buying centre must be examined. First, the management level is determined by the five purchase-specific variables discussed above. Second, the functional area composition of the buying centre varies with the product being purchased and the buyphase. Third, roles accorded to members in the buying centre must be examined. Webster and Wind (1972) identified the roles of user, influencer, buyer, decider and gatekeeper in the purchasing decision process.

Roles can be conceived fairly easily for the purchasing of products such as production materials. It is more difficult to specify roles for services, such as who within the firm is the user of transportation for inbound materials or outbound products, who is the gate-keeper, or who has the decider role. Fourth, there is the question of interaction which is mainly concerned with identifying who is involved in the decision process. The contribution of the interaction of members of the buying centre is of greater value when the identity of those involved is determined. Finally, the purchasing department through greater professionalism has become an important part of the firm's management team for product planning. Negotiating skills make the purchasing department a key element during the interorganizational steps of the purchasing process.

Decision criteria for industrial buying

The numerous stages involved in industrial buying mean that a cascading hierarchical dependency exists among the choice criteria. It is likely that numerous different sets of buying criteria are involved (Möller and Laaksonen, 1984). First, buyers use one set of criteria for selecting potential suppliers to submit bids (Figure 16.4). Because the intention

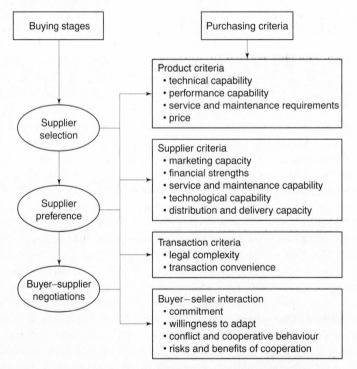

Figure 16.4 Buying stages and purchasing criteria in industrial markets.
Source: adapted from Möller, K. K. E. and Laaksonen, M. (1984) 'Situational dimensions and decision criteria in industrial buying: theoretical and empirical analysis', *Proceedings of the International Research Seminar on Industrial Marketing*, Stockholm School of Economics, 29–31 August.

is to restrict or screen suppliers, criteria based on supplier reputation, technical specifications and delivery capacity dominate. In evaluating bids the same set of criteria may be used, but now a rank order of preference among the suppliers is established. The relative importance of the criteria may change as those left meet the criteria imposed.

At the stage involving negotiations with one or two potential suppliers a third set of criteria may be used that contains only the most important attributes still having some variation across the bidders after the first two stages. At this stage in the negotiations the buyer's aim is often to get the best possible price without jeopardizing quality and delivery.

Numerous stages in the industrial buying process are more in evidence for high-value and complex buying situations where competitive offers are available. In simpler routinized buying situations the above stages will not normally be used. The stages phenomenon is complicated further by the presence of the buying centre influence on the criteria. The interaction of buying stages and buying centre members should also be assessed.

Assessing competitive positions

Segmenting industrial product markets

The practice of industrial market segmentation has lagged behind many of the theoretical developments in the field. Even a simple framework, such as a two-dimensional relationship of price against the cost of serving customers, can help to discover behavioural segments in industrial markets (Rangan *et al.*, 1992, p. 82). Customers that demand and receive high levels of services for low prices must have alternatives, just as customers that pay high prices must find the product attractive even though they do not obtain the full list of services. Even a simple segmentation scheme such as this can assist the industrial products firm as it internationalizes. Segmenting industrial markets internationally can pay large dividends to the company. In a study of industrial segmentation in international supply chain management in the car components industry, Dyer *et al.* (1998, p. 74) discovered that the Japanese car manufacturers Toyota and Nissan segment suppliers by dividing them into groups with whom they establish partnerships and others they keep at arm's length, an approach which gives them a major differential advantage over competitors, whereas US and Korean firms do not segment suppliers and hence miss important marketing opportunities.

Industrial product markets are highly heterogeneous, complex and often hard to reach because of the multitude of products and uses as well as a great diversity among customers. Formulating a coherent marketing strategy can be extremely difficult in such an environment (Kluyver and Whitelark, 1986). The need for market segmentation becomes very important in such circumstances. As seen in Chapter 9, market segmentation is the process of dividing a potential market into distinct subsets of consumers or users and selecting one or more segments as a market target to be reached with a distinct marketing programme.

Failure to segment an industrial market properly can result in missed opportunities and even business failures (Hlavacek and Reddy, 1986). It is also particularly important for the firm in international markets, because the benefits that accrue from standardizing elements of the marketing strategy are realized only when similarities among countries are identified. Universal needs and similarities in buying processes are far more evident in industrial markets than in consumer markets (Day *et al.*, 1988).

Before attempting to segment international markets, Day *et al.* (1988) recommend that the company should screen world markets in a preliminary manner in order to assess similarities among countries, thus making the task of segmentation more focused and less complex. They propose the use of economic variables as a method of determining the level of economic development and hence the level of demand and the type of products needed. Scores are allocated to each country for each of the economic variables chosen. The factor scores thus represent the degree to which each country can be described by each of the underlying constructs. Subsequently, through cluster analysis countries are grouped according to similarities exhibited by the factor scores. The more favourable clusters are then selected for detailed examination. There are certain limitations to this approach, i.e. subjectivity in selecting the type and number of variables needed to cluster countries and the difficulty in finding accurate data on international markets being the more important. Once this process has been completed a typical segmentation technique can be employed.

Various market segmentation approaches have been proposed. Macro variables such as type of industry, size of customer and product usage are relevant. These segments may be subdivided on the basis of micro variables such as the characteristics of the decision-making unit. Such an approach captures all the variables that help to make a particular segment unique. Hlavacek and Reddy (1986) propose a four-step method:

1. identification;
2. qualification;
3. attractiveness;
4. monitoring.

The identification phase involves classifying the particular product and segmenting the market for it on the basis of typical end uses employing industry classification codes such as the SITC or BTN (Figure 16.4). Once a segment is selected there is continuous monitoring of both competitive and technological changes which could dramatically change the boundaries and attractiveness of segments (Figure 16.5). An example of the need for monitoring may be found in the X-ray film market. DuPont concentrated on and achieved a large market share in the X-ray film market, but recent developments in magnetic resonance imaging (MRI) technology has replaced part of the need for X-rays.

Developing market positions

In developing a marketing strategy to enter foreign industrial markets the firm must pay attention to how it wishes to be positioned in the market. A positioning strategy implies a frame of reference for the firm's image among its target customers, the reference point usually being the competition. A positioning strategy can provide a focus for the development of a promotional campaign.

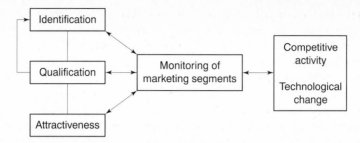

Figure 16.5 Monitoring industrial market segments
Source: Hlavacek, J. D. and Reddy, N. M. (1986) 'Identifying and qualifying industrial market segments', *European Journal of Marketing,* **20** (2), 8–21.

The strategy is usually conceived and implemented with reference to the firm's attributes, the competition and types of customers involved and branding, to name the more important. While there are many ways of measuring buyers' reactions to suppliers involving detailed lists of evaluative factors, managers frequently seek a parsimonious approach which would give useful managerial information in summary form. In a study of industrial buyers, using a multidimensional scaling techniques, Bradley (1986) identifies the preferences of 20 buyers of electric and electronic components used in industrial markets (Figure 16.6). The analysis used here is based on a multidimensional scaling technique which elicits from respondents, in this case industrial buyers, their preferred positions on the two most important latent evaluative buying criteria: product innovation and price.

The 20 buyers, A–T, are positioned at their point of preference around the diagram. Ten buyers are located in cell 3, five in cell 2, four in cell 4 and only one, Buyer H, in cell 1. The positions of the companies are similarly evaluated and reflect buyer preferences. Thus the average position for French companies falls in cell 1, while Swiss and Italian companies fall in cell 2. The majority of companies fall in cell 3, while German companies fall in cell 4.

From this study of preferences it appears that the French firms are preferred by a segment dominated by Customer H, while Swiss and Italian firms are preferred by a segment containing five customers. The Italian firms, on average, are most preferred in this segment. German firms located in a very different market segment are preferred by a segment containing four customers. The largest segment, which contains 10 customers, prefers to work with Dutch, Swedish, US and UK firms, with UK firms being the most preferred and Swedish firms the least preferred of this group.

A number of important lessons arise from this study. First, the relative competitive positions are established. Second, the size and identity of the key market segments become evident. Third, the match or fit of customer segments and supplier firms is specified. It becomes a managerial decision for the firm to choose to change position or otherwise to alter it in the light of the information supplied by the analysis.

Research on branding in industrial markets is not very extensive but a number of papers are beginning to address some of the problems of industrial products brands. In a small group study of industrial buyers Thompson *et al.* (1998) report that 13 brand

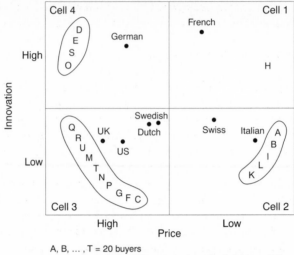

A, B, ... , T = 20 buyers
● = average position of companies in each of eight countries

Figure 16.6 Multidimensional scaling of buyer preferences for suppliers.
Source: Bradley, M. F. (1986) 'Developing communications strategies for foreign market entry', in P. W. Turnbull and S. J. Paliwoda (eds), *Research in International Marketing*, London: Croom Helm, pp. 35–61.

attributes are important in buyer choice and these may be divided into three groups. According to these authors the first group of attributes constitute parity criteria that can be satisfied by a large number of potential suppliers capable of meeting the technical and service criteria which determine the supplier's fitness for purpose. The next set of requirements are differentiators which serve to screen out all suppliers who have a solid reputation in the key areas. However, as these requirements become essential they are insufficient prerequisites for success and the key differentiating criteria between suppliers has become: who will make the best partner over time? This is an interrelated scheme which integrates traditional product attributes that can be branded with relationship factors which contribute to the establishment and maintenance of a long term mutually beneficial partnership. Branding in industrial marketing has moved beyond querying the trustworthiness of the products and services themselves to assessing whether the buyer can trust the company behind them. Branding of industrial products is still in it infancy, however, and while the potential power of industrial brands is great its value in terms of competitive positioning remains largely unexplained and untapped (McDowell Mudabi *et al.*, 1997, p. 445).

Routes to international markets

The path to internationalization of the industrial products firm may follow any one of four different routes (Andersen *et al.*, 1997, p. 240). The firm may follow its customers abroad, it may go abroad by being integrated into the supply chain of a large international company, it may be part of a domestic or foreign system supplier or it may internationalize as an independent firm.

Following domestic customers abroad is a route used by suppliers whose products are of strategic importance to the customer. As the customer expands the foreign business, the market position may be strengthened, thereby requiring more product adaptation to local needs. As a consequence, the supplier firm finds itself increasingly in competition with local suppliers in the foreign market. If successful in the adaptation, the supplier becomes an indirect exporter and the firm adapts to the requirements of international markets. Eventually, the supplier may be encouraged first to locate service facilities and, subsequently, production facilities in the foreign market.

For firms whose products are not of strategic importance to customers, the situation may turn out to be quite different. These firms may reach the stage of being indirect exporters, at which point the customer may discover alternative suppliers in the foreign market who are better in some important way. These suppliers could easily fall out of the business system in the international and domestic markets.

The second way an industrial products company can internationalize its activities is by integrating itself into the supply chain of a large international company. If successful with one division of the international customer, such business can rapidly lead to introductions to other divisions in other countries. As more and more customer companies outsource their requirements, additional opportunities arise for suppliers. International firms in the car industry, electrical businesses, computers and electronics generally are constantly searching for smaller supplier firms who can support areas of key competence – usually skills which complement the core competence in the customer firm.

Being part of a system recognizes that, for the business system to function properly, several fields of competence must be brought together. Frequently, firms internationalize through collaboration with other specialized firms located in different countries. Indeed, the design and management of the system assembly may be the responsibility of a company located in one country with numerous suppliers located in other countries, all focused on providing a system for use by a customer in another country. Specialized small firms find this approach to internationalization attractive as it allows them to concentrate on their key skills while sharing resources and information on a need basis with others in the business system.

Motives to internationalize as an independent firm usually arise because of a stagnant or mature domestic market. Occasionally, specialized firms do not wish to share trade secrets and other technical information with companies which could subsequently become competitors. In such cases, they may prefer to develop new business abroad independently of others. This is the approach adopted most frequently by traditional companies. A major disadvantage of this approach to internationalization, especially for the small industrial products company, is the cost of establishing a sufficiently broad base of customers. Networks of relationships and customers are easier to establish under the previous approaches to internationalization outlined above.

Commitment to international markets

The commitment of the firm to international markets may be measured by the way in which the firm organizes its resources to reach the market. The character of the marketing organization through formal and informal marketing networks indicates commitment to the market and the strategic choices open to the firm (Hallen, 1986, p. 242). This author identifies three basic types of marketing organization related to the degree of investment in the market. For major customers in international markets, direct selling from the home base may be the most appropriate organizational form. Alternatively, access to the market with only minor investments may be obtained by the use of agents. To obtain a long-lasting presence in the market, however, a sales subsidiary, perhaps with local production facilities, may be used according to Hallen. In a study of 120 suppliers located in France, the Federal Republic of Germany, Sweden and the United Kingdom, Hallen (1986) found a preponderance of direct selling in domestic markets (Table 16.1).

In export markets the use of direct selling is less common, although there is some variation among the countries represented. High commitment, extensive experience or strategic ambitions are reflected in the establishment of subsidiaries. Regarding the choice between agents and subsidiaries the United Kingdom and Swedish suppliers were very different, while the French and German were somewhere in the middle of the strategic spectrum. The dominance of agents in the United Kingdom relationships reflects recent internationalization of these firms, while the dominance of subsidiaries among Swedish firms reflects their well-established position in international markets (Hallen, 1986, p. 243). In general the greater the use of subsidiaries the greater the investment in, and hence commitment to, the market in question.

Although somewhat dated, the Johnston and Czinkota (1982) study of US industrial products exporters identifies a number of motivations for going abroad. In a survey of 300 companies, these authors discovered that the following factors were the most important:

Table 16.1 International marketing organization in selected European countries

Country	Market	Direct selling (per cent)	Agents (per cent)	Subsidiaries (per cent)
France	Domestic	87	4	9
(43 firms)	International	12	42	47
Germany	Domestic	67	7	27
(30 firms)	International	21	46	33
Sweden	Domestic	62	5	33
(20 firms)	International	8	17	75
United Kingdom	Domestic	100	0	0
(27 firms)	International	9	64	27

Source: adapted from Hallen, L. (1986) 'Comparison of strategic marketing approaches', in P. W. Turnbull and J. P. Valla (eds), *Strategies for International Industrial Markets*, London: Croom Helm, p. 242.

- profit advantage;
- product uniqueness;
- technological advantage;
- managerial urge;
- competitive pressure.

Exporters in this study were motivated by the above proactive or internal factors which did not change over time. Proactive firms appeared to have larger sales volumes and were more service oriented than reactive firms and they were also more marketing and strategy oriented. Reactive firms were more concerned with operational issues (Johnston and Czinkota, 1982, p. 17). In a more recent study of industrial firms in international marketing Morgan and Katsikeas (1998, p. 173) recommend that industrial firms:

- seek assistance to ensure that exporting strategy is based on a well-founded approach to market planning,
- visit export markets to gain personal understanding of customers, their preferences and idiosyncracies,
- work closely with specialized industrial agents and distributors to develop a win–win position for all parties,
- recruit specialized people who understand industrial products exporting and have a proven track record in international marketing and
- select markets which are not adversely affected by likely future exchange rate movements.

Sources of international competitive advantage

Companies manufacturing capital goods and equipment have moved aggressively abroad in recent years in search of lower costs, more rapid growth or diversification or simply to follow their customers who have already moved abroad for similar reasons. Currency strength also encourages industrial products companies to internationalize as materials, components and factories are cheaper abroad when the home currency is stronger. As industrial products firms are very diverse, it is very difficult to identify common competitive factors which more than a few share. Some industrial products firms succeed internationally by establishing strong local operations in key strategic markets while others continue to export. Danfoss, a Danish company, combines these two features with technical capability to become a world leader in its field (Exhibit 16.3). Another Nordic company, Ericsson, has an international competitive advantage because it is so entrenched in each of its markets that it is considered a local firm in most countries where it has a presence. Many people do not know that it is Swedish. Other firms continue to export. Because of their dependence on export sales, industrial products firms with higher levels of exporting intensity better understand the mechanisms, operational complexities, and decision-making parameters of the exporting process and have demonstrated that they are capable of overcoming many of the limitations imposed by strategic and tactical export marketing activities (Morgan and Katsikeas, 1998, p. 172).

========= **Exhibit 16. 3** =========
Danfoss – a global industrial products company

Danfoss is changing from a solid Danish owned export company to a dynamic player on the world stage. Factories and R&D facilities located near key markets, and a high level of effectiveness have helped the company become one of the world's ten most effective. Since taking over as President, the 49 year old Jørgen Mads Clausen has put the company into a higher gear. The financial results for the accounting year 1996-97 showed the highest turnover and biggest profit the company has ever made, and the trend is expected to continue. The workforce in 1996–97 was 18,300 (8,700 in Denmark), turnover was DKK 13 billion and profit before tax was DKK 900 million. Jørgen Mads Clausen's father, Mads Clausen, founded Danfoss in 1933. Since April 1996 Jørgen M. Clausen, the eldest son, runs the company as President and CEO. 'We are only about 25 percent global right now, says Jørgen Mads Clausen. But as far as planning is concerned we are a long way into the process. What we need to do now is implement the plans we have made'. The company is already world leader in some product fields such as radiator thermostats, refrigeration and hydraulics.

Danfoss's core market is still the EU, but the opportunities for further growth are limited. The focus has been expanded to other potential markets. In eastern Europe, for example, Danfoss buys or builds its own factories. The potential for growth is huge, and in Poland and the Czech Republic Danfoss is thriving. In North America Danfoss has acquired or established its own facilities and is continuing to expand into South America – one of the fastest growing markets. 'An important megatrend is that we need to be close to our clients. We need to be able to service American clients from our factory in the U.S. so that we get quick feedback and can react quickly to client needs'.

Danfoss has expanded into the global market with more than 50 subsidiaries round the world. By building and buying production facilities in countries with low wage levels the company has ensured that it is able to increase its ability to meet still tougher competition. Furthermore, local factories experience a synergy effect and increased local sales of other products which Danfoss produces.

Source: adapted from Thaysen-Lowth, J. (1998) 'Danfoss – a truly global company', *News*, (Copenhagen Airport), March–April–May, pp. 8–11.

The United Kingdom company Psion, best known for its palmtop computers, is capitalized on the London Stock Exchange at about £300 million and is a world leader in mobile digital computing and communications. Its competitive advantage is based on a clear long-term vision and a software systems approach. According to David Potter, founder of Psion, there are lessons to be learned from the Psion story for other technical and industrial products companies attempting to internationalize (Potter, 1998, p. 17):

• European companies can be innovative and compete in new high technology markets, e.g. SAP in Germany, Baan in the Netherlands and Nokia and Ericsson in digital cellular technology markets are increasingly global and very competitive.

- There is a continuous struggle pursuing change and innovation in high-technology markets; innovation drives high-technology markets, not money.
- Companies that succeed and survive in the long run are not based on one product or one idea but are those which continuously introduce new products and services.
- Through growth, a company, its founder and management have to change and learn progressively as they evolve through different company sizes.

In their study of industrial products companies, Morgan Stanley (1996) discovered that there were three sources of competitive advantage which were obvious and universal: strong management, low costs and financial strength. These competitive advantages can be elaborated into a longer list of elements which give many industrial products companies an internationally sustainable competitive advantage:

- low-cost manufacturing;
- global distribution strength;
- product quality and reliability;
- large installed customer base;
- technological leadership;
- dominance of narrow product niche;
- coherent corporate culture.

By addressing industrial products companies active in international markets on these criteria, Morgan Stanley identified a list of companies in different countries, whose sustainable advantage ranged from 5 to 30 years (Table 16.2). Most of those firms obtained a relatively high proportion of their revenues from foreign markets.

Table 16.2 Sustainable competitive advantage in industrial products firms

Company	Where they stand out	Country	Sustainable advantage (years)	Foreign market revenues (per cent)
General Electric	Cost–technology leadership in global markets for power-generation equipment, aircraft engines, medical imaging systems and engineered plastics.	US	10–30	38
United Technologies	Global presence and leadership in Otis Elevators and Carrier air conditioning, which together, produce 47 per cent of profits. Competitive advantage through strong local identity.	US	10–30	55
Caterpillar	Exceptionally strong distribution supports high market shares. Superior	US	10–20	46

Table 16.2 *continued*

Company	Where they stand out	Country	Sustainable advantage (years)	Foreign market revenues (per cent)
	products, premium prices, high resale value and low total cost of ownership.			
Deere	Large scale US farms, strong distribution, excellent products, and strong brand loyalty support high global market share in large equipment. Premium prices, high residual values.	US	10–20	25
Emerson Electric	Global market and technology leader and 'best-cost producer' in instruments and values used to control and optimize processing operations; also air conditioning components, especially compressors.	US	10–20	44
MAN	MAN Roland is the leader in web printing machinery used by newspaper industry. Complex technology for colour offset printing, plate making, and high-speed paper folding.	US	10–20	34
Sandvik	Biggest maker of cutting tools made from cemented carbide and steel. Strengths in global manufacturing and distribution, high R&D for new products, size relative to competition.	Sweden	10–20	41
Valmet	Largest manufacturer of paper machinery.	Sweden	10–20	49
ABB	One of the top three manufacturers of power generation, transmission, and distribution equipment; industrial and building systems; rail transportation equipment.	Swiss/ Swedish	5–10	34
Technip	Plant engineering for hydrocarbon and petrochemicals. Experience in lump-sum turnkey projects in emerging markets. Wide network of subsidiaries, good at complex financing and flexible proposals.		5–10	69

Source: The Competitive Edge, London: Morgan Stanley.

Pricing, selling and promoting industrial products

Pricing industrial products

International pricing has to take many variables into consideration. It is rare to have the same price prevail in all world markets because of currency fluctuations, different factor costs, different product requirements and government regulations, standards and official limits on pricing and discounting. At best this differential may be contained within a few percentage points across different markets. Otherwise, there is the ever-present danger of parallel exports taking place.

Fluctuating values in currencies pose considerable problems to the international firm. Because of fluctuations in currencies many companies seek to use forward foreign exchange markets. Foreign currency is sold either at the spot rate, which is the daily rate prevailing on the day of the requested exchange transaction, or for any number of months ahead, usually three, six or nine. The rate of exchange is specified and known to the exporter when the forward contract is made. Thus the buyer is relieved of exchange risk.

Government interventions and political interference are a second issue that can cause concern to the firm. Government legislation and regulations directly affect price. National government regulations concerning maintenance of good trade balances, development of national resource bases, promotion of national security and provision of employment can all have a considerable impact on prices. Industrial goods are particularly susceptible since they are often the cannon fodder of economic wars being waged to win the political allegiance of developing countries (Rahman and Scapens, 1986). As a result, international marketing firms are sometimes confronted with impossible price competition because prices are shaded by a foreign government for political rather than economic reasons.

Dumping is the third concern which affects prices and revenues in international markets. This is an unfair trade practice, based on international price discrimination, which occurs when a product is sold abroad for a lower price than the seller charges for the same product in the home market. This normally occurs when the home country's demand is less elastic than is the foreign market.

The fourth concern is transfer pricing, which refers to the prices at which products and services are transferred within the corporate family across national frontiers as they move globally, division to division or to a foreign subsidiary or joint venture (Burns, 1980). Transfer pricing sometimes becomes a problem within the company. Where a profitable international division is an intermediary there will be an inevitable conflict over price when products move from the manufacturing division to the international division and from there to the foreign subsidiary. For the manufacturing division the price should be high enough to encourage a flow of products for export and build up an export trade. Low prices result in poor returns for the manufacturing division, and losses can have a very bad effect on morale. From the viewpoint of the international division, however, the transfer price should be low enough to enable it to be both competitive and profitable in the foreign market.

Market price is by far the most usual method of transfer pricing, followed by standard unit full cost plus a fixed mark-up. Seven reasons may be identified which are likely to induce high transfer price above arm's length prices for flows from parents to foreign subsidiaries:

1. corporate income tax higher than in parent's country;
2. pressure from workers to obtain greater share of profits;
3. political pressure to nationalize or expropriate high-profit foreign firms;
4. political instability;
5. high inflation rate;
6. price of final product controlled by government but based on production cost;
7. desire to mask profitability of subsidiary operations to keep competitors out.

Selling industrial products

Personal selling is the most important method of promoting and selling industrial products. The reason that personal selling is so important in the industrial markets is inherent in the types of purchases that are made. The need for sales personnel who are well trained and experienced within their individual technical discipline when marketing high-technology industrial products is well documented in the literature and in trade journals. Most such purchases are large and processing the sale often takes considerable time. Often the purchaser is not exactly sure of what is available in a company's product line or requires a special item for which specifications need to be worked out and a price and delivery date negotiated. Those operating in another culture need to be familiar with various negotiation strategies employed there and how the negotiation process is similar to and different from that which exists in their own culture.

By dealing with a salesman, many of the final details concerning the product can be resolved. For new, maintenance, repair and operating service products end-users often determine which products are purchased and are most influenced by advertising, but closing a sale may still require many calls from the salesman to the organization's gatekeepers (Berkowitz, 1986).

Promoting industrial products

Trade journals are the principal communications medium used by industrial products firms. Trade fairs are also a valuable means for reaching the hidden buying influences not reached by regular salesmen or by trade publications. A salesman can talk to more prospects in a three or four day trade show than could be reached by personal calls in a much longer period. Other members of the buying centre frequently attend trade shows. In the marketing of high-technology industrial products, exhibitions and trade shows play a very important role at the interest–awareness stage as well as the evaluation and selection stage. Having reviewed an extensive list of articles, Rice (1992, p. 33) summarizes the benefits of international trade shows as follows:

- lower customer contact cost than sales call;
- examine opportunities before investing in foreign markets;

- monitor regional–global competition efficiently;
- identify new product opportunities in discussion with visitors;
- evaluate reactions to a new product;
- build relationships with existing and potential customers.

Mail brochures are popular, especially for technical products. While it is unknown what percentage of mail brochures are read or taken seriously, a low sales response rate is often sufficient to cover the cost of the mail campaign. Although often irritating to customers, it has remained a promotional technique for this reason. Improved targeting of customers can improve effectiveness of mail brochures.

In a recent study of a large sample of US industrial firms the internet website was discovered to have only a very modest initial impact on sales and profits but a very significantly improved public relations and communications effect among suppliers, customers and employees (Honeycutt *et al.*, 1998, p. 71). These authors conclude that a website allows industrial products firms to enter the world of electronic commerce inexpensively as part of their marketing effort. This would allow industrial firms to communicate internationally in a direct and effective way with selected customer groups.

Product sampling is a very effective way to introduce and stimulate interest among end-users and influencers for industrial supply items which are relatively inexpensive. More expensive products, however, may be promoted in this way by offering a free trial period. Various restrictions are imposed on the industrial marketing firm's chosen communication mix in international markets. The EU directive on product liability influences the content of a particular communication mix.

Summary

There are very great differences between marketing consumer products and industrial products. Industrial marketing is far more complex in that organizational buying involves a more intricate network of buying influences, the product is normally much more technical and therefore quite complex, the size of the purchase is greater in money terms and the buying relationship is more involved and continuous in nature. These differences influence how industrial products are marketed internationally. The complex interaction process is made even more complex when operating within different cultures.

Discussion questions

1. Describe the main characteristics of industrial markets facing the international firm.
2. What are the key purchasing criteria in industrial products marketing? Are they different in domestic and international markets?
3. What effect have international product standards on the sale of industrial products abroad?
4. Outline the industrial buying process and demonstrate how it is complicated in international marketing.

5. What role do cultural influences have on the marketing of industrial products in international markets?

6. How might you apply segmentation analysis to international industrial markets?

7. How would the industrial products firm establish a position in international markets?

8. The pricing, selling and promotion of industrial products in international markets are complicated by the intervention of governments and multinational regulatory authorities. Discuss.

References

Andersen, P. H., Blenker, P. and C. and Rind, P. (1997) *Generic Routes to Subcontractors' Internationalization*, Copenhagen: Handelshøjskolens Forlag, pp. 231–55.

Axelsson, B. (1993) 'Understanding industrial systems: critical issues in describing, analysing and acting in business networks', *Advances in International Marketing*, **5**, 221–34.

Berkowitz, M. (1986) 'New product adoption by the buying organization: who are the real influencers?' *Industrial Marketing Management*, **15** (1), 33–43.

Bradley, M. F. (1986) 'Developing communication strategies for foreign market entry', in P. W. Turnbull and S. J. Paliwoda (eds), *Research in International Marketing*, London: Croom Helm, pp. 35–61.

Burns, J. O. (1980) 'Transfer pricing decisions in the US MNCs', *Journal of International Business Studies*, **11** (2), 23–28.

Cammerota, D. A. (1984) 'Developing trade patterns for advanced materials', in *Proceedings of the International Research Seminar on Industrial Marketing*, Stockholm School of Economics, Sweden, 29–31 August, pp. 78–89.

Chumpitaz, R. (1998): 'Determinants of client satisfaction in business to business', in P. Andersson (ed.) *Track 1, Market Relationships, Proceedings, 27th EMAC Conference*, Stockholm 20–23rd May, pp. 167–86.

Czinkota, M. R. and Johnston, W. T (1981) 'Segmenting US firms for export development', *Journal of Business Research*, **9**, 353–65.

Day, E., Fox, R. J. and Huszagh, S. M. (1988) 'Segmenting the global market for industrial goods', *International Marketing Review*, **5** (3), 14–27.

De Burca, S. (1994), 'The network perspective: theoretical foundations, assumptions and characteristics', *Working Paper, 94–5*, Centre for Quality and Services Management, University College Dublin, Dublin, Ireland.

Dyer, J. H., Cho, D. S. and Chu, W. (1998) 'Strategic supplier segmentation: the next "best practice" in supply chain management', *California Management Review*, **40** (2), 57–77.

Easton, G. (1990) 'Relationships among competitors', in G. Day, B. Weitz and R. Wensley, (eds) *The Interface of Marketing and Strategy*, Greenwich, CT: JAI Press.

Easton, G. and Aruajo, L. (1994) 'Market exchange, social structures and time', *European Journal of Marketing*, **28** (3), 72–84.

Forsgren, M. and Johanson, J. (eds) (1992) *Managing Networks in International Business*, Philadelphia, PA: Gordon and Breach.

Fox, H. W. and Rink, D. R. (1978) 'Purchasing's role across life cycle', *Industrial Marketing Management*, **7** (3), 186–92.

Haas, R. W. (1986) *Industrial Marketing Management*, Boston, MA: Kent Publishing Co.

Håkansson, H. and Snehota, I. (1989) 'No business is an island: the network concept of business strategy', *Scandinavian Journal of Management*, **5** (3), 187–200.

Hallen, L. (1986) 'A comparison of strategic marketing approaches', in P. W. Turnbull and J. P. Valla, (eds), *Strategies for International Industrial Markets*, London: Croom Helm, pp. 235–49.

Hlavacek, J. D. and Reddy, N. M. (1986) 'Identifying and qualifying industrial market segments', *European Journal of Marketing*, **20** (2), 8–21.

Honeycutt, E. D., Jr., Flaherty, T. B. and Benassi, K. (1998): 'Marketing industrial products on the Internet', *Industrial Marketing Management*, **27**, 63–72.

Jackson, R. W. and Cooper, P. D. (1988) 'Unique aspects of marketing industrial services', *Industrial Marketing Management*, **17** (2), 111–18.

Johanson, J. and Mattsson, L. G. (1986) 'International marketing and internationalization processes – a network approach', in P. W. Turnbull and S. J. Paliwoda (eds), *Research in International Marketing*, London: Croom Helm, pp. 234–65.

Johnston, W. J. and Czinkota, M. R (1982) 'Managerial motivations as determinants of industrial export behaviour', in M. R. Czinkota and G. Tesar (eds), *Export Management: An international context*, New York, NY: Praeger, pp. 3–17.

Jüttner, U. and Schlange, L. E. (1996) 'A network approach to strategy', *International Journal of Research in Marketing*, **13**, 479–94.

Kluyver, C. A. de and Whitelark, D. B. (1986) 'Benefit segmentation for industrial products', *Industrial Marketing Management*, **15** (4), 273–86.

Mattson, M. R. (1988) 'How to determine the composition and influence of a buying centre', *Industrial Marketing Management*, **17** (3), 205–14.

McDowell Mudabi, S., Doyle, P. and Wong, V. (1997): 'An exploration of branding in industrial markets', *Industrial Marketing Management*, **26**, 433–46.

McQuiston, D. H. (1989) 'Novelty, complexity and importance as causal determinants of industrial buyer behaviour', *Journal of Marketing*, **53** (2), 66–79.

Möller, K. K. E. and Laaksonen, M. (1984) 'Situational dimensions and decision criteria in industrial buying: theoretical and empirical analysis', in *Proceedings of the International Research Seminar on Industrial Marketing*, Stockholm School of Economics, 29–31 August.

Morgan, R. E. and Katsikeas, C. (1998) 'Exporting problems of industrial manufacturers', *Industrial Marketing Management*, **27**, 161–76.

Morgan Stanley (1996) *The Competitive Edge*, London: Morgan Stanley.

Ozanne, U. B. and Churchill, G. A. (1971) 'Five dimensions of the industrial adoption process', *Journal of Marketing Research*, **8**, 322–8.

Perrino, A. C. and Tipping, J. W. (1989) 'Global management of technology', *Research Technology Management*, **32** (3), 12–19.

Porter, M. E. (1980) *Competitive Strategy*, New York, NY: Free Press.

Porter, M. E. (1985) *Competitive Advantage: Creating and sustaining superior performance*, New York, NY: Free Press.

Potter, D. (1998): 'Entrepreneurship: Psion and Europe', *Business Strategy Review*, **9** (1), 15–20.

Rangan, K., Moriarty, R. T. and Swartz, G. S. (1992) 'Segmenting customers in mature industrial markets', *Journal of Marketing*, **56** (4), 72–82.

Rice, G. (1992) 'Using the interaction approach to understand industrial trade shows', *International Marketing Review*, **9** (4), 32–45.

Robinson P. J, Faris, C. W. and Wind, Y. (1967) *Industrial Buying and Creative Marketing*, Boston, MA: Allyn and Bacon.

Smith, D. and Taylor, R. (1985) 'Organizational decision making and industrial marketing', *European Journal of Marketing*, **19** (7), 56–71.

Thompson, K. E., Knox, S. D. and Mitchell, H. G. (1998): 'Business to business brand attributes in a changing purchasing environment', *Irish Marketing Review*, **10** (2), 25–32.

Webster, F. E. and Wind, Y. (1972) 'A general model for understanding buying behaviour', *Journal of Marketing*, **36**, 12–19.

Wind, Y., (1978) 'Organizational buying center: a research agenda', in G. Zaltman and T. V. Bonoma, (eds), *Organizational Buying Behavior*, American Marketing Association, pp. 67–76.

17

The services firm

There are three reasons, stemming from the international marketing of products, why service firms have grown and internationalized. First, a manufacturing firm which pursues an international strategy requires detailed information on the size, composition and trends in foreign markets – information which is usually provided by specialized firms. Second, where it is essential to modify the product the firm will require engineering and design services and, frequently, after-sales maintenance and servicing facilities. Third, as products moving across borders meet more obstacles than sales within the domestic market, e.g. distance, language, customs, laws and regulations, there is a growing demand for services to remove these barriers. Many of the added costs of internationalizing in manufacturing are service costs. Services are independent of, but related to, developments in product markets.

Services in international marketing

Services differ from products in that international marketing transactions frequently require consumers and providers to be at the same place at the same time. One result of this is that restrictions on market access for services may involve barriers to the international exchange of services and policies affecting the actual entry of service providers into the markets where the customers are located. Because services tend to be intangible and non-storable when they are traded, they must be embodied in products, information flows or people which are transported from one country to another (Feketekuty, 1988). Furthermore, it is frequently necessary for providers and consumers of services to cooperate if the service is to be provided. The interaction or exchange requirement can be met through a wide set of modes of service delivery (Sampson and Snape, 1985).

International services differ from domestic services in two respects, therefore: (a) they involve something crossing borders and (b) they interact with a foreign culture. They are similar to international products in this respect. Because services depend on people for their provision and delivery, cultural sensitivity is more critical. For these reasons, international services have been defined as 'deeds, performances, efforts, conducted across national boundaries in critical contact with foreign cultures' (Clark *et al.*, 1996, p. 15).

Internationalizing the service firm

In many cases the service offering is not conducive to 'going international' nor is it necessary to start out 'large', e.g. the airline industry and some corporate banking activities. The international service marketing firm often cannot draw from small-scale domestic experience whereas the product marketing firm can usually develop the domestic market first – before going abroad. The services firm wishing to internationalize its business must be reasonably flexible regarding the definition and nature of the service provided, be prepared to learn from initial experiences and attempt to develop reliable international networks and systems for the delivery of the service (Mathe and Perras, 1994).

The product marketing firm can also 'test the waters' – start into foreign markets initially by exporting a limited or reduced product line. Gradually, as success gathers momentum, the full product line can be introduced abroad. Market commitment can be extended by setting up overseas production units and subsidiaries. The process continues, constantly building from a position of strength. It is very different for the service marketing firm. It will have to 'plunge straight in', as a service cannot be exported. Normann (1984) explains that few services can be exported without also exporting the full 'service delivery system'. Basically, the service offering must be available in full from the day of entry to the market. In a marketing environment of increased international competition, slower growth in the domestic market and mature markets a system perspective is central to the creation of a climate and culture of relationship orientation in a service business and, through a relationship orientation, customer retention is the key to profitability in the long term (Schneider *et al.* 1997, pp. 19–20).

As was seen in earlier chapters, among the many reasons why product marketing firms go international are stagnant domestic market, growth in the market abroad, matching domestic competitors as they internationalize, opportunism, counteracting foreign firm action, i.e. threat in the domestic market, and exploiting a competitive advantage. These reasons also apply to service firms as they attempt to enter and develop international markets. Normann (1984) highlights two additional reasons: (a) a personal challenge to senior people in the firm; (b) the need to service customers who have internationalized. Unless three conditions are fulfilled, however, the full potential of international markets can never be realized (Normann, 1984):

1. A competitive advantage must exist in the service management system.
2. There must be a strong desire or ambition among senior management to internationalize.
3. The service firm must provide adequate commitment of time and resources.

The involvement of people in the process usually means that there is a degree of variability not experienced by the product marketing firm. Cultural diversities and social norms quickly come into focus in service marketing. The effect of these elements obviously varies with the degree of intangibility of the service offering and the extent of the contact involved.

Nature of services

A service firm develops a system to organize the production and implementation of a set of services for customers. A service may be described as any activity or benefit that a supplier offers a customer that is usually intangible and does not result in the ownership of anything. The provision of a service may or may not be tied to a physical product. Services, according to the International Standard Industrial Classification (ISIC), include the following: wholesale and retail trade, restaurants and hotels; transport, storage and communications; financial, insurance, real estate and business services; personal, community and social services; government services. The key asset managed by the firm in each of the above businesses is a system for interfacing people and machines or equipment.

These systems are developed by the firm over many years and are the result of investment in human, financial and physical resources. The unique blend of these assets in a system gives the service firm its competitive advantage.

> The effective service management system is characterized by harmony and by the good fit between its components. All the components enhance each other; and they must all promote the fundamental ideas which constitute the basic logic and success factors in any business. (Normann, 1984, p. 96)

Normann develops these points by noting that it is the unique corporate culture in service firms which sets them apart. He notes the dangers which can arise when firms attempt to extend or transfer service systems to new markets or new customer groups. The corporate culture in the firm embraces people, values and skills which can be confused when extended to new situations:

> it is difficult to mix service management systems which represent delicate formulas for poised success without destroying or disturbing something valuable in the process. If diversification is to be devised, it must be done with the utmost sensitivity, so as to maintain the integrity of the existing service management systems. (Normann, 1984, p. 98)

One of the principal factors causing an increase in the level of services is the change from 'in-house' to 'arm's length' provision of services. This has occurred at two levels. At the household level it is reflected in increased participation by women in paid employment. At the level of the firm there has also been a pronounced shift to arm's length sourcing of services as manufacturing industry reorganizes to take account of the changes in the working environment mainly brought about through technological change.

The service growth phenomenon

The growth in services internationally may be attributed to two principal factors: changing life styles affected by affluence, leisure time and women in paid employment and the changing world affected by the increased complexity of life, ecological concerns and the variety and complexity of products available on the market (Figure 17.1).

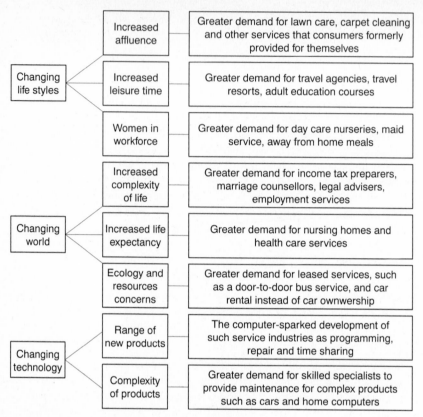

Figure 17.1 Reasons for growth in service businesses
Source: adapted from Scheol, W. F. and Ivy, J. J. (1981) *Marketing: Contemporary concepts and practices*, Boston, MA: Allyn and Bacon, p. 277.

Services can be either commercial or non-commercial (Figure 17.2). Commercial services are now the most dynamic in world trade. They include business services, distribution services and financial services and personal services such as private health care. Non-commercial services are provided principally by government agencies or are strongly influenced by public policy. Growth in these areas is still much lower than in commercial services. Non-commercial services include education, cultural services, public service and public health service.

In general, the production of services and products are very closely linked. Telecommunications services cannot be produced without the support of extensive technical equipment. Distribution services are essential for manufacturing to take place. To some extent the difference in the relative importance of services in developed and developing countries may be due to the lower prices of many services in developing countries. Services are very important in the gross domestic product (GDP) of most countries. In 1970 services represented 55 per cent of the GDP in developed countries and 45 per cent in developing countries. By the mid-1990s these proportions had risen to 70 per cent and

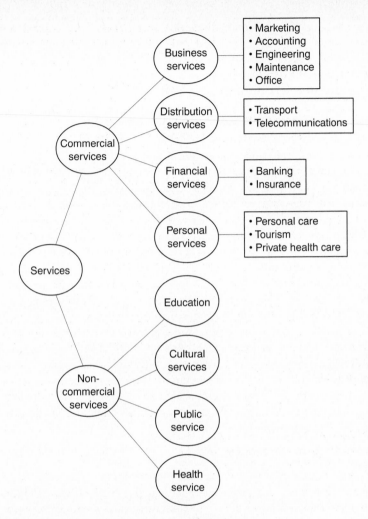

Figure 17.2 Commercial and non-commercial services

55 per cent, respectively. Among developed countries it appears that services are proportionately more important in the smaller countries. In some countries the shift to a service economy has not been pronounced but the composition of services has changed dramatically. Finance, business and government services have gained share at the expense of personal and distribution services.

Marketing of services

The usual way of examining services in marketing has been to attempt to overlay the success formulae of product marketing on service industries with little or no adjustment.

The approach led one commentator to claim that 'service industries remain dominated by an operations orientation that insists that each industry is different' (Lovelock, 1983, p. 10). Early attempts to develop a discipline of service marketing went astray. The relentless pursuit of segmentation, adaptation and differentiation as if such were a prerequisite for the recognition of service firms' unique needs, was a failure to recognize the linkages between products and services and the need to treat both uniformly and within the same analytical framework. Not only were boundaries and demarcations being drawn up between services and products but also among service industries. This left early enthusiasts open to attack from traditional marketing academics.

The development of service industries is also being hindered considerably by the failure to recognize commonalities among service industries. To date, they are treated as heterogeneous. The literature is replete with separate treatments of banks, airlines, insurance and hotels, to name the more common. It is not necessary, however, to consider various service industries as unique and separate from each other (Grönroos, 1987). By recognizing the common features of many service industries, a service marketing theory could develop more rapidly and, as Lovelock (1983) points out, such an approach would be conducive to some useful cross-utilization of concepts and strategies.

Defining a pure service business as one in which the service is the primary component on offer (similarly for a pure product), it becomes clear that few, if any, pure products or services exist. Products are not marketed. Only the benefits they offer are marketed and these include both tangible and intangible elements. By deduction, the same applies to services. Following along these lines, Levitt's (1972) view that 'everyone is in service' becomes more acceptable. Levitt is saying that everyone is in services, not that everyone is in products, and hence the focus of attention should be on the service component of the 'thing' being marketed and this can only improve our understanding of service marketing.

Role of technology in the services firm

Technology has the potential to make service industries more cost effective and it also supports quality control. Other potential benefits highlighted by Cowell (1984) include the ability to handle large volumes of certain kinds of services and to offer a wider range of services and potential increases in management efficiencies. Employees also benefit considerably. Technological improvements enhance the status and motivation of employees (Normann, 1984). For example, secretarial work has become less tedious since the introduction of microcomputers.

Services involve social actions and considerable customer interactions. Both are heavily dictated by cultural and social norms. With the introduction of technology, social interaction may be removed. The potential benefits from employing new technology will only be realized if they are favourably perceived by potential customers. For instance, many customers have reacted adversely to the introduction by banks of 'faceless' ATMs. The banks may have a more efficient and controlled service but, in many cases, customers do not welcome such developments.

Once again, it is necessary to be constantly aware of the delicately balanced service process and management system. Any changes must be skilfully introduced and positioned to increase the likelihood of their trouble-free acceptance. If this could be achieved, i.e. 'if the new technology could be skilfully employed to enhance and promote rather than to disturb the kind of social process that typifies effective service organizations, then the potential will be very great' (Normann, 1984, p. 71). The successful introduction of new technology is highly sensitive to different cultures and the way different societies adopt innovations.

Productivity in services

Higher services productivity is the key to securing a rising national standard of living. Moreover, it is a critical factor in improving a country's competitiveness and shrinking the trade deficit. Services are just as productive as manufacturing, or are becoming so. Services traditionally were protected by restrictive practices but are now being liberalized and freed to competition.

It is often argued that they are not susceptible to international marketing and competition. It is difficult to envisage dry cleaning, services, financial advice and hotel accommodation being the subject of international marketing. However, many services are tradeable and more are becoming so. Through cross-border sales, joint ventures and foreign direct investment, companies providing financial, legal and business services, and consultancy, telecommunications and recreation services experience international marketing opportunities. Indeed, by combining or incorporating services in products, companies have discovered that it is easier to export services. Two sources of labour productivity in services are high technology investment and international competition (Figure 17.3).

It is generally believed that while both investment in technology and international competition contribute to improved productivity in services, the latter is the more effective. It is often argued that productivity in services lags that in manufacturing but it is not certain whether this is a measurement issue, or a lack of technology or a lack of competition. The level of technology available to workers has risen dramatically in recent years and has resulted in a shake-out in services industries. Furthermore, services have until recently been sheltered from international competition. Much of the shake-out in services has been due to government deregulation in industries such as telecommunications and airlines and increased foreign direct investment in services. Productivity differences in services are due as much to open international competition and improved labour configurations as investment in technology.

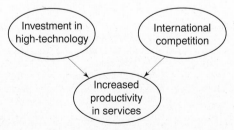

Figure 17.3 Sources of labour productivity in services

Thomas (1978) discusses the apparent difficulty in service-based offerings using economies of scale. The perishable quality of a service creates a need to decentralize the service production process to a local level. However, a little imagination provides considerable scope, i.e. by introducing wide-bodied jets, airlines are able to fly twice as many passengers with the same number of high-salaried pilots.

Service systems

Service systems with high customer contact are more difficult to control and to rationalize than those with lower customer contact (Chase, 1978). In high-contact systems, the customer can affect the time of demand, the exact nature of the service and the quality of the service since, by definition, the consumer becomes involved in the process itself. In fact it is frequently better to view the marketing of services as the marketing of a system. The system consists of products which produce explicit benefits and services which produce tacit benefits (Figure 17.4). Emphasis on individual components is associated with transportation, financial and personal services. Emphasis on the system itself arises in education and professional services.

In services where the customer must be present, satisfaction with the service will be influenced by interactions between customers and the service facilities themselves, and perhaps also by others using the system (Lovelock, 1983). At the opposite end, where the customer does not come into contact with the service facility, the outcome of the service remains important but the process of service delivery may be of little interest. e.g. bank credit cards.

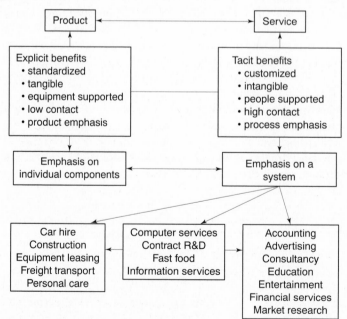

Figure 17.4 Services marketing is marketing a system

International marketing of services

Types of services in international marketing

Services marketing is heterogeneous and consists of many disparate activities. Services are provided by private and public firms which use low- and high-skilled labour. Services provided are sold to final consumers and to the industrial market. Three types of services have been described by Stern and Hoekman (1987, p. 40) which are relevant in international marketing:

- no movement of providers or customers;
- movement of providers only;
- movement of customers only.

The first category covers the separated services (Sampson and Snape, 1985) which are 'pure' or independent services, in that they can be traded like products without any requirement for a physical presence in the foreign country. Many separated services complement trade in products, especially industrial products. The second type of service requires the physical proximity of customer and provider. Capital and/or labour must move internationally for provision to be feasible. The transfer modality may be through foreign direct investment or some form of competitive alliance. It is not necessary that all factors move abroad; management may remain in the home country but support foreign production through management, manufacturing and marketing guidelines. In the third stage the services are provided in the home country of the providers. Tourism, education and medical services are prime examples. The Uruguay Round of GATT in its basic agreement uses a variant of the Stern and Hoekman approach to define the scope of services as:

- services supplied from the territory of one party to the territory of another,
- services supplied in the territory of one party to the consumers of any other,
- services provided through the presence of service providing agents of one party in the territory of another, and
- services provided by nationals of one party in the territory of any other.

An example of the second type listed is tourism, while banking and financial services generally would fit the third category. Construction and engineering projects and management consultancy are examples of the fourth category.

International marketing potential

The unique status of the marketing in services offers rich potential for creative new approaches and analysis. Interest in services marketing has reached a considerable height. Unless service marketing is perceived by managers to be at least as important as product marketing, opportunities in the international market place will continue to be lost. The problems in service marketing which are especially pronounced in international marketing and which frequently arise are due to a number of factors:

- physical display is impossible;
- patent protection is impossible;
- demonstration gives the service away;
- provision of warranties is difficult;
- packaging is marginal.

Classifying services

Interest in developing classification schemes for services may be found in practically every publication on services. Many have been criticized for not being based on 'a sufficiently comprehensive theoretical foundation and strong definitional basis that clearly delineates between products and services' (Uhl and Upah, 1983). There are general marketing concepts, approaches and theories of universal applicability which must be adapted to suit different circumstances.

Although the marketing concepts and many of the techniques are universal, marketing practices are often unique to particular situations. It must be remembered, however, that because both product marketing and services marketing are derived from the same general marketing theory, it follows that there are also many areas of commonality. Nevertheless, a number of differences do arise. Observing the wide range of literature devoted to analysing differences between manufacturing and services led Swartz *et al.* (1992) to argue for more research attention to analysing the substantial differences which exist within the services sector.

In the literature four major characteristics of services distinguish services from products: (a) intangibility; (b) inseparability, i.e. simultaneous production and consumption; (c) heterogeneity, i.e. less standardization and uniformity; (d) perishability, i.e. services cannot be stored. To these Cowell (1984) has added a fifth: (e) ownership.

The view of most researchers is that intangibility is the critical product–service distinction from which all other differences emerge. It is wrong to imply that services are just like products except for intangibility. Shostack (1977) explains: 'By such logic, apples are just like oranges except for their "appleness". Intangibility is not a modifier, it is a state'. Intangibility is the key differentiating characteristic from which the others are derived.

The intangibility creates several marketing implications (Patterson and Cicic, 1995, p. 60):

- services cannot be easily displayed or communicated;
- without inspection, buyers rely on cues, communications experience and word of mouth to make judgements;
- the greater the intangibility, the more difficult it is to differentiate the services and, hence,
- the higher the costs required to build a corporate image;
- the more intangible the service, the higher the perceived costs and risks in internationalization.

The more intangible the service, the greater the difficulty in exporting. Financial, engineering and medical services, for example, 'do not enjoy the same opportunities for learning from the gradual experience as the goods firm, e.g., via indirect or casual exporting. The international marketer of services has got no choice but to deal directly with the foreign customer' (Nicoulaud, 1989, p. 58). Such service firms must choose from a reduced set of foreign market entry modes. Only those services that are embedded in goods may be directly exported, e.g. software, videos, because their production and consumption can be decoupled by being produced in one country, embodied in the tangible product, e.g. disk, training manual, and exported in the traditional manner (Patterson and Cicic, 1995, p. 61).

Product service continuum – intangibility

The simplest approach in attempting to develop a continuum of services is to distinguish between pure service businesses on one hand and product-oriented businesses on the other (Thomas, 1978). A market offering is classified as a service or a product on the basis of whether the essence of what is being bought is tangible or intangible. In this way, a continuum can be developed with varying degrees of dominance towards a product in one direction and a service in the other.

In this way, Shostack (1977) has developed a 'molecular model' classifying products and services according to the degree to which ownership of a tangible object is transferred from buyer to seller in the market transaction: 'This broader concept postulates that market entities are in reality combinations of discrete elements which are linked together in molecular-like wholes'. This enables all 'market-entities' or 'product–service hybrids' (Uhl and Upah, 1983) to be positioned along the continuum, according to the weight of the mix of elements that constitute them.

For example, an apple is almost totally dominated by a tangible object, i.e. a product, whereas intangibility dominates in an airline flight. Many market offerings fall in between, e.g. food served in a restaurant has a considerable service component. Wilson (1972) uses the concept of tangibility to distinguish between producer and consumer services which are essentially intangible and those which are tangible (Table 17.1).

In tandem with Shostack's exposition, it is possible to represent the definitions of other researchers on a similar continuum. Services may be treated in a spectrum of people based or equipment based services (Thomas, 1978). According to Thomas, as a service business evolves, it moves along the spectrum from people based to equipment based (Table 17.2). The middle ground is covered by the many businesses that are in more than one type of business, i.e. nearly all banks operate multiple service businesses, some equipment based; and some people based.

The extent of required customer contact in the creation of the service is another way of examining services (Chase, 1978). Customer contact is defined as the physical presence of the customer in the system. Extent of contact is defined as the percentage of time the customer must be in the system relative to the total time it takes to serve him (Table 17.2). At the 'high-contact' end of the scale, it is likely that supply will seldom match demand for the service, given the customized nature of each delivery. At the opposite end of the continuum the potential for supply and demand to match exactly, is much greater.

Table 17.1 Application of the concept of tangibility to services marketing

Degree of tangibility	Producer services	Consumer services
Services that are essentially intangible	Security communications systems, franchising, mergers, acquisitions and valuations	Museums, employment agencies, auctioneers, entertainment
Services providing added value to a tangible product	Insurance contract maintenance, engineering, consultancy, advertising, packaging, design	Launderettes, repairs, personal care, insurance
Services that make available a tangible product	Wholesaling, transport, warehousing, financial services, architecture, factoring, contract R&D	Retailing, automatic vending, mail order, hire purchase, charities, mortgages

Source: adapted from Wilson, A. (1972) *The Marketing of Professional Services*, London: McGraw-Hill, p. 8.

Table 17.2 Alternative view of the provision of services

	Tangibility	Equipment	Contact
Production	Tangible dominant	Equipment based	Low contact
	Salt	Automated	Manufacturing
	Soft drinks	Unskilled operators	
	Cars		
	Cosmetics		Quasi manufacturing
	Fast-food restaurants	Skilled operators	
	Advertising agencies		
	Airlines	Unskilled labour	Mixed services
	Investment management	Skilled labour	
	Consultancy	Professional	Pure services
	Teaching		
Performance	Intangible dominant	People based	High contact

Sources: adapted from: Chase, R. B. (1979) 'Where do customers fit in a service operation?' *Harvard Business Review*, November–December; Shostack, G. L. (1977) 'Breaking free from product marketing', *Journal of Marketing*, April, 73–80; Thomas, D. R. E. (1978) 'Strategy is different in service business', *Harvard Business Review*, July–August, p. 161.

Standardization and customization of services

Services comprise the 'core service' and 'auxiliary or supporting services' so the core service obviously cannot be left out (Grönroos, 1987). The other kind, auxiliary and support services, is optional but may be used to customize the service. Increasingly, core service products that are sold globally are more likely to be standardized than customized – McDonald's Veggie Burgers should be seen as an exception rather than a trend (Lovelock and Yip, 1996, p. 82). The international services company should, however, seek ways of customizing the service package to meet local requirements.

These can be added to the service offering to increase its total value to make it more attractive. It is here that the competitive advantage may be found where the service marketing firm can differentiate its service from all other services but also, with some measure of imaginative application, standardize these peripherals and obtain some degree of standardization.

Grönroos further distinguishes auxiliary services into facilitating services and supporting services forming his 'basic service package'. Facilitating services are defined as additional services often required in order for the consumer to use the core service, e.g. a ticket issuer at a cinema. From these he distinguishes support services which are only there to increase the services' value and to differentiate them from the services of competitors, e.g. a restaurant in an hotel. Supporting services are competitive tools.

Services are usually designed around the specific requirements of the individual customer. The degree of standardization possible in a service depends largely on the extent to which the service is 'people based' or 'equipment based'. A service such as an automatic car wash raises the level of standardization as it removes the human element, which has considerable bearing on the viability of the service function. Because of the inseparability factor, the service sector is one which is highly labour intensive. Investment in people and training is, therefore, one approach to quality control. The difficulty of producing services of uniform quality which is necessary for successful branding, advertising and other mass-marketing activities makes the successful and sustained marketing of services that much more difficult than is the case for products (Uhl and Upah, 1983).

Standardization and customization are simultaneously possible to achieve with services. By using local nationals as providers, the 'foreignness' of a standardized service may be overcome, e.g. the use of local cabin crews by international airlines (Lovelock and Yip, 1996, p. 72). According to these authors, the practice of augmenting a core service with many supplementary elements makes it relatively easy to provide a globally standardized core service augmented and differentiated by nationally customized supplementary service elements.

Travel-related services, especially airline passenger services, benefit from global advertising and positioning, although the communications task may vary by country. One way of achieving the objective of global positioning while being locally sensitive is to develop a dual campaign like that of British Airways – 'The World's Favourite Airline' with a smaller budget to customize marketing mix elements for local customers including items such as schedules, prices and special offers. In contrast, Singapore Airlines satisfies both objectives simultaneously. A number of years ago, when Singapore Airlines did not have the large aircraft to compete with the big carriers, it concentrated on service backed by the advertising theme of the 'Singapore Girl', a unique way of customizing and differentiating a service.

Contact-based services are the purest of the international services because they exhibit all the classical service characteristics – intangibility, heterogeneity, perishability and inseparability.

For many services, the provider must be in face-to-face contact with the customer. Many services fit this category – engineering projects, management consulting and tourism. These require a high degree of contact between the client and the provider. Other services, particularly financial services, medical diagnosis and telecommunications, may be delivered by technology and are not high contact. For high-contact services, there are a number of marketing implications. A high degree of contact requires a local presence in the foreign market and customization. People delivering such services need high technical skills, but also they need culturally sensitive interpersonal skills, since they are involved directly in the provision and marketing of the service. For the services that require little contact, standardization is a possibility and a presence in the foreign market may not be required. Such services are not culturally sensitive and so marketing costs are lower. Such services may easily be provided to many customers, whereas high-contact services may have to be restricted to a fewer number of customers. The extent of personal contact involved and the number of customers served in a given time period are factors which influence the international marketing of services (Figure 17.5).

Professional services involve very extensive personal contact and a small number of customers served. At the other extreme mass services such as banking through ATMs and credit cards typically involve much less personal contact but much larger numbers of customers served. Between these extremes are service shop operations such as car hire. The degree of personal contact and the number of customers served have clearly defined consequences for attempts to internationalize a service business.

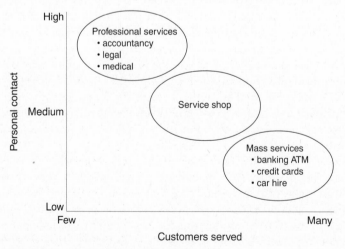

Figure 17.5 Personal contact and customers served

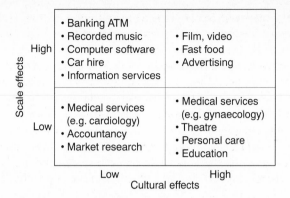

Figure 17.6 Scale and cultural effects in international services marketing

Scale and cultural effects

Certain scale and cultural effects in the international marketing of services must be considered when diversifying into international markets. Some services businesses respond to scale operations, while others do not. The provision and marketing of some banking services, recorded music, films, video, computer software, information services and some forms of advertising are examples of services having associated scale effects (Figure 17.6). Medical services, legal and accountancy services, market research, theatre, personal care and education are examples of services where the scale effects are low.

The important point, however, is that services are also influenced by cultural factors. Some are highly culture bound and demand is strongly influenced by society. Many medical services, personal care, education programmes, films, video and selected advertising are strongly influenced by culture. Many banking services, computer software, some medical services and professional services are not so strongly affected.

Managing services marketing

Service marketing is complex since it involves a number of relationships: between the organization and the external customer, between the service provider and the external customer, and between the organization and the service provider or internal customer (Glynn, 1994, p. 8). In purchasing products, the product and its features provide enough evidence of what is being offered. In the case of a service, the 'management of evidence' is vital (Shostack, 1977). This refers to the tangible cues surrounding the seller's capabilities to deliver the service. The literature is extensive on the importance of situational characteristics in purchase decisions for services (Berry, 1980; Shostack, 1977). Such things as the physical, environmental setting, e.g. doctor's waiting rooms, and the appearance of service, e.g. clothes and presentation, should receive very high management priority.

The importance of price should also be discussed. The tendency for customers to use the price of a product as an indicator of its quality is well known. For services, it is even more pronounced. Berry (1980) explains that lawyers, consultants and even hairdressers can contradict signals they wish to communicate regarding quality by setting their prices too low. This is another 'evidence' which must be managed carefully. Great emphasis is placed on ensuring that the distribution of products occurs at the 'right time' in the 'right place'. With services, it is necessary to add: 'in the right way'. The 'how' of service distribution is vital to get right. 'How . . . doctors, lawyers . . . conduct themselves in the presence of the customer can influence future patronage decisions. Washing machines can't be rude or careless – but people providing services can and sometimes are' (Berry, 1980).

The whole issue of trust arises in service marketing but is seldom ever mentioned. Berry (1980) refers to it in what he terms the need for 'internal marketing', particularly in high-contact service industries. He defines internal marketing as the need to apply the philosophy and practices of marketing to the people who serve the external customer so that (a) the best people possible can be employed and retained and (b) they will be the most effective in their work. Presumably, by deduction, such employees exude an air of trust-worthiness and reliability on which the customer places confidence and also, in the case of long-term relationships, a degree of loyalty.

Market entry modalities for services

Using the concepts of tangibility and contact, it is possible to devise a framework which separates services in international marketing into four groups (Figure 17.7). Firms that

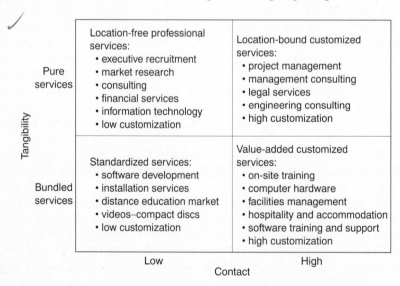

Figure 17.7 Tangibility and contact in international services marketing
Source: adapted from Vandermerwe, S. and Chadwick, M. (1989) 'Internationalization of services', *The Services Industry Journal*, January, p. 85 and Patterson, P. G. and Cicic, M. (1995) 'A typology of service firms in international markets: an empirical investigation', *Journal of International Marketing*, **3** (4), 67.

sell pure services which require very little contact have been labelled 'location free' by Patterson and Cicic (1995, p. 67). Executives in these firms need only travel to the foreign country from the domestic base for relatively short periods to conduct an assignment. Then they return home. They do not require a permanent presence in the foreign market. The client is not expected to visit the company to obtain these services nor does the company spend much time with the client abroad. These are low-contact standardized pure services, such as market research, transportation and insurance.

Where contact is high and the company is dealing with pure services, a customized service is required. These 'location bound' services require relatively continuous contact with the client for successful delivery of the service. As such, services are customized. Staff providing them must exercise more executional discretion and adaptation during service delivery. Major engineering projects, long-term management consulting and project management services fall into this category.

Firms which sell standardized services tend to bundle the service with products. Because they are bundled and require little personal contact, these services tend to be exported in the traditional manner.

Lastly, value-added customized services require a high degree of supplier–client interaction for successful service delivery. These services are highly customized in that the service component adds considerable value to the product component. High-contact bundled services include technical training and support, associated with major installations such as a telecommunications network or the building of a holiday resort.

Coterminality of production and consumption of services

In general, the production of services and the production of products are usually closely linked. It has been argued by Vandermerwe and Chadwick (1989, pp. 89–90) that modes for service internationalization are influenced by a combination of the nature of the service, i.e. the degree of interaction between service provider and service consumer, and the way in which it is delivered, i.e. the degree to which the services are embodied in, or delivered through, goods. For example, telecommunications services cannot be produced without the support of extensive technical equipment. Distribution services are essential for manufacturing to take place. For international exchange to occur in services that require the physical proximity of provider and consumer, it is necessary that one visit the other.

The coterminality in production and consumption of many services, requiring both the supplier and consumer to be present for the service transaction to take place, has made them difficult to trade by conventional means (Miles, 1993, p. 667). If physical proximity is not required, other possibilities exist. The interaction requirement may be met through physical movement, through the use of telecommunication and computer technology or the mail services. Computer- and telecommunications-based information technology makes it possible to separate the location and timing of the provision of a service and its delivery which gives rise to a 'mode of presence' range on a continuum from greater to lesser intimacy (Miles, 1993, p. 668). The greatest degree of intimacy is obtained with foreign direct investment and the least with exporting.

Because of the frequent need for temporary visits by providers of foreign direct investment in competing in foreign markets, the international marketing of services involves a greater number of dimensions than is the case with products. Market access for services may involve the full range of market entry modalities, whereas access for products can be achieved through one, e.g. exporting. In health services, for example, where the customer–patient must be present, satisfaction with the service will be influenced by the interactions between customers and the health service facilities themselves and perhaps also others using the system (Bradley, 1990). In purchasing products, the product and its features provide enough evidence of what is being offered. In the case of a health service, the management of the evidence is vital. This refers to the tangible cues surrounding the healthcare provider's capabilities to deliver the service. The 'how' of service distribution, as emphasized by Berry (1980), is vital to get right. The distribution and delivery of medical services is a particularly difficult issue to manage across cultures and requires a high degree of cultural sensitivity in the management of health services.

Choosing the entry mode

With respect to market entry strategies, the options open to the service firm are similar to those available for the product marketing firm:

- exporting;
- competitive alliances;
- acquisitions–direct investment.

Exporting has already been shown to be difficult for the services firm since the delivery system must accompany the service. By embodying services in a product, it may be easier to access foreign markets. This is a particularly attractive option when barriers to trade in services are greater than barriers on merchandise trade. By embodying services in products, the company is moving towards the tangible dominant part of the product–service continuum (Shostack, 1977). Service contracts sold as part of an equipment purchase package are an example: Levi Strauss embodies a design service in the famous denim jeans which are branded and sold in many markets. Benetton similarly embodies design and style in clothing sold through leading retailers throughout the world. Forms of competitive alliance such as joint ventures abound and are used more often than in product marketing due to the cultural element of services and the different people involved. Locals can overcome many barriers confronting the service marketing firm.

The licensing of a service operation has never been as widespread as it is for products but, as seen in Chapter 13, franchising of services operations is growing. Many are of the opinion that because of the very nature of services, a service firm cannot have patents or exclusive 'manufacturing' processes to protect its offering, and hence it is considered unsuitable for licensing. To overcome this problem, Winter (1970) demonstrates the need for the service firm to offer a substantial quid pro quo in return for the licence fee. He suggests that, to avoid the foreign counterpart 'taking the idea and going it alone', an acceptable arrangement should include the following:

- a strong name;
- a well-designed marketing strategy;
- a complete manualized operation system;
- substantial opportunity for profit.

The name of the firm and the goodwill attached to the trademark are crucial elements in the service offering process. When a product is taken to international markets, these markets are generally familiar with the product. For a service marketing firm such will not be the case; the firm's name and reputation are critical to selling the service successfully and these must be given much attention and be advertised or communicated in some way to the new market before purchase of the service can begin. The confidence of the prospective client or customer must be won initially. The firm's name and existing experience may not be sufficient, however. The conditions in the marketing environment must be conducive. Sears Roebuck discovered that its experience was not relevant to international trading and so dropped its aspirations in that direction. The firm acquired specialized firms to perform the tasks and reverted to consumer products in which it had experience.

In designing an international licensing agreement minimum sales performance standards should be included. Otherwise, the licensee is unlikely to put much effort into the programme. The distance factor, language barriers and differences in business customers can often cause problems between the licensor and licensee.

Franchising appears to be even better for service companies, affording a greater degree of control over the elements of the service component, as described in the Grönroos model. Franchising is frequently used in the fast food industry.

Acquisitions and foreign direct investment decisions for service firms, in the form of a branch or subsidiary, must consider the costs of the investment compared with other market entry modes, on the one hand, and the obvious scope for greater control, particularly quality control, on the other.

Restrictions on international marketing of services

Restrictions by governments and public agencies are much more common for service firms than for product firms. After primary resources, host governments see services as a way by which foreign companies can 'take the most out of a country and leave little' (Carman and Langeard, 1979). The special nature of some services prompts governments into taking action – particularly when the service has some cultural, political or security sensitivity. Staltson (1985) illustrates the extent of government regulation of services in the United States by drawing attention to 'a voluminous inventory compiled by the Office of the US Trade Representative'. She also highlights the service equivalent to tariff barriers used against products. Services can be controlled by measures such as licences, fees and special taxes. Administrative and investment-related barriers are quite common and are examined in detail in Cowell (1984). Administrative barriers may be in the form of:

- delays in granting licences;
- failure to certify certain professional services;

- discriminatory implementation of statutory regulations;
- inadequate access to local judicial bodies.

Investment-related barriers include:

- employment requirements that control the personnel practices of the foreign firm;
- restrictions on the extent of foreign ownership permitted;
- biased government regulation against foreign service companies;
- limitations on the firm's access to advertising and communications failures;
- discriminatory practices against specific service industries, i.e. higher reserve requirements for foreign bank subsidiaries or special capital requirements for foreign insurance firms.

Exporting services

When a firm has selected its target international markets, the next important step is to decide what form of representation to use for developing the service business abroad. The main alternatives are:

- direct sales, using a domestically based representative;
- indirect sales, using a local agent in the foreign market;
- appointing a local company as a full-time representative;
- opening a branch office with full-time representatives;
- entering into a joint venture with a local firm;
- establishing a new company in the market, or acquiring an existing one;
- licensing or franchising a local company;
- forming a bidding consortium with other firms.

Different approaches suit different types of services and markets. In general, the most appropriate form of representation depends on:

- the nature of the services – personal–professional or delivered on the basis of some form of hardware;
- the location of delivery – is the service performed in the domestic market or at another fixed location?;
- the regulations of the market in question – local partners may be required;
- the distance and cultural characteristics of the target market;
- the need for long-term customer support services.

The main issue is the extent to which the firm needs to establish a long-term presence in the selected markets. In this context, it is important for the company to understand that:

- it is difficult for third parties to sell another firm's services;
- obtaining a good flow of information on service or project opportunities is impossible without local representation, and/or frequent market visits;
- where services are delivered locally, firms may lack credibility unless they have a local base.

Lastly, the firm must consider how to promote its services abroad. When the form of representation is selected, the next step is to identify suitable candidates for the task. This can be difficult, and it is best to use multiple sources of information and advice.

The nature of the promotional techniques used by firms varies widely according to the type of service they offer. There is no single formula for success and the approach needs to be tailored to the characteristics of the market in question. According to the Irish Trade Board, the range of promotional activities available to most firms exporting services may be classified as interactive, indirect, based on public relations or on a combination of these forms:

Interactive:
- sales calls;
- proposals;
- current contacts with important customers;
- participation in trade fairs and exhibitions;

Indirect marketing:
- advertisements in trade and specialist journals;
- advertisements in other media (diaries, year books, directories, etc);
- brochures, videos and other corporate literature;
- direct mail;
- participation in joint promotions;

Public relations:
- invitations to visit the firm's premises;
- invitations to view other projects being managed by the firm;
- seminars and lectures;
- participation in conferences.

Internationalization in selected service industries

Advertising services in international markets

Any service marketing firm attempting to tackle the complexities of advertising un-equipped with a thorough understanding and appreciation of the uniqueness and abstract nature of a service is bound to pay a very heavy price as it attempts to advertise.

The product marketing firm enters the arena with a principal, tangible product to which the advertising process adds abstract qualities to enhance and sell the product. The service marketing firm enters with an intangible offering which cannot be physically evaluated or accessed. When combined with further abstract and intangible qualities by the advertising process, the result may be confusion, even a 'money-for-nothing' image (Shostack, 1977). Shostack urges the service marketing firm to understand the need to make the service offered more 'concrete' through advertising, rather than more 'hazy'. Merrill Lynch has developed a strong association between itself and the bull symbol. Also, its advertisements show photographs of tangible physical booklets and the TV screenings of most advertisements finish by inviting customers to write for them. In this regard Merrill Lynch successfully associated its intangible service with some 'tangible evidence' working against the media's abstracting qualities. In a similar vein Singapore Airlines attempts to convey a sense of tangible customer service in its press advertising with the Singapore Girl as the theme. Both domestic and international services marketing firms are well advised to acquaint themselves with Shostack's concluding principle: 'Effective media representation of intangibles is a function of establishing non-abstract manifestations of them' (Shostack, 1977, p. 80).

The advertising agency world has gone through a number of changes in recent years, many of which can be attributed to international market trends and company responses. Many advertising agencies find that to service their clients properly they must follow them abroad. In examining the motives for internationalization among advertising agencies, Whitelock *et al.* (1993) report that the initial interest of a senior executive is important and entry mode choice is restricted, with the most popular means being wholly owned subsidiaries and joint ventures.

It is not only the large agencies which have internationalized. Many smaller firms are also seeking partners and other ways into international markets. The smaller agencies seek partnerships principally because of the squeeze placed on them by the size of their clients, on one hand, and the size of the international media groups, on the other.

The concentration of advertiser strength and the development of large media groups are together forcing many small- and medium-sized advertising agencies to internationalize by seeking competitive alliances abroad. Other factors are also important in opening up international markets to advertising agencies. Deregulation of the television industry in Europe indicates that further growth in advertising is expected. Liberalization tends to increase the size of the market rather than simply drawing advertising away from other media such as newspapers or magazines. Satellite television also contributes to the growth in the international advertising market. Advertisers have access through satellite television to new and wider markets. The market in Europe is, however, at different stages of maturity depending on country. The United Kingdom is still the largest market for advertising.

It will continue to be difficult to consolidate the European advertising industry for two reasons. Many of the advertising agencies sought as partners are private companies and therefore difficult to acquire through share purchases. Furthermore, mergers or cooperative alliances between advertising agencies are intrinsically difficult to establish and maintain. Manufacturers of industrial or consumer products combine to serve a common purpose: to sell a product. The advertising agency is a service business where success depends greatly on its next campaign. There is no product to hold potential partners together. The need is greater for a coalition of people and perceptions and how they work together. It is the human factor and the nature of the business which can cause disharmony and instability in such partnership relations. A further complicating factor is that joining with another agency to serve a particular market can easily fall into the trap of a conflict of interest among customer groups. Rarely will competitor clients agree to being served by the same agency. In such circumstances, the newly formed joint groups frequently lose valued customers.

Financial services in international markets

For financial services the ability to engage in international marketing of such services and the ability to establish a physical presence in foreign markets are important, as some financial services require establishment whereas others do not (Hoekman, 1992, p. 714).

Acquisitions and mergers in financial services have increased quite dramatically in recent years. The purpose of these acquisitions and mergers appears to be a broadening of the product range and market expansion. Financial institutions are able, through mergers and acquisitions, to offer quickly their customers an international network based on a wider range of services and at the same time to reduce costs of operation.

Scale economies are not a key determinant of acquisitions in financial services as labour and interest expenses represent the most important costs of operation. Nevertheless, the EU is attempting to liberalize the financial services market. Mergers and acquisitions, however, are not the easiest way of obtaining the benefits of integration of large financial markets such as the EU. Friendly competitive alliances involving cross-selling of selected products or joint ventures could be an attractive alternative.

Many financial services are based on information and such services can be produced in one part of the world and delivered through electronic channels for consumption elsewhere. According to Lovelock and Yip (1996, p. 83) information technology is emerging as a key globalization driver for such services; in mutual funds, for example, offers can be pieced together from elements created in many different countries and, unlike physical goods, the logistics of service assembly and delivery tend to be much simpler once the necessary infrastructure and network are in place.

Internationalizing accountancy services

Accountancy firms are also going through a dramatic period of change for similar and different reasons. The growth of individual firms among the 'Big Six' accountancy firms has led to much comment. Two firms in the Big Six have very strong positions in Continental Europe: KPMG and Coopers & Lybrand. The merger between Ernst & Whinney and Arthur Young made the new firm dominant in the US market but only the third largest in the world. Price Waterhouse has a strong base in the United Kingdom and the United States but very little representation elsewhere in Europe. Since audits change very infrequently among companies, success by Price Waterhouse in attracting such firms as Befec in 1990, formerly part of the BDO Binder Group, complete with its own client bases, is a key way of building market position in the core accountancy business in Europe.

Constraints on the growth of the international service firm

International service industries are fragmented. There are low entry barriers to service businesses as manifested by the many small firms sharing each market. There are few scale economies in many services owing to the relatively simple process involved, e.g. warehousing, or the inherently high labour content, e.g. personal care. In service businesses there are frequently high transportation costs since services are usually produced at the customer's premises or the customer must visit the provider; because inventory is impossible, service businesses must usually be frequented. The problem is exacerbated for services with fluctuating demand. Firms with large-scale facilities have no advantage.

In many instances diseconomies of scale exist in service businesses. Small firms are more efficient where personal service is the key to the business. Individualized, responsive service declines with size after reaching a threshold, e.g. beauty care and management consulting.

Market needs with regard to services are diverse. Buyer tastes for many services are fragmented. This fragmentation arises because of local and regional differences in market needs. There is considerable need for customized products and services, e.g. most fire engines sold are unique. The problem with fragmentation in the marketing of services is that an industry in which no firm has a significant market share means that no firm can strongly influence the industry outcome. There is also considerable indeterminancy in the industry since there are no market leaders with the power to shape industry events.

It is the accessibility of the service that counts. A service may be intangible but the resources, human and equipment, influencing its accessibility transform the service into a concrete offering. A number of simple illustrations, as follows, demonstrate how accessibility is evaluated by customers, which varies by country, in comparison with competing offerings:

- location of a bank and its interior;
- means of transportation and their condition;
- exterior of a restaurant and the waiters.

Stressing accessibility isolates direct distribution as just one way of reaching customers:

- insurance vending machines;
- hotel and restaurant franchising.

As with all aspects of marketing it is necessary for the service firm to research the market, to identify its target customers very carefully and to aim its products and services at customer needs. People are very important in service marketing. The administration of human resources is a key way of competing. Most people in a service firm act in a selling capacity; all are engaged in the personal market communication effort of the firm. In such circumstances marketing training, especially in the areas of communications and selling, is essential for success. As all people in the service firm are engaged in marketing tasks, the firm must recognize the internal marketing task of service firms. The service must be successfully marketed to the people in the firm itself. This helps to avoid the possibility that the service might fail in its ultimate target markets. The staff are simultaneously the producers and sellers of the service.

Summary

The unique status of marketing in services offers rich potential for creative new approaches and analysis. Interest in service marketing has reached a considerable height.

Unless service marketing is perceived by managers to be at least as important as product marketing, however, opportunities in the international market place will continue to be lost. The key characteristics of services are as follows:

- intangibility;
- direct contact between supplier and customer;
- customer participates in the production of the service;
- production and consumption occur simultaneously.

The problems in service marketing which frequently arise are due to the following:

- physical display is impossible;
- patent protection is impossible;
- demonstration gives the service away;
- provision of warranties is difficult;
- packaging is marginal.

In recent years there has been a very considerable growth in the international marketing of services. Many of the motives for international product marketing can be found in services marketing. Most of the growth which has occurred in international services has been concentrated in a few key sectors such as advertising, accounting and financial services.

Discussion questions

1. A service has been described as any activity or benefit which a supplier offers a customer, which is usually intangible and does not result in the ownership of anything. Discuss.
2. The growth in services internationally has been attributed to changing life styles and a changing world. Do you agree ?
3. Why are services more important to the economies of some countries than to others? How reliable are statistics on services in different countries?
4. The problems and approaches to marketing of products and services are similar and there is no need to develop a separate treatment of services. Discuss.
5. For the firm in international markets is there any classification framework for its activities which is more appropriate than others?
6. What market entry options does the services firm have if it wishes to internationalize?
7. There are fewer barriers to international services marketing than to international product marketing. Do you agree?
8. Discuss the recent trends in the internationalization of firms in advertising and financial services businesses.
9. How useful can information technology be in removing constraints on the growth of the international services firm?

References

Berry, L. L. (1980) 'Service marketing is different', *Business*, May–June, 24–8.

Bradley, F. (1990) *Trade in Health Services in Developing Countries: A Discussion Document*, Technical Cooperation Programme, Department of Marketing, University College Dublin, December, 24 pp.

Carman, J. and Langeard, E. (1979) 'Growth strategies for the service firm', *Eighth Annual Meeting of the European Academy for Advanced Research in Marketing*, Groningen, The Netherlands, 10–12 April.

Chase, R. B. (1978) 'Where does the customer fit in a service operation', *Harvard Business Review*, **56** (6), 137–42.

Clark, T., Rajaratnam, D. and Smith, T. (1996) 'Towards a theory of international services: marketing intangibles in a world of nations', *Journal of International Marketing*, **4** (2), 9–28.

Cowell, D. W. (1984) *The Marketing of Services*, London: Heinemann.

Feketekuty, G. (1988) *International Trade in Services: An overview and blueprint for negotiations*, Cambridge, MA: Ballinger Publications.

Glynn, W. J. (1994) 'Services marketing and the concept of exchange', *Working Paper No 94-1*, Centre for Quality and Services Management, University College Dublin.

Grönroos, C. (1987) 'Developing the service offering – a source of competitive advantage', *Working Paper 161*, Swedish School of Economics and Business Administration, Helsinki, Finland.

Hoekman, B. (1992) 'Market access through multilateral agreement: from goods to services', *World Economy*, **15** (1), 707–27.

Levitt, T. (1972) 'Production-line approach to services', *Harvard Business Review*, **50** (September–October), 41–52.

Lovelock, C. H. (1983) 'Classifying services to gain strategic marketing insights', *Journal of Marketing*, **47**, 9–20.

Lovelock, C. H and Yip, G. S. (1996), 'Developing global strategies for service businesses', *California Management Review*, **38** (2), 64–86.

Mathe, H. and Perras, C. (1994) 'Successful global strategies for service companies', *Long Range Planning*, **27** (1), 36–49.

Miles, I. (1993) 'Services in the new industrial economy', *Futures*, (July–August), 653–72.

Nicoulaud, B. (1989), 'Problems and strategies in the international marketing of services', *European Journal of Marketing*, **23** (6), 55–66.

Normann, R. (1984) *Service Management*, Chichester: Wiley.

Patterson, P. G. and Cicic, M. (1995), 'A typology of services firms in international markets: an empirical investigation', *Journal of International Marketing*, **3** (4), 57–83.

Sampson, G. and Snape, R. (1985) 'Identifying the issues in trade in services', *The World Economy*, **8**, 171–81.

Schneider, B., Schoenberger White, S. and Paul, M. C. (1997): 'Relationship marketing in an organizational perspective', in T. A. Swartz, D. E. Bowen, and D. Iacobucci (eds) *Advances in Services Marketing and Management*, London: JAI Press, **6**, 1–22.

Schoel, W. F. and Ivy, J. J. (1981) *Marketing: Contemporary Concepts and Practices*, Boston, MA: Allyn and Bacon.

Shostack, G. L. (1977) 'Breaking free from product marketing', *Journal of Marketing*, (April), 73–80.

Staltson, H. (1985) 'US trade policy and international services transactions' in R. P. Inman (ed.), *Managing the Service Economy*, Cambridge: Cambridge University Press.

Stern, R. M. and Hoekman, B. M. (1987) 'Issues and data needs for GATT negotiations on services', *World Economy*, **10** (1), 39–59.

Swartz, T. A., Bowen, D. E. and Brown, S. W. (1992) 'Fifteen years after breaking free: services then, now and beyond', in T. A. Swartz, D. E. Bowen and S. W. Brown (eds), *Advances in Services Marketing and Management: Research and Practice*, Vol. 1, Greenwich CT: JAI Press.

Thomas, D. R. E. (1978) 'Strategy is different in service business', *Harvard Business Review*, **56** (July–August), 158–65.

Uhl, K. P. and Upah, G. D. (1983) 'The marketing of services: why and how it is different', *Research in Marketing*, **6**, 231–57.

Vandermerwe, S. and Chadwick, M. (1989) 'The internationalisation of services', *Services Industries Journal*, **9** (1), 79–93.

Whitelock, J., Woodruffe, H. R. and Khalidi, F. A. (1993) 'A study of advertising agencies in the international environment: motivation and internationalisation', in L. Moutinho, R. Whipp, E. Ogbonna and R. Morgan (eds), *Proceedings, Managing Innovation in Services Conference*, Cardiff Business School, University of Wales, Cardiff, UK, 5–7 April.

Wilson, A. (1972) *The Marketing of Professional Services*, New York, NY: McGraw-Hill.

Winter, E. L. (1970) 'How to license a service', *Columbia Journal of World Business*, **5** (September–October), 83–5.

18
International distribution channels

Although recognized as a subject of study in its own right it is important for the firm to avoid functional myopia by integrating decisions on distribution and channels with other key management decisions. Access to international markets is the key decision area facing companies in the new millennium. Companies which have invested heavily in developing new products and processes will need to seek international markets in which to exploit these developments. Accelerating product life cycles and increasing capital requirements for research and development in many product areas require rapid international market entry to numerous markets. The ability to maximize the number of markets successfully entered requires the international firm to have access to a highly developed distribution system characterized by coordination between marketing and production.

Nature of international channels of distribution

Definitions of business using the traditional product-market concept ignore the levels of business at which the firm should operate. Donnelly Mirrors, a manufacturer of prismatic rear view mirrors for road vehicles, and supplier to many well-known models, integrated forwards to enter the French market for prismatic mirrors for cars. Other companies, Cannon, Rank Xerox and IBM, for example, have established retail shops to reach small business customers. There is a trade-off between the increased control and the return gained from vertical integration in international distribution channels compared with the increased risk and loss of flexibility associated with the investment involved in the integrated system.

International distribution channels are changing rapidly as is the role of the various intermediaries in the channel. There is now a greater emphasis on direct distribution from point of manufacture to point of use or consumption. Border transit documents and procedures have been simplified and other controls have virtually been eliminated, all of which affects the strategies of international marketing companies. The strategic options for the company include a combination of consolidation of manufacturing, use of centralized distribution centres, just-in-time delivery and the creation of non-traditional distribution channels. The behaviour of marketing channels and intermediaries must also be considered. Within channels of distribution participants or intermediaries use various forms of influencing strategy and sometimes conflict between partners arises. Channels are also characterized by communications and information exchange, commitment and trust. Each of these factors contributes to the success of the international marketing channels and must be considered.

There are four important roles for international marketing intermediaries:

- they coordinate or assemble demand by buyers and product availability of sellers to achieve economies of scale or scope and they reduce bargaining asymmetry between buyers and sellers in different countries;
- they protect buyers and sellers from the opportunistic behaviour of other participants in a market by becoming an agent of trust which is essential in a cross-cultural context;
- they facilitate the market by reducing operating costs;
- they match buyers and sellers.

With regard to the first point, the intermediary aggregates the demand of many customers or the products of many suppliers and so avoids the situation where each customer would have to negotiate individually with a corresponding supplier. The potential benefits include a reduction of transactions costs, achieving the advantages of scale economies and reducing asymmetries in the bargaining power of customers and suppliers located in different countries. On the second point, intermediaries may be able to prevent parties to a market exchange or relationship from behaving opportunistically. Because of their experience in the market, intermediaries have significant incentives to ensure that market exchanges are completed and that both the supplier and the customer comply with their agreement.

With regard to facilitation information, exchange between companies is expensive especially if it involves implicit contextual knowledge that cannot easily be explicated. In these instances, the intermediary can facilitate the exchange of information by coordinating the process and translating the information that moves between supplies and customer. This is a particularly important function in international marketing where cultural, language and different business practices intervene. Because of the differences in a number of companies and customers, intermediaries can also reduce the overall processing and coordination costs.

Finally, the need of customers to locate an appropriate supplier and for suppliers to locate appropriate customers can be accommodated by an intermediary that becomes the focal point of this match. Intermediaries can provide a better price discovery mechanism and acquire better knowledge of the market demand and supply characteristics that individual customers and suppliers like.

Establishing channel relationships

The management of international channels of distribution refers to the myriad relationships which arise in the transfer of products and services from a provider located in one country to a customer located in another. Marketing channels have been defined as 'sets of interdependent organizations involved in the process of making a product or service available for use or consumption' (Stern and El-Ansary, 1988). There are many alternative channels for the firm in international markets to choose from (Kahler, 1983) and many decision areas which need to be managed (Figure 18.1).

One of the more important differences between establishing a domestic or international system is the complexity of the variables involved (Slater, 1978, p. 243). In attempting to manage these issues the firm frequently finds that it must service each foreign market with a different distribution system. Thus, the key success factors which promote profitability in one market may not be transferable to another. Distribution networks in different countries may, however, have much in common so that planning should be based on observed similarities rather than differences (Goldstucker, 1968). Goldstucker argues that the distribution strategy should be modified to suit the country rather than attempting to change it completely. He further argues that culture also exerts an indirect influence on the costs of distribution through its direct effect on the marketing programme, an argument supported by Kale and McIntyre (1991, pp. 43–4), who suggest that national cultures have a systematic impact on behavioural relationships within a distribution channel.

Much of the literature on international channels of distribution seems to focus on the exporter or supplier, an emphasis which may be misplaced. Intermediaries, importers or distributors are frequently considered as silent partners in the international marketing process. They are sometimes treated as passive recipients of what the exporter has to offer and cast in the role of providers of intermediary services. This is a very one-sided view of a two-sided exchange and potential long-term relationship. The initiative is often taken by importers who choose exporters and exporting countries, rigidly specifying all export marketing functions in the import country and even entering into joint ventures with exporters (Liang and Parkhe, 1997, p. 520). In a study of trade between Greece and Britain, it was the British importers, not the Greek exporters, who decided the product

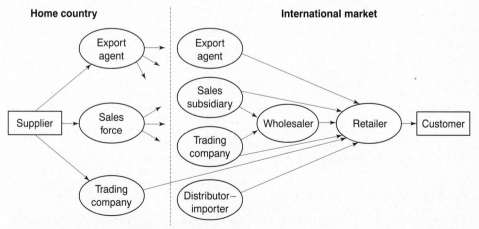

Figure 18.1 International marketing channels

mix, the selling price, the sales force, the organization, promotional efforts and inventory levels (Katsikeas and Piercy, 1992). Importers play a much stronger role than is often acknowledged.

Because of the greater complexity and uncertainty in international marketing and the associated higher search costs and the difficulty of choosing from a wide range of suppliers, importers may choose exporters not on the basis of rational choice but, rather, on the basis of solving a problem in which global sourcing becomes a sequential search process (Liang and Parkhe, 1997, p. 521).

Channel interactive management

By examining channel interactions, Frazier (1983) characterizes channel behaviour as occurring in three interactive processes: the initiation process, the implementation process and the review process (Figure 18.2). The initiation process focuses on the reasons why and the methods by which firms establish channel relationships with other firms. Key aspects of this relationship include the need and motive for exchanges, perceptions of deserved rewards, a search for a prospective partner and negotiations (Frazier, 1983). Frazier lists a number of reasons that start the initiation process, replacing an unsatisfactory distributor and adding a new distributor for a market being the two more important.

The implementation process refers to the way in which independent firms manage and coordinate continuing channel relationships. It starts with the exchange of products, services and information in particular. Other aspects of the implementation phase deal with the interaction itself: role performance for the manufacturer and distributor; the need for influence; the choice of influence strategies.

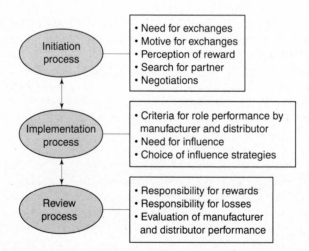

Figure 18.2 Interactive processes in channel behaviour
Source: adapted from Frazier, G. L. (1983) 'Interorganisational exchanges behaviour in marketing channels', *Journal of Marketing*, Fall, 68–78.

The review process examines the rewards and losses achieved by each firm in the relationship. The important aspect of such evaluation is the attribution of responsibility for the rewards and losses and a detailed evaluation of managerial performance on both sides.

Supplier–intermediary commitment

Commitment and trust are related in international marketing channels. Commitment, defined as 'an exchange partner believing that an on-going relationship with another is so important as to warrant maximum effort at maintaining it, that is, the committed party believes the relationship is worth working on to ensure that it endures indefinitely' (Morgan and Hunt, 1994, p. 23), is believed to be essential to effective marketing channel relationships. Commitment also appears to be enhanced by dependence on a relationship (Andaleeb, 1995) where dependence is defined as the degree to which a firm needs the resources of a partner firm to achieve its goals.

Trust is also an essential ingredient in effective channel relationships and one that gives rise to special problems in international marketing. Trust has been defined as 'existing when one party has confidence in an exchange partner's reliability and integrity' (Morgan and Hunt, 1994, p. 23). Trust, like commitment, is believed to be positively affected by dependence (Kumar et al., 1995), which suggests that the more dependent a partner is on a relationship, the more trust is developed. Trust may be built on shared values regarding the business system in which the partners operate. Trust is developed through interpersonal relationships and is directly related to cooperation. Morgan and Hunt (1994) report that cooperation is a positive function of trust.

Types of channel commitment

Commitment to a channel partner has been defined as a channel member's intention to continue the relationship (Anderson and Weitz, 1989). Several different kinds of motivation underlie this intention, the most common being affective commitment and calculative commitment (Geyskens et al., 1996, p. 304). Affective commitment refers to an underlying motive to maintain a channel relationship because of a high regard for and attachment to the company. In this situation, channel members desire to continue the relationship because they like the partner and enjoy the partnership. A sense of loyalty and trust has been established between the two.

In contrast, calculative commitment is the extent to which channel members perceive the need to maintain the relationship given the significant expected switching costs associated with severing the partnership. It results from a cold calculation of costs and benefits.

In their research, Geyskens et al. (1996, p. 315) discover that, given their choice between developing closeness through affective or calculative commitment, the company should strongly cultivate the former. Building trust should be of greater importance than altering the dependence structure through changing costs or benefits. Working to develop trust pays handsome dividends. Dependence imbalances that would exist, for example between a well-endowed intermediary and a small supplier, are of relatively minor importance if trust can be developed.

In international distribution, communication and information exchange between part-ners promote good interfirm relationships and reduces sources of conflict. Information exchange between partners may be divided into three categories: initiating behaviour, signalling behaviour and disclosing behaviour (Leuthesser and Kohli, 1995). Initiating behaviour involves effort to understand better the partner's needs and to help the partner to add more value in the business system. Signalling behaviour refers to the provision of advance information to the partner about changes in marketing plans for the country, product design or packaging, for example. Disclosing behaviour refers to the extent to which a partner is perceived to reveal sensitive information. Communication and infor-mation exchange have a positive influence on cooperation in the channel (Metcalf *et al.*, 1990) and communication also affects commitment to the relationship where commit-ment is defined as a 'desire to develop a stable relationship, a willingness to make short term sacrifices to maintain the relationship, and a confidence in the stability of the relationship' (Anderson and Weitz, 1992, p. 19).

Marketing channel design

In designing a marketing channel the firm operates on a number of basic criteria which apply in many circumstances. First, the choice of intermediary for manufacturers and the choice of supplier for middlemen is frequently very restricted owing to the nature of the business and the size and geographical distribution of customers. To achieve sales volume and scale effects a new manufacturer would probably have to compete for private label business in most marketing situations. Similarly, wholesalers and retailers may find them-selves cut off from suppliers because of marketing policies to bypass such institutions.

Second, the number, size and geographical concentration of customers have a direct effect on the design of the marketing channel. For industrial products, customers are likely to be few, large and geographically concentrated. Hence, a direct channel design might be appropriate. Microsoft's European distribution centre in Dublin provides warehousing and distribution services for its European customers and removes the need to carry inventory in each country. According to Bernard Vergnes, president of Microsoft Europe,

> Microsoft is a software company, not a distributor and if we are to continue to be successful we must focus on this. In the past five years we have seen Europe move towards being a single market with more companies wanting to do business at a pan-European level.

For consumer products with a diffuse market the opposite may be the case. A cumbersome distribution task calls for the use of intermediaries.

Third, perishable products require direct marketing or the use of intermediaries who can ensure rapid merchandise turnover and protected delivery. Manufacturers and pro-ducers of bulky products normally attempt to minimize shipping distance and handling costs, which also implies a direct selling approach. Non-standard products calling for technical expertise in selling require direct selling to allow for specialized attention by or on behalf of the manufacturing company. In contrast, non-perishable, non-bulky, standardized products indicate the use of indirect channels of distribution. Fourth, the characteristics of the environment facing intermediaries, competitors and the firm itself also influence channel design. Having assessed the constraints implied by these four criteria the firm must make two decisions, as follows:

- determine the way in which products and services will be made available to designated user markets;
- determine the number of intermediaries or suppliers the firm in the channel wishes to work with.

Needs of channel members

Manufacturers and intermediaries in international channels have very different perspectives. It is necessary to achieve a subtle blending of the needs and objectives of all parties in the system: manufacturer, intermediary and consumer. These perspectives are manifested in the criteria that each uses to select the other (Figure 18.3).

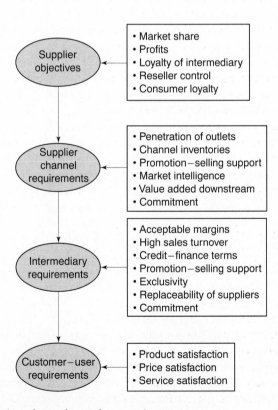

Figure 18.3 Balancing channel member requirements

The factors important to the manufacturer in selecting intermediaries usually involve final consumer considerations, company strategic issues and financial returns. The manufacturer usually evaluates potential channel partners on the basis of their contacts and relationships with customers in target markets and their capabilities, reputation and past performance in respect of sales and service. The manufacturer normally checks that the functions provided by the intermediary complement those provided by the manufacturer. In this regard the manufacturer also evaluates the potential contribution of the product or service to the intermediary's needs; profit; contribution; and gaps in product line. Here the manufacturer is attempting to determine the probability of effective long-term working relations. Finally, it is necessary to examine the potential intermediary's financial status and management ability.

Factors important to intermediaries in establishing relationships with manufacturers usually involve the manufacturer's product and/or brand image, the support and assistance provided and the compatibility of the product with the intermediary's existing line. The intermediary is also concerned with the trade reputation of the manufacturer and the potential profit contribution of the product to the intermediary. Sometimes it is difficult for a manufacturer to break into a distribution system for reasons known only to the intermediary. The manufacturer will be concerned with the expected reaction of channel members to the attempted entry by the manufacturer to the channel system. Lastly, intermediaries examine the estimated investment costs closely in adding the new product to the existing business.

A thorough review of the literature has identified one dominant factor which is essential to suppliers and one factor which is essential to intermediaries. For suppliers, it is value added in the downstream channel and, for intermediaries, it is supplier replaceability (Kim and Frazier, 1996, p. 21). From the suppliers' point of view, the extent of value added in the downstream channel is the most crucial for the existence of a channel system and the achievement of channel goals. For intermediaries, the extent to which suppliers are easily replaceable with other alternative suppliers is the most important.

Value added in the downstream channel is the contribution which intermediaries make to completed exchanges with end-customers (Kim and Frazier, 1996, p. 21). Value-added activities include basic economic values such as the reduction of transaction costs, but they also include social values, such as mutual support and trust. Members of Japanese channels of distribution consider social as well as economic factors in developing and managing channel relationships. When the value added in downstream activities is high, suppliers take a greater interest in enhancing cooperation and coordination with channel partners. When value added is low, suppliers are less likely to be worried about relationships with intermediaries.

Replaceability of suppliers refers to the ease with which suppliers can be changed. Supplier replaceability reflects the general value of supplier relationships to intermediaries. When suppliers are easy to replace, intermediaries are unlikely to commit strongly to them. When suppliers are difficult to replace, for whatever reason, intermediaries are likely to be more concerned about their relationship with them (Heide and John, 1988). Suppliers may be difficult to replace because of social concerns, loyalty and reputation factors experienced by intermediaries (Czinkota and Woronoff, 1986).

Structure and function in channels of distribution

Distribution channels vary enormously from one country to another on a number of dimensions. Traditions, culture, customs and legal requirements influence both the structure of distribution channels and the functions performed in the system. There are, however, a number of things usually common to all channels, irrespective of product category or market. Actors in the channel usually include manufacturers, distributors and wholesalers, retailers and consumers. The nature of the activities and their direction are also usually constant (Figure 18.4). The activities specified in the right-hand side of this diagram are found in all channels of distribution.

Distribution channel structure

In this section the structure of distribution channels in the United States for rattan furniture is examined as an example of a distribution channel. Furniture made from rattan includes chairs, tables and occasional pieces, sold in the casual furniture market. The selection of import channels is greatly influenced by the specifications of the product offered (component or finished product) and the target market segment (upper or lower) (Figure 18.5). The principal import channels which supply components and semifinished furniture to the middle and upper market segments are manufacturers and specialized importers. Distributors and retailers supply the lower segment. Department stores and buying groups are less significant.

There are a number of features of distribution channels that the firm must consider. From the example examined above it is clear that the product influences the choice, as does the kind of market. Smaller European markets for specialized products are very

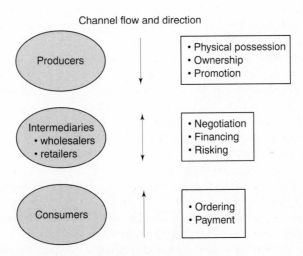

Figure 18.4 Marketing flows in distribution channels

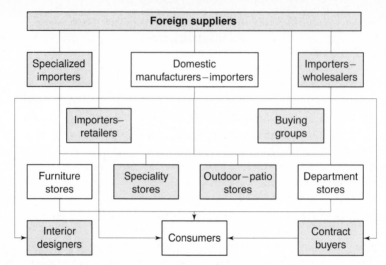

Figure 18.5 Distribution channels in the US for rattan furniture
Source: International Trade Centre (UNCTAD/GATT) (1985) *Monograph on Trade Channels: Rattan Furniture in the United States of America,* Geneva.

different from the large US market. Similarly, the role played by the various types of importer is a key consideration.

The role of the specialized importer in the distribution of rattan furniture in the United States is very important. Because of the physical size of the country, transportation costs are high. The specialized importer exploits the large volume of business and holds large inventories, which allows it to compete successfully. The specialized importer in the United States generally supplies the middle and more exclusive segments of the market: finished furniture of high quality. Specialized importers, because of their knowledge of the market, frequently influence new product development and design. They often seek exclusive arrangements with the foreign firm.

Some major manufacturers also import a complementary range of products to supplement their own product range. A number of US furniture manufacturers import unfinished rattan components for assembly, finishing and upholstering. Firms in this category dominate the upper market segment for rattan furniture.

Manufacturers who import pose a potential threat to the foreign supplier. There is a distinct possibility that future growth could be limited owing to the possible conflict of interests between competing products manufactured by the importing manufacturer and those manufactured by the foreign supplier.

Many different types of retailers import directly. The principal types are department stores, specialized retailers, mail order houses and catalogue firms. Department stores are interested primarily in volume business because of the size of their own market and the financial terms involved. For many consumer products department stores have recently become active importers in their own right. Many large department stores maintain sophisticated buying departments and are constantly looking for attractive merchandise for their customers. These outlets plan their purchasing requirements up to one year in advance of seasons and make early commitments for their requirements. Quality of merchandise and adherence to delivery dates are key factors when supplying to this type of foreign customer.

Effectiveness of international distribution channels

In deciding a distribution strategy for international markets or in assessing existing channels the firm must consider the cost of the alternative chosen, the barriers to entry in the market, the orientation of intermediaries, the ability of the channel to distribute the range of the firm's products and the characteristics of the product or service and the customer.

One very effective framework to analyse this situation is based on the Five Cs: coverage, character, continuity, control and cost (Cateora, 1993). This framework allows the firm to establish its strategic goals with respect to channel management (Table 18.1).

Considerations of market coverage usually refer to the firm's objectives regarding market penetration and market share or merely sales. The firm attempts to find that channel which is optimal in terms of sales and the ability of the channel to service the product or product line.

In most cases the firm is intimately interested in the character or suitability of the channel for its particular product or product line. Occasionally this becomes an issue of whether the intermediary fits the overall positioning strategy for the product. Here concern lies in determining the suitability of the channel in the overall market positioning of the product. The character of the channel addresses the broader aspects of managing the channel.

Distributors frequently change their loyalties depending on the returns they receive. The contribution the intermediary receives is the principal determinant of the continuity

---

Table 18.1 Analysing channels of distribution: the Five C's framework

Coverage	Ability of channel to reach targeted customers to achieve market share and growth objectives
Character	Compatibility of channel with the firm's desired product positioning
Continuity	Loyalty of channel to the firm
Control	Ability of the firm to control total marketing programme for the product or service
Cost	Investment required to establish and maintain the channel – variable associated with sales level. Fixed costs required to manage the channel: inventories, facilities, training of salesforce

Source: Cateora, P. (1993) *International Marketing*, 8th edn, Homewood, IL: Irwin.

of the channel. Small-scale exporters frequently complain of the lack of continuity in international channels.

Generally, control diminishes with the length of the channel. Control may be increased by investing in control systems which send information back to the firm; it is usually proportional to the capital intensity in the channel. Longer distribution channels which are frequently found in developing country markets are typically weak with regard to control. Generally, the more different and distant is the foreign market entered the less likely that the firm will invest in company-owned sales operations and other assets likely to give greater control of the operations (Gronhaug and Kvitastein, 1991).

The firm tries to reduce or optimize the effect of cost. Here the firm is concerned with the capital cost, which refers to the expenditure by the firm on salesforce training, the investment in safety stocks and the initial marketing and distribution costs. These costs are generally fixed or at least periodic. The firm is also concerned with the cost or investment required to develop and maintain the distribution channels. Firms aim to minimize these costs, which are usually variable and associated with the level of sales.

Complicated channel systems which are long and involve margins at each stage are sometimes considered as barriers to entry to the market in question. In other situations multitiered distribution systems which have evolved over many generations make it very difficult for the international firm to penetrate. Sometimes foreign governments claim that such distribution structures prevent trade and are, therefore, a barrier to international competition. Sometimes it is a question of understanding the origins of the system. For many US firms, for example, the Japanese distribution system is archaic but is now beginning to be understood. When the Taiwanese company Acer Computers decided to enter the Russian market it first considered assembling in Russia and selling locally but decided instead to assemble in Finland and use Russian intermediaries who imported the completed product into Russia (Exhibit 18.1).

Exhibit 18.1

Laptops from Lapland

When Acer Computers, a Taiwanese firm, decided in 1995 that it needed to 'localise' assembly of its computers for a growing Russian market, it was Lappeenranta, Finland, rather than Russia, to which it turned. Acer believed that it could do even better in Russia if it assembled computers locally, instead of shipping them in from distant plants.

Finland, with its law-abiding business environment and highly developed infrastructure offered a vision of everything Russia was not. Valuable goods that went into airport cargo terminals also came out again. Public utilities worked. The law of contract counted for something. Acer struck up a partnership with Wilson Finland, a subsidiary of a Swedish-owned international freight firm, which was a big carrier of goods between Finland and Russia and stood to benefit from the business Acer would create.

The key to Acer's strategy was a plan to sell its computers to Russian distributors 'at the factory gate' in Finland. Across the border within Russia, Acer's Moscow office would be on hand with support and advice. But it was for the distributors to arrange import procedures, and to cope with customs formalities and border taxes on the computers to which they held title. This division of labour allowed Acer to reconcile the contradictory imperatives confronting it in Russia. So Acer let its distributors worry about the routes and wheezes for clearing customs. In a quite literal sense, these would be none of Acer's business.

Such were the considerations that encouraged Acer to opt for Finland. And such is Finland, everything went according to plan. The first computers emerged from Lappeenranta at the start of 1996, and they were brought into Russia by the half-dozen main distributors with which Acer had established close ties. The decision to assemble in Finland, as a low-risk route to expanding Russian sales, still offers a model of its kind. It recognises that Russia, for the next couple of years at least, is not a market like any other, but a place in which many things are simply too dangerous or difficult for all but the most massive and ironclad of foreign firms to attempt.

Source: adapted from *Economist*, 6 September 1997, pp. 71–2.

Using representatives – agents or distributors

Companies may appoint agents or distributors in the foreign market who serve as the local representative for the company. The success and reputation of the company abroad depend to a great extent on the calibre of the agent or distributor selected. It is important that every care is taken in making the choice and in defining the relationship between the company and the representative to avoid future disputes and confusion of tasks. There are important differences between agents and distributors which must be considered.

The agent abroad is an independent contractor who knows the market, acquires orders and carries out other tasks, making the agent in effect the company's salesperson in the foreign market. The agent introduces the company into direct contact with customers to whom the company supplies the product, raises the invoice and is the person from whom the company collects the price of the goods sold. It is the company and not the agent which sets the prices and if the customer does not pay it is not possible to sue the agent. If the company fails to deliver or commits any other breach of the sales contract the customer may sue the company, not the agent. Once the goods are sold the agent is entitled to a commission of anything between 2 and 15 per cent depending on the nature of the product and nature of the service provided. Many payments arrangements are found in practice; the most common is, perhaps, a commission on orders received plus fee where the fee is paid to motivate and compensate for any extra effort required, as found for example, in launching a new product in the market. An agent typically does not need more than a good communications system to operate successfully. The agent, however, must be extremely knowledgeable about trends in the market. Apart from getting paid the agent has no other financial interest in the sale. It is the company's responsibility to deliver the goods on time according to the agreed specifications and to collect payment from the customer. The company usually seeks the following essential characteristics when appointing an agent:

- the agent is a foreign-based sales representative, a key member of the company's team but not an employee;
- the agent's skill derives from market knowledge, business contacts, experience of working in the market;
- the agent neither sees nor handles the goods and acts as a salesperson only while the company ships directly to the customer;
- the agent is not involved in promotion and does not invest capital in stock apart from showroom samples.

A distributor on the other hand is the company's customer who does not take a commission on sales but buys and imports the goods, stores them and makes a profit by selling them on to a third party at a mark-up of up to 33 per cent, to a retailer, for example. A distributor typically has warehousing facilities, a sales and distribution network and an after-sales service capable of providing technical assistance if necessary. In many respects appointing a distributor is a much stronger arrangement for representation abroad and easier to make. The distributor buys the company's products, takes title to them and stocks them. The problem of finding customers and getting paid fall to the distributor. Appointing a distributor is most effective where there is large number of relatively small customers for the company's products. Using distributors is less suitable in more concentrated industrial markets where technical sales and servicing can only be provided by the company's qualified staff.

Because distributors face the cost of holding inventory and providing a salesforce, sole and exclusive distribution rights in a defined territory are usually expected. This, however, may not be legally possible under local or EU competition laws.

Appointing an agent or a distributor depends on the a nature of the product and the expected sales volume. Distributors provide a stronger presence in the market, a capability to keep product supplies available to customers and, because they take title to the goods, relieve the exporting company of the task of debt collecting from the ultimate customer. Usually distributors handle large volumes of fast-moving goods such as are sold in supermarkets or department stores. They also handle standard industrial items such as building materials, components, low-cost machinery and smaller items of equipment where the customer is relying on a ready supply in the market. Clothing, footwear and textiles and the more expensive customized items of capital equipment are more usually the business of agents. There are a number of things the company should consider when appointing an agent or a distributor:

- geographical area and market segments covered;
- range of products and companies already represented;
- retailers sold to and trade contacts used;
- size of salesforce and sales training available;
- distribution channels used;

- growth in business in recent years;
- experience in the application of systems in which the company's products are used;
- servicing and after-sales service;
- showroom, office suitability and storage facilities;
- financial standing of potential agent or distributor;
- period of appointment and notice for termination of agreement;
- form of commission.

Many of the above points are obvious but one, after-sales service, requires particular attention by both parties. In Chapter 10 the importance of after-sales service in international marketing was noted. Ultimately, after-sales service is delivered mostly through intermediaries so a firm's attempt to provide after-sales service can be foiled by uncooperative intermediaries (Asugman *et al.*, 1997, p. 25). These authors advise that the firm should select intermediaries so that it can effectively compel them to support its after-sales service. It may be possible at the recruitment stage to select intermediaries who understand the importance of after-sales service and are committed to serving customers. The international firm may also be in a position to reinforce and reward the intermediary's role in the successful delivery of after-sales service in the market.

Frequently situations arise where it is not clear whether the company's representative is acting as an agent or a distributor. In some cases a representative may be an agent in respect of some of the company's products and a distributor in respect of others. In such cases it is as well for the company to note that the legal relationship between it and its agents and distributors is a matter of contract. It arises from the actual nature of the relationship, agreements with them and the provisions of the appropriate law. It does not simply depend on the title conferred on them or used in practice. That title, however, may greatly affect the legal relationship with third parties who take it at face value without understanding the private arrangements between the company and the foreign market representative.

It is also of great importance that agents or distributors do not acquire the legal status of employees which can arise by implication of law unless the contract appointing them is clearly expressed. Contracts of whatever kind usually confer legal rights and responsibilities on each party and can come into being by and exchange of letters or a phone call or, as one expert in the business once noted, 'by an enthusiastic discussion over a business lunch'. It is usually advisable, therefore, in establishing representation in foreign markets to seek legal advice.

When the company has appointed an agent or a distributor it is important the company supports them in carrying out the tasks expected of them. There are many ways of doing this, among which the more important measures the company can take are:

- to provide an ample supply of catalogs, sales brochures and promotional materials written in the local language;
- to visit the agent or distributor regularly and to visit customers together;
- invite agents–distributors to company premises regularly;
- to ensure that the price structure provides a genuine financial incentive;
- to provide updates on products, markets and company developments.

Appointing and managing foreign market representation is a process, not an event. The agent or distributor, although independent, is part of the company's team. It is essential to monitor performance, to relate to the representatives and to seek ways of improving the economic circumstance of all parties concerned. It is essential that the company continually seeks ways of motivating the agent or distributor, otherwise the relationship will wither.

Performance of the marketing channel

There are a variety of ways of improving the performance of distributors. The basic ways of improving general business performance also apply to intermediaries who are profit motivated. As in other parts of business, distributor performance is improved by the prospects of greater profits, less capital investment, fewer user complaints, lower training costs and more repeat business.

Small distributors, like small retailers, may need assistance in accounting, financing and inventory control. Manufacturers who can provide such assistance, especially by way of computer software geared at re-ordering the manufacturer's products, can easily gain a strong competitive advantage in this sector.

The provision of various kinds of information to intermediaries can strengthen the position of the manufacturer. The firm usually tries to ensure the provision of regular information regarding the firm's products, margins, credit terms and advertising support available. Successful firms provide such information for specific intermediaries or groups of intermediaries on a regional basis.

As a matter of dealing with contingencies, successful firms pay immediate personal attention to distributor grievances in international markets. The R & A Bailey & Company Limited, manufacturers of Baileys Original Irish Cream, recognize that excessive delegation of such tasks is dangerous. For this reason the Dublin-based marketing sales executives travel immediately to all major customers on discovery of problems similar to those outlined here.

By monitoring the distributor's sales volume, customer base and market penetration, the firm can improve the performance of the international marketing channel. By making distributors accountable for operational and economic results, while providing them with the freedom to select the most efficient and effective local marketing actions, export productivity is enhanced (Bello and Gilliland, 1997, p. 34). Close monitoring is particularly important for firms that export a highly technical product, since they are exposed to the risk of opportunistic behaviour on the part of their intermediary. In such cases, exporters attempt to influence the process by which intermediaries sell their products. They do so in various ways to ensure that the correct technical benefits are emphasized and that only appropriate applications are allowed.

Integrated international distribution

The issue of deciding which activities should be performed by the firm itself and which should be performed by others outside the firm was discussed from the point of view of firm size and growth in Chapter 4. Here the same issue is discussed from the point of view of effective control and cost regarding the international channel. Internalizing international distribution within the firm gives rise to a trade-off between cost and control. Some firms, especially strong brand companies, insist on owning their international distributors where possible. This is the policy followed to ensure complete control of brand positioning in each international market. The choice of approach can be interpreted as a transactions costs problem (Ruekert *et al.*, 1985). The balance of control and cost evaluated in terms of transactions costs determines whether international distribution should take place through subsidiaries of the firm or through independent distributors.

In calculating the transactions costs the firm also examines many other factors. Transactions costs are closely linked to psychic distance of markets and experience already obtained in international markets (Klein and Roth, 1990, pp. 30–2). Integration offers the benefit of having a captive outlet in each international market entered. Such extensive control implies the commitment of many resources, which means that failure is thereby much more expensive. In contrast, the use of an independent distributor implies specialization and associated benefits. Ready-made access to markets means that learning costs are low and entry is quickly and effectively expedited.

As already mentioned, the value of independent distributors with regard to channel loyalty and control of the marketing programme is questionable. Benetton, an Italian knitwear manufacturer, believes in distributing its products through its own agents wherever possible. This has allowed the firm to standardize its promotions and distribution: inventories; type of outlet; shipment; types and sizes. Sometimes, success depends on combining two moves at the same time. Hiram Walker, a whisky firm, whose principal brand is Ballantine's, combined advertising and distribution decisions to achieve the desired effect. Success in the US market for the Ballantine brand depended on good advertising and the use of the best distributors available. In distributing its products in new markets the Guinness Group increasingly combines heavy advertising with the concept of the Irish Pub which it encourages local retailers to build from independently supplied kits. By ensuring access to the customer Guinness builds a strong franchise in new markets such as Asia for its well-known brand (Exhibit 18.2).

Firms are sometimes advised to use independent distributors if the market is competitive. Other influencing factors include the cost of monitoring the performance of the intermediary, the stage of the life cycle for the product and the degree of standardization applied to the marketing programme. Integration of services within the firm is more likely for US firms where the market entered is culturally similar, where the firm's product is innovative or highly differentiated, where the salesforce is specialized and where the firm wishes to control the marketing of its products closely (Anderson and Coughlan, 1987). In a study of 94 US overseas distributors these authors also found that the initial channel choice was very influential on all subsequent decisions.

Occasionally a firm may choose a dual strategy of distributing through its own distributors and through an independent company. This allows the market to be differentiated into two or more segments to be served differently. Problems sometimes arise if there is a delay in production or supply is limited for a period. In such circumstances integrated distributors tend to be favoured. The oil industry in the 1970s is an example of this situation: the major oil companies favoured their own outlets over independents when supplies were short.

Exhibit 18.2
Betting on the luck of the Irish

Delaney's and Gaelic Inns entered the Asian market with the help of an Irish 'kit' pub programme that is flogged in tandem by Guinness Brewing Worldwide and the Irish Pub Company (IPC), a Dublin-based design-and-build firm. Since IPC entered the region in 1995, it has set up 28 pubs and aims to have another 100 operating in Asia within the next three years. Most of the Irish pubs in Asia see a profit within 20 months, according to IPC officials.

Clayton Parker, managing director of Delaney's International, says that he believes Irish theme pubs are successful in Asia because they are a well-defined concept. Many English pubs in Asia try to offer something for everyone and have lost their style and identity, he says. Irish Pubs, however, thrive on their uniqueness. To maintain their uniqueness, pub owners serve up Irish food and music. They also import Irish staff. Delaney's, for instance, has a permanent Irish band based in Hong Kong to play at its pubs. Irish pub owners also say that their food is a big draw. Guinness pie, chaps and farls (meat pies, chips and thin, round cakes) are packing in lunch and dinner crowds from Tokyo to Bangkok. 'Fine dining is on the way out; people now want casual dining and entertainment. That's why the Hard Rock Café and Planet Hollywood do so well', says Parker.

Then there is something called 'craic' (pronounced crack), a Gaelic word that means atmosphere. In this case the atmosphere is formed when the Irish decor, music, food, drink and hospitality are thrown together, says Parker. From Muddy Murphy's in Singapore to the aptly-named O'Kim's in Seoul, pub owners credit 'craic' with being the secret to success. The secret ingredient certainly helps sell beer. And Guinness, the mother of all Irish brewers, knows this is the market to push 'craic', rustic pubs and whatever else will continue to boost already-soaring sales. Guinness Brewing Worldwide, part of Guinness PLC, lists the Asia-Pacific region as its second most profitable market. This region delivered the company £58 million in profit last year out of a worldwide total profit of £283 million.

There is no franchise fee involved. IPC takes its profit from the usual design and build fees. Guinness, which has poured about £2 million over the past 18 months into promoting the concept in Asia, collects profit purely from the increase in beverage sales. While Irish pubs have proved successful in the Asian market, operators say that in some cities, the bulk of their patrons are expatriate Westerners. But, as Guinness' figures attest, Asian consumers are acquiring a taste for Irish culture and drink, and pub owners say the make-up of their clientele is changing.

Source: adapted from *Asia Business*, July 1977, pp. 34–6.

International direct distribution

Four sets of factors influence the firm's decision regarding direct distribution: the resources of the firm; the characteristics of the product or service; the market segments served; the marketing programme developed by the firm.

With regard to the first factor, successful direct distribution presumes that the firm has sufficient resources available to support a direct marketing approach, e.g. establishment of a sales force. It is also necessary that the firm already possesses experience in the marketing of similar products to comparable market targets, i.e. that direct channels exist. There must also be sufficient time available to develop direct distribution before potential competition becomes a threat, e.g. patent protection.

Direct distribution is likely to be possible where the manufacturer's personnel are required to sell and service the product or service because of its complexity, e.g. computer sales and service.

Width of product line sufficient to support a direct marketing approach is another concern, e.g. Avon, Tupperware. In situations where product application assistance is required, direct distribution may be appropriate, e.g. cosmetics and skin care products. The Avon distribution system has been very successful in Asia but the company suffers from an old-fashioned image in its country of origin. The company's quaint human distribution system may return to fashion, however, as consumer values change in the US (Exhibit 18.3). Finally, when product technology is changing rapidly, direct distribution may be favoured, e.g. computer turnkey services.

The direct distribution decision is also influenced by the nature of the market segments served. Market segments with relatively few customers, where the unit purchase is large in terms of quantity or price and where customers are concentrated geographically, tend to favour direct distribution. There must also be a sufficient margin to support personal selling or frequent mail shots. Finally, when the purchase decision is a major long-term commitment by the buyer, direct distribution may be an attractive proposition.

The marketing programme developed by the firm influences the decision to distribute directly. It is favoured where personal selling is a major component in the marketing programme and where intermediary functions are not needed, e.g. storage, local credit inventory and packaging. Where these services can be efficiently provided by the manufacturer, direct distribution may also be favoured. In most distribution channels there is a series of direct distribution relationships which characterize the situation described.

Intermediaries and the internet

An electronic market is an interorganizational information system that allows participating buyers and sellers in some markets to exchange information about prices and offerings (Bailey and Bakos, 1997, p. 11). These authors conclude that, while some of the traditional roles of intermediaries may become less important as information technology facilitates communication between customers and suppliers, the need for intermediaries is not likely to be eliminated in the near future. Intermediaries in electronic markets are likely to assume important roles that will include aggregating information goods,

Exhibit 18.3

Scents and sensibility

Many companies have a different image at home and abroad. Few are as Janus-like as Avon. To would-be Avon ladies in Asia, Eastern Europe and Latin America, the brand is an exciting opportunity to cash in on an American icon. In the US and especially in the internet age, Avon's direct sales force of 445,000 seems distinctly passé. Many of its customers have full-time jobs and so are not at home to take the Avon Lady's call. Avon's customers are ageing, too: young cosmetics users seem to prefer hipper brands, such as Body Shop, L'Oréal and Estée Lauder, that they can find in stores. As a result of Avon's wrinkled image, the number of customers using its products has been flat in America and falling in Western Europe.

Developing countries might have been designed for Avon. First, the retailing infrastructure tends to be underdeveloped, and, apart from a very basic distribution network, Avon needs no infrastructure. Second, the products sold by local vendors tend to be of poor quality. Third, women in most developing countries are eager to work to supplement the family income: they call on three or four times as many clients as their Western counterparts. Can Avon tie its developing- and mature-market strategies together? Whereas most of the firm's products cater to local preferences (largely in skin tones and packaging), Avon now wants to focus on a number of global brands it can sell the world over. So far it has created six lines – including Far Away perfumes and Anew skin products.

By consolidating its brands, Avon has been able to improve quality and to reduce the number of suppliers, thereby cutting costs. This and other economies, such as uniform ingredients and packaging, mean that gross profit margins on Avon's global brands are up to four percentage points higher than those of its other lines. Also, just as global products such as 'No 5' have boosted Chanel's worldwide brand recognition, Avon is positioning its new brands to raise its profile around the world.

Moreover, there is just a chance that Avon's most obvious anachronism – its quaint human distribution system – might be coming back into fashion in developed markets. American women's incomes are increasing, but they have less time to spend it. They might shun the cosmetics counter and opt to buy direct from a salesperson who comes to them. Until they do, Avon will remain a company with two faces.

Source: adapted from *Economist*, 13 July 1996, pp. 57–8.

providing trust relationships and ensuring the integrity of the market, matching customers and suppliers and providing marketing information to suppliers (Bailey and Bakos, 1997, p. 18).

In consumer markets, characterized by a large number of products and infrequent purchases, the matching role of intermediaries is usually more important. Markets with fewer suppliers and customers and frequent purchases, such as the machine tools or car components markets, have less need for matching intermediaries. Intermediaries should also be able to provide information that allows suppliers to customize their products based on their marketing strategy and on the needs of their customers. The movement to electronic markets does not seem to result in the elimination of intermediaries, as electronic markets require intermediation services, albeit in ways that differ from traditional physical markets (Bailey and Bakos, 1997, p. 19).

The growing use of the internet is likely to have very significant implications for companies active in international marketing. The internet has demonstrated its power for building relationships in the physical world of goods and services. The emphasis on creating value in the business system receives a further endorsement from use of the internet. Suppliers and customers seek value in any exchange on the internet and the ability of the firm to provide value is emerging as a core marketing capability. Audiences are attracted to the internet by information that adds value in both form and substance, but the information must reach visitors to the web site in a time period commensurate with the perceived value of the information (Eighmey and McCord, 1998, p. 193). In the future, the internet may allow suppliers to concentrate on a very wide range of customer product experiences as customers interact with the company at different points in time and also interact with competitors. Competition may be driven, not only post-purchase value added but by the competition for first purchase through the provision of simulated experiences (Klein, 1998, p. 201).

The internet sets new standards for total relationship management in both breadth and depth (Cartellieri *et al.*, 1997, p. 58). For these authors, breadth means that the relationship will increasingly last for the entire ownership experience including the time before and after the purchase of the product or service, while depth refers to the degree of interaction with consumers at any given point in their experience of the product. The book retailer, amazon.com, for example, uses the information it gleans from customers to create value-added services such as suggestions about books that a particular reader might enjoy. The challenge for the international marketing company is to adapt to the new information and communication technologies and to cope with customers in different countries and cultures. The collaboration of many publishers with amazon.com to enable books to be sold on line and to reduce return rates has forced category killers like Borders and Barnes and Noble to enter the on-line arena (Bucklin *et al.*, 1997).

According to Kotha (1998, p. 220), there are several industry conditions, location and proximity to supplies being the more important, that may be the key for the successful pursuit of an on-line book retailing strategy – first mover advantages may be critical for the success of on-line retailing. Although contrary to the literature, Kotha's (1998) study of amazon.com suggests that for on-line markets, especially those who sell physical products and are intermediaries in the value chain, location can be a source of competitive advantage because of the need to acquire rapidly the product for distribution to the customer and the cost saving from not having to carry large inventories. This would certainly limit the potential of the internet in international markets. This author discovered that many of the mechanisms used by the company were outgrowths of in-house programming – i.e. amazon.com already possessed many of the skills needed. One of the most important was the ability to attract and hold human capital to do the job properly. According to Kotha (1998), Barnes and Noble's entry and that of others had no negative impact on amazon.com as brand names established in other media do not appear to transfer easily to the internet, at least for books.

The challenge of using the internet is magnified, therefore, when it is realized that so many competitors, and large ones, are already well established on the internet. The challenge is how to be noticed by browsers. The low barriers to entry to the internet are both an attraction and a limitation. Almost anybody can create a site on the internet, so everybody is difficult to find. This gives an advantage to the big brands, particularly among people in international markets as they begin to use the internet. These people tend to go first to the brand names familiar from the real world. Indeed, these brands are quite adept at promoting their web sites in the more traditional media.

Cooperation and conflict in international channels of distribution

Cooperation is an essential ingredient of distribution because of the multiplicity of firms, many of which are usually independent decision makers and not under common ownership. The situation is complicated by culture, distance, legal factors and different business practices in international markets. Functional interdependence in the marketing channel requires a certain minimum level of cooperation to accomplish the channel task. Because of the complexity and number of levels in international distribution the issue of cooperation is crucial.

Channel conflict arises when one channel member perceives another to be impeding the achievement of its goals. Frustration arises from a restriction of role performance. There are three sources for such conflict:

- incompatible goals between large manufacturers and small retailers,
- domain conflict where manufacturers compete with wholesalers, and
- incongruent perceptions of reality attributable to technical communication problems which produces a different basis for action in response to the same situation.

Some conflict in the channel is manageable but coping with too much is difficult. If conflict becomes destructive, i.e. pathological moves are made which impede the performance of the conflicting parties and the system itself, then the channel system is likely to disintegrate, even though channel objectives are attained in the short run. Channel conflict is highly positive so long as it does not pass the malignant threshold and impair the output of the system. The question of conflict in the channel has been examined by Rosson and Ford (1980), who found that there was strong empirical support for the hypothesis that low levels of conflict are associated with high performance in the channel.

Specifying channel tasks

By clearly specifying channel roles, cooperating firms in the marketing channel can reduce the potential for conflict and improve the situation of the channel system in its entirety.

Roles define appropriate behaviour for firms occupying each position in the system: the firm selects a channel position which is a function of its goals, expectations, values and frame of reference. For example, a 20 per cent return on investment objective may suggest manufacturing as a more attractive position than, say, retailing. Role prescriptions are determined by the norms the channel members set for each other; they indicate what each member desires from all channel members, including itself, relative to their respective degree of participation in the channel marketing functions. Role consensus enables channel members to anticipate the behaviour of others and to operate collectively in a unified manner. Power may be used to achieve effective role congruence and performance and to keep conflict within the functional range. Power is the ability of one channel member to get another to do what the latter would not otherwise have done. It is important that the firm knows where power lies in the channel and is able to note changes in its location over time. In some industries there is evidence that power lies at a particular location. It is generally accepted, for example, that retailers possess the power in the apparel and furniture industries. In alcoholic beverages, cars and some appliances, especially washing machines and microwave ovens, manufacturers have established brand names and greater relative power. Firms discover that it is strategically wise to avoid channels with undesirable power balances. Changes in power structure can have strategic implications: legislation for generic drugs shifted power to retail pharmacies.

Power in distribution channels

Firms use power in bargaining. Firms make commitments and concessions, provide rewards, make threats and sometimes compromise, all part of a strategy to manage conflict. Channel leadership is often based on power relationships. One of the primary functions of the channel leader is to provide leadership. Channel leaders use power to coordinate and to specify and implement channel synergy. Power is correlated with asymmetrical dependence believed to arise from five sources (Table 18.2).

Rewards refer to the belief by one firm that the second has the ability to mediate rewards for it, e.g. wider margins, promotional allowances in fast-moving consumer products. Coercion refers to the belief that punishment will ensue if the firm fails to conform, e.g. margin reduction, slowing shipments, reduced territory rights. Frequently, manufacturers squeeze the margins of intermediaries who are not performing well. New agents are appointed to cover markets poorly served by established agents.

Expertise refers to the firm's perception that another possesses special knowledge: manufacturers providing managerial training for marketing intermediaries or detailed technical manuals for the salesforce of sophisticated industrial or medical product are examples of this form of power. As in human relations it is believed that firms sometimes wish to identify with other firms. The attraction of being associated with the other may stem from the worldwide reputation of the other firm or its well-known brands in particular markets. This is referent power, in that the responding firm expects that the benefits of the association will have positive and important effects in the local market. The power of legitimacy stems from values internalized by one firm which produce the feeling that another firm has a right to exert influence, and that the first firm has an obligation to accept it.

Table 18.2 Sources of power in distribution channels

Rewards
- wider margins
- promotional allowances

Coercion
- reduced margins
- slow deliveries
- restricted market coverage

Expertise
- training for intermediaries
- manuals for salesforce

Referent
- affiliation

Legitimacy
- value system

A supplier–exporter doing business with a smaller foreign intermediary may be tempted to influence that intermediary coercively, which may lead to an unstable relationship and an inability on the part of the exporter to influence a much larger intermediary. Where the choice of intermediary is limited, the exporter may face a decision between forming a relationship with one intermediary that is totally compatible with the exporter or consider a different form of market entry, since, if the goals of the parties are not aligned, the relationship may be unstable and prove to be unsatisfactory in the longer term (Karuaratna and Johnson, 1997, p. 28). Research evidence, however, suggests that firms rely mostly on non-coercive approaches because they are generally more supportive of continuing a cooperative relationship whereas the opposite applies in the case of coercion (Frazier and Rody, 1991). The argument is based on the assumption that a degree of dependence and trust exists in the relationship which makes non-coercion a feasible approach to influencing the other party. The use of coercive influence makes partners less satisfied (Richardson *et al.*, 1995).

Control of distribution channels

The ability of the firm to control its intermediaries internationally is a key part of any distribution strategy. Control in particular is an issue where the channel used is independent rather than integrated. Channel control is characterized by the degree of congruence between distributor goals and those of the supplier, the amount and relevance of market information feedback from the channel and whether the distributor conforms to certain standards determined by the supplier.

Smaller firms have particular problems in this area and often find that they must trade off control with the cost of that control. One example is Alltech Biotechnology, a

Kentucky-based biotechnology firm, whose rapid expansion within the US market led it to consider international markets only three years after its creation. Because it was small and had few resources, the company's desire to exploit as many markets as possible was limited and it was forced to use independent agents, whereas it would ideally have chosen to use an internal distribution network. In order to control these agents the company tries to form a special relationship with them. Where the agent does not work closely with Alltech the agent is dropped.

Channel service quality may be used as an element of power to influence and control the decisions and behaviour of channel partners (Keith *et al.*, 1990). This may be even more applicable to international channels owing to distance, diversity of channel levels, time zones and risk (de Ruytner *et al.*, 1996, p. 22). In international channels, producers have less control over service levels, so a quality service may convey a manufacturer's intention to cultivate and maintain strong partnerships in addition to traditional power dependence themes. Two dimensions characterize the perceived service quality in international marketing channels – service elements controlled by the company which are strategic in nature and service elements controlled by the intermediary which are tactical or operational in nature (de Ruytner *et al.*, 1996, p. 32).

From a strategic perspective, most businesses establish channel service policies which are uniformly applied to all intermediaries, but this may be suboptimal. The results of the de Ruytner *et al.* (1996) study suggest that, because customers in different geographic segments are different, they require different distribution services, so different quality service levels should be provided. Competitive advantage may be gained by differentiating service quality by market segment. Astute use of the perceived quality variable significantly affects the closeness of exporter–importer relationship, which constitutes the power impact of perceived service quality. In such relationships, striving for service, quality and partnership benefits from mutual reinforcement.

Distribution channels in the European Union

An efficient distribution and marketing system is one of the most valuable assets a country can have. In recent years, the European Commission has attempted to promote a single competitive market throughout the European Union. In doing so, it has had to deal with restrictive agreements among manufacturers, wholesalers and retailers or so-called 'vertical restraints'. Some vertical restraints may reduce competition, but others may benefit consumers. A manufacturer may attempt to force all retailers to sell its products at the same price or it might require distributors who sell its products to refrain from selling those of rivals. The European Commission and most national governments treat such instances on an industry by industry basis.

There is one form of vertical restraint the European Commission is determined to stamp out – territorial protection. The Commission will block any arrangement that grants a retailer exclusive rights to serve customers in its area (European Commission, 1997). Exclusive territories arise because manufacturers wish to maintain a brand's image by selling only through a high-class retailer or because a high level of customer services is desired. To accomplish these objectives, manufacturers may require retailers to invest in special training and equipment. Since this often involves large commitments by both parties, the manufacturer may insist that its retailers may not sell a rival's products. When such practices provide an adequate combination of service and prices, consumers benefit. Under this arrangement, there is an incentive for the manufacturer to raise prices and/or to contract with another retailer nearby. In this way, the manufacturer gets a larger share of the profits or encourages greater sales through competition at retail level. With an increased number of retailers, the manufacturer is free to raise prices to all. To protect itself from the possibility of such behaviour, the retailer will seek an exclusive territory before making any commitments. In these circumstances, territorial monopolies can be beneficial to all parties. Retailers understand that manufacturers cannot exert power over them and manufacturers realize that their products will be treated loyally and that both parties can serve customers well and make profits in the process.

In some circumstances, however, retailer monopolies can raise prices to consumers. This occurs in many parts of Europe where regulations inhibit potential competitors from entering the market. These retailers can demand exclusivity from the manufacturer as a price for carrying the products but leave consumers with a restrictive choice.

The situation is particularly aggravated in the European Union, when potential sales outlets are all tied up by competitors. The task facing the European Commission is to determine the negative impact of territorial protection on a case by case basis, depending on industry structure and the particular country market. If there is not much competition among rival brands, exclusive territories strengthen the monopolist's position and reduce benefits to consumers. If there are many rival brands, however, a territorial monopoly in a single brand may do little harm to consumers. With many specialized retailers, one for each brand of car, for example, customers would be able to shop around easily both nearly and even across European borders (see Figure 15.6).

The European Commission, in attempting to integrate 15 national markets, is interested in introducing directives designed to improve marketing and distribution arrangements within the European Union. In general, its effect to date has been beneficial in this regard as attested by a recent survey of companies throughout the EU and in nearby countries.

With the exception of Luxembourg, Malta, Portugal and Switzerland, companies elsewhere in Europe report that marketing has remained unchanged or become easier over the past five years (Table 18.3). Furthermore, more small and medium-sized companies have found it easier to distribute to customers over the past five years, particularly in Ireland and Austria. A different scene exists in Malta, Norway and Switzerland, the non-EU countries who did not join the EU during the recent wave of entry.

Direct cross-border shipments in Europe

With the removal of trade barriers in Europe and other areas the costs of transport and distribution are expected to fall. The abolition of border checks, expensive administration form-filling procedures and circulation restrictions are each expected to significantly

Table 18.3 Impact of membership and organization of the EU on marketing and distribution

| Country | Impact of EU Changes on (per cent) | | | | | |
| | Marketing | | | Distribution | | |
	Easier	More difficult	No change	Easier	More difficult	No change
Austria	19	10	49	37	5	32
Belgium	13	13	46	28	11	39
Denmark	15	0	60	32	2	44
Finland	16	6	65	26	2	54
France	17	15	40	14	11	40
Germany	9	7	43	29	2	33
Greece	28	20	27	23	9	35
Ireland	22	8	42	39	4	37
Italy	10	8	46	17	5	47
Luxembourg	17	21	37	21	9	40
Netherlands	11	7	52	31	5	39
Portugal	6	24	42	22	11	39
Spain	35	14	31	30	5	40
Sweden	6	6	62	23	3	46
United Kingdom	11	7	59	17	5	56
EU Average	*15*	*11*	*45*	*23*	*6*	*43*
Malta	8	9	22	1	2	29
Norway	5	4	54	2	11	48
Switzerland	5	11	33	5	9	34
Turkey	17	13	27	18	4	33
Survey Average	*15*	*11*	*44*	*22*	*6*	*43*

Note: The residuals are 'don't knows' or unstated reasons, e.g. in the case of Austria, 22 per cent fell into this category in marketing and 26 per cent in distribution.

Source: European Business Survey (1997) London: Grant Thornton International Business Strategies Ltd, London, May, pp. 33–4.

improve the distribution of goods in the EU. Under the old regime manufacturers exported goods from one European country to another. Under the new regime it may be possible to dispatch the goods. Under such a regime, direct cross-border shipping becomes increasingly attractive for many firms that have historically consolidated shipments to replenish inventories in local national warehouses (Figure 18.6a). The alignment of warehousing operations with natural service areas irrespective of national border is an expected result of this improved situation (Figure 18.6b). Companies in Europe are now better positioned to secure benefits from a reconfiguration of market logistics. To obtain

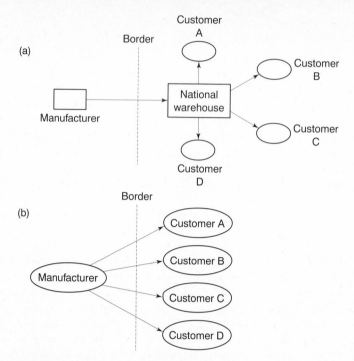

Figure 18.6 Alternative cross-border shipping methods:
(a) Traditional cross-border shipment in Europe;
(b) Future direct cross-border shipment in Europe
Source: O'Laughlin, K. A., Cooper, J. and Cabocel, E. (1993) *Reconfiguring European Logistics Systems,*
Oak Brook, IL: Council of Logistics Management.

the benefits companies must ensure that regional or country marketing and sales work
effectively with logistics when the change from a geographic-based structure to a market-
based structure is implemented.

The transportation infrastructure available to the company varies widely according to
country and region. Highly developed countries and those with large centres of urban
population tend to have well-developed multimodal transportation systems which provide
a wide range of services. Developing countries tend to have a poorly developed
transportation system owing to the level of economic development and the sparsely popu-
lated regions to be served. In such cases rail transportation may be available and often
government subsidies are required to maintain such services.

Island economies are particularly vulnerable in terms of transportation services.
Efficient transportation system to serve islands can be very expensive as an efficient ferry
and air transport system is required. In Europe the central land mass of France, Germany
and Northern Italy is well served by all modes of transportation: road, rail, air, waterway
and pipeline. Countries like the UK and Ireland, being island economies and on the
periphery are less well served. One of the objectives of the Channel Tunnel is to integrate

the UK economy with that of continental Europe. Distance too has an impact. The cost of transportation of goods from Greece and Portugal to German and French markets, for example, can be very high.

The task facing the company is to select from among the available alternatives the combined transportation mix that best fits its market logistics needs. The selection of the transportation mix must be fully integrated into the overall market logistics configuration in order to design a cost-effective service-balanced system

Underlying the transportation decision is a complex system of national government regulations and EU directives which affect rate structures and restrictions which must also be considered. Regulations on driving times, rate charges and prices, restricted access to cities and environmental protection all affect the modal choice available.

Summary

Access to international markets is one of the key areas of management in the new millennium. Gaining and holding access to markets relies heavily on good distribution channel management, which must be seen as an interactive process between manufacturer and the intermediary who may dominate the path to the final consumer. The relationship is further complicated in international markets where different historical developments give rise to different distribution structures. The first task facing the firm in international markets is to understand the distribution channel for its products and services. This means understanding the needs of channel members as well as the needs of final users or consumers.

Increasingly, firms are paying close attention to ensuring that channels perform according to objectives. Agreements between manufacturer and distributor involve a range of factors including physical performance criteria related to the sale of the product or service and financial criteria related to profits and return on investment. Because objectives may be different at different stages in the distribution channel, conflict between the members can arise. The resolution of conflict requires one or a subset of channel members to use power to bring about interorganizational harmony for the good of the entire channel. Specifying channel roles in advance can minimize channel conflict. It is not an easy task, however. The large consumer brand companies pay very close attention to control in distribution channels. The primary objective of this interest is in maintaining the position of their brand in the market. Frequently they go to the extreme of buying up their distribution partners to ensure this control.

Discussion questions

1. What is meant by a marketing channel? Describe the differences which exist between domestic and international channels of distribution.

2. What criteria should the firm apply when selecting channels of distribution?

3. Explain why different countries have different channel structures.

4. A number of examples of distribution channels were outlined in the text. What are their common elements? How are they different?

5. How can the firm motivate channel members?

6. Discuss the need for control and market coverage in selecting and managing a distribution channel.

7. Why does channel conflict occur? Is conflict more likely to occur in international marketing?

8. What role has innovation in international channel management? How can a firm maintain or gain market share by innovating in the channel of distribution?

References

Andaleeb, S. S. (1995) 'Dependence relations and the moderating role of trust: implications for behavioural intentions in marketing channels', *International Journal of Research in Marketing*, **12** (2), 157–72.

Anderson, E. and Coughlan, A. T. (1987) 'International market entry and expansion via independent or integrated channels of distribution', *Journal of Marketing*, **51**, 71–82.

Anderson, E. and Weitz, B. A. (1989) 'Determinants of continuity in conventional industrial channel dyads', *Marketing Science*, **8** (Fall), 310–23.

Anderson, E. and Weitz, B. A. (1992) 'The use of pledges to build and sustain commitment in distribution channels', *Journal of Marketing Research*, **29** (February), 18–34.

Asugman, G., Johnson, J. J. and McCullough, J. (1997) 'The role of after-sales service in international marketing', *Journal of International Marketing*, **5** (4), 11–28.

Bailey, J. P. and Bakos, Y. (1997) 'An exploratory study of the emerging role of electronic inter-mediaries', *International Journal of Electronic Commerce*, **1** (3), 7–20.

Bello, D. C. and Gilliland, D. I. (1997) 'The effect of output controls, process controls, and flexibility on export channel performance', *Journal of Marketing*, **61** (January), 22–38.

Bucklin, C. B., Thomas-Graham, P. A. and Webster, E. A. (1997) 'Channel conflict: when is it dangerous?', *McKinsey Quarterly*, **3**, 37–43.

Cartellieri, C., Parsons, A. J., Rao, V. and Zeisser, M. P. (1997) 'The real impact of internet advertising', *McKinsey Quarterly*, **3**, 44–62.

Cateora, P. R. (1993) *International Marketing*, 8th edn, Homewood, IL: Irwin.

Czinkota, M. R. and Woronoff, J. (1986) *Japan's Market: The Distribution System*, New York, NY: Praeger.

Eighmey, J. and McCord, L. (1998) 'Adding value in the information age: uses and gratifications of sites on the World Wide Web', *Journal of Business Research*, **41** (3), 187–94.

European Commission (1997) 'Green Paper on vertical restraints', January.

Frazier, G. L. (1983) 'Interorganisational exchange behaviour in marketing channels: a broadened perspective', *Journal of Marketing*, **47** (Fall), 68–78.

Frazier, G. L. and Rody, R. C. (1981) 'The use of influence strategies and their application within distribution channels', *Journal of Marketing*, **55** (January), 52–69.

Geyskens, I., Steenkamp, J.-B. E. M., Scheer, L. K. and Kumar, N. (1996) 'The effect of trust and interdependence on relationship commitment: a trans-Atlantic study', *International Journal of Research in Marketing*, **13**, 303–17.

Goldstucker, J. L. (1968) 'The influence of culture on channels of distribution', *AMA Proceedings*, **28**, 468–73.

Gronhaug, K. and Kvitastein, O. (1991) 'Distributional involvement in international strategic business units', in *17th Annual Conference*, European International Business Association, Copenhagen, 15–17 December.

Heide, J. B. and John, G (1988) 'The role of dependence balancing in safeguarding transaction-specific assets in conventional channels', *Journal of Marketing*, **52** (January), 20–35.

International Trade Centre (UNCTAD/GATT), (1985) *Monograph on Trade Channels: Rattan Furniture in the United States of America*, Geneva.

Kahler, R. (1983) *International Marketing*, 5th edn, Cincinnati, OH: Southwestern Publishing Co.

Kale, S. and McIntyre, R. P. (1991) 'Distribution channel relationships in diverse cultures', *International Marketing Review*, **8** (3) 31–45.

Karunaratna, A. R. and Johnson, L. W. (1997) 'Initiating and maintaining export channel intermediary relationships', *Journal of International Marketing*, **5** (2), 11–32.

Katsikeas, C. and Piercy, N. F. (1992) 'Exporter–importer and exporter domestic customer relationships: power considerations', *Management Decision*, **30** (4), 12–19.

Keith, J. E., Jackson, D. W. Jr. and Crosby, L. A. (1990) 'Effects of alternative types of influence strategies under different channel dependence structures', *Journal of Marketing*, **54** (July), 30–41.

Kim, K. and Frazier, G. I. (1996) 'A typology of distribution channel systems: a contextual approach', *International Marketing Review*, **13** (1), 19–32.

Klein, L. R. (1998) 'Evaluating the potential of interactive media through a new lens: search versus experience goods', *Journal of Business Research*, **41** (3), 195–203.

Klein, S. and Roth, V. J. (1990) 'Determinants of export channel structure: the effects of experience and psychic distance reconsidered', *International Marketing Review*, **7** (5), 27–38.

Kotha, S. (1998) 'Competing on the Internet: the case of amazon.com', *European Management Journal*, **16** (2), 212–22.

Kumar, N. Scheer, L. K. and Steenkamp, J-B. E. M. (1995) 'The effects of perceived interdependence on dealer attitudes', *Journal of Marketing Research*, **32** (August), 348–56.

Leuthesser, L. and Kohli, A. K. (1995) 'Relational behaviour in business markets: implications for relationship management', *Journal of Business Research*, **34** (3), 221–33.

Liang, N. and Parkhe, A. (1997) 'Importer behaviour: the neglected counterpart of international exchange', *Journal of International Business Studies*, **28** (Third Quarter), 495–530.

Metcalf L. E. , Frear, C. R. and Krishnan, R. (1990) 'Buyer-seller relationships: an application of the IMP interaction model', *European Journal of Marketing*, **26** (2), 27–46.

Morgan,, R. M. and Hunt, S. D. (1994) 'The commitment–trust theory of relationship marketing', *Journal of Marketing*, **58** (July), 20–38.

O'Laughlin, K. A, Cooper, J. and Cabocel, E. (1993) *Reconfiguring European Logistics Systems*, Oak Brook, IL: Council of Logistics Management.

Richardson, L. D., Swan, J. E. and Hutton, J. D. (1995) 'The effect of the presence and use of channel power sources on distribution satisfaction', *International Review of Retail, Distribution and Consumer Research*, **5** (2), 185–201.

Rosson, Ph. J. and Ford, I. D. (1980) 'Stake conflict and performance in export marketing channels', *Management International Review*, **20** (4), 31–7.

Ruekert, R., Walker, O. and Roering, K. (1985) 'The organisation of marketing activities: a contingency theory of structure and performance', *Journal of Marketing*, **49**, 13–25.

de Ruyter, K., Wetzels, M. and Lemmink, J. (1996) 'The power of perceived service quality in international marketing channels', *European Journal of Marketing*, **30** (12), 22–38.

Slater, A. G. (1978) 'International logistics strategies', *International Journal of Physical Distribution and Materials Management*, **8** (4), 228–44.

Stern, L. W. and El-Ansary, A. (1988) *Marketing Channels*, 3rd edn, Englewood Cliffs, NJ: Prentice Hall.

19

Selling and negotiating in international markets

Marketing strategy is implemented through the marketing team and the salesforce, which is key to the growth and survival of the firm since it is they who directly interact with customers in the market and become the eyes and ears of the company. In international markets, the salesforce must work with an additional constraint. In most circumstances communication, especially through personal selling, is more difficult owing to differing cultures and language and the interaction between the familiar and unfamiliar. The role of the salesforce is emphasized since personal selling is a key function in most firms actively involved in international markets. In international marketing most exchanges are between firms. The supplying firm in one market deals directly with a purchasing firm in another, but only indirectly with the consumer market. The strategy is one of pushing products and services down through the channel from producer to agent or intermediary or industrial user. Rarely does the international firm sell directly to the consumer mass market internationally although with the growth in direct marketing and the internet this occurs in some areas but yet accounts for only a small proportion of total international sales. Frequently, it sells directly to industrial users. Hence, much of the emphasis on personal selling in this chapter applies to international business-to-business marketing.

Marketing exchange through selling and negotiating

Marketing exchanges which occur internationally refer to the transfer of a wide range of assets and myriad marketing agreements which arise in exporting, competitive alliances and foreign direct investment. The marketing exchange involves at least two parties, in this chapter referred to as the buyer and seller for convenience. Also for the sake of convenience the exchange of assets is referred to as buying and selling but at all stages it is recognized that a wide range of activities is involved in the process.

Marketing is concerned with exchange activities and the manner in which the terms of such exchange are established. We distinguish between discrete exchanges where only weak relationships are established between the parties and negotiated exchanges where buyers and sellers are actively involved in a process which may result in the formation of longer-lasting and deeper marketing relationships.

Negotiations have a number of distinguishing features. At least two parties are involved and there may be a conflict of interests. Buyers and sellers, however, come together in a voluntary relationship concerned with the exchange of tangible and intangible assets. Negotiation has been defined as

> any sequence of written and or verbal communication processes whereby parties to both common and conflicting commercial interests and of differing cultural backgrounds consider the form of any joint action they might take in pursuit of their individual objectives which will define or redefine the terms of their interdependence.
>
> (McCall and Warrington, 1989, p. 15)

The negotiations process is a sequence of activities involving the presentation of demands by one or both parties, their evaluation, possible concessions and counter proposals, closing with an agreement which, in an ideal situation, benefits both parties. There are two basic types of negotiation. The first is referred to in the literature as a 'win–lose' (or distributive bargaining) situation whereby the goals of one party are usually in direct conflict with those of the other party. In this situation resources are perceived as fixed and each company attempts to maximize its share of the resources. As a result each company uses a set of strategies to maximize the share of resources to be obtained. Generally, companies do not willingly enter into 'win–lose' situations in international marketing. In most circumstances companies in international markets seek 'win–win' (or integrative negotiations) where the goals of the parties are not mutually exclusive – one party's gain is not necessarily at the other party's expense. It is possible for both parties to achieve their objectives. It is

> a problem solving approach, where both parties perceive the process of negotiation as process to find a solution to a common problem [where] it is possible for both parties to achieve their objectives and one party's gain is not dependent upon the other party's concession.
>
> (Ghauri, 1996, p. 4)

According to this author there are a number of features which distinguish negotiations of this form:

- open information flows between the parties; both sides disclose their objectives and listen to the other party's objectives in order to find a match between them;
- a search for a solution that satisfies both sets of objectives;
- an understanding that parties have common and conflicting objectives;
- the task is to find common and complementary objectives acceptable to both sides;
- both parties must sincerely attempt to understand the viewpoint of the other.

To avoid strategic errors in international marketing negotiations, companies must have access to information that is as complete as possible, including information on how to cope with cultural differences, how to assess management processes and styles, and how to understand the political economy of the target country (Marshall *et al.*, 1998, p. 19). In this chapter we are primarily concerned with these matters in a 'win–win' context and attempts by parties through international marketing negotiation to achieve them.

Figure 19.1 Nature of marketing exchanges or relationships

Nature of marketing exchanges

Marketing exchanges are events and processes which arise between two or more parties, organizations, firms or individuals. Behind every marketing exchange is a network of individuals and groups who contribute in various ways to its implementation. In a marketing exchange we are concerned with the transfer of assets which may consist of products, services, ideas, information or rewards associated with the transfer of industrial and consumer products, licensing and joint venture agreements, distribution and agency agreements and information. Marketing exchanges are central to marketing, as they represent the point of convergence of the selling process and the buying process. Concern also involves understanding the process of exchange including personal selling, marketing negotiations and managing the resulting relationships. The selling and buying firms are linked through these products and processes (Figure 19.1).

Foundations of international marketing negotiation

Fundamental to success in international marketing is an ability to communicate across different cultures, languages and business backgrounds. Communication refers to the extent to which the parties to an exchange openly share information and expectations (Anderson and Weitz, 1992), which also applies to cross-cultural exchanges in international marketing (Graham *et al.*, 1994). Open sharing of expectations and information as well as increased communication enable business partners to enjoy satisfying, productive, rewarding and effective business relationships and this communication is even more critical when it crosses national boundaries, because of the increased difficulty of understanding the needs of remote customers (LaBahn and Harich, 1997, p. 34).

Buyer–seller communications

Communication is defined as a 'process of convergence in which two or more participants share information in order to reach a better mutual understanding of each other and the world in which they live' (Barnett and Kincaid, 1983). Communication is at the heart of buying and selling negotiations in international markets. Effective communication is essential for understanding, cooperation and completing exchanges. The importance of good communication is emphasized in buying and selling in face-to-face meetings (Graham, 1985).

Communication is a two-way process of interaction (Kotler, 1997, p. 605; Schramm, 1971, p. 4) involving a sender, a message and a receiver (Figure 19.2). Both the sender and the receiver play an active role in the transmission and reception of the message. The message may be conveyed verbally or otherwise by means of a code (Cooley, 1983), which includes oral and written language accompanied by a set of paralinguistic features, such as stress and loudness. It also contains non-verbal phenomena such as gestures and facial expressions. Coding and decoding are the ways in which participants in the buying and selling process negotiate and define new knowledge, new understanding, new joint priorities and new values as a key to understanding the intercultural communication process. Throughout the communications process, especially in international marketing, many opportunities exist for distortion and loss of messages. In this regard the overlap between the fields of experience of the sender in the home country and the receiver in the foreign country establishes how effective the communication is likely to be. If there is little common experience or culture, successful communication will be very difficult. Striving to understand the field of experience of the counterpart is a necessary step in facilitating a more successful communication process. With some common ground in experience and culture, buyers and sellers will share similar expectations of a situation, the decisions to be made and the implications of those decisions, will understand the style and pattern of communication to be used, will plan to discuss similar topics and may choose to use similar forms of communication (Schuster and Copeland, 1996, p. 152). The more each partner understands the other's situation, perspective and culture, the easier it is to create verbal and non-verbal symbols that can be encoded and decoded similarly by both.

Two principal factors causing a distortion in a verbal communication, and thereby affecting the buyer's or seller's ability to understand what the other is saying, have been identified (Gourlay, 1987). The first of these is filters, the second is referred to as 'noise'. Filters refer to forms of internal psychological distorting mechanisms which alter the counterpart's message. A number of examples will illustrate. In buying and selling in international markets it is easy for a buyer or seller to assume that they know instinctively what the counterpart seeks. Expectations can also lead to difficulties. If the seller expects the buyer to be difficult the seller may distort the buyer's communications to fit the expectation.

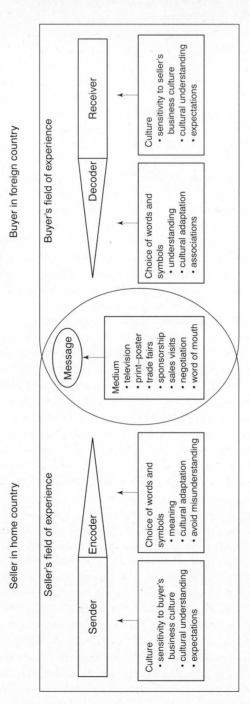

Figure 19.2 Factors affecting shared meaning in international marketing

Another set of distorting factors which act as filters, called double messages, make listening difficult because one party picks up more than one message from the other. The listener should be concerned with what is genuinely meant, not necessarily with the words themselves. This is particularly difficult in cross-cultural communications especially where one party incorrectly uses the paralanguage of the other. The double messages which result are a great source of mistaken understanding and confusion. It is one of the reasons why television advertising attempts to rely on messages with universal meanings and avoids themes which may be interpreted differently in different countries.

The second set of factors, referred to as 'noise', in the system relates to background distraction which has nothing to do with the substance of the message but can complicate the communication process. Such 'noise' is present in all markets, domestic and international, and includes physical noise, the presence of other people, a poor telephone connection and the habits and idiosyncrasies of the communicators. In an international marketing exchange the effect of such noise is exacerbated. Cross-cultural noise derives from gestures, behaviour seeming overly or insufficiently courteous, clothing, office surroundings and the speaking distance between the parties to the exchange. Noise may lead to conflict with expectations and may result in a misinterpretation of the situation, a change of intent on the part of the counterpart or even a change in the meaning of the message itself.

A key decision facing the selling company is the extent to which communications should be standardized across markets or customized to address better communication needs within individual markets. The firm's ability to standardize communications messages depends on the kind of message involved. An advertising campaign, using an emotional appeal, for example, may be difficult to standardize across countries since the success of an emotional appeal depends on viewers bringing similar cultural values to the situation (Ueltschy and Ryans, 1997, p. 491). This supports the Samli *et al.* (1993) view that overlap in the sender's and receiver's culture is necessary for successful cross-cultural communications. Brand names also pose considerable problems in international marketing. Simple straightforward names like Kodak travel well, but others, especially the brand names used on Japanese cars, must be changed to carry any meaning in target markets (Exhibit 19.1).

Culture and communication

Communication, whether inter- or intracultural, can only take place when the participants in the process share a set of affective meaning symbols. Such symbols are learnt: the whole range of symbols used in communication, from the more basic such as language to non-verbal cues and sets of ideological principles, beliefs, values and norms, are acquired and attributed meaning on the basis of experience. Interpersonal communication is at its most effective when those involved attribute very similar or identical affective meaning to the various communicative stimuli which feature in the process. The more divergent the experiences of individuals, the more difficult it is for effective communication to take place. It is important, therefore, to be sensitive to the national business culture of potential business partners. Sensitivity to national business culture refers to the firm's understanding of and adaptation to its exchange partner's domestic business practices as

========= Exhibit 19.1 =========

A Bongo Friendee by another name

Somewhere between the Nissan factory in Tochigi, Japan, and the Port of Los Angeles, the Leopard J Ferie sedan loses its first and last names. In America, it's sold by Infiniti dealers as the J – the J30 to be precise. Other Nissans that leave their badges at home include the Sunny, which becomes the Sentra, and the Fairlady Z, which appears as the 300ZX.

Names, it seems, don't travel very well – in either direction. Take Toyota's flagship Avalon, which was conceived, built, and named in the US. 'We wanted something elegant and upscale, and this was highly rated in clinics with intended buyers', says Sherilyn K Marshall, strategic planning manager at Toyota Motor Sales USA Inc in Torrance, California. 'But we had a difficult time selling the idea to executives in Japan.'

No surprise. In Japanese, Avalon's 'V' is pronounced 'B' and the 'L' indistinguishable from the 'R'. So the word, 'Avalon' could come out sounding a lot like that shellfish, the abalone. Mazda Motor Corp's American-bred Miata, from the old high German word for 'reward' sounds suspiciously like Miyata, a prominent Japanese bicycle company. So in Japan, the sporty little number is called the Eunos Roadster. A Mazda spokesman says that Eunos is a made-up word, meaning 'happy number.'

In Japan, Toyota's car names almost always start with 'C' – there's Crown, Celica, Carina, Cressida, Celsior, Century, Corona, Corolla, and Camry. Legend has it a fortune-teller told founder Kiichiro Toyoda that names starting with 'C' would sell better. He also told him that a name written with 8 brush strokes was luckier than one written with 10, which is why the company is named Toyota instead of Toyoda.

Most Japanese car names, both at home and abroad, are derived from Latin roots, easy to say in Japanese. Some English derivations also are fashionable. Mazda's 4×4 the Proceed Marvie, combines all of these elements and includes the Spanish *mar* for ocean and the French *vie* for life. Its Bongo Friendee van picks up the word 'friendly' but drops the difficult 'L'.

Sometimes, something is lost in translation: Mitsubishi Motors Corp's Starion, the Colt Starion in Europe, obviously was supposed to be a frisky 'stallion'. Funny things happen, it seems, even on the way to the global marketplace.

Source: adapted from *Business Week*, 19 February 1996, p. 46.

perceived by the partner (LaBahn and Harich, 1997, p. 31). Furthermore, sensitivity to national business culture is an important prerequisite for the cross-cultural adaptation necessary to lessen misunderstanding and disagreement (Reardon and Spekman, 1994).

Symbolic meaning systems are, effectively, frames of references used to interpret information emanating from the environment or from the other human beings. It is these 'networks of shared meanings' (culture) which Schramm (1971) refers to in his discussion of the conditions necessary for effective communication. The Schramm model conceives of participants in the communicative process as having separate frames of reference. As may be seen in Figure 19.2, effective communication can only take place in the area of overlap between the two frames of reference. The greater the degree of overlap, the broader the range of issues about which the individuals can communicate. The area of common frames of reference also determines the possible depth of communication.

Cultural barriers militate against effective communication and increase the likelihood of total breakdown in communication. The reason for this is that such barriers lead one of the parties to ignore or fail to respond correctly to all of the cues in the situation – from the environment or from the other person. 'Denial of critical cues from the environment and distortion of verbal or non-verbal cues from the other person' are the primary causes of communications breakdown (Barlund, 1979). Cross-cultural communication problems arise because of language and language behaviour, non-verbal behaviour, different value systems and different cognitive styles or thought patterns. Misunderstandings at the level of language are usually very obvious and easy to correct but at the higher levels of values and cognitive styles they are not so obvious and therefore often go uncorrected.

Three sets of constraints (Fisher, 1980, p. 13) cause some of the normal features of thought and perception to become booby traps in communication when two or more cultures are involved:

1. information processing,
2. internal consistency, and
3. projection of meaning.

In buying and selling negotiations the human mind is an information processor which receives, stores, analyses and uses information. Although born with this capacity people also learn to behave in a certain way. Effective communication depends on there being a reasonable similarity of such learning among buyers and sellers. To a large extent, however, the cultural impact on learning is dominant. Where cultures differ, communication is more difficult and buyer–seller convergence is likely to be slower or distorted.

Within a culture it is necessary to have a certain degree of internal consistency among beliefs, images and the way we understand phenomena around us in order to experience efficient communications. Because the mind resists disturbance to this consistency it attempts to fit new pieces of information into the existing framework of ideas or beliefs. In some circumstances it may be impossible to understand something that conflicts with the way we expect to see it. Buying and selling negotiations in international markets almost certainly mean having to cope with new and inconsistent information and very different behaviour by the counterpart to the negotiations.

The third difficulty arises when we assume that implicit assumptions and habitual ways of thinking about our own circumstances have universal applicability. This self-reference criterion trap gives rise to many problems in international marketing (Hall, 1960; Lee, 1966). As a consequence, confusion turns full circle in cross-cultural communications, when the mind not only places its own stamp of meaning on an incoming message but begins to project that same meaning to the counterpart in the negotiations (Fisher, 1980, p. 15). One form of unconscious projection that wreaks havoc in negotiations, according to Fisher, is attribution of motive. Motives attributed reflect the buyer's or seller's experience in dealing with another. An example of an assumed motive that does not need to be thought through to complete an exchange when operating in single culture would be: 'he is hesitating because he thinks that the price is too high or that my offer could improve'. In such circumstances the probability of being correct in assuming motives is relatively high. The probability falls rapidly when a cross-cultural situation is encountered and declines further when the subject matter is complex.

Impact of culture on cognitive structure

A crucial aspect of the influence of culture on communication is the context in which it takes place (Hall, 1976). By context Hall refers to situation-specific factors such as the roles of participants, their power and status, the physical environment and the subject of interest. The content of communication can be understood only in the context of these factors. For Hall the relevance of context also applies to negotiations. In high-context countries the content of the communication used in negotiation is not as important as the role of participants. In such situations communications depend greatly on the context or non-verbal aspects of the communications. In low-context countries focus of attention is on the content or words used. In this respect Campbell *et al.* (1988, p. 57) reports that context makes a difference in France. In a negotiations simulation involving business people they found that the role of the negotiator in France appeared to influence negotiation results, whereas in Germany role or context had no importance, leading these authors to claim support for Hall's (1976) characterization of Germany as a low-context culture.

Cultures vary in the extent to which communication is influenced by context. In high context communication, much of the meaning is internalized by the individual whereas in low context communication, meaning is derived from the coded explicit part of the message (Hall, 1976). Culture is also influenced by the degree to which the society is individualist or collectivist and these factors also influence communications. Individualist societies allow more freedom of expression, expect people to take care of themselves, whereas collectivist societies are more group oriented and take the group into account in making decisions (Hofstede, 1991). Building on the work of others, including Hall and Hofstede, Bush and Ingram (1996) develop a comprehensive framework which captures the general comparative characteristics of culture and allows us to apply them to international marketing phenomena (Table 19.1).

At a more general level it is accepted that there are pronounced differences in cognitive structures or intellectual styles which influence international communications. For example, it is generally believed that there is a wide gulf between the ways in which people in the West and East think. Western cognition tends to be logical and uses sequential connections and abstract notions of reality to represent universals. The emphasis is on causes rather than outcomes.

Oriental cognition, on the other hand, tends to be intuitive with more reliance on sense data. It is concrete and not abstract. It is non-logical in the Cartesian sense, with emphasis on the particular rather than the universal, and highly sensitive to context and relationships and expresses a concern for reconciliation, harmony and balance in relationships.

Table 19.1 Comparative characteristics of culture

Characteristic	Low context / individualistic	High context / collectivistic
Communication and language	Explicit, direct	Implicit, indirect
Sense of self and space	Informal handshakes	Formal hugs, bows, and handshakes
Dress and appearance	Dress for individual success, wide variety	Indication of position in society, religious rule
Food and eating habits	Eating is a necessity, fast food	Eating is a social event
Time consciousness	Linear, exact, promptness is valued, time = money	Elastic, relative, time spent on enjoyment, time = relationships
Family and friends	Nuclear family, self-oriented, value youth	Extended family, other oriented, loyalty and responsibility, respect for old age
Values and norms	Independence, confrontation and conflict	Group conformity, harmony
Beliefs and attitudes	Egalitarian, challenge authority, individuals control destiny, gender equality	Hierarchical, respect for authority, individuals accept destiny, gender roles
Mental process and learning	Linear, logical, sequential, problem-solving	Lateral, holistic, simultaneous, accepting life's difficulties
Work habits	Task oriented, rewards based on achievement, work has value, Protestant ethic	Relationship oriented, rewards based on seniority, work is a necessity

Source: Bush, V. D. and Ingram, T. (1996) 'Adapting to diverse customers: a training matrix for international marketers', *Industrial Marketing Management*, **25**, 373–83.

Oriental cognition is influenced by Confucianism and Buddhism, which leads to an emphasis on loyalty and harmony and an adherence to group norms whereby the individual is subordinated to the welfare of the group (Dubinsky *et al.*, 1997, p. 196). The converse is true in the West where culture reflects a Judeo-Christian value system where people have an individualistic approach towards everything that affects them leading them to place their own self-interest ahead of the organization or group.

For marketing and sales people the analysis of social structure in high-context countries is essential to obtain useful insights to a selling or buying situation. In such circumstances the firm must obtain sufficient knowledge of the culture to communicate understandably and acceptably.

As an example of the negotiations process it is instructive to examine Chinese cognitive structure and its effect on international negotiations. In business negotiations the Chinese tend to elicit as much information as possible before disclosing their hand to avoid losing face or displaying ignorance. In 1985 Boeing negotiated a deal with the Chinese, taking eight months to obtain an agreement in principle, i.e. the agenda for the negotiations was agreed. It is generally accepted that the Chinese assimilate data in intuitive lumps or bundles and understand in terms of systems. In such circumstances appreciation of technologies may be limited until they have grasped how the diverse elements fit into an entire system.

Establishing the negotiation range may be unimportant where the assimilation of information is a major element in the interaction. The problem-solving element assumes a greater importance for the development of the relationships between the negotiators. It is not a gradual move, but one of attaining an agreed position in one well-considered step. In such a buying–selling regime foreign negotiators must make their points as cogently as possible within the relationships that they can establish and hope that their package is accepted.

Following these guidelines suggests that the international firm should present a summary close involving a simple package, which would be more suitable than a concession close, provided that the timing is right. Finally, it is important to note that, in dealing with the Chinese, business relations are based on harmony and friendship. The Chinese accept contracts as a basis of business relationships rather than in any strictly legal sense, as would be the case in the West.

Buyer–seller interaction

The reality of international markets, especially for industrial products, is that the supplier cannot usually determine its product offering unilaterally. For this reason an interaction approach based on a longer-term relationship between buyer and seller seems more appropriate (Turnbull, 1987). Aspects of product development, product quality, delivery and service criteria, price and other factors are all subject in many cases to a process of negotiation and adaptation. This negotiation and change process, whereby suppliers and customers adapt to each other, takes place through a complex interaction framework. Interaction can only occur where relationships have been established between people, and thus the challenge is often to establish relationships with potentially new partners, as well as to defend existing relationships (Cunningham and Homse, 1982). In the traditional view of marketing, the firm has a simple contract with a single unit within the customer company (Figure 19.3a). This naive view must be modified for international markets to recognize that complexity of the buying decision is often manifested by a large number of people being devoted to serving customers (Figure 19.3b).

Industrial products firms in international markets generally emphasize close, even contractual, relationships rather than market relationships. The value of these in terms of cost reduction or increased sales acts to reduce the incentive of both buying and selling companies to seek additional or substitute partners (Ford, 1984). For consumer products firms the same may be said, since in most cases the marketing exchange is between two independent firms located in different countries and hence has many of the trappings of an industrial market.

The interaction approach as discussed in Chapter 2 is particularly relevant in the

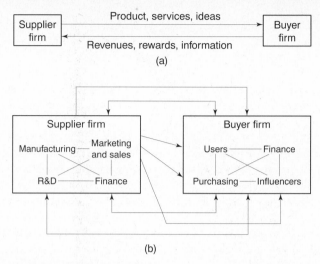

Figure 19.3 Evolution of marketing relationships in international marketing:
(a) Simple seller–buyer interface recognized;
(b) Marketing relationships recognized
Source: adapted from Turnbull, P. W. (1987) 'Interaction and international marketing: an investment process', *International Marketing Review,* **4** (4), 7–19.

international context. The development of relationships across national boundaries is often a very time-consuming and resource-intensive process. The seller is likely to be faced with considerable modifications to the products and services on offer to suit a foreign buyer. The demonstration of commitment may involve considerable travel costs and perhaps the establishment of an overseas sales and service subsidiary. The selling firm is usually faced with the task of overcoming the 'business distance' which exists between itself and the buyer.

International customer firms expect extremely high commitment from their suppliers. Attributes used to select suppliers in France, Germany, Italy, Sweden and the United Kingdom were examined by Ford (1984), who found that there is a strong association between a buyer's assessment of the technical and commercial skills of its suppliers and the extent of commitment to it. Technical skill refers to the buyer's view of the seller's technical abilities in the area of product performance, production quality or development. Commercial skill refers to the seller's commercial ability in the provision of sales service, in delivery and delivery information. Such types of commitment are especially important for international industrial markets where there are differences, for example, in national standards and procedures between the United States and Europe.

Selling and negotiating strategies

In international marketing personal selling is the dominant demand-stimulating factor in the communications mix. This is especially true for industrial products and for products and services transferred between two firms in different international markets. In such situations sales people work primarily to stimulate demand while also providing a range of other customer services. Such services are frequently crucial to the buyer–seller relationship.

In recent years the approach to selling has changed significantly. From once being an adversarial function selling has recently become much more cooperatively and collaboratively driven. Noting this trend for industrial products has led Hutt and Speh (1989, pp. 521–2) to refer to consultative selling, negotiative selling, systems selling and team selling. In consultative selling the sales person assumes the role of a consultant helping to improve the client's profitability. Here face to face contact is important and questioning and listening are crucial skills. The sales person provides analysis and problem-solving assistance in an attempt to offer more value than competitors. A negotiations style is adopted to optimize the benefits of a marketing transaction for both the buyer and seller. The objective is to establish a partnership between buyer and seller with common objectives, mutually beneficial strategies and a common defence against outsiders. Negotiation means talking about a relationship before doing something about it. Negotiations are mixed motive situations: each party has a motive to enter into negotiation to reach a mutually acceptable solution while, simultaneously, each may have a motive for competition.

In systems selling recognition is given to the likelihood that most buying and selling situations require a perspective beyond the product itself. A systems approach to selling would require a comprehensive package of products, recommendations on use and facilities, information and advice and even training and maintenance programmes. In team selling the firm provides a group of people with functional expertise that matches the specialized knowledge of key buying influences in the customer firm. The team is formed to serve the buying and selling process and members may contribute to that process in different ways at different times.

Changing role of the salesforce

Marketing is an interactive function in the firm. The traditional emphasis on selling and purchasing as separate processes, often in conflict, is an inaccurate reflection of the task facing the firm.

Marketing as interaction in the systems exchange framework allows the company to embrace the resources of supplier and customer organizations to achieve mutually beneficial targets. The interaction perspective treats the development of relationships with other organizations as a necessary condition for the effective harnessing of resources across organizations. These relationships are established through the negotiation process. For the purposes of this chapter negotiation situations are confined to those where buyers and sellers attempt to settle the basis of their future behaviour across national and cultural boundaries without the intervention of third parties. As was seen in Chapter 6, cultural boundaries include micro cultures, e.g. corporate philosophies and styles, and macro cultures, e.g. national, political and linguistic frameworks. It is argued that these cultural boundaries act as barriers to communication between the firm and its international customers.

A permanent presence in a foreign country requires a greater knowledge of both national and micro cultures of individual firms and organizations. Where the stage of growth in international markets relies on the use of intermediaries, knowledge at the national culture level probably suffices but may be limiting. However, for the high-technology and high-value capital products manufacturer whose specialist marketing people deal with a few customers in each of a number of countries, a knowledge of the micro culture at company level is essential.

Many companies are beginning to give the salesforce more marketing autonomy. A rapidly changing marketing environment, especially in Europe, is allowing firms to reassess the role of the salesforce. In many instances firms have reorganized to give marketing autonomy to the product-market salesforce. This shift to a new organization form has broadened the role of the salesforce. From calling on distributors, retailers, industrial users and their customers the salesforce is now spending more time meeting country-based agency creative directors and media buyers to develop local advertising campaigns. The converted salesforce is better able to obtain good deals locally, which results in more effective marketing. The salesforce by its nature can move quickly to respond to local conditions. In such circumstances the role of the salesforce is changing from concentrating on discrete marketing exchanges to the development of broad-based marketing relationships requiring sophisticated negotiation skills. In developing relationships the values possessed by the salesforce can be of paramount importance. As was seen in Chapter 6 'values represent basic beliefs which serve to define the salesforce and ultimately guide and motivate behaviour' (Jackson and Tax, 1995, p. 35) and they also influence a plethora of attitudes and behaviours (Beatty *et al.*, 1985). Success in international markets requires an unstructured and flexible disposition on the part of the salesforce. Sales people who emphasize the values of accomplishment and excitement are more likely to be entrepreneurial than sales people who perceive these values to be less important (Weeks and Kahle, 1990).

In marketing, the salesforce is given a focal position in the implementation of strategy. It negotiates relationships with its counterparts in customer firms and with their constituents and influencers. It seeks information about the needs and preferences of customers prior to formal negotiations. Sales people employ skills to elicit information in the course of a negotiation, which is valuable in determining the source and location of power in the marketing relationship being established.

Convergence of buying and selling

Individuals, companies and organizations are constantly seeking solutions to various problems which can only be solved by becoming involved in the buying and selling process. Potential buyers must search for information and they try to keep this search as simple as possible. Sellers are rarely passive in such circumstances. They frequently intervene with information to assist the buyer. The search is influenced by the background of the buyer and by a host of other intervening factors, including the role of the potential seller. Motivated by the need to reduce uncertainty or to avoid conflict, companies and organizations frequently seek satisfactory solutions rather than optimal solutions. Individual buyers may seek optimal solutions in their buying. The interaction between buying and selling is acknowledged by firms that recognize the convergence of buying and selling processes to provide a solution.

The convergence of the buying and selling processes in international markets is greatly influenced by the ability of the parties to the exchange to communicate. At almost every stage in the buying and selling process there is a need to communicate. Buyers attempt to learn what is available that can solve their perceived problems, and the buying process involves many people at many stages. Similarly, sellers must communicate with potential buyers to obtain their attention to convey offers and to prescribe possible solutions to identified problems. Hence there are many opportunities for communications breakdown.

Stages in the buying process

The anatomy of the buying process consists of five discrete phases (Figure 19.4). First, buyers must recognize the need to buy: Stage One. At this stage the buyer identifies and defines a need. Need recognition may arise within the organization, e.g. the need for supplies of components. Alternatively, need recognition may be stimulated through promotion by salespeople or advertising.

A new need is the most difficult of the three buying situations identified: Stage Two; this frequently arises from a very significant change in the operation of the company or

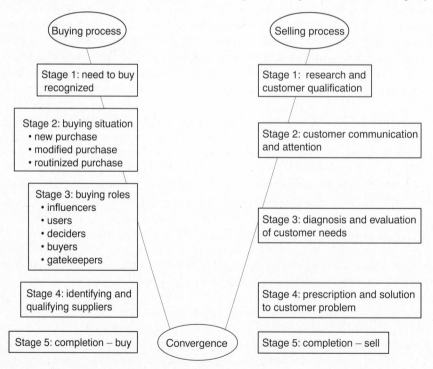

Figure 19.4 Convergence of buying and selling processes

organization. The introduction of a new product may require new materials, components, packaging and even capital equipment. The solution to such buying problems is usually complex and time consuming. The amount of interaction between the buyer and seller is also usually quite significant and takes place at several points in the respective organizations.

A change in a production process or in internal accounting procedures may give rise to a modified buying situation. The buyer may have to search for a new solution but, because of a high degree of familiarity with the situation and experience, the decision process is much simpler than the first time such a purchase was made.

Buying needs also reflect the buying situation and decision process. A routinized buying situation results in the purchase of a product that has been bought many times before. The buying process is simple and often automatic. Both buyer and seller know the solution to the buying problem.

Buying roles depend very much on the buying situation: Stage Three. A new need may require a number of people both within and outside the firm to be involved in the buying decision. For example, the purchase of a new aircraft by an airline would require considerable involvement from purchasing, engineering, finance, senior management, outside consultants, banks, leasing firms and even government departments. At the other extreme, for a routinized need, it is probably only necessary for the buyer to become aware that a purchase needs to be made. Depending on the situation, therefore, the buying decision will involve one or several people. In such circumstances it is important that the seller understands that there are important differences in the way in which different people search for information and make buying decisions.

Before buyers begin to search for information they develop criteria by which the information collected can be evaluated: Stage Four. The criteria serve as a guide in the search process. For the seller it is important to know and understand the buying criteria used. The search process is directed at identifying and qualifying potential suppliers.

Buyers frequently shortlist potential suppliers, particularly for industrial products. Selection criteria including credit rating, financial strength, management skills, experience in the product market and quality control and performance standards are used to shortlist potential suppliers. Often at the same time the buying firm compares actual products on offer.

Specifications are prepared which establish criteria in terms of product performance, characteristics, quality, acceptable price ranges, repair, maintenance, installation and advice. The final step involves a comparison of competing offers to choose the best possible package of price, quantity, delivery, quality and service in making the purchase decision: Stage Five. At all stages there are valuable opportunities for interaction by the selling firm which assist in the problem solving process outlined.

Stages in the selling process

The selling process may similarly be divided into five definable but interdependent stages. The first step is to qualify the customer to prepare for the ultimate sale: Stage One. At this stage the seller is interested in identifying possible problems in the customer firm. This also means attempting to specify a set of selling objectives which take account of the marketing environment and the specific situation in the customer firm. The selling firm begins to identify the nature and range of issues to be resolved in a possible encounter with the buyer. Intangible issues are also identified. At this stage, too, it is important to plan the negotiation strategy, to incorporate trade-offs and to allow for contingencies. The seller or salesforce will also establish authority limits for dealing with the potential customer. All activity at this stage is carried out before meeting the customer.

The attention phase is critical in international selling: Stage Two. Getting the buyer's individual attention is critical to success. Very often the sales person has very little time to do it and many factors can interfere in the process. The sales call may be in person, by telephone, at an exhibition stand in a trade fair or even at the potential customer's premises. Many legitimate distractions and disruptions can interfere with obtaining the potential customer's individual attention. All subsequent stages in the selling process depend on successful completion of this one. Cross-cultural communications and differences in cognitive styles add to the possible distractions or interference in the communication between buyer and seller which reduces attention.

In the first communications with the potential customer the seller must complete a number of tasks. At this stage the selling firm attempts to test the limits to which it may go with the buyer in order to isolate key issues. At this stage, too, factors which affect the relative power of the parties are identified. The seller and the buyer begin to determine how best to approach the negotiation. Indeed, if the work of the first stage is not carried out accurately it may be decided not to proceed further. Both sides also attempt to establish the needs and preferences of the other party. Face-to-face communication is normal at various points in this stage of the process.

In Chapter 9 attention was given to ways of diagnosing customers and evaluating their needs and buying situation: Stage Three. This stage consists primarily of collecting facts and qualitative information about the potential customer and analysing these to arrive at a diagnosis of the customer. Real needs, rather than perceived needs, are identified. It is important at this stage to establish the buyer's primary concerns in terms of the product or service sought. The seller must also attempt to identify the buyer's dominant buying urge, i.e. the reason for buying the product or service. Diagnosis and evaluation clearly indicate the problem solving aspect of selling.

At this stage, which should be highly interactive with a great deal of interpersonal communication, buyers and sellers become aware of the other's problems. This stage is very demanding on interpersonal skills, especially those concerned with communicating and influencing. It is important to maintain flexibility, and experienced buyers and sellers keep issues linked as proposals and counter proposals are made. It may be necessary at this stage to reformulate objectives and strategies in the light of new information on tangible and intangible issues.

The next step in the selling process is to begin to prescribe a range of possible solutions: Stage Four. A well-prepared and executed selling programme will convince the potential buyer of the seller's purpose and that (s)he is the target. The seller at this point demonstrates that (s)he understands the buyer's problem and that her/his range of products and services can help solve that problem. The seller attempts to influence strongly the buyer–seller negotiations by assuming a knowledgeable role and concern for and proper understanding of the buyer's problem.

At this stage it is necessary for both parties to consider details of the exchange package. It is important to determine how issues interact and to establish the effect of the interaction on results. The seller moves toward an agreement conditional on acceptance of a package of products, services and conditions for their exchange. It is essential to test the other side for understanding and agreement. Good negotiators attempt to keep options open and rarely allow the process to degenerate to the point where only a very limited number of factors are examined. Research on negotiation has shown differences between average and skilled negotiators (Exhibit 19.2).

Having obtained acceptance for the prescription offered, the seller must convince the buyer as to the appropriateness of the proposed solution. This means explaining the purpose, use, features and benefits of the product or service so clearly that the buyer completely understands and accepts what is said.

The final stage is to close the sale, which means employing an effective approach to direct the buyer to the point of decision and also means recognizing when the buyer has made such a decision: Stage Five. The objective of closing is to influence the buyer to make a decision to purchase the product or service and to ensure that all formalities are completed. At this stage the seller resorts to an appropriate closing technique. In some situations it is more appropriate to close a sale by summarizing the agreement, while in other circumstances making a concession to the buyer is more appropriate. The choice depends on the situation, the product market and the circumstances.

In closing, the seller normally draws up an agreement which reflects the mutual understanding of the parties. It may also be necessary to acknowledge the basis for legal interpretation if such is warranted. Finally, good marketing relationships usually call for the provision for revision when circumstances change.

Domain of international marketing negotiation

As already indicated, this chapter is concerned with international marketing negotiations leading to mutual net benefits to the parties in the relationship. For success in developing 'win–win' solutions both parties must be willing to reveal their true objectives and to listen to the other side carefully. At the same time it is recognized that negotiators differ with regard to their values and preferences – what one party needs and wants may or may not be what the other party needs and wants. Where there is a convergence between the needs and wants of both parties and the expected benefits are high both parties will be intimately involved in managing the relationship (Figure 19.5). Where the needs and wants of the seller dominate or the expected net benefits are higher than the buyer's, the seller is likely to manage the relationship. The same is true for the buying firm when its needs and wants are met or the expected net benefits are higher.

Throughout the process of sharing information about preferences and priorities the parties endeavour to understand what the other side really wants to achieve. Because of cultural differences and different business practices this usually means probing below the surface of the counterpart's position to discover latent needs. Good negotiators create a

========= Exhibit 19.2 =========
What distinguishes the good negotiators from the crowd

According to research conducted by Neil Rackman and others of the Sheffield-based Huthwaite Research Group into actual negotiating performance, there are significant differences of technique between good and merely average negotiators:

- The skilled negotiator considered twice the number of outcomes or options for action compared with the average negotiator, and three times as much attention to common ground.
- The average negotiator took a shorter term view. Only one comment in 25 met the criteria of a long-term consideration. The skilled negotiator made twice as many long-term comments.
- The researchers also asked negotiators about their objectives and recorded whether their replies referred to single point objectives or to a defined range. Skilled negotiators were significantly more likely to set their objectives in terms of a range. Average negotiators, in contrast, were more likely to plan their objectives around a fixed point.
- Skilled negotiators show marked differences in their face-to-face behaviour. They avoid irritating words and phrases like 'generous offer' used by a negotiator to describe his own proposal. When the opposition puts forward a proposal, they generally avoid immediately making a counter-proposal.
- Average negotiators seem to believe that there is some special merit in quantity. Having three reasons for doing something is considered more persuasive than having only one reason. In contrast, skilled negotiators used fewer reasons to back up their arguments. They also do considerably more checking out, testing their understanding and summarising thoroughly during the negotiation and reviewing it afterwards.

Over two-thirds of the skilled negotiators claimed that they always set aside some time after a negotiation to review it and consider what they had learned. Just under half of the average category made the same claim.

Source: adapted from *International Management*, May 1987, p. 69.

free and open flow of information and they use their desire to satisfy both parties as the perspective from which to structure their discussions. This is the essential ingredient of a 'win–win' situation in international marketing negotiations.

In establishing a marketing relationship involving buying and selling it is necessary to recognize that a range of outcomes is possible. By examining the mutual expected net benefits of a marketing relationship, we can observe that in some situations the seller attempts to dominate and manage the relationship, while in other situations the buyer

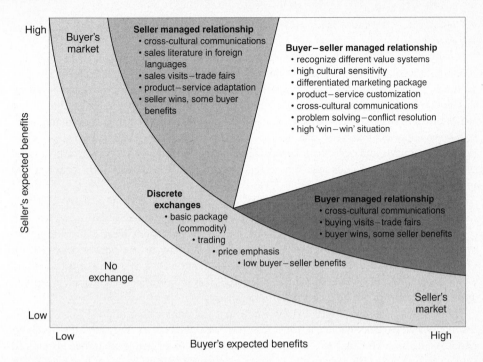

Figure 19.5 Domain of buyer–seller relationships
Source: adapted from Dwyer, F. R., Schurr, P. M. and Oh, S. (1987) 'Developing buyer–seller relationships', *Journal of Marketing,* **51** (April), 15.

attempts to dominate and manage the relationship (Dwyer *et al.,* 1987). In other situations the relationship will be jointly managed (Figure 19.5). Where the expected net benefit from the relationship is equally high for both parties a joint arrangement is likely to operate. The seller manages where the pay-off is high for the seller but neither high nor low for the buyer. The buyer manages where the pay-off is high for the buyer and neither high nor low for the seller. A relatively large area remains which is designated as a buyer's or seller's market depending on the relative benefits, which are likely to be dominated by discrete exchanges. In circumstances where the benefits or pay-offs are low to both parties it is unlikely that any exchange will occur.

Marketing exchanges may be concerned with discrete transactions which lie in the realm of selling or relationships which lie more in the area of negotiations. The latter involve a degree of interdependence and once well developed lead to loyalty and repeat business. There is an increasing tendency for marketing exchanges to be conditioned by longer-term contractual or semicontractual relations which bond buyers and sellers together (Arndt, 1979). Discrete transactions which fall into the selling mode are usually characterized as exchanges involving the transfer of money for an easily identified and quantified product. They usually involve limited communications and detail concerning the product or service exchanged. A one-off purchase of a machine tool component by a United States company from a German company closely represents such a discrete transaction.

Firms that have developed a strong customer franchise or have become recognized as reliable and sought-after suppliers have established marketing relationships. The key factor for such firms is that the basis for further collaboration may be supported by implicit and explicit assumptions and planning. Firms at this end of the continuum can be expected to derive complex, personal, non-economic satisfactions and also to engage in social exchanges. Observing that duties and performance in such circumstances are relatively complex and occur over time led Dwyer *et al.* (1987, p. 12) to conclude that the parties to this type of exchange may direct much effort toward carefully defining and measuring the items of exchange.

Close relationships between two parties in a marketing exchange usually lead to a degree of customization of products and services leading to differentiation, which can create barriers to switching and hence a competitive advantage. Close relationships also reduce uncertainty and significantly increase joint benefits to the parties arising from effective communication and collaboration to attain mutual objectives, i.e. profit for one and satisfaction for the other. This emphasizes the importance of a problem-solving approach in an effort to collaborate by both parties.

Sometimes, however, conflict occurs between the parties that is not always easy to resolve. When participants in a conflict are from the same culture, they are more likely to perceive the situation in basically the same way and to organize their perceptions in similar ways. The people involved in cross-cultural conflicts must be careful, however, not to assume that the perception and values of the counterparts or adversaries in the conflict are the same. Conflict in international markets can be difficult to resolve. The methods used by society for dealing with conflicts reflect the basic values and philosophy in that society. In the West, particularly in the United States, assertive styles tend to be more common. In the Arab world it is mediation – confrontation almost never works. The Chinese, on the other hand, have learned to internalize conflict and seem to ignore it – for the Chinese conflict is not constructive. Considerable assistance in avoiding or reducing conflict may derive from an understanding of buyer–seller styles, as was studied in the preceding section.

Cultural familiarity and negotiation styles

Many authors have examined buying and selling styles from different cultural and business perspectives. The cultural perspective, particularly the need for cultural sensitivity in negotiations, has been examined by many authors including Francis (1991), Lewicki *et al.* (1994) and Weiss (1993, 1994a, 1994b) while the business perspective has been examined by Blake and Mouton (1976) and by McCall and Warrington (1989). This section attempts to integrate the contributions of these authors to derive an understanding of the importance of cultural familiarity in buyer–seller negotiations in international marketing. The framework of the analysis considers the two dimensions – concern for the counterpart to the negotiations, whether buyer or seller, and concern for the product or service, whether bought or sold (Figure 19.6). Concern for the counterpart in the other

Figure 19.6 Cultural familiarity and styles of negotiation

country measures the extent to which the buyer or seller seeks to satisfy the counterpart's objectives, while concern for the sale or purchase of the product or service seeks to satisfy the buyer's or seller's own objectives (Figure 19.6).

With regard to the cultural perspective many writers on the subject assume implicitly that the best way to manage cross-cultural negotiations is to be sensitive to the cultural norms of the other party to the negotiation and to modify strategy to be consistent with behaviours manifested in that culture. In addition, international salespeople must recognize that foreign customers judge performance on cultural accommodation as well as on the more established notions of customer orientation, communication effectiveness and dependability (Harich and LaBahn, 1998, p. 97). This approach may be contrasted with the less culturally sensitive view that 'business is business and a good deal carries the day'. In the latter approach the assumption is that the counterpart adapts to your style of negotiating. Flexibility may also be an important dimension of cross-border negotiations. In negotiating the successful acquisition of Labelmetal AG, a division of the German conglomerate MAN, the Italian company Societa Metalurgia Italiana SpA (SMI) answered the question 'how much did national cultural differences matter?' by stating that 'they might have mattered a great deal, had we, as potential Italian owners, not taken pains to be very flexible' (Sebenius, 1988, p. 38).

Although it is important to avoid cultural traps when negotiating it is not clear that the best approach is to modify strategy to match the counterpart's approach in all circumstances. Several factors indicate that cross-cultural negotiators should not make large concessions to their approach (Lewicki *et al.*, 1994, p. 429):

- Negotiators may not be able to modify their approach effectively – it takes years to understand another culture and there may not be time to gain this understanding.
- Even if negotiators can modify their approach effectively, it does not mean that it will translate automatically into a better negotiation outcome – it is possible that the other side will modify their approach too. With each side trying to act like the other 'should' be acting and both sides not really understanding what the counterpart is doing, negotiations can easily collapse in failure.
- Moderate adaptation may be more effective than either no adaptation or very large adaptations.

A negotiator may be able to choose from eight different culturally responsive strategies (Weiss, 1994a). According to Weiss, when choosing a strategy the negotiators should be aware of their own and the counterpart's culture in general, understand the specific factors in the current relationship and predict or attempt to influence the counterpart's approach. Weiss's culturally responsive negotiation strategies may be arranged into three categories based on familiarity that the negotiator has with the counterpart's culture: low familiarity; moderate familiarity; high familiarity.

In situations where the company is not familiar with the counterpart's culture it may be advisable to hire an agent or advisor who is familiar with the culture of both parties. Agents and advisors may be effective for companies that have little awareness of the other's culture and little time to become aware. As an alternative, it may be possible to introduce a mediator. Mediators who make introductions and then withdraw are quite common. More frequently, however, mediators are present throughout the negotiation and take responsibility for orchestrating the negotiation process. Throughout Europe interpreters and language schools often play the role of mediator, providing both parties with a deeper understanding of the cross-cultural negotiation process. Neither of these approaches involves a full-blown commitment to cross-cultural negotiation but they represent a starting point and may evolve into something more substantial. In this situation the parties to the exchange may still be avoiding substantial engagement with the other or they may be following a very competitive style of negotiation.

A slightly more aggressive approach is to attempt to induce the counterpart to follow your approach. There are many ways of doing this, ranging from a polite request to asserting strongly that your way is the best; it can also be done more subtly by continuing to respond in your language to the requests of counterparts because 'you cannot express yourself well enough in their language' (Lewicki *et al.*, 1994, p. 431). Two can play this game, however, as the counterpart may have a strategic advantage and may attempt more extreme tactics and, if they do not work, excuse them on the basis of 'cultural ignorance'.

When the company is moderately familiar with the counterpart's approach it may be possible to be more accommodating and to make conscious changes to the negotiation approach so that it is more appealing to the counterpart. Rather than trying to act like the counterpart, adapting to the counterpart's approach means maintaining a firm grasp on the preferred approach but making modifications to help relations with the counterpart. The challenge in adapting to the other party is to know which behaviours to modify, which to eliminate and which to adopt. Furthermore, it is not clear that the counterpart will interpret your modifications in the way intended.

Another approach used when both parties are moderately familiar with the other's culture is to coordinate adjustments mutually to find a common process for negotiation. This approach usually involves an explicit recognition of the need to agree the approach to be adopted and requires some facility in each other's language.

As the company becomes more experienced in doing business abroad and becomes very familiar with negotiating in different foreign cultures it may begin to adopt a win–win or collaborative style in its negotiations. One way of doing this is to embrace the counterpart's approach, which requires the negotiator to be completely bilingual and bicultural. In essence the negotiator using this approach does not 'act like a Roman' but is a Roman (Francis, 1991; Weiss, 1994a). This is an expensive strategy and places the negotiator under considerable stress. There is much to be gained by this approach, however, since counterparts can be approached and understood completely on their own terms.

As an alternative to embracing fully the counterpart's approach both parties may customize or improvise an approach to suit a specific situation. In improvising an approach both parties must be very familiar with the counterpart's culture and have a strong understanding of the individual characteristics of the other party. This is a very flexible approach.

Lastly, a very collaborative negotiation style is witnessed when both parties attempt to 'transcend exclusive use of either home culture by exploiting their high familiarity capabilities'(Weiss, 1994a, p. 58). This approach has been referred to as a symphony as it involves both parties working together to create a new approach that may include aspects of either home culture or adopting practices from a third culture. Use of this strategy is complex and involves a great deal of time and effort. It works best when both parties are very familiar with each other, familiar with both home cultures and have a common structure for the negotiation (Lewicki *et al.*, 1994, pp. 432–3; Weiss, 1994a, pp. 58–9). This is the negotiation approach used by professional diplomats.

Turning to the business perspective, a low level of concern for both parties leads to an avoiding style, where the product or service is expected to sell itself or where the purchase is a very routine affair in the customer firm. Neither buyer nor seller emphasizes any aspect of the exchange. Avoiding behaviour frequently results in a breakdown of the exchange relationship and no exchange is likely to result. An accommodating style means an attempt to understand the counterpart, to be responsive, to think in terms of establishing and developing personal relationships and in general to emphasize people rather than things. Such a style displays a high concern for the counterpart and a lower concern for the sale or purchase. In these circumstances the buyer or seller enters the negotiation with a trusting posture and expects cooperative gestures to be reciprocated. If the other party is cooperative the relationship will flourish. An accommodating style usually results in immediate agreement through acceptance of this behaviour by the counterpart.

The competitive style revolves around the hard sell, pressure on the buyer or seller for better terms, disregard for the other side and emphasis on the product or value of the deal. The competitive buyer or seller enters the negotiation to take advantage of the other party and is usually suspicious and untrustworthy. The outcome of an exchange based on a competitive style turns upon location of power in the relationship. A competitive style by one party to the exchange must be matched by complete accommodation by the other side, otherwise agreement is unlikely. A competitive style implies exploiting the exchange situation, especially when the other party is cooperative. The competitive style is often associated with the adversarial approach in buying and selling.

The collaborative style to buying and selling is based on consultation with a focus on customer benefits and the need to find a good result for both parties. Concern is high for both sides. The collaborative style seeks both a good purchase and a good selling decision. Emphasis is on solving problems; a joint problem solving operation provides the best mutually attractive result. In collaborating, both parties recognize the possibility of increasing the shared benefits. Collaboration relies on believing that business negotiations lead to longer-term relationships when the benefits are shared on a win–win basis.

How the above translates into practice in different countries is, of course, the question of interest. The impact of culture on negotiation style varies greatly between different countries (Exhibit 19.3). In a study of the differences in negotiation styles in the United States and Japan, Kamins *et al.* (1998, pp. 26–8) make three recommendations for doing business in Japan:

- since situational factors such as status and role in a business negotiation are extremely important in Japan, negotiators should attempt to learn as much as possible about the individuals who will be on the other side of the negotiations – understanding their roles and relative positions in the company is essential;
- an effective way of gaining knowledge about the other company in the negotiation involves asking questions to uncover what is expected;
- it is necessary to adjust the style of business interactions to fit the hierarchical social and business system in Japan – deliver detailed and comprehensive presentations, be prepared to listen more and defer to the wishes of Japanese buyers.

═══ Exhibit 19.3 ═══
Negotiation style – impact of culture

The French pride themselves on reasoned discussion. They dislike being rushed into decisions, preferring instead to examine various options in decisions. Negotiations are likely to be in French unless they occur outside France. Punctuality is expected. They tend to be formal in their negotiations and do not move quickly to expressions of goodwill until the relationship has existed for some time.

In Japan, business often goes to the party respected the most. Recognising who is deserving of such respect takes more time than most. Westerners are inclined to give with pleasure. Moreover, the Japanese consult with all parties involved before they make decisions. If a delivery date is specified, they are likely to check with the managers responsible for ensuring that it can be met before they will agree to it. They spend considerable amounts of time asking detailed questions about financial, market, manufacturing, and structural issues relevant to the negotiation, as well as questions that some outsiders would perceive as irrelevant. The Japanese also tend to spend time becoming acquainted with the potential partner before developing the framework for a partnership.

American negotiators usually operate as if today is the last day of their lives. They negotiate with conviction and interpret delays and hesitation as signs of stalling or ineptitude. Most do not speak languages other than English. Ford, for example, has a complex alliance with Mazda, but has not dedicated to the relationship an employee who speaks fluent Japanese. Though they are capable of developing long-term relationships, characterised by respect and mutual consideration, American negotiators exhibit words and behaviours that are often perceived as tough or insensitive. Winning is part of their psyche. Once they are assured that they will not lose, it is possible to redirect their attention to mutual gains.

Creating the right environment in Sweden, however, is not the same as doing so in Italy. For example, the Swedes tend to be formal in their relationships, dislike haggling over price, expect thorough, professional proposals without flaws, and are attracted to quality. Italians tend to be extremely hospitable, but are often volatile in temperament. When they make a point, they do so with considerable gesticulation and emotional expression. Impressed by style, they tend to dress well themselves. Moreover, they enjoy haggling over prices.

Of course, these are stereotypes that individual Swedes or Italians may violate. They demonstrate, however, that business people of different cultures come to the negotiation setting with different expectations and different styles of conducting business. Blind to these differences, the foreign negotiator can expect to create a negative impression. Once that impression is formed, it is difficult to establish positive rapport.

Bridging differences such as these is not accomplished without effort. It begins with a strong desire to make things work for both parties and requires the ability to see differences for what they are – the product of diverse cultures rather than sure signs of incompatibility or threats to one's own control.

Source: adapted from Reardon, K. K. and Spekman, R. E (1994) 'Starting out right: negotiation lessons for domestic and cross cultural business alliances' *Business Horizons*, **37** (1), 72–3.

Language in international marketing

With increased internationalization of business and travel, language also travels. Many modern languages borrow from neighbouring language groups. English is perhaps one of the greatest borrowers. A difficulty which can arise in cross-cultural communication under such circumstances occurs when the precise meaning of words used is not the same for the the two speakers. In this regard it is generally advised that if the sales person does not have a reasonable command of the counterpart's language they should consider not using it at all.

In attempting to be flexible there is the added danger of interference from the para-linguistic features of another tongue. The length of pauses between sentences uttered by orientals can be misleading, for example. In the East the time between conscious thought and speaking can be much longer than in the West. In other instances a seeming degree of exaggeration or overassertion of certain words may appear be misinterpreted. For example, in Arabic the apparent assertion of certain phrases and words is a natural means of expression.

The managers of a subsidiary or sales firm are key figures since they absorb the culture of the subsidiary and the wider national culture and interpret it for headquarters. Where response to the market and its culture is deemed to be more important than communication between the person in the field and headquarters, a national of the country is usually employed.

The key prerequisites for successful communication in international markets in an ideal world are awareness of the selling and negotiating process, the ability to understand and use influencing behaviour and empathy for the culture with which the sales person is dealing.

In dealing with the real world, stereotyping of approaches to selling and negotiating may sometimes be used to characterize the likely responses of counterparts. In this regard Fisher (1980) poses the following questions: is there a national style in choosing nego-tiators and what kind of people are likely to be chosen to conduct business with foreign counterparts? He provides a series of answers for the United States, Japan, Mexico and France which demonstrate the differences involved. His approach relies on the choice of technical or social competence as a qualification for conducting business in international markets (Exhibit 19.4).

Fisher concludes that most negotiators will need a mix of technical competence and social competence. The mix tends to vary in emphasis, however, from place to place. Counterparts from traditional societies may operate much more on the basis of their social competence, i.e. who they are, their connections and social class. Most Americans tend to believe in technical competence when credentials are being checked. Thus Americans frequently find they are dealing with counterparts who place more stock on their social competence than seems reasonable to Americans. An underlying difference in this role definition helps explain some of the feeling of social distance in achieving rapport both within and without the negotiation process.

Role of language in selling and negotiations

Increasingly, international companies are developing a match between the firm's language ability and its marketing strategies. Successful international marketing firms employ more foreign language specialists than do less successful firms and the foreign language skills within successful firms are more closely aligned with their major international market (Enderwick and Akoorie, 1994, p. 16). By developing a language profile within the firm and among its customers, the international company is better placed to evaluate the potential for convergence in negotiations and other communi-cations.

Exhibit 19.4
Analysing the negotiating team

Is there a national style in choosing negotiators; what kinds of people qualify to occupy positions that call for conducting business with foreign counterparts; how does their bureaucratic or business culture determine the team members' relationship with each other? This sets the internal dynamics of the team. For Americans technical competence is basic. It is the position in the firm that supplies the authority for team members whose background is an egalitarian society. Competence is the key; team members are not judged by other factors, e.g. negotiators' social egos are not placed on the line. For the Japanese the team presents much more of a closed circle. Cultural conditioning that stresses orderliness in group dynamics rules the relationships among the members and defines their relationships with the non-Japanese world. The progression to leadership and status is by professional competence but also very much by seniority and experience. The team leader might be only marginally competent in the specific subject matter under negotiation but still be the obvious boss. For Mexicans, individuals on a negotiating team stand out. The factors which bring them into a negotiating position are much more likely to reflect their personal qualities and social connections or leverage inside a political–business system in which personality is paramount – 'ubicacion' – how the individual is 'plugged in' in the system. Leaders of such teams do see their social egos more on the line. For the French it is the social status or high academic qualification for entering the system that then stresses competence and adherence to standards. Typical senior negotiators in foreign business deals is likely to have studied at one of three or four business schools. Preparatory work will be done carefully. Typically self-assured in international negotiations because their system prepared them for it and backs them up – it gives them prestige and authority – 'the French have a highly sophisticated ability to make their opponents feel inadequate'. The understanding of the above 'national identities' is important because it helps to define a problem that often plagues international negotiation: conflicting expectations in role behaviour – a particularly useful conceptual tool in cross-cultural analysis.

Source: based on Fisher, G. (1980) *International Negotiation*, Chicago, IL: Intercultural Press, pp. 17–26.

The connection between strategy and language is through people. Company policies, technical information, sales brochures and other communications relating to strategic implementation must be translated into various languages. The company is critically dependent on its people, their language competence, and coping responses which are clearly linked to human resource policies in the company (Marschan *et al.*, 1997, p. 596).

In international marketing, language can be a facilitator of communication or an impediment. Impediments may take two forms, filtration, where messages are only partially transmitted, and distortion, where the intended meaning is altered during the transmission of the message (Marschan *et al.*, 1997, p. 595). The two faces of language, as facilitator or as impediment, may emerge in a range of situations between the company and its customers, all of which affect the company's ability to communicate.

On average, about two-thirds of small and medium-sized businesses in Europe have at least one manager who is able to conduct business negotiations in another language. There is, however, considerable variation in the possession of language skills (Table 19.2). Smaller companies in Ireland, the UK and France have by far the fewest number of executives able to negotiate in another language. For Ireland and the UK, this partly reflects the role of English as the language of international business, and partly the fact that much of the UK's trade is with the US and a large, but declining, proportion of Ireland's is with the UK. In contrast, more than 90 per cent of companies in Malta, Belgium, Luxembourg and the

Table 19.2 Negotiation and communication resources and skills

Country	Language skills (per cent)	Email (per cent)	Information Technology		
			Internet: information (per cent)	Internet: to sell (per cent)	Internet: to buy (per cent)
Austria	86	38	33	15	16
Belgium	91	38	27	12	10
Denmark	90	43	31	4	4
Finland	87	50	44	21	15
France	45	36	8	4	3
Germany	67	25	22	8	11
Greece	86	17	20	6	5
Ireland	31	38	31	12	8
Italy	67	27	25	12	9
Luxembourg	95	43	23	2	2
Netherlands	91	35	33	15	10
Portugal	83	33	23	3	1
Spain	70	34	18	6	8
Sweden	85	46	39	11	11
United Kingdom	38	39	32	11	7
EU Average	*66*	*32*	*24*	*9*	*9*
Malta	96	54	55	13	18
Norway	89	42	41	12	19
Switzerland	82	50	40	18	21
Turkey	68	23	22	6	6
Survey Average	*67*	*33*	*25*	*9*	*9*

Notes: Language skill is defined as the proportion of executives able to negotiate in more than one language; information technology is defined as the proportion of executives having and using information technology

Source: European Business Survey (1997), London: Grant Thornton International Business Strategies Ltd, May, pp. 30–1.

Exhibit 19.5
Euro-tongues wag in English

Europeans are becoming ever more polyglottal. More than half the European Union's people say they speak at least one European language other than their mother tongue. One in three now speaks English well enough to get along in conversation, making it the Union's *lingua franca*. French is spoken by 15% of the EU citizens (outside France), while 9% of them (excluding Germans) say they speak German. Only 5% of non-Spaniards in the Union claim to speak Spanish.

Multi-lingualism varies hugely within Europe. Not surprisingly, those from small places – Luxembourg, the Netherlands, Denmark – do best, with the Luxembourgers winning the prize for Europe's linguistic paragons. Their official language is Letzeburgisch, a German–French mishmash, but 86% of people in the duchy also speak French and 77% German as their second languages, while nearly half can chat in English and a tenth in Italian.

The Dutch are fine linguists too. Only 14% of them admit to knowing no second tongue: 79% speak English, two-thirds German, and nearly a quarter French. Eurosceptic though many Danes may be, they are no linguistic slouches: more than three-quarters can rattle along in English, just over half know German, a fifth can talk Swedish, and a tenth French. The British and Irish are the duds – two-thirds of people in both countries speak English only. But then the ability to speak a language may not be the same as willingness to do so.

Cross the border into Central Europe and the picture changes sharply. Russian still supplants English as the most common foreign tongue. The outlook across the continental board is clear: English is rampant, German making steady advances on the eastern front, while French is losing ground, especially outside the Union.

Source: adapted from *Economist*, 25 October 1997, p. 48.

Netherlands are able to negotiate business in another language, reflecting perhaps the small size of their domestic market and the pressure to export a large proportion of production (Exhibit 19.5).

Related to negotiation and the role of language is the place of information technology among managers. On average, a third of European managers in small and medium-sized companies have e-mail. Maltese, Finnish and Swiss companies are most likely to have e-mail. In contrast, less than a quarter of Greek and Turkish companies have it, while the proportion in Germany and Italy is noticeably low.

A quarter of small and medium-sized companies have the internet and use it to collect information. This is especially true in Malta, Finland and Norway, where over 40 per cent of companies gather information from the internet. In France, however, fewer than 10 per cent have the internet, but it must be remembered that Minitel has achieved very high penetration in France, which possibly explains the low awareness and use of the internet there.

Selecting the sales team

For the international sales person to succeed it is necessary to have a comprehensive knowledge of the business culture as well as an ability to adapt to a foreign culture if necessary. A number of skills have been identified as important in adapting to a new culture (Hutton, 1988). Most important among these are the following:

1. tolerance of ambiguity and a willingness to change objectives;
2. a low task orientation to allow flexibility to different circumstances;
3. open-minded non-judgemental view of life;
4. empathy;
5. ability to communicate across cultures;
6. self-reliance.

Flexibility does not mean that the salesforce relinquishes its own ways of doing business and goes 'native' in the face of different circumstances. In such circumstances the role of language becomes important. A facility in the counterpart's language is a basic ingredient for successful interpersonal relations and affects results.

The firm has three choices when selecting a sales team. It can hire expatriates, host country nationals or third country nationals. Expatriates are home country sales people and are favoured by industrial products firms because of their technical competence and ability to provide after-sales service (Boyacigiller, 1990). While there are many benefits in using expatriates, there are also many costs. Many expatriates do not cope easily in a foreign culture and so are ineffective. They are also more expensive than locals. Comprehensive training in and sensitivity to the foreign culture are required before sending expatriates abroad. This means providing detailed knowledge of the area's language and culture as cultural alienation renders a sales person ineffectual.

The second option, hiring a host country national, has the benefit of acquiring extensive market and cultural knowledge, language skills and familiarity with business customs. Locals tend to be less expensive, except for some advanced economies, such as Japan, the US and Germany. The adjustment period is shorter as a local sales person can be effective in a relatively short period. There are, however, some disadvantages in using locals. They may not have the detailed product knowledge required and they do not understand the company and its culture.

The third option open to the firm is to hire third country nationals. Third country nationals, if selected from the region, may be culturally sensitive and have the language required. This is certainly true in European countries and in Asia. Third country nationals are a welcome compromise for regionally focused companies. There are, however, some disadvantages in hiring third country nationals. They may feel that they do not belong to the company or the host country and they may feel that their career path within the firm is ill defined and uncertain. They may also cost more than the others. The advantages and disadvantages of each type of sales person have been identified by Honeycutt and Ford (1995) and are summarized in Figure 19.7.

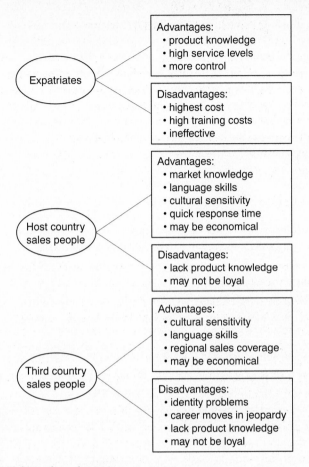

Figure 19.7 Picking the sales team

Summary

Selling and negotiation strategies are developed by the firm to implement marketing strategy. The firm implements its strategy through the sales and marketing team. The interaction between buyer and seller in international marketing is a very complex activity. The marketing exchange may refer to a simple discrete transaction or, alternatively, it may refer to a long-standing, well-developed relationship between two firms operating in two very different cultures to attain mutually beneficial objectives. Understanding the selling and negotiations process is important whichever situation is present.

Where sophisticated marketing relationships are involved it is important to understand the multifaceted aspects of the relationships.

The role of the salesforce in international markets is changing to include a deeper understanding of marketing and an acknowledgement of a degree of marketing autonomy in local markets. In deciding appropriate roles for the salesforce it is necessary for the firm to acknowledge the existence of both a buying process and a selling process which converge to produce a satisfactory result to both parties to the exchange.

The successful outcome of these processes of convergence is dependent, to a large extent, on there being a high degree of cultural understanding and affinity between the partners. This affinity arises through communications between the parties involved. The international marketing aspect adds a new and complex dimension to the communications process. Successful buying and selling strategies are based on establishing mutually beneficial marketing relationships.

Discussion questions

1. Describe what is meant by marketing exchanges in international marketing. To what extent are marketing exchanges confined to products and services?

2. What is the role of the salesforce in the firm in international markets? Do you expect any changes in its role in the future?

3. A distinction was drawn in the chapter between discrete exchanges and exchanges which occur as a result of a longer-term relationship. What is your opinion regarding this distinction?

4. What is meant by the convergence of buying and selling processes?

5. Discuss the importance of communications in buying and selling in international marketing. What is the effect of culture on communications?

6. In developing a selling or negotiating strategy the firm may use a particular buyer–seller style. Outline the more important of these and discuss their relevance to the firm in international markets.

7. What are the key factors to consider in picking the international sales team?

References

Anderson, E. and Weitz, B. (1992) 'The use of pledges to build and sustain commitment in distribution channels', *Journal of Marketing Research*, **29** (February), 18–34.

Arndt, J. (1979) 'Towards a concept of domesticated markets', *Journal of Marketing*, **43** (Fall), 69–75.

Barlund, D. C. (1979) 'A transaction model of communication', in D. Mortensen (ed.), *Basic Readings in Communications Theory*, New York, NY: Harper and Row.

Barnett, G. A. and Kincaid, L. D. (1983) 'Cultural convergence: a mathematical theory', in W. B. Gudykunst and B. Hill (eds), *Intercultural Communication Theory*, London: Sage Publications, Chapter 10.

Beatty, S. E., Kahle, L. R., Homer, P. and Misra, S. (1985) 'Alternative measurement approaches to consumer values: the list of values and the Rokeach value scale', *Psychology and Marketing*, **2** (Fall), 181–200.

Blake, R. R. and Mouton, J. S. (1976) *The Grid for Sales Excellence: Benchmarks for Effective Salesmanship*, New York, NY: McGraw Hill.

Boyacigiller, N. (1990) 'The role of expatriates in the management of interdependence, complexity and risk in multinational corporations', *Journal of International Business Studies*, **21** (3), 357–81.

Bush, V. D. and Ingram, T. (1996) 'Adapting to diverse customers: a training matrix for international marketers', *Industrial Marketing Management*, **25**, 373–83.

Campbell, N. C. G., Graham, J. L., Jolibert, A. and Meissner, H. G. (1988) 'Marketing negotiations in France, Germany, the United Kingdom, and the United States', *Journal of Marketing*, **52**, 49–62.

Cooley, R. E. (1983) 'Codes and contexts: an argument for their description', in W. B. Gudykunst and B. Hill (eds), *Intercultural Communication Theory*, London: Sage Publications, Chapter 13.

Cunningham, M. T. and Homse, E. (1982) 'An interaction approach to marketing strategy', in H. Håkansson (ed.), *International Marketing and Purchasing of Industrial Goods: An Interaction Approach*, Chichester: Wiley, 358–69.

Dubinsky, A. J., Kotabe, M., Lim, C. U. and Wagner, W. (1997) 'The impact of values on salespeople's job responses: a cross-national investigation', *Journal of Business Research*, **39**, 195–208.

Dwyer, F. R., Schurr, P. H. and Oh, S. (1987) 'Developing buyer–seller relationship', *Journal of Marketing*, **51**, 11–27.

Enderwick, P. and Akoorie, M. E. M. (1994) 'The employment of foreign language specialists and export success – the case of New Zealand', *International Marketing Review*, **11** (4), 4–18.

Fisher, G. (1980) *International Negotiation*, Chicago, IL: Intercultural Press.

Ford, I. D. (1984) 'Buyer–seller relationships in international industrial markets', *Industrial Marketing Management*, **13**, 101–12.

Francis, J. N. P. (1991) 'When in Rome? The effects of cultural adaptation on intercultural business negotiations', *Journal of International Business Studies*, **22** (Third Quarter), 402–28.

Ghauri, P. (1996) 'Introduction', in P. N. Ghauri and J.-C. Usunier (eds) *International Business Negotiations*, Oxford: Pergamon, pp. 3–20.

Gourlay, R. (1987) 'Negotiations and bargaining', *Management Decision (UK)*, **25** (3), 16–27.

Graham, J. L. (1985) 'The influence of culture on the process of business negotiations: an exploratory study', *Journal of International Business Studies*, **26** (1), 81–96.

Graham, J. L., Mintu, A. T. and Rodgers, W. (1994): 'Explorations of negotiations behaviours in ten foreign cultures using a model developed in the United States', *Management Science*, **40** (January), 72–95.

Hall, E. T. (1960) 'The silent language of overseas business', *Harvard Business Review*, **38** (May–June), 81–98.

Hall, E. T. (1976) *Beyond Culture*, New York, NY: Anchor Press/Doubleday.

Harich, K. R. and LaBahn, D. W. (1998) 'Enhancing international business relationships: a focus on customer perceptions of salesperson role performance including cultural sensitivity', *Journal of Business Research*, **42** (1), 87–101.

Hofstede, G. (1991) *Cultures and Organisations: Software of the Mind*, London: McGraw-Hill.

Honeycutt, E. D. Jr. and Ford, J. B. (1995) 'Guidelines for managing an international sales force', *Industrial Marketing Management*, **24**, 135–44

Hutt, M. D. and Speh, T. W. (1989) *Business Marketing Management*, 3rd edn, Chicago, IL: Dryden Press.

Hutton, J. (1988) *The World of the International Manager*, Oxford: Philip Allan.

Jackson, D. W. and Tax, S. S. (1995) 'Managing the industrial salesforce culture', *Journal of Business and Industrial Marketing*, **10** (2), 34–47.

Kamins, M. A., Johnston, W. J. and Graham, J. L. (1998) 'A multi-method examination of buyer-seller interactions among Japanese and American businesspeople', *Journal of International Marketing*, **6** (1), 8–32.

Kotler, P. (1997) *Marketing Management*, 9th edn, Englewood Cliffs, NJ: Prentice Hall International.

LaBahn, D. W. and Harich, K. R. (1997): 'Sensitivity to national business culture: effects on U.S.–Mexican channel relationship performance', *Journal of International Marketing*, **5** (4), 29–51.

Lee, J. A. (1966) 'Cultural analysis in overseas operations', *Harvard Business Review*, **44** (March–April), 106–11.

Lewicki, R. J., Litterer, J. A., Minton, J. W. and Saunders, D. M. (1994) *Negotiation*, 2nd edn, Chicago, IL: Irwin.

Marschan, R., Welch, D. and Welch, L. (1997) 'Language: the forgotten factor in multinational management', *European Management Journal*, **15** (5), 591–98.

Marshall, G. W., Brouthers, L. E. and Lamb, C. W. Jr. (1998) 'A typology of political economies and strategies in international selling', *Industrial Marketing Management*, **27**, 11–19.

McCall, J. B. and Warrington, M. B. (1989) *Marketing by Agreement*, Chichester, Wiley.

Reardon, K. K. and Spekman, R. E. (1994) 'Starting out right: negotiation lessons for domestic and cross-cultural business alliances', *Business Horizons*, **37** (1), 71–80.

Samli, A. C., Still, R. and Hill, J. S. (1993) *International Marketing*, New York, NY: MacMillan.

Schramm, W. (1971) 'How communication works', in W. Schramm and D. F. Roberts (eds), *The Process and Effects of Mass Communications*, Urbana, IL: University of Illinois Press.

Schuster, C. and Copeland, M. (1996) 'Cross-cultural communication: issues and implications', in P. N. Ghauri and J.-C. Usunier (eds) *International Business Negotiations*, Oxford: Pergamon, pp. 131–52.

Sebenius, J. K. (1998) 'Negotiating cross-border acquisitions', *Sloan Management Review*, **40** (Winter), 27–41.

Turnbull, P.W. (1987) 'Interaction and international marketing: an investment process', *International Marketing Review*, **4** (4), 7–19.

Ueltschy, L. C. and Ryans, J. K. Jr. (1997) 'Employing standardised promotion strategies in Mexico: the Impact of language and cultural differences', *International Executive*, **39** (4), 479–95.

Weeks, W. A. and Kahle, L. R. (1990) 'Social values and salespeople's effort', *Journal of Business Research*, **34** (March), 183–90.

Weiss, S. E. (1993) 'Analysis of complex negotiations in international business: the RBC perspective', *Organization Science*, **4**, 269–300.

Weiss, S. E. (1994a) 'Negotiating with "Romans" – Part 1', *Sloan Management Review*, **38** (Winter), 51–61.

Weiss, S. E. (1994b) 'Negotiating with "Romans" – Part 2', *Sloan Management Review*, (Spring), 55–99.

20

Managing international marketing operations

Managing international marketing operations means ensuring that the programme developed for each international market is implemented and controlled. This means that in planning the programme the firm must pay attention to difficulties that may arise subsequently in implementing plans in the market. Successful firms institute control systems to complement and support their planning. The key issues arising in implementing international marketing plans and systems for controlling implementation are examined in this chapter. A hierarchy of control systems is introduced. First, we examine how firms develop and use operational control systems. This is followed by a section dealing specifically with financial control. Finally, the appropriate role for strategic control in the firm is discussed. The chapter ends with a short section on the need to review performance standards periodically as they apply to the management of international marketing operations.

Effective implementation of the international marketing task

Measuring marketing performance

The objective of the firm in international markets is to create a multidimensional management process capable of identifying and responding to diversity, dynamism and complexity in the international environment. Only effective firms survive in this environment.

Effectiveness derives from the management of demands of the various interest groups upon which the firm depends for resources and support (Pfeffer and Salancik, 1978, pp. 2–3). As was seen in many earlier chapters the firm is linked to its environment through customer–supplier relationships, competitive relationships and relationships with firms that complement the company, with the cultural and political–legal framework which defines and controls the nature and boundaries of these relationships within the business system. The behaviour of the firm depends upon the firm itself, its structure, its leadership, its procedures and its goals. It also depends on the environment and the particular contingencies and constraints deriving from that environment. The firm must manage these relationships. For the firm in international markets the task is more complex and difficult since:

> achieving a coherent view of the output or performance measures of marketing has remained a difficult and generally unrewarding business. Indeed, perhaps no other concept in marketing's short history has proven as stubbornly resistant to concep-tualization, definition or application as that of marketing performance.
>
> (Bonoma and Clarke, 1988, p. 1)

Managers bring four implementation skills to the marketing task: interacting, allocating, monitoring and organizing (Bonoma, 1984, p. 75). Bonoma suggested that the marketing task by its nature is one of influencing others inside and outside the firm. There are internal and external conditions over which the manager has no direct control but which must be influenced. The manager must also allocate time, assignments and resources among the various tasks involved in implementing marketing strategy. Monitoring is a task which must be done; some firms cope very poorly with it, spending too much time collecting data and not enough time developing managerially useful information. Finally, good implementation means having the ability to develop informal networks and relationships both within the firm and outside it to address problems as they arise. According to Bonoma (1984, p. 75), customized informal organization facilitates good implementation. Many of the issues which must be considered in implementing marketing strategies apply also for the firm in international markets. In assessing marketing performance, firms are concerned with measuring the efficiency of the use of marketing inputs, the influence of mediating factors and the nature and level of marketing outputs (Bonoma and Clarke, 1988). Many of these, which Bonoma and Clarke derived from an extensive literature search, are already familiar. These authors identified a number of input measures, a list of mediating factors divided into market characteristics, product characteristics, customer characteristics and task characteristics, and a set of output measures (Figure 20.1). Very few firms measure all the variables outlined. Many use a subset of these variables and monitor their behaviour over time. How they are measured and the value placed on them is the subject of the following sections in this chapter.

Review of international marketing tasks

The firm in international markets faces two major sets of tasks. First, it must analyse and understand its customers, actual and potential. Second, it must provide products and services through a marketing programme to produce satisfaction for the customer and profits for the company. Managing international marketing operations is the planning and coordinating of all the activities implied above to arrive at a successful integrated marketing programme which may involve numerous and different foreign markets. The implementation, management and control of the firm's marketing programme in different international markets is complex and requires sophisticated analytical and managerial skills.

Success in international markets requires a strategic orientation on the part of the firm.

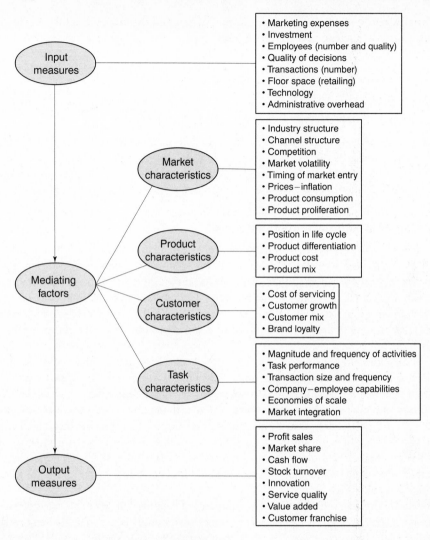

Figure 20.1 Measures of marketing efficiency
Source: adapted from Bonoma, T. V. and Clarke, B. H. (1988) *Marketing Performance Assessment*, Boston, MA: Harvard Business School Press, pp. 35–7.

The process of strategic marketing means working in the context of a corporate strategic plan with specified mission statements, objectives and component strategies. The strategic marketing process, therefore, implies deciding the marketing strategy based on a set of objectives, target market segments, positioning and policies. The firm in international markets is especially aware that its markets are dynamic, needs and wants change continuously, product markets evolve and resources are not fixed.

There are three key components in formulating a marketing strategy:

- it is necessary to analyse the firm itself, the market and the competition to understand the market and the competitive environment,
- international marketing operations must have institutional support, i.e. organizational structures and processes, incentives and value systems, to allow strategic thinking to occur and
- strategic thinking which refers to creative, entrepreneurial insights into the firm, the industry and the market must be the basis of the approach.

As seen in Chapter 4, international marketing strategy is an integrated set of activities which take account of the firm's resources and are designed to increase the long-term well-being of the firm through securing a sustainable competitive advantage with respect to the competition in serving customer needs in one or more international markets.

Financing international market expansion

Many firms following a growth strategy in international markets do not fully understand that profitability and solvency, although related, frequently follow very different paths during an expansionary phase. The firm entering international markets for the first time or seeking to expand there must remain solvent. That is the firm's first financial objective. Its second is to ensure that funds for expansion are available when needed. This means deciding the sources of the funds and the capital and ownership structure of the firm in the longer term.

In costing the international marketing strategy the firm must identify costs under a number of headings: management; time; reorganization required; new staff employed and their training. It is also necessary to allow for the acquisition of know-how, development costs and any capital investment associated with expansion abroad. The firm must also ensure that production, distribution and marketing costs, any income forgone through reduced prices and a contribution to overheads are met. Finally, the firm must decide whether the new international strategy involves an investment which is a budget item or an annual investment matter, or whether it should be considered part of the long-term development plan of the firm.

Expansion through self-financing has a number of benefits: the firm pays no interest on the money used although the opportunity cost of such money is relevant, the firm retains control over the financial strategy and it is possible to retain the existing capital structure of the firm. In some instances, however, it may be desirable or necessary to seek external finance, especially for a new international marketing venture or an expansion in an existing international market. External financing requires the firm to estimate the feasibility of a number of possible growth rates and to judge the level and source of finance required to service such sales. In making the decision whether to finance a strategy internally or externally the firm must recognize the need to support its marketing strategy at every point with an appropriate financial strategy.

Meaning of management control

In preceding chapters the emphasis on developing strategies for the firm in international markets focused on controlled expansion into foreign markets and controlled growth.

The need to pursue growth opportunities selectively raised the issue of finding an agreed strategic framework for international marketing control. Unfortunately, there has been very little interaction of concepts and theories in international marketing strategy and planning with those of finance and managerial accounting. While the importance of market share objectives, market size and growth rates, and the importance of good forecasts have been recognized, procedures for marketing control have not yet been successfully related to these key factors (Hulbert and Toy, 1984, p. 452). Good control systems are necessary for implementation of management strategies. A framework for control

> provides a system for attempting to ensure that 'things don't go wrong' during the implementation of strategies. During implementation, control should be continuously exercised through the application of the framework. The basis of this application is the achievement of organizational and business objectives, with profits being extracted for separate attention.   (Greenley, 1989, p. 369)

Control and implementation are serious and complex management issues faced by the firm. In international markets they mean added complexity and are frequently very central to the growth and survival of the firm. Many international companies attempt to control implementation of their marketing strategies by changing the structure of the organization. Organizational change can result in efficiencies and considerable savings. The downside of moving toward a global organization, as Ford Motor Co. attempted to a few years ago, can be considerable. When a company centralizes all product development, however, a mistake which could have been confined to a single country or region could become a global disaster. 'If you misjudge the market, you are wrong in 15 countries rather than in one', says one European executive of Ford (*Business Week*, 23 May 1994, p. 30).

Larger firms take a greater interest in how they organize to implement strategies in various international markets. The emphasis appears to be away from country managers and marketing activities organized on a country basis to management for a region or group of countries on a product line basis. Much of this interest in re-designing organizational structures relates to the growth of large market groups, as has occurred with the completion of the EU market and the opening of markets in Eastern Europe.

Organization and control

In earlier chapters, the issues of standardization and customization of international marketing strategies were discussed. It is appropriate to return to these issues, since they have a direct impact on the firm's approach to strategic and operational control. Standardization leads directly in some companies to centralized control, because of the perceived benefits with regard to implementation of strategy. On the other hand, customization would indicate a degree of autonomy in implementation. The stress and conflict between these two positions has given rise to the catch cry, 'think global, but act local'. This is advice which is very difficult to heed. A number of research studies have addressed the matter and provide some guidance.

The advocates of global standardization of marketing strategies claim a superior performance for the firm doing so. The evidence does not exist, except in anecdotal fashion, to support such a claim. The critical issue of superior performance, through global standardization, which follows the theoretical underpinning of market segmentation, is not supported (Samiee and Roth, 1992). The fact that Coca-Cola or Guinness sells a number of their brands in over 100 countries does not mean that they have developed a high degree of global standardization for all of their products. Brand names may have the best chance of becoming global, but the presence of a global brand implies a global position. Baileys have achieved a global position for their brand, and as a leader in its product category it may be considered a global brand. Achieving a global position for the brand may be neither easy nor beneficial. Global branding is very expensive and may be a mistake. Even when brands achieve global status, however, better performance might result from positioning them differently in different markets (Samiee and Roth, 1992). Unilever's Domestos household cleaner brand succeeded only after management abandoned its uniform positioning strategy (Kashani, 1989). While the reasons given in the literature in support of global standardization appear intuitively acceptable, they usually refer to cost advantages (Daniels, 1987) but ignore or downplay customer interests. In the long term, global standardization may be myopic.

Creating an international marketing organization is a very challenging management task because the interests of the company as a whole are not perceived in the same way by each of the affected constituents. Different perspectives arise from the production side and the marketing side. Financial and accounting considerations may differ. Even people outside the organization will have to be considered: suppliers and customers. Complementary service providers such as agents, financial institutions and advertising agents will also have a view. If, however, the company is to be an international force, it should be in everybody's interest to participate and share in an international organization, rather than to seek local independence. The challenge is to blend cultural and human considerations so that the benefits of whatever organizational structure emerges is accepted by all concerned. Finding the proper balance between responsiveness to local needs and home country control is a most challenging task facing management (Blackwell *et al.*, 1991). Following these authors, the level of international coordination may be divided into six categories in descending order of home-country control:

1. control;
2. direction;
3. coordination;
4. coordinating mechanisms;
5. cooperation;
6. autonomy.

There are four marketing areas which are immediately susceptible to decisions regarding control: sourcing of raw materials and components, product development, product management and sales. By combining these elements of marketing with the six control categories, we derive matching levels of international coordination (Table 20.1).

Global standardization does not contribute to control and companies pay little attention to this matter (Samiee and Roth, 1992). Control may be more important in

Table 20.1 Levels of international marketing coordination

	Sourcing	Product development	Product management	Sales
1. Home country control	Fully centralized	New products created in home country	Home country management	Home country management
2. Home country direction	Home country negotiates contract; locals have option to use	Home country development; local brand decisions	International brands, home country campaigns, where desired by local managers	Major accounts managed from home country
3. Home country coordination	Supplier deals in lead countries for all units	Some shared developments in prime mover markets	International brands, local campaigns	Coordinated approach to international customers
4. Coordinating mechanisms	Regular sourcing meetings, sharing details of prices, etc.	Local development, some product swapping	Some international brands, sharing of market research	International sales performance standards
5. Informal cooperation	Sourcing managers meet yearly, informal network	Local development with some development meetings	Some meetings, sharing of research	International sales meetings
6. Market autonomy	All local sourcing	Entirely local initiatives and products	National brands only	Local sales force and channel management

Source: adapted from Blackwell, N., Bizet, J.-P., Child, P. and Hensley, D. (1991) 'Creating European organizations that work', *McKinsey Quarterly*, **24** (2), 32.

administering certain elements of the marketing mix, such as advertising and packaging. According to Samiee and Roth (1992), the ability of firms to pursue global standardization may depend on their international business philosophies and organizational structures. A firm organized in a multidomestic way is less likely to implement a standardized strategy, whereas firms that follow a geographic market expansion strategy are better able to consider a global standardization strategy because they can centrally coordinate and implement the necessary changes.

Centralized control has been advocated for other reasons and benefits: to facilitate sales forecasting, to determine changes in government regulations, to increase the likelihood of government contracts, to share marketing experiences and to manage the strategic product portfolio from country to country (Daniels, 1987). Because of variations and differences between areas of the world, Daniels advocates a regional approach as an enduring pragmatic way of dealing with control.

Operational control in international markets

Many companies active in international markets acknowledge that a reliance on financial measures alone can undermine the marketing strategies the company must pursue for long-term survival. Non-financial measures such as quality, customer satisfaction, market share, innovation, organization learning and human resources issues are now recognized as important. In terms of human resources it seems most important for international marketing companies that international growth and expansion strategies are explicitly linked to the competences of staff. This means that these competences are measured, benchmarked and publicized within the company. It is necessary to link each area of the business to the international marketing strategy in the company. This means taking into consideration traditional measures and other broader based measures which focus on the longer-term position of the company.

Sales quotas and controls

Sometimes firms monitor foreign sales from one year to the next and use the trends to judge performance, good or poor, depending on the trend. Other firms adopt a more formal sales control approach, where sales might be classified by country or region of a foreign market, by customer and by product group. The next step would be to decide appropriate criteria to decide the sales level which should fall into each category. The firm might develop an index to measure the importance of each of the categories used. An analysis of previous sales might be used to establish quotas which, over time, are adjusted to accommodate changes in the market. Usually, effective sales control systems require a variable standard, as implied here. If economic activity in a particular country is very high and developing rapidly, sales in that market might also expect to grow. Similarly, a decline in the market should be reflected in a downward adjustment of the quota. The assumption behind such a sales control system is that factors causing an expansion or contraction in the market beyond the influence of the firm should not be used in evaluating sales performance.

Current earnings and profits

The managers of foreign operations evaluated on the basis of current earnings are likely to emphasize short-run profits and to neglect long-run profits. This is particularly true if managers are frequently moved from market to market or are repatriated, which would allow them to avoid the longer-term consequences of their actions. These actions could involve reducing advertising and general marketing expenditures, reducing research and development work under their control and not spending sufficient sums on staff training and development. Because circumstances can be different in different foreign markets and outside management control, performance measures based on sales, profits or return on investment can be misleading at best and inaccurate at worst. For this reason firms frequently compare actual results with budgeted estimates. Variances in costs and revenues can then be examined to determine whether these are affected by outside events such as changes in the exchange rate or caused mainly by management intervention.

Financial control in international marketing

Having decided to enter or expand in international markets the firm must ensure that the strategy to be followed is costed properly. The firm must also decide how to finance the strategy, from internal resources or from selected external sources. Finally, good financial management dictates that the expansion strategy should not jeopardize the survival and growth of the firm.

As emphasized elsewhere in this chapter, growth and expansion in international markets are associated with considerable cost. The costs of entering and expanding in slow-growth markets are particularly high. Expansion for the firm in international markets, even in industries which are not capital intensive, requires large cash outlays, the postponement of income and skilful marketing and financial management. For success it is thus necessary to coordinate marketing strategies and financial planning. Where the firm does not properly relate its marketing strategy to its financial resources this lack of coordination can lead to collapse.

The costing and financial control of international marketing strategies are difficult tasks for most firms and can be very complicated. International marketing strategies can be difficult to quantify; they refer to the longer term and consist of numerous steps with varying impacts. It is difficult in costing strategies to separate costs into fixed costs, variable costs and cash flow projections. To overcome these difficulties, successful international firms attempt to ensure that control rests with financial, marketing and general management people, since such a team effort is likely to understand better the cost implications of an international marketing strategy.

Importance of cash flow in international markets

The significance of cash flow to the firm in international markets may be gleaned by observing the difference between profits and cash flow. A brief review of these concepts will illustrate the point. There are two reasons why cash flow is very unlike profit. First, there is a lapse of time between obtaining raw materials and employing labour to produce the product for sale and the time of the actual sale of the product. The second is the influence of credit. Cash is not necessarily paid out for the materials and labour at the time they are used. Similarly, cash may not be received at the time the sale is made.

In contrast, profit is the difference between two sums: the price the customer pays and the total of prices the firm agrees to pay for all the inputs used in preparing the product or service for sale. Profit is the difference between agreed prices.

Cash flow is money lodged to a bank account, less cash withdrawals from that account in any given period. Most deposits arise when customer receipts are received for products and services previously sold.

Disbursements generally arise when the firm pays for the goods and services previously purchased. Cash flow is the difference between money lodged in the bank and the money withdrawn from the bank. The size of the cash flow and its direction, positive or negative, depend absolutely as much upon when the money is lodged or withdrawn as upon how much is deposited or withdrawn.

Profit is therefore very different from cash flow. As will be seen, it is possible to have a very profitable business but still to fail owing to poor cash flow performance. The significance arises most dramatically as the firm expands into international markets. A major benefit of examining the firm's cash flow requirements related to an expansion is that the amount of financing required to carry out the anticipated expansion programme is determined. Associated with most international expansions are larger purchases of raw materials and other inputs, more sophisticated machinery, access to sources of finance and additional sales people. An instinctive urge to grow through international market expansion has led many firms into the growth trap. Herein lies the dilemma for many international firms. The firm operationalizes international strategies, not just for increased sales in world markets; many firms also require the cash flow generated in world markets to support new product development, to support the acquisition of new technologies and to invest in international marketing channels of distribution. According to Hamel and Prahalad (1985, p. 145), this is a real problem; companies that remain in the domestic market are likely to find themselves at a resource and cost disadvantage which will also prevent them from defending the home market.

In general a faster growth in sales should produce an attractive increase in profits. There may, however, be an adverse impact on cash flow. The firm may experience impressive growth in many of its international markets with an equally impressive growth in earnings and at the same time face severe financial constraint. Sales growth in most businesses consumes cash. As seen above, cash is needed to purchase items such as raw materials, services and merchandise when preparing the product or service for sale. Growth in sales requires that greater quantities of these items be bought in anticipation of future sales. Cash is also needed to support the business at its now larger size while awaiting payment from customers for larger sales. Consequently, during periods of rapid growth the cash flow is characteristically negative.

Timing of cash flows for international sales growth

The firm that introduces its products to a new foreign market usually finds that, initially, sales growth is slow, the firm incurs losses and cash flow is negative. While customers may be innovative there are few of them and the firm needs a lot of money to develop the market. At this stage the firm is attempting to move potential customers from awareness to adoption. Initial success brings with it rapid sales growth which requires considerable amounts of cash to service it. At this stage the firm may have to lower prices slightly and to incur extra costs to improve the product in an effort to penetrate distribution channels. The costs of such expansion to establish preferences for the firm's products can be high. Such developments exacerbate the pressure on cash flows in the firm.

While it is not possible to be precise about the exact nature of the relationships between sales, profits, cash flow and bank balances for all businesses, there are some general principles that apply and that can be examined (Figure 20.2).

Sales growth is generally believed to follow the traditional path of a life cycle, starting off relatively slowly and then rising rapidly in the new and growing phase, slowing down to the growth in population for consumer products and to the replacement sales rate for industrial products in the mature and stable phase and falling off rapidly in the decline phase. The life cycle of the profit–loss curve is thought to parallel the sales curve starting out as a loss and only becoming positive in the growth phase. Greatest profits are believed to occur in the mature and stable phase of the market evolution.

These early losses give rise to a problem encountered by many entrepreneurial firms which expand into international markets without adequate financial resources. Early losses, or negative cash flow, may cause a significant drain on cash resources in the company's bank. As sales increase, investment by the firm in cash, debtors and stocks must grow proportionately and fluctuations in sales, for whatever reason, would be followed by similar fluctuations in current asset requirements (Weston and Copeland, 1988, p. 243). For the small- to medium-sized company the working capital management policy is likely to depend on the banking system. Assuming no external financing the cash flow position is likely to be negative for a considerable period of time, only becoming positive in the late period of the new and growing phase of the life cycle. Further expansions and the extra demands on cash, as discussed above, are likely to be reactivated, thereby pushing the cash flow curve down again. The process continues in such a cyclical fashion throughout the earlier phases of the life cycle, which causes great demands on the firm's cash resources. Under the conditions assumed the result on the company's bank balance is likely to be traumatic.

With the initial flurry of sales and first orders and sales perhaps being made out of inventory, bank balances are likely to be positive. The continued pressure on cash flow will, however, rapidly cause bank balances to become negative. While the cyclical pattern is likely to be repeated in the bank balances, most of the activity is likely to occur below the line in the negative or loss area (Figure 20.2). The size of the negative bank balance is indicative of the amount of external cash that must be injected into the business. The behaviour of the four variables sales, profits, cash flow and bank balances and their

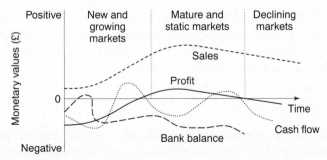

Figure 20.2 Relationship among sales growth, cash flow and bank balance: expansion into new foreign markets

interrelation may be cited in support of government financial subsidy schemes for smaller businesses attempting to internationalize. The peculiar pattern of these four key variables also raises the important issue of adequate equity in the firm contemplating an expansion in international markets.

Size of firm and cash flow

The problem is greater for smaller than for larger firms. Smaller firms need proportionally more external financing and typically have much more difficulty obtaining it. It is relatively easy to double sales in one year if what is being doubled is small. It is a much more difficult task to double sales in one year if existing sales are large. A small firm entering international markets for the first time could easily find itself in a position of doubling its sales if it chooses. Consequently, smaller firms are more likely to have a continuous and urgent need for proportionally more cash to overcome negative cash flow than larger firms.

Larger firms frequently find it easier to obtain additional money under conditions of rapid growth. They usually have long-established relationships with banks and suppliers, good reputations and historical evidence of their ability to survive. Lenders and investors feel reasonably safe in dealing with large firms that are growing profitably.

Smaller firms, and entrepreneurial firms especially, usually find that the additional money needed is difficult to obtain. They seldom have long-established relationships; they may have little or no reputation, and they may have only narrow evidence of their ability to manage the larger enterprise they hold as an aspiration for their firm. In such circumstances lenders and investors find it difficult to do business with smaller firms. Consequently, money that is made available to smaller firms often takes longer to procure, costs more and has conditions of control over management attached to it which may be unattractive. This is one of the major reasons behind the many government-sponsored export promotion and industrial development schemes involving financial incentives for smaller firms.

Implementing performance standards

Most companies still use profit-based measures to evaluate performance. Cash flow measures are not seen as so important, which reflects on emphasis on shareholder value. Other measures beginning to be used in more progressive organizations are customer service, market share and improvements in business processes.

Financial performance criteria

For the firm in international markets measuring the relevant returns on foreign operations is a difficult task, since differences can arise between foreign market cash flows and cash flows back to the firm itself owing to tax regulations and exchange controls. Furthermore, adjustment in transfer prices and credit can distort the true profitability of an investment by shifting profits and liquidity from one location to another (Shapiro, 1985). Firms use a variety of ways of measuring returns including foreign earnings, dividends, royalties and fees, interest, commissions and profits on exports. The key considerations in measuring returns in most circumstances are that they are incremental.

While non-financial criteria such as market share or sales growth may be used in determining the value of a foreign market investment, many firms employ a version of return on investment (ROI) as the means of measuring the long-run profit performance of their foreign operations. We usually associate the former approach with Japanese firms and a virtual complete dependence on ROI by US and other Western firms.

Where return on investment is used, a number of comparisons are possible: comparisons with similar firms in the foreign market, with other foreign operations controlled by the firm, with the firm's operations in the domestic market or with targets established before entering the foreign market. Unless historical measures such as the above indicate the relative returns to be expected from future investments there is no point in using any of the above measures. The most important comparison that can be made is between actual results and *ex ante* budgeted figures, since a post-investment audit can help a firm to learn from its mistakes as well as its successes (Shapiro, 1985).

The appropriate measures to use in evaluating and controlling foreign operations depend on the nature of the business. For marketing-oriented firms, market share, sales growth or the costs associated with generating a unit of sales revenue may be the most relevant measures. These measures would seem appropriate for the industrial products firm, the consumer products firm and the service firm operating abroad in most circumstances. They are especially relevant when entry to foreign markets is made by exporting.

A firm that enters foreign markets through foreign direct investment, however, may be more concerned about unit costs of production, quality control and labour productivity and labour-related matters. Firms that enter foreign markets through the foreign direct investment mode and equity-based competitive alliances may find return on assets or a working capital to sales ratio most helpful.

The important point is to use those measures which experience has shown are the key indicators to evaluate the performance of the foreign business. An important objective in deciding on the approach to performance valuation is to ensure that managers are motivated to attain the firm's corporate objectives. A well-designed marketing strategy which does not capture the imagination and support of managers is likely to fail. It is thus necessary, in selecting the performance criteria, to anticipate managerial reaction. Ultimately, all performance measures are subjective since the choice of which measure to stress in particular circumstances is a matter of judgement for the individual firm (Shapiro, 1985, p. 231).

Return on international investments

Financial analysis based on return on investment is frequently used by firms to measure annual performances of foreign operations. A detailed financial analysis can decompose the elements that affect the firm's return on investment. In order to examine these issues it is necessary to recall that the formula for return on investment can be decomposed into two subratios, one which measures cost control in the firm and the second which measures marketing effectiveness:

return on investment = (cost control) × (marketing effectiveness)
or in ratios

$$\frac{\text{net income}}{\text{total assets}} = \frac{\text{net income}}{\text{sales}} \times \frac{\text{sales}}{\text{total assets}}$$

The first ratio to the right of the equals symbol, net income divided by sales, measures cost control in the firm, i.e. the amount of gross profit the firm obtains in the market. The second ratio, sales divided by total assets, measures marketing effectiveness in the firm, i.e. the level of sales the firm obtains from the total resources at its disposal. This formula owes its origins to the DuPont Company which developed it to measure new wealth created, i.e. net income, compared with all the resources the firm could employ in the creation of that wealth, i.e. total assets.

By plotting the firm's cost control performance against its marketing effectiveness we derive the firm's return on investment. Numerous combinations of cost control effort and marketing effectiveness produce a given return on investment. By plotting the ratios over a number of years the firm can determine whether its emphasis on marketing effectiveness or cost control has been more fruitful. To illustrate the principles involved, the short historical performance of two hypothetical firms, ABC Technologies and XYZ Textiles, adapted from Mobley and McKeown (1987a, 1987b), is shown in Figure 20.3.

As can be seen, ABC Technologies, which entered a nearby foreign market for the first time during Year l, experienced a decline in cost control between Year 1 and Year 2, while marketing effectiveness did not change to compensate for this loss. Understanding the costs of entering a market, and particularly the costs of product adaptation in high-technology firms, is a common problem. The result is that return on investment declined to 20 per cent. For such a business let us assume that a return of 20–25 per cent would be

Figure 20.3 Cost control and marketing effectiveness for balanced growth
Sources: Mobley, L. and McKeown, K. (1987a) 'ROI revisited', in *Intrapreneurial Excellence*, American Management Association, pp. 1 and 4, and Mobley, L. and McKeown, K. (1987b) 'Balanced growth plans – an ROI breakthrough', in *Growth Strategies*, American Management Association, p. 3.

much too low and that the firm should attempt to raise its return to at least 40 per cent to satisfy profit and development requirements fully. Acknowledging this problem and the need for greater profits, ABC Technologies might, therefore, plan a balanced growth of its operations to obtain a return on investment in Year 3 of 40 per cent. As shown in Figure 20.3 it can reach its target by improvements on the cost side and by improved marketing effectiveness.

The returns on investment in Year 2 for ABC Technologies and XYZ Textiles were the same: 20 per cent. XYZ Textiles, however, achieved its 20 per cent ROI through a much more effective marketing effort; it made £3 of sales for every £1 of assets. The marketing effectiveness performance of ABC Technologies was £1 of sales for each £1 of assets but its cost effectiveness or productive efficiency was 25 per cent compared with 5 per cent for XYZ Textiles. As a result of this analysis and a decision to seek balanced growth, ABC Technologies might decide in Year 3 to increase its return on investment to 40 per cent.

The foreign operation, which is evaluated on the basis of return on investment, can, however, produce undesired results. In such an evaluative system longer-term performance may be ignored by managers. In order to boost returns essential equipment may not be replaced even when such investment is required for longer-term growth. This is so because new investments increase the asset base, the denominator in the equation above, and also because return on investment measured on a historical cost basis will be greater than investment measured on a replacement cost basis.

Strategic control of international marketing operations

Periodically, the firm in international markets decides to undertake a critical review of its overall marketing effectiveness in its various markets. Because marketing suffers from rapid obsolescence of objectives, policies, strategies and operational programmes, the firm must continuously monitor and control marketing activities (Kotler, 1997, p. 765). Strategic control for Kotler means auditing the firm's marketing activities to evaluate its marketing effectiveness. According to Kotler the marketing effectiveness of a firm is reflected in the degree to which it exhibits five major attributes of a marketing orientation: customer philosophy; integrated marketing organization; adequate marketing information; strategic orientation; operational efficiency.

Successful entry to and performance in international markets usually means developing a marketing strategy involving a combination of initiatives by the firm under each of the above headings:

- new or redesigned products,
- different distribution channels,
- expanded or improved production facilities with an emphasis on cost competitiveness in international markets,
- pricing with an emphasis on the ability to retaliate to influence the behaviour of competitors, and
- the acquisition or establishment of associated companies in the target market, in some cases.

All such initiatives require increased marketing expenditures.

Some of the above initiatives may be managed within the firm's long-term strategy, while others would fit into annual marketing plans. Some marketing expenditures and price changes would be tactical matters, the concern solely of a local manager or salesperson. It is the combination of these initiatives which the firm uses to expand in international markets and which therefore constitute the cost of the strategy.

The manner in which firms cost international marketing strategies varies according to the size and nature of the expansion, size, corporate culture and structure of the firm, and the type of management involved. Sometimes the chief executives of very large firms take the decision to internationalize and develop and monitor the marketing strategies developed. In other cases, even small subsidiaries of international firms are required to prepare detailed cost analyses of international market expansion strategies.

Planning and control

It is generally believed that there is a positive correlation between planning and financial performance in the firm. Recall that marketing planning must answer six key questions for the firm:

- Where are we now?
- How did we get here?
- Where are we going?
- What must be done?
- Who should do it?
- When should it be done?

Answers to these questions should help to improve the firm's marketing performance in all aspects of its activities. The value of marketing planning stems from the observation that international marketing is complex and life cycle properties result in changes in marketing programme requirements in the firm over time. In the context of rapid growth and expanding markets as face the firm on first entry to international markets, many firms may initially be profitable but experience cash flow problems as outlined elsewhere in this chapter.

The day-to-day operational aspects of the business dominate at this stage in the development of the firm. As the market stabilizes and a more mature situation reigns, survival and continued growth may depend on the extent to which the firm has anticipated these changes, has recognized their present and future implications and has developed strategic as well as operational skills to cope with them (Bracker *et al.*, 1988, p. 593).

Most strategic planning starts with a static view of the firm, its customers and the competition: a static analysis means assessing the attractiveness of the market and the company's position compared to competitors. As seen in earlier chapters, Chapter 10 particularly, many companies are myopic in this regard. Companies, especially those defending domestic positions, are often shortsighted about the strategic intentions of their competitors. It has been argued that such companies do not understand their own vulnerability until they understand the intentions of their rivals and then reason back to potential tactics (Hamel and Prahalad, 1985, p. 143). With no appreciation of strategic intent these authors argue that defensively minded competitors are doomed to a perpetual game of catch-up. Key issues and problem areas are also identified at this stage. The next stage involves a dynamic analysis which is sometimes based on subjective judgements but usually supported by research. The firm must examine sets of factors in deciding probable future outcomes. A series of factors affect customers, competitors and the environment which impact on costs and financial performance, which must be considered in a dynamic analysis of the firm (Figure 20.4).

Meeting and reviewing performance standards

Designing an effective implementation and control system is not an easy task. A range of possible controls were discussed in preceding sections. A comprehensive treatment of the subject would mean an evaluation of the effectiveness of the firm in international markets on the following criteria (Newman and Logan, 1976, p. 512):

1. profitability (per centage of sales and return on investment);
2. market position;
3. productivity (costs and sales improvements);
4. leadership in technological research;
5. development of key people (technical and managerial);
6. attitudes (employees and public).

The above list places considerable emphasis on strength for future company growth and current profitability. As may be judged, therefore, real control of marketing strategy implementation in the firm is more comprehensive than a simple examination of how well the firm performed in the past. Unless corrective action is taken when performance

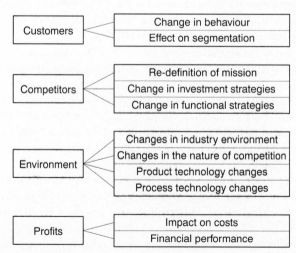

Figure 20.4 Factors analysed in a dynamic analysis of the firm, customers and competitors

standards are not met or when new opportunities appear, the process of implementation and control in the firm is an empty exercise. As soon as a deviation from standard is detected, the causes of the variation should be investigated. A number of causes may be identified: obstacles arising in operating conditions, poor communications leading to misunderstanding, inadequate training, lack of required basic skills or inadequate incentives (Newman and Logan, 1976, p. 509). Corrective action sometimes leads to a change in the targets. An evaluation of operating conditions, leadership training and motivation may reveal unrealistic standards in relation to the firm and its markets. In such circumstances it would be important to revise the standards. This may be true especially for the firm new to international marketing. In circumstances where the performance evaluation indicates results better than expected, new higher standards might be established if improved circumstances are likely to continue. This may be true for the more confident firm already with a number of years of successful experience in international markets. Successful firms are innovative even in the area of performance measurement. Better performing firms gain a competitive advantage by using advanced monitoring systems to measure their international marketing performance (Subramanian and IsHak, 1998, p. 21). At the same time the successful international marketing company must not lose sight of its core business and what it takes to be successful.

Summary

Implementing international marketing strategy means paying attention to a number of closely related areas. First, it is important to understand the dimensions of effective implementation of strategy in the firm in international markets. Second, the firm must decide on the best approach to operational control in its markets. Finally, there is the issue of implementing performance standards in the firm. In examining the issue of implementation there is the added dimension of short-run tactical controls on implementation and long-term strategic control on the direction of the firm.

Measuring marketing performance is not an easy task. Numerous measures of efficiency can be applied to marketing inputs, intermediary factors and marketing outputs. Firms select a number from these which they monitor over time. Among the more common measures are sales quotas and controls, asset earnings and profits, market share and market growth. In addition, firms seek financial control in their international markets. One of the key variables to be managed in this regard is cash flow. The timing and sequencing of events in international markets are such as to put great pressure on cash flow. The effect is usually greater on smaller firms.

Financial controls in the form of return on investment which are short term in nature are also used by firms. They have the advantage, however, that if applied over time the firm can monitor its performance and attribute any deviation from standard to cost or marketing factors.

Most firms attempting to develop and grow in international markets apply strategic controls to their international operations. Strategic control involves a much broader set of factors related to marketing, customers and competitors and distinguishes the more successful companies from the less successful. It is also recognized that not only do strategies change from time to time but so too do performance standards. With more experience of international markets the firm may revise the performance standards it uses.

Discussion questions

1. Why is the firm concerned with measuring marketing performance?
2. What is meant by strategy implementation for the firm in international markets? Describe the relationship between marketing strategy and its implementation.
3. Expansion into international markets must be accompanied by a financial strategy. Discuss.
4. Describe the more important operational controls which could be applied in international markets.
5. Short-term financial performance measures identify the likelihood of long-term survival in international markets. Discuss.
6. Most of the measures of strategic control are inappropriate, difficult to apply and too expensive. Discuss.
7. Increasingly, firms in international markets organize themselves on the basis of information networks to serve customers and compete. Discuss.
8. Marketing strategies evolve with time and circumstances so why not performance standards and approaches to implementation too?

References

Blackwell, N., Bizet, J.-P., Child, P. and Hensley, D. (1991) 'Creating European organizations that work', *McKinsey Quarterly*, **25** (4), 155–65.

Bonoma, T. V. (1984) 'Making your marketing strategy work', *Harvard Business Review*, **62** (March–April), 69–76.

Bonoma, T. V. and Clarke, B. H. (1988) *Marketing Performance Assessment*, Boston, MA: Harvard Business School Press.

Bracker, J. S., Keats, B. W. and Pearson, J. N. (1988) 'Planning and financial performance among small firms in a growth industry', *Strategic Management Journal*, **9**, 591–603.

Daniels, J. D. (1987) 'Bridging national and global marketing strategies through regional operations' *International Marketing Review*, **4** (Autumn), 29–44.

Greenley, G. E. (1989) *Strategic Management*, New York, NY: Prentice Hall.

Hamel, G. and Prahalad, C. K. (1985) 'Do you really have a global strategy?, *Harvard Business Review*, **63** (July–August), 139–48.

Hulbert, J. M. and Toy, N. E. (1984) 'A strategic framework for marketing control', in B. A. Weitz and R. Wensley, (eds), *Strategic Marketing*, Boston, MA: Kent Publishing Company, pp. 452–65.

Kashani, K. (1989) 'Beware the global pitfalls of global marketing', *Harvard Business Review*, **67** (September–October), 91–9.

Kotler, P. (1997) *Marketing Management*, 9th edn, Englewood Cliffs, NJ: Prentice Hall International.

Mobley, L. and McKeown, K. (1987a) 'ROI revisited', in *Intrapreneurial Excellence*, American Management Association, pp. 1 and 4.

Mobley, L. and McKeown, K. (1987b) 'Balanced growth plans – an ROI breakthrough', in *Growth Strategies*, American Management Association, p. 3.

Newman, W. and Logan, J. P. (1976) *Strategy, Policy and Central Management*, 7th edn, Cincinnati, OH: South Western Publishing Company.

Pfeffer, J. and Salancik, G. R. (1978) *The External Control of Organizations*, New York, NY: Harper and Row.

Samiee, S. and Roth, K. (1992) 'The influence of global marketing standardization on performance' *Journal of Marketing*, **56** (April), 1–17.

Shapiro, A. C. (1985) 'Evaluation and control of foreign operations', in Vernon – H. Wortzel and L. C. Wortzel, (eds), *Strategic Management of Multinational Corporations: The essentials*, New York, NY: Wiley, pp. 225–39.

Subramanian, R. and IsHak, T. (1988): 'Competitor analysis practices of U.S. companies: an empirical investigation', *Management International Review*, **38** (1), 7–23.

Weston, J. F. and Copeland, T. E. (1988) *Managerial Finance*, 2nd edn, London: Cassell Educational.

Glossary

Absolute advantage: The ability to produce a good or service more cheaply than it can be produced by competitors elsewhere.

Agents: Representatives that fully represent a company in a particular market. They do not, however, take title to the products.

Andean pact: In November 1969 the Cartagena Agreement established the basic framework of this act which sought to harmonize the trade and investment regimes of its members – Venezuela, Columbia, Bolivia, Peru and Ecuador.

Balance of payments: The account that details all the economic transactions involving goods, services and investments that occur between one nation and other nations in a given period.

Balance of trade: The merchandise account that records a nation's imports and exports.

Barter: The exchange of goods or services of approximately equal value without transfers of money.

The Caribbean Common Market (CARICOM): In 1973 a common market for trade and to promote other forms of economic cooperation was established among its 13 English-speaking member states.

Comparative advantage: A theory that world trade occurs because a nation has the ability to produce a good or service more cheaply than is possible in other countries.

Competitive advantage: Corporate competencies demanded by the market place that competitors cannot easily match, except at high cost and/or over an extended period.

Competitive assessment: A research process which requires matching corporate strengths to markets and providing an analysis of the best potential for specific offerings.

Corporate culture: The values and beliefs shared by the members of a company and the rules of behaviour (social norms) they follow. It provides a general frame of reference for the members of the organization that may be used to interpret events and facts in the company's environments.

Corporate strategy: Determines the general nature of a company's relationships with its environments and how business is conducted.

Counterfeiting: The intentional and illegal use of a name, product shape or packaging that differs from the original but that the consumer will associate with the original.

547

Country-of-origin effect: The transfer of a particular country's image to products made there. In the minds of customers products are often assigned values on the basis of where they are made.

Cultural complexity: The degree to which the understanding of the conditions within a culture is dependent on the possession of data and information which places it in context.

Cultural universals: Manifestations of the total way of life of any group of people.

Customs union: A type of cooperative agreement in which members dismantle barriers to trade in goods and services. In addition a common trade policy with respect to non-members is enforced.

Deregulation: A movement toward relaxing anti-trust rules and laws, along with supporting the privatization of businesses.

Direct investment: Establishing or expanding international operations by means of capital flows, involving a degree of control by the investor.

Distribution system: The agents, dealers, wholesalers and retailers, as well as all the tools and facilities used in transferring the good or service from the producer to the customer.

Distributor: An intermediary, especially a wholesaler who has a formalized, continuing relationship with the manufacturer, with exclusive sales rights for specific geographic areas.

Diversification: A market expansion policy characterized by growth in a relatively large number of markets or market segments. This growth is achieved by increasing the range of the company's products or investing money in several different securities.

Domestication: Government demands that partial ownership and management responsibility of a foreign company is transferred to them, with or without compensation.

Dumping: An unfair trade practice, based on international price discrimination where goods are sold in other countries at a price lower than in the exporter's home market, or at a price below the cost of production, or both.

Economic union: Member states are fully integrated economically and adopt a common unit of currency.

Ethnocentric: The tendency to regard one's own culture as superior; tending to be home market oriented.

European Coal and Steel Community (ECSC): A common market for coal, iron and steel only which was established by a treaty signed in Paris on 18 April 1951. The treaty came into force on 23 July 1952. The original signatories of the treaty were Belgium, France, Federal Republic of Germany, Italy, Luxembourg and the Netherlands. Denmark, the Republic of Ireland and the UK became members on I January 1973; Greece was admitted in 1981.

European Community (EC): A common market whose members are Belgium. Denmark, France, Germany, Greece, Ireland, Italy, Luxembourg, The Netherlands, Portugal, Spain and the United Kingdom.

European Currency Unit (Ecu): A common monetary unit based on a basket of the European Community currencies to facilitate transactions.

European Economic Community (EEC): A common market for all products except those covered by the European Coal and Steel Community (ECSC). It was established by the Treaty of Rome signed on 25 March 1957. Its membership is the same as that of the ECSC.

European Free Trade Association (EFTA): A free trade area established in 1960 under the

Stockholm Convention. Current members are Norway, Sweden, Switzerland, Austria, Liechtenstein, Iceland and Finland. Since 31 December 1966, all duties imposed by EFTA on imports from member countries have been abolished and there are no export restrictions between member states. The agreement does not cover agriculture although individual agreements are permitted. Former members Denmark, Portugal and the UK subsequently joined the EU.

European Monetary System (EMS): A system created in 1979 to guarantee the internal and external stability of currencies of member countries. It also attempts to coordinate their economic policies.

European Union (EU): New title for the EEC used since the ratification of the Maastricht Treaty.

Exchange rate risk: Risk arises from the need to conduct the transaction in more than one currency where a future payment could be more expensive, or a future receipt less valuable than was expected.

Exclusive distribution: A limit placed on the number of partners in a distribution channel for representing a producer of speciality goods or services.

Experience curve effects: Increased efficiency due to economies of scale and increased effectiveness due to accumulated knowledge.

Expropriation: A company is seized by the government supposedly in the 'public interest'. Compensation is frequently at a level lower than the investment value of the company's assets.

Foreign direct investment (FDI): A market entry strategy in which a company invests in a subsidiary or partnership in a foreign market. Foreign direct investment entails some degree of control by the investor.

Franchising: An indirect market entry technique in the form of licensing that gives a distributor or retailer the exclusive right to sell a product or service in a specified area. This technique is used by organizations that want to establish a market presence rapidly with limited capital risk.

Free trade area (FTA): An area in which all barriers to trade among member countries are removed, although sometimes only for certain goods or services.

General Agreement on Tariffs and Trade (GATT): An international code of tariffs and trade rules signed by 23 nations in 1947; headquartered in Geneva, Switzerland; currently has 100 members. The Uruguay Round of GATT completed in 1994 has achieved the greatest trade liberalization to date.

Geocentric: Tending to take a world view; oriented toward global market place.

Geocentric firm: A company committed to developing worldwide opportunities for coordination and concentration of its business interests.

Global brand: A brand that is used by a global company in all the national markets it serves.

Global marketing: An approach to marketing that concentrates on product markets, emphasizing their similarities, regardless of the geographic area in which they are located.

Grey market: A market entered in a way not intended by the manufacturer of the goods. It describes that part of a national economy that operates outside the officially regulated structure of business activities.

High-context cultures: Cultures in which cultural nuances are an important means of conveying information because human behaviour is covert and implicit.

Import substitution: A policy for economic growth adopted by many developing countries encourages domestic production of goods which were formerly imported.

Importers: Retailers and wholesalers that fulfil the same functions as distributors. Generally do not have exclusive rights to the product.

Income elasticity of demand: A means of describing responsiveness to a change in demand relative to a change in income.

Incoterms: Terms of sale developed in international trade over the years that have been precisely phrased by the International Chamber of Commerce and are now regarded as standard.

Industrial policy: Official planning for industry as a whole or for a particular industry.

Industry analysis: The assessment of the potential attractiveness of a market. It involves analysing a particular industry, including competing firms, intermediaries, suppliers and the labour force.

Intangible asset: Something that is owned by a person or company but which cannot be seen, tasted or touched in a conventional sense. It can, however, be assigned a value on the basis of its usefulness. It is that characteristic of services which most strongly differentiates them from products.

Integration: Control of different organizations merges through the building of a tight network of interrelationships between a business and its partners.

Intensive distribution: The representation of a company in as many outlets as possible.

International competitiveness: The ability of a company, an industry or a country to compete in the international market place while maintaining a stable or rising standard of living.

Joint venture: An agreement in which a company joins forces with a local partner to enter a particular market.

Legal environment: The set of laws established by a society to govern the behaviour of its members.

Licensing agreement: An agreement by which one firm permits another to use its intellectual property in return for compensation.

Low context cultures: Cultures in which most information is conveyed overtly and explicitly rather than through cultural nuances.

Macro economic approach: An analysis dealing with the economy as a whole with respect to total output, income, employment and other aggregate economic variables.

Management contract: An international business alternative in which the company sells its expertise in running a company. In doing so it avoids the risk or benefit of ownership.

Managerial commitment: The willingness of management to act on an idea.

Market attractiveness: An approach to building a product portfolio which considers market growth, degree of competition, relative market size and corporate competencies.

Market imperfections: Departures from the strict assumptions of competitive economic theory.

Marketing infrastructure: Facilitating marketing agencies in a country, for example distribution networks.

Material culture: The standard of living or level of economic development which a society has achieved.

Mercosur: Latin America's largest planned common market. It was formed on 26 March 1991 when the governments of Argentina, Brazil, Paraguay and Uruguay signed the Treaty of Asunción.

Micro economic approach: An analysis concerned with outputs and prices in individual markets.

Multilateral agreements: Agreements that regulate trade between two or more countries.

Multilateral trade negotiations: Trade negotiations held among more than two parties.

Multinational firms: Those companies that view selected foreign markets as at least as important as the domestic market.

North American Free Trade Agreement (NAFTA): In August 1992, the United States, Canada and Mexico signed a free trade agreement to establish an open market across the North American continent.

National firms: Companies that focus their business interests on domestic markets.

National sovereignty: The supreme right of nations to determine national policies, free from any external controls.

Newly industrialized countries (NICs): Highly competitive, export-oriented manufacturing countries which are characterized by low rates of inflation and unemployment and by high rates of economic growth.

Norms: A society's underlying set of beliefs about what it considers to be acceptable behaviour.

Objectives: Performance measures that permit evaluation of results, to determine whether the company has determined its mission.

Organization for Economic Cooperation and Development (OECD): A multinational forum based in Paris that allows the major industrialized nations to discuss economic policies and events.

Physical distribution: A strategic tool used in global marketing that includes customer service, inventory management, warehousing, storage, shipping and receiving, transportation. All associated documentation is also included.

Political risk: The risk of loss of assets, earning power or managerial control by an international corporation, as a result of political actions.

Political union: An advanced form of economic cooperation in which the agreement among the signatories results in the formation of a new nation.

Polycentric firm: A company which regards international markets as a series of domestic (or national) markets.

Portfolio analysis: A firm determines how its strategic business units are distributed in relation to various factors that influence business success and to various measures of success.

Positioning: The perception by consumers of a company's product in relation to its competitors' products.

Positioning analysis: Research used to determine whether a desired position has been established in the mind of the customers and whether the company is achieving this goal more successfully than its competitors.

Positioning strategy: A marketing strategy that highlights the benefits which are attractive to customers in the target market and which distinguishes the product or company from its competitors.

Product differentiation: An attempt by the company to build unique differences or improvements into its products.

Product improvement: Attempts by the company to augment the capabilities and reliability of its products, by extending warranties and services related to the products and applying new technologies.

Product life cycle: A theory that portrays the sales history of products as passing through four stages: introduction, growth, maturity, decline.

Protectionism: The use of legal controls by governments to protect specific domestic industries or businesses against foreign competition.

Public relations (PR): A non-personal form of communication in which the organization tries to convey a favourable image of the organization to various publics.

Rationalization: The change that occurs within an industry to compensate for some form of imbalance, such as the need to achieve greater economies of scale.

Regiocentric: Tending to be oriented toward regions larger than individual countries as markets.

Self-reference criterion: The unconscious reference to ones own cultural values and experiences when considering a market in another culture.

Social stratification: The division of a particular population into classes.

Sociocultural factors: A wide variety of patterns of living, including behaviour norms such as those regarding diet or styles of dress.

Standard of living: The level of material affluence of a group or nation. It may be measured as a composite of quantities of goods and their quality.

Strategic alliances: A new term meaning joint ventures, i.e. to join forces with a local partner to enter a particular market.

Strategic business unit (SBU): A single business or a collection of related businesses that can be planned separately from the rest of the company. It is organized around the customer groups that will be served, the customer needs that will be met and the products or services that will satisfy those needs.

Tariffs: Taxes on imported goods and services, levied by foreign governments as a means to raise revenue and/or to protect domestic companies.

Technology transfer: The transfer of knowledge necessary for the manufacture of a product, the application of a process or the rendering of a service.

Trade creation: The benefit to a particular country when a group of countries trade a product freely among themselves while maintaining common barriers to trade with non-members.

Trade diversion: The cost to a particular country when a group of countries trade a product freely among themselves while maintaining common barriers to trade with non-members.

Trade fair: Exhibitions designed to display products for the purpose of promoting sales and use of a product or service,

Trademark: The distinctive identification of a product or service. It may take the form of a name, logo, letter, picture, or other device to distinguish it from similar offerings. It protects the exclusive rights to use the brand name and mark.

Trademark licensing: A form of licensing which permits the names or logos of recognizable individuals or groups to be used on products.

Trading company: A company which is involved in importing, exporting, countertrading, investing and manufacturing, e.g. Japanese sogoshosha.

Transfer cost: The costs incurred in transferring technology to a licensee and all ongoing expense of maintaining the licensing agreement.

Transfer price: A price set in an intracompany transaction involving goods or services.

Triad: The United States, Japan and the European Union.

Value-added chain: A marketing approach used in analysing product competitiveness in which a product is viewed as a bundle of related services and production is viewed as a bundle of processes.

World Bank: Another name for the International Bank for Reconstruction and Development.

World Trade Organisation: An institution comprising the GATT, a legal entity with privileges and immunities similar to those of the specialized agencies of the United Nations.

Acronyms

CIF: carriage, insurance and freight
Ecu: European Currency Unit
EEC: European Economic Community (obsolete)
EFTA: European Free Trade Association
EMS: European Monetary System
EU: European Union
FAS: free alongside ship
FDI: foreign direct investment
FOB: free on board
GATS: General Agreement on Trade in Services
GATT: General Agreement on Tariffs and Trade
MFN: most favoured nation
NAFTA: North American Free Trade Association
NIC: newly industrialized countries (e.g. Brazil, Malaysia, Mexico, South Korea)
NTB: non-tariff barrier
OECD: Organization for Economic Cooperation and Development
SBU: strategic business unit
TNC: transnational corporation

Irl£: punt (Irish)
Lire: Italian lire
NZ$: New Zealand dollars
Peso: Mexican peso
Ptas: Spanish pesetas
Rouble: Russian rouble
Sch: Austrian schilling
Sfr: Swiss franc
S$: Singapore dollar
Stg£: Pound sterling (British)
¥: Japanese yen

Company index

Name index

Aaker, D.A. 247, 248, 250, 389
Abdel-Malek, T. 291
Abegglen, J.C. 329
Abernathy, W.J. 42, 50, 95
Abramson, N.R. 76
Adams, J. 324
Agarwal, S. 277
Akoorie, M.E.M. 518
Albaum, G.S. 269
Alexander, M. 92
Amin Gutiérrez de Piñeres, S. 126
Andaleeb, S.S. 465
Andersen, O. 291
Andersen, P.H. 418
Anderson, E. 228, 329, 330, 465, 466, 477, 494
Anderson, P.F. 47, 50
Arndt, J. 511
Aruajo, L. 408
Asugman, G. 258, 475
Attiyeh, R.J. 210
Atuahene-Gima, K. 319
Axelsson, B. 409
Ayal, I. 107, 109, 212, 267, 269, 279, 280
Ayling, D. 323, 325
Ayling, R. 313

Bailey, J.P. 479, 480, 481
Bakos, Y. 479, 480, 481
Bamossy, G.J. 331
Banks, A.S. 146
Barabba, V.P. 42, 52
Barnett, G.A. 495

Barney, J.B. 40, 59
Barnlund, D.C. 499
Bartels, R. 33, 104
Beatty, S.E. 505
Becker, H. 292
Bello, D.C. 476
Bennett, P. 145
Berkowitz, M. 426
Bernard, D. 96
Berry, C.A. 273, 276
Berry, L.L. 445, 446, 448
Bilkey, W.J. 44, 72, 80, 218, 289, 290, 292
Bilsky, W. 146, 147
Bini-Smaghi, L. 176
Blackwell, N. 532, 533
Blake, R.R. 512
Boddewyn, J.J. 13, 378
Bonaccorsi, A. 292
Bonoma, T.V. 528
Boyacigiller, N. 522
Bracker, J.S. 542
Bradley, F. 23, 33, 51, 54, 72, 75, 78, 79, 80, 81, 190, 191, 291, 295, 296, 298, 417, 418, 448
Brandenburg, M. 323
Brandenburger, A.M. 49, 51
Brenes, E.R. 126
Brennan, K.L. 192
Bridgewater, S. 132
Brouthers, K.D. 166, 267, 331
Brown, L.G. 228
Brozin, R. 14

557

Subject index

Note: Page numbers in *italics* refer to Figures; those in **bold** refer to Tables